CONTEMPORARY MUSICIANS

ISSN 1044-2197

CONTEMPORARY MUSICIANS

PROFILES OF THE PEOPLE IN MUSIC

LAURA HIGHTOWER

LEIGH ANN DeREMER, Project Editor

VOLUME 28
Includes Cumulative Indexes

GALE GROUP

Detroit
New York
San Francisco
London
Boston
Woodbridge, CT

STAFF

Leigh Ann DeRemer, *Project Editor*
Luann Brennan, *Contributing Editor*

Laura Avery, Aaron J. Oppliger, *Associate Editors*

Laura Hightower, *Senior Sketchwriter*

Gerald E. Brennan, Gloria Cooksey, Francis E. McKinley Jr., Ann M. Schwalboski,
Jane E. Spear, Julie Sweet, Nathan Sweet, *Sketchwriters*

Bridget Travers, *Managing Editor*

Maria L. Franklin, *Permissions Manager*
Margaret Chamberlain, *Permissions Specialist*

Mary Beth Trimper, *Manager, Compostion and Electronic Prepress*
Dorothy Maki, *Manufacturing Manager*
Stacy Melson, *Buyer*

Robert Duncan, *Imaging Specialist*
Randy Bassett, *Image Database Supervisor*
Dean Dauphinais, *Senior Editor, Imaging and Multimedia Content*
Pamela A. Reed, *Imaging Coordinator*
Michael Logusz, *Graphic Artist*
Cover illustration by John Kleber

27500 Drake Rd.
Farmington Hills, MI 48334-3535

Printed in the United States of America

ISBN 0-7876-3253-8
ISSN 1044-2197

Contents

Introduction ix

Cumulative Subject Index 271

Cumulative Musicians Index 297

Barry Adamson 1
Pop musician turned film composer

Daevid Allen 5
Casts a spell with eccentric music

Fiona Apple 8
Powerful bluesy-pop

Hoyt Axton 11
Multi-talented entertainer

Bad Religion 15
Intelligent, blistering punk

Bardo Pond 19
"Art rock" band

Beat Happening 22
Respected, low-end production pop group

Belle and Sebastian 26
Acclaimed Scottish folk octet

Tito Beltrán 29
Chilean tenor on a mission

Jeb Bishop 32
Creativity beyond jazz scene

Peter Blegvad 35
Master of poetic wordplay

Blonde Redhead 39
Find artistry in punk rock

Johnny Bond 42
Humorous singing cowboy

The Boredoms 46
Prominent Japanese "noise band"

Can 49
Broke rock and roll mold

Vicki Carr 53
Mexican-American success story

Vic Chesnutt 57
Lyrics capture painful realities

Billy Childish 61
Prolific British rock performer

Christian Death 64
Goth-rock with loyal following

Charlotte Church 68
Welsh operatic prodigy

Cibo Matto 71
Pop with international flair

Cobra Verde 74
"Avant-glam" experiment

Creed 77
Rock within the lines

D.O.A. 80
Enduring Canadian punk band

Jeff Dahl 83
Prolific punk soloist

Death in Vegas 86
Big beat rock out of England

Dave Edmunds 89
Quintessential musician's musician

Eminem 92
Gritty hip hop

The Ex 95
Punk driven by socialist agenda

Filter 98
Rode Short Bus to fame

The Flying Luttenbachers 101
Extreme musical sounds

The Folk Implosion 105
Reluctant rock stars

Kenny Garrett 108
Lets music do the talking

The Go-Betweens 111
Themes of love and loneliness

Gogi Grant 114
Premier vocalist of the '50s and '60s

Tom Harrell 117
Electrifying jazz trumpeter

Penelope Houston 120
Surprising musical transformation

Jay-Z 124
Hard knocks formed rap voice

Eyvind Kang 127
Wide-open curiosity

Stacey Kent 130
Uncluttered jazz vocals

Lambert, Hendricks and Ross 133
Masters of vocalese

Fred Lane 136
Catalog of styles

Lyle Lovett 139
Classic country storyteller

The Magnetic Fields 143
Eccentric pop of the '90s

Johnny Mandel 146
Musician turned arranger

Mercury Rev 149
Experimental pop

Monks of Doom 153
Heavy and hip rock

Dave Murray 156
Avant-garde jazz giant

Neurosis 160
Metal takes the road less traveled

NOFX 163
Punk royalty

Olivia Tremor Control 166
Upheld home-town tradition

Evan Parker 169
Improvisational jazz standout

The Promise Ring 172
"Emocre" outfit

Roswell Rudd 175
Blasted into new jazz dimensions

Saint Etienne 178
Established indie-dance genre

David Sanborn 181
Saxophone great avoids cliches

Pharoah Sanders 184
Resonating, rough-edged sound

Mongo Santamaria 188
Music explores Cuban roots

Randy Scruggs 191
Made mark on country music

George Shearing 195
Prominent British composer/arranger

Sloan 199
Canadian radio staple

Elliott Smith 202
Impressive songwriting talent

Tommy Smith 206
Elevated jazz in Scotland

Smog 209
Lo-fi movement pioneer

Britney Spears 212
Pop superstar got early start

Ronnie Spector 215
From Ronettes to solo success

Sunny Day Real Estate 219
Melodic punk-metal

Super Furry Animals 223
Innovative Welsh pop band

Teri Thornton 226
"Greatest jazz voice since Ella Fitzgerald"

Trick Daddy 230
Lives Southern rap

Ken Vandermark 233
Musical democrat

Caetano Veloso 237
Dominant Brazilian pop force

Velvet Crush 241
Melodic power-pop trio

Arcadi Volodos 244
Award-winning piano virtuoso

Joe Louis Walker 246
Explosive jazz style

The Wedding Present 249
Lovelorn lyrics with edgy flavor

Margaret Whiting 253
Classic pop songstress

Willem Breuker Kollektief 256
Unpredictable musical humor

John Williams 259
Legendary film music composer/conductor

Nancy Wilson 264
Timeless, sultry jazz vocals

Introduction

Fills the Information Gap on Today's Musicians

Contemporary Musicians profiles the colorful personalities in the music industry who create or influence the music we hear today. Prior to *Contemporary Musicians,* no quality reference series provided comprehensive information on such a wide range of artists despite keen and ongoing public interest. To find biographical and critical coverage, an information seeker had little choice but to wade through the offerings of the popular press, scan television "infotainment" programs, and search for the occasional published biography or exposé. *Contemporary Musicians* is designed to serve that information seeker, providing in one ongoing source in-depth coverage of the important names on the modern music scene in a format that is both informative and entertaining. Students, researchers, and casual browsers alike can use *Contemporary Musicians* to meet their needs for personal information about music figures; find a selected discography of a musician's recordings; and uncover an insightful essay offering biographical and critical information.

Provides Broad Coverage

Single-volume biographical sources on musicians are limited in scope, often focusing on a handful of performers from a specific musical genre or era. In contrast, *Contemporary Musicians* offers researchers and music devotees a comprehensive, informative, and entertaining alternative. *Contemporary Musicians* is published three times per year, with each volume providing information on about 80 musical artists and record-industry luminaries from all the genres that form the broad spectrum of contemporary music—pop, rock, jazz, blues, country, New Age, folk, rhythm and blues, gospel, bluegrass, rap, and reggae, to name a few—as well as selected classical artists who have achieved "crossover" success with the general public. *Contemporary Musicians* will also occasionally include profiles of influential nonperforming members of the music community, including producers, promoters, and record company executives. Additionally, beginning with *Contemporary Musicians 11,* each volume features new profiles of a selection of previous *Contemporary Musicians* listees who remain of interest to today's readers and who have been active enough to require completely revised entries.

Includes Popular Features

In *Contemporary Musicians* you'll find popular features that users value:

- **Easy-to-locate data sections:** Vital personal statistics, chronological career summaries, listings of major awards, and mailing addresses, when available, are prominently displayed in a clearly marked box on the second page of each entry.

- **Biographical/critical essays:** Colorful and informative essays trace each subject's personal and professional life, offer representative examples of critical response to the artist's work, and provide entertaining personal sidelights.

- **Selected discographies:** Each entry provides a comprehensive listing of the artist's major recorded works.

- **Photographs:** Most entries include portraits of the subject profiled.

- **Sources for additional information:** This invaluable feature directs the user to selected books, magazines, newspapers, and online sources where more information can be obtained.

Helpful Indexes Make It Easy to Find the Information You Need

Each volume of *Contemporary Musicians* features a cumulative Musicians Index, listing names of individual performers and musical groups, and a cumulative Subject Index, which provides the user with a breakdown by primary musical instruments played and by musical genre.

Available in Electronic Formats

Diskette/Magnetic Tape. *Contemporary Musicians* is available for licensing on magnetic tape or diskette in a fielded format. The database is available for internal data processing and nonpublishing purposes only. For more information, call (800) 877-GALE.

Online. *Contemporary Musicians* is available online as part of the Gale Biographies (GALBIO) database accessible through LEXIS-NEXIS, P.O. Box 933, Daton, OH 454012-0933; phone: (513)865-6800, toll-free:800-543-6862.

We Welcome Your Suggestions

The editors welcome your comments and suggestions for enhancing and improving *Contemporary Musicians.* If you would like to suggest subjects for inclusion, please submit these names to the editors. Mail comments or suggestions to:

The Editor
Contemporary Musicians
Gale Group, Inc.
27500 Drake Rd.
Farmington Hills, MI 48334-3535

Or call toll free: (800) 347-GALE

Barry Adamson

Composer, guitar, piano

Photograph by Martyn Goodacre. Corbis. Reproduced by permission.

British composer Barry Adamson began his musical career as a member of the avant-garde pop band Magazine and honed his skills playing piano and guitar for Nick Cave and the Bad Seeds before realizing that his true musical calling stood beyond the rock and roll genre. Drawn to and inspired by the cinema early in life, Adamson left the confines of pop music to pursue a solo career writing evocative, jazzy instrumentals. Composing scores for both real and imaginary film soundtracks, "Adamson's muse has always revealed a colorful debt to insurgent pulp fiction, smoky film intrigue and other manifestations of high-spy thrillers," wrote Mitch Myers of *Magnet.* In addition to writing music for several films, including *Gas Food Lodging* in 1992 and *Lost Highway* in 1996, Adamson also penned songs for solo works such as his debut album *Moss Side Story.* Released in 1989, the autobiographical thriller revealed themes from a film that never existed.

As a solo artist and soundtrack composer, Adamson further enjoyed exploring the dual nature of humanity (goodness versus evil and sin versus salvation) and man's eternal struggle with himself in his music. "The big question is how the soul can be the house of both incredible joy and such abject misery," Adamson told Myers, discussing his eclectic 1998 solo release *As Above, So Below.* "Can one reach a place of acceptance that puts everything in balance? The darkness is there for a reason, and the lightness is there for a reason. We walk through life with both of these things in check, and it's the very humanness that I'm talking about."

Born on June 1, 1958, in England, Adamson grew up in Manchester's Moss Side, where he developed an early fascination with the relationship between film and music. "I guess the influence of film came before I got into music, so a lot of the people were from the late '60s," he revealed to Myers. "Henry Mancini, Ennio Morricone, Quincy Jones, John Barry—these people were at the height of their powers at that time. It's different now, but those people were so powerful in the way they talked about the world of a film on a musical and emotional level. It had a profound effect on me then and still does today."

Despite his later jazz and film-inspired compositions that approached music from a cinematic perspective, Adamson spent most of the 1970s and 1980s playing with rock, punk, and pop bands. In 1977, Adamson joined his first band, an art-punk group that refused to honor musical boundaries, led by singer/lyricist and ex-Buzzcocks member Howard Devoto called Magazine. With Magazine, which became Manchester's most influential pop group of the time, Adamson learned to play

For the Record . . .

Born June 1, 1958, in England.

Left Nick Cave and the Bad Seeds to pursue solo career, signed with Mute Records, 1987; released debut album *Moss Side Story*, 1989; penned soundtracks for *Delusion*, 1991; and *Gas Food Lodging*, 1992; contributed to soundtrack for the David Lynch film *Lost Highway*, 1996; released first solo album utilizing his vocals, *As Above, So Below*, 1998.

Addresses: *Record company*—Mute Records, 140 W. 22nd St., Ste. 10-A, New York City, NY 10011, phone (212) 255-7670, fax (212) 255-6056. *Website*—Barry Adamson at Mute Records, http://www.mutelibtech.com/mute/adamson/adamson.htm.

bass guitar literally overnight. While the group started out playing harder-edged material, exemplified in Magazine's 1978 debut entitled *Real Life*, they eventually gravitated to more melodic, pop tunes by the release of their third album in 1980, *The Correct Use of Soap*. In 1981, after recording five albums together, the band dissolved, although Adamson, guitarist John McGeoch (who left Magazine in 1980 to join Siouxsie and the Banshees), and keyboardist Dave Formula continued to play in a side project, the synth-pop band Visage, until around 1984. Adamson also worked briefly with Pete Shelley, another former Buzzcocks member, after the disbanding of Magazine.

From 1982 until 1983, Adamson played bass for the Birthday Party, a punk band led by vocalist Nick Cave and guitarist, drummer, and keyboardist Mick Harvey. Despite the group's festive name, Birthday Party—propelled by Cave's poetic, yet disturbing lyrics that often centered around love, death, and religion—created some of the darkest and most violent music of the time. The band's debut and follow-up album, *Prayers on Fire* released in 1981, and *Junkyard* released in 1982, earned both popular and critical acclaim. When Birthday Party dissolved in 1983, Adamson joined Cave, Harvey, and Blixa Bargeld to form Nick Cave and the Bad Seeds. He played both piano and guitar for the Bad Seeds from 1984 until 1986 and recorded three albums with the ensemble before deciding that rock music was too restricting a format for his other musical ideas—specifically, writing songs inspired by classic film music composers like Morricone and Barry.

In 1987, Adamson signed with Mute Records as a solo artist and released his first EP in 1988, *The Man With the Golden Arm*. In preparation for his debut album, Adamson returned to the streets of Manchester's worst neighborhoods. The result was the dark, moody autobiographical thriller *Moss Side Story*, issued in 1989. Nurturing his desire to compose scores similar to his cinematic influences, Adamson's first effort contained various themes from an essentially non-existent film. According to Adamson's website at Mute Records, "the album set a precedent for inventive forms and thinking through echoes of cinema past." Divided into three acts with each act containing four movements, *Moss Side Story* traveled through a range of musical styles from jazz to neo-classical to industrial, showcasing Adamson's diversity as a composer. While his debut failed to earn substantial commercial attention, *Moss Side Story* received critical recognition, and Adamson's experimental sound techniques influenced a younger generation of British trip-hop acts, especially Portishead and DJ Food.

After recording a four-song EP entitled *Taming of the Shrewd* (also released in 1989), which included the epic song "Diamonds" and illustrated Adamson's solid grasp of the jazz style, he received his first opportunity to write music for actual films. His first cinematic soundtrack was for Carl Colpaert's witty, neo-noir independent film *Delusion* in 1991. Here, Adamson put seriousness aside and revealed a playfulness usually lacking in his solo work. For the composer's work on *Delusion*, as noted by Doug Broad and Ira A. Robbins in the *Trouser Press Guide to '90s Rock*, "Adamson drenches the grooves with menacing organ, flamenco guitar and spaghetti western sass that perfectly evokes the film's double dealings." Next, Adamson shared scoring duties with Dinosaur Jr.'s J Mascis for the acclaimed Alison Anders film *Gas Food Lodging* in 1992. Along with Adamson's work, the soundtrack featured a diverse collection of instrumental and vocal pieces from various Mute recording artists.

Returning to solo aspirations and film scores of the imagination, Adamson released the album *Soul Murder* in 1992. Another eclectic blend of musical styles, the work contained hints of jazz, ska, electronica, and orchestral wanderings punctuated by samples (including one from the television prison documentary *Scared Straight*) and spoken-word narratives. One track, for instance, offered the Fall's Marcia Schofield telling the gruesome story "A Gentle Man of Colour," a tale of a young black man falsely accused of raping a white woman. Another highlight included Adamson's reinterpretation of the James Bond film series theme entitled "007, A Fantasy Bond Theme," on which the composer alternated between rock/ska and big band music. Adamson's next release, 1992's *Cinema Is King,* presented one track from each of his prior solo collections, minus his first EP, and film music.

The following year saw the release of the six-track, album-length *The Negro Inside Me,* a blend of hip-hop, French pop, jazz, and funk. It is considered one of Adamson's most accessible recordings. The ideas for the album resulted after Adamson traveled to Los Angeles to produce for the band Ethyl Meatplow. Again, Adamson took samples from innovative sources, such as from a message left on an answering machine from his publicist in "The Snowball Effect."

Desiring to learn more about the cinema, Adamson spent the next few years studying film in New York and recovering from reconstructive hip surgery. He returned in 1996 with the release of *Oedipus Schmoedipus,* which Adamson named "the third part in a personal trilogy," according to his website. With this album, Adamson revisited the darkness of *Moss Side Story* and enlisted appearances by Cave, Billy MacKenzie (former frontman of the Associates), and Jarvis Cocker (of the band Pulp). *Oedipus Schmoedipus* brought Adamson widespread acclaim for his vision, insight, and musical innovation. The release also caught the attention of renowned filmmaker David Lynch, who asked Adamson to contribute to the soundtrack of his forthcoming film, 1996's *Lost Highway.*

Adamson would later consider the *Lost Highway* soundtrack (produced by Nine Inch Nails' Trent Reznor) his most satisfying and appropriate cinematic project. He ended up penning four songs for the film. "It all made sense when Lynch and I started talking about *Lost Highway,*" Adamson proudly revealed to Myers. "I realized that I'd been connecting with a similar kind of scene in my own work, and Lynch noted that as well. We connected artistically with where he wanted to go with the film, so I was really pleased by that." And when asked how it felt to finally be viewed as a bona fide film scorer, Adamson replied, "It's a nice little story, you know. You get a push to do something and you think everything's against you. Then you decide, 'Well, what the hell—I'll do it anyway.' And some force outside of your awareness is assembling itself because you've taken the risk against the odds. There's a payoff there, and it gives me a nice warm feeling in my belly."

In 1998, Adamson released his sixth solo album, *As Above So Below,* which extensively featured his vocal ability for the first time. "I think [singing] was where I personally needed to go," he explained, as quoted by Myers. "I had laid enough ground, and it was to the point where I lost interest in the ambiguity of what I was trying to say. I think ambiguity is very powerful in asense of suspense, but to make suggestions with words, the palette was broadened." Aimed to broaden his fan base in the United States from a cult following as well, the album proved another critical favorite and provided noteworthy tracks such as the danceable "Can't Get Loose," the abstract "Jesus Wept," and the hip-hop tune "Still I Rise." Also that year, Adamson performed live with a full band for the first time in over ten years and found time to score the music for the BBC television drama series *City Central.*

In 1999, Adamson released a collection of previously released songs representative of his solo career entitled *The Murky World of Barry Adamson.* The album also included three new songs: "Walk the Last Mile," "Mitch and Andy," and "Saturn in the Summertime."

Selected discography

The Man With the Golden Arm, (EP), Mute, 1988.
Moss Side Story, Mute/Restless, 1989.
The Taming of the Shrewd, (EP), Mute, 1989.
Delusion, (soundtrack), Mute, 1991.
Cinema Is King, (EP), Mute 1992.
(With others) *Gas Food Lodging* (soundtrack), Mute, 1992.
Soul Murder, Mute, 1992.
The Negro Inside Me, Mute, 1993.
(With others) *Lost Highway* (soundtrack; produced by Trent Reznor), nothing, 1996.
Oedipus Schmoedipus, Mute, 1996.
As Above, So Below, Mute, 1998.
The Murky World of Barry Adamson, Mute, 1999.

Sources

Books

MusicHound Rock: The Essential Album Guide, Visible Ink Press, 1999.
Robbins, Ira A., editor, *The Trouser Press Guide to '90s Rock,* Fireside/Simon and Schuster, 1997.

Periodicals

Arizona Republic, July 23, 1998, p. 30.
Daily Telegraph, May 30, 1998; May 8, 1999, p. 12.
Independent, March 7, 1997, p. 14; May 29, 1998, p. 11.
Independent on Sunday, August 11, 1996, p. 16.
Magnet, November/December 1998, p. 25.

Online

Barry Adamson at Mute Records, http://www.mutelibtech.com/mute/adamson/adamson.htm (December 15, 1999).
Rolling Stone.com, http://www.rollingstone.tunes.com (December 15, 1999).

—*Laura Hightower*

Daevid Allen

Progressive rock musician, guitar

Daevid Allen, the impetus for the success of the classic "Flying Teapot," was never impressed with and was often daunted by stardom, though success with Soft Machine and Gong made celebrity something he had to confront. When Allen started out as a poet and musician in the 1950s in his native Melbourne, Australia, the scene was full of the energy that he needed. By 1958 when he discovered the legendary jazz artist Sun Ra, Allen's course was drawn. The inspiration of Sun Ra and the entire mood he brought into the jazz world with his Myth Science Arkestra eventually gave birth to Allen's pursuit with Gong.

According to an article in the *Los Angeles Times* in June of 1999, reporter Jon Matsumoto noted that "Gong's main support base was always in Europe. The band initially kicked up its heels in Paris in 1970. The brainchild of Australian beatnik and ex-Soft Machine vocalist-guitarist Daevid Allen, Gong was largely an experimental unit that mixed free-jazz improvisation with trippy psychedelic rock, folk and ambient electronic music." But for a group and its creator whose names were not well-known in the United States, Allen managed to survive both obscurity and stardom, still casting his spell with eccentric music for over 30 years.

Allen was born January 13, 1938, in Melbourne, Australia. He talked about his family and upbringing with Mitch Myers of *Magnet* in 1999. "I'm a third-generation Australian," he explained. "My great-great-grandfather was brought out from England because he had a reputable wood-cabinet business. He was a drunken maniac and would burn up all his money and then go out and make some more and burn it up again. The family never recovered, and our motto has been, 'Oh God! No money!' We're all very good at spending money, that's for sure." Though he seemingly came from an offbeat family, his father did try to steer him into a more normal way of life. When Allen was a teenager, his father placed him in a department store as a junior executive. It had a very particular effect on him, even if it was not the intended one. "All that did was show me that the whole commercial system is a complete illusion," he told Myers. "My survival kit has always been to stay away from any big-business organization. If I received all the money that I've earned according to my contracts over the years, I'd be a millionaire instead of having no house and only half a car. People say, 'Oh, you're afraid of money.' Wrong. I know exactly what I'm doing. Whenever fame comes too close, I vanish, sabotage, whatever. For this reason, I'm known in the business as a very bad bet, and this suits me fine."

Allen went to England in the early 1960s where he rented a room in Canterbury. The teenage son of the homeowners, Robert Wyatt, would team with Allen a few years later to form Soft Machine. Until then, Allen moved to London where he, Wyatt, and Hugh Hopper started the Daevid Allen Trio, concentrating on free jazz. Few were impressed with the music they created. Though they lost their gigs, they started gaining notoriety. When Allen moved on to Paris shortly afterward, he met some of the famed characters that comprised the Beat movement, and whom writer Jack Kerouac made known through his writings, including the book that was considered the gospel for the some baby boomers, *On the Road.* In addition to poet Allen Ginsburg, Peter Orlovsky and Brion Gysin—all a part of the Greenwich Village and San Franscisco underground literary movement—William Burroughs had been living in the Beat Hotel. When Burroughs met Allen, he told him he was looking for a jazz band to play during his dramatization of his book called *The Ticket That Exploded.* Burroughs hired Allen, and the performance happened. According to Allen, "We put on the show and there was the weirdest collection of people in the audience.... Terry Riley [considered one of the "founding fathers" of modern minimalism] came, and we ended up playing together outside in the street with motorscooter motors, electric guitar and poetry. It was wild," Allen told Myers.

In 1964, Allen met Gilli Smyth, his life partner for many years who eventually joined him in Gong as a vocalist. In 1966, after Allen experienced a mystical vision that

For the Record . . .

Born on January 13, 1938 in Melbourne, Australia.

Founder, vocalist, and guitarist of groups including Soft Machine (1966-67), Gong (1967-75, 1991-), Planet Gong (1977), New York Gong (1979-80), Gong Maison (1988-91), Magick Brothers (1992-), and the University of Errors (1999-); also recorded several solo albums including *Banana Moon*, 1971; *Now is The Happiest Time of Your Life*, 1977; *N'Existe Pas*, 1979; *Divided Alien Playbax*, 1981; *Alien in New York*, 1983; *Stop/ Don't* (with David Tolley), 1986; *Australia Aquaria*, 1990; *Dreaming a Dream*, 1996; and *Money Doesn't Make It* (as Daevid Allen's University of Errors), 1999; has published several books.

Addresses: *Record company*—InnerSpace Records, P.O. Box 411241, San Francisco, CA 94141-1241. *Website*—http://www.gong-gas/GAShome.html.

mapped out his life in detail—including his future musical pursuits— he formed Soft Machine with Wyatt, Kevin Ayers, and Mike Ratledge. Allen was part of the group for about a year, after which time Gong became his focus. When Gong was formed in 1969, the group lived communally while they made their music. Eventually they moved on to rural England, still living in the same arrangement. "Living communally was very important," Didier Malherbe, Gong saxophonist-flutist, told Matsumoto. "That creates ties on a composition level. It makes things very interesting, obviously. We don't live communally anymore. I live in Paris with my wife. But when we come back with Gong, those ties are still very vivid and lively, and it's a pleasure."

When Gong dissolved in 1980 after a slow dissipation of its momentum, the group still had not realized mainstream success. The breakup process had been gradual, and the group went out with little noise. Allen left for Majorca in 1976 and joined a local acoustic band, Euterpe, on an album called *Good Morning.* He followed with some solo albums, including *About Time*, capturing an influence of the newly-emerging punk movement in music. Smyth had left Gong and Allen in 1978 to form her own performance with "Mothergong," which she said represented the feminine side of Gong. In 1981 Allen made it home in time to see his father in Australia before he died. That same year he dropped out of professional music and drove a cab until 1989.

Though not actively creating music, Allen's fans followed him in a cult-like adulation that helped to prompt his return. By 1990, he went on to new projects using the Gong name recognition with Planet Gong and New York Gong. In 1992 the group came together for an official reunion and released *Shapeshifter*, the first studio album they had done in 14 years. In celebration of their 25th anniversary in 1995, they released an album recorded live at their London Forum concert. For Allen, Gong was as much a spiritual journey as a musical group. "Gong has this supernatural quality for me," he told Myers. "I've had this communication from somewhere else that's been giving me instructions. The instructions say that in the year 2032, there will be a bunch of people from the Planet Gong dimension appearing on [Earth's] physical plane. One thing about Gong is that there's a great deal of playfulness. Usually, with spiritual things, everyone is very solemn, but the whole point about Gong is that we maintain this aura of silliness to get rid of the people who are too serious. However, Planet Gong does exist and they run on the laws of music. Everything they do derives from notes, intervals, scales and octaves. It's very real for me because every day I meditate for hours, and during that period they connect with me and tell me what to do."

Gong original members, Allen, Smyth, Malherbe and bassist Mike Howlett have been joined by newcomers: Chris Taylor on drums and guitarist Mark Hewins. As with Allen and his University of Errors, the others have continued to pursue music outside of Gong, yet they have continued to tour together. Many changes throughout the years have been a part of the group's "karma," Malherbe explained. Allen has also been involved in other Gong incarnations including Gong Maison in the late 1980s and Magick Brothers in the early 1990s.

By 1999 Allen and rock archivist and musician Billy James, also known as "Art-Bee," became friends. Allen's work has been the inspiration for James on his own album, *Electronic Church Muzik.* Also in 1999, Allen continued to make news among his select fans in a small Berkeley, California, club known as Starry Plough. With his "University of Errors," a group of San Francisco Bay area musicians who also go by the name of "Mushroom," Allen continues to build on his past vision. His musical legacy has been described as "psychedelic" by those wound into his unique brand of exploration. The group's drummer Patrick O'Hearn told Myer that, "The thing about Daevid is that he brings out the best in his musicians, and he also lets us play whatever the hell we want."

Whatever else may happen with Gong, Allen remains clear about his own motivation. "For me, the most important thing is the spirit and the spark," he told Myer. "I'm trying to do something unusual, but the actual spirit of what's happening is consistent. From beginning to end, there's that silver line of Gong's spirit that I represent. It remains unchanging, but the clothes do change. I'm all for respecting the inner being rather than getting hung up on the clothes."

Like his master inspiration, Sun Ra, Allen has stayed open to his dream with little regard to what outside forces or audiences would try to do to influence him. His scope pierces deeper and deeper into the essence of a truth he has seen very clearly. He told Jason Rubin in a 1991 interview, as quoted in *Contemporary Musicians*, volume 24, explaining the Radio Gnome Invisible Trilogy, "There was the first level, which was the playful silliness and just having fun. But it is also the code both for a political manifesto and a spiritual teaching. But what is interesting is that while the story that we told originally appears to be just talking about little green men with pointed hats, every single thing in the Planet Gong mythology has a deeper meaning for those who want to peel away the layers and get to the chocolate center."

Selected discography

Albums

Banana Moon, BYG/Virgin, 1971.
Good Morning, (w/Euterpe), Virgin, 1976.
Now Is The Happiest Time of Your Life, Affinity/Charly, 1977.
N'existe Pas! Charly, 1979.
Divided Alien Playbax 80, Charly, 1981.
The Death of Rock and Other Entrances, (EP), Shanghai, 1982.
Alien in New York, Charly, (EP), 1983.
Stop/Don't (w/David Tolley) Shanghai, 1986; Demi-Monde, 1990.
The Australian Years, Voiceprint, 1990.
Stroking the Tail of the Bird (w/Harry Williamson, Gilli Smyth), AMP, 1990.
Australia Aquaria/She, Demi-Monde, 1990.
Seven Drones, Voiceprint, 1991.
Live at the Witchwood 1991 (w/the Magick Brothers) Voiceprint, 1992.
Who's Afraid? (w/Kramer) Shimmy Disc, 1992.
Twelve Selves, Voiceprint, 1993.
Je Ne Fum' Pas Des Bananes (w/ Banana Moon Band, Gong) KZL/Legend, 1993.
Voiceprint Radio Session, Voiceprint, 1994.
Daevid Allen Trio: Live 1963, Voiceprint, 1994.
Hit Men (w/Kramer), Shimmy Disc, 1995.
Dreaming a Dream, GAS, 1996.
Eat Me Baby, I'm a Jelly Bean, GAS, 1999.
22 Meanings (w/Harry Williamson), Gliss, 1999.
The Children's Crusade, (as Brainville) Shimmy Disc, 1999.
Money Doesn't Make It (as Daevid Allen's University of Errors), Innerspace, 1999.

Sources

Books

Allen, Daevid, *If Words Were Birds,* Outposts Publicaations, 1964.
Allen, Daevid, *Gong Dreaming part 1*, Gong Appreciation Society, 1995.
Allen, Daevid, *Gong Dreaming part 2,* Gong Appreciation Society, 1996.
Allen, Daevid, *A Pocket Introduction To The Planet Gong,* Byg, 1971.
Contemporary Musicians, Volume 24, Gale Research, 1998.
Cutler, Chris, *File Under Popular,* Autonomedia, 1994.
Joynson, Vernon, *Tapestry of Delights: The Comprehensive Guide to British Music of the Beat, R & B, Psychedelic, and Progressive Eras, 1963-1976,* Borderline Productions, 1996.
King, Michael, *Wrong Movements: A Robert Wyatt History,* S.A.F., 1994.
Miller, Bill, *Listening To The Future: The Time of Progressive Rock 1968-1978,* Open Court, 1998.
Smyth, Gillian, *The Nitrogen Dreams of A Wide Girl,* Outposts Publicaations, 1966.
Thompson, Dave, *Space Daze: The History and Mystery of Electronic Ambient Space Rock,* Cleopatra, 1996.
Woodstra, Chris, editor, *The All Music Guide to Rock,* Miller-Freeman, 1995.

Periodicals

Los Angeles Times, June 2, 1999.
Magnet, 1998.
New York Times, Sept. 4, 1998; Sept. 8, 1998.
Village Voice, New York, Sept. 22, 1998.

Online

"Daevid Allen," http://www.alpes-net.fr/~bigband/musicians/daevidallen.html (April 2000)."
"Daevid Allen" *NetBeat*, http://www.netbeat.com/artists/daevid_allen_467.html (April 2000).
"Daevid Allen," *Spaceboy Music*, http://www.spaceboymusic.com (April 2000)."
"Daevid Allen discography," *CDDB*, http://www.cddb.com (April 2000).

—Jane Spear

Fiona Apple

Singer, songwriter, piano

Photography by Ken Settle. Reproduced by permission. ©

Confident of her own creative abilities and sure of her originality as a female solo pop artist, singer-pianist Fiona Apple began her career young and powerfully. Her bluesy-pop sound of naked emotion was unique in a developing field of mid-nineties female artists. Continually compared to Tori Amos and Alanis Morrisette, Apple's wise-for-her-years maturity maintained her composure as an artist. She explained to an *Associated Press* journalist that "I realized over the years that you develop as a human being, you develop your personality, and people get to know you and you make your own name. I think that experience has prepared me for this, because otherwise I might be sitting here going, 'I'm not Alanis Morrisette's little sister.'" Apple smoothly launched into the vanguard of contemporary pop at age 19 with the release of her first album, *Tidal*. The sultry, soulful voice showcased on *Tidal* pushed the release to outstanding commercial success. Continuing her career, Apple moved through aggravations that accompany life, success of her music, complications of youth, and strove to live with honesty. She continued her career by accepting the aggravations that accompany life and striving to understand the success and complications of youth.

Apple grew up in New York, on Manhattan's Upper West Side, as the daughter of an artistic set of parents. Her father was an actor and her mother a multi-talented woman—singer, dancer, nutritionist, fitness trainer, and cook. She began playing piano at eight years old. As for singing, she explained in her recording label (Epic Records) biography that it seems as if she has always sung. She revealed, "I'd come home from school and hang up my keys on a key chain that was right beside my mirror. I would look in the mirror and realize I was singing. I sang all the time." Growing up to the sounds of jazz standards influenced Apple's style, as some connoisseurs recognized reflections of legends such as Nina Simone, Carole King, and Billie Holiday.

Concepts for songs were forged amidst tremendous conflict during Apple's early years at home. She began her expressive exercises by leaving household fights and writing letters about her feelings. She described her reactions in the *Fiona Online* biography, "I resorted to not participating in any fighting. I used to leave the room and write a letter that would make my point." In addition to being born into tumultuous family dynamics, Apple has admitted to sexual abuse as a pre-teen and found relief through pushing her traumatic defilement by talking about it. In an interview with Jane Stevenson of the *Toronto Sun* she said, "I remember hesitating and thinking this is probably going to ruin me ... I just didn't want to keep it a secret." Apple fell into turmoil

For the Record . . .

Born c. 1978 in New York, NY; daughter of an actor (father) and a multi-talented mother.

Started playing piano at eight years of age; released debut album, *Tidal,* Clean/Slate/Epic, 1996; at age 18; released *When The Pawn...,* Clean/Slate/Epic, 1999.

Awards: Triple platinum status for *Tidal*, 1996; MTV Video Music Award for Best New Artist In A Video for "Sleep to Dream," 1997; Grammy Award for Best Female Rock Vocal Performance, 1998; MTV VMA for Best Cinematography in "Criminal" video, 1998.

Addresses: *Record company*—Epic Records, 2100 Colorado Ave., Santa Monica, CA 90404, phone: (310) 449-2746, fax: (310) 449-2848. *Websites*—Epic Records: http://www.epicrecords.com; Fiona Apple Online: http://members.aol.com/FionaAO/wtpspecial/.

without an escape except her mind. Like many artists, she survived the amazing frustration and pain of her life situation by creating. Piano scores and emotional letters were the outlets which latter became her lifeline.

Apple moved from New York to Los Angeles when she was 16. She wanted to spend time with her father, finish her high school education, and make a demo. She planned to record lots of copies and distribute them widely. However, similar to many of the experiences which Apple had been thrust into over her short life, her entrance into the pop music scene was sudden, almost as if she had no choice in the matter. She traveled to New York to visit friends over the Christmas holidays. A three-song demo tape was given to a friend who was baby-sitting for a music industry executive. The friend passed the demo along to the exec, who then played it for a holiday party guest, producer and manager Andrew Slater. Slater contacted Apple soon thereafter and they worked together for more than four years.

Tidal, the debut album, was released in July of 1996 on Clean Slate/Work/Epic. Apple ignored reviews because she didn't want to gauge herself by anything she was hearing or reading. A statement from *Fiona Apple Online* explained her philosophy about art, "The way I feel about music—any song, any style—is that there is no right and wrong, only true and false. If the music and lyrics are conceived out of honesty and if the production of the song goes along with its original message, then what has been expressed is art regardless of what anyone's opinion is of it. So things are a lot simpler if you just tell the truth." Even though the album name was drawn from how life's experiences ebb and flow like the ocean tides, *Tidal* hit like a tsunami, blasting onto the pop scene. The popularity of "Shadowboxer'" received heavy videoplay on MTV and VH1 and landed *Tidal* on the Top 40 albums chart. "Sleep to Dream," and "Criminal," were the other primary components of the wave which hit the United States. The album went gold within six months and triple platinum within three years.

The instant success surprised the young singer. Despite playing the piano from her early years and writing songs about many of her personal experiences, Apple had yet to perform her expressions. Boldly taking the next step as a musician, she vowed in the *Fiona Apple Online* biography, "I'll be nervous, but what else can I do? I won't go backwards." She met that challenge by doing her first gig in Paris, appearing on Saturday Night Live guest spots, touring with Chris Isaak, exciting crowds as a headlining act on the 1997 Lilith Fair tour, and entertaining sold-out audiences with concert hall performances. Apple spoke to Alan Light of *Spin* magazine about her confidence on stage and her performance style. She expressed that she strived to be authentic while on stage: "I feel totally in control when I'm singing the songs. As soon as I'm not, I don't know how to act. But I would rather not be contrived, even if it makes me look better."

Apple's success soon placed her in yet more disturbing situations. After winning the 1997 MTV Video Music Award for Best New Artist In A Video for "Sleep to Dream," she turned infamous by blasting the music industry while accepting the award. After quoting Maya Angelou about how humans can create opportunities, she took her opportunity and decried, to everyone watching, "this world is bullshit," and that everybody knew that to be true. In an interview posted on *Fiona Apple Online*, she explained her anger displayed while accepting the award. She felt there was too much manipulation of Nineties' youth through fabricated music star images. She explained that people should think for themselves and not model their lives on what pop stars tell them is cool. "Go with yourself," she instructed. She went on to win other awards, including the 1998 Grammy Award for Best Female Rock Vocal Performance, and the 1998 MTV VMA for Best Cinematography in her "Criminal" video. However, making the video was another experience of violation for Apple. Saying that she regretted doing the video, she revealed her frustration, "what f***in' bullshit did I really win that night. I won ... because it was controversial. I won for being in my underwear on MTV. That made me so ashamed of myself." She said the videographers were telling how beautiful she looked during filming, but afterward, she just felt stupid.

Obviously, Apple was tired of the exploitation and humiliation that had repeatedly occurred in her life.

Angst-ridden Apple sought to further clarify her thoughts on her sophomore album which was released in late 1999. Responding in frustration to a November 1997 article about herself in *Spin* magazine, she wrote a poem which she began reciting onstage during the *Tidal* tour. Following her own advice to the youth of the day, Apple went with herself and chose the 90-word prose as the title of her 1999 release. The longest album title ever, *When the Pawn Hits the Conflicts He Thinks Like a King What he Knows Throws the Blows When He Goes to the Fight and He'll Win the Whole Thing 'Fore He Enters the Ring There's No Body to Batter When Your Mind Is Your Might So When You Go Solo, You Hold Your Own Hand and Remember That Depth Is the Greatest of Heights And if You Know Where You Stand, Then You Know Where to Land And if You fall It Won't Matter, 'Cuz You'll Know That You're Right*, was a collection of songs uncovering the angst about the selfish, greedy, self-serving, and voracious part of the world she has experienced. The sound of the second album was more upbeat and rocked a little harder than her debut. Rob Sheffield, from *Rolling Stone,* described Apple's music as a spiritual sister to Korn and Limp Bizkit. Apple found success in expressing that part of human experience which has been used, hurt, abused, pushed to anger, manipulated, and confused as evidenced by her second album hitting gold status in two months. Sheffield further wrote that she had a promising future: "[When the Pawn...] makes you hope that she'll find a way to use her talent as a connection to the world ... she's an artist who deserves a shot at growing up."

Selected discography

Tidal, Clean Slate/Work/Columbia, 1996.

When the Pawn Hits the Conflicts He Thinks Like a King What he Knows Throws the Blows When He Goes to the Fight and He'll Win the Whole Thing 'Fore He Enters the Ring There's No Body to Batter When Your Mind Is Your Might So When You Go Solo, You Hold Your Own Hand and Remember That Depth Is the Greatest of Heights And if You Know Where You Stand, Then You Know Where to Land And if You fall It Won't Matter, 'Cuz You'll Know That You're Right, Clean Slate/Epic, 1999.

Sources

Books

MusicHound Rock, The Essential Album Guide. Visible Ink Press, 1999.

Periodicals

Spin, December 1999, p. 82; January 2000, pp. 59-64.

Rolling Stone, November 25, 1999, pp. 97-98.

Online

"Fiona Apple Bio," *Epic Center,* http://www.epicrecords.com, (November, 1999).

"Fiona Apple," *Rolling Stone.com,* http://rollingstone.tunes.com, (December 21, 1999).

"Happily Ever After," *Fiona Apple Online*, http://members.aol.com/FionaAO/wtpspecial/, November, 1999; (December 16, 1999).

"Fiona Apple," *Jam! Showbiz,* http://www.canoe.ca/JamMusicArtistsA/apple_fiona.html, January, 1997; October 28, 1997; (December 18, 1999).

"Some Girls," *Miami News Times.com*, http://www.miaminewstimes.com, (December, 1997).

—*Nathan Sweet*

Hoyt Axton

Singer, songwriter, guitar

Photograph by Roger Ressmeyer. Corbis. Reproduced by permission. ©

Throughout his 30-year career as a musician and actor, the songs of entertainer Hoyt Axton left few, if any, untouched in some way. In addition to penning Three Dog Night's number one hit "Joy to the World," which became a modern folk-rock standard, Axton also wrote songs for recording artists such as Ringo Starr ("No No Song"), Steppenwolf ("The Pusher"), and the Kingston Trio ("Greenback Dollar"), among others. His film credits include *The Black Stallion* and *We're No Angels,* while his appearances on television included work in the 1960s for episodes of *Bonanza* as well as roles in the 1980s on *Murder She Wrote.* Known for his sense of humor, his large physical stature, and his generous nature, Axton felt most at home writing songs and performing his music on stage.

Born in Duncan, Oklahoma, on March 25, 1938, Hoyt Wayne Axton came by his talent and ambition naturally. His mother, Mae Boren Axton, also worked in the music industry and was widely known in Nashville, Tennessee, for mentoring struggling musicians and songwriters. Among those she helped secure recording and publishing deals included Willie Nelson, Dolly Parton, and Mel Tillis. A successful songwriter as well, Mae Axton penned several hit songs that were recorded by country stars such as Patsy Cline, Faron Young, Hank Snow, and Conway Twitty. Her biggest hit, "Heartbreak Hotel" (co-written with Thomas Durden), was Elvis Presley's first single for RCA Records and held the number one spot on the *Billboard* magazine charts for eight weeks. Although she originally intended to work as a journalist, graduating from the University of Oklahoma in that subject, she broke into the music business when comedienne Minnie Pearl started introducing Mae Axton, at the time a freelance writer, to friends as a songwriter. When her son's career took off, she occasionally joined him on stage to sing duets. Influenced by his mother's interests, Axton studied classical piano as a child and also learned to play guitar. However, Axton's father, John Thomas Axton, also played an important role in his son's development. A high school football coach, he encouraged Axton to participate in athletics. After graduating from high school, Axton attended Oklahoma State University on a football scholarship.

However, in 1958, Axton dropped out of college, realizing that singing and songwriting, rather than sports, were his true calling. After serving time with the United States Navy from 1958 until 1962, Axton concentrated solely on performing and began his musical career as a country-flavored folk singer in the Southern California coffeehouse/folk club circuit. After a memorial service held in Santa Ana, California, shortly after the songwriter's death, keyboard player David Jackson and guitarist David Brooks recalled watching Axton perform early on

For the Record . . .

Born Hoyt Wayne Axton on March 25, 1938, in Duncan, OK; died on October 26, 1999, at his home in the Bitterroot Valley near Victor, MT; son of John Thomas (a high school football coach) and Mae Boren Axton (songwriter); married Kathy Roberts, 1963 (divorced, 1973); married Donna, 1980 (divorced, 1991); married Deborah Hawkins, April 28, 1997; children: Mark Roberts, Michael Stephen Axton, April Laura (Axton) Ruggiero, Matthew Christopher. *Education*: Attended Oklahoma State University, 1957-58. Served in the U.S. Navy, 1958-62. Member of the Screen Actors Guild, American Federation of Television and Radio Artists, American Federation of Musicians, Country Music Association, Broadcast Music Inc., and the Oklahoma Cattlemen's Association.

Started performing on the Southern California coffeehouse/folk club circuit, early 1960s; Kingston Trio recorded Axton's "Greenback Dollar,"1962, which became a hit in 1963; Three Dog Night recorded the Axton original "Joy to the World (Jeremiah)," which became a number one hit, 1971; released hit song "Boney Fingers" with Linda Ronstadt, 1974; released *Road Songs*, 1977; performed as many as 300 shows per year during the 1970s and 1980s; made numerous film, television, and commercial appearances (for McDonald's, Pizza Hut, and Busch Beer) from the 1960s through the 1990s; chairperson, Jeremiah Records, 1975-late 1990s; spokesperson for American Heart Association, 1975, and Unicef, 1975-76; active in Democratic political campaigns of Eugene McCarthy, George McGovern, Edmund Brown, and David Borean; fundraiser for INTERPLAST, Free Clinics, Redwing Foundation, and Bread and Roses Foundation.

Awards: Bread and Roses Foundation Award, 1984.

in his career. "I first went to see him at a place called Mon Amie in Tustin," Jackson, who joined Axton's band as a teenager, told *Los Angeles Times* reporter Randy Lewis in 1999. "Man, after that I ran off and joined the Hoyt—not the circus. I joined the Hoyt, because he was the trapeze act and the elephant all in one." Brooks, who frequently opened for Axton's band in the 1960s, noted that the showman was always willing to share the spotlight. "Sometimes I think songwriters are a little too sensitive about not getting more press," Axton revealed in a 1982 interview with the *Los Angeles Times*. "When you consider there are about a million songs out there, it does nothing but make the inside of my brain shine when somebody records one of my songs."

The now-defunct Golden Bear nightclub in Huntington Beach, California, as well as the Troubadour in West Hollywood, were two of the key venues where Axton earned a reputation for his memorable tunes that often reflected his wry sense of humor. "At one point I think I did about 30 weekends straight [at the Golden Bear]," Axton told the *Los Angeles Times* in a 1982. "It was literally my home away from home." While honing his skills on stage, Axton made his first significant mark as a songwriter with the song "Greenback Dollar." In 1963, the single became a hit for the Kingston Trio and has since been recognized as a modern folk standard. Another Axton original, "The Pusher, " was recorded in 1964 by Steppenwolf for their debut album and became an instant hit; the song was also featured prominently in the acclaimed 1969 film *Easy Rider*. In 1967, Steppenwolf recorded another song written by Axton entitled "Snowblind Friend."

Axton recorded for several small labels beginning in 1961, including Horizon, Vee-Jay, and Exodus, but saw little chart action until the mid-1970s. In the meantime, as the 1960s came to an end, Axton started opening shows for the group Three Dog Night. They recorded two of Axton's songs, "Joy to the World (Jeremiah)" in 1971 and "Never Been to Spain" in 1972. "Joy to the World," originally written for a children's television program though never used, reached number one on the pop charts, where it stayed for six weeks, and sold more than one million copies in 1971. Likewise, "Never Been to Spain" climbed to the number five position the year of its release. Chuck Negron of Three Dog Night and a longtime friend of Axton recalled that the songwriter was never crazy about "Joy to the World" until a new arrangement led to its success. "Then he called and said, 'They're playing this song too damn much—I hope I never hear this song again,'" Negron told Richard Skanse of *Rolling Stone* in 1999. He went on to call the singer/songwriter "a wise man and a cool man. The guy seemed to have done everything. He was big as life, not just physically. Great stories, funny man."

Axton's own recording career flourished in the early 1970s. He recorded for Capitol, A & M, MCA, and later for his own label, Jeremiah. During these years, much of Axton's work focused on country-rock music. His greatest success as a recording artist occurred in 1974 with his top ten country hit "Boney Fingers," a duet performed with singer Linda Ronstadt. Two other top 20 hits followed: "Della and the Dealer" and "A Rusty Old Halo." Axton's most recognized full-length album, *Road Songs,* was released in 1977. Two years earlier, in 1975, Axton produced his first album, *Tales from the Ozone,* for Commander Cody and His Lost Planet Airmen. Still widely covered by some of the industry's biggest stars, Axton's songs were recorded by the likes of Ronstadt, John Denver, Waylon Jennings, Glen Campbell, Joan Baez, Ringo Starr, and others. In the early 1980s, Axton signed with the Elektra label, but his later songs and albums saw little chart success.

During the 1970s and 1980s, Axton continued to tour and record. An entertainer who would at times perform up to 300 shows a year, Axton thrived on touring and an active lifestyle. "I like everything about touring," he revealed to the *Los Angeles Times* in 1988. "I like the traveling, the cheeseburgers and the French fries, the starry nights and rolling out of town in the dark." In addition to music, Axton also enjoyed a side career as an actor, usually playing character roles such as the portly good ol' boy, for both television and in film. He made appearances in several made-for-television movies, miniseries, and episodic series, including the 1960s television series *Bonanza.* Axton's film credits included roles in *The Black Stallion* in 1979, *Gremlins* in 1984, and *We're No Angels* in 1989. After playing the role of Sheriff Henault in the 1989 film *Disorganized Crime,* Axton moved to Montana, where the movie was filmed. However, Axton rightfully admitted that music, not acting, brought him the most fulfillment. As he explained to the *Los Angeles Times,* "The freedom of songwriting and the spontaneity is wonderful.... There's a certain blending of melody and lyric, there's a harmony to it that just strikes a chord, and that's what I really like—that contact with heaven."

Axton died of heart failure on October 26, 1999, at the age of 61 at his home in the Bitterroot Valley near Victor, Montana. Two weeks prior to his death, he suffered a heart attack at his home and another while undergoing surgery. In addition, Axton had never fully recovered from a stroke he suffered in 1996, which left him confined to a wheel chair much of the time. His fourth wife Deborah Hawkins, aged 46 at the time of Axton's death, told *People* magazine that her husband was happiest making music and never gave up hope of walking again. Years of drug use and compulsive overeating had also taken a toll on Axton's health, and he eventually sought help through a drug rehabilitation program in 1991. Axton was survived by Hawkins and his five adult children. He divorced third wife Donna Axton in 1990, though they remained friends after the breakup. Donna Axton, the mother of four of Axton's children (he had one child out of wedlock), also played piano for Axton's touring band. Despite personal vices, Axton was beloved by all who knew him and was known for his generous nature, as well as for his girth and songwriting achievements.

Selected discography

Albums

Joy to the World, Capitol, 1971.
Less Than the Song, A & M, 1973.
Life Machine, A & M, 1974.
Southbound, A & M, 1975.
Fearless, A & M, 1976.
Road Songs, A & M, 1977.
A Rusty Old Halo, Jeremiah Records, 1979.
Spin of the Wheel, 1990.
Snowblind Friend, MCA, 1977; reissued, 1995.
Free Sallin', MCA, 1996.
Hoyt Axton, Youngheart Music, 1996.

As Songwriter

(With Ken Ramsey) "Greenback Dollar," recorded by the Kingston Trio, 1962.
"The Pusher," recorded by Steppenwolf, 1964.
"Snowblind Friend," recorded by Steppenwolf, 1967.
"Joy to the World (Jeremiah)," recorded by Three Dog Night, 1972.
"Never Been to Spain," recorded by Three Dog Night, 1972.
"Ease Your Pain," 1973.
"When the Morning Comes," recorded by Linda Ronstadt and Axton, 1974.
"Boney Fingers," recorded by Linda Ronstadt and Axton, 1974.
"Lion in the Winter," 1974.
"The No No Song," recorded by Ringo Starr, 1975.
"Flash of Fire," 1976.
"You're the Hangnail in My Life," 1977.

Sources

Books

Contemporary Theatre, Film, and Television, Volume 18, Gale Research, 1998.
Kingsbury, Paul, editor, *Encyclopedia of Country Music,* Oxford University Press, 1998.
MusicHound Rock: The Essential Album Guide, Visible Ink Press, 1999.

Periodicals

Atlanta Journal-Constitution, October 27, 1999.
Chicago Tribune, October 27, 1999.

Los Angeles Times, April 11, 1997; October 27, 1999; October 30, 1999; November 1, 1999; November 2, 1999; November 8, 1999.
New York Times, October 27, 1999.
People, November 15, 1999, p. 69.
Publishers Weekly, October 14, 1996.
Rolling Stone, December 9, 1999, p. 24.
Variety, November 1, 1999, p. 105.
Washington Post, April 11, 1997; October 27, 1999.

—Laura Hightower

Bad Religion

Punk rock band

Photograph by Freddie Patterson. Archive Photos. Reproduced by permission.

Combining the brief, rapid-fire sonic assault of 1980's Southern California hardcore punk, with highly intelligent lyrics which often addressed issues such as religion, politics, and ecology, Bad Religion forged songs that rang listeners' ears as well as their heads. The Southern California hardcore punk band, according to Seth Hindin of *Rolling Stone,* was "one of the most influential and commercially successful American punk groups of all time." Influenced by The Clash, the Buzzcocks, and Bad Brains, their two-pronged attack of a tight, blistering sound and sharp, compelling lyrics attracted a wide variety of fans. The group even awarded research grants for college students studying cultural and natural sciences in 1998 and 1999. Listeners from the United States and abroad, especially in Europe, helped keep Bad Religion going for more than twenty years. Perhaps the band's success at making their music exactly the way they wanted through a band member's label was key in promoting their career. Bad Religion maintained their powerful, raw performance with sophisticated content throughout their 20-year history.

Erupting out of the northern suburbs of Los Angeles, California, in 1979, the members of Bad Religion burned with frustrations similar to their colleagues Black Flag, the Descendants, Fugazi, the Circle Jerks, and Minor Threat. Greg Graffin, imported from Wisconsin, found several El Camino High School classmates that were also aggravated about their teenage culture. "Mr. Brett" Gurewitz, Jay Bentley, and Jay Ziskrout joined Gaffin to spew forth their righteous anger as they learned how to play their instruments. Bentley admitted that Kiss' *Alive! one,* and the Sex Pistols' *Never Mind The Bullocks,* were two of the albums that changed his life and lead him to join the Los Angeles punk rock scene. Bad Religion soon gained a small following and by 1981 put out a self-titled EP. The release was through their own label, Epitaph Records, which would play a vital role in their success. Thus began the story of the longest lasting band from the Southern California hardcore scene of the early 1980s.

Members developed their musical abilities over the year following their EP. Peter Finestone was added as a new drummer, they refined their timing as a group, hammered out melodies, tightened grooves, and even delved into piano. Hard work reaped rewards and the debut full-length album, *How Could Hell Be Any Worse,* was released in 1982. Produced by Jim Mankey, who would eventually work with Concrete Blonde, album sales shot to more than 10,000 units within a year. Hugh Hackett of *The Rough Guide to Rock,* stated, "*How Could Hell Be Any Worse,* can be considered the genesis of the American punk revival that culminated with the stellar success of the likes of Green Day and Offspring."

For the Record . . .

Members include **Brian Baker**, guitar; **Jay Bentley**, bass; **Peter Finestone**, drums; **Tim Gallegos**, bass; **Greg Graffin** (*Education*: UCLA, Cornell University), lead vocals; **Brett Gurewitz**, guitar, vocals; **Greg Hetson**, guitar, vocals; **Bobby Schayer**, drums; **Jay Ziskrout**, drums.

Formed in Los Angeles, CA, in 1979; Gurewitz started the prominent independent label, Epitaph; released *Into the Unknown*, 1983; *Back to the Known*, 1984; *Suffer*, 1988; *No Control*, 1989; *Against the Grain*, 1990; *80-85*, 1991; *Recipe for Hate*, 1993; *Stranger than Fiction*, 1994; *All Ages*, 1995; *The Gray Race*, 1996; Total, 1997; *NO Substance*, 1998; provided research grants for college students studying the natural sciences; band toured with the 1998 Vans Warped Tour.

Awards: *Maximum RockNRoll and Flipside* Album of the Year for *Suffer*, 1988.

Addresses: *Record company*—Epitaph Records, Epitaph Records, 2798 Sunset Blvd., Los Angeles, CA 90026, phone: (323) 413-7353, fax: (323) 413-9678, website: http://www.epitaph.com. *Website*—Bad Religion homepage: http://www.badreligion.com.

Perhaps inspired by new wave sounds, Bad Religion plugged in synthesizers and ventured into a new area with the release of 1983's *Into The Unknown.* The 1970s keyboard-pop collection of ballads turned the punk listeners away. A breakup ensued and the album became the major skeleton of Bad Religion's closet. Eventually, however, the disowned second album grew into a collector's item. Meanwhile, Graffin and Finestone used the down time by segueing into higher education. Bentley continued his musical efforts through Wasted Youth and TSOL.

Prepared for Take-Off

A little time away from Bad Religion provided members a new focus that the band needed to proceed. Upon Graffin's return to Los Angeles in 1984, the artistic energy began to take the familiar hardcore punk shape again. Because Gurewitz had to recover from debilitating substance abuse, Graffin was the only original member prepared to make music. He quickly gathered a handful of fellow punkers and lead the group into Bad Religion's next album, an EP entitled *Back to the Known.* The 1985 release was recorded by Graffin, the former Circle Jerks guitarist Greg Hetson, who had played with Bad Religion in the past, drummer Pete Finestone, and bassist Tim Gallegos. Punk rock was what Bad Religion knew, so that was what they recorded. Many previous Bad Religion fans forgave the band for *Into the Unknown* and savored the five-song EP of hardcore punk. It would be the last release for three years, while Graffin completed a Master's degree in geology from UCLA during the hiatus.

Bad Religion reassembled and began their run for lift-off in 1987 by performing reunion concerts throughout California. The crew included Graffin, Gurewitz, Bentley, Finestone, and Hetson. Flight was attained with their 1988 release *Suffer.* The *MaximumRockNRoll* and *Flipside* album of the year established Bad Religion as a significant member of the American hardcore punk community. Songwriting was shared by Graffin and Gurewitz this time and each wrote according to his own style. Graffin's style showcased the speed and sonic power of underground punk of the 1980s, the roots of American hardcore punk. Gurewitz wrote songs that were wrapped in a pop sound that glistened with rock overtones. This style laid some of the initial building blocks for the bridge connecting underground hardcore punk to mainstream "modern music" and pop-punk of the 1990s. *The Trouser Press guide to '90s rock* described the album as "ablaze with unusual hooks (sea chanteys seem to be a primary source for song shapes, which give the band an abiding folk-roots undercurrent), pointed riffs and pretentious pseudo-erudition." Warp speed attacks and alluring melodies tickled the ears of listeners and created a punk rock classic. Bad Religion was back and ready to soar.

According to a writer from *The Trouser Press guide to "0s rock,* Bad Religion continued quality hardcore with 1989's *No Control,* yet another Epitaph release. Dubbing it "perhaps one of the best hardcore albums ever" the offering highlighted vocal harmonies, the usual insightful lyrics, and machine-gun musical delivery. Bad Religion emerged as a leader in hardcore punk and an inspiration for many up-and-coming bands. Those groups inspired by Bad Religion would churn out pop-punk tunes across the world. Bad Religion spread their religion by "evangelizing" an international crowd. European listeners greatly appreciated Bad Religion's art and welcomed them with high regard during their tour.

Against the Grain was released in 1990. It was hard-hitting sonically and lyrically, addressing topics such as the anti-abortion movement with especially aggravated sound. Pete Finestone departed in 1991 to play with Fisherman and was replaced with another drummer,

Bobby Schayer. In the meantime Epitaph cranked out a compilation entitled *80-85,* pulling together unreleased material and songs from *Bad Religion, How Could Hell Be Any Worse?,* and *Back to the Known. Into the Unknown* was completely omitted. *Against the Grain,* and their following release in 1992, *Generator,* a darker expression, turned out to be considered disappointing to many. The group's reputation had been established, however, especially overseas. Two concerts in London, England, were sold out with no advertising. Fans in Germany considered Bad Religion a band of superstars.

Turbulent Air

Bad Religion continued their flight through turbulence. Graffin was working on his PhD in zoology at Cornell University in New York. Gurewitz was operating Epitaph in Los Angeles, where Bentley also worked. Despite the many extra-curricular commitments of Bad Religion members, another respected album was released in 1993, *Recipe for Hate.* Alternative rock was accepted by the mainstream by that time, so Bad Religion and Epitaph were in promising positions to ride the alternative rock wave and changes were inevitable. Eddie Vedder of Pearl Jam even joined the punk veterans for a duet on *Recipe for Hate.* Bad Religion's huge following along with the growing popularity of modern rock caught the attention of a major recording company, Atlantic Records. A deal with Atlantic re-issued the previous Epitaph release *Recipe for Hate.* Thus began the realignment of Bad Religion's flight.

The major label debut, *Stranger than Fiction,* from 1994, which included an outside co-producer, Andy Wallace, was the last Bad Religion album on which Gurewitz played. Epitaph was requiring more attention with the success of "Smash" from the Offspring and releases from the band Rancid. It had become one of the largest independent labels in the States. Gurewitz's full-time attention to Epitaph allowed the label to grow to enormous success. As stated by *Rolling Stone's* Seth Hindin, "originally Bad Religion's vanity imprint, [Epitaph] has grown into perhaps the largest, best-known punk label in the world." The label included acts such as Offspring, Rancid, NOFX, and Pennywise.

Brian Baker of Minor Threat, Dag Nasty, and Junkyard filled the open rhythm guitar position for the *Stranger than Fiction* tour and stayed with the band for their successive releases. One band member claimed the *Stranger than Fiction* tour was, "the most pleasant experience of the last three years." Ironically, the album outsold previous releases, perhaps due to the popularity of aggressive rock and the greater marketing capacity of Atlantic Records. Epitaph released *All Ages* in 1995, which was a compilation of songs from the four albums released between 1988 and 1992. Only two tracks were pre-1985.

Cruising at Speed

The Gray Race appeared in 1996, along with other offerings from Bad Religion relatives. De-popped *Gray Race* tunes were written by Graffin and co-produced by Ric Ocasek of the Cars. Not even Baker's guitar playing could prevent critics' comments that the release mainly consisted of filler material. Perhaps major label recording demands stifled creativity. Graffin, meanwhile, found an outlet for his other musical tastes. He offered a solo album, *American Lesion,* in late 1996. Its sound stepped away from the rapid-fire sonic attacks of Bad Religion and ventured through several slow piano ballads. Gurewitz also did some work in the studio. The Daredevils was a studio group that released a CD single of "Hate You" and "Rules, Hearts". Critics recognized a familiar sound from the Daredevils even though some ill-feelings toward Bad Religion emerged from the project.

A live album, *Total,* was released in 1997. It was a collection of live performances and contained many hits from Bad Religion. *NO Substance* was released in 1998 and accurately portrayed the dynamic intensity and powerful drive of Bad Religion's live performance. After recording much of the album in Graffin's house in upstate New York, the group tested it at several small club shows in New York City.

Bad Religion's powerful sonics and Graffin's insightful writing on how he sees American society as a community of robots lacking substance proved appealing. Bad Religion later headlined the 1998 Vans Warped Tour. In late 1999, Graffin was a speaker on the politically and socially charged Spitfire Tour. The band continued after *No Substance* by signing Todd Rungren as producer for their next album. As for the remaining band members, Brian Baker released a solo album entitled *Troublizing.* In addition, he joined other punkers in Lickety Split to record and perform. Hetson co-founded an independent label, Porterhouse Records, which released efforts by Speed Buggy and Rosemary's Billy Goat.

Selected discography

Bad Religion, Epitaph, 1981.
How Could Hell be Any Worse?, Epitaph, 1982.
Into the Unknown, Epitaph, 1983.
Back to the Known, Epitaph, 1984.
Suffer, Epitaph, 1988.

No Control, Epitaph, 1989.
Against the Grain, Epitaph, 1990.
80-85, Epitaph, 1991.
Generator, Epitaph, 1992.
Recipe for Hate, Epitaph, Epitaph/Atlantic, 1993.
Stranger than Fiction, Atlantic, 1994.
All Ages, Epitaph, 1995.
The Gray Race, Atlantic, 1996.
No Substance, Atlantic, 1998.

Sources

Books

*MusicHound Rock: The Essential Album Guide,*Visible Ink Press, 1999.

Robbins, Ira A., editor, *The Trouser Press Guide to '90s Rock,* Fireside/Simon and Schuster, 1997.

Online

"BadReligion," *RollingStone.com,* http://rollingstone.tunes.com, (December 27, 1999).

"Bad Religion," *The Rough Guide to Rock,* http://www-2.roughguides.com, (January 4, 2000).

"Bad Religion,"*Allmusic Zine,* http://allmusic.com/zine/, (January 18, 2000).

Bad Religion home page, http://badreligion.com/, (January 4, 2000).

"Bad Religion," *Atlantic Records,* http://www.atlantic-records.com/, (January 7, 2000).

"Bad Religion Sponsors Scholarship, Demo Competition," *Billboard,* http://billboard.com/, (January 4, 2000).

"Todd Rungren to Produce Next Big Bad Religion Record," MTV.com, http://www.mtv.com/, (January 4, 2000).

—Nathan Sweet

Bardo Pond

Art rock band

Bardo Pond can literally be considered an "art rock" band, given the fact that the members of this Philadelphia, Pennsylvania-based group all graduated from art school and continued to work odd jobs at museums and galleries as their musical career escalated. Bass player Clint Takeda and brothers Michael and John Gibbons, who both play guitar (the latter plays occasional saxophone as well), dedicated time at institutions such as the University of Pennsylvania's Institute of Contemporary Art, the Moore College of Art and Design, and Goldie Paley Gallery; Takeda, a painter and sculptor who regularly showed work at Philadelphia art galleries, created the illustration for the band's 1996 album, *Amanita.* Vocalist, flutist, and violinist Isobel Sollenberger worked as a finisher for a local furniture company, while drummer Joe Culver took a break from touring from 1998 until 1999 when his doctorate work and research duties precluded a regular performance schedule. Drummer Ed Farnsworth stepped up in Culver's absence for live shows. Although inspired by several classic and contemporary artists, including Dutch painter Vincent Van Gogh, sculptor and Sonic Youth cohort Mike Kelly, psychedelic painter Sigmar Pole, and the late Fluxus member Joseph Boyce, Bardo Pond found the music world more accepting than the art community. "The art world is smaller than the music world—it's very intense, and critics get all over everything you do," Michael Gibbons told Teresa Gubbins of the *Dallas Morning News* in June of 1998. "Music criticism isn't quite as vicious, maybe because of the nature of music. It's more open-ended."

Despite earning a reputation for constructing rock songs rather than for creating paintings and sculptures, Bardo Pond nonetheless maintained a connection to the art world. "Our friends are more artists than musicians," guitarists Michael Gibbons acknowledged to Teresa Gubbins in a September 1996 profile for the *Dallas Morning News.* Gibbons, along with brother John, turned to music when they realized that pursuing a career in art seemed just as much about the hustle as about creativity. "I was so burned out, and I loved music," Michael Gibbons acknowledged. "We started playing noise—just making sounds. We didn't know how to play, but it didn't matter. We didn't want to know—we were almost dogmatic about not knowing how to play our instruments." However, they relented after jamming with some skilled musicians. "This one guy, [Dave] Nolski, was a great guitar player, not flashy, but good—he had a soulful sound," recalled Michael Gibbons. "'You should learn how to play,' he said, and he showed me some things. We always thank him on our records." For both brothers, the transition from art to music felt natural. "Everything I learned from painting is in our music," said Michael Gibbons. "It's more about the process. The art I was interested in was about the process of making a painting. And our sound is more about how it's made. It's more about the sound than a song—but the song is there."

Music on the Margins of Rock

Since forming in Philadelphia in 1992, Bardo Pond—the name taken from the Tibetan Book of the Dead—have released more than a dozen singles and full-length albums, composed of mostly drawn-out, undulating tracks that hold the listener's attention with ravishing flute melodies and crashing guitars and drums. Critics described their sound as wispy and experimental, much like Sonic Youth and My Bloody Valentine, but with the added metal influence of Black Sabbath. "It is this wide crevasse between the ethereally light and the heavily distorted muck that this band thrives," wrote Brendan Doherty in *Weekly Wire,* available through the band's unofficial website. "Lilting over the murk of bashed bass and smashing drums is Isobel Sollenberger's voice, a siren amongst a swirling gale force of guitar storms. Plenty of guitar-based bands have tried the heavily group-oriented song improvisations, only to end their super-ego super-distorted post-hippie rock

For the Record . . .

Members include **Joe Culver**, drums; **Ed Farnsworth**, drums; brothers **John Gibbons**, guitar, and **Michael Gibbons**, guitar; **Isobel Sollenberger**, vocals, flute, violin; **Clint Takeda**, bass.

Formed band in Philadelphia, PA, 1992; released debut album, *Bufo Alvarius, Amen 29:15,* 1995; released *Amanita,* 1996; performed at Terrastock music festival, 1997 (in Providence, RI) and 1998 (in San Francisco, CA); released *Lapsed,* 1997; released *Set and Setting,* 1999.

Addresses: *Home*—Bardo Pond, 1801 N. Howard St., Philadelphia, PA 19122. *Record company* —Matador Records, 625 Broadway, 12th Fl., New York City, NY 10012, phone (212) 995-5882, fax (212) 995-5883. *Website*—Bardo Pond at Matador Records: http://www.matador.recs.com. The Unofficial Bardo Pond Homepage: http://www.mindspring.com/~threelobed/bardo/bardo.htm.

love-ins for something more glam. Not this band. This is where rock is interesting—on its margins."

Armed with their passionate outlook on making music and a blend of vintage hard rock and psychedelic bliss, Bardo Pond quickly made a name for themselves around their hometown. They regularly opened at a popular Philadelphia punk-rock club, Khyber Pass, long before they earned critical acclaim and gained a huge cult following in the United States and Europe. "We've opened for the Grifters, Guided By Voices—we were immediately getting high-profile gigs when nobody knew who we were," said Gibbons, as quoted by Gubbins. "Or else everybody thought we were nuts."

Throughout their time together as a band, Bardo Pond have remained committed to a united goal that Takeda described as "a backward approach" to making music, as quoted by Fred Mills of *Magnet* magazine, and have preferred not to strive for commercial success or celebrity status. "In a sense, we're purely driven by the making of sounds," he said, "of getting into this neighborhood of the music we'd all been listening to that really got us off. Instead of approaching it in terms of what's gonna sell, what's gonna get played on the radio, we think if we do the best we can artistically, then that might lend itself to people—maybe that group of people isn't huge—who want to hear us."

Mix of Sounds on Debut Release

The band's first album, *Bufo Alvarius, Amen 29:15,* was released on the independent label Drunken Fish in 1995. Known for endorsing the use of illicit substances, as well as for displaying an unpretentious, easygoing nature, Bardo Pond borrowed the album's title from the Latin name of the hallucinogen-secreting Colorado River toad. One of the tracks, "Amen 29:15," clocks in at close to 30 minutes long, as the title implies. However, Sollenberger provided a buffer to the lengthy onslaught of hard-rock aggression and psychedelic references with her flowing vocals and skillful flute. Her vocals, asserted David Sprague in the *Trouser Press Guide to '90s Rock,* "bear a passing resemblance to those of renaissance art-rock songbird Annie Haslam," while Sollenberger's flute playing "is so striking that it just about absolves the flute for the sins of Ian Anderson." 1995 also saw the release of the group's second effort, the EP *Big Laughing Jym,* a seven-song collection of album outtakes and home-studio work which showcased the Gibbons' guitar rumblings, especially in "Dispersion" and "Clearhead."

In 1996, Bardo Pond returned with a double album that spanned more than 70 minutes, entitled *Amanita,* produced and engineered by Jason Cox and named after an obscure hallucinogenic mushroom. With the album, the group illustrated their increasing dimensionality. Psychedelic rock tracks included "Sentence," "Tantric Porno," and "Be A Fish," while references to the blues resonated through "Wank," "Yellow Turban," and "Rumination." Although the songs were more concise than those on the band's debut release, "Limerick," "The High Frequency," and "RM" gave way to *Bufo Alvarius, Amen 29:15*' s spaciousness and improvised quality.

Bardo Pond's next album, 1997's *Lapsed,* also produced by Cox, saw additional influences creeping into the band's overall sound and featured more focused, less sprawling songs. According to Michael Gibbons, Japanese bands such as Mainliner and High Rise, as well as avant-garde jazz artists like Alice Coltrane and Archie Schepp, provided substantial inspiration in the recording of *Lapsed.* "Those bands just sort of crept into what we were doing," he told Sara Sherr in an interview for the band's unofficial website, explaining the gentleness of tracks like "Pick My Brain" and "Aldrin." Another highlight included the song "Tommy Gun Angel," which begins with intensity instead of building up to a climax. "We were just really interested in pure, distorted sound, with Isobel's voice on top of it, or in it," recalled Gibbons in an interview with *Addicted To Noise* writer Chris Nelson, available through the band's unofficial website. "A lot of our songs peak, but this one cuts to the chase. I was interested in starting a song at that point. Let's get that dense sound of us peaking on a jam and start with that, then mix it with less of an improv thing so that it's a tight all around sound."

Two years later in 1999, Bardo Pond released *Set and Setting,* marking yet another stage in the band's development. The band worked on the entirely self-produced album (the title taken from a line in Timothy Leary's classic *The Psychedelic Experience*) for more than a year at their home studio in Philadelphia. After recording numerous improvisational jam sessions, they sifted through the resulting collage to pick the most pertinent moments to include on *Set and Setting.* "One thing is that we were interested in making a 40- to 45-minute statement this time," Michael Gibbons recalled to Mills, revealing the group's initial plan for the record. "We did *Amanita,* which is a double album, and shit, we've got enough to put out three albums. But when it's shorter, you tend to get all the differences and you're thinking about [what you've heard] more. If it's longer, you tend to forget about the first things on it."

Hash Jar Tempo

In addition to recording music as Bardo Pond, the band has also released two albums with guitarist Roy Montgomery (of the band New Zealand) as Hash Jar Tempo. Bardo Pond's collaboration with Montgomery began in 1994 when Drunken Fish owner Darren Mock urged Montgomery to attend a Bardo Pond show at the Cooler in New York City. "I think they have a delicacy and subtlety that isn't contrived, and (they) trust in their intuitions," Montgomery told Mills. Recalling the first time he saw Bardo Pond on stage, Montgomery further noted, "It was great to see and hear something as 'resinous' as they, going against the grain of tempo and speed as was the norm at the time." Montgomery and Bardo Pond's efforts as Hash Jar Tempo, *Well Oiled* and *Under the Glass,* were issued in 1996 and 1999 respectively by Drunken Fish.

In 1997, Bardo Pond participated for the first time in Terrastock, a spring music festival sponsored by the psychedelic music magazine *Terrastock.* That year, the concert was held in Providence, Rhode Island, and Bardo Pond returned in 1998 for the festival in San Francisco, California. "That whole scene is so important, and the vibe is so warm," Gibbons informed Gubbins. "Ghost played, Damon and Naomi, Alistair Galbraith from New Zealand, Nick Saloman (the Bevis Frond), the Deviants, Cul De Sac, Roy Montgomery, who did a set and did a song with us. It was like three days of being in a dream. When it was happening I realized: We're in the right place at the right time. It's a rush every time I think about it."

Although critics noted Bardo Pond's musical progression over the course of their albums, the band members themselves insisted that they have not changed much since 1992. "I swear, it seems like we're the same as we were back then," Michael Gibbons told Mills. "I mean, there have been things we've done, touring the country a couple of times, meeting so many cool people and being part of that world. Just the fact that we've been able to keep going." Sollenberger further added, "To be able to record music, that's the most gratifying process. I want to keep doing it for the rest of my life."

Selected discography

Albums

Big Laughing Jym, Compulsiv, 1995.
Bufo Alvarius, Amen 25:15, Drunken Fish, 1995.
Amanita, Drunken Fish/Matador, 1996.
Tests for New Swords,(EP), Siltbreeze, 1996.
Well Oiled, (as Hash Jar Tempo), Drunken Fish, 1996.
Lapsed, Matador, 1997.
Set and Setting, Matador, 1999.
Under the Glass, (as Hash Jar Tempo), Drunken Fish, 1999.

Sources

Books

Robbins, Ira A., editor, *Trouser Press Guide to '90s Rock,* Fireside/Simon and Schuster, 1997.

Periodicals

Dallas Morning News, September 13, 1996, p. 40; June 12, 1998, p. 63.
Gannett News Service, November 19, 1999.
Magnet, October/November 1999, pp. 45-49.

Online

Bardo Pond at Matador Records, http://www.matador.recs.com (December 22, 1999).
The Unofficial Bardo Pond Homepage, http://www.mindspring.com/~threelobed/bardo/bardo.htm (December 22, 1999).

—*Laura Hightower*

Beat Happening

Pop band

One of the most influential and respected bands to come from the underground music scene, Beat Happening and its concoction of minimalist, low-end production pop music emerged in the capitol town of Olympia, Washington, in the 1980s, during the same time the grunge rock movement was taking hold in nearby Seattle. At the center of the former phenomenon, which demonstrated that punk music's rebel spirit could defy rock's conventions as well as society's ideals, stood Calvin Johnson, his band, and a label he founded called K Records. Adopting a musical attitude with little interest in traditional standards of vocalization or instrumentation, Johnson helped to create a new punk/ indie rock community that would become the lo-fi pop sound in America. Groups such as Teenage Fanclub, Nirvana, Sonic Youth, and Fugazi all claimed to have been influenced by the musical attitudes of Beat Happening.

Johnson, a native of Olympia, resided for a total of six of his first 17 years in the small community located just outside of Seattle. He lived in a variety of other places during his early years as well, including suburban Washington, D.C., where he graduated from high school. At the time of his graduation, his sister, and brother Streator Johnson, who studied at the University of Washington, encouraged their brother to move back to the Northwest. Desiring to study at a smaller, less bureaucratic school, Johnson chose to enroll at Evergreen State College, located in his former hometown of Olympia. A school of approximately 3,000 students nestled in the woods, Evergreen State was not a typical American university. Here, professors did not award grades to students, and the curriculum did not consist of specific majors, although students needed to take a few required courses in order to graduate with either a bachelor of arts or bachelor of science degree. Not one to follow established ideas, Johnson seemed suited for such as environment.

Prior to forming a band, Johnson, who grew up admiring the Doors, the Stooges, and the Velvet Underground, had long since held an interest in music. In 1977, for example, he started donating time to a Seattle-based fan magazine called *Sub Pop,* the same organization that became an influential designer record label in the 1990s. By the time the 1980s got underway, Johnson was booking local shows and also started his own record label, K Records. The idea for creating his own label arose out of what he believed was a necessity: to issue records by lesser-known bands that no other company would have otherwise released. At the same time, Johnson worked at KAOS-FM, the Evergreen State College radio station. Because the station mandated the deejays to play independent music, Johnson's interest in starting his own label seemed possible. "I just started putting out stuff by my friends," he told Patti Schmidt for a Canadian Broadcasting Company (CBC) radio profile in 1995, "which is exactly what I still do...."

From Cool Rays to Beat Happening

In 1981, Johnson formed his first band, the Cool Rays. While the band only lasted a short time, one of their tracks was included in an early Sub Pop compilation album. After the demise of the Cool Rays, an early form of what would become Beat Happening started to take shape in 1983. The new group started playing at record stores, birthday parties and social events, and any small venue that would let them perform, so long as the club welcomed audiences of all ages, a stipulation that Beat Happening insisted upon. In the beginning, Johnson played guitar and sang baritone vocals, Heather Lewis (a fellow Evergreen State student whom Johnson had met through his roommate at the time) added female vocals and played drums, and various other musicians filled in on third guitar until they met Bret Lunsford.

Although Lunsford later attended Evergreen State, the guitarist, uncertain about his future, decided not to enroll in college straight out of high school. Instead, in 1983 he was living in Tucson, Arizona, collecting unemployment and spending most of his time going to watch bands. Although he wasn't living in a major city, Lunsford recalled that a number of well-known acts, including

For the Record . . .

Members include **Calvin Johnson** (born in Olympia, WA), guitar and baritone vocals; **Heather Lewis**, drums and vocals; **Bret Lunsford**, guitar. *Education:* All attended Evergreen State College in Olympia, WA.

Johnson founded K Records, early-1980s; formed Beat Happening in Olympia, WA, 1983; released debut album, *Beat Happening,* 1985; released *Jamboree,* 1988; Johnson and K Records hosted the International Pop Underground Convention, 1991; released last album, *You Turn Me On,* 1992; Johnson founded Dub Narcotic studios, 1994.

Addresses: *Record company*—K Records, P.O. Box 7154, Olympia, WA 98507, phone: (360) 786-1594, fax: (360) 786-5024, email: promo@kpunk.com; Sub Pop, 1932 1st Ave., Ste. 1103, Seattle, WA 98101, phone: (206) 441-8441, fax: (206) 441-8245, email: hello@subpop.com. *Websites*—Beat Happening at K Records: http://www.kpunk.com, Beat Happening at Sub Pop: http://www.subpop.com.

Hüsker Dü and Minor Threat (one of the best live bands he had ever seen up to that point) played in Tucson on their way to and from Los Angeles. In the fall of 1983, Lunsford returned to Washington state to visit friends. One night, while at the Smithfield Café in Olympia, Lunsford saw a band that struck a chord with him called Beat Happening. Watching the trio together on stage, "I just knew something was brewing," Lunsford said to Schmidt. Soon thereafter, Johnson and Lewis asked the guitarist to join the group on a permanent basis.

In early 1984, Johnson's K label issued the band's first recording, a self-titled, five-song tape EP of juvenile ramblings and sex tales. Later that year, the trio recorded another tape, the five-song EP *Three Tea Breakfast,* while visiting a friend who was an exchange student in Japan. During his stay in Japan, Johnson picked up an early tape by Shonen Knife (*Burning Farm,* released in Japan on the Zero label in 1983), which he brought back to the United States. Shonen Knife, an all-female, American-styled pop-punk Japanese group, would become a favorite of such underground heroes such as Nirvana, Fugazi, and Sonic Youth after Johnson released the tape in 1985 on K Records.

Debuted with *Beat Happening*

That same year, Beat Happening made their monumental, full-length album debut. The self-titled release, produced by Greg Sage of the Wipers, included one-take pop songs such as "I Spy," "Down at the Sea" and the Cramps-inspired "Bad Seeds." Although amateurish in terms of production quality, *Beat Happening* nonetheless charmed critics with its ingenuity and invention. In 1988, following the release in Great Britain of the EP *Crashing Through* and a 12-inch split with the Screaming Trees (one of the most influential and underrated bands to spring from the Northwest), Beat Happening released their second album, *Jamboree.* This time boasting the production team of Mark Lanegan and Lee Conner, both members of the Screaming Trees, and Steve Fisk of Pell Mell, Beat Happening and their latest album left critics at a loss for an appropriate description of their sound. The music press made some obvious references to acts like the Velvet Underground, the Cramps, Jonathan Richman, the Pastels and the Vaselines (two Scottish bands), and the Australian group the Cannanes, and labeled Beat Happening's music with phrases such as "proto-punk," "minimalist rock," "love-rock" "sub-folk," "basement trash," and others. Overall, most writers seemed confused by the group's brand of stripped-down pop,which included a lot of rudimentary, yet clever, boy-girl songs told through the escapist language of a child. "People expect certain things that we haven't always given them," Johnson told Schmidt, acknowledging the band's reductionist tendencies. "We don't have a bass player. A lot of people were offended by that. I don't know why, it's really weird."

Beat Happening returned in 1989 with their third album, *Black Candy,* which failed to earn the same recognition as their previous collection. With the exception of two standout songs, "Black Candy" and "Cast a Shadow," the release was described with words such as "disappointing" and "more careless than casual," as Ira A. Robbins concluded in the *Trouser Press Guide to '90s Rock.* Nevertheless, such a setback didn't deter Beat Happening's growing fanbase, a following they established not through publicity, but by extensive touring. The group's next album, 1991's *Dreamy,* which featured roughly three chords and tin can beats, endeared Beat Happening to the college radio crowd. A substantial improvement over *Black Candy, Dreamy* included several notable songs: the ominous "Me Untamed," the Shonen-Knife sounding "Hot Chocolate Boy," and the 1960s-like "Cry for a Shadow."

Earned Indie Credentials

By the late 1980s, Beat Happening had earned indie credentials—bands as diverse as Sonic Youth, Fugazi, Teenage Fanclub, and Nirvana were claiming the group as an important influence on their own music. In 1991, Johnson and his staff at K Records hosted a gathering in Olympia called the International Pop Underground Convention. During the alternative music festival, Johnson and K featured more than 50 bands whose only ties were a mutual lack of support by major labels, referred to as "the corporate ogre," on Beat Happening's website at Sub Pop Records. Among the bands in attendance included L7, Fugazi, the Melvins, Scrawl, Thee Headcoats, the Pastels, Jad Fair, Bikini Kill, the Fastbacks, Seaweed, Mecca Normal, and Nation of Ulysses.

Also in 1991, Beat Happening recorded their last full-length album together entitled *You Turn Me On.* Released in 1992, the record departed somewhat from Beat Happening's usual style. Produced with more clarity, yet not to excess, by Fisk and Stuart Moxham (from the 1970s new-wave minimalists the Young Marble Giants), *You Turn Me On* revealed longer, seemingly more thought out songs and arrangements. Aside from the album's title track, critics applauded the effort, calling attention to numbers such as "Pinebox Derby," "Bury the Hammer," "Tiger Trap," and "Sleepyhead." However, with *You Turn Me On* the strategy remained the same since the group's inception; Beat Happening always refused to embellish their songs and forbid the use of over dubs. According to Johnson, growing larger in popularity, as well as in song complexity, never fit into Beat Happening's agenda. "It's not that we don't want to get better, it's just not the main focus," he explained to Schmidt. "The main focus is to write cool songs and play shows that are fun. I don't need to be a guitar virtuoso. Playing a really hot guitar solo has nothing to do with what we're doing."

Although Beat Happening never officially broke-up, insisting that they would one day record together again, the band concentrated on other projects after releasing *You Turn Me On.* Lewis went on to record tracks with the Land of the Loops' album *Bundle of Joy,* released on theSeattle-based Up label, while Lunsford joined the group D+ and formed the Know-Yr-Own label, which he ran from his home in Anacortes, Washington. Meanwhile, Johnson continued with his work at K and in 1994 founded his Dub Narcotic studios, a sort of lo-fi community center located in the basement of his home in Olympia. One of the first projects recorded at the studio was the Halo Benders' debut album *God Don't Make No Junk.* Johnson formed the group with Built to Spill's Doug Martsch and Fisk. The trio released two other LPs: *Don't Tell Me Now* and *The Rebel's Not In,* released on K in 1996 and 1998 respectively. In addition to playing with the Halo Benders, Johnson also released work with a rotating cast of musicians from his studio under the name Dub Narcotic Sound System. In addition to releasing a handful of EPs, Dub Narcotic Sound System released two albums, 1995's *Rhythm Record Vol. One: Echoes From the Scene Control Room* and 1996's *Boot Party.*

Selected discography

Beat Happening

Beat Happening, (EP), K, 1984.
Three Tea Breakfast, (EP), K, 1984.
Beat Happening, K, 1985; reissued, 1996.
Beat Happening/Screaming Trees, (EP), K/Homestead, 1988.
Crashing Through, (EP), (U.K.) 53rd & 3rd, 1988.
Black Candy, K, 1989; reissued, K/Sub Pop, 1992.
1983-85, K/Feel Good All Over, 1990.
Dreamy, Sub Pop, 1991.
You Turn Me On, K/Sub Pop, 1992.

Dub Narcotic Sound System

Hands on the Dial, Punk in My Vitamins?, 1994.
Industrial Breakdown, (EP), Soul Static Sound/K, 1995.
Rhythm Record Vol. One: Echoes From the Scene Control Room, K, 1995.
Ridin' Shotgun, (EP), 1995.
Boot Party, K, 1996.
Ship to Shore, (EP), 1996.

Halo Benders

God Don't Make No Junk, K, 1994
Don't Tell Me Now, K, 1996.

Sources

MusicHound Rock: The Essential Album Guide, Visible Ink Press, 1999.
Robbins, Ira A., *Trouser Press Guide to '90s Rock,* Fireside/Simon and Schuster, 1997.

Periodicals

Los Angeles Times, April 10, 1998.
Washington Post, August 28, 1998.

Online

Beat Happening Profile, http://www,geocities.com/Paris/1618/bh.html (February 6, 2000).

K Records, http://www.kpunk.com (February 6, 2000).
Sub Pop: Beat Happening, http://www.subpop.com/bands/bhappening/bhappening.html, (February 6, 2000).

—Laura Hightower

Belle and Sebastian

Folk rock group

While the Scottish folk-pop octet Belle and Sebastian appeared to guard their anonymity, giving media interviews on only rare occasions and often refusing photo opportunities, those close to the band and the members themselves insist that their shyness is not contrived. "There is this sort of myth, and we're not really comfortable with it, because some of the effects are a bit embarrassing, painting [lead singer and songwriter] Stuart [Murdoch] out to be some sort of enigma," drummer Richard Colburn revealed to David Daley in *Magnet* magazine. "He's just this guy that writes songs, you know. When the band started, it was to make records. It wasn't to talk about the records. We think we should get on to making another one rather than talk about ourselves."

"Everyone's a bit elusive, likes to keep a bit to themselves," bassist Stuart David revealed to Angela Lewis in *Independent.* "That's what most of us have in common." Despite shunning the press, Belle and Sebastian nonetheless captivated fans in their native Britain, winning the Brit Award for 1998's best new band in 1999, and in the United States as well, although band members continue to view their rise in popularity with amazement. "I still don't think of us as being a particularly successful band," Colburn told *Magnet* in early 1999. "We were quite taken aback by the response (in the United States). I don't think when we recorded *Tigermilk* we went, 'Let's sit back and watch them praise us.' We've only played maybe 20 gigs. Then one day you'll get a letter from Brazil, and someone on the other side of the world likes your record. It doesn't seem feasible."

Singer, songwriter, and guitarist Stuart Murdoch and bassist Stuart David formed Belle and Sebastian at an all-night café in Glasgow, Scotland, in January of 1996. The name of the band came from a short story written by Murdoch, inspired by the French children's story about a boy named Sebastian and his dog, Belle. Soon, they enlisted six other musicians: Stevie Jackson on guitar and vocals; Richard Colburn on drums; Chris Geddes on keyboards; Isobel Campbell on viola, cello, guitar, and vocals; Sarah Martin on violin; and Mick Cooke on trumpet. At the time, Murdoch and Colburn were sharing a flat above a Glasgow church, for which they were also the caretakers. After the octet recorded some demo tapes together, Belle and Sebastian were contacted by a Jeepster (the British record label) talent scout who was participating in the Stow College Music Business Course in Glasgow. Each year, the course (run by multi-instrumentalist Alane Rankine, a former member of the Associates) produces and releases one record—usually a single—on a college label called Electric Honey Records for promising new bands. While most incoming groups approached by the course students have a limited supply of written music to work with, Belle and Sebastian had already composed an unusually vast amount of material, enough to support a whole album.

Thus, rather than release a debut single, Belle and Sebastian instead made a full-length LP, the elusive *Tigermilk,* which took just three days to record and contained songs mostly penned by Murdoch. Shane Harrison of the *Atlanta Journal and Constitution* described the debut effort as "a blend of gentle folk, low-key '60s psychedelia and a bruised, occasionally caustic, lyrical wit.The sum of those parts is a very distinctive, though not easily described, sound." Electric Honey issued a limited edition (1,000 copies) of the album available on vinyl only in mid-1996, not anticipating *Tigermilk*'s overwhelming success. Before long, the release became a huge collector's item and brought in ridiculous prices. In the summer of 1998, for instance, one band member auctioned an autographed copy to donate the proceeds to charity and raised more than $1,200. Later, in early 1999, Belle and Sebastian allowed their record company (Jeepster/Matador) to reissue *Tigermilk* on CD.

In August of 1996, Belle and Sebastian signed with Jeepster. They released their second album, the acclaimed *If You're Feeling Sinister,* in November of that year. Soon thereafter, Belle and Sebastian gave their debut performance in London, first as the support slot for the Tindersticks, followed by a headlining show at the

For the Record . . .

Members include **Isobel Campbell** (also solo artist as the Gentle Wave), viola, cello, guitar, vocals; **Richard Colburn**, drums; **Mick Cooke**, trumpet; **Stuart David** (also member of Looper with wife, Karn), bass, vocals; **Chris Geddes**, keyboards; **Stevie Jackson**, guitar, vocals; **Sarah Martin**, violin; **Stuart Murdoch**, guitar, lead vocals.

Formed band in Glasgow, Scotland, released *Tigermilk* for a college course, signed with Jeepster label, released *If You're Feeling Sinister* in the U.K., 1996; released *The Boy with the Arab Strap,* 1998.

Awards: Brit Award for 1998's best new group, 1999.

Addresses: *Record company*—Matador Records, 625 Broadway, 12th Fl., New York, NY 10012, phone (212) 995-5882, fax (212) 995-5883. *Website*—Belle and Sebastian at Matador Records: http://www.matador.recs.com; Belle and Sebastian Official Fan Club: http://www.jeepster.co.uk/belleandsebastian/main/index.shtml.

Borderline. In February of 1997, Belle and Sebastian released the album to American audiences on the Virgin subsidiary label Enclave. *If You're Feeling Sinister,* regarded as Belle and Sebastian's most satisfying folk-pop album for its infectious musical arrangements built around charming stories, made several top ten lists in the United States, including the *Village Voice*'s annual critics poll of 1997.

Throughout the summer of 1997, Belle and Sebastian set out to release a string of EPs, the first of which, *Dog On Wheels,* hit in late April. The record contained early demos of the band, previous to the six other band members joining Murdoch and David, including a version of "The State I Am In." The song, played by Radcliffe on *Tigermilk,* appealed to fans without a copy of Belle and Sebastian's limited edition debut and reached number 59 on the British singles chart.

The second EP, *Lazy Line Painter Jane,* was recorded at a show at the Union Chapel in Islington, London, and released in late July of 1997. Despite the poor sound quality, the band encouraged the crowd, many of whom were seeing Belle and Sebastian perform for the first time, to dance in the aisles and pews of the chapel. *Lazy Line Painter Jane* barely missed the United Kingdom top 40, but managed to peak at number 41, much to the amusement of keyboardist Geddes who had made a bet with Jeepster executive Mark Jones that the EP would not enter the top 40.

After playing two more gigs in Oxford and Colchester in England, the band traveled to New York City for the first time in September of that year and took part in the *CMJ* (*College Music Journal*) festival. Afterwards, Belle and Sebastian gave two performances at the Angel Organization Foundation Center for the Arts in Greenwich Village. Fans became so excited at the venue (another old chapel) that parts of the ceiling crumbled down on to the stage while the band played, according to Belle and Sebastian's website at Matador Records. Returning to Europe, the group performed in late September 1997, at the Barcelona (Spain) BAM festival, where Belle and Sebastian captivated yet another audience. The venue setting this time was in an ancient courtyard at the Plaza Del Rai beneath a moonlit sky.

The group's third summer EP, *3..6..9 Seconds of Light,* was issued on Jeepster in mid-October 1997, leading the British music press to acknowledge the band's popularity and importance. Both *Melody Maker* and *NME* (*New Musical Express*) named the title-track single of the week, and despite a lack of radio support, the single became the band's first United Kingdom top 40 hit, debuting at number 32 on the charts. The group concluded 1997 by working on music for their third full-length album, as well as playing two gigs at the Manchester (England) Town Hall in December.

In the late summer of 1998, Belle and Sebastian released the album *The Boy with the Arab Strap*. In response to the band's third effort, Magnet noted, "Perhaps *The Boy with The Arab Strap* (Matador) doesn't feel as decisively crafted or immediately captivating as its predecessors, but it's always winning, always pretty, with highlights like the rollicking title track and the breathtaking 'Is It Wicked Not To Care.'" The fall of that year, the group returned to American soil for their first proper tour of the United States, headlining shows up and down the East Coast that concluded with two sold-out gigs at the Supper Club in New York City.

In addition to playing with Belle and Sebastian, two of the group's members started side projects as well. David, for one, recorded an album with his wife, Karn, under the namesake Looper entitled *Up A Tree* (released on Sub Pop in the United States in 1999). Whereas Belle and Sebastian's music centered around Murdoch's youth-inspired fantasies and melodic instrumentation, Looper combined pop playfulness with electronic beats. "[Belle and Sebastian] is how Stuart Murdoch likes the world to sound—I like it to sound this way," David told Matthew Fritch of *Magnet*, explaining his decision to form Looper. Cellist Campbell pursued a solo effort as the Gentle Waves with *The Green Fields of Foreverland* (issued by Jeepster/Never in 1999), full of mostly melancholy songs that nevertheless offered a sense of optimism.

Selected discography

Belle and Sebastian

Tigermilk, Electric Honey, 1996.
If You're Feeling Sinister, Jeepster/Enclave, 1997.
Dog On Wheels, (EP), Jeepster, 1997.
3..6..9 Seconds of Light, (EP), Jeepster, 1997.
Lazy Line Painter Jane, (EP), Jeepster, 1997.
The Boy with the Arab Strap, Matador, 1998.

Gentle Waves (Isobel Campbell)

The Green Fields of Foreverland, Jeepster/Never, 1999.

Looper (Stuart and Karn David)

Up A Tree, Sub Pop, 1999.

Sources

Periodicals

Atlanta Journal and Constitution, October 27, 1998, p. F03.
Independent, July 26, 1997, p. 25; September 11, 1998, p. 20; March 12, 1999, p. 13.
Magnet, November/December 1998, pp. 33-35; January/February 1999, p. 40; August/September 1999, p. 18.
Toronto Sun, July 17, 1999, p. 50.

Online

Belle and Sebastian at Matador Records, http://www.matador.recs.com/bands/belle_and_sebastian/belle-biography.html (December 17, 1999).
Rolling Stone.com, http://www.rollingstone.tunes.com (December 17, 1999).

—*Laura Hightower*

Tito Beltrán

Tenor

Tito Beltrán is a man with a mission—to spread the beauty of the opera to the youth of the world, and especially to those in his homeland of Chile. He loves to sing above all else, and his wish is for the opera experience to reach around the globe. Throughout his career, Beltrán, a native of Patagonia, has used every opportunity to return to Chile and perform for his fellow countrymen who are disadvantaged culturally because of their remote location. Passionate and politically involved, Beltrán immigrated to Sweden in 1986 in a self-imposed exile to protest the repressive political regime of August Pinochet. Beltrán remained politically active, and opera became at once his passion and an instrument of reform, by which he resolved to propagate a message of classical beauty and hope.

Beltrán was born c.1965 in Punta Arenas, Chile, just off of the coast of the Tierra del Fuego archipelago. Punta Arenas is situated in a remote peninsular location on the tip of the mainland in the desolate region of Patagonia. It was in this area, unusually isolated from world culture, that Beltrán spent his youth. Remarkably, it was also the place that he first learned of the opera as well.

Even as a youth in Chile, Beltrán found gratification and enjoyment in singing. At the age of 16 he embarked on a professional singing career performing popular tunes. His interests, however, changed dramatically one day when his father showed him a videotape of a 1951 MGM video called *The Great Caruso.* The movie, starring the late Mario Lanza, proved inspirational to Beltrán, and ignited the young tenor's interest in classical singing. So impressed and inspired was Beltrán that he set out immediately to expand his repertoire, adding especially those classical songs associated with Mario Lanza. As voice teachers were not available on the barren Chilean plateau where Beltrán lived, he continued to nurture his career as previously, performing at the same popular venues, yet updating his programs to include some of the old classical pieces like "Ave Maria."

As the Chilean nation entered the 1980s, Beltrán became disenchanted with the oppressive regime of the country's dictator August Pinochet. Through the assistance of an uncle living in Sweden, Beltran immigrated to that country in 1986 in what he termed a self-imposed exile. Following his move to Sweden, Beltrán embarked on a serious course of classical voice training with a goal of becoming a professional opera singer. His first teacher, an elderly diva in her 80s, taught him proper breath control and other lyric techniques. Beltrán, who was then 20 years old, fought the drudgery, but eventually came to appreciate the importance of self-discipline. He attended the Göteborg Academy of Theater and Opera, and he spent some time studying in London, England. Through his studies he learned of the late Swedish tenor, Jussi Bjorling, and looked to the memory of the celebrated singer for a role model. Sweden celebrated no living classical tenors at that time, thus as Beltrán's talent matured and he developed his skills during those early years of his career, the Swedes respected Beltrán much as they had respected Bjorling.

As Beltrán's classical repertoire expanded, he traveled the world, yet repeatedly he realized his greatest satisfaction when he performed in Chile. In 1992 he sang the role of the Duke of Mantua in Verdi's *Rigoletto* at Teatro Municipal in Santiago, and he returned to Santiago in September of 1997 in the same role. Beltran's 1997 performance prompted Enzo Berio of *Opera News* to call Beltrán "a highly competent Duke, his lyric voice ringing out to advantage." During that same visit to Chile, Beltrán visited his hometown of Punta Arenas where he performed a fund raiser for the Lion's Club. In the summer of 1999, he sang once more in Santiago, as Rodolfo in Puccini's *La Bohème,* a role that he sang originally as a student of music in Sweden.

Beltrán's European performance venues included Convent Gardens with the Royal Opera Company where he appeared as Rodolfo, and as the Italian Tenor in *Der Rosenkavalier.* In 1993 he sang as a finalist in the Singer of the World competition at Cardiff, Wales, England, and in the spring of 1996, Beltrán graced the North American

For the Record . . .

Born c. 1965 in Punta Arenas, Chile; married to Malin; three children. *Education*: Göteborg Academy of Theater and Opera, Sweden.

Started professional singer career at age 16; immigrated to Sweden, began classical voice training, 1986; released first album, *Tito Beltrán*, 1995; has performed in the U.S., Europe, and South America; roles include: Duke of Mantua, *Rigoletto,* Teatro Municipal in Santiago, Chile, 1992; Geneva (December 1996, January 1998), Michigan Opera Theatre (April 1997); Toulouse (June 1997); Santiago, San Francisco Opera (December 1997, 1998); Oregon (October 1998); Rodolfo, *La Bohème,* Leeds (February 1996), Michigan Opera Theatre (May 1996), London, (October 1996), Bordeaux (May 1998); Santiago (July 1999); Italian Tenor, *Der Rosenkavalier*; Nemorino, *L'Elisir d'Amore,* Florida (November 1996), Pittsburgh Opera (November 1998); Edgardo, *Lucia di Lammermoor*; Ruggero, *La Rondine*; Alfredo Germont, *La Traviata*; Ismaele, *Nabucco*; Tybalt, *Romeo et Juliette*. Member of the Royal Danish Opera in Copenhagen and San Francisco Opera.

Awards: Finalist, Singer of the World Competition, Cardiff, Wales, England, 1993.

Addresses: *Record company*—Silva Screen Records America, Silva Classics, 1600 Broadway, Suite 910, New York, NY 10019.

continent with his debut as Rodolfo, at the Michigan Opera in Detroit, Michigan. Despite his relative youth as a classical singer, by the end of the 1990s, Beltrán's appearances spanned Europe—from Iceland to Sweden to Toulouse—as well as to the Opera North in England and across the Atlantic to North America where he sang to critical acclaim in a variety of roles. He performed his Rodolfo at the San Francisco Opera, and also brought the role to Convent Garden, the Hamburg State Opera, and Rio. He performed as Verdi's Duke in Monte Carlo, Geneva, and Sweden, and in April of 1997 he returned to the Detroit Opera House in that role. Jeffrey Smith in *Opera News* said that the tenor's voice as Duke was "often forceful and metallic...."

In December of 1997, Beltrán reprised his Duke role for the San Francisco Opera, and critics noted Beltrán's ability to emote. His Nemorino in *L'Elisir d'Amore*—which he performed in Sweden, Florida, and again later with the Pittsburgh Opera—earned more accolades for the singer. It was the Orlando, Florida production in 1997 that prompted Tim Smith to note in *Opera News* that Beltrán was a "combination nebbish and teddy bear ... [he] brought an intriguing earthiness in the character." Early in his career he sang Edgardo in *Lucia di Lammermoor* with the Icelandic Opera and performed in the *Rosenkavalier* tenor role at Copenhagen's Royal Danish Opera, and in San Francisco as well. His other roles include Ruggero in *La Rondine,* Alfredo Germont in *La Traviata,* Ismaele in *Nabucco,* and Tybalt in *Romeo et Juliette.*

Soulful and talented, Beltrán is small in stature and possesses a voice best suited for lyric roles. As Beltrán came to prominence, he evoked comparison to Caruso because of the strength and quality of his voice. Some called him the Chilean Caruso, and he proved worthy of that reputation. Among his most impressive performances, one evening as a stand-in for Nemorino in Donizetti's *L'Elisir d'Amore,* the plucky tenor amazed all present with his creative antics when he performed one aria, live on stage, while walking around the set on his hands. The gymnastic display, according to Beltrán, was completely impromptu and highly effective for its spontaneity. It served to demonstrate not only the tenor's agility, but also the strength and control of his melodic voice.

Beltrán released his first album in 1995. The recording, called *Tito Beltrán,* featured Robin Stapleton conducting the Royal Philharmonic Orchestra. Selections on the recording included classic operatic arias from *La Bohème, La Traviata,* and Bizet's *Les Pêcheurs de Perles (ThePearlfishers).* Stapleton and the Philharmonic were heard again on Beltrán's *Romantica* in 1996, an album that included songs from around the world. In 1999 Beltrán released a recording called *Tenor at the Movies,* wherein he paid tribute to Mario Lanza not only through the selection of songs, but also by emulating the style of the great American tenor. Additionally, the chairman of the British Mario Lanza Society contributed an introduction to the recording. Beltrán recorded the album with Paul Bateman conducting the City of Prague Philharmonic Orchestra and the Crouch End Festival Chorus. Arthur said in *American Record Guide* that Beltrán has a "fine lyric tenor voice with splendid top notes, and sings with intelligence and sincerity." The album, recorded in high-quality sound, includes operatic arias, plus music from the movies *Titanic* and *Love Story.* Also in 1999 Beltrán recorded the first Spanish-language version of "My Heart Will Go On" from the film *Titanic.*

Amid the accolades, Beltrán has received criticism for singing compositions that are too sophisticated for his relative youth as a classical singer—songs with too much range, that might strain his developing voice. Likewise, Beltrán's managers constantly encourage him to rest his voice to avoid the risk of a strain that might put a valuable career in jeopardy. Critically, the apprehension was valid, in consideration of the dearth of young tenors at the dawn of the twenty-first century. The arena of Beltrán's generation remained limited when compared to a previous generation of opera talent that included the legendary Three Tenors—Carreras, Pavarotti, and Domingo—who shared the spotlight for years. Beltrán responded to critics by singing continually on and off stage, for the sheer joy of the music. Not singing was punishment for him, according to the tenor who upheld a serendipitous stance regarding his place in history as a rising new voice.

Beltrán makes his home in Kungsbacka, Sweden with his wife, Malin, and their three children. He performs regularly on mainstream Swedish television.

Selected discography

Tito Beltrán (with the Royal Philharmonic Orchestra), Silva Classics, 1995.
Romantica (with the Royal Philharmonic Orchestra), Silva Classics, 1996
Tenor at the Movies, Silva, 1999.

Sources

Periodicals

American Record Guide, November/December 1996, p. 272; March/April 1998, p. 24; September/October 1999, p. 325.
Americas, March/April 1996, p. 56.
Musical Opinion, April 1, 1999, p. 150.
Opera News, January 25, 1997, p. 47, September 1997, p. 66; January 17, 1998, p 50.

Online

"Tito Beltrán," *Operabase,* http://operabase.com/showart.cgi?lang=en&id=none&name=Beltrán&forename=Tito (February 11, 2000).
"Tito Beltrán," *San Francisco Opera Artist Biographies*, 1999-2000 Season, available at http://www.sfopera.com/bios/bios_a-f/Beltrán.htm (February 11, 2000).
"Tito Beltrán," *Silva Screen Records America, Inc.*, http://www.silvascreen.com/titobio.html (February 11, 2000).
"Tito Beltrán can even sing while walking on his hands," *ONLINE POST-GAZETTE*, November 13, 1998, http://www.post-gazette.com/magazine/1998113Beltrán4.asp (February 11, 2000).

—*Gloria Cooksey*

Jeb Bishop

Trombone, guitar

In the late 1990s, Jeb Bishop became one of the most visible figures in creative music. In addition to recording two projects as a band leader, 1999's *98 Duets* and *Jeb Bishop Trio,* he played trombone in four groups led by cellist Fred Lonberg-Holms, a free jazz tentet led by saxophonist and clarinetist Peter Brötzmann, and an experimental jazz ensemble called the Vandermark 5, for which he also doubled on guitar. A former member of various punk and indie rock bands as well, Bishop does not limit his talents to the jazz genre. He often performs with the avant-classical group Ensemble Noamnesia, and he has guested on albums by numerous indie and avant-garde bands, including Stereolab, Superchunk, Tortoise, David Grubbs, and Jim O'Rourke.

Born around 1962 in Raleigh, North Carolina, Bishop left his hometown in 1980, relocating to Chicago to study orchestral music at Northwestern University. However, after studying classical trombone for two years, feelings of disillusionment led him back to Raleigh. Upon his return, he temporarily packed his instrument away in the attic of his parents' home and started playing bass guitar for various Southeastern punk and pop combos, including a local hardcore band called the Stillborn Christians. He also enrolled at North Carolina State University to pursue a degree in engineering. Still indecisive about this field of study, as well as his future in music, Bishop traveled to Belgium for a brief time to study philosophy at the University of Louvain, where he enrolled in graduate courses. It was here that Bishop had the opportunity to witness an impressive display of jazz artists from across the globe, taking in performances by American jazz innovators such as saxophonists Anthony Braxton and Steve Lacy. While in Belgium, Bishop also met European trombonist Garrett List and visited the musician's free jazz improvisation class at the conservatory in Liège.

Bishop, energized with a new sense of purpose and a growing interest in jazz, returned to North Carolina in 1985. Despite his experiences overseas, Bishop decided to focus on rock music rather than jazz, forming the experimental pop band the Angels of Epistemology. The group released one album, *Fruit,* on the Merge label before disbanding. Bishop spent the late 1980s taking philosophy courses in Tucson, Arizona, deciding to let go of his musical aspirations, aside from dabbling in self-taught classical guitar and playing for a short time in a noisy Tucson rock band. Nevertheless, from 1989 until around 1992, Bishop never picked up his trombone.

In 1990, Bishop moved back to his adopted home of Chicago to further his graduate studies at Northwestern. Unable to ignore the variety of music the city offered, Bishop began to contemplate a musical career again. Soon after his arrival, he met and developed a friendship with saxophone/clarinet player Ken Vandermark. Vandermark has become one of the world's most respected post-modern, free jazz musicians, often combining elements of rhythm and blues and rock into his compositions. In addition to establishing contact with Vandermark, Bishop, in 1992, joined a punk-jazz ensemble called the Flying Luttenbachers playing bass, further establishing a course for himself in free jazz. By 1993, Bishop had quit his studies in order to give his full attention to music.

Around the same time, Bishop retrieved his trombone again, but would not play the instrument in public until 1995, the year he joined Vandermark's quintet, known as the Vandermark 5. In this ongoing ensemble, Bishop played both trombone and electric guitar. "He's been on the scene a short amount of time, and the velocity of his development is astounding," Vandermark said of Bishop's talents, as quoted by Bill Meyer in *Magnet* magazine. "Being around him and seeing how intense he is about his instrument is inspiring." The quintet's first album, *Single Piece Flow,* arrived in 1996, and from that moment, Bishop became a much sought-after backing musician. However, Bishop's appeal was not limited to the jazz scene. Following the release of *Single Piece Flow,* he made an acclaimed appearance on Stereolab's *Dots and Loops* album and the EP *Miss Modular* (both released in 1997) that provided him a strong reputation within Chicago's post-rock community. He guested on

For the Record . . .

Born c. 1962 in Raleigh, NC. *Education*: Studied orchestral music and classical trombone, and later graduate-level philosophy, at Northwestern University; studied philosophy at the University of Louvain in Belgium; studied engineering at North Carolina State University.

Moved to Chicago to pursue graduate studies and struck a friendship with Ken Vandermark, 1990; joined punk-jazz ensemble called the Flying Luttenbachers, 1992; joined Vandermark's quintet, the Vandermark 5, 1995; appeared on Stereolab's album *Dots and Loops*, 1997; released debut as a bandleader with *98 Duets*, 1998; released *Jeb Bishop Trio*, 1999.

Addresses: *Record company*—Okkadisk, email: info@okkadisk.com. *Website*—Jeb Bishop at Okkadisk, http://www.okkadisk.com/artists/bishop.html.

several other non-jazz releases in 1997, including Jim O'Rourke's acclaimed *Bad Timing,* Last Time I Committed Suicide's self-titled LP, and Cheer Accident's *Enduring the American Dream.*

In 1998, Bishop released his debut as a bandleader, *98 Duets,* on the independent label Wobbly Rail Records, a subsidiary of Merge Records founded by Superchunk front man Mac McCaughan (McCaughan and co-member of Superchunk Laura Balance operate Merge together). He started the imprint after realizing that numerous talented, under-appreciated jazz musicians, both old and young, needed a way of getting their music to the public. For *98 Duets,* Bishop documented his spontaneous, experimental side with a backing band that included Vandermark, cellist Fred Lonberg-Holm, drummer Hamid Drake, bassist Josh Abrams, trumpeter Leo Smith, and saxophonist Mats Gustafsson. "Their explorations," concluded Meyer, "take in breathy abstractions, gorgeous celebrations of sound and fragile, lyrical statements." According to Bishop, his attraction to unusual sounds was nothing new. "From an early age, I've been attracted to stuff that was dissonant or somehow outside," as quoted by Meyer. "A lot of what I've done is always dealing with stuff that strikes me as somehow outside some kind of boundaries."

In addition to releasing his debut, the album *Destroy All Music* with the Flying Luttenbachers, and the album *Target or Flag* with the Vandermark 5, Bishop appeared on other jazz and indie rock albums that year, including Gastro del Sol's *Camofleur,* David Grubbs' *Thicket,* and Loren Mazzacan Connors' *Hoffman Estates.* Several other guest appearances came the following year. Bishop, along with Vandermark and Lonberg-Holm, played on Superchunk's 1999 release *Come Pick Me Up.* "And we didn't use them like you'd usually hear them," Superchunk's guitarist McCaughan told Steve Dollar of the *Atlanta Journal-Constitution.* "We told them to try and play like the E Street Band." Other album appearances by Bishop that year included the Vandermark 5's *Simpatico,* Vandermark's solo release entitled *Straight Lines,* Peter Brötzmann's *The Chicago Octet/Tentet,* multi-instrumentalist Joe McPhee's *The Brass City* (which included compositions by Bishop as well), Simon Joyner's *Lousy Dance,* and the Aluminum Group's *Pedals.*

The year 1999 also saw the release of another Bishop solo effort, *Jeb Bishop Trio,* recorded in Chicago in November of 1997 with bassist Kent Kessler and drummer Tim Mulvenna (who also played with Vandermark's quintet). According to Bishop, the impetus for starting the trio resulted from working with the inspiring rhythm section, led by Kessler and Mulvenna, of the Vandermark 5."With Ken's music, the blowing space is constrained by the overall form, which is usually pretty complicated," Bishop reported, as quoted by his website at Okkadisk. "I wanted something that would let everyone stretch out, including me. And to have the interest of the music come from seeing how we deal with that space."

The album, issued by the established Okkadisk label, included seven tracks, all but one ("Anticipation of an Embrace" by Lisle Ellis) composed by Bishop. In contrast to *98 Duets, Jeb Bishop Trio* centered around melody rather than experimental sounds, although both projects earned critical praise. "Eschewing avant garde trickery, Bishop applies his robust tone to the business of no nonsense jazz improvisation," according to the Summer 1999 issue of the *Wire,* as quoted by Bishop's website. "Strong melodies supply the impetus, but the group takes its time, delving and probing, working through the options." With two acclaimed albums that secured his status as a commanding improviser and respected instrumentalist, Bishop continued to collaborate with other musicians and planned to compose more work for both large and small ensembles.

Selected discography

98 Duets, Wobbly Rail, 1998.
Jeb Bishop Trio, Okkadisk, 1999.

Sources

Books

Cook, Richard and Brian Morton, editors, *Penguin Guide to Jazz on Compact Disc*, Penguin Books, 1998.

Swenson, John, editor, *Rolling Stone Jazz and Blues Album Guide*, Random House, 1999.

Periodicals

Atlanta Journal-Constitution, June 18, 1999.

Chicago Tribune, January 29, 1997; September 19, 1997; December 16, 1998; December 19, 1998.

Magnet, April/May 1999, p. 18.

University Wire, May 13, 1999.

Online

All Music Guide, http://www.allmusic.com (January 26, 2000).

Jeb Bishop at Okkadisk, http://www.okkadisk.com/artists/bishop.html (January 26, 2000).

—*Laura Hightower*

Peter Blegvad

Composer, lyricist, singer, guitar

Although recognized more widely for his weekly comic strip, *Leviathan*, for the British newspaper the *Independent*, American-born musician and artist Peter Blegvad also pursued a songwriting career beginning in the 1970s, that revealed some of the most poetic wordplay to ever find its way into song. He played and composed songs for numerous bands, including Slapp Happy from 1968-74, Faust in 1973, Slapp Happy/Henry Cow from1974-75, the Lodge from 1982-88, and the Golden Palominos from 1985-87, and enjoyed an acclaimed solo career as well. His most highly-acclaimed effort, *King Strut and Other Stories,* was released in 1990 and became a testament to his hard work and clear vision.

Peter Blegvad was born on August 14, 1951, in New York City, to a Danish father and American mother. He was raised in Connecticut until his parents moved the family to England in 1965. They moved as a result of what they perceived as the deteriorating social climate in the United States at the time, following the assassinations of President John F. Kennedy and civil rights leader Martin Luther King, Jr. They also wanted to prevent their two sons, Peter and his brother Kristoffer, from being drafted to serve in the war in Vietnam. Before leaving America, Blegvad had already developed an interest in music and art and started writing his first songs at age 13, which were largely influenced by the Beatles and Bob Dylan.

In England, Blegvad attended a free-thinking, alternative boarding school, St. Christopher School, Letchworth, located in Hertfordshire. Here he met his future musical collaborator, pianist Anthony Moore. The two started playing together with another of Blegvad's friends, Neil Murray, an aspiring drummer who later moved to bass guitar and became accomplished on that instrument. The trio went by several names, including Slapp Happy and the Dum-Dums. At first, the group mostly played blues and rock and roll tunes, but later on, Blegvad steered them toward more experimental music, such as the music of Pink Floyd and Soft Machine. Even in those days, Murray's taste laid more with conventional rock, while Blegvad and Moore were increasingly drawn to the avant-garde. Blegvad focused on his other talents as well at the St. Christopher School, including artwork, and when Murray edited the school's magazine in 1967, he devoted a whole section, eight pages, to surrealistic drawings by Blegvad that told a story.

Also during his school days, Blegvad discovered poetry, a passion that would later affect his own writing. He drew the greatest inspiration from Irish poet William Butler Yeats. "I often think my life was saved or perhaps my character was radically changed by adolescent confrontation with W.B. Yeats," he told *Hearsay* magazine in an online interview. "Yeats's interest in mysticism, symbolism and the toughness and economy of his later poems, when he was influenced by Ezra Pound, that was an enormous influence. The entire spectrum of his interests—but maybe less the political thing—really fascinated me."

Formed Slapp Happy

In 1971, during a stay in Hamburg, Germany, Blegvad started his first official band, Slapp Happy, with Moore, who had already released two experimental solo albums for the Polydor label, and Moore's then girlfriend and future wife, singer Dagmar Krause. The trio recorded their debut album, *Sort Of,* in the spring of 1972, with the members of the German group Faust serving as the backing band. The album was released later that summer in Germany on Polydor. Faust joined Slapp Happy again to record a follow-up album in 1973, but after Slapp Happy signed with Virgin Records, the project was re-recorded at Virgin's Manor studios in the United Kingdom with British sessions musicians. Robert Wyatt, an enduring British musical artist and former member of Soft Machine, along with members of the group Henry Cow, had suggested a re-make after hearing the Slapp Happy/Faust demo tape. The resulting album, *Slapp Happy,* appeared in May of 1973, while the original version with Faust was eventually released in 1982 as *Acnalbasac*

For the Record . . .

Born on August 14, 1951, in New York, NY; son of a Danish father and American mother; siblings: brother Kristoffer.

Formed first band, Slapp Happy, 1971; signed solo contract with Virgin Records, released debut album *The Naked Shakespeare,* 1983; released most acclaimed album, *King Strut and Other Stories,* 1990; began *Leviathan* cartoon series for *Independent,* 1992; released *Just Woke Up,* 1995. Member of past bands including Slapp Happy (1968-74), the Lodge (1982-88), and the Golden Palominos (1985-87).

Addresses: *Record company*—East Side Digital (ESD), 530 N. 3rd. St., Minneapolis, MN 55401, phone: (612) 375-0233, email: esd@noside.com. *Website*—Peter Blegvad on East Side Digital (ESD), http://www.noside.com/esd/blegvad.html.

Noom. Despite the split with Faust, Blegvad managed to preserve the relationship and performed with the band for a few months in the fall of 1973 for a British tour with Henry Cow. By the end of the tour, Faust had signed with Virgin as well.

The tour also led to the merger of Slapp Happy with Henry Cow, beginning in 1974, to record the album *Desperate Straights,* issued by Virgin in 1975. Soon thereafter, Henry Cow fully absorbed the Slapp Happy trio into their band and released 1975's *In Praise of Learning.* However, the association between Blegvad, Moore and Henry Cow proved incompatible by the time they had completed recording their second album. Consequently, Moore left the band and Blegvad, who admitted his inability to play Henry Cow's music, was ejected shortly afterwards.

Taking a leave from music, Blegvad returned to New York where he took a job drawing background scenes for the nationally syndicated *Peanuts* cartoon series. A few months after he arrived in the United States, though, Blegvad met with John Greaves, also a former member of Henry Cow, to collaborate on an album. Blegvad and Greaves, joined by vocalist Lisa Herman, released the dense *Kew. Rhone* album on Virgin in May of 1977. Over the next few years, Blegvad retreated from music again, except for his involvement in several short-lived bands, until his return to England in 1982.

Began Solo Career

Upon his arrival, Blegvad reunited briefly with Slapp Happy, recording the single "Everybody's Slimmin,'" released in May of 1983, and playing the trio's first live performance at the Institute of Contemporary Arts in London. Also in 1983, Blegvad signed a contract with Virgin to record solo work, and in October of that year, the label released his debut, *The Naked Shakespeare,* with Andy Partridge of the band XTC as producer. Blegvad also sought contributions from other musicians, such as Greaves and the Eurythmics' Dave Stewart, to help write music for the record. However, while critics pointed to some fine moments on *The Naked Shakespeare,* the record overall received little recognition. Blegvad's follow-up effort, 1985's *Knights Like This,* however, was a greater disappointment. Virgin, who wanted to release a Blegvad album with more commercial appeal, hired producer David Lord to make the musician a pop sensation. Consequently, Blegvad's songs, originally intended to be performed by his regular backing band (his brother Kristoffer and Chris Stamey on guitar and Carla Bley guesting on organ), wound up buried under Lord's over-arrangement. However, more stripped-down versions of songs from the album were later released under the title *Just Woke Up,* which critics called a masterpiece, on East Side Digital in 1995.

Following the failure of *Knights Like This* and news that Virgin wished to discontinue their relationship with the songwriter, Blegvad moved back to New York and hooked up with various musicians, including drummer Anton Fier and his collective band the Golden Palominos. Blegvad's songs, including versions of "Not Weak Enough" and "When the Work Was New" from his forthcoming project, helped shape the identity of that group's 1986 album *Blast of Silence.* Around the same time, Blegvad began work on a third solo album with Chris Cutler, Henry Cow's former drummer. After three years of struggling through financial difficulties to complete the project, he released the uncompromised *Downtime* on Cutler's Recommended label in 1989 (issued in the United Kingdom on the ReR label in 1988) to favorable reviews.

Meanwhile, another collaboration with Greaves and his band called the Lodge came to fruition with an album recorded in New York and released in 1988 by Island Records entitled *Smell of a Friend.* In addition to Greaves and Blegvad, the Lodge consisted of Kristoffer Blegvad on lead vocals, Jakko Jakszyk (who played on Blegvad's first two solo outings) on guitar and vocals, and Fier on drums; Herman joined the ensemble to sing lead vocals and play piano for the song "Swelling Valley." Also that year, the Lodge performed one show at the Bataclan in Paris, adding keyboardist Lyndon Collin and drummer Gavin Harrison to replace Fier. In 1989, the group played another show at London's Institute of Contemporary Arts. For this performance, keyboardist Steve Franklin (of the band In Cahoots) and drummer Nic France (of the groups Nucleus and Loose Tubes) replaced Collin and Harrison.

After this, Blegvad agreed to record his next solo effort with the Silvertone label and obtained a larger recording budget. In July of 1990, he released *King Strut and Other Stories* in the United Kingdom to critical acclaim. Produced by Stamey, who previously played with Blegvad's band and the Golden Palominos collective, the album consisted of short stories set to music and was regarded as the songwriter's most accomplished solo outing. The following year, the members of Slapp Happy reunited, in a sense, when British television commissioned an hour-long opera entitled *Camera,* with music composed by Moore and a libretto written by Blegvad, performed by Krause. The television opera aired in 1994.

Created *Leviathan*

In 1992, Blegvad resumed his career as a cartoonist, accepting an offer to draw a weekly comic strip called *Leviathan* for the *Independent on Sunday* that brought him unanticipated fame. Consequently, he became more widely known for his comic series, rather than for his music. Nonetheless, Blegvad continued to pursue his songwriting. He collaborated again with Greaves for two more projects: 1992's *Dr. Huelsenbecks Mentale Heilmethode* and 1995's *Unearthed,* a set of Blegvad's stories (many of which had been published in 1994 in his book *Headcheese*) recited over a variety of musical backdrops.

The year 1995 saw the release of Blegvad's first proper American release of his career with *Just Woke Up,* recorded in 1992 and 1993 and issued on East Side Digital. Performed as a trio with Greaves and Cutler, *Just Woke Up,* which many critics hailed a masterpiece, featured new versions of three songs from *Knights Like This,* as well as the song "Something Else," originally recorded by the Golden Palominos. Guest musicians for the release included Kristoffer Blegvad on guitar and pedal steel player B.J. Cole. The group made their live debut in July of 1996 at the MIMI Festival in Avignon, France, followed by a tour of the United States. In April of 1998, Virgin's subsidiary label, V2, released a new Slapp Happy compilation album that earned critical acclaim entitled *Ça Va.*

In addition to writing music for other musicians, pursuing a solo career, and creating his weekly comic strip, Blegvad also contributed his artwork to numerous albums and singles by other artists. Some of these included Greaves's 1992 album *Accident,* as well as his 1997 CD *Little Bottle of Laundry,* Pere Ubu's 1993 CD *Story of My Life,* and many others.

Selected discography

Solo

The Naked Shakespeare, Virgin (U.K.), 1983.
Knights Like This, Virgin (U.K.), 1985.
Downtime, Virgin (U.K.), ReR, 1988.
King Strut and Other Stories, Silvertone (U.K.), 1990.
Just Woke Up, East Side Digital, 1995.

Peter Blegvad and John Greaves

Kew. Rhone, Virgin (U.K.), 1977; reissued, Europa, 1977.
Unearthed, Sub Rosa (Belgium), 1995.
Dr. Huelsenbecks Mentale Heilmethode, 1992.

Slapp Happy

Sort Of, Polydor (Germany), 1972.
Slapp Happy, Virgin (U.K.), 1973.
Acnalbasac Noom, Recommended (U.K.), 1982; reissued, Cuneiform, 1988.
Casablanca Moon/Desperate Straights, Virgin (U.K.), 1993.

Henry Cow/Slapp Happy

Desperate Straights, Virgin (U.K.), 1975; reissued, ReR (U.K.), 1982.

Henry Cow

In Praise of Learning, Virgin (U.K.), 1975; reissued, Red, 1979; reissued, East Side Digital, 1991.

Lodge

Smell of a Friend, Island, 1988.

Sources

Books

MusicHound Rock: The Essential Album Guide, Visible Ink Press, 1999.
Robins, Ira A., editor, *Trouser Press Guide to '90s Rock,* Fireside/Simon and Schuster, 1997.

Periodicals

Chicago Tribune, September 11, 1998.
New York Times, November 11, 1997; September 9, 1998.

Online

"Discography: Peter Blegvad," http://www.reality.sgi.com/relph/music/blegvad.peter (January 22, 2000).
Hearsay Online, http://www.hearsaymagazine.demon.co.uk/peter.htm (January 22, 2000).
"Peter Blegvad," http://www.alpes-net.fr/~bigbang/musicians/peterblegvad.html (January 22, 2000).
"Peter Blegvad on East Side Digital," http://www.noside.com/esd/blegvad.html (January 22, 2000).

—Laura Hightower

Blonde Redhead

Punk rock band

Although the New York-based trio Blonde Redhead made a connection with the art world in late 1998 when they performed at the Andy Warhol Museum in Pittsburgh, Pennsylvania, to celebrate an exhibit by Japanese artist Mariko Mori, the members of the group refused to define their music as "art rock." "We always totally avoid seeming pretentious or arty," vocalist/guitarist Kazu Makino revealed to *Magnet* magazine's Matthew Fritch. "I think arty bands are never arty.... To me, the most artistic band is a punk-rock band. There's a big difference between an art band and a band that has a concept of its music. That's what's really artistic; it's not about dropping weird stuff in and making weird noises and having awkward pauses in the music. I never wanted to be categorized as that." Though Blonde Redhead's sound often includes odd harmonies, pulsating funk rhythms, and punk music, the band has become admired most for their ability to create direct-hitting, rather than avant-garde, rock.

Taking their name from a song by one of their favorite bands, DNA, a 1980s New York avant-garde post-punk band, Blonde Redhead formed around 1993 after a chance meeting at a New York City restaurant. Two of the group's members, Makino (who previously collaborated with Marc Ribot) and bassist Maki Takahashi (who left the group in 1994) were Japanese-born art students, while twin bothers Simone (drums, keyboards) and Amedeo Pace (guitar, vocals) were born in Milan, Italy. The Pace brothers emigrated to Canada at age 13, then came to the United States to attend the prestigious Berklee College of Music in Boston, Massachusetts. From the onset, the band members, especially Makino, Amadeo, and Simone, realized an instant connection to each other that strengthened into a deep friendship. "I think we have a desire to be together as much as possible. In some ways we want to be separate, but in some ways, we have this burning desire to be the same thing, one person," Makino told Fritch. "We've made ourselves be so close," Amadeo further revealed. "And a relationship like this, to be in a band, even though you want to be an individual, it's almost impossible. You kind of have to give up certain things."

Blonde Redhead debuted in 1993 with the seven-inch single "Big Song," issued by the Oxo label. The song, along with constant performing, caught the attention of Steve Shelley, the drummer for Sonic Youth and owner of the independent label Smells Like Records, who offered to produce and release records for the band. In 1994, Blonde Redhead released a second single, "Vague," followed by their self-titled debut album that drew comparisons, though not without cause, to Shelley's own band. Produced by Shelley, the eight-song *Blonde Redhead* took obvious cues from Sonic Youth by implementing similar guitar sounds and song structures, such as in the warped pop tune "Sciuri Sciura" and the convulsive guitar foray "I Don't Want U." However, Blonde Redhead found a way to differentiate their sound from the Sonic Youth ethic. "Blonde Redhead have earnestly studied that band's method of fusing disparate peals of guitar into frail, blinking melodies," concluded the *Ink Blot* magazine website, "but they adeptly avoid mere mimicry by providing their arrangements with a welcome degree of flexibility." For example, Makino and Amedeo Pace alternated providing the lead vocals throughout the guitar-dominated album, and whereas Sonic Youth often buries the vocal delivery of Kim Gordon and Thurston Moore within instrumentation, Blonde Redhead opted to give Makino's singing greater attention.

Shortly after *Blonde Redhead*'s release, bassist Takahashi left the band, and the group started working on their follow-up, 1995's *La Mia Vita Violenta,* as a trio. Since Takahashi's departure, the bass position for Blonde Redhead remained unfilled, although some later recordings would feature guest bassists. For their second album, Blonde Redhead distinguished their sound even further, allowing their own personalities to take the lead. Pace's singing appeared fuller, while Makino began to develop her passionate, high-pitched vocals that critics would often compare to the Icelandic singer Björk. With improved guitar playing, tracks such as the catchy punk song "(I Am Taking Out My Eurotrash) I Still Get Rocks

For the Record . . .

Members include **Kazu Makino** (born in Japan), guitar, vocals; twin brothers **Amedeo Pace**, guitar, vocals; and **Simone Pace**, drums, keyboards (both born in Milan, Italy; emigrated to Canada at age 13; attended Berklee College of Music in Boston, MA); **Maki Takahashi** (born in Japan; left band in 1994), bass.

Formed band c. 1993 in New York City, NY, and released first seven-inch single, "Big Song;" signed with Smells Like Records, released debut album Blonde Redhead, 1994; released La Mia Vita Violenta as a trio, 1995; released first album for Touch and Go Records, Fake Can Be Just As Good, 1997; released In An Expression of the Inexpressible, performed at Andy Warhol Museum in Pittsburgh, PA, 1998.

Addresses: *Record company*—Touch and Go Records, P.O. Box 25520, Chicago, IL 60625, (773) 388-3888, email: info@southern.com. *Website*—Blonde Redhead at Touch and Go, http://www.southern.com.

Off" and the sitar-laced, melodic "Harmony," became noted critical favorites. Also in 1995, Blonde Redhead released three singles: "Flying Douglas," "10 Feet High," and a split with the group Sammy.

In 1997, Blonde Redhead released their first album for the larger independent label Touch and Go Records entitled *Fake Can Be Just As Good,* co-produced by technical engineer John Goodmanson. Still lacking a permanent bassist, Blonde Redhead invited Vern Ramsey of the band Unwound to participate in recording sessions. The album yielded notable tracks such as "Ego Manic Kid," "Pier Paolo," and "Oh James." Touch and Go also issued its first single for Blonde Redhead in 1997, "Symphony of Treble." In addition to playing the East Coast and other United States dates that year, the group also traveled to Europe, where they maintained devoted fans. After one show at London's Upstairs at the Garage, Mark Luffman of *Melody Maker* observed, "Blonde Redhead are a fantastically insular band. Their brittle, tightly strung music carried no flab, and takes neither prisoners nor joyriders."

After releasing another single, "Slogan," Blonde Redhead returned with their fourth full-length album, 1998's *In An Expression of the Inexpressible.* Deciding to again record solely as a trio at a 5,000-square-foot studio in Hoboken, New Jersey, Blonde Redhead called upon Goodmanson to produce the album and Guy Picciotto to lend his vocals to the geometric punk track "Futurism vs. Passeism Part 2." "This is the band," Simone Pace told Fritch, explaining the decision not to bring in a guest bassist. "We don't have a bass player, so why should we put a bass on the record?" Filled with punk rock songs such as "Luv Machine," "L-Zero," and "Distilled," as well as high-end funk numbers like "Missile," *In An Expression of the Inexpressible* earned rave reviews. "It's rock torn from a cleanly digitised womb and thrown into the howling fizz of a high-frequency hurricane," wrote Neil Kulkarni in *Melody Maker.* "This record pierces the skull and affords itself no bassed-out relief. It's all here ... and it's astonishing."

Touring constantly, usually dressed in matching uniforms, Blonde Redhead spent the remainder of the year playing rock clubs with bands such as Fugazi, Unwound, and Shellac. The band also insisted on making their shows available to younger audiences, booking 18 of their 19 dates for early 1999 at all-ages venues. In spite of the social problems that plague America, Makino described the young adults they meet on tour as "intelligent" and "really beautiful and completely focused and completely sensitive," as quoted by Fritch. "I just hope these kids can get to survive—in terms of their sensitivity and intelligence... (The kids) really impress me." Blonde Redhead, in spite of their rising popularity, likewise insisted upon maintaining their independence, opting to stay with a hands-off, cooperative label such as Touch and Go, as well as handling booking and management duties themselves.

Selected discography

Singles

"Big Song," Oxo, 1993.
"Vague," Smells Like, 1994.
"Flying Douglas," Rough Trade, 1995.
"10 Feet High," Smells Like, 1995.
"Symphony of Treble," Touch and Go, 1997.
"Slogan," Touch and Go, 1998.

Albums

Blonde Redhead, Smells Like, 1994.
La Mia Vita Violenta, Smells Like, 1995.
Fake Can Be Just As Good, Touch and Go, 1997.
In An Expression of the Inexpressible, Touch and Go, 1998.

Sources

Books

Robbins, Ira A., editor, *Trouser Press Guide to '90s Rock,* Fireside/Simon and Schuster, 1997.

Periodicals

Magnet, November/December, 1998, pp. 45-47.
Melody Maker, November 29, 1997; September 26, 1998.
Washington Post, January 29, 1999.

Online

Blonde Redhead at Touch and Go Records, http://www.southern.com (January 25, 2000).
Ink Blot magazine, http://www.inkblotmagazine.com (January 25, 2000).
Rolling Stone.com, http://www.rollingstone.tunes.com (January 25, 2000).
Yahoo! Music, http://www.musicfider.yahoo.com (January 25, 2000).

—Laura Hightower

Johnny Bond

Singer, songwriter, guitar

Although he composed hundreds of songs including "I Wonder Where You Are Tonight," "Love Gone Cold," "Your Old Love Letters," "Tomorrow Never Comes," and "Those Gone and Left Me Blues," during his entertainment career that endured for more than 30 years, the humorous, self-depreciating singing cowboy Johnny Bond was best remembered for his western classic "Cimarron." In addition to songwriting, recording, and performing, Bond also landed numerous roles in B-western films, often appearing as the musical sidekick for stars such as Gene Autry, Charles Starrett, and others. A successful radio and later television personality as well, Bond was a mainstay on Autry's popular radio show, *Melody Ranch,* from 1940 until the show's cancellation in 1956 and hosted his own television show called *Town Hall Party.*

Born Cyrus Whitfield Bond on June 1, 1915, in Enville, Oklahoma, to a poor farming family, Bond discovered his musical talents at a young age. He started out as a boy playing trumpet, his first instrument, but also learned both guitar and ukulele along the way. Largely inspired by the playing of Jimmie Rodgers, the first performer inducted into the Country Music Hall of Fame and often referred to as the father of country music, as well as western swing bandleader Milton Browne and his Light Crust Doughboys, Bond started entertaining for the first time at local dances during his teens. Upon graduating from high school in 1933, Bond continued to perform locally until he left his rural hometown in 1937, moving to Oklahoma City, Oklahoma, to try and establish a radio career. He first broadcasted under the name Cyrus Whitfield and later as Johnny Whitfield before settling with Johnny Bond. Around the same time, Bond also met and formed a trio with Jimmy Wakely and Scotty Harrell. They originally called themselves the Singing Cowboy Trio, but later changed their name to the Bell Boys after their radio sponsor, the Bell Clothing Company.

The Bell Boys, whose influences were heavily drawn from cowboy singers such as Gene Autry and the Sons of the Pioneers, started out broadcasting from WKY radio in Oklahoma City and cutting transcription discs at KVOO in Tulsa, Oklahoma. Bond, who would go on to a prolific songwriting career, was already penning songs of his own, writing his first classic, "Cimarron," in 1938. Regional success followed, and they soon caught the attention of Hollywood, California, then the center of country music. Autry himself also expressed interest in using the Bell Boys in his radio show, *Melody Ranch,* after hearing them perform during one of his tours in the late 1930s. The trio got their first taste of Hollywood in 1939, when they were brought out for an appearance as the Jimmy Wakely Trio in a B-western, singing cowboy film for Republic Pictures called *The Saga of Death Valley,* which starred cowboy singer Roy Rogers, the most popular western film star of all time.

Trio Arrived in Hollywood

Although Autry, whose film success helped to launch the entire B-western genre, in addition to Rogers, would remain the most prominent of the singing cowboys, their success undoubtedly paved the way for others, and the taste of movie work struck a chord with both Wakely and Bond. By May of 1940, the Wakely Trio—at this time consisting of Bond, Wakely, and Dick Reinhart— and their families had arrived in Hollywood in Wakely's Dodge with the words of Autry still ringing in their ears: "If you boys ever get to California, look me up," as quoted in the *Illustrated History of Country Music.* Almost immediately upon their arrival, the group joined Autry and became regulars on his Sunday afternoon radio show for CBS, a national broadcast called *Melody Ranch.* The move marked an important boost to the careers of Bond, who continued to play on the show for 16 years until its cancellation in 1956, and Wakely, as well as for the development of the country music scene in California. And with their music now reaching millions of listeners, the Wakely Trio became an instant hit across the country. As record offers came pouring in, the trio pulled a clever musical scam, recording as the

For the Record . . .

Born Cyrus Whitfield Bond on June 1, 1915, in Enville, OK; (died on June, 12, 1978, in Burbank, CA) to a poor farming family.

Moved to Oklahoma City, OK, 1937; formed the Bell Boys (later named the Wakely Trio), 1937; penned classic song "Cimarron," 1938; appeared in first B-western, The Saga of Death Valley, 1939; moved to Hollywood, CA, with the Wakely Trio, joined Gene Autry's Melody Ranch radio show, 1940; signed solo recording contract with Columbia Records, 1941; made final film appearance in Song of the Wasteland, 1947; recorded top ten hit "Oklahoma Waltz," 1948; recorded top ten hit "Love Song in 32 Bars," 1950; became host and writer for *Town Hall Party* television show, 1950; signed with the Starday label, 1960; recorded new version of "Ten Little Bottles."

Awards: Inducted into the Country Music Hall of Fame, September 22, 1999.

Jimmy Wakely Trio for the Decca label and as Johnny Bond and the Cimarron Boys for Columbia.

Also in 1940, the group made a second appearance for Republic, this time credited as Jimmy Wakely and His Rough Riders, in the film *The Tulsa Kid,* starring Don "Red" Barry. The group's subsequent film, 1940s *Pony Post,* starring Johnny Mack Brown, came next for Universal. In addition to recording and making film appearances, the group played numerous concerts at ballrooms and clubs throughout Southern California. Along with Harrell, who the group welcomed back into the lineup when he joined them later in Hollywood, the Wakely Trio continued to work together in various configurations for the next two years until Bond—the first group member to receive a solo contract in 1941—and Wakely broke up the trio to move on to broader horizons. Wakely, a handsome man who patterned himself after Autry, formed his own band after leaving *Melody Ranch* and the Wakely Trio and started performing at promotor Forman Phillips' popular "Los Angeles County Barn Dance" at the Venice Pier, one of the major stops for touring country stars. He became so popular that he formed a backing trio, The Saddle Pals, was featured in more than 30 B-westerns, and eventually signed with Monogram Pictures to star in his own western series.

Steady Solo Career

But whereas Wakely experienced meteoric success as an entertainer, Bond enjoyed a steadier career over the years. In 1941, Bond signed with Columbia Records, for which he became a mainstay over the next 14 years. Art Satherly, who had also signed Autry, Tex Ritter, Leadbelly, and other music legends to Columbia, took responsibility for sealing the deal. Bond's first solo recording sessions occurred by August of that year, yielding a hit song entitled "Those Gone and Left Me Blues." He entered the studio again in April of 1942 to record covers of the Carson Robinson, who wrote songs about news events such as "1942 Turkey in the Straw," "Mussolini's Letter to Hitler," "Hitler's Reply to Mussolini," and "Hitler's Last Letter to Hirohito," a series of humorous, insulting numbers inspired by World War II, though Columbia decided not to issue Bond's renditions. Around this time, Bond started earning recognition for his own songwriting skills, as his "I Wonder Where You Are Tonight" and "Cimarron" went into publication. He recorded more work, backed by a band that included bandleader Spade Cooley on violin, including the originals "You Let Me Down" and "Love Gone Cold." Like Wakely, Bond became popular in the Los Angeles country ballroom scene and was usually backed by the Cass County Boys, Autry's own touring band. He also frequently played with Autry on tours and on record throughout the forties and fifties.

Although monetary shortages during the wartime era interrupted Bond's singing career over the next few years, he resumed sessions again in June of 1945, recording three originals including "Heart and Soul," "Gotta Make Up for Lost Time," and "Sad, Sad and Blue." However, Bond kept busy while away from the studio by appearing on Autry's show and other programs, as well as performing on behalf of the war effort. In addition, he worked in 38 films as both a musical sidekick in B-westerns for stars like Autry, Wakely, and Ritter and in musical sequences built around non-singing actors like Johnny Mack Brown and Ray "Crash" Corrigan. He also found work in other types of films, such as in the 1941 comedy *Six Lessons from Madame La Zonga,* starring Leon Errol and Lupe Velez, as well as a rare supporting role appearance for a major film, David O. Selznick's 1946 film *Duel In the Sun.* His last movie appearance came a year later in Wakely's final western, 1947's *Song of the Wasteland.*

All the while, Bond found time to work with other West Coast entertainers, including leading Ritter's studio band, the Red River Valley Boys. And with the end of his movie career, Bond found more energy to focus on his songwriting recording several country hits in 1947 such as "So Round, So Firm, So Fully Packed, "Divorce Me C.O.D.," and "The Daughter of Jole Blon." In 1948, he recorded the top ten hit "Oklahoma Waltz," and recorded two more hits the following year with "Till the End of the World" and "Tennessee Saturday Night." Another top ten hit arrived in 1950 entitled "Love Song in 32 Bars," while "Sick, Sober and Sorry" made the charts in 1951. Also in 1950, Bond became the emcee and a writer for the popular Los Angeles country music television show on KTTV called *Town Hall Party.* He worked on the program for nearly a decade.

Rock 'n' Roll's New Beat

By the 1950s, though, the new sounds of rock and roll began to overshadow country in terms of mainstream popularity. However, unlike many of his comrades, Bond never felt threatened by such changes, and because he realized that country and rock shared close ties, he sometimes tried to combine elements of rock and roll into his songs with some success. Nonetheless, Columbia declined to renew his contract in 1957. By this time, Bond had penned 123 songs, many of which were covered by both country and non-country artists alike for years to come. For example, not only did "Cimarron" become a country standard through recorded versions by the Sons of the Pioneers, Bob Wills, and Jimmy Dean and with concert renditions by Johnny Cash and Chet Atkins, the song was also recorded by musicians from other genres such as Les Paul, Harry James, and Billy Vaughn.

Despite his departure from Columbia, Bond continued to pursue his singing and songwriting career, spending a brief period with Autry's Republic Records label. For Republic, he recorded the song "Hot Rod Lincoln," a crossover tune that sold well and went on to become a rock and roll standard. In 1960, Bond moved to the Starday label, where he remained for the next 11 years. For Starday he recorded a new version of a previous song, "Ten Little Bottles," which became Bond's greatest hit of his career, reaching the number one spot on some charts. However, most of his other songs for Starday, largely a repertoire of drinking songs that made Bond seem a one-note performer, failed to sell with the same success. Ending his relationship with Starday in 1969, Bond, aided by Ritter's influences, signed with Capitol Records. He recorded one album for the label in 1969 with longtime friend Merle Travis, a Delmore Brothers tribute entitled *Great Songs of the Delmore Brothers,* which again failed to sell. By the end of 1969, he was dropped by Capitol and picked up again by Starday. He remained with his former label until he left Starday permanently in 1971. During the early 1970s, Bond recorded songs for the Lamb & Lion label, then signed with Wakely's Shasta label in 1974. His work with Shasta included just one session, which resulted in remakes of some of his older songs and a cover of Woody Guthrie's "Oklahoma Hills."

After enjoying a prolific entertainment career, Bond turned to writing in his later years. He wrote a brief autobiography, in addition to a biography of his old friend Tex Ritter. Bond died on June, 12, 1978, in Burbank, California, and had written more than 400 songs at the time of his death. On September 22, 1999, Bond was inducted into the Country Music Hall of Fame during the 33rd Annual Country Music Association (CMA) Awards.

Selected discography

That Wild, Wicked But Wonderful West, Starday, 1961, reissued by Shasta, 1994.
Live It Up, Laugh It Up, Starday, 1962.
Songs that Made Him Famous, Starday, 1963.
Johnny Bond's Best, Harmony, 1964.
Hot Rod Lincoln, Starday, 1965.
Ten Little Bottles, Starday, 1965.
Famous Hot Rodders I Have Known, Starday, 1966.
Bottled in Bond, Harmony, 1967.
Bottles Up, Starday, 1968.
The Man Who Comes Around, Starday, 1968.
Branded Stock of Johnny Bond, Starday, 1969.
Great Songs of the Delmore Brothers, Longhorn, 1969.
Drink Up and Go Home, Starday, 1970.
Ten Nights in a Barroom, Starday, 1970.
The Best of Johnny Bond, Starday, 1971.
Something Old, New, Patriotic and Blue, Starday, 1971.
Here Come the Elephants, Starday, 1972.
How I Love Them Old Songs, Lion & Lamb, 1974.
Johnny Bond Rides Again, Shasta, 1975, reissued by CMH, 1992.
The Way They Were Back Then, Shasta, 1975.
The Best of Comedy, Richmond, 1996.
Truckstop Comedy, King, 1996.
The Very Best of Johnny Bond, Varese, 1998.
1999—Country Music Hall of Fame, King, 2000.

Sources

Books

Carr, Patrick, editor, *The Illustrated History of Country Music,* Doubleday, 1979.
Kingsbury, Paul, editor, *The Encyclopedia of Country Music,* Oxford University Press, 1998.

Periodicals

Atlanta Journal-Constitution, June 18, 1999.
USA Today, June 17, 1999; September 22, 1999.

Online

"Johnny Bond," *All Movie Guide*, http://www.allmovie.com, (January 12, 2000).
"Johnny Bond," *All Music Guide*, http://www.allmusic.com, (January 12, 2000).

—Laura Hightower

The Boredoms

Alternative rock/noise band

Since forming in the mid-1980s, the Boredoms, known for their sometimes unlistenable creations, have become Japan's most prominent "noise" bands. According to Stephen Thomas Erlewine of the *All Music Guide* website, "Unless you have an extreme amount of patience or enjoy listening to the soothing sounds of heavy machinery, chances are you won't be able to tolerate the Boredoms. Which is exactly what they want, by the way." Inspired by the early output of Sonic Youth and with the support from that band as well as Nirvana behind them, the Boredoms arrived on the alternative/college music scene in the United States in the early 1990s. The group did not speak English fluently, but lyrics were seldom an issue in their compositions, which mixed hardcore punk, free jazz, and sometimes ambient music. Although many felt that the band failed to differentiate themselves enough from their primary influences, namely Sonic Youth, the Boredoms themselves declined to concern themselves with others' opinions, believing that their music did have something new to offer. And according to numerous other critics, the group had, by the time Americans discovered the Boredoms, established a sound that was uniquely their own.

Even those who reacted with less enthusiasm to the Boredoms' noise-rock experiments admitted to their tireless and inventive work ethic, and the band's willpower and high-reaching special effects using pedals and amplifiers endeared such albums as 1994's *Chocolate Synthesizer* to many alternative music fans across Japan, Europe, and the United States. By this time in the band's career, their albums had become more accessible to mainstream listeners, though the band always remained less interested in commercial Japanese pop, which is often as bland, rehearsed-sounding, and mechanical as the Boredoms' creations are eccentric and unpredictable. In addition to holding Sonic Youth in high esteem, the Boredoms also looked toward legendary jazz artists, as well as rap, pop, punk, and rock and roll musicians to serve as inspiration.

The Boredoms included the following members: vocalist Eye Yamataka; drummer, percussionist, trumpeter, keyboardist, and vocalist Yoshimi; guitarist Seichi Yamamoto; vocalist Toyohito Yoshikawa; bassist Hilah; percussionist E-da; and drummer ATR. These various names illustrate one aspect of the Boredoms' playfulness with image and language. Similarly, the group named its 1999 album *Super ae*—the "ae" digraph, pronounced like "eye," was once common in Latin and Latinate English but is now seldom used. The name confused some Americans and other English-speaking people unfamiliar with the ligature, who thought that the album title was actually "Super Ar" or "Super Are."

An ever-evolving bundle of energy based in Osaka, Japan, members began creating wild music together in the early 1980s. At that time, the group consisted of Eye on drums, Yamamoto on guitar, Hira on bass, and an unnamed female singer performing vocals, and they called themselves Acid Maki & Combi and Zombie. Upon that band's demise, the remaining members and others mutated into the Boredoms. Obviously drawing from the early work of Sonic Youth, the group also combined the sounds of other acts from a diverse range of styles. Some of those influences included the free jazz style of Sun Ra, the Beastie Boys, and the Residents, and the guitar stylings of Funkadelic. Eye, who also designed most of the artwork for the group's album covers, said that Funkadelic not only inspired the Boredoms musically, but also cited them as a jacket art influence.

In 1986, along with co-frontman Toyohito Yoshikawa, Eye led the Boredoms to their first Japanese release, *Anal by Anal,* which included songs like "Anal Eater" and "Born to Anal." Two years later in 1988, the group arrived with an even weirder album, *Osorezan to Stooges Kyo,* an outer-space, sonic whirlwind of eclectic songs such as "Call Me God" and "Feedbackf**k" that covered both quirk-rock humor and death-metal posing simultaneously. Both of these records were combined and released in Japan in 1989 as *Onanie Bomb Meets the Sex Pistols;* Warner Brothers later issued the album with different packaging in the United States in 1994. Also in 1988, as

For the Record . . .

Members include **ATR** (also known as Atari), drums; **E-da**, percussion; **Hilah** (formerly Hira), bass; **Eye Yamataka**(formerlyYamatsuka), vocals; **Seichi Yamamoto**, guitar; **Toyohito Yoshikawa**, vocals; **Yoshimi** (also known as Yoshimi P-Wee and P-We YY), drums, percussion, trumpet, keyboards, vocals.

Formed band in Osaka, Japan around1986; released debut album *Anal by Anal*, Trans (Japan), 1986; sophmore release *Osoreazan to Stooges Kyo*, Selfish, 1988; also released *Pop Tatari*, WEA 1992, rerelease on Warner Bros., 1994; initiated a self-funded American tour, also toured with Sonic Youth and Nirvana, 1993; released *Chocolate Synthesizer* in Japan, toured with Lollapalooza '94, 1994; released a more tempered album entitled *Super ae*, 1999.

Addresses: *Home*—Osaka, Japan. *Record company*—Birdman.

the group's name and music spread throughout their native Japan and caught the attention of European audiences and recording artists, the Boredoms earned the opportunity to meet and perform with their idols, Sonic Youth, for a live show in Japan.

The Boredoms' next project, 1989's *Soul Discharge*, revealed more concrete, albeit minimal, reference points. For instance, the song "52 Boredom" made reference to the pop sounds of the B-52s, while "JB Dick + Tin Turner Pussy Badsmell" recalled the grooves of Funkadelic. A daunting album by most accounts, *Soul Discharge* made use of guitarist Yamamoto's accomplished improvisational technique, especially during interludes with drummer Yoshimi. After the initial release of the album, *Soul Discharge* went through several subsequent pressings for which bonus tracks, both new and alternate versions of previously released songs, were added.

In 1992, the Boredoms released their first record for WEA, a major Japanese label, entitled *Pop Tatari*. In the United States, Reprise Records issued the album the following year. According to the band's biography on the Yahoo! Music website, one critic analogized *Pop Tatari* as the "least commercially viable album released by a major label since *Metal Machine Music*, the Lou Reed album." But despite the album's disinterest in mainstream appeal, it nevertheless was considered by many reviewers to represent the apex of the Boredoms' output. With *Pop Tatari*, the Boredoms put forth an endless show of their audio noise spectacle, self-depreciating, humorous conceit, and a surprising display of their grasp of free-jazz. The band's drummers also figured prominently throughout the album, pushing the band forward as well as setting up blocks in the music's path, especially for "Bod" and "Okinawa Rasta Beef (Mockin' Fuzz2)." Likewise, singer Yamatsuka highlighted such tracks as "Heeba" and "Telehorse Uma." An excessive work by all accounts, the album ended with a ten-minute song that includes sounds that more or less document the entire history or rock and roll entitled "Cory & the Mandara Suicide Pyramid Action or Gas Satori." By now, the Boredoms had started to distance themselves from comparisons to Sonic Youth.

In order to further their cause and market *Pop Tatari* in the United States, the Boredoms set out on a self-funded American tour in 1993. Another American tour followed later in the year when Sonic Youth, Nirvana, and others asked the Boredoms to join them for a series of live performances. In the meantime, the group released two more records in Japan: the LP *Wow-2* and the EP *Super Roots* issued by Reprise Records in 1994, which initiated the Boredoms' *Super Roots* series. All of these albums, *Super Roots 2* EP, *Super Roots 3, Super Roots 5,* and *Super Roots 6,* were dominated by unedited musical encounters among the band members, with the later volumes combining both ambient and hardcore sounds and often consisting of just one long piece. For example, *Super Roots 5*, released in Japan by WEA in 1995 consisted of a 64-minute, 19-second single entitled "Go!"

According to Eye, the band approached these records from a different standpoint in comparison to other releases. "The *Super Roots* series doesn't have any part in rehearsing when making songs," he explained in an interview interpreted from Japanese for the internet magazine *Alles*. "We go to the studio, discuss what we'll do in the studio facilities, and have fun realizing on the spot what we have thought of, jokes and so on, normal song making, recording a product that's already finished inside your head is boring. Not that it's boring, but while making songs the usual way, we also wanted to record jingle-like stuff.... Like placing between songs little amusing pieces."

Both 1994 and 1995 proved significant years for the Boredoms. After releasing *Chocolate Synthesizer* in Japan, a more accessible work that earned praise by many music professionals, the band joined America's most prominent rock/pop summer event, Lollapalooza '94, with acts such as the Beastie Boys, George Clinton, and the Smashing Pumpkins. In the fall of that year, the Boredoms toured Europe, followed by a triumphant return tour through 13 cities in Japan and the release of *Super Roots 3* as the year came to a close. After returning to the U.S. and Europe in 1995, the Boredoms released *Chocolate Synthesizer* in May of that year in America. Capturing the attention of alternative and college-aged listeners across the U.S., the album rose to number ten on the *College Music Journal* (*CMJ*) chart. Following the release in 1995 of *Super Roots 5*—there is no fourth volume— in Japan, the Boredoms returned in 1996 with *Super Roots 6* released on Reprise.

In 1999, the Boredoms released a more tempered, yet not exactly mellow album entitled *Super ae* that emphasized groove, a world beat style, and chant over sonic aggression. "Traditional music is always in our heart," the group's vocalist Eye revealed to Mark Jenkins of the *Washington Post* in 1999. Nonetheless, he insisted that the band did not consciously intend to tone down their sound. "It just happened to be like that," he said. "We never [plan] on something." For the album, Eye mentioned that American and European influences like the hardcore punk band the Minutemen and Soulfly, a Brazilian American band that combined heavy metal and Afro-Brazilian drumming, figured prominently. Notable tracks from the album included a tuneful rock song entitled "Super Shine," which resembled the Rolling Stones' "Sing This All Together," as well as the tracks "Super You," "Super Are," and "Super Are You." The Boredoms supported the release by touring in both Japan and the U.S., including a performance at the Bell Atlantic Jazz Festival in New York City in June of 1999.

Throughout their time together, the Boredoms played with various affiliated or side project bands. As of 1999, Eye was also a member of the hardcore punk band 1, Yoshimi played in a band called Ooioo, and Hilah and E-da were members of the group AOA. Yamamoto, meanwhile, was affiliated with a list of bands too numerous to mention. According to Eye, Yamamoto himself even had trouble remembering all the groups he played with. Prior to his membership with 1, Eye worked on other projects, including the groups UFO or Die and Hanatarash, a band often compared to Einsturzende Neubauten and known for involving bulldozers, fire, circular saws, and other tactics during live performances. Eye also collaborated several times with New York-based avant-garde saxophonist John Zorn. In 1999, the singer published a collection of artwork entitled *Nanoo,* which he described to Jenkins as "my mind-expanding-song book with collages and drawings."

Selected discography

Anal by Anal, (Japan) Trans, 1986.
Osorezan to Stooges Kyo, (Japan) Selfish, 1988.
Onanie Bomb Meets the Sex Pistols, (Japan) WEA, 1989; Warner Brothers, 1994.
Soul Discharge, Shimmy-Disc, 1989.
Pop Tatari, (Japan) WEA, 1992; Reprise, 1993.
Wow-2, (Japan) Avant, 1993.
Super Roots, (EP), (Japan) WEA, 1993; Reprise, 1994.
Chocolate Synthesizer, (Japan) WEA, 1994; Reprise, 1995.
Super Roots 2, (EP), (Japan) WEA, 1994.
Super Roots 3, (Japan) WEA, 1994.
Super Roots 5, (Japan) WEA, 1995.
Super Roots 6, Reprise/Warner Brothers, 1996.
Super ae, Birdman, 1999.

Sources

Books

Robbins, Ira A., editor, *Trouser Press Guide to '90s Rock,* Fireside/Simon and Schuster, 1997.

Periodicals

New York Times, June 11, 1999.
Washington Post, June 11, 1999, p. N15; June 15, 1999, p. C09.

Online

All Music Guide website, http://www.allmusic.com, (February 16, 2000).
"Alles Interview Boredoms," *Internet Voice Magazine alles,* http://www.express.co.jp/Alles7/bor1.html, (February 16, 2000).
"Boredoms," *browbeat—issue numero uno—boredoms,* http://www.browbeat.com/browbeat01/boredoms.htm, (February 16, 2000).
"Boredoms Profile," *Internet Voice Magazine alles,* http://www.express.co.jp/ALLES/7/bor_p.html, (February 16, 2000).
"Boredoms," *RollingStone.com,* http://www.rollingstone.tunes.com, (February 16, 2000).
"Boredoms Biography," *Yahoo! Music,* http://www.musicfinder.yahoo.com, (February 16, 2000).

—Laura Hightower

Can

Avant-garde rock group

Although the Can never boasted more than a cult following during their career, the German combo would later be acknowledged as the leading avant-garde rock band to emerge from the 1970s. Always ignoring the trends of contemporary pop music, Can desired to explore other areas of music by breaking traditionally held concepts about rock and roll. In describing the group's sound, rock historians often named Frank Zappa or the Velvet Underground as Can's closest contemporaries, but also noted that in contrast to these artists, Can created a much more serious and inaccessible style of music. "Instead of recording tight pop songs or satire," stated *All Music Guide* contributor Stephen Thomas Erlewine, "Can experimented with noise, synthesizers, nontraditional music, cut-and-paste techniques, and, most importantly, electronic music; each album marked a significant step forward from the previous album, investigating new territories that other rock bands weren't interested in exploring." By the end of their career, Can, whose core members included Irmin Schmidt, Jaki Liebezeit, Michael Karoli, and Holger Czukay, had produced some of the most respected examples of experimental rock ever recorded. The group's groundbreaking, as well as challenging, music would later influence such bands as Public Image Limited, the Fall, Einsturzende Neubauten, and numerous others.

In 1968, the people of Germany felt divisions in both a political and a cultural sense. Aside from the obvious tensions resulting from the East/West split, a decentralized sense of culture prevailed that caused local fixations of various music scenes. However, the late 1960s were nonetheless rebellious, watershed years for youth culture around the world, and changes would arise, especially in music, that would also touch intellectual and artistic activity in Germany. The germ cell of a band that would make history later on as Can felt the new vibrations as well in June of 1968, when five young musicians, together searching for a new musical concept and under the spell of innovative artists such as Jimi Hendrix, the Velvet Underground, and the Mothers of Invention, held a meeting at Irmin Schmidt's apartment in Cologne, West Germany.

Schmidt, a 31-year-old pianist and conductor at the time, along with a then 30-year-old double-bassist named Holger Czukay and an American flautist named David Johnson, received formal classical training in music. Schmidt and Czukay had previously studied with classical avant-garde musician Karlheinz Stockhausen. Abandoning promising careers in academia and classical pursuits to form their own avant-garde rock group, the three men enlisted one of Czukay's students, then 19-year-old Michael Karoli, to play guitar. The band found a fifth member in then 30-year-old jazz percussionist and drummer Jaki Liebezeit, who nominated himself for the position after responding to Schmidt's inquiry about the availability of local drummer.

Adopting the name Inner Space Productions, the group started out working within the German film industry composing and recording soundtrack music. Meanwhile, a wealthy local art patron donated the band free rehearsal and recording space at his castle, Schloss Narvenich, situated near Cologne. It was at this location that Inner Space held their first gig, an improvised show that produced a spectacular collage of rock music and tape samples. The 1968 performance was documented on a cassette tape entitled *Prehistoric Future.*

Can Debuted

Toward the end of 1968, a black American sculptor named Malcolm Mooney arrived in Cologne to visit Schmidt and his wife and Can's longtime manager Hildegarde. During his stay, Mooney linked up with the band as vocalist, leading the band with his intuitive drive closer to rock music. One of the first sessions with Mooney adding vocals yielded the track "Father Cannot Yell." Around the same time, another lineup change occurred; Johnson, whose involvement with the band was more limited than the other members, departed in December of 1968. Shortly thereafter, Mooney and Liebezeit thought up a new name for the group—Can—

For the Record . . .

Members include **Reebop Kwaku Baah** (born in Konongo, Ghana; died c. mid-1980s; former member of Traffic; joined band in 1977), percussion; **Holger Czukay** (born March 24, 1938, in Danzig, Germany; married artist/musician U-She; left band in 1977), bass, vocals, electronics; **Rosko Gee** (former member of Traffic; joined band in 1977), bass; **David Johnson**, flute, electronics; **Michael Karoli** (born April 29, 1948, in Straubing, West Germany), guitar, violin, vocals; **Jaki Liebezeit** (born May 26, 1938, in Dresden, Germany), drums, reeds, vocals; **Malcolm Mooney** (joined band in 1968, left band in 1969), vocals; **Irmin Schmidt** (born May 29, 1937, in Berlin, Germany; married Hildegarde), keyboards, vocals; **Kenji "Damo" Suzuki** (born January 16, 1950, in Japan; joined band in 1970, left band in 1973), vocals.

Formed band in 1968 in Cologne, West Germany; released debut album *Monster Movie*, 1969; released *Tago Mago*, founded Inner Space Studios, 1971; released *Ege Bamysi*, which included the German hit "Spoon," 1972; had a U.K. hit with the single "I Want More," 1976; dissolved band, 1979; Spoon Records released *Can Box*, 1999.

Addresses: *Record company*—Mute Records, 140 W. 22nd St., Ste. 10A, New York City, NY 10011, phone: (212) 255-7670, fax: (212) 255-6056, email: mute@mute.com. *Website*—Can at Spoon Records, http://www.spoonrecords.com.

and the band began work on their debut album, 1969's *Monster Movie*. A unique cosmos of sound recorded with two-track technology, *Monster Movie* shattered numerous well-worn production and musical concepts, and introduced the Can ethic of playing and recording spontaneously against a backdrop of repetitive rhythms.

In December of 1969, Mooney, suffering from paranoia and a psychological breakdown, left the band and returned to the United States. Although his involvement with Can lasted only one year, he would be forever remembered for participating in the band's groundbreaking debut. Mooney also appeared on a few tracks for the project *The Can Soundtracks* (released in 1970), which featured Can's film scores from 1969 through 1970. His era was also extensively documented on the 1981 release *Delay 1968*, a collection of then-unreleased material. Following Mooney's departure, in May of 1970, Can invited Japanese singer Kenji "Damo" Suzuki to join the band when they spotted him on a street corner in Munich, Germany, one afternoon prior to a scheduled Can show. Suzuki immediately accepted Can's offer and gave an impromptu performance with the band that night. In addition to making a living as a traveling street performer, Suzuki had also worked as a cast member for the musical *Hair*. The extraordinary gig, a pandemonium of feedback and ingenious, chaotic noise experiments held at Munich's Blow Up club, became one of the most notable live performances in the band's history.

With Suzuki fronting the band, Can, early in 1971, recorded again on a two-track machine their second official offering, the legendary psychedelic double album *Tago Mago*. Released later that year and illustrating new departures for the skilled collective, the record caught the immediate attention of critics in both England and France. Describing the energy captured on *Tago Mago*, Mills asserted, "the five-pronged Can assault—Liebezeit's volcanic-but-precise cyclical drumming, Czukay's impulsively jabbing bass, Karoli's psychedelicised splatter guitar, Schmidt's pan-topographical keyboards, Suzuki's free-form vocal incantations—was further shaped by Czukay's tape-editing wizardry, and the group was able to lay down lengthy jams from which to whittle its unique studio recordings."

Founded Inner Space Studios

As *Tago Mago* steadily earned acclaim, the band, in December of 1971, officially founded the Inner Space Studios in an old movie theater in Weilerswist, a town near Cologne. After taking up residence at Inner Space to make *Tago Mago*, Can recorded and produced all subsequent projects at their new studio, known as the Can Studio since 1978. In an interview with *Magnet* in 1989, Karoli reflected upon Can's early days and the creation of Innerspace: "We were into instant creation," he recalled. "Because we couldn't afford to pay studio fees, we built our own studio. We didn't have proper technology, just two microphones and not even a real mixing desk. But we got so skilled and the discipline was so tight, that we produced stuff that sounded like it was produced in a proper studio."

During the early 1970s, Can earned a reputation for their highly developed and entertaining live performances as well, creating different arrangements of songs so as not to reproduce an exact replica of a track recorded in the studio. One of Can's performances at the Cologne Sporthalle on February 3, 1972, featured vaudeville artists and other acts in addition to the group's own music. Prominent cameramen, including Martin Schaefer, Robbie Muller, and Egon Mann, were also on location, and captured the show on tape for Peter Przygodda's film *Can Free Concert.*

The band's third album, *Ege Bamysi,* released in October of 1972, included Can's first and most prominent chart success in Germany, the song "Spoon," also the title track for the crime thriller *Das Messer.* Another substantial achievement, *Ege Bamysi,* prompted *Melody Maker* that year to conclude, according to Can's website, "Can are without doubt the most talented and most consistent experimental rock band in Europe, England included." In 1973, Can returned with a proto-ambient classic entitled *Future Days,* the last album recorded with Suzuki. Despite the band's increasing international popularity, Suzuki left the band that year to follow the religious group the Jehovah's Witnesses. After Suzuki's departure, Can's music changed and the remaining members continued more or less as a quartet with Karoli taking on vocal duties at first. Later, various other singers, among them Tim Hardin, joined Can for brief interludes.

In 1974, Can released the album *Limited Edition* and also held the longest concert in the band's history in Berlin, lasting from eight o'clock in the evening until eight thirty the next morning. That same year, the band recorded *Soon Over Babaluma,* an album marking the end of Can's technique of recording straight onto one track. However, this change also gave rise to new discoveries for the band, evidenced on the track "Quantum Physics," Can's first entirely ambient composition. The year 1975 saw the release of the double album *Unlimited Edition,* an extended version of *Limited Edition* that included unreleased session material. For their next album of new material, 1975's *Landed,* Can abandoned two-track recording altogether. Although critically hailed as one of the most advanced rock units after *Landed's* release, Can nonetheless suffered consequences by availing themselves to newer technology.

According to the band, Can's spontaneity and creativity as a collective slowly started slipping away. "In the beginning, when we only had a two-track recorder, we all had to be there together," Liebezeit told Mills. "Later, we had a multi-track machine, so we didn't work together so much in the studio. One would come to the studio and do some overdubbing, and the other ones would stay home. And I think that was not good for the group." Nonetheless, the band prevailed for a while longer, and using more advanced recording methods, Can recorded the musically versatile *Flow Motion* (released in 1976), an album featuring David Gilmour's "I Want More," which became a disco hit single and reached number 30 on the British chart.

Can Disbanded

Around the same time, Czukay developed interests in non-rock instrumentation, including short-wave radios and Dictaphones as primitive samplers, and introduced such elements into Can's music. Not only did these new methods alter the group's sound, but it also necessitated that the band hire a new bass player to cover Czukay's former role. Thus, the well-known rhythm duo of bassist Rosko Gee and percussionist Reebop Kwaku Baah, both former members of the band Traffic, joined Can for 1977's *Saw Delight.* Now retired from the bass position, Czukay for this album served as the "special sounds" engineer. Although *Saw Delight* was well-received, the record's funkier sound and Czukay's new musical process was at odds with the other members' interests in rock music.

Consequently, Czukay departed from Can in May of 1977, and the remaining members recorded two more albums: 1978's disappointing album *Out of Reach* without Czukay and 1979's self-titled release, which was edited by Czukay. The group also issued in 1978 a "best of Can" compilation double album entitled *Cannibalism.* In 1979, realizing that the magic had come to an end, Can finally dissolved. The various members went on to work on solo and collaborative projects, though Czukay enjoyed the most prolific post-Can career. Can played their final show in Lisbon at the end of May of that year before a crowd of more than 10,000 fans. The original Can lineup reunited briefly in 1988 with Mooney at Karoli's new studio near Nice, France, called Outer Space Studio to record another album, 1989's *Rite Time.* The above mentioned members, minus Czukay, came together again in 1991 at the old Can Studio to record the track "Last Night Sleep" for the Wim Wenders film *Until the End of the World.*

Meanwhile, in 1980, Schmidt's wife established the Spoon label—distributed by Mute Records— to start reissuing the group's catalog. Because of her efforts, many of Can's records were later made available on compact disc. In 1997, the label released the remix album *Sacrilege,* followed in 1999 by an impressive and highly recommended box set entitled *Can Box.* "[*Can Box*] was an expensive project and very difficult to organize," Hildegarde Schmidt, who worked tirelessly on the project, revealed to Mills. "The hours and hours of live tapes; the video itself, which was difficult to put together;

and the book, which I did with (German journalist) Wolf (Kampmann)." The finished product included two live discs, a 130-minute video of concert and documentary footage, and a 500-page book with text in French, English, and German.

Selected discography

Monster Movie, United Artists, 1969; reissued on CD by Spoon/Mute.
The Can Soundtracks, Liberty, 1979; reissued on CD by Spoon/Mute.
Tago Mago, Liberty, 1971; reissued on CD by Spoon/Mute.
Ege Bamyasi, United Artists, 1972; reissued on CD by Spoon/Mute.
Future Days, United Artists, 1973; reissued on CD by Spoon/Mute.
Limited Edition, United Artists, 1974.
Soon Over Babaluma, United Artists, 1974; reissued on CD by Spoon/Mute.
Landed, Virgin, 1975; reissued on CD, Virgin, 1987; reissued on CD by Spoon/Mute.
Unlimited Edition, Virgin, 1975; reissued on CD by Spoon/Mute.
Flow Motion, Harvest, 1976; reissued, Virgin, 1987; reissued on CD by Spoon/Mute.
Saw Delight, Virgin, 1977; reissued on CD by Spoon/Mute.
Out of Reach, EMI/Electrola, 1978; reissued Magnum/Thunderbolt, 1988.
Cannibalism: 1968-1974, United Artists, 1978; reissued, Spoon, 1980; reissued on CD by Spoon/Mute.
Can, EMI/Electrola, 1979; reissued, Magnum/Thunderbolt, 1985; reissued on CD by Spoon/Mute.
Delay 1968, Spoon, 1981; reissued on CD by Spoon/Mute.
Only You, (cassette tape), Pure Freude, 1982.
Prehistoric Future, (cassette tape), Tago Mago, 1984.
Rite Time, Phonogram, 1989; reissued on CD by Spoon/Mute.
Cannibalism 2, Spoon, 1992; reissued on CD by Spoon/Mute.
Cannibalism 3, Spoon, 1994; reissued on CD by Spoon/Mute.
Can Anthology 25 Years, Spoon, 1994; reissued on CD by Spoon/Mute.
Peel Sessions, Strange Fruit, 1995.
Radio Waves, Sonic Platten, 1997.
Sacrilege, Spoon/Mute, 1997.
Can Box, Spoon/Mute, 1999.

Sources

Periodicals

Magnet, April/May 1999, p. 87; August/September 1999, pp. 35-38.

Online

All Music Guide, http://www.allmusic.com (February 17, 2000).
"Can," *Rolling Stone.com*, http://www.rollingstone.tunes.com (February 17, 2000).
"Can History," *Can Site Map*, http://www.spoonrecords.com/sitemap.html (February 17, 2000).
"His 'n' Listen," *Third Ear +*, http://www.tribeca.ios.com/~jpayne/ThirdEar.html (February 17, 2000).
Holger Czukay website, http://www.czukay.de/can/index.html, (February 17, 2000).

—Laura Hightower

Vikki Carr

Singer

One of the great success stories of modern day entertainers is Mexican-American Vikki Carr, born Florencia Bisenta de Casilias Martinez Cardona on July 19,1942 in El Paso, Texas, to Carlos and Florencia Cardona. She is the eldest of seven children and has been called the "Calias" of contemporary music, a lady who sings with her heart and has released more than 50 best selling recordings including 17 gold albums embracing two languages. Deeply proud of her Mexican heritage and her Mexican-American parents, she always shares her lengthy christened birth name with her audiences.

Raised in a strict family, her father was often referred to as "the priest" because of his sermons to his children. He was very supportive of her career development, installed a strong work ethic in his children and although very stern, when it came to music he would allow her to participate in any endeavor. Although the Cardona family was very rich in love, concern and care for one another and others, when food was in short supply her mother would go into the San Gabriel Valley and retrieve wild growing berries from young cactus plants to feed her

AP/Wide World Photos. Reproduced by permission.

For the Record . . .

Born Florencia Bisenta, De Casillas Martinez Cardona, July 19, 1942, in El Paso, Texas; daughter of a Mexican American family headed by Carlos Cardona, a self taught construction engineer and Florencia, nee Martinez, a homemaker; married Dan Moss, (divorced); married Michael Neilson (divorced); married Dr. Pedro De Leon, June 1993.

Made her debut as an angel singing "Silent Night" and "Adeste Fidelis" in Latin at a children's school Christmas play in 1947;, employed as a bank clerk for in Los Angeles, CA, late 1950s; worked as a singer in nightclubs in and around the Los Angeles area, late 1950s; hired by Pepe Callahan's Mexican-American band that led to a tour on the Nevada lounge circuit; released single "He's a Rebel," 1960; released "It Must Be Him," 1961.

Awards: Three Grammy Awards for "It Must Be Him," 1961; Woman of the Year Award, Los Angeles Times 1970; Star on the Hollywood Walk of Fame, 1981; Nosotros Golden Eagle Award, 1981; Woman of Year Award Hispanic Women's Council 1984; Hispanic Woman of the Year by the Los Angeles Hispanic Women's Council, 1986; Silver Achievement Award, YWCA 1989; Golden Eagle Award, Nosotros 1989; Founder of Hope Award 1990; YWCA Silver Achievement Award 1990; Girls Scouts of America Award 1991; Hispanic Heritage Award, Washington, D. C. 1996; 17 Gold/Platinum Albums

Addresses: *Management*—Vi Car Entertainment, 6245 Vance Jackson Rd., San Antonio, TX 78230.

family. Carr first learned to sing in the school choir and school plays and regularly heard her father singing and playing a guitar among friends. By the time she graduated from high school, she was singing with local bands around the Los Angeles and the San Gabriel Valley. After she graduated from high school with college preparatory courses, she was forced to seek permanent employment to help her family financially and became employed with a Los Angeles bank as a bookkeeper.

She continued to sing in local bands and while her father was shopping at an automobile dealership, he came across an old friend who mentioned he knew of a band looking for a bilingual singer. She quickly learned a few songs in Spanish that led to a successful audition with Pepe Callahan's Mexican-Irish Band. She made her professional debut at the Chi Chi Club in Palm Springs, California with Callahan under the adopted stage name, "Carlita", after her father Carlos.

Carr left the Pepe Callahan band and went solo in Reno, Nevada, traveling the lounge circuit with the Fabulous Woodsons, a vaudeville troupe. This was followed by Las Vegas and Lake Tahoe, where she joined the Chuck Leonard Quartet, singing a mix of old favorites and more contemporary material on the lounge circuit. After one last tour on the lounge circuit with an act billed as the Andrini Brothers, she took 25 dollars and with the continued encouragement of her father and an accordion playing friend, she made recordings of popular songs and won a recording contract with Liberty Records in 1961.

One evening while singing at the Sands Hotel in Las Vegas, she became discouraged by the party atmosphere, occasional rudeness and obvious lack of attention to her performance. After she returned to her dressing room, there was a knock at the door and there stood a very tall man. It was Nat King Cole. He apologized for the group's discourtesy and bad manners but strongly encouraged her to continue her career and never stop singing. "I was only a kid and he made a lasting impression," she said.

Her rise to stardom began in Australia in 1960, where she recorded "He's a Rebel" that became a major hit. That was followed by a another number one hit in England, "It Must Be Him;" the following year it was released in the United States and earned Carr three Grammy Award nominations. In the 1990s, the song was again used in the 1987 Academy Award winning motion picture, *Moonstruck* that starred Cher and Nicolas Cage. A string of hits followed including "With Pen in Hand" for which she received her fourth Grammy Award nomination, "The Lesson," "Can't Take My Eyes Off of You" and "For Once in My Life."

In 1966, she went to Vietnam with performer Danny Kaye to entertain United States servicemen and women. For two weeks she sang for the troops in combat areas before thousands of appreciative fans and stage locations were sometimes changed because of battle conditions. Since it was a very small entertainment troupe, she and Kaye were allowed to visit locales where only a few soldiers were entertained at a time. She also entertained more than 10,000 soldiers at one time including those from the the 101st First Calvary as well as others on the United States aircraft carrier, Kittyhawk. The following year, she appeared in a critically acclaimed performance in *South Pacific* at the starlight Theater in Kansas City and in 1969 in the *Unsinkable Molly Brown* with the John Kenley Players in Ohio.

Carr has performed at the White House for Presidents Richard Nixon in 1970, Gerald Ford in 1974 and sang for George Bush, Ronald Reagan and a 1967 Royal Command Performance for the Queen of England. Carr has tremendous international appeal and many of her sold out performances have occurred in Japan, Germany, Spain, Mexico, France, England, Australia, and Holland. She is one of the most popular and beloved recording artists in many Latin American countries. She has been a frequent guest star on major network television shows, including Perry Como, Dean Martin, Ray Anthony, Jackie Gleason, Carol Burnett and numerous other shows including many in the United Kingdom. She was also a regular guest host for Johnny Carson on the *Tonight Show* and Michael Jackson's ABC radio show as well. In recent years she has made two guest appearances on television's *Baywatch* series.

In 1998, Carr performed at New York's Carnegie Hall in a special tribute to Judy Garland. Vikki Carr and friends also performed a 1998 television special for the Public Broadcasting System special entitled "Vikki Carr, Memories, Memorias". In addition to the popular songs listed throughout, additional hits include: "It Must Be Him," "San Francisco," "Nowhere Man," "My Heart Reminds Me," "Santiago," "For Those Who Are Young," "With Pen in Hand," "For Once in My Life," "Yesterday I Heard the Rain," "Don't Break My Pretty Balloon," "Eternity," "So Nice," and "He's a Rebel." She has recorded more than 13 albums in Spanish and more 55 best selling recordings including 17 gold records.

In 1976, the Vikki Carr Scholarship Foundation was formed, which provides higher education scholarships to Hispanic teens. It has funded college tuition for more than 300 students totaling over a quarter of a million dollars. " My voice is a gift and a gift is nothing unless you can share it. I didn't like what I was reading and hearing about the image of Latinos and in particular Mexican-Americans. My publicist and friend told me to do something about it. The Foundation seeks to help young Latino students achieve their goals through a college education, something I myself was never able to do", she said. Her humanitarian efforts have complimented such charities as The United Way, The American Lung Association, Cystic Fibrosis, Cerebral Palsy, The Muscular Dystrophy Association, and St. Jude's Hospital.

Selected discography

CDs

Memories, Memoiras, Universal 012-15306-2.
Vikki Carr, Greatest Hits, Curb D2-77677.
The Unforgettable, Vikki Carr, EMI 7243-8-34468-2-7 Import.
It Must Be Him, The Best of Vikki Carr, Liberty 0777-7-93450-2.

Albums

Discovery! Miss Vikki Carr, Liberty LRP 3354.
Don't Break My Pretty Balloon, Liberty LST 7565.
For Once in My Life, Liberty LST 7604.
From the Heart, Pair PDL 2-1082.
The Golden Songbook, United Artists UA LA-089-F2.
That's All, Sunset SUS 5228.
Unforgettable, Pickwick SPC- 3613.
The Very Best of Vikki Carr, United Artists, UA LA 244G.
The Very Best of Vikki Carr, United Artists UA LA 385-E.
Vikki Carr Live at the Greek Theater, Columbia KG 32656.
The Ways to Love a Man, Springboard SPB 4027.

Sources

Books

Gammond, Peter, *The Oxford Companion to Popular Music,* Oxford University Press, 1993.
Kaplan, Mike, *Variety Who's Who in Show Business,* Garland Publishing, 1983.
Larkin, Colin, *The Guiness Encyclopedia of Popular Music,* Guiness Publishing, 1992.
Lax, Roger and Frederick Smith, *The Great Song Thesaurus,* Oxford University Press, 1989.
Maltin, Leonard, *Movie and Video Guide 1995,* Penguin Books Ltd., 1994.
Morino, Marianne, *Hollywood Walk of Fame,* Ten Speed Press, 1987.
Osborne, Jerry, *Rockin Records,* Osborne Publications, 1999.

Online

"Vicki Carr," *All Music Guide,* http://www.allmusic.com/cg/x.dll, (January 1999).
"Vicki Carr," *Hot Comedy Productions,* http://www.hotcomedy.com, (October 1999).
"Vicki Carr," *The Orleans Showroom,* http://www.orleanscasino.com/entertainment/vikki_carr.html, (October 1999).
"Vicki Carr," *Verio,* http://www.tvshowbiz.com/vikkicarr.html (October 1999).

Additional information was obtained in an interview with Vikki Carr on October 11, 1999.

—Francis D. McKinley

Vic Chesnutt

Singer, songwriter, guitar

Corbis. Reproduced by permission.

While numerous artists can produce convincing stories of alienation, guilt, remorse, self-effacing misery, and overall heartbreak through song, few, if any, accomplish the talk with the same bitter pleasure, honesty, left-handed wit, or charm of songwriter and Athens, Georgia, resident Vic Chesnutt. Singing in an unsteady voice and strumming simple chords on an acoustic guitar from his wheelchair (a confinement that resulted from a paralyzing car accident), Chesnutt mastered the skill of turning predictable emotions inside out by using sublime and intentionally unpolished lyrics. A colorful idealist and storyteller as well, Chesnutt was not afraid to confront his own shortcomings, as well as the world's in general, through his music. His poignant, despairing and mordant yet humorous poetry led reviewers to compare his lyrics to southern author Flannery O'Connor. "In a bleak corrosion of Chesnutt's tender idealism," Ira A. Robbins asserted in the *Trouser Press Guide to '90s Rock,* "a highly literate mind in a ruined body becomes a willful primitive with a ferocious and highly developed sense of irony. His skilled songwriting burns with reality's pain while glowing with imagination." Thanks in a large part to the encouragement and support of one famous fan and frequent producer, Michael Stipe of the Athens-based band R.E.M., who had been taken by Chesnutt's music since the early 1980s, the songwriter's popularity continued to broaden throughout the following decade.

Chesnutt was born in 1965 in Jacksonville, Florida, where he spent his early childhood with his adoptive parents. Besides curiosities about his genetic makeup (he insisted that because of his craving for Guinness beer, he must have at least some Irish blood), Chesnutt never felt driven to seek out his biological parents. After moving with immediate family to Athens, Georgia, Chesnutt still maintained close ties with his native state, spending summers with his extended family who lived in the town of Live Oak, also located in northern Florida. Later on, the southern United States, including Florida, would figure into Chesnutt's songwriting. The song "Betty Lonely," for instance, "is totally a Florida love song ... a love song for Florida," he told Gavin Foster in an interview for the online magazine *Ink Blot.* However, along with the state's wildlife and natural beauty, Chesnutt also drew attention to how man destroyed much of the land. "But they [developers] have raped Florida in a major way, just completely ... by digging canals and draining the wetlands," he continued. "It's a fascinating history Florida has... like the turn of the century cattle farms ... I'm completely tied to it in my imagination."

Language and its usage has also fascinated Chesnutt and influenced his lyrical output. "I've always been interested in the evocative nature of language," he said

For the Record . . .

Born in 1965 in Jacksonville, FL.

Began performing at clubs in Athens, GA, caught the attention of Michael Stipe of R.E.M., early 1980s; signed with Texas Hotel Records and released debut album *Little*, 1990; released *West of Rome*, Texas Hotel, 1992; released *Drunk*, Texas Hotel, 1994; released *Is the Actor Happy?*, 1995; released *Nine High a Pallet*, Capricorn, 1995; released and recorded with various artists *Sweet Relief II: Gravity of the Situation*, 1996; signed with Capitol Records and released *About to Choke,* 1996; signed with Capricorn Records and released *The Salesman and Bernadette,* 1998.

Addresses: *Record company*—Capricorn Records, 83 Walton St., Atlanta, GA 30303, phone: (404) 954-6600, fax: (404) 954-6687.

to Thor Christensen of the *Dallas Morning News.* "One song I remember really liking [growing up] was the Beatles 'Cry Baby Cry,' which is kind of an adult nursery rhyme with surreal lyrics." Other creative spirits that influenced Chesnutt included Austrian writer Franz Kafka. "The things he was writing about were so surreal and insane, but he always had this calm tone, which inspired me a great deal."

From an early age, Chesnutt began to contemplate other subjects that would impact his musical creativity, such as his personal notion of reality (or lack thereof), idealism, and spiritual longing. All of these emotions and perspectives culminated in 1983 when Chesnutt, then 18 years old and playing keyboards in an Athens band called the La De Das, was driving under the influence, lost control of his car, and ended up in a ditch. The accident left him a paraplegic confined to a wheelchair, a condition that impacted his art, though mostly in a physical sense. "One hand is paralyzed, and the other has big problems," Chesnutt, who strums his guitar with a pick attached to his arm, explained to *Boston Globe* writer Jim Sullivan. "So it definitely affects the notes I play and how I play 'em. I'm physically impaired. I've got to be a little wily to play." In contrast, Chesnutt believed that the debilitating injury resulted in few overall differences in his songwriting. "I've gained insights into the human condition, maybe from the way I am now, from the times in the hospital and being relegated to handicapped parking spaces," continued Chesnutt. "I've been writing songs my whole life, even before I was in a wheelchair, so I still think about the same things I did before." And despite the public celebrity he enjoyed in his later career, the irreverent singer declined to serve as a spokesman for people with similar conditions. "I don't really talk about 'disabled issues' or whatever you call it. Most of the time, my political views on the issues are a little different than the norm."

Soon after recovering from the accident, Chesnutt struck out on his own, playing contemporary acoustic folk music on guitar and singing in clubs around Athens. One of the town's most renowned citizens, Michael Stipe, became a huge fan of Chesnutt after seeing one of his shows at the 40 Watt Club and encouraged the local hero to start a recording career of his own. After some prodding, Chesnutt agreed, and Stipe helped produce the singer's debut album and worked on landing Chesnutt a record contract. Recorded in one day in 1988 at Stipe's offices in Athens, featuring a trace of synthesizer on the track "Speed Racer" and a small acoustic band for "Stevie Smith," *Little* was eventually picked up by the Texas Hotel label and released in 1990. Other songs on the album included "Rabbit Box," which told the story of Chesnutt, as a child, catching a rabbit and a possum, then setting the animals free and breathing a sigh of relief, and the passing along of the unfortunate story of Joan, a newspaper girl who hung herself entitled "Mr. Riley." In the song, Chesnutt revealed, "They found her by the frozen lake but it wasn't frozen enough to skate but by the look on her face it must have been awful tempting."

For Chesnutt's follow-up album, 1992's *West of Rome* (also issued on Texas Hotel), Stipe incorporated a handful of musicians to play cello, bass, drums, and keyboards for a more ambitious production. More accomplished in his vocalization, Chesnutt put his naked emotions on the line for the challenging album. He focuses jealousy and romantic hurt in "Where Were You," stumbles into an abyss of self-loathing in "Stupid Preoccupation," and discovers that raw pain is beyond his control in "Withering." Chesnutt, known for his clever play on words, engages this skill on the songs such as "Lucinda William" and "Sponge." Other noteworthy songs included "Florida," which Chesnutt declares the "perfect place to retire from life," "Soggy Tongues," an attack on malicious gossips, and "Steve Willoughby," a song that displays Chesnutt's guarded optimism.

After recording his first two albums, Chesnutt started to enjoy a building cult audience, and other famous rock musicians took notice of his intimate work. In 1994, Chesnutt took a significant leap forward in sound—at times more eclectic than acoustic—songwriting, and vocal development with the release of *Drunk,* his first accessible album. Chesnutt revealed later that he came up with the album's name because the term described his state throughout the recording process—a heavy drinker in his younger days, Chesnutt quit consuming alcohol altogether in the late 1990s; years of excess had by then all but destroyed his liver. He brings forth his southern charm in songs like "Kick My Ass" and "Dodge," which includes the lines: "I bent over backwards to misbehave/It's a holy wonder I didn't just flip over into an early grave," a reference to his life-altering accident.

Delving further into his personal experiences, the singer in *Drunk* also recalls his hospital days in "Gluefoot" and "Supernatural," all the while maintaining a sense of amusement about his own misfortunes. "I worry that there's nothing universal in my songs," the singer admitted to Ira Robbins in *Newsday* in 1994. "But I really don't care. I don't beg people to be listening to me or nothing." According to Chesnutt, who also toured with the popular rock band Live that year, found satisfaction elsewhere: "I feel the best when I'm writing a tune." For some people—the songwriter believes—listening to his music was similar to watching a movie. "Even if they don't relate to it personally, they might appreciate my story, or just the circumstance around it," Chesnutt continued. "A lot of my songs are rather vague, 'cause I try to hide my specific meaning in metaphors and [stuff] like that. It's what writers do.... Language is a heavy deal to me."

Chesnutt's fourth album for Texas Hotel, *Is the Actor Happy,* appeared in 1995 and saw the songwriter entering into the realm of commercial readiness. Under the guidance of producer John Keane of the Athens-based group Widespread Panic, a low-key backing trio and Chesnutt delivered the artist's eccentric songs with empathy, such as for the far-away vision of "Thailand" and the close-up revelations of "Thumbtack." He also illustrated his aptitude for balancing self-mocking humor and determination in "Gravity of the Situation," taking the serious aspects of life in stride without assigning blame. Around the same time, Chesnutt dedicated time to a side project called Brute with the members of the group Widespread Panic, including Keane, David A. Schools, Michael Houser, Todd Nance, John Hermann, Johnny Hickman, and David Lowery. Brute released the country-soul-rock flavored album *Nine High a Pallet* in 1995.

The following year, Chesnutt's fanbase exploded with the release of a tribute album by various artists entitled *Sweet Relief II: Gravity of the Situation.* Up to that point, "I mainly just relied for my living on people liking my songs and telling other people," Chesnutt told Sullivan. The first "Sweet Relief" album, released in 1993, paid tribute to the music of Victoria Williams, who suffered from multiple sclerosis. With the proceeds from that album, the Sweet Relief Musician Fund was established to aid artists who need medical assistance and remain uninsured. Likewise, sales of Chesnutt's tribute, along with private contributions, helped expand and sustain the same trust. In addition to Stipe and his band R.E.M., other artists who performed Chesnutt's songs for the release included Madonna, Live, Hootie and the Blowfish, the Smashing Pumpkins, Red Red Meat, Cracker, the Indigo Girls, Nanci Griffith, Garbage, Soul Asylum, Kristin Hersh, Sparklehorse, Joe Henry, and Mary Margaret O'Hara. "I just love Vic. I think his music is so good, he's written so many great songs," Cracker's David Lowery said to David John Farinella of *Billboard* magazine. "I'm a big fan. That's why I wanted to do it."

Soon after the songs of Chesnutt's benefit album hit stores in 1996, the singer signed with a major label, Capitol Records, and released About to Choke that same year. Although a critical success, the album remained a bit too dark and enigmatic to garner substantial mainstream record sales. "A lot of people look at me and hear my music and think it's too depressing, which I can't understand," Chesnutt told Christensen. "Every song of mine has something funny in it." Nonetheless, Capitol released the musician from his contract shortly before he was scheduled to record his second album for the label. "They pretty much gave the record to me and said, 'Go find somebody who cares,'" he recalled to Steve Dollar of the Atlanta Journal-Constitution in 1998. Around the same time, in spite of the setback, Chesnutt made his acting debut for a small role in the Billy Bob Thornton *Sling Blade* and was featured in a documentary of his life entitled *Speed Racer,* produced and directed by Peter Sillen. The film aired on PBS and was made available on video.

After leaving Capitol, Chesnutt accepted an offer to sign with Atlanta's Capricorn Records, releasing his next album, The Salesman and Bernadette, in 1998. Another critical favorite, the album received an eight out of ten stars from Spin magazine reviewer Eric Weisbard, who wrote, "With a trembling quiver that's loose, self-possessed and amply self-mocking, plus music that dips and flows just as thoroughly, Chesnutt's oeuvre is passive/aggressive indolent: The same song can put you to sleep, then beat you up," as quoted by Dollar in the Atlantic Journal and Constitution. For the album's opening track, "Woodrow Wilson," Chesnutt sang with country superstar Emmylou Harris. Meeting Harris, admitted Chesnutt, who grew up listening to albums by Dolly Parton and Hank Williams, made him somewhat nervous at first. "This was life-changing, meeting her," he said to Steve Knopper of *Newsday* in 1999. "Now I was like, 'I can't suck now. I've met Emmylou." " Moreover, *The Salesman and Bernadette* placed the singer before the public eye like never before, earning Chesnutt appearances on NBC's Late Night with Conan O'Brien and for the PBS concert series *Sessions at West 57th.*

Selected discography

Little, Texas Hotel, 1990.
West of Rome, Texas Hotel, 1992.
Drunk, Texas Hotel, 1994.
Is the Actor Happy?, Texas Hotel, 1995.
(With Widespread Panic) Brute, *Nine High a Pallet*, Capricorn, 1995.
(Various artists) *Sweet Relief II: Gravity of the Situation (The Songs of Vic Chesnutt),* Columbia, 1996.
About to Choke, Capitol, 1996.
The Salesman and Bernadette, Capricorn, 1998.

Sources

Books

Robbins, Ira A., editor, *Trouser Press Guide to '90s Rock,* Fireside/Simon and Schuster, 1997.

Periodicals

Atlanta Journal-Constitution, April 15, 1997; August 19, 1997; December 18, 1998, p. P04..
Billboard, June 22, 1996, pp. 12-14; October 5, 1996, p. 18.
Dallas Morning News, January 22, 1999, p. 63.
Denver Rocky Mountain News, March 24, 1997, p. 14D.
Entertainment Weekly, August 2, 1995, p. 58; January 10, 1997, p. 58.
Newsday, June 26, 1994, p. 23; January 7, 1999, p. C01.
New York Times, October 30, 1998.
People, August 19, 1996, p. 23.
Playboy, January 1997, pp. 30-32.
Washington Post, July 16, 1999, p. N08.

Online

"Vic Chesnutt,"*All Music Guide*, http://www.allmusic.com, February 10, 2000.
"Symposium with Vic Chesnutt," *Ink Blot Magazine*, http://www.inkblotmagazine.com, February 10, 2000.

—Laura Hightower

Billy Childish

Singer, songwriter

Although an admitted commercial and critical failure, British musician, writer, and artist Billy Childish has become one of the most prolific performers in rock history. In fact, a complete discography of his solo work and projects as a member of his various bands would take up countless pages. As of late 1999, he had released between 100 to 150 albums as a solo artist and as a member of bands such as Thee Headcoats, and also worked with and produced records for bands such as Mudhoney and the New Bomb Turks. A singer, songwriter, artist, poet, critic, fanzine editor, and guitarist who suffers from severe dyslexia, Childish, it would seem, gets little rest. However, many have never heard of Childish, listened to his songs, viewed his estimated 1,800 paintings, or read his excess of 40 books of verse and two novels that spanned his long, uninterrupted career. A cherished underground musician, Childish has remained obscure to the mainstream. Nevertheless, Childish started recording in 1979, playing a rough, punk-inspired form of music commonly called garage rock for its lo-fi production techniques. Although his music varied in substance and coherency over the years, the consistent element of Childish's work was that it always sounded as though it was recorded and mixed in about an hour. "When we record, I take the song along and teach the others, and then we do one take," he explained to Jim Sullivan in a 1996 interview with *San Francisco Weekly.* "A lot of it we can't play live, because I don't know the words. We know it for about three minutes, when we record it."

Thus, Childish values immediacy and intensity over technicalities, and he often seems in a hurry to move on to the next song, as well as the next band. Considered a primitive talent because of his learning disability and lack of a completed formal education, Childish made music based on pure emotion and even revealed that he never learned to play guitar properly. But despite such setbacks, Childish remained unfailingly sure of himself and his vision, and even his worst critics declared that his music was as honest and direct as one was ever likely to hear. For this reason, Childish became a cult hero for many across Europe, the United States, and Japan. And while critics called Childish everything from a mad genius to a goofball, his followers insisted that he was one of the most under-appreciated musicians of his generation. Childish has also inspired a younger generation of musicians; some of his most loyal supporters included the late Kurt Cobain, Beck, Jon Spencer, and Graham Coxon of Blur. Years after releasing his first single, the Sex Pistols-inspired "Fun in the U.K.," Childish continued to produce material at an amazing rate, epitomizing the endurance and determination of the archetypal rock outsider.

Billy Childish was born Bill Hamper in 1958 in Chatham, Kent, England, where he would continue to reside and work throughout his life. Art, as well as a love for music, came to Childish early in life. He loved to paint from as far back as he could remember, and enjoyed listening to the Beatles and the Rolling Stones. When Childish reached his teens, he discovered punk music and became a fan of the Sex Pistols, the Kinks, and the Clash. Around the same time, the young artist also started listening to blues and rock music; some of his favorite performers included Bo Diddley and Jimi Hendrix.

Lacking the necessary skills and determination to excel at school, Childish dropped out at age 16,and at age 17, took a job working in the local dockyard. However, making a living as a laborer only lasted for a short time. "I decided I didn't want to do it," he recalled to Sullivan. "I've always been a bit single-minded about that." In 1977, Childish won acceptance into St. Martins College of Art after submitting 600 of his own drawings, but only lasted in the program half a term. Around the same time, Childish was drawn more and more to the British punk scene. According to Childish, taking on an alias was meant as a tribute to punk's earlier days. "We used to go to the shows up in London," he recalled. "I started writing a punk fanzine. Everyone seemed to have a weird and wonderful name, so I wanted one. I was called Gus Claudius, and a friend said, 'you're not Gus Claudius, you're Billy Childish.'"

Like many unemployed British artists and musicians, Childish spent much of his life living on government

For the Record . . .

Born Bill Hamper in 1958 in Chatham, Kent, England. *Education*: Studied at St. Martins College of Art for half a term, 1977.

Formed the Pop Rivets, 1976; band mutated into the Milkshakes, 1982; disbanded the Milkshakes and formed Thee Mighty Caesars, started recording blues-oriented solo work, mid-1980s; formed Thee Headcoats, 1989; released two-CD sampler *I Am the Billy Childish,* 1991; Thee Headcoats broke up when bassist Johnny "Tub" Johnson left the band, 1999; has published around 40 collections of poetry and two novels, released 100-150 solo and collaborative albums, and has created an estimated 1800 paintings.

Addresses: *Websites*—Thee Billy Childish: http://www.billychildish.com, Stuckism: http://www.stuckism.com.

handouts and admitted to neglecting to pay taxes for his art-related income, known as "working on the black" in England, because his earnings were usually so meager. Not until the mid- to late-1990s did he start earning any mentionable income, primarily from his paintings. Childish arrived on the punk scene in 1979 with his first band, the Pop Rivets, an enthusiastic mod-punk combo that recorded three self-produced studio albums. At first, Childish provided just vocals and finally learned to play guitar at about 20 years of age. By 1982, the band had mutated into the Milkshakes (also known as Thee Milkshakes and originally Mickey and the Milkshakes). A more competent band than the Pop Rivets, the Milkshakes played energetic garage rock infused with the spirit of Bo Diddley and the early Kinks. Although not so impressive as their inspirations, the Milkshakes fascinated many by the amount of work they produced. For example, in 1984, the band's most productive year, the Milkshakes released at least seven albums, and four of those recordings came out on the same day.

Meanwhile, Childish, by now playing guitar as well as singing, and Milkshakes partner Mickey Hampshire served behind-the-scenes with their sister group, the Delmonas, who originally convened as the backing singers for the Milkshakes but ended up releasing several records of their own. Around the mid-1980s, Childish retired the Milkshakes and started a similar sounding band called Thee Mighty Caesars. His new band's original lineup consisted of the Milkshake rhythm section, and like their predecessors, Thee Mighty Caesars enjoyed a prolific output. Childish released most of their records on his own imprint label, Hangman. He also used the publishing arm of the label to begin issuing dozens upon dozens of volumes of his poetry. Also during Thee Mighty Caesars years, Childish started producing solo and side projects at an astounding rate under various assumed names and with other musicians. A small portion of his earlier work, which brought forth the singer's blues side, included *I've Got Everything Indeed, i remember,* and *The 1982 Cassettes,* all released in 1987. *Poems of Laughter and Violence*—a spoken-word, ambient project—was released in 1988, while 1990's *50 Albums Great* was a retrospective collection of solo versions of songs from previous releases.

In 1989, Childish established a new vehicle for his punk and rock impulses with Thee Headcoats, a trio formed with drummer and backing vocalist Bruce Brand, who also performed with the Pop Rivets, the Milkshakes, and Thee Mighty Caesars. Johnny "Tub" Johnson, who replaced original member Ollie Dolat, joined the lineup on bass and backing vocals. Considered the most successful and accessible of Childish's undertakings, Thee Headcoats continued the singer's propensity for releasing massive amounts of work. Some of the group's more recognized albums included 1993's *Beached Earls* CD, which combined the *Beach Bums Must Die* and *The Earls of Suavedom* vinyl-only albums, both released in 1990, and emphasized the band's 1960s lo-fi garage tendencies; *Heavens to Murgatroyd*, released in 1990, and *Headcoatitude*, released in 1991, offered both rhythm and blues as well as pop songs; and *Bo in Thee Garage*, released in 1991, was a careless, yet compelling, Bo Diddley tribute. The band also recorded numerous live albums, including *Live! At the Wild Western Room* and *The Sound of the Baskervilles,* released in 1994 and 1995 respectively. These recordings were made with Thee Headcoats' all-female counterparts, Thee Headcoatees (which included members of the Delmonas), whose own albums were largely written and produced by Childish. Some of the musician's other diversions around this time included the Black Hands, a band which featured Childish's leftist sentiments deceptively set to an upbeat accordion, banjo, and trumpet, as well as the Singing Loins and the Natural Born Lovers.

By 1999, Thee Headcoats broke up after Johnson left the band. In that year alone, the band had released ten albums, including *In Tweed We Trust* and *Knights of the Baskervilles,* and Childish started tentative arrangements for two new bands, the Buff Medways and

Swedish Erotica. Childish has also published two novels: *Notebooks of a Naked Youth* and *My Fault.* As of late 1999, the artist/musician had also published 40 collections of poetry and had released an estimated 100 to 150 albums as a solo performer and with his various bands. He also helped an artist society called Stuckism, an anti-conceptual art movement. Because of Childish's lengthy discography and his insistence of making all his recordings available to his public, album reviewers recommend the following as an introduction to the songwriter's work: the two-CD sampler *I Am the Billy Childish,* released in 1991, features 50 tracks, each from a different Childish project, and the 18-track *Native American Sampler,* a benefit project for the tribal rights organization Survival International released in 1993, collects previously released cuts from Childish-affiliated bands.

Selected discography

Billy Childish

The 1982 Cassettes, Hangman, 1987.
i remember..., Hangman, 1987.
I've Got Everything Indeed, Hangman, 1987.
(With the Black Hands) *Captain Calypso's Hoodoo Party,* Hangman, 1988.
Poems of Laughter and Violence, Hangman, 1988.
50 Great Albums, Hangman, 1990.
I Am the Billy Childish, Sub Pop, 1991.
(With the Black Hands) *The Original Chatham Jack,* Sub Pop, 1992.
The Sudden Fart of Laughter, Dog Meat, 1992.
(With the Singing Loins) *At the Bridge,* Hangman, 1993.
Hunger at the Moon, Sympathy for the Record Industry, 1993.
(With the Black Hands) *Live in the Netherlands,* Hangman, 1993.
Native American Sampler—A History 1983-1993, Sub Pop, 1993.
Made With a Passion, Sympathy for the Record Industry, 1996.
Devil in the Flesh, Sympathy for the Record Industry, 1998.
Cheeky Cheese, Damaged Goods, 1999.
Crimes Against Music: 1986-99, Sympathy for the Record Industry, 1999.
In Blood, Wabana, 1999.

Thee Headcoats

Headcoats Down!, Hangman, 1989.
The Earls of Suavedom, Crypt, 1990.
The Kids Are All Square—This Is Hip!, Hangman, 1990.
Beach Bums Must Die, Crypt, 1990.
Heavens to Murgatroyd, Already, 1990,
Even! It's Thee Headcoats, Sub Pop, 1990.
Headcoatitude, Shakin Street, 1991; reissued, Get Hip, 1993.
Bo in Thee Garage, Hangman, 1991; reissued, Get Hip, 1993.
Beached Earls, Crypt, 1993.
The Good Times Are Killing Me, Japan, 1993.
(With Thee Headcoatees) *The Kids Are All Square/Girlsville,* Damaged Goods, 1993.
(With Thee Headcoatees) *Live! At the Wild Western Room,* Damaged Goods, 1994.
Conundum, Hangman's Daughter, 1994.
(With Thee Headcoatees) *The Sound of the Baskervilles,* Overground, 1995.
In Tweed We Trust, 1999.
Knights of the Baskervilles, 1999.

Sources

Books

Robbins, Ira A., editor, *Trouser Press Guide to '90s Rock,* Fireside/Simon and Schuster, 1997.

Periodicals

Chicago Tribune, July 15, 1998.
Daily Telegraph, November 29, 1999.
New York Times, July 10, 1998; July 14, 1998.
San Francisco Weekly, August 1996.
Tampa Tribune, October 22, 1999, p. 17.
Village Voice, June 15, 1999.

Online

Stucksim, http://www.stuckism.com (January 28, 2000).
Thee Billy Childish, http://www.billychildish.com (January 28, 2000).

—Laura Hightower

Christian Death

Goth-rock band

During the 1980s, Christian Death became one of the few bands to cultivate a sizable and extremely loyal following while at the same time averting the media. The group's dark, brooding style of music—described with terms like gothic, death metal, and goth-rock—would serve as an important catalyst for other bands for years to come. Both Trent Reznor of Nine Inch Nails and Marilyn Manson cite Christian Death as an influence. Over the years, Christian Death earned a reputation as one of the most prolific and enduring of the goth-rock bands, in spite of numerous lineup changes and altercations within the band. Christian Death's founder and former lead vocalist Rozz Williams, who committed suicide in 1998, was known as an extremist throughout his career, dabbling in bisexuality and cross-dressing, as well as Satanism and even Christianity. Although recognized for spawning the goth rock genre, Williams himself, believing that being pigeonholed as goth did not fully represent his work, preferred the description death rock over gothic.

Christian Death, then known as the Upsetters, was formed in 1979 in Los Angeles, California, under the leadership of an androgynous teenage street performer and vocalist named Rozz Williams. The other original band members, who shared Williams's passion for the hardcore rock music that had penetrated the Los Angeles club scene, included former member of the Adolescents Rikk Agnew on guitar, James McGearly on bass, and George Belanger on drums. After spending some time establishing a local audience, the Upsetters officially changed their name to Christian Death and released their debut album, *Only Theatre of Pain* in 1982. Along with Williams, Agnew, McGearly, and Belanger, the studio recording also featured guest vocalists Eva O. and Ron Athey. According to the *Rough Guide to Rock* website, *Only Theatre of Pain* presented "an unpromising display of self-aggrandizing doom rock with total ghastliness averted only by the strong musicianship of those concerned." While not one of the group's best efforts by critical accounts, the band's debut became one of their most controversial and served as a cornerstone of the death rock movement. Not only was *Only Theatre of Pain* one of the original "goth" albums, but Williams also used satanic imagery and lyrics, in addition to backwards vocals, for intended shock value. Although Christian Death would not include such overt references to Satanism in subsequent albums, the band's later work continued to question religion and spirituality.

The Second Christian Death

Soon after issuing their debut, Christian Death returned with a six-track EP entitled *Deathwish,* which was, in fact, recorded prior to *Only Theatre of Pain.* However, these two records would come to represent the only recordings by the original lineup. In the two years that passed between *Only Theatre of Pain* and a full-length follow-up, the band fell apart. Following the release of the above mentioned records, L'Invitation au Suicide owner Yann Farcy licensed the album and EP in France and invited Williams and his band to relocate to Paris to record a new album. Meanwhile, Williams had formed friendships with singer/keyboardist Gitane DeMone, guitarist Valor Kand, and drummer David Glass, all members of a local band called Pompeii 99. Intrigued by Williams's vision and notoriety, the members of Pompeii 99 offered to join the singer in Europe, thus giving rise to a new Christian Death lineup.

Once the new group arrived in Paris, they were immediately influenced by their surroundings. Williams idolized several French artists and literary figures from Rimbaud, Genet, and Lautremont, to Marcel Duchamp and Rene Magritte. As a result, the album *Catastrophe Ballet,* released in 1984, sounded more surreal in comparison to Christian Death's brash debut, though it maintained a portion of the band's trademark dark lyrical content. Based around songs such as "Sleepwalk," a song first recorded by the original band in 1983 and eventually released on 1993's *Invocations: 1981-1989,* and "The Drowning," a song written for the original band's aborted second LP, *Catastrophe Ballet* was recorded at Rock-

For the Record . . .

Members include **Rikk Agnew** (former member of the Adolescents; left band c. 1984), guitar; **George Belanger** (left band c. 1984), drums; **Gitane DeMone** (joined band c. 1984; former member of Pompeii 99), vocals, keyboards; **David Glass** (joined band c. 1984; former member of Pompeii 99), drums; **Valor Kand** (joined band c. 1984; former member of Pompeii 99) vocals, guitar; **James McGearly** (left band c. 1984), bass; **Rozz Williams** (born Roger Alan Painter, c. 1964; left band in 1985; committed suicide on April 1, 1998), vocals, lyrics.

Williams formed band (originally called the Upsetters) with Agnew, Belanger, and McGearly, 1979; released debut album *Only Theatre of Pain* as Christian Death, 1982; original lineup disbanded and new band (consisting of Williams, DeMone, Glass, and Kand) released *Catastrophe Ballet*, 1984; Williams left band, 1985; both Williams and the second version of band released albums under the name Christian Death from the mid-1980s to the mid-1990s.

field Studios in Monmouth, Wales, England, the same location where Bauhaus recorded two classic albums.

Following an extensive European tour that lasted through 1984, Christian Death returned to Los Angeles to record *Ashes*, released in 1985. This time, according to critics, Williams's lyrics, which were sometimes performed in German, seemed somewhat more convincing, despite their overwhelming focus on medieval savagery, and diehard fans considered the album Christian Death's masterpiece. However, Christian Death, in the midst of contemplating further personnel changes, performed only one show together in support of *Ashes.* The extravagant event, entitled "The Path of Sorrows" and held at Hollywood's Roxy Theater on Easter, 1985, included spectacular visuals, films, and four costume changes for Williams. Stylist Kristina Fuller, known for her work for major films such as *Batman and Robin*, supervised and coordinated Williams's wardrobe.

Williams Left Band

Near the end of the night, during the band's final song, Williams announced his decision to leave Christian Death, which came as a shock to the group's obsessed fans. Feeling that he had outgrown his band and the confines of the goth genre, Williams wanted to pursue solo and side projects. At first, the split between Williams and the remaining Christian Death members appeared amicable; DeMone, Kand, and Glass agreed to tour Europe in support of *Ashes*, but would call themselves Sin and Sacrifice and only perform songs that they helped write. However, according to Williams and his loyal supporters, his former band mates failed to keep their word, igniting a battle over name rights that would continue throughout the band's remaining history. As the Sin and Sacrifice tour progressed across Europe, fans reported that the band was still using the name Christian Death. Moreover, word circulated that Valor was singing Williams's lyrics, including songs like "Cavity" and "Romeo's Distress," composed for *Only Theatre of Pain* two years before Kand and Williams ever met. When the group, now fronted by Kand, released the 1985 EP *The Windkissed Pictures,* the name The Sin and Sacrifice of Christian Death appeared on the cover; but by the time their first full-length album, 1986's *Atrocities,* arrived, the band listed themselves as Christian Death and continued to tour and record under that name.

With Kand now taking over songwriting duties, as well as the general direction of the band, the third version of Christian Death released several albums throughout the later 1980s and into the 1990s. As leader of the trio, Kand's chief ambition, as indicated in the *Rough Guide to Rock,* "seemed to be to castigate the church and religious institutions at every conceivable opportunity—not in itself a bad thing, but it soon became abundantly clear that Kand was not the man to articulate the concept." Some of Christian Death's other post-Williams efforts included the lyrically pompous *The Scriptures* released in 1987, the semi-musical, yet shocking —the cover included a picture of Jesus injecting drugs on the cross—*Sex and Drugs and Jesus Christ* released in 1988, as well as *All the Love All the Hate Part One: All the Love* and *All the Love All the Hate Part Two: All the Hate* (which included samples from the Third Reich and the Ku Klux Klan), both issued in 1989. Overall, critics agreed that the Kand-led Christian Death repeatedly acted in poor judgement.

Williams's Solo and Side Projects

On his own and with other musicians, Williams recorded and performed under several guises, including Shadow Project, Heltir, and Premature Ejaculation. His solo releases, *Every King a Bastard Son* released in 1992, and *Whorse's Mouth* released in 1996, were both nightmarish, spoken-word journeys. For the project Daucus

Karota, Williams teamed with bassist Mark Barone, drummer Christian Omar Madrigal Izzo, and guitarist Roxy, abandoning his goth tendencies in favor of glam-rock. That band's EP, *Shine,* was released in 1994 and became a critical favorite. Williams also worked with Demone for one album, and also formed the band Heltir for an album that was a collage of samples and instrumental loops. With the dark, heavy rock band Shadow Project, Williams was joined by Agnew on guitar and vocalist Eva O., along with an unstable rhythm section, to recapture the intensity of the original Christian Death. The collaboration also led to the recording of new Williams-led Christian death albums: *The Iron Mask* released in 1992, which included remakes of past Christian Death songs that Williams later denounced as a mistake, *The Path of Sorrows* released in 1992, a collection of new songs that was well-received by both critics and the public, and *The Rage of Angels,* a more angry, aggressive album.

By the mid-1990s, two versions of Christian Death were making records and performing. As the battle persisted, Williams claimed that he deserved name rights for forming the band in the first place, but Valor believed that because he was the most constant of band members over the longest period of time, he should own the name. Nonetheless, most fans sided with Williams, given his higher profile.

Williams took his own life by hanging on April 1, 1998, at his apartment in West Hollywood, California, at the age of 34. Although he was known to have struggled with bouts of depression and drug dependency, Bruce Duff of Williams's label at the time, Triple X Records, told *NME* (*New Musical Express*) that the singer/songwriter had not seemed depressed in the days just before his death. "I saw him a week ago, I was hanging out in a club with him and he was partying and everything was fine. Most people I know were caught off guard: he didn't leave a note, I don't think there was any real warning, and you can only speculate as to why."

Selected discography

Christian Death

Only Theatre of Pain, Frontier, 1982.
Death Wish, (EP), L'Invitation au Suicide (France), 1984.
Catastrophe Ballet, L'Invitation au Suicide, 1984; Contempo (Italy), 1987; Nostradamus, 1990.
Ashes, Nostradamus, 1985; Normal (Germany), 1988.
The Wind Kissed Pictures, (EP), Supporti Fonografici (Italy), 1985; Nostradamus/Chameleon, 1985.
The Decomposition of Violets, ROIR, 1985; Contempo, 1990.
An Official Anthology of "Live" Bootlegs, Nostradamus (U.K.), 1986.
Atrocities, Normal (Germany), 1986.
Jesus Christ Proudly Presents Christian Death, Normal, 1987.
The Scriptures, Jungle (U.K.) , 1987.
The Wind Kissed Pictures (past and present), Supporti Fonografici, 1988.
Sex and Drugs and Jesus Christ, Jungle, 1988; Nostradamus/Dutch East India Trading, 1989.
The Heretics Alive, Jungle, 1989; Nostradamus/Dutch East India Trading, 1990.
All the Love All the Hate Part One: All the Love, Jungle, 1989.
All the Love All the Hate Part Two: All the Hate, Jungle, 1989.
Jesus Points the Bone at You, Century Media, 1991.
The Iron Mask, Cleopatra, 1992.
Skeleton Kiss, (EP), Cleopatra, 1992.
The Path of Sorrows, Cleopatra, 1993.
Iconologia: Apparitions Dreams and Nightmares, Triple X, 1993.
Sleepless Nights: Live 1990, Cleopatra, 1993.
Invocations: 1981-1989, Cleopatra, 1993.
The Doll's Theatre, Cleopatra, 1994.
Sexy Death God, Nostradamus, 1994.
The Rage of Angels, Cleopatra, 1994.
Tales of Innocence: A Continued Anthology, Cleopatra, 1994.
Death in Detroit, Cleopatra, 1995.
Prophecies, 1996.
Pornographic Messiah, 1999.

Rozz Williams

Every King a Bastard Son, Cleopatra, 1992.
(With Gitane Demone) *Dream Home Heartache,* Triple X, 1995.
Whorse's Mouth, Triple X, 1996.

Shadow Project

Shadow Project, Triple X, 1991.
Dreams for the Dying, Triple X, 1992.
In Tuned Out—Live '93, Triple X, 1994.

Premature Ejaculation

Necessary Discomforts, Cleopatra, 1993.
Estimating the Time of Death, Triple X, 1994.

Daucus Karota

Shrine, (EP), Triple X, 1994.

Rozz Williams/Heltir

Neue Sachlichkeit, Triple X, 1994.

Gitane Demone

A Heavenly Melancholy, (EP), Cult Music (Holland), 1992.
Lullabies for a Troubled World, (EP), Cult Music, 1993.
Facets of Blue, Cleopatra, 1993.
With Love and Dementia, Cleopatra, 1995.

Eva O.

Past Time, Cleopatra, 1993.

Eva O. Halo Experience

A Demon's Fall for an Angel's Kiss, Cleopatra, 1994.

Sources

Books

Robbins, Ira A., editor, *Trouser Press Guide to '90s Rock,* Fireside/Simon and Schuster, 1997.

Periodicals

New York Times, April 14, 1998.
Rolling Stone, May 28, 1998, p. 52.
Washington Post, August 16, 1996.

Online

80s Music Site, http://www.80music/tqn.com (January 25, 2000).
All Music Guide, http://www.allmusic.com (January 25, 2000).
"Christian Death," *Rough Guide to Rock,* http://www-2.roughguides.com/rock/entries/entries-c/CHRISTIAN_DEATH.html (January 25, 2000).
"Christian Death singer dies—8 April 1988," *NME.com*, http://www.nme.com/newsdesk/19980308125248news.html (January 25, 2000).
Discography of Christian Death, http://www.olga.net/resources/discographies/c/christian_death (January 25, 2000).
RozzNet, http://www.rozznet.com (January 25, 2000).

—Laura Hightower

Charlotte Church

Soprano

Photograph by Suzanne Plunkett. AP/Wide World Photos. Reproduced by permission.

Welsh-born soprano prodigy Charlotte Church virtually hip-hopped to fame with the same ease as other children her age might bounce on a pogo stick. She progressed from an impromptu audition over the telephone at age eight, to a spontaneous show stopping performance on British ITV's *Big Big Talent Show* at age ten. By the age of twelve she unwittingly found herself immersed in a world of popcorn, pigtails, and Puccini, having earned legitimacy in the recording industry as a classical soprano. By her thirteenth birthday, she had accommodated a series of command performances at the request of a queen, a pope, a president, and a prince respectively. Yet she took her fame in stride and has remained, by all reports, a perfectly normal, albeit talented teenager. Church, who debuted in the United States in January of 1998, earned name recognition by the summer of that year. Later, in October, she performed at the invitation of His Royal Highness, Charles, Prince of Wales, at his fiftieth birthday party, and her "Christmas at the Vatican" concert marked a command performance for Pope John Paul II.

Church was born in Llandaff in Cardiff, Wales, on February 21, 1986, the only child of James and Maria Church. Her father worked at a security firm, and her mother managed a housing project prior to supervising her diva daughter's career. After a brief debut when she was a toddler—singing "Ghostbusters" to a resort crowd with her cousin—Church first auditioned for a children's television show at age eight. She called the show in response to a broadcaster's solicitation and sang an impressive rendition of Andrew Lloyd Webber's "Pie Jesu" over the telephone line for the production personnel. She began voice lessons at the age of nine, and her voice matured with unusual speed and grace. She was not quite eleven years old when she literally stole the spotlight from her own aunt during a talent show performance, again singing Webber's "Pie Jesu." When a clip of Church's solo on the talent show fell into the hands of Jonathan Shalit of Shalit Entertainment in the fall of 1997, the agent recognized her potential within moments of starting the videotape. He signed Church and arranged for an audition with Sony Music in the United Kingdom.

Charlotte Church was not yet a teenager when she entered into a five-record contract with Sony, and she insisted that the recording company include a critical provision in the contract—a trip to Disneyland. She was eleven years old at the time, and her career blossomed within the year, long before she entered her teens. Her first album, *Voice of an Angel,* was released in March of 1999. The recording includes "Ave Maria," and what by then was her signature song, "Pie Jesu," from *Requiem. Voice of an Angel,* recorded with the orchestra of the Welsh National Opera, earned not only the number one

For the Record . . .

Born on February 21, 1986, in Llandaff, Cardiff, Wales; daughter of James and Maria Church.

Contracted with Sony Music, 1997; albums: *Voice of an Angel,* 1999; *Charlotte Church,* 1999; spokesperson for Ford Motor Company's "Face of the Millennium" campaign, 2000.

Addresses: *Record company*—Sony Music Entertainment, Inc., c/o Sony Classics, 550 Madison Ave., New York, NY 10022-3211; website: SonyMusicOnline@sonymusic.com. *Management*—William Morris Agency: ced@wma.com.

slot on the British classical chart, but rose to number ten on the British pop chart, even before its release in the United States. The album sold more than three million copies globally by the year 2000. Other selections on her debut album include "Danny Boy," "Amazing Grace," and selections from Franck, Orff, and *Hansel and Gretel* by Humperdinck. In reviewing the album, J. D. Considine of *Entertainment* cited her "well-schooled vibrato."

As her album paid testament to her exceptional talent, she received invitations to perform at the finest venues in Britain, including Wales's Cardiff Arms Park, London's Palladium, Royal Albert Hall, and at the Lyceum Theatre. She appeared in command performances for England's Queen Elizabeth and Prince Charles and went on to sing in Washington, D.C. before the President of the United States. She sang also for Pope John Paul II at the Vatican, and the pontiff impressed the young soprano by his peaceful piety.

Unlike many classical singers who find a limited audience among opera fans, Church has achieved name recognition beyond the spectrum of classical music. Paul Burger, a spokesman for Sony Classics, Church's record label, noted that the adolescent soprano marketed easily as a crossover artist. She appeals in many ways as a popular singer, despite the classical nature of her repertoire. Burger said of Church, "This girl is a pop star, and she happens to sing classical music," according to *Billboard.* Regardless of labels, her youth combined with her mass appeal inspired *Toronto Sun's* Jim Slotek to call her "a walking dichotomy of classic versus pop culture."

Overall Church shies from nothing; her repertoire includes "La Pastorella" by Rossini, "O mio Babbino caro," by Puccini, and Mozart's "Voi che sapete." She is ranked as the best-selling female classical artist worldwide according to a report in January of 2000. Ivor Geraghty in *World of Hibernia* was impressed that at just 12 years old, Church is "the possessor of a voice more befitting a singer twice her age.... She could well become one of the world's finest sopranos." He said of her "Panis Angelicus:" "Church makes this well-known piece her own." *Opera News* called Church "this undeniably talented nascent singer," and added, "Charlotte Church is a plucky young woman who will no doubt survive the maelstrom of a publicity juggernaut whose existence is not her fault."

In the wake of her sudden fame, Church's schedule included appearances on the *David Letterman Show,* the *Today* Show, *Good Morning America,* and with Rosie O'Donnell, Jay Leno, and Oprah Winfrey. Church accepted an invitation for January of 1999 to perform at a convention of the National Association of Recording Merchandisers (NARM). She made an acting debut on CBS-TV on *Touched by an Angel* and scheduled an appearance at the rugby World Cup finals in Cardiff, Wales. Ford Motor Company also coaxed Church into a million-dollar contract to appear as the company's "Face of the Millennium." The millennium promotion not only furthered the reputation of Ford automobiles, but provided added exposure for Church's second album, *Charlotte Church,* released late in 1999. On the Ford commercial, Church sang the album's single release, "Just Wave Hello." Also in 2000, Church signed with the William Morris Agency, and her family assumed greater control of her career which by then had earned for the child star approximately $10 million (about six million pounds) in 1999 alone. Prior to severing ties with Shalit, Church signed a deal with Time Warner to publish her memoir.

By January of 2000, Church's records had sold over two million copies in the United States alone. She surpassed three million records by her fourteenth birthday in February of 2000. Additionally, she was the youngest musician ever to have an album reach the number one position on the classical music charts in the United Kingdom, a distinction that earned her a mention in the *Guinness Book of Records.*

Church attends school in Wales, and although she spends much of her time with a tutor when her career takes her on tour, her time is well spent, as she scores high grades in her classes—including music, French, and history. Church, who wears glasses when she's not on stage, enjoys typical teenager pastimes, including video games, pajama parties, and listening to the Spice Girls. Church readily admits to her admiration of other popular singers—such as Gloria Estefan, Puff Daddy, and Celine Dion—and opera virtuosos as well. She loves to shop for clothes, as much as her monthly allowance of approximately $100 per month (50 pounds) permits. As for Church's dislikes, she hates the traditional ballroom attire that she wears for her classical performances. She nonetheless looks toward a future where one of her greatest accomplishments will be to one day perform as the 15-year-old heroine in the title role of Puccini's *Madame Butterfly.* It is Church's further ambition to sing the part of Butterfly at La Scala Opera House in Milan, Italy. Church, who is neither proud nor haughty, dreams of standing ovations nonetheless.

Despite her broad travels, her well publicized royal command performances, and her appearances before a president and a pope, Church maintained that the greatest thrill of her career occurred at the MTV Music Awards when she had the opportunity to meet the popular rap singer and movie actor Will Smith.

Selected discography

Voice of an Angel (includes "Pie Jesu"), Sony Classical, March 1999.

Charlotte Church and the London Symphony Orchestra (includes "Just Wave Hello"), Sony Classical, 1999.

Sources

Periodicals

Billboard, January 30, 1999, p. 11.
Biography, October 1999, p. 63.
Entertainment, April 23, 1999, p. 60.
Newsweek, February 1, 1999, p. 67.
Opera News, September 1999, p. 98.
People, April 12, 1999, p. 146; December 31, 1999, p. 118.
Telegraph, January 13, 2000.
Time, June 21, 1999, p. 77.
Toronto Sun, February 3, 2000, p. 57.
World of Hibernia, Spring 1999, p. 1952.

Online

"Charlotte Church," *Sony Classical,* http://www.sonyclassical.com/music/64356/bio.html (March 7, 1999).

"Charlotte Church: bio," *Yahoo! GeoCities,* wysiwyg://57/http://www.geocities.com/Vienna/State/6542/bio.html (March 7, 2000).

—*Gloria Cooksey*

Cibo Matto

Pop duo

Cibo Matto founders Yuka Honda and Miho Hatori made the world a smaller place by means of their swank and upbeat flair for combining international concepts and musical forms with charismatic results. The pair formed an act with an Italian name and flavored their recordings with juxtaposed French and broken English peppered with Spanish and Japanese. They borrowed likewise from Latin and African jazz rhythms along with whatever else suited the moment. Although each of the Japanese-born duo emigrated to the United States independently, they met by chance in New York City and joined forces. As their music evolved, they attracted the attention of respected musicians, including Beatle offspring Sean Lennon who came to be accepted as a de facto member of the group.

Cibo Matto co-founder and keyboardist Yuka Honda moved to New York City from Tokyo in 1987 as a result of a friendship that developed between her and Lounge Lizard member Dougie Bowne. The two met earlier in Tokyo when the Lounge Lizards performed there; they remained friends and eventually married and subse-

Photograph by Chris Pizzello. AP/Wide World Photos. Reproduced by permission.

For the Record . . .

Members include **Miho Hatori** (born in Japan; immigrated to the United States in 1993; former member of Kimidori); **Yuka Honda** (born in Japan; immigrated to the United States in 1987; former member of the Brooklyn Funk Essentials).

Debut release, "Birthday Cake," 1995; signed with Warner Bros., 1996; released *Viva! La Woman,* 1996; released *Stereotype A,* 1999; tours: Europe and Japan; Lilith Fair, 1999; formed a second band, Butter 08, that included Mike Mills, and Russell Simins.

Addresses: *Record company*—Warner Bros. Records Inc., 3300 Warner Boulevard, Burbank, CA 91505-4694.

quently divorced. Upon her arrival in the United States, Honda blended easily into the musical society of the East Village. She performed at sit-in sessions and collaborated with Dave Douglas of Masuda; hip-hop artist Sha Key; John Zorn, and other prominent locals. Honda herself became a member of the acid jazz group Brooklyn Funk Essentials, and in time her musical aspirations evolved from keyboard styles to sampler experimentation. It was the sampler, a pseudo-instrument, that expanded Honda's creative horizons. Critics noted that the essence of Honda's compositional talent rests in her ability to employ the sampler as an instrument of itself. She effectively manipulates the machine into a workshop of sound, from which she develops the basis of her creative compositions. She later transposes the substance of each arrangement to the keyboard, and polishes the song for performance. Cibo Matto vocalist Miho Hatori was formerly a member of a Tokyo-based hip-hop and rap group called Kimidori. Additionally, she worked in a record store and as a DJ. She moved to New York City in 1993, and inevitably crossed paths with Honda because of their overlapping interests.

Prior to their individual moves to New York, Honda and Hatori had never met, although they did not live far apart even in Japan. They crossed musical paths in 1994 and began to work together under the name of the Leitoh Lychee (frozen lychee nut). As a duo the pair quickly connected with the locals of New York's East (Greenwich) Village in their serendipitous quest to establish a unique niche in the music world. Even at the outset, the collaboration between Honda and Hatori was improvisational in nature, and punk jam in genre. Not surprisingly, their music caught the ear of the Village denizens, and as Leitoh Lychee gained popularity the two musicians reinvented their act under the name of Cibo Matto, which when translated from the Italian means "crazy food." Food, according to Honda, was always a keyword for the duo, and she was quoted in *Time* as saying that the food thing evolved because "[W]e love to eat—it was a mutual obsession." When they abandoned Leitoh Lychee and adopted a new name, the choice of Cibo Matto proved a comfortable fit.

Linguistics and cuisine notwithstanding, the words Cibo Matto quickly came to evoke the band's unique affinity for "techno" improvisational styles. Essentially Hatori and Honda composed musical arrangements punctuated with clipped and broken narratives, meandering between French and English, with Spanish and Japanese ad lib inserted. Honda's talent thrived as she set to developing intricate melodies to set off the song lyrics of her vocalist friend Hatori, who also performed jazz violin styles—sometimes in dissonance against Honda's distorted jazz guitar. As their music evolved into a trademark style, during the transitional time when Cibo Matto took shape, it was Hatori who attempted to write song lyrics in her non-native English and unwittingly spawned the duo's trademark affinity for performing songs about food. Thus Hatori compensated for her poor English skills by building lyrical metaphors based on her favorite edibles. With her cultural roots in Japan, a country of highly evolved culinary traditions and one where international cuisine abounds, the food-related lyrics flowed easily for Hatori.

Improvisational jazz moods permeated Cibo Matto music in the mid-1990s as Hatori and Honda developed their uniquely detached and untempoed sound. In 1995 they released their first recording, a mini CD with five songs, including "Birthday Cake," and the groups flagship food song, "Know Your Chicken." The record, issued through a Japanese label called Error Records, also featured Bowne along with drummer Russell Simins of Jon Spencer Blues Explosion. The CD earned airplay and brought the pair sufficient recognition. By 1996, Warner Brothers signed the two musicians to a contract.

Hatori and Honda officially adopted the stage name of Cibo Matto in anticipation of their first album release on the Warner Brothers label. The album, called *Viva! La Woman,* featured classically trained funk keyboard artist Bernie Worrell, Bowne, and Lee of "Key," among others. A follow-up European tour by the group helped to promote the release, which earned the musicians a following among collegiate aficionados and FM radio listeners in the United States, Europe, and Japan. Cibo Matto's sound evolved and collaborative efforts expanded as the pair toured with Lennon and Simins. A mini CD followed, called "Super Relax," issued under the Warner Brothers label, and in 1999 Cibo Matto released a second album, *Stereotype A,* cited by *Arizona Republic* as one of the "Top Musical Milestones" of 1999. *Stereotype A* features percussionist Duma Love with Timo Ellis on drums, and Cibo Matto's perennial partner, Lennon.

Because of their many professional affiliations Hatori and Honda formed a second "food" band called Butter 08. Colleagues Simins and Lee joined them, along with bassist Mike Mills. Butter 08 contributed to the soundtrack for the movie *Half Baked.* Meanwhile Cibo Matto collaborations with Sean Lennon were so extensive that he gained public acceptance as a member of the group. Additionally, Honda collaborated behind-the-scenes with Lennon in producing his 1998 album, *Into the Sun.*

Although sex appeal is far from Cibo Matto's agenda, the broken speech and lightness of tones combined to create a package that in many ways fit squarely with mainstream media's projections of female sex appeal. With the release of their 1999 album, *Stereotype A,* Cibo Matto discarded some of the cutie-pie reputation and diminished the "food" obsession as well. Instead the pair came to be seen in a more serious vein, as musicians who take complete artistic control of their work and tend to every detail from editing to presentation while maintaining a reputation for acute perfectionism. The two share writing lyrics, mixing, producing, and performing. In essence they are full-service professionals whose efforts accomplish very unique results. The 1999 album not only dwelt less emphatically on cuisine but also veered from Cibo Matto's earlier musical styles with the inclusion of highly spirited dance tunes.

In late spring and summer of 1999, Cibo Matto toured extensively on an itinerary that included a dozen shows in New York City to promote *Stereotype A,* followed by a Lilith Fair appearance in July. Cibo Matto's plans for the summer of 2000 included an appearance at Perry Farrell's benefit, Jubilee 2000, in West Hollywood, California. Through touring engagements Cibo Matto travels frequently to Japan and Europe. Additionally, Hatori and Honda accompanied Lennon's mother, Yoko Ono, on a tour with the Tibetan Freedom Concert, and the duo has appeared elsewhere with Jon Spencer Blues Explosion, Patti Stipe, The Beastie Boys, and Natalie Merchant.

Hatori and Honda developed their style from a myriad of sounds to invent the unique and spontaneous Cibo Matto. In a *Rolling Stone* review at CDNOW, Arion Berger called the group "more levelheaded and masterful than their musical sisters," such as Japanese girl groups Shonen Knife and Pizzicato Five. With bossa nova rhythms, riffs, disco beats, even heavy metal, unpredictability became the byword of Hatori and Honda's art—nothwithstanding the whimsical food fixation that pervaded their first album. Assorted critics have noted their "quirky" nature, and "pastiche" along with their maturity.

Selected discography

Viva! La Woman, Warner Bros. Records, 1996.
Stereotype A (with Duma Love, Timo Ellis, and Sean Lennon), Warner Bros. Records, 1999.

Sources

Periodicals

Arizona Republic, December 30, 1999, p. 39.
Billboard, May 1, 1999, p. 13.
Fortune, June 21, 1999, p. 56.
People, June 7, 1999, p. 37.
Time, February 12, 1996, p. 79.
Vibe, June/July 1999, p. 194.

Online

"Cibo Matto," *CDNOW,* http://www.cdnow.com/cgi-bin/mserver/s..l/ArtistID=CIB+MATTO/select=biography (February 6, 2000).
"Shibuya River Japan Gallery By: W. Dire Wolff," available at http://www.wdirewolf.com/JapCibo3.htm (February 6, 2000).

—Gloria Cooksey

Cobra Verde

Glam rock band

Cobra Verde define themselves as an "avant-glam" experiment, according to their official website, that explores and spans a wide range of sounds and styles. Drawing from music both old and new and often using lo-fi production techniques, Cobra Verde successfully combined the classic style of the Rolling Stones, Led Zeppelin, and the Who with the contemporary drama of David Bowie, Pere Ubu, and Birthday Party into a fresh, modern sound. "I think one thing that was great about music in the '70s was that rock had hit a certain point where you could imagine equal doses of loud guitars, doo-wop, pop, harmonies, driving backbeat, avant-garde stylings on a synth, some guitar-noise feedback chaos and throw on some sappy strings at the end," lead singer and guitarist John Petkovic explained to Fred Mills of *Magnet* magazine. "It all seemed like there was some sort of conglomeration that rock hadn't rejected but accumulated. I wanted music with that large sound, an expansive sound, not one that's limiting things."

Petkovic was born around 1966 to Serbian immigrant parents who had escaped Yugoslavia and settled in middle-class Cleveland, Ohio. During a family vacation to Europe, Petkovic was exposed to many things that his peers in Cleveland had only read about. As a result, he explained to Mills, "I was drawn to weird shit, to punk rock, to absolute concepts in art and politics." Like other 1970s Cleveland bands, such as Pere Ubu, Devo, and the Dead Boys, Cobra Verde was influenced by the Velvet Underground, Roxy Music, and Alex Harvey, as well as lo-fi production. But unlike many who are drawn to lo-fi because elaborate equipment is not necessary, Petkovic said he was inspired for other reasons. After hearing bands such as the Velvet Underground, the Rolling Stones, and Alice Cooper, Petkovic recalled, "I was inspired by the greatness of the music, the other-worldliness," as quoted by Mills.

In 1984, Petkovic formed his first band, a theatrical rock group called Death Of Samantha. Along with friends Doug Gillard on guitar, Dave Swanson on bass, and Steve-O on drums, vocalist Petkovic released four records as Death of Samantha for the Homestead Records label before the band dissolved five years later. Throughout their time together, Death of Samantha won favorable criticism for their music and gained a following of fans in their hometown. Robert Griffin, a veteran Cleveland-area musician and owner of Scat Records, attended the group's shows numerous times and recalled, as quoted by Mills, "They always came on strong, completely in overdrive. Rock 'n' roll chaos at its best." Incidentally, Griffin would later persuade Petkovic to return to music.

After Death of Samantha disbanded, Petkovic spent the next five years in a self-imposed absence from the music scene, but kept productive with other interests. During this time, he served as an aide to the exiled Crown Prince Alexander of Yugoslavia, hosted a political panel show for National Public Radio (NPR) in the United States, worked as a correspondent for a Bosnian-Serb news agency, and started writing an entertainment column for the *Cleveland Plain Dealer,* his hometown's daily newspaper, where he continued to work full-time after resurrecting his music career. His column centers not only on music, but also on area exhibitions, books, and film. "It's a strange way to moonlight," Petkovic acknowledged to Kieran Grant of the *Toronto Sun.* "I'll read reviews of my records and catch myself going, 'Ah, what do you know, you're just some hack... hey, wait a minute, so am I.'"

However, music beckoned, and Griffin eventually convinced Petkovic to record some songs at a local studio, promising to release the results on his label. By mid-1994, Petkovic's new band, Cobra Verde, came into existence. The group's lineup initially consisted of Petkovic on guitar and vocals, Gillard on guitar, Swanson, who switched from bass to drums, and the studio's owner and engineer, Don Depew on bass. That same year, Scat issued Cobra Verde's debut album, *Viva La Muerte,* a collection of literate songs reflecting various eras of rock influence, from the melodious "Was It Good"

For the Record . . .

Members include **Don Depew**, bass, engineering; **Doug Gillard** (left band in 1997; former member of Death Of Samantha; member of Gem and Guided By Voices), guitar; **Dave Hill** (joined band in 1999; former member of Sons of Elvis; member of Upton Sinclair), bass; **Mark Klein** (joined band in 1997; member of Ether Net), drums; **John Petkovic** (born c. 1966; son of Serbian immigrant parents; former member of Death Of Samantha; member of Einstein's Secret Orchestra), guitar, vocals; **Chas Smith** (joined band in 1997; member of Einstein's Secret Orchestra), theremin, synthesizer; **Ched Stanisic** (joined band in 1997), keyboards; **Dave Swanson** (left band in 1997; former member of Death Of Samantha), drums; **Frank Vazzano** (joined band in 1999; member of Quazi Modo), guitar.

Formed band, signed with Scat Records, released debut album *Viva La Muerte,* 1994; collaborated with Guided By Voices on Mag Earwhig! album, 1997; signed with Motel Records, released Nightlife, 1999.

Addresses: *Record company—Motel Records,* 210 E. 49th St., New York City, NY 10017, phone (888) 755-6347, fax (212) 755-6092. *Management*—Autotonic, phone (901) 276-2225, fax (901) 276-6554, email, press@autotonic.com. *Email*—waxpigs@aol.com. *Website*—Official Cobra Verde Website: http://www.cobraverde.com.

to the guitar-riffed "Gimmie Your Heart," that made a lasting impression on the music press. According to the band's official website, *Rolling Stone* picked *Viva La Muerte* as one of the year's best releases. Highlights from the album also included expansive tracks such as "Montenegro," "Already Dead," and the epic "I Thought You Knew (What Pleasure Was)," in addition to energized songs like "Until the Killing Time" and "Cease to Exist" (not the Charles Manson song). Cobra Verde spent the summer of 1994 supporting their debut, joining the Scat-sponsored "Insects Of Rock" tour headlined by the Dayton, Ohio, band Guided By Voices, led by songwriter Robert Pollard.

After this, Cobra Verde returned to other projects (Gillard also had a band called Gem that released the album *Hexed* on Restless in 1995) and day jobs, deciding not to make touring a priority for the band. In 1996, Cobra Verde released a six-track EP entitled *Vintage Crime,* which also received favorable mention for its more accomplished, controlled, and diverse songs. With *Vintage Crime,* Petkovic also expressed his cynical disgust at public trends in "Media Whore," performers in "Every God for Himself," the future in "World Doesn't End," and alienation in "Wish I Was Here." Cobra Verde's second album, a singles compilation entitled *Egomania (Love Songs),* hit store shelves in 1997.

That same year, Pollard, who had separated from his previous backing band, invited the members of Cobra Verde to join him in an overhauled Guided By Voices. Thus, Cobra Verde put plans for their forthcoming album on hold to accept Pollard's offer. Along with Pollard, Cobra Verde co-produced Guided By Voices' *Mag Earwhig!* album and toured. Despite the success of the album, though, the union between Guided By Voices and Cobra Verde was destined to come undone and resulted in unforeseen consequences. First, Pollard unexpectedly dissolved the collaboration in the midst of touring; the members of Cobra Verde initially discovered the news from an online magazine interview given by Pollard. And second, Pollard asked guitarist Gillard to rejoin his band several months later when he started assembling a new Guided By Voices lineup. Although Gillard said he would still contribute to Cobra Verde as time permitted, Petkovic, who was anxious to record Cobra Verde's next project, declined his offer. "The record was going in a different direction, and at some point, time means something," Petkovic, remaining diplomatic, explained to Mills. "You just have to allocate more time to one project and get that done."

For unrelated reasons, Swanson left Cobra Verde as well, and Petkovic continued working with Depew, in addition to new members Ched Stanisic on keyboards, Mark Klein on drums, and Chas Smith on synth and theremin. Saxophonist Ralph Carney, known for his work with Tom Waits and Oranj Symphonette, joined Cobra Verde for a number of sessions, while guitarist Frank Vazzano and bassist Dave Hill joined the band sometime in 1999.

In the fall of that year, after signing a contract with Motel Records, the reconfigured Cobra Verde released their third album, *Nightlife.* Produced by Petkovic, Klein, and Depew, the album provided further examples of Cobra Verde's diversity. For the opening track, "One Step Away from Myself," the band started off with pulsating synthesizers, then merged into a tribute to pop-rock. One of the record's most noted highlights and one of the five songs that featured Carney on saxophone, "Crashing in a Plane," showcased the band's ability to play speed-driven rock, while "$2 Souvenir" provided a taste of glam-rock. Cobra Verde left rock behind altogether for the cabaret-inspired "What Makes a Man a Man" and "Pontius Pilate." Like the prior releases, *Nightlife* gathered critical praise. Scott Woods, in a review for the *Village Voice* concluded, "Pretension and silliness abound all over *Nightlife* ... and with any luck at all aspiring four-track kids across the nation will soon be scouring used bins for Silverhead albums and their mothers' closets for silver stilettos."

As for Cobra Verde's future, Petkovic insisted that the band will perform live more often and that plans for the next album are already underway. "I actually make up songs while driving," he admitted to Grant. "It's a half-hour from my house to the studio. It's kind of like working on deadline." Petkovic was also contemplating the release of a Death Of Samantha boxed set. In addition to writing his column, Petkovic also created an online magazine in 1999 called "Scamcity 2000: A Journal of American Anti-Culture and a Guide to Millennial Panic," located at http://www.scamcity2000.com. Likewise, the other members of Cobra Verde pursued other projects and careers as well. Smith taught courses about rock and roll at Cleveland State University and played with Petkovic in a side project called Einstein's Secret Orchestra; Vazzano played in the band Quazi Modo; Klein continued to work as a studio engineer and played in the band Ether Net; and Hill, a former member of Sons of Elvis, dedicated time to his writing, composing, and artwork. He composed the theme for an HBO show entitled "Reverb," for which he also writes, and played in the group Upton Sinclair.

Selected discography

Singles

"Leather," Scat, 1996.
"One Step Away From Myself," Sub Pop, 1996.

Albums

Viva La Muerte, Scat, 1994.
Vintage Crime (EP), Scat, 1996.
Egomania (Love Songs), Scat, 1997.
(With others) *Why We Came Together* (compilation), Yakuza, 1997.
Nightlife, Motel, 1999.

Sources

Periodicals

Boston Globe, October 7, 1999.
Chicago Tribune, June 13, 1997; December 13, 1999.
Los Angeles Times, May 18, 1997.
Magnet, April/May 1999, pp. 39-43.
Toronto Sun, August 26, 1999, p. 61.
Village Voice, November 9, 1999.
Washington Post, July 11, 1997.

Online

Official Cobra Verde Website, http://www.cobraverde.com (January 16, 2000).

—*Laura Hightower*

Creed

Rock band

Creed is a modern rock band of grassroots troubadours that performs highly inspirational music with a message, within the lines of a simple and unaffected genre called "new-era" rock. The band, led by vocalist Scott Stapp, features Mark Tremonti on guitar, Brian Marshall on bass, and Scott Phillips on drums. The four musicians are clean-cut and wholesome and qualify easily as "the boys next door." Creed's "formula" for success—if indeed they have one—is embodied in their independence from corporate ties. The band eschews conglomerate involvement, relying instead on writing and self-publishing their own songs and touring incessantly to popularize their music. They record and perform without gimmicks, and mind the business operations of their band, relying extensively on the Internet for communications as well as for advertising. Creed uses its website not only to promote songs, concerts, and albums, but for mutual correspondence between its fans and the band members.

Creed originated in Tallahassee in 1995 with a chance meeting between Stapp and Tremonti, two former school-

Photograph by Roy Tee. Corbis. Reproduced by permission.

For the Record . . .

Members include **Brian Marshall** (born April 24, 1973), bass; **Scott Phillips** (born February 22, 1973), drums; **Scott Stapp** (born August 8, 1973, in Orlando, FL; one son, Jagger), vocals; **Mark Tremonti** (born on April 18, 1974), guitar.

Released *My Own Prison,* 1997; *Human Clay,* 1999; produced and performed (with others) soundtrack for film *Scream 3;* performed at Woodstock '99.

Awards: Rock Artist of the Year, *Billboard* magazine; songwriting award for "My Own Prison," by Scott Stapp and Mark Tremonti, BMI Pop Music Awards, 1999.

Addresses: *Record company*—Wind-up Records, 72 Madison Avenue, 8th Floor, New York, NY 10016; e-mail: windup@wind-upnet.com.

mates from Orlando, Florida. Before long the two musicians recruited drummer Phillips and bassist Marshall from among the ample mélange of otherwise unskilled workers in north Florida. Between the four of them, before uniting to form their band, the future Creed members shucked oysters, fry cooked, and washed dishes to earn a living. Stapp himself was on the rebound from a series of injudicious career decisions and minor catastrophes. After performing poorly in school due to lack of interest, he abandoned his pre-law studies at Florida State University, job-hopped, and lived in his car for lack of income. It was, in fact, his lack of general prudence that inspired much of his music.

The members of the neophyte group invested their own money, a modest $6,000, into recording *My Own Prison,* an album that featured an assortment of songs, written by Stapp during the months after he abandoned his education and wandered aimlessly in search of a purpose. Most notably he wrote "My Own Prison," which became the title track of the debut album, in contemplation of the difficulties he courted by his own choices in life. Despite the bitter undertone of the song, it brought him to an epiphany about self-determination, as he wrote "No time for mourning, Ain't got no time, So I held my head up high...." Another song on the album, "What's This Life For?" was a collaborative effort by Stapp and Tremonti, the result of their reflection on the suicides of two mutual friends. Songwriters Tremonti and Stapp published their own works through Tremonti/Stapp Music of BMI, while a secondary publisher, Wind-up's Dwight Frye Music, assumed the administrative functions for the pair.

Creed released *My Own Prison* on August 26, 1997, on the Wind-up label, and the album had moved halfway up the Billboard 200 chart less in than three months. The title song became a hit single, and by November 22 reached number two on the rock-track chart of most-played hits. The album, which sold more than four million copies, went into successive releases, and other hits emerged—including "Tom," "What's This Life For?" and "One." Each of the single releases from *My Own Prison* attained number one hit status on *Billboard* Rock Radio.

The members of the band collectively invested a portion of the royalties from *My Own Prison* to acquire a parcel of land, away from urbana and city life, where they might relax and find inspiration for future creative endeavors. They retired to their newly acquired hideaway, and set to work on *Human Clay,* their second album. The tone of *Human Clay,* which was released on October 1, 1999, evoked an uplifting atmosphere, in direct contrast to Creed's original, *My Own Prison. Human Clay* featured assorted ballads, soothing and melodic, yet interspersed with energetic and fast-paced compositions. Two months later, in early December, *Human Clay* achieved double platinum sales (over 2 million copies sold), and Anthony Bozza of *Rolling Stone* dubbed Creed the best-selling hard-rock band in America. Additionally, their albums ranked in the top 12 in 1999, according to radio play and sales statistics. Additionally, Creed's international appeal extended to remote continents; the group sold 80,000 albums in New Zealand alone in 1999.

With two best-selling albums to their credit, the band expanded its horizons and contributed to the movie soundtracks of *Faculty* and *Dead Man on Campus.* The soundtrack for *Scream 3,* which Creed self-produced, includes original Creed compositions "What If" and "Is the End." For that album, Creed solicited contributions from a number of their fellow recording artists and comrades from Wind-up Records, including Orgy and Static-X. A total of 17 "heavy rock" bands contributed to the album.

Between recording sessions, Creed tours extensively. The band attracts audiences composed primarily of teen-agers and young adults, 14 to 34 years old. In 2000, the band remained a young and evolving musical entity, at times unpolished because of its newness. Regardless, Creed persisted in projecting a positive image as was evidenced in July of 1999 when the band performed in Rome, New York, at *Woodstock 99,* a reprise festival of the original festival by the same name. The 1999 concert, held in celebration of the 30-year anniversary of the original festival in 1969, differed drastically in mood from the original concert in the 1960s. When a catastrophic outbreak of violence instigated by concertgoers marred the end of the 1999 festival, Stapp responded to the chaotic outburst and vented his embarrassment during Creed's performance.

The four Creed band members are extremely close in age, and all enjoy the music of Led Zeppelin. The senior member of the group, drummer Scott Phillips of Madison, Florida, was born in February of 1973. Phillips began playing the drums in his late teens. Guitarist Mark Tremonti was born in April of 1974 and is the youngest member of the group. He played guitar for approximately ten years before joining Creed. Bassist Brian Marshall was born on April 24, 1974, approximately one week before Tremonti. Marshall is a native of Fort Walton Beach in Florida. He started playing the bass in his mid-teens. Creed founder and vocalist, Scott Stapp, was born and raised in Orlando, Florida, the son of a Pentecostal minister. He was born on August 8, 1973, and is the second oldest member of the group. During adolescence his musical affinities veered toward U2, Elvis, Led Zeppelin, and the Doors, and according to critics, the circumstances of Stapp's childhood are evidenced in many of his song lyrics. Stapp, who repeatedly disavowed such interpretation of his music, nonetheless intimated that his parents were not only devoutly religious, but rigid and strict, and highly antagonistic toward rock music and electric guitars. Stapp moved with his family to Tallahassee, Florida, in the mid-1990s. He wrote the song "With Arms Wide Open" in honor of the birth of his eldest child, a son named Jagger.

As Creed's media presence continually evolves, their presence on the Internet is secure. "We're on our Web site almost every day, especially when we're on tour. The Internet is such a cool medium. It's definitely the future of how bands will know what their fans are thinking," Stapp told *Billboard* in September of 1999. Creed's plans for the new millenium included more touring and a live album, along with an acoustic album. Their schedule included appearances in Las Vegas in December of 1999, and contract negotiations to play in Edmonton, Canada in the year 2000.

Selected discography

My Own Prison, Wind-up Records, 1997.
Human Clay (includes "Higher"), Wind-up Records, 1999.
Scream 3 soundtrack (with other bands), 1999.

Sources

Periodicals

Billboard, November 22, 1997; December 20, 1997, p. 97; September 4, 1999, p. 18.

Campus Life, September-October 1998, p. 32.

Telegraph (Sydney, Australia), January 14, 2000.

Rolling Stone, September 16, 1999, p. 38; October 28, 1999; pp. 99-100; December 9, 1999, p. 34.

Online

"Info About the Band Creed," available at http:/xrs.nct/unified/info.html (February 4, 2000).

"Lyrics and Meanings Behind Songs," available at http:/xrs.nct/unified/lyrics-myownprison.html (February 4, 2000).

—Gloria Cooksey

D.O.A.

Punk band

Arguably the best and most enduring hardcore punk band to emerge from Canada, D.O.A. of Vancouver, British Columbia, not only established themselves as a leading force in their native country, but in Europe and North America as well. For more than 20 years, D.O.A.'s singer and guitarist, Joey "Shithead" Keithley led the band with his dedicated work ethic and level head, ignoring stylistic detours that tempt many longtime performers, not to mention the creative exhaustion that often accompanies years of touring. Although the D.O.A. family suffered personal tragedies over the years, as well as a shifting lineup, Keithley remained the mainstay member, earning respect by those who stayed true to the D.I.Y (Do It Yourself) concept that defined early punk rock. In addition to fronting the band, Keithley also founded his own record label, Sudden Death Records, in the late-1990s and even ran for public office in 1996 as a Green Party candidate in his hometown.

Unabashedly anti-mainstream, Keithley, after more than two decades in the music business, still considered the world a mess and never backed away from his musical and his political/activist roots. "I see myself, at my ripe old age, as the fly in the ointment. A tiny counterweight to the bullshit of the corporate world," Keithley commented to Pieter Hofmann in a 1998 interview for *Drop Dead Magazine.* Neither the onset of middle age, nor fatherhood, altered too much the ideals of Keithley's youth. "I have three kids now and that does make you think differently. I don't think it's mellowed me out, though," he continued. "If anything, it makes me more pissed off at the world now. This place will be f***ed up even more for the kids if someone doesn't stand up to the bullshit of globalization, environmental degradation and the mass media push to corporatization. Just look around you. You see people wearing companies' logos on their t-shirts. There's something inherently wrong with that."

Formed in 1978 (some sources say 1977) in Vancouver, D.O.A. started off as a trio, consisting of Keithley on vocals and guitar, Randy Rampage on bass, and Chuck Biscuits on drums. Eventually considered hardcore punk's most recognized percussionist, Biscuits, following his stint with D.O.A., went on to work with the Circle Jerks, Black Flag, and Danzig. From the onset, D.O.A.'s message, true to the punk formula established by the genre's English and American archetypes, was both menacing and confrontational. Financed by Keithley's first wife's unemployment checks, the band's debut, an abrasive and political EP entitled *Disco Sucks,* arrived in 1978. The trio emerged with another EP, *Triumph of the Ignoroids,* in 1979, firmly planting the seeds for fellow Canadian punk groups such as the Dishrags and Subhumans.

In 1980, D.O.A. released their first album, *Something Better Change,* followed in 1981 by *Hardcore 81.* Both early albums established the band's dynamic formula: fast, rousing rock guitar backed by accusatory lyrics. While their verbal assault lacked the puritanical quality of peers such as Minor Threat, D.O.A, in the same vein as the Dead Kennedys, the Avengers, and Black Flag, nevertheless placed a similar emphasis on social unrest, injustices, and collapse.

Signing with the Alternative Tentacles record label, D.O.A. next released the eight-song EP *Waron 45* in 1982. Stronger and better produced than their previous efforts, the record won D.O.A. new converts in Europe to add to their secure Canadian/ Northwest American fanbase. By this time, however, the band's lineup had changed. Along with Keithley, a second guitarist, Dave Gregg, was added, while Rampage and Biscuits were replaced by bassist Brian Roy Goble and drummer Gregg James. In 1984, the band released a career anthology up to that point entitled *Bloodied But Unbound* that recaptured the exhilarating rush of the group's early output.

In 1985, the release of *Let's Wreck the Party,* an album which included two of the four Peel sessions tracks from that year's *Don't Turn Yer Back* EP, marked D.O.A.'s peak in both popularity in form. "Here the clean, professional production showcased their trademark rhythmic

For the Record . . .

Members include **Chuck Biscuits** (left band c. 1982; later member of the Circle Jerks, Black Flag, and Danzig), drums; **Brian Roy Goble** (former member of the Subhumans), bass; **Dave Gregg** (left band c. 1990), guitar; **Gregg James**, drums; **Ken Jensen** (joined band c. 1992; died in a fire at his home in January of 1995), drums; **Joey "Shithead" Keithley**, vocals, guitar; **Kuba** (former member of the Sweater, Scum Element, and Ted), bass; **Ken "Dimwit" Montgomery** (died c. mid-1990s), drums; **Brien O'Brien** (former member of Stick Monkey, Bif Naked, and the Real McKenzies), drums; **Fred Pier** (joined band c. 1995), guitar, keyboards; and **Chris Pohom** (joined band c. 1990), guitar; **Randy Rampage** (left band c. 1982), bass.

Formed band in 1978 in Vancouver, BC, Canada; debuted with EP *Disco Sucks,* 1978; released first album, *Something Better Change,* 1981; released *Let's Wreck the Party,* the band's career peak, 1985; D.O.A. temporarily disbanded, 1990; released *13 Flavors of Doom,* 1992; band dedicated *The Black Spot* to Jensen, 1995; Keithley established Sudden Death Records and released D.O.A.'s *Festival of the Atheists,* 1998.

Addresses: *Home*—Joe Keithley, Burnaby, BC, Canada, email: suddend@concentric.net, website: joey@suddendeath.com, phone: (604) 439-9046. *Record company*—Sudden Death Records, c/o Moscrop, P.O. Box 43001, Burnaby, BC, Canada V5G 3H0. *Management*—Brandon, email: javabxxx@hotmail.com. *U.S.A. Promotion*—Bob Cutler, email: corn@direct.ca, website: bobc@suddendeath.com, phone: (604) 874-9871.

attack at its best," declared *Rough Guide to Rock* contributor Alex Ogg. "Unlike their rivals, however, DOA refrained from crossing the sonic and ideological borders between punk and heavy metal." Later, in 1991, Alternative Tentacles reissued the record in *The Dawning of a New Error,* a 33-track album augmented with the complete set of songs from *Don't Turn Yer Back* and selected early singles.

With *True (North) Strong & Free,* released in 1987, the band again garnered critical approval and also allowed more variety, humor, and maturity to enter into the repertoire. Topics revealed in the album ranged from the domestic growth of fascism in "Nazi Training Camp" (a remake of the song from the debut EP) to Canada's cultural domination by the United States in "51st State." Moreover, the band donated royalties from such songs as "Ready to Explode" to the ANC (African National Congress). For the band's next effort, 1990's *Murder,* released on Restless Records, a new guitarist, Chris Pohom, replaced Gregg. The album lacked the fire of previous records, but retained some inspiration, noted by the recognition of South African leader Nelson Mandela's release for a rewrite of the song "The Midnight Special."

That same year, D.O.A. moved to adjourn, and a live album of the group's farewell show at a Vancouver club was released entitled *Talk Minus Action Equals Zero.* Subsequently, Keithley formed a short-lived band called Joey Keithley's Instinct, but was soon back re-creating D.O.A. This time around, he enlisted former bassist/singer Goble (a former member of the Subhumans) and new drummer Ken Jensen to complete the D.O.A. lineup. In 1992, the group released the well-received album *13 Flavours of Doom.* Issued on Alternative Tentacles and produced by John Wright (of NoMeansNo), *13 Flavors of Doom* recaptured the inspiration lacking from *Murder.* Focusing on guitar power and taking a serious lyrical stance, the album revealed notable songs about governmental and economic injustice ("Death Machine" and "Legalized Theft"), environmental and health issues ("Hole in the Sky" and the safe-sex number "Use Your Raincoat"), and a diseased culture ("Beatin' Rock 'n' Roll to Death"). Keithley also acknowledged his own imperfections with the song "I Played the Fool."

Following the more lighthearted five-song EP entitled *It's Not Unusual... But It Sure Is Ugly!,* D.O.A. returned in 1993 with *Loggerheads.* Released on Alternative Tentacles and keeping on track with social concerns, the album featured songs about North America's trade imbalance in "Logjam," religious hypocrisy in "I See Your Cross," conformity in "That Turbulent Uneasy Feeling," environmentalism in "The Only Thing Green," and urban decay in "I Can't Take Much More." In an unprecedented move to elevate their musical ambitions, D.O.A. capped the record with a mind-boggling, Melvins-speed cover of a Johnny Cash cover, "Folsom Prison Dirge."

In January of 1995, drummer Jensen died in a fire at home, and the album *The Black Spot,* issued on Essential Noise/Virgin, was dedicated to his memory. Recorded by Keithley, Goble, new guitarist/keyboardist Ford Pier, and Wright guesting on drums, the album also eulogized five other past band members, including drummer Ken Montgomery (also known as "Dimwit") and others who died of various causes in the 1990s. In 1996, D.O.A. released *Alive & Kickin'* on the Polo label, followed by *Festival of the Atheists* in 1998 on Keithley's own Sudden Death Records. Packaged as a CD-ROM and featuring old D.O.A. videos, *Festival of the Atheists* was the first release issued by Keithley's label. In early 2000, Sudden Death released *The Lost Tapes,* a collection of previously unreleased tracks by the original lineup covering the years 1978 through 1984.

D.O.A.'s latest lineup consisted of Keithley, drummer Brien O'Brien (a past member of Stick Monkey, Bif Naked, and the Real McKenzies) and bassist Kuba (a former member of the Sweaters, Scum Element, and Ted). They continued to perform as a popular attraction, especially in their native Canada, as well as in Europe and in North America.

Selected discography

Disco Sucks, (EP7), (Canada) Sudden Death, 1978; (Canada) Quintessence, 1978.
Triumph of the Ignoroids, (EP), (Canada) Friend's, 1979.
Something Better Change, (Canada) Friend's, 1980.
Hardcore 81, (Canada) Friend's, 1981.
War on 45, Alternative Tentacles, 1982.
Bloodied But Unbowed, CD Presents, 1984; reissued, Restless, 1992.
Don't Turn Your Back (on Desperate Times), (EP), Alternative Tentacles, 1985.
Let's Wreck the Party, Alternative Tentacles, 1985.
True (North) Strong & Free, Rock Hotel/Profile, 1987.
Murder, Restless, 1990.
Talk Minus Action Equals Zero, Restless, 1990.
The Dawning of a New Error, Alternative Tentacles, 1991.
13 Flavors of Doom, Alternative Tentacles, 1992.
It's Not Unusual...But It Sure Is Ugly!, (EP), Alternative Tentacles, 1993.
Loggerheads, Alternative Tentacles, 1993.
The Black Spot, Essential Noise/Virgin, 1995.
Alive & Kickin', Polo, 1996.
Festival of the Atheists, (CD-ROM), Sudden Death, 1998.
The Lost Tapes, Sudden Death, 2000.

Sources

Books

Robbins, Ira A., editor, *Trouser Press Guide to '90s Rock,* Fireside/Simon and Schuster, 1997.

Periodicals

Billboard, January 27, 1996; October 19, 1996.
Boston Globe, May 2, 1996; May 9, 1996.
Los Angeles Times, October 2, 1996.
Maclean's, March 27, 1995.
Stereo Review, April 1996.

Online

All Music Guide, http://www.allmusic.com (March 1, 2000).
D.O.A. (unofficial site), http://www.conspiracy.com/DOA (March 1, 2000).
"DOA," *Rough Guide to Rock*, http://www.roughguides.com/rock/entries/entries-d/DOA.html (March 1, 2000).
"Interview: D.O.A.'s Joe Keithley, May 1996," Drop-D Magazine, http://www.dropd.com/issue/8/JoeKeithley/index.html (March 1, 2000).
"Interview: D.O.A.'s Joe Keithley, March 1998," *Drop-D Magazine*, http://www.dropd.com/issue/91/DOA/index.html (March 1, 2000).
"July 21, 1999: Bloodied But Unbowed: A Tour of '80s Hardcore Punk Legends," *Las Vegas Weekly*, http://www.scopemag.com/departments/07_21_99/sound_punk.html (March 1, 2000).
"Punk perennials: 7 Seconds and D.O.A. bring back the loud/fast rule," *The Oregonian*, January 15, 1999, http://www.olive-live.webnet.advance.net (March 1, 2000).
Sudden Death Records Online, http://www.suddendeath.com (March 1, 2000).

—Laura Hightower

Jeff Dahl

Singer, songwriter, guitar

From his ranch-style home in the desert town of Cave Creek, Arizona, punk legend Jeff Dahl has been self-producing and recording, usually by himself, albums since the early 1990s. Also known for his role as the former lead vocalist for the West Coast underground punk outfit the Angry Samoans and as the founder of the punk-metal band Powertrip, Dahl the solo artist has enjoyed a prolific career, battling drug and alcohol addiction to release, on average, at least one album every year, not to mention a myriad of EPs and seven-inch singles. Influenced by the Stooges, the New York Dolls, T. Rex, and the MC5, Dahl's output combines elements of classic rock and roll, 1970s glam-rock, 1950s rockabilly, metal, and punk, making his music difficult to place in a single category. Although working as an underground performer never made Dahl a wealthy man, he has nonetheless managed to enjoy a comfortable career as a well-known cult hero. His success arrived without a major-label contract, videos airing on the MTV network, or performing in stadium-sized venues.

Born in 1955 in Stuttgart, Germany, Dahl, the son of an Army officer, spent his first five years overseas. In 1960, Dahl and his family left Germany and settled in Hawaii, where he lived until graduating from high school. Drawn to the music of the time from an early age, by 1966, Dahl was already attending concerts on a regular basis. Some of the first shows he witnessed included the Doors, Jimi Hendrix, Humble Pie, Jefferson Airplane, and Blue Cheer. A few years later, in 1969, Dahl purchased his first albums by the Stooges and the MC5, bands that would later represent two of his greatest influences. Around the same time, he learned to play drums and performed with various combos as a teenager.

Although the Hawaiian islands seem a paradise to many, Dahl found the decidedly un-rock and roll atmosphere too confining. Thus, after graduating from high school in 1973, he enlisted in the United States Army. Between the years of 1974 and 1977, Dahl was stationed primarily at the Pentagon heliport in Washington, D.C., as an air traffic controller—not the most common position for a future punk rocker. However, in an interview with *Agree to Disagree* #6, Dahl (who "dug" his job with the Army) pointed out that in those days the rebellious punk ethic had not yet been established, noting, "there wasn't even a Ramones record out at that time! There was no 'punk.' As far as being 'unpunk,' punk is about no rules. I made my own."

In 1976, Dahl bought his first guitar, an instrument he had never picked up before. Within a week, he recorded a few songs, including the first song he ever wrote, a punk-sounding tune called "Rock 'n' Roll Critic," at a four-track studio in Virginia. According to Dahl, because all of the musicians he knew at the time played jazz and felt his simple compositions were beneath them, he ended up playing all of the instruments himself. "When I recorded it there was no DIY [Do It Yourself], the idea of putting out your own single was completely alien...," he recalled in an interview with *Carbon 14 #13.* Subsequently, an independent Washington, D.C., label called Doodley Squat heard "Rock 'n' Roll Critic" by chance at the same Virginia studio and asked Dahl if they could release it. He agreed, and in 1977 Doodley Squat issued the song as a seven-inch single (now available only on bootlegs). A pivotal record in paving the way for Dahl's international popularity, "Rock 'n' Roll Critic" became a hit among the punk-rock-starved youth of Europe.

After completing his service with the Army and a brief return to Hawaii, Dahl moved to Los Angeles, California, in 1977 where he made a few abortive attempts to form a band. Finally succeeding in 1979, Dahl formed the group Vox Pop in Los Angeles with then-future/current members of the Germs, 45 Grave, Dream Syndicate, and Nervous Gender. Darby Crash, a member of the Germs who later committed suicide, called Vox Pop the worst band he had ever seen. In 1980, after Vox Pop folded, Dahl accepted the offer to replace Angry Samoans co-founder and lead vocalist Mike Saunders during his absence from the band. Although the Angry Samoans, a punk/rock critic combo, helped lead the Los

For the Record . . .

Born in 1955 in Stuttgart, Germany; married Sylvia, c. 1974.

Served in the U.S. Army, 1974-77; learned to play guitar, recorded first original song, "Rock 'n' Roll Critic," 1976; lead vocalist for the Angry Samoans, 1980-82; fronted Powertrip, 1982-84; formed Jeff Dahl Group, 1987; started recording as a soloist, released *I Kill Me,* 1990; established fan magazine *Sonic Iguana,* 1999.

Addresses: *Home*—Jeff Dahl, c/o Ultra Underground, P.O. Box 1867, Cave Creek, AZ 85327. *Record company*—Triple X Records, P.O. Box 862529, Los Angeles, CA 90086, phone: (323) 221-2204, fax: (323) 221-2778. *Website*—Dahlhaus—The Official Web Site of Jeff Dahl, http://www.lastbandit.com/jeffdahl/. *Email*—DAHL@aol.com.

Angeles underground music scene, working with the group wasn't the most ideal situation for Dahl. "People hated us," he commented, smiling, to Phoenix New Times Online contributor Brian Smith. "There was no legendary status; we were hated. We couldn't play anywhere at the time." The band also suffered internal problems as well, and because of what Dahl described as the intense hatred the band members felt toward one another, he left the Angry Samoans in 1982.

Dahl formed his next band, Powertrip, in 1982, hoping to merge the proto-punk music of the Stooges with the harder-edged sounds of Motörhead. A pioneering speed-metal quartet, Powertrip, from 1982 until its demise in 1984, toured the United States twice, played extensively up and down the West Coast, shared billing with other newly established metal bands like Metallica and Slayer, and released a single on Mystic Records and an album on the Public label. However, plagued by the members' self-destructive drug problems, Powertrip only lasted two years. During his stint as the group's front man, Dahl injured his knee and hand, shattered his tailbone, bit off a chunk of his tongue, and all but destroyed his liver, which doctors informed him was only functioning at 15 percent capacity. He was the only group member to survive and overcome his addictions; unfortunately, the other three original members all died from drug-related causes.

Determined to change his lifestyle, Dahl bailed out of Powertrip and drug use. Over the next couple of years, he removed himself from the music scene, sobered up, and began writing new songs. Resurfacing again in 1987, he formed the Jeff Dahl Group, and started recording seven-inch singles at a furious pace. The singles were distributed worldwide, from Europe and Japan to Australia and the United States. In 1988, the Jeff Dahl Group released the competent, though undistinguished album *Vomit Wet Kiss,* followed in 1989 by *Scratch Up Some Action,* an album that included both covers and Dahl originals. Dahl's new band became a headlining fixture in Los Angeles and San Francisco, California, and their reputation took hold overseas as well. Despite the welcomed attention, Dahl disbanded the group in 1990 to record as a solo artist.

Relocating to the Arizona desert after folding his band, Dahl next landed a record deal with an upstart independent label, Triple X, out of Los Angeles and decided to use different musicians and/or bands for different sessions. "Anything to confuse people," Dahl joked on his official website. For his first true solo effort, *I Kill Me,* released in 1990, Dahl enlisted the aid of ex-Dead Boy guitarist Cheetah Chrome, the Angry Samoans, and the Lazy Cowgirls and included some tracks from *Vomit Wet Kiss.* Since then, he has released a steady flow of about one full-length album per year and a myriad of singles and EPs. He also started conducting annual tours of Europe and Japan, where his popularity remained strong.

For his follow-up solo album, made back in Los Angeles, he enlisted drummer Dave Nazworthy of Chemical People and guitarist Paul Cutler of 45 Grave and Dream Syndicate to join the recording sessions. The resulting *Ultra Under,* released in 1991, unleashed Dahl's brand of Detroit-inspired punk originals, spirited rock covers (the Runaways' "Cherry Bomb"), and even a piano ballad entitled "Just Amazin'." He followed this with 1992's *Wicked,* which followed a similar approach. Both albums were well-received by critics. Some of his most recognized subsequent albums included 1993's *Wasted Remains of a Disturbing Childhood* and *Moonchild,* 1994's *Leather Frankenstein,* 1995's *Bliss,* and 1996's *French Cough Syrup.* During the late-1990s, Dahl's output included *Heart Full of Snot,* released in 1997, and *All Trashed Up,* released in 1999.

Around the same time he decided to focus on his health, Dahl also discovered a replacement for drugs and alcohol in a former pastime: running. Before long, the musician was competing in marathons, as well as triathalon. One event, the Fountain Mountain Triathlon, brought Dahl to the Phoenix area for the first time. Remaining sober throughout the 1990s and beyond, Dahl continued to participate in cross-country events non-competitively as the decade came to a close. "With the running, I had to do something to ease my mind," he explained to Smith. "If I was still getting f***ed up, I would be accomplishing about a tenth of what I am doing now."

At his home in Cave Creek that he shares with wife Sylvia, Dahl's high school sweetheart whom he married around 1974, the glitter-punk rocker assembled a do-it-yourself empire of sorts. In his studio dubbed Devil Tree Ranch, Dahl usually records, produces, engineers, and often plays all the instruments by himself for each recording. While tours across Europe and the Americas often leave him in the black upon his return, Dahl's semi-thriving worldwide mail-order business called the Dahlhaus (from which Dahl sells his own records and merchandise, as well as limited-edition merchandise from other like-minded punk and glam-rock heroes) provides a steady income, and his records sell well enough to help keep him afloat.

In 1999, Dahl established his own irreverent fan magazine called *Sonic Iguana.* Published three times a year by Jeff Dahl/Ultra Underground, the fanzine covered areas of music such as punk, trash, powerpop, glam, garage, rockabilly, and blues. He does direct-mail orders to stores by himself, and hired a distributor to make *Sonic Iguana* available internationally in Japan, Australia, Israel, South Africa, Malaysia, Tahiti, and all over Europe and the United States. "I have offers for bigger distribution and people interested in upping the circulation. But I want to keep it at this level," Dahl, who used to read *Rolling Stone* and *Creem* when those publications were still underground ventures, revealed to Smith. "This underground is like a real word-of-mouth thing, too. The thing I like about it is that it is not at all casual music fans. It is people to whom music still means something."

Selected discography

(With the Jeff Dahl Group) *Vomit Wet Kiss,* Sympathy for the Record Industry, 1987.
(With the Jeff Dahl Group) *Scratch Up Some Action,* Dog Meat, 1989; reissued, Triple X, 1993.
I Kill Me, Triple X, 1990.
Ultra Under, Triple X, 1991.
Wicked, Triple X, 1992.
Have Faith, (EP), Triple X, 1992.
Wasted Remains of a Disturbing Childhood, Triple X, 1993.
Moonchild, Triple X, 1993.
Leather Frankenstein, Triple X, 1994.
Bliss, Triple X, 1995.
French Cough Syrup, Triple X, 1996.
Heart Full of Snot, Triple X, 1997.
All Trashed Up, Triple X, 1999.

Sources

Books

Robbins, Ira A., editor, *Trouser Press Guide to '90s Rock,* Fireside/Simon and Schuster, 1997.

Periodicals

Arizona Republic, March 25, 1999, p. 38; November 18, 1999, p. 42.

Online

All Music Guide, http://www.allmusic.com (February 28, 2000).
"Cave Creek Dahl," *Phoenix New Times Online*, http://www.phoenixnewtimes.com/issues/1990-08-26/music.html (February 28, 2000).
Dahlhaus—The Official Web Site of Jeff Dahl, http://www.lastbandit.com/jeffdahl/ (February 28, 2000).
"Jeff Dahl I from C14," *Carbon 14 #13*, http://www.c14.com/Music/dahl/dahl.html (February 28, 2000).
Jeff Dahl—All Trashed Up, http://www.glitzine.com/recensioner/jeffdahl_alltrashedup.htm (February 28, 2000).
Jeff Dahl Interview,"*Agree to Disagree #6,* http://www.members,xoom.com/_XMCM/a2d/jeffdahl.htm (February 28, 2000).
"Jeff Dahl," *Noise for Heroes,* http://www.members.webgalaxy.com/nkvd/jeffdahl.htm (February 28, 2000).
"Valley of the Dahls," *Aversion.com Interviews,* http://www.aversion.com/bands/interviews.cfm?f_id=20 (February 28, 2000).

—Laura Hightower

Death in Vegas

Rock band

Born out of the re-ignited dance club scene that swept through London, England, during the mid-1990s, Death in Vegas formed in 1994 and spent three years perfecting tracks for their debut album, *Dead Elvis*. Dubbed the next great big beat act by club enthusiasts and the British press, the band quickly gained acceptance in America, with their video for the single "Dirt" gaining regular airplay on MTV (Music Television) and a tour of the United States. But despite the group's success with dance music, Death in Vegas decided to dedicate their follow-up album, *The Contino Sessions,* issued in 1999 by Time Bomb/Concrete, to trance rock. Though the record, which featured a cast of well-known guests vocalists, including the legendary rocker Iggy Pop, failed to secure a home on night club dance floors, *The Contino Sessions'* more experimental British rock sound nonetheless captured the attention of both the music press and psychedelic rock enthusiasts. "Death in Vegas' quirky debut, *Dead Elvis,* was rather pretentious, a mish-mash of live instruments-play-techno big beat and youth/rave-nation trendiness," wrote Fred Mills of *Magnet* magazine. However, the group's follow-up,

Photograph by Steve Double. Corbis. Reproduced by permission.

For the Record . . .

Members include **Richard Fearless** (born c. 1971), DJ, artwork; **Steve Hellier** (left band in 1998), production, engineering; **Tim Holmes** (became a full-time member in 1998), production, engineering.

Formed band and signed with Concrete Records, 1994; released debut album, *Dead Elvis*, 1997; released *The Contino Sessions*, which featured live instrumentation and guest vocalists, 1999.

Addresses: *Record company*—Time Bomb Recordings, 31652 2nd Ave., Laguna Beach, CA 92651. *Website*—Death in Vegas at Time Bomb Recordings, http://www.timebombrecordings.com.

continued Mills, "is both diverse and intensely focused ... a rock 'n' roll record through and through."

Death in Vegas began to take shape in the early 1990s when graphic artist, amateur photographer, and night club DJ Richard Fearless and producer Steve Hellier, at the time a BBC World Service engineer, started recording demo tapes. Fearless, a former member of bands such as Joy Club and Moral Panic and a resident spinner at the Heavenly Social in London (the same club made famous by the internationally successful techno duo the Chemical Brothers), pursued art as well as music throughout his life. At age 13, he won an art scholarship to attend a fine arts boarding school and later earned a graphic design degree from the London College of Printing. His creative aspirations seemed to run in the family and developed naturally; Fearless's mother made a living as an art teacher, while his sister designed shoes. His collaborator enjoyed a musical and artistic background as well. Hellier, the son of a painter, noted that his earliest memories consisted of jazz musicians dropping by the family home for impromptu jam sessions.

In 1994, the pair's early demo tapes came to the attention of the British label Concrete Records. After signing a contract that year with Concrete, which included a clause stating that Fearless would use his skills as a graphic designer for album sleeves and other visuals (including advertisements) related to the band, Death in Vegas released their debut single, "Opium Shuffle," in 1995 in the United Kingdom. At that time, Fearless and Hellier were known as Dead Elvis, a name that didn't go over well with Elvis Presley fans and led many club goers to show up at gigs expecting a Presley tribute performance. Thus, they changed the name to Death in Vegas, maintaining their fascination with the pop culture's obsession with the rock and roll legend.

March of 1996 saw the release of the duo's second British single and their first outing as Death in Vegas entitled, "Dirt," which became a popular club scene song. According to the group's official website at Time Bomb Recordings, the early singles led many to view Death in Vegas as "something of a dance music anomaly; a mixed up clattering garage band with a love of dirty basslines, dub reggae, Vegas-era Elvis, '60s pop art and James Ellroy thrillers." However, witthe release of their first album, 1997's *Dead Elvis,* "it became clear that Death in Vegas were much more than a couple of good-time studio boffins with a neat line in mashed up breakbeats and Studio One samples." Influenced by New York art school bands, ska, hip-hop, and techno, *Dead Elvis,* although not intended to become just another dance record, enjoyed instant success among clubbers.

Consequently, the album was lumped in with the big beat genre, also due in part to Fearless's continued residency at the Heavenly Social. Nonetheless, Death in Vegas started to see their audience widen. The macabre, disturbing video for "Dirt," which featured an eight-armed soldier in a garter belt, received regular rotation on MTV's Buzz Bin program, and Death in Vegas toured the United States for the first time with the techno group Crystal Method in addition to the Chemical Brothers. American audiences were entranced by Death in Vegas' live shows. Rather than using samplers and sequences for performances as do most electronica outfits, Death in Vegas opted for an array of live instruments, guitars, and vocals (by guest vocalist Rankin Roger during 1997). Likewise, the stunning visuals implemented during Death in Vegas gigs attracted attention: a collage of pop culture images projected behind the band on grainy 16 millimeter film.

Fearless himself made headlines for the act's supporting artwork. Encouraging the misguided assumption that the name Death in Vegas suggests a death metal sound, Fearless, along with his graphic artist cohort William Beaven, designed the album sleeves in the spirit of Americana trash culture—complete with gothic lettering, twisted spines, and skulls and x-rays. Fearless and Beaven's artwork gained so much attention around the time of *Dead Elvis'* release that the designs were exhibited at *Dazed & Confused* magazine's gallery in London. *Dead Elvis* earned critical accolades as well, spending the year near the top of several British music press polls.

In the two years between releasing their debut and subsequent album, Death in Vegas remained active within music, art, and entertainment circles. Fearless continued to DJ at the Heavenly Social, in addition to other venues throughout the world, and produced tracks for Scottish solo artist Dot Allison, former vocalist for the group One Dove. Fearless and Allison began dating while working together. In addition, Fearless delved further into filmmaking and won a showing at one of London's Kentra film nights. He also continued to exhibit his artwork the world over in cities such as San Francisco, Paris, and Tokyo. Another one of Fearless's many non-musical, on-going projects included a collection of photographs detailing his travels.

During this time, Hellier departed Death in Vegas to concentrate on producing, and Fearless set up his own recording and design studio, which he christened "The Contino Rooms." Tim Holmes, who helped Hellier and Fearless engineer *Dead Elvis,* stepped in full-time in 1998 as Hellier's replacement. Together, Fearless and Holmes recorded Death in Vegas' second album, appropriately titled *The Contino Sessions*, which earned the band worldwide critical acclaim.

The Contino Sessions, released in 1999 on Time Bomb/ Concrete, revealed a wide range of influences, from rock bands such as the Rolling Stones, the Velvet Underground, Can, and Iggy Pop's the Stooges, to techno acts like Underground Resistance and Primal Scream. Death in Vegas also invoked the music of 1980s neo-psychedelic bands such as My Bloody Valentine, Loop, and Spaceman 3, the groups that so enthralled Fearless as a teen, to figure into *The Contino Sessions'* overall sound. "I'm still excited by dance music, but we were trying to get away from the whole 'electronica' thing, which seemed to be exploding in America," Fearless said to Simon Reynolds in *Spin,* explaining the reasoning behind taking Death in Vegas in a new direction. "It would have been too easy to make an album that rode on that wave." The group also used live musicians for the album, which further separated the album from Death in Vegas' debut. "What I love about the best techno is how hypnotic and monotonous it is," continued Fearless. "When there *is* a change [in musical structure], you notice it so much more. That's what we tried to do, but using live musicians. We get the guys to play along to the tracks, and then we sample, rework, and loop the best bits."

In addition to implementing live instrumentation, Death in Vegas also contacted various rock and roll heroes to add vocals to selected songs, and to Fearless's surprise, all were willing to participate. As a result, Iggy Pop appeared reciting a morbid tale for the song "Aisha," Primal Scream's Bobby Gillespie added vocals reminiscent of Bob Dylan for "Soul Auctioneer," and the Jesus and Mary Chain's Jim Reid sang for the punk/rock track "Broken Little Sister." "I wanted to work with three male vocalists who were very in tune with each other," said Fearless in an interview with Liza Ghorbani for Rolling Stone.com. "And there was a parallel line there, not just in lyrical content, but there's a dark edge to them. You think Mary Chain, Primal Scream and the Stooges, and there's some territory there. Certainly the Mary Chain and Primal Scream were influenced by the Stooges." Other guest vocalists included the London Community Gospel Choir, as well as Allison for the track "Dirge." While Fearless himself named the space rock song "Neptune City" as his favorite track on the album, several reviewers called attention to "Aladdin's Story," which Rob Sheffield in *Rolling Stone* in 1999 described as "one of the strangest, loveliest songs you'll hear all year."

Selected discography

Dead Elvis, (includes "Opium Shuffle" and "Dirt"), Concrete, 1997.

The Contino Sessions, (includes "Aladdin's Story"), Time Bomb/Concrete, 1999.

Sources

Periodicals

Independent, December 5, 1997, pp. 16-17; November 9, 1999, p. 9.

Magnet, October/November 1999, p. 71.

Rolling Stone, October 14, 1999, p. 36.

Spin, October 1999, pp. 125-126.

Toronto Sun, November 20, 1999, p. 54.

Online

Death in Vegas at Time Bomb Recordings, http://www.timebombrecordings.com (December 24, 1999).

Death in Vegas Unofficial website, http://www.cgocable.net/~jgage/bio.htm (December 24, 1999).

Rolling Stone.com, http://www.rollingstone.tunes.com (December 24, 1999).

—*Laura Hightower*

Dave Edmunds

Singer, songwriter, producer, guitar

Photography by Ken Settle. Reproduced by permission. ©

Considered by many as the quintessential musician's musician, British retro revivalist Dave Edmunds has gained recognition not only as an accomplished guitarist, songwriter, and solo performer, but also for his efforts as a producer, sideman, frontman, vocalist, and as a member of the band Rockpile—a second-tier supergroup that also included Nick Lowe on bass, drummer Terry Williams, and Billy Bremner on guitar. Edmunds, more of a knowledgeable stylist than a purist, has worked in several forms of music as well, from traditional American rock and roll and pop to country, but has never fallen back on mere genre-mongering. "There's nothing fancy about Edmunds' chosen music," commented *Newsday* reporter David Herndon in 1994. He displayed his talents best in these styles, always emphasizing impeccable taste, craft, and a good-time vibe.

Throughout his 30-year career as a singer, guitarist, and producer, Edmunds usually invested a greater amount of his own energy in comparison to most modern-day musicians. In addition to producing for most of his own projects, Edmunds also built a myriad of production credits for other artists; a few examples include the Stray Cats' first two British albums, the Everly Brothers' comeback effort entitled *EB '84,* and Lowe's *Party of One.* Edmunds has also produced albums for the Fabulous Thunderbirds and k.d. lang.

Born on April 15, 1943, in Cardiff, Wales, Edmunds began his career in music in the late 1960s with his first real band, a psychedelic blues trio called the Love Sculptures. Most of that group's output—a total of two albums—approached "headache-inducing guitar music," according to *MusicHound Rock* contributor Leland Rucker. However, the band did produce one hit with "Sabre Dance." Following his tenure leading the Love Sculptures, Edmunds struck out on his own. Soon thereafter, he scored his biggest success, "I Hear You Knocking," a number one British single in 1970 that also reached number four on charts in the United States. More than a dozen British hits would follow his initial accomplishment, including songs penned by Elvis Costello ("Girls Talk"), Bruce Springsteen ("From Small Things, Big Things Come"), and Graham Parker ("Crawling From the Wreckage).

After "I Hear You Knocking," Edmunds released his first two solo efforts, *Rockpile*, released in 1972, and *Subtle as a Flying Mallet*, 1975. Both of these patchy, yet enjoyable albums saw Edmunds acting largely as a one-man studio band covering Chuck Berry-styled rock and roll, rockabilly, and the blues. Despite his British roots, Edmunds had, in his younger years, already adopted the regional styles of Louisiana and Memphis, Tennessee, and blended them with the sounds of 1960s pop radio

For the Record . . .

Born April 15, 1943, in Cardiff, Wales.

Began career in music with a psychedelic-blues trio called the Love Sculptures, late-1960s; "I Hear You Knocking" became a number one U.K. single, 1970; released first two solo albums, *Rockpile*, 1972; and *Subtle as a Flying Magnet*, 1975; played in Rockpile, 1976-81; released *D.E. 7th*, 1982; released comeback album *Plugged In*, 1994; has produced albums for the Stray Cats, the Everly Brothers, Nick Lowe, the Fabulous Thunderbirds, and k.d. lang.

Addresses: *Record company*—Pyramid, 1208 Lula Lake Rd., Lookout Mountain, GA 37350.

hits. Some of his favorite hit makers from that era included the Beach Boys and Phil Spector, although Chuck Berry remained his greatest songwriting influence throughout his career. "He was it. He's the poet," Edmunds asserted to Herndon. As for his guitar inspirations, Edmunds cited Chet Atkins, Scotty Moore, and James Burton. While working on his first two albums, Edmunds also recorded several rock and roll oldies covers for the 1974 movie *Stardust.* Coincidentally, the band credited with six of the seven tracks on the soundtrack album was called the Stray Cats, and Edmunds later produced for an unrelated trio by the same name in the 1980s.

Later on, Edmunds' earlier work was compiled to form various releases. *The Early Edmunds,* released in 1991 in Britain by EMI, included both albums by the Love Sculptures and their hit single, Edmunds' solo *Rockpile* album, as well as a rare single by Edmunds' short-lived band prior to the Love Sculptures called Human Beans. Two other compilations, 1997's *Dave Edmunds, Rocker: Early Works 1968-1972* and 1980's *Dave Edmunds & Love Sculptures Singles A's & B's,* also covered the first phase of the singer's recording career.

During the next period of Edmunds' career, the musician worked extensively with bassist/singer Nick Lowe, guitarist Billy Bremner, and drummer Terry Williams in a live/studio outfit called Rockpile. The collaboration proved a beneficial arrangement for Edmunds, who found a sympathetic writing partner in Lowe. The four men formed the rootsy, new-wave pop group in 1976 in London, England, and adopted a relaxed approach to their music-making. "We'd meet at the bar at the London airport and go on tour," he recalled to Herndon, adding that he still considered the band's eventual break-up over a contractual dispute a "bitter disappointment."

Although the group worked together until they disbanded in 1981, Rockpile only released one album, 1980's *Seconds of Pleasure,* as a collective unit. However, during the years spent with Rockpile, Edmunds recorded with the band and himself produced for the Swan Song label three of his best projects. *Get It*, released in 1977, included the tracks "I Knew the Bride (When She Used to Rock 'n' Roll)," "Get Out of Denver," and "JuJu Man." His next offering, *Tracks on Wax 4*, released in 1978, was Rockpile's hardest rocking album, while *Repeat When Necessary*, released in 1979, showcased the band's sharp and consistent work ethic at a time when Rockpile was also busy working on Lowe's impressive *Labour of Lust* album. The 1981 sampler/compilation album *The Best of Dave Edmunds* reflected his years with Swan Song and Rockpile.

While saddened over Rockpile's demise, Edmunds at the same time began to concentrate more on his guitar technique. "I didn't learn a thing on guitar during the '70's," he admitted to Kevin Ransom in a 1994 interview for *Guitar Player.* After joining Rockpile, Edmunds said, "I just wasn't sitting down and picking anymore." Furthermore, he rediscovered the Chet Atkins roots of his earlier days. "He's the guy who got me interested in the guitar in the first place," Edmunds said. "I've been developing that finger-picking thing quite seriously the last several years, and I've become a lot more proficient at it." Edmunds would later utilize these skills in his surprise 1994 comeback album.

During the 1980s and 1990s, Edmunds continued to release records with mixed results, but his first post-Rockpile effort, 1982's *D.E. 7th,* hit the mark. This collection of rollicking rock songs (none of which were penned by Edmunds) disclosed the Springsteen song "From Small Things, Big Things Come," a cover of NRBQ's "Me and My Boys," and a little-known Chuck Berry original entitled "Dear Dad." Following this, Edmunds teamed unsuccessfully with machine-pop wizard Jeff Lynne for the albums *Information*, released in 1983, and *Riff Raff*, released in 1984. Sharing songwriting and production duties, Lynne employed techniques that were inappropriate for Edmunds' style which made for two poor collections. Devoted fans of Edmunds saw both releases as dreadful examples of the musician's work. Although his next release, 1990's *Closer to the Flame,* was an improvement over his previous two efforts, hinting again at both rhythm and blues and rockabilly, it nonetheless failed to excite his fans.

Between recording *Riff Raff* and *Closer to the Flame,* Edmunds took time away from working on solo projects, using this break to produce for numerous other artists. However, he did take on working on the soundtrack for the 1985 teen-movie sequel *Porky's Revenge.* Earning acclaim for his efforts, Edmunds contributed three new songs for the film soundtrack and also played on tracks by former Beatle George Harrison, guitarist Jeff Beck, Clarence Clemons, and former Led Zeppelin vocalist Robert Plant. In 1987, Columbia Records released another greatest hits album of sorts entitled *The Dave Edmunds Band Live: I Hear You Rockin,'* with music taken from various live performances.

After the disappointment of *Closer to the Flame,* Edmunds again went on a hiatus from recording his own albums, but emerged in 1994 with the critically acclaimed *Plugged In.* He recorded the entire album himself and played all the instruments, building songs track by track in his new studio in Los Angeles, California. "Booking a studio and going in with a band and a bunch of songs just isn't as much fun as doing it all myself," he explained to Ransom. Reminiscent of his best work from the 1970s and 1980s, *Plugged In* returned to rockabilly, country-inspired leads, and rock and roll rhythms. Notable tracks from the album included a cover of Jerry Reed's "The Claw," and a remake of "Sabre Dance."

After more than three decades as a viable and consistent participant in the rock and roll business, Edmunds felt fortunate about his longevity. "I've lived a life of music I choose to like and record," he said to Herndon. "I haven't had to join the rest of the human race in their social jail on the nine-to-five corporate ladder, and I'm very grateful." And although mainstream popularity in the United States continued to elude him throughout his accomplished career, Edmunds insisted that earning stardom to him was no big thing. "I'm not out to prove anything, as if there's a goal," Edmunds added. "The traveling is the goal."

Selected discography

Rockpile, MAM, 1972.
(With others) *Stardust,* (soundtrack), Arista, 1974.
Subtle as a Flying Mallet, RCA, 1975.
Dave Edmunds, Rocker: Early Works 1968-1972, (France) Parlophone/EMI, 1977.
Get It, Swan Song, 1977.
Tracks on Wax, Swan Song, 1978.
Repeat When Necessary, Swan Song, 1979.
Dave Edmunds & Love Sculptures Singles A's & B's, (U.K.) See for Miles, 1980.
(Rockpile) *Seconds of Pleasure,* Columbia, 1980.
Twangin..., Swan Song, 1981.
The Best of Dave Edmunds, Swan Song, 1981.
D.E. 7th, Columbia, 1982.
Information, Columbia, 1983.
Riff Raff, Columbia, 1984.
(With others) *Porky's Revenge,* (soundtrack), Columbia, 1985.
The Dave Edmunds Band Live: I Hear You Rockin', Columbia, 1987.
Closer to the Flame, Capitol, 1990.
The Early Edmunds, (U.K.) EMI, 1991.
The Dave Edmunds Anthology (1968-90), Rhino, 1993.
Plugged In, Pyramid, 1994.

Sources

Books

MusicHound Rock: The Essential Album Guide, Visible Ink Press, 1999.
Robbins, Ira A., editor, *Trouser Press Guide to '90s Rock,* Fireside/Simon and Schuster, 1997.

Periodicals

Boston Globe, June 19, 1998.
Guitar Player, October 1994, p. 123; December 1994, pp. 38-39.
Los Angeles Times, January 30, 1997; April 25, 1998.
Newsday, September 9, 1994, p. B25.
Playboy, June 1990, p. 20.

—Laura Hightower

Eminem

Hip hop, rap artist

Photograph by Ron Frehm. AP/World Wide Photos. Reproduced by permission.

If his message is misunderstood by parents of teenagers across America, that is not stopping Eminem from earning sweeping popularity. Though his lyrics can be gritty, racy, and carry violent overtones, fans of all races have responded to his honest anger. Eminem's *Slim Shady* LP took home a Grammy Award on February 23, 2000 as the Best Rap Album of the year for 1999. His solo, "My Name Is," won the award of Best Rap Solo Performance. For a young man who grew up in a less than ideal setting in suburban Detroit, fame arrived after several years of hard work, and, as he said, "paying his dues."

Eminem reflects his own harsh life experiences in his music, experiences common to many teenagers. In a July1999 article for the *Washington Post*, Alona Wartofsky summarized his appeal when she commented that "a large part of Eminem's meteoric rise can be explained by the appeal of being profoundly expletived up. Both Eminem and his alter ego, Slim Shady, represent the perennial loser, the class clown who's going nowhere fast. The guy who gets beat up in the bathroom, keeps flunking the same grade and can't even keep a $5.50-an-hour job. So he checks out—blows off school and gets wasted with whatever drug he can get his hands on. It's not just his white skin and bleached blond hair that set him apart from the hip-hop pack. Unlike most rappers, he's harshly self-deprecating." If other white kids were listening to rap before he came on the scene, they were listening even harder when Eminem appeared.

Marshall Mathers III was born in Kansas City, Missouri, on October 17, 1974, and spent his early childhood between there and Detroit, primarily in Macomb County, just northeast of the city. He was raised by a single mother, Debbie Mathers-Briggs. When he was 12, they settled on the east side of Detroit permanently, but life got no easier. Mathers never knew his father, although his mother contended that the two of them were married at the time of Mathers' birth. Aggravated by having to move and difficulties making friends, Mathers retreated into television and comic books. He attended Lincoln Junior High School and Osbourne High School where he started listening to LL Cool J and the 2 Live Crew. He made friends, and went off against other rappers. He quickly gained a reputation of some notoriety at his skill for rhyming. Mathers did skip too much school, and failed the ninth grade. Eventually, he dropped out of school before getting a diploma. Working odd jobs, Mathers worked on his craft, his art of rapping. He told *Rap Pages* in 1999 that, "I tried to go back to school five years ago, but I couldn't do it. I just wanted to rap and be a star."

Mathers did continue his rapping. Working with different groups that included Basement Productions, the New

For the Record . . .

Born Marshall Mathers III on October 17, 1974, in Kansas City, MO; married: wife Kim; children: daughter, Hailie Jade, born December 25, 1995.

Has worked with groups such as Basement Productions, the New Jacks, and Sole Intent before going solo with the release of *Infinite,* 1997; released *Slim Shady,* 1998; released *The Marshall Mathers LP*, 2000.

Awards: Grammy Awards for Best Rap Album of the Year, *Slim Shady;* Best Rap Solo Performance, "My Name Is," 1999.

Addresses: Interscope Records, 10900 Wilshire Blvd., Suite 1230, Los Angeles, CA 90024. *Website*—http://www.eminem.com.

Jacks and Sole Intent, he finally went solo in 1997. His album, *Infinite*, was released through FBT Productions, a local Detroit company. The local hiphop community did not take to him, but he ignored the criticism and tirelessly promoted himself through radio stations and freestyle competitions across the country. People started taking notice. He was honored with a mention in the *Source's* key column, "Unsigned Hype." By the end of the year he won the 1997 Wake Up Show Freestyle Performer of the Year from Los Angeles disc jockeys, Sway and Tech. Mathers took second place in *Rap Sheet* magazine's "Rap Olympics," an annual freestyle competition.

His *Slim Shady EP* in early 1998 not only made him an underground star, it also got the attention of the famed Dr. Dre, creator of The Chronic and N.W.A., and president of Aftermath Entertainment. Dr. Dre was so impressed that he signed Mathers to his label. When *Slim Shady LP* finally came out, it debuted at number three on the *Billboard* Album Chart. He also had been invited to appear on underground MC Shabam Sahdeeq's "Five Star Generals" single, Kid Rock's Devil Without a Cause and other rap releases in the interim. His songs depicted rape, violence and drug use. They horrified some people, to be sure. Some of his lyrics were even directed at his own mother, as well as the mother of his daughter who was three at the time of the song's release. The song, "97 Bonnie and Clyde," has Mathers fantasizing about killing the mother of his child. Writing for *USA Today,* Edna Gunderson reviewed the album that was causing the uproar. "The first release on Dr. Dre's Aftermath label is a marvel of entertaining contradictions. The white rapper kicks himself mercilessly on one track, lashes out against the cruel world in the next, then vacillates between rage and apathy in razor-sharp tunes that visit a host of suburban miseries and comedies. He's unquestionably offensive, but the antidote for that venom can be found in the music's stinging humor and tight grooves."

Mathers defended himself and his lyrics to those who not only loathed his message, but also those who were still not prepared to welcome a white rap artist into a field that seemed to be the domain of blacks since its beginnings. Mathers told *Source* that, "I do feel like I'm coming from a standpoint where people don't realize there are a lot of poor white people. Rap music kept my mind off all the bullshit I had to go through." He went on to say that, "I'm white in a music started by black people. I'm not ignorant to the culture and I'm not trying to take anything away from the culture. But no one has a choice where they grew up or what color they are. If you're a rich kid or a ghetto kid you have no control over your circumstances. The only control you have is to get out of your situation or stay in it." Maybe because of that, his music resonated with teens especially, all over America and the world, no matter what their race or economic status.

His music was certainly not popular with some people. In the spring of 1999, *Billboard* editor-in-chief, Timothy White accused Eminem and the music industry promoting him of "exploiting the world's misery," in an editorial. The harshest criticism came in the form of a lawsuit—from his own mother! On September 17, 1999, Mathers-Briggs filed a lawsuit in Macomb County, Michigan Circuit Court, charging that her son, the rapper, made "defamatory comments about her in interviews, including descriptions of her as 'pill-popping' and 'lawsuit happy,'...claiming emotional distress, humiliation, and damages that included the loss of her mobile home in the summer of 1999," according to Carla Hay, writing in *Billboard.* Although the outcome of the lawsuit was still pending, Paul Rosenberg, Eminem's attorney issued a statement saying, "Eminem's life is reflected in his music. Everything he said can be verified as true—the truth is an absolute defense to a claim of defamation. The lawsuit does not come as a surprise to Eminem—his mother has been threatening to sue him since the success of his single, 'My Name Is.' It is merely the result of a lifelong strained relationship between him and his mother. Regardless, it is still painful to be sued by your mother, and therefore the lawsuit will only be responded to through legal channels."

Eminem's United States tour that began in the spring of 1999 met with a lot of kudoes and cajoles. According to Jon Dolan in *Spin* in August of 1999, that tour did not go too well in most cities. Fans disappointed at his mere 25-minute stage performance booed him offstage. A date in San Francisco was "cut even shorter," Dolan noted, "after he leapt into the crowd to beat down a heckler." Actor Dustin Hoffman surprised a lot of concertgoers and the star himself during the Los Angeles performance when he appeared onstage, wrapped up like the mummy on the cover of *Slim Shady LP*. Yet Dolan also noted that, "he delivered Motor City madness that would do Ted Nugent proud ... appropriately ... Slim was playing for his peeps—young, Midwestern hip-hop kids from urban dead zones and their first-ring suburbs."

As he continued to plan for the debut of his latest album in the spring of 2000, *Marshall Mathers LP*, the controversy continued to rage. From his fall 1999 tour of Europe, tongues were still wagging with criticism. British writer, Peter Robinson, in *Melody Maker*, had said that, "By far the most distressing thing about the *Slim Shady LP* is how seductive it is—largely due to Dr Dre's production work, it captivates and thrills, and this is an unavoidably amazing body of work. There are tracks here 10 times better than 'My Name Is,' hence the generous mark at the end of this review. But the spite, the sheer nastiness, is revolting. But is it funny?" In an interview for *Melody Maker* later, in November of 1999, Robinson posed the question to Mathers that, "Does the fact that you made a success of the album entirely negate the principle of being an anti-hero?" "Kind of," responded Mathers. "Me rappin' about shootin' up with heroin and bein' broke and this and that, it's like a pun on the album. It's like, my family and people around me always told me that I would grow up to be nothing and my teachers in school and everyone said it. I dropped out of high school, I failed ninth grade three times, I couldn't keep a job, people said that I wouldn't amount to anything. And I portray myself as the biggest loser in the world.... Look at me now."

Whatever else Mathers might project, his affection and love for his daughter Hailie Jade, born on Christmas Day in 1995 when he was only 21 himself, is clear. She lives in Detroit, but sometimes accompanies him on tour. Mathers and his daughter's mother, Kim, spent most of their eight-year relationship breaking up and making up. He says that while his daughter has listened to the album with the song about him killing her mother, and loves it, she does not yet understand it. "When she gets old enough, I'm going to explain it to her," he says. "I'll let her know that Mommy and Daddy weren't getting along at the time. None of it was to be taken literally."

Dr. Dre commented to *Rolling Stone* that "If he remains the same person that walked into the studio with me that first day, he will be ... larger than Michael Jackson." For a person still in his mid-twenties, who was also named Best New Artist by MTV during their awards in September of 1999, that is a lot to live up to.

Selected discography

Infinite, FBT Productions, 1997.
The Slim Shady LP, Aftermath/Interscope, 1998.
*Just Don't Give a F****, Aftermath/Interscope, 1998.
The Marshall Mathers LP, Aftermath/Interscope, 2000.

Sources

Periodicals

The Atlanta Constitution, (Georgia) Apr. 20, 1999; Aug. 1, 1999.
Billboard, Oct. 2, 1999.
The Los Angeles Times, Dec. 26, 1999.
Melody Maker, (London) May 1, 1999; Aug. 14, 1999; Nov. 10-16, 1999; Nov. 17-23, 1999.
The New York Times, Aug. 22, 1999; Sept. 11, 1999; Nov. 14, 1999.
Rolling Stone, Apr. 29, 1999; May 27, 1999; Dec. 16-23, 1999.
Spin, Aug. 1999.
Time, June 21, 1999; Oct. 4, 1999.
USA Today, Dec. 28, 1999.
The Washington Post, July 27, 1999.

Online

Official Eminem website, http://www.eminem.com (April 2000).
EminemWorld, http://eminemworld.com (April 2000).

—Jane Spear

The Ex

Post-punk band

A legendary force across the Netherlands and a well-known act in Europe, the Ex, out of Amsterdam, Holland, have used a hybrid of punk music and experimental rock to advance their liberal socialist agenda for over two decades. During the 1980s, the Ex released a vast amount of recorded work, as well as propaganda that supported their anarchist stance, leading the group to the forefront of Holland's punk scene. Distributed either by various Dutch labels or by the band members themselves—the group scrupulously avoided the music industry from the onset—the early Ex albums focused mainly on rhythmic guitar and energized anger. However, the same musical formula eventually ran its course, and with all of the Ex's recordings beginning to sound alike, many supposed that the group's artistic tether was destined to come to a close. Despite such assumptions, the Ex expanded their vocabulary in the early 1990s, a period that saw the group embrace other styles such as industrial and improvisation along the lines of Einsturzende Neubauten and Test Dept. Further expanding their fanbase overseas, the Ex , despite rarely performing in the United States, have attained legendary status in the underground hardcore community. The band has also collaborated and performed with jazz artists, such as drummer Han Bennink, clarinetist Ab Baars, and avant-garde cellist Tom Cora, a musician often described as the best thing the cello has to guitar legend Jimi Hendrix.

While the Ex stretched beyond their punk roots in the 1990s, they nevertheless consistently held true to the protocol of the punk movement. Unlike many of their punk-era peers, the Ex never handed over control to a major label and continued to issue their own material under the band's name or through non-threatening independent labels. The group maintained their sense of political consciousness. Always outspoken about their causes, the band backed the issues they championed, including liberation and human rights struggles around the world. Taking action to support funds and inform others, the Ex held regular benefit concerts and also stuffed record sleeves with educational texts.

Veteran producer Steve Albini, a fan of the Ex since 1982 who also recorded the band's 1998 album *Starters Alternators,* explained that "they have not lost their original inspiration, and they have found an evolving and engaging way to develop along unexplored avenues without making their original abilities and perceptions become trivial," as quoted by Bill Meyer in a 1999 Ex profile for *Magnet* magazine. "For many people, evolution is a continual discarding of the past, with a corresponding disdain for its attitudes and expression—an after-market cheapening of history," Albini continued. "This is a trap of trends that the Ex have avoided by not serially embracing ludicrous positions—which they would feel obliged to disregard and disown—and not mistaking their past inspiration for delusion. No pirate outfits, no drum 'n' bass, no heavy-metal apologies, no 'unplugged.'"

By the later 1990s, the Amsterdam-based band consisted of five politically and musically like-minded members known by their first names only. Two of the groups founding members, vocalist Jos (who goes by the name G.W. Sok on record sleeves and book spines) and guitarist Terrie focused on the Ex since its inception, while bassist Luc and drummer Katrin both joined in 1984. Until that time, various other bassists and drummers came and went. A full decade later, the band added a fifth member, Andy, the only non-Dutch participant in the Ex lineup. The Scottish guitarist played with the group for the first time in 1990 during a break from his previous band, the Dog Faced Hermans. Then in 1994, when the Dog Faced Hermans disbanded, Andy joined the Ex on a permanent basis.

The story of the Ex began in April of 1979. Four young Dutch anarchists, heavily involved in the political environment of the time and the squatters movement, formed a band, calling themselves the Ex. Reportedly, they opted for a name that could be easily spray painted within seconds onto a wall. As the 1970s came to a close, the Ex played their first gig, established themselves in the underground clubs of Amsterdam, and recorded their

For the Record . . .

Members include **Andy** (born in Scotland; joined band in 1994; former member of the Dog Faced Hermans), guitar; **Jos** (born in Holland; also known as G.W. Sok), vocals; **Katrin** (born in Holland; joined band in 1984), drums; **Luc** (born in Holland; joined band in 1984), bass; **Terrie** (born in Holland), guitar.

Formed band in Amsterdam, Holland, in April of 1979; released debut album, *Disturbing Domestic Peace,* 1980; formed Ex Records, 1988; released *Scrabbling at the Lock* with cellist Tom Cora, 1991; signed with Touch and Go Records, released *Starters Alternators,* 1998.

Addresses: *Record company*—Touch and Go Records, P.O. Box 25520, Chicago, IL 60625, (773) 388-3888. *Website*—The Ex: http://www.southern.com/southern/band/EX000/.

debut album, *Disturbing Domestic Peace*, released in 1980. The group's follow-up effort, *History is What's Happening,* appeared in 1982, followed by four releases in 1983: two albums, *Tumult* and *Blueprints for a Blackout*; a singles collection, *Dignity of Labour*; and an EP entitled *Gonna Rob the Sperm Bank.* Although the band lacked technical prowess early on—most songs saw Jos condemning society's ills over choppy electric guitars and brittle rhythms—they used such shortcomings to their advantage. "Instead of familiar notes and chords," wrote Meyer, "the guitar and bass generated massive sound slabs that toppled through the open spaces in the drummers' stark patterns."

All the while, the Ex were earning a reputation for their ferocious, kinetic live performances. According to Jos, the group duplicated the same physical energy for studio work. "The movement is necessary," he revealed to Meyer. "Andy and Terrie couldn't get their sounds without it." Unfortunately, and in spite of the group's obvious commitment, the band's live energy failed to reveal itself in the same way for two straight-ahead rock albums *Pokkeherrie*, released in 1985, and *Too Many Cowboys,* released in 1987. After forming their own label, Ex Records in 1988, to release a compilation of their three Peel Sessions on that year's *Hands Up! You're Free,* the band redeemed themselves with *Joggers & Smoggers,* an epic double-album released in 1989. Here, the band broadened its sound, reining in their heavy guitars to make way for a variety of vocalists and guest musicians (16 in all, including Thurston Moore and Lee Ranaldo of the band Sonic Youth on guitars) playing instruments such as trombone, saxophone, and bagpipes. Some of the less traditional "instruments" used included rattling bird cages and bamboo sticks.

The Ex kicked off the 1990s with other major undertakings. First, they released a series of singles in 1991 and 1992 known as the *6* series. One of those efforts, *6.4,* was a double seven-inch single that excerpted a live performance with guest appearances by the Dog Faced Hermans and free-jazz drummer Hans Bennink. Another, *6.2* (featuring the single "Millîtan"), was recorded with Kurdish folk musician/protest singer Brader. Then, the band released what *Trouser Press Guide to '90s Rock* contributor Douglas Walk called "the Ex's first genuinely great album," 1991's *Scrabbling at the Lock.* A collaboration with avant-garde cellist Tom Cora, a solo recording artist who had also played with Curlew and the Skeleton Crew, the album saw the Ex exploring the different ways a punk band could sound by exploring improvisation and traditional music. Highlights from *Scrabbling at the Lock* included a second and improved version of "Hidegen Fujnak a Szelek" (the original was recorded for the *6* series), "State of Shock," and "Batium," an arrangement of a piece written by the late Turkish composer Ismet Siral.

After touring the world with Cora, the Ex released another album with the cellist entitled *And the Weathermen Shrug Their Shoulders*, released in 1993. A more dense and dark album than its predecessor, the second Cora collaboration nonetheless earned favorable recognition as well. In 1995, the Ex returned with *Mudbird Shivers*, an abrasive, daring album featuring guest vocalist Han Buhrs. That same year, the band released another collaborative effort entitled *Instant,* a 32-track improvisational double CD that won critics and fans over. Joined by Buhrs again on harmonica and "toffee-tin" bass, the Ex also enlisted a variety of guest improvisers, among them Bennink, cellist Tristan Honsinger, clarinetist Ab Baars, and Michael Vatcher.

Tapping into their rising popularity in the United States, the Ex in 1998 signed with the independent label Touch and Go Records to distribute their next album. Recorded with ubiquitous producer Steve Albini, *Starters Alternators* was released in October of 1998. Returning to their roots for this record, the Ex with the aid of Albini found a way to capture the dynamics of their life set. "On its new songs, the Ex sounds like a five-piece drum corps, with the separate rhythms of voices and guitar combining into complex polyrhythms," wrote Meyer, describing the essence the group's highly acclaimed work. "Each instrument also takes its turn at articulating the songs' intertwined melodies." Unfortunately, earlier in April of

1998, the group's ongoing partnership with Cora ended when the jazz great succumbed to cancer; the Ex had to cancel rehearsals for a third record with the cellist when he was first diagnosed. At the time of his death, the Ex had played nearly 100 concerts with Cora.

Following the release of *Starter Alternators,* the Ex toured the United States with Fugazi, recorded a collaborative album with the band Tortoise, continued to perform the world over, and Luc and Andy also played with jazz musicians Mats Gustafsson and Vatcher. For their next album, the Ex planned to include songs from around the world from countries like Greece, Cambodia, and Ethiopia. "There is always a new adventure," Terrie told Meyer with enthusiasm. "That makes it worthwhile."

Selected discography

Singles

"All Corpses Smell the Same," Ex, 1980.
"New Horizons in Retailing," Ex, 1980.
"Weapons for El Salvador," Gramschap, 1981.
"Villa Zuid Moet Blijven," Ex, 1981.
"Gonna Rob the Sperm Bank," Ex, 1983.
"The Red Dance Package," Ex, 1983.
"Enough is Enough," Gramschap, 1984.
"Destroy Fascism!," Loony Tunes, 1987.
"Rara Rap," Ex, 1988.
"Lied Der Steinklopfer," Ex, 1990.
"Keep on Hoppin," Clawfist, 1991.
6.1, ("Slimy Toad"), Ex, 1991.
(With Brader) *6.2,* ("Millîtan"), Ex, 1991.
6.3, ("Hidegen Fujnak a Szelek"), Ex, 1991.
6.4, (double-seven-inch single), Ex , 1991.
6.5, ("This Song Is in English"), Ex, 1991.
6.6 (12-inch single "Euroconfusion"), Ex, 1992.

Albums, EPs, and tapes

Disturbing Domestic Peace, Verrecords, 1980; reissued, Ex, 1995.
History Is What's Happening, More DPM, 1982; reissued, Ex, 1995.
Dignity of Labour, VGZ, 1983; reissued, Ex, 1995.
Gonna Rob the Spermbank, (EP), Sneeelleeer, 1983.
Tumult, FAI, 1983; reissued, Fist Puppet, 1994.
Blueprints for a Blackout, Pig Brother Productions, 1983; reissued, Fist Puppet, 1994.
1936: The Spanish Revolution, (EP), Ron Johnson, 1985.
Pay No More Than 6 Fr., (tape), 1985.
Pokkeherrie, Rockabilly, 1985; reissued, Ex, 1995.
Live in Wroclaw, Red, (tape), 1987.
Too Many Cowboys, Mordam, 1987; reissued, Fist Puppet, 1994.
Hands Up! You're Free, Ex/Fist Puppet, 1988.
Aural Guerilla, Ex, 1988; Homestead, 1989.
Joggers & Smoggers, Ex, 1989; reissued, Fist Puppet, 1994.
Dead Fish, (EP), Ex, 1990.
(With Dog Faced Hermans) *Treat,* (tape), Damon Radge, 1990.
Ample, (tape), 1991.
(With Tom Cora) *Scrabbling at the Lock,* Ex, 1991; reissued, Fist Puppet, 1994.
(With Tom Cora) *And the Weathermen Shrug Their Shoulders,* Ex/Fist Puppet, 1993.
Ample 2, (tape), 1995.
(With guests) *Instant,* Ex, 1995.
Mudbird Shivers, Ex/Crosstalk, 1995.
Starters Alternators, Ex/Touch and Go, 1998.

Sources

Books

Robbins, Ira A., editor, *Trouser Press Guide to '90s Rock,* Fireside/Simon and Schuster, 1997.

Periodicals

Magnet, January/February 1999, pp. 29-31.

Online

All Music Guide, http://www.allmusic.com (March 3, 2000).
The Ex at Touch and Go/Southern Records, http://www.southern.com/southern/band/EX000/ (March 3, 2000).
Rolling Stone.com, http://www.rollingstone.tunes.com (March 3, 2000).

—*Laura Hightower*

Filter

Rock band

Filter's use of electronic sound is one of the characteristics that sets the band apart from the rest. The group expressed their philosophy about technology and artistry on the back of their 1996 debut, *Short Bus*: "There is a certain subset of musicians who for reasons unknown adhere to the false premise that 'electronic' music or the tools involved imply a lack of creativity or inspired performance. Technology in the hands of creative, intelligent individuals is a tool for art, not a hindrance. Filter, being members of the current millennia, admit freely to the use of such devices."

Filter founder Richard Patrick began experimenting with electronic sound on a small eight-track in his parents' basement in Cleveland, Ohio. While at the University of Chicago, fellow Filter member Brian Liesegang did some of his own electronic sound experimentation in his small studio situated across the hall from Bob Mood, the inventor of the modern synthesizer. The band originally featured Patrick on vocals, guitars, bass, programming, and drums, and Brian Liesegang on programming, guitars, keyboards, and drums. After Liesegang's departure from the band in 1997, Patrick continued to work with bass player Frank Cavanaugh and guitarist Geno Lenardo, both of whom he and Lesegang worked with on tour.

Patrick began his musical career as a guitarist in the original touring band for Nine Inch Nails. Lead singer for Nine Inch Nails, Trent Reznor, introduced Patrick to Liesegang during a shoot for a Nine Inch Nails video. After the lengthy tour ended, Patrick left the band in 1994 and began recording industrial rock with Liesegang, incorporating the influences of bands such as Nine Inch Nails and Ministry. In the summer and fall of 1994, Patrick and Liesegang produced, recorded, and engineered *Short Bus* in a small brick house in the outskirts of Cleveland. *Short Bus* was released in 1995 as Filter's debut album. The album, recorded solely by the two band members, proved a challenging endeavor; however, Filter managed to reach the mainstream, earning platinum album status. There was some controversy over the name of the album which refers to the short bus that transports "challenged" students to school. The biography on the *Rolling Stone* website stated that the title was in no way a sarcastic joke to poke fun at the expense of others; instead, "Filter believes there is much to be learned from the special and the different. Difference is just that, and it is only through the vision, ambition, and drive of those with an outlook and perspective outside the norm that original thought and real change can actually occur."

"Hey Man, Nice Shot," a career launching hit off of *Short Bus* also led to controversy. Patrick, inspired by the suicide of indicted Pennsylvania treasurer R. Budd Dwyer, wrote the song in 1991. The event of Dwyer's death was captured on live television in several United States markets, including Cleveland where Patrick watched. The Filter record label received an angry call from Dwyer's widow demanding an explanation. To this day, however, some believe the song was about Nirvana lead singer Kurt Cobain, who took his own life around the same time. The accusations angered Patrick. He told Blair Fischer in *Rolling Stone,* "when it started to come out that it was about Kurt Cobain, that really freaked me out because the last thing in the world I want is Courtney Love or Krist Novoselic or Dave Grohl to think that I'm pushing my song's success just by saying it's about [him]. That's a horrible thing. That just drove me crazy."

After the release of *Short Bus,* Filter spent the next two years touring and promoting the album. Patrick and Liesegang were joined by bass player Frank Cavanaugh from Outface, Chem Lab guitarist Geno Lenardo, and drummer Matt Walker for the tour. Apart from Filter, Patrick also toured with the Smashing Pumpkins in 1996. Filter lost drummer Walker to the aforementioned band shortly thereafter. Although Patrick respected the talent Walker brought to the group, he admitted that Walker was spread a little thin. "I want to record with Matt, but I don't know if I want to tour with him," Patrick told *RollingStone.com.* "I need a real go-getter. [Matt] is a married guy with a baby. Plus, he's working with three bands.... He's been touring non-stop for three years." Filter also contributed to several soundtracks during the

For the Record . . .

Members include **Frank Cavanaugh**, bass; **Steve Gillis**, drums; **Geno Leonardo**, guitar; **Brian Liesegang**, programmer, guitar, keyboard, drums; **Richard Patrick**, vocals, programmer, songwriter, guitar, bass, drums; **Matt Walker**, drums.

Patrick founded band while attending the University of Chicago; released debut album, *Short Bus,* in 1995, which reached platinum status; released *Title of Record,* 1999; Filter contributed to several movie soundtracks, including *Crow 2, Spawn, City of Angels, The Cable Guy,* and the *X Files.*

Addresses: *Record company*—Reprise Records, 75 Rockefeller Plaza, New York, NY 10019, (212) 275-4500. *Website*—Reprise Records: http://www.Reprise.Rec.com.

time between recording. The soundtracks for the *Crow 2* and *Spawn* both reached platinum album status. Patrick's cover of the Three Dog Night track, "One," was contributed to the *X-Files* movie soundtrack, which went gold.

Meanwhile, tension built between Patrick and Liesegang while working on Filter's next album. Liesegang wanted to record some of his own songs for inclusion on the next album. At the time, Patrick felt the songs were too experimental within the context of Filter. Patrick said on the official website, "when it came time to write songs, [Liesegang's] songs weren't very good. All I wanted him to do was to program and co-produce. When it came time to do the record, I told him to assume the position behind the computer. He wasn't about that, and obviously, it wasn't going to work." In late 1997, Liesegang severed his relationship with Patrick and Filter to pursue his own recording career.

Patrick spent the next two years writing songs and preparing for a new album, joined again by Cavanaugh and Lenardo. Filter also enlisted a new drummer, Steve Gillis, who replaced Walker. In 1999, Filter released their second album, *Title of Record,* which basically reflected Patrick's life for the previous four years. Fischer said the album was filled with "bitter anger" which seemed to permeate the album including the first cut, "Welcome to the Fold." The song tells the story of people trying to steal his money. Patrick says the song was inspired by an audience member in Arizona who sued him after claiming that she was hit in the head by a beer can that Patrick allegedly threw from the stage. "Some girl got hurt," Patrick told Fischer. "Got a combat boot in the face out in the desert playing some gig and, 'hey, I got hurt.' It's all about the lawsuit and you take my money.... Welcome to the fold."

"I'm Not the Only One" reflected a devastating ending of a two and a half year relationship with his girlfriend. "The title says it all. I'm not the only one," Patrick told Jon Wiederhorn of *Allmusic Zine*. "I found out she had slept with someone.... I couldn't hit her, so I smashed the platinum record that was on the wall and broke my hand.... Before they took me to the [hospital] I'm like, 'Put me in front of the mic now.' And that was the whole first verse of 'I'm Not the Only One'," Patrick confessed to Fischer.

Patrick admits his emotions were running high while making the album. In fact, he also confessed that he spent a lot of time drinking. Patrick said he was under a lot of pressure and "it's not necessarily the best thing to be going through [in your late 20s]," Patrick told Wiederhorn. "So I had to make a choice; Was I gonna drink all the time, or was I gonna get my shit together? And I decided I wanted to get my shit together. So I made some rules, and I stuck by them.... I just don't believe in wasting a lot of time anymore."

After the break with Liesegang, Patrick was leery to allow any of the other band members to contribute to the album; however, Lenardo wanted to contribute more to Filter than just showing up for the recording, rehearsals, and performances. Lenardo respected Patrick as the driving force of Filter which enabled Patrick to let go of some of the control. "Geno wanted to write for the band and I was put off by that," Patrick said on the website. "But his attitude was 'You're the boss, and I'm gonna do what I can to realize your musical vision' ... His songwriting embodies the spirit of *Short Bus* with a completely different vibe over it. He didn't demand to be in videos or interviews. He came through the back door, the proper door, and said, 'This is my music, can you work with it?' I'm proud to say he is in the band."

Patrick felt that his individuality and dedication to Filter are what make the fans responsive to his music. "Fans of Filter are fans because I am my own person," Patrick said on the official website. "They don't give a shit about what I'm wearing, or what I think is cool. My life is about Filter. If the kids dig it, great. If they don't dig it because I'm not wearing a gold chain, I don't care.... All I believe in is writing music and articulating my own opinion out of millions of opinions and seeing if anyone else agrees."

Moreover, Patrick believes it is important for musicians to remember their responsibilities as artists and performers. He stated on the official website, "Every word that you hear on this album, I lived through personally. I think that's what is lacking in music today, the lack of the human emotion. Being a musician gives you the responsibility to create musical journeys.... If there's a kid in Ames, Iowa, who hears my record and says, 'I can do that,' I'm stoked that I was a catalyst for him. I have a responsibility; and it's not to talk bullshit."

Selected discography

Short Bus, Reprise Records, 1995.
Title of Record, Reprise Records, 1999.

Sources

Books

MusicHound Rock: The Essential Album Guide, Visible Ink Press, 1999.

Robbins, Ira A, editor, *Trouser Press Guide to '90s Rock,* Fireside/Simon and Schuster, 1997.

Periodicals

Rolling Stone, August 24, 1999.
Spin, October 1999, pp. 45-46.

Online

"Filter," *All Music Guide,* http://allmusic.com/cg/x.dll?UID=7:28:42IPM&p=amg&sql=B143752 (February 13, 2000).

"Filter," *Rolling Stone,* http://rollingstone.tunes.com/sections/artists/text/bio.asp?afl=&LookUpString=117 (February 13, 2000).

"Filter...About the Band," Official Web Site, http://www.officialfilter.com/band5.html (February 13, 2000).

"Filter Smokes," *Rolling Stone,* http://rollingstone.tunes.com/se.../newsarticle.asp?afl=&NewsID=4317&LookUpString=11 (February 13, 2000).

"Filter: Songs Written in a Moment of Crisis," *Allmusic Zine,* wysiwyg://main.25/http://allmusic.com/zine/filter_interview.html (January 4, 2000).

"Reviews" *The Limelight,* http://www.mtv.com/mtv/music/reviews/archive/alive/filter_lime.html (Feburary 13, 2000).

"Take Another," *Rolling Stone,* http://rollingstone.tunes.com/se.../newsarticle.asp?afl=&NewsID=3438&LookUpStrings=11 (February 13, 2000).

—*Julie Sweet*

The Flying Luttenbachers

Free jazz/punk/metal group

Photograph by Samn Gaddis. Reproduced by permission.

Weasel Walter is a man on a quest. He is on a search for that elusive mix of extreme musical sound that will heighten existence. "What I am interested in," he told *Contemporary Musicians*, "is creating an abstract music with superhuman qualities. I'm trying to realize a medium in which I can attempt to transcend the mediocrity of the human condition that surrounds me." The vehicle for that quest is the Flying Luttenbachers. Along the way the band has morphed repeatedly from free jazz to no wave, punk jazz, industrial sound collage, and death metal. The Flying Luttenbachers have also passed through a series of band line-ups that have included the cream of Chicago's recent improv scene, including Ken Vandermark, Jeb Bishop, and Hal Russell. Walter provides the only constant, and the history of the band is the story of his demanding musical nature.

The founding member of the Flying Luttenbachers is multi-instrumentalist Walter, who grew up playing drums, guitar, and saxophone in Rockford, Illinois. From the beginning, Walter was attracted to the more *outré* and extreme musical forms. He played in a series of local bands, punk and otherwise, in Rockford. At the same time, he was devouring Albert Ayler and any other free jazz he could track down in suburban Illinois.

In the fall of 1990, he moved to Chicago to attend college where, with his friend Bill Pisarri, he founded a precursor to the Flying Luttenbachers, the Sound Improvisation Collective. The Collective seems to have been something of a musical terrorist group. Its usual venue was the dorm lobby where the group let loose a flurry of music and designed sounds to provoke and antagonize bystander and listener alike. Police were summoned regularly to break up performances. The flyer Walter posted for the Collective's single public performance, cited as the Fortress of the Flying Luttenbachers, offers a description of the group's music: "the eczema of dada, Ornette, No Wave, Partch, Punk, Ayler, Company and Beefheart."

As the 1991-92 school year began, Walter was accepted for private study with Hal Russell. Russell was a legendary underground jazz figure in Chicago whose recordings had excited Walter back in Rockford; Walter had been drawn to the school specifically because Russell was on the faculty. Walter took his sax to the first lesson, and when the two engaged in a fiery improvised duet, something clicked. Russell suggested they form a duo in which both could give free rein to their multi-instrumental proclivities. On December 6, 1991, Walter and Russell christened the group the Flying Luttenbachers, Luttenbacher being Russell's family name. Saxist Chad Organ, a mutual acquaintance of both Walter and Russell, had also been invited over to play the day the band was birthed, and it was decided that he should join the group as well.

For the Record . . .

Members include **Jeb Bishop**, bass; **Michael Colligan**, reeds; **Chuck Falzone**, guitar, vocals; **Kurt Johnson**, bass; **Fred Lonberg-Holm**, cello; **Chad Organ**, sax, moog synthesizer, vocals; **Bill Pisarri**, bass, vocals; **Dylan Posa**, guitar; **Hal Russell**, sax; **Ken Vandermark**, reeds; **Weasel Walter** (born May 18, 1972, *Education*: B.A. Music Composition, Columbia College, Chicago, Illinois), drums, percussion, saxes, clarinet, vocals; **Tatsuya Yoshida**, vocals.

Walter formed Sound Improvisation Collective with Bill Pisarri, 1991; Walter, Russell and, Organ formed the Flying Luttenbachers, 1991; Vandermark joined group, 1992; *546 Seconds of Noise* released, July 1992; Bishop joined group, March 1993; Dylan Posa joined group, May 1993; Vandermark left band, April 1994; Walter dissolved band, August 1994; Walter launched solo Luttenbachers, October 1994; Falzone and Pisarri joined band, May 1995; *Revenge of the Flying Luttenbachers* and *Gods of Chaos* recorded, 1996; Flying Luttenbachers European tour, January-February 1998; Walter dissolved band once again, March 1998; performed with various Luttenbacher line-up loosely grouped around Colligan and Johnson, 1998; Lonberg-Holm joined group, 2000.

Addresses: *Home*—Weasel Walter, Chicago, Illinois; e-mail: weaselw@juno.com. *Record company*—ugEXPLODE Records, P.O. Box 82, Chicago, IL 60690-0082; Skin Graft Records, P.O. Box 257546, Chicago, IL, 60625, website: http://www.skingraftrecords.com. *Website*—Official Luttenbachers website: http://www.ripco.net/~nailhead.

The group rehearsed together regularly during the first half of 1992. They held their only public performance at WNUR, the Northwestern University student radio station, a show that was saved for posterity on *Live At WNUR 2-6-92*, an album released on ugEXPLODE, the label Walter founded around that time. The record presents a manic free jazz performance, with Russell and Organ dueling on sax, and Walter caterwauling on drums, chopsticks and smashing jars.

Unfortunately, as 1992 progressed, Russell was devoting increasingly more time to other projects. The situation came to a head when a new label, Quinnah Records, expressed interest in doing a Luttenbacher 7 inch. In early July 1992, just days before the recording session was to take place, Russell told Walter, in so many words, that he wasn't interested in doing the record. Unwilling to let the opportunity to record pass, Walter phoned Ken Vandermark, a musician he had met earlier that spring at an Anthony Braxton workshop. With Vandermark in the line-up, the Luttenbachers cut *546 Seconds of Noise*—without the benefit of a single full group rehearsal. The record presented a new Luttenbacher sound. The Russell ensemble had played music that was clearly free jazz. With Vandermark on board, the band's music was more primitive, beat-driven, even danceable. It was the birth of punk jazz.

By the end of the summer of 1992, the Flying Luttenbachers were playing regularly in Chicago clubs. According to Walter, however, the musical chemistry between the players was fragile. "Ken and Chad would often butt heads musically in the improvisations," Walter wrote on the Luttenbacher website, "trying nervously to accommodate each other's respective level of ability, while trying to maintain the high energy level set by Weasel's merciless—and sometimes numbing—bashing." At the same time, Vandermark, who was going through a difficult time in his career, had doubts about the direction Walter and the group were following. They continued to rehearse and perform, however, and the group's recordings showed little evidence that these problems affected the Luttenbachers' performances.

By the end of 1992, however, Walter was becoming dissatisfied with the limitations of the Luttenbachers' sax-sax-drums line-up and the musical cul-de-sac he felt they had entered. He wanted the band to continue to forge ahead into new, unexplored territory. The answer, he believed, might be adding a new member, perhaps a bass or cello. In February of 1993, after the band recorded the EP *1389 Seconds of Noise*, it auditioned Jeb Bishop. His presence gave the Luttenbachers the extra dimension Walter was looking for. "Bishop's sympathetic bass playing helped buffer the horn players mutual differences," Walter wrote, "and made it possible for the improvisation to gain new depth."

By the time spring 1993 rolled around, Vandermark had become active in a plethora of musical activities in Chicago that conflicted with his commitments to the Luttenbachers. To ensure that the band would always have a full performing complement, Walter invited guitarist Dylan Posa to join. Posa, who had auditioned unsuccessfully to become the band's bassist, was interested in the modern and avant garde classical repertoire, and added a whole new factor to the Luttenbacher mix. The guitar and bass created a sonic assault of orchestral proportions. Each instrument provided interesting new textural backgrounds and a heightened level of interplay in improvisations. While it was just a unrelenting as earlier Luttenbacher incarnations, the new line-up was in many ways the band's most accessible.

The Flying Luttenbachers were in the vanguard of the Chicago No Wave and the improvised music scenes, both of which were in full swing in 1993. Walter was very active himself: he was playing in the group Ectomorph with Vandermark, Bishop and Kevin Drumm, in the Rev Trio with Bishop and saxist Joe Vajarsky, and on top of that he was running a weekly series, the Improvised Music Workshop. In October, the band went into the studio to cut an LP, *Constructive Destruction*.

Ken Vandermark, in the meantime, was playing in at least seven other ongoing musical projects. In April of 1994 the inevitable occurred: He announced he was leaving the Luttenbachers. In May, he played on one last record with the group, the LP *Destroy All Music*, half of which was recorded live in the studio, the rest comprised of tapes made on various occasions. In the summer, the Flying Luttenbachers set off on an East Coast tour. Their performances made Walter act on his own dissatisfaction with the group. On the way home he announced that he would not be playing with that line-up any longer. It was time to move on. "He was seeking to create an aggressive, merciless ensemble," Walter later wrote of himself, "that unsympathetically synthesized the more extreme and nihilistic characteristics of free jazz and punk."

Walter had given up his band but he wasn't ready to give up the Flying Luttenbachers. He was already giving thought to a new collection of musicians that would include Bishop, Joe Vajarsky and reedist Michael Colligan. Events were moving faster than he could. Before he was able to get a band together, he was asked to contribute some Luttenbacher material to various 7 inches. In less than two months in late 1994, completely on his own, he recorded three new tracks, "Logic Negation System," "Modulation Decay Unit," and "Deception," all of which appear on the anthology *Retrospektiw III*. The new work was harsher, with a threatening electronic-industrial edge absent from earlier Luttenbacher work. In winter 1995, with the aid of a Walkman, Walter began performing as a solo Flying Luttenbacher. Preparing the tapes to accompany each show consumed a great deal of time, however, and by May he had reached a scheduling impasse. His back against the wall, he called two old friends, Chuck Falzone and Bill Pisarri, and asked them to join the band.

Guitarist Falzone was Walter's childhood friend from Rockford, where they had stormed together through a series of bands, in and out of school. Pisarri, Walter's main collaborator in the Sound Improvisation Collective, was an artist, not a trained musician. He was playing gigs only days after he obtained his first bass guitar. He didn't so much play bass in any traditional sense, as in play *with* the bass, but instead scratched and pounded the strings to coax out a variety of feedback and other sounds. This latest version of the Luttenbachers was also the most democratic. Unlike the other bands, for whom Walter had done virtually all the composing and arranging, both Falzone and Pisarri contributed music. The music was elemental and darker than ever, a sort of ambient music from Hell, hinted at by the pentagram displayed at the Luttenbacher concerts of the time and the 666 that graced their T-shirts. The band recorded two albums in 1996, *The Revenge of the Flying Luttenbachers* and *Gods of Chaos*. The latter was the Flying Luttenbachers' destruction myth, the musical story of the destruction of humankind which for the Luttenbachers end, not ironically, in total silence.

The band toured Europe in early 1998. When they returned to Chicago, Walter's creative impatience rose to the surface once again. The music was no longer moving forward, and he dissolved the band. He put together various temporary line-ups in early 1998, with reed player Michael Colligan and bassist Kurt Johnson at their core. A high point came in the summer when cellist Fred Lonberg-Holm and Tatsuya Yoshida of the Ruins joined for a performance of "De Futura," a 20-minute piece by Magma, a band for which Walter has tremendous admiration. By the time the Luttenbachers released their next album in June of 1999, the group had settled around Colligan and Johnson. The record, provocatively titled *"...The Truth is A F***ing Lie..."* marked a return to the complexities of a more all-out free jazz sound. But the music was denser than earlier Luttenbacher free jazz, even modernist sounding at times, and held together by Johnson's bass guitar. In early 2000, Lonberg-Holm joined on a regular basis. His experience in a wide range of jazz and pop bands brought the Luttenbachers to a new level of complexity as they were preparing their next record, tentatively titled *Alptraum*, German for "nightmare." *Alptraum* promised to be the most uncompromising, demanding music the Flying Luttenbachers have ever released.

Selected discography

Live at WNUR 2-6-92, ugEXPLODE Records, 1992; reissued on Coat-tail/ugEXPLODE, 1996.

546 Seconds of Noise, (EP), Quinnah/ugEXPLODE, 1992; included on *Retrospektiw III*.

1389 Seconds of Noise, (EP), Quinnah/ugEXPLODE, 1993; included on *Retrospektiw III.*
Constructive Destruction, (LP), Quinnah/ugEXPLODE, 1994; reissued on (Quinnah/ugEXPLODE), 1996.
Destroy All Music, (LP), ugEXPLODE, 1995.
Revenge of the Flying Luttenbachers, (LP/CD), Skin Graft/ ugEXPLODE,1996.
Live at the Middle East Cafe, Bourgeois Chimp, 1996.
Gods of Chaos, ugEXPLODE/Skin Graft, 1997.
Retrospektiw III, ugEXPLODE/Quinnah, 1998.
*"...The Truth is A F***ing Lie...,"* ugEXPLODE/Skin Graft, 1999.

Sources

Periodicals

Carbon 14, February 1998.
Destroy Amerikkka, # 2.
Earshot Online Magazine, Winter 1997.
Mole #11, Summer 1998.
Mutiny # 7.
Skug Magazine #34, Spring 1998.
Trust Magazine #69, Spring 1998.
U.S. Rocker, March 1998.

Online

Flying Luttenbachers website, http://pages.ripco.net/~nail-head/ (April 2000).

Additional information was provided by Weasel Walter.

—*Gerald E. Brennan*

The Folk Implosion

Retro rock band

After Lou Barlow received the boot in 1989 as bass guitarist for the indie group Dinosaur Jr., he turned his misfortune around and settled into a respectable career path with Sebadoh, a group which stood the fine line between selling out to commercialism and the freedom of indie territory that produced a consistent flow of notable records. In 1993, in addition to making solo records as Sentridoh, Barlow started a second project, the Folk Implosion, with solo recording artist John Davis. While both musicians felt an aversion to the mass music industry, they nevertheless found themselves on the modern rock charts when a song entitled "Natural One" became an unexpected hit. After coming to terms with the popular success of the single, the Folk Implosion shed their association with the lesser-known Communion label (which issued the pair's first two albums) in favor of a contract with the established Interscope Records.

Barlow was born around 1966 and spent his younger life in and around Boston, Massachusetts. He experienced indie-level celebrity at an early age as the bassist for Dinosaur Jr., an influential underground rock band formed in 1984 (the group disbanded in 1997) in Amherst, Massachusetts, under the direction of lead guitarist and vocalist J Mascis (born Joseph D. Mascis). During Barlow's stint with Dinosaur Jr., the young guitarist and vocalist joined forces with percussionist and songwriter Eric Gaffney to record homemade tapes as Sebadoh. In 1989, the pair's work, recorded in various living rooms and bedrooms between 1986 and 1988 and entitled *The Freed Man,* was picked up by Homestead Records. That same year, Dinosaur Jr. fired Barlow, who left the group under less than friendly conditions. According to Barlow, Masics's unrelenting control made working with Dinosaur Jr. difficult, though Mascis blamed Barlow's inept social skills as the cause for his dismissal. Nonetheless, Barlow seemed well on his way to establishing a respectable career with Sebadoh, as two more albums followed in 1990: *Weed Forestin,* as well as *The Freed Weed,* which compiled 41 tracks from the first two projects.

With the addition of a third songwriting voice and bassist, Jason Lowenstein, who officially joined Sebadoh in 1989, the group started playing live. During performances, audiences witnessed the conflicting musical styles that would become Sebadoh's signature as Gaffney's noise-rock experiments shared the stage with Barlow's acoustic numbers. Personal differences plagued the band as well, and Gaffney departed and returned on numerous occasions between 1990 and 1993, the year he left Sebadoh for good. Upon his departure, Bob Fay, the regular fill-in for Gaffney during his frequent absences, became Sebodah's full-time drummer. Despite such turmoil, Sebadoh forged ahead, releasing *Sebadoh III* for Homestead in 1991, signing with the well-established indie label Sub Pop Records, and recording the albums *Smash Your Head on the Punk Rock* in 1992 and *Bubble and Scrape* in 1993. The following year, 1994's *Bakesale,* Sebadoh's first commercial success, rendered the modern rock hit "Rebound," while their next release, 1996's *Harmacy,* became the group's first album to chart in the United States (Ironically, Barlow was known for his contempt for the standard music business, refusing high-profile gigs and subverting Sebadoh's pop material with sonic experimentation). Sebadoh returned with a new drummer, Russ Pollard, in 1999 for the release of *The Sebadoh.*

In the meantime, Barlow was enjoying success as a solo artist (releasing work under the name Sentridoh) and with his side project the Folk Implosion, a band he formed with a former Sebadoh fan named Jon Davis. Davis, who had released solo records as well, was a noted performer known for his minimal guitar technique that backed his songs primarily about childhood memories. The two first met in the late 1980s when Davis, then a high school student in Boston, sent Barlow some tapes he had made at his home. In the fall of 1993, Barlow and Davis joined forces, writing and recording songs at Davis's home that appeared on several EPs, including *The Electric Idiot* in 1994 and *Walk Through This World with the Folk Implosion* in 1994, in addition to their debut album, *Take a Look Inside the Folk Implosion* in 1995, for the Communion

For the Record . . .

Members include **Lou Barlow** (born c. 1966; former bassist for Dinosaur Jr.; vocalist, guitarist, and songwriter for Sebadoh), vocals, guitar; **John Davis,** vocals, guitar.

Formed band, 1993; released debut album *Take a Look Inside the Folk Implosion,* 1995; single "Natural One" from the *Kids* soundtrack became a top 40 hit, 1995; released *Dare To Be Surprised,* 1997; released *One Part Lullaby,* 1999.

Addresses: *Record company*—Interscope Records, 10900 Wilshire Blvd., Los Angeles, CA 90024, phone (310) 208-6547, fax (310) 208-7343. *Website*—Folk Implosion at the Communion label: http://www.midheaven.com, Folk Implosion at Interscope Records: http://www.folkimplosion.com.

label. Noteworthy tracks from *Take a Look Inside* included the punk title track, the John Lennon-inspired "Slap Me," and the Residents-styled "Sputnik's Down." Shortly thereafter, the Folk Implosion scored a commercial success when "Natural One," a song created for Larry Clark's acclaimed 1995 film *Kids* about New York teenagers, became a top 40 radio hit.

After recording the *Kids* soundtrack, Barlow and Davis started working with engineer Wally Gagel in the summer of 1995 at his studio, Bliss, located in Boston. Because of the studio's relaxed atmosphere and low hourly cost, not to mention the promotional distractions resulting from the popularity of "Natural One," the Folk Implosion averaged three days a month in the studio over the course of a year before arriving at a finished product. Consequently, *Dare To Be Surprised,* issued in 1997 by Communion, was the result of ever-changing musical intentions. At first, Barlow and Davis wanted to focus on garage band/new wave elements, but as the winter and early spring of 1996 approached, they found themselves adding groove-oriented sounds as well. The album earned favorable critical reviews, with tracks such as "Barricade" and "Ball and Chain." As Ivan Kreilkamp of the *Village Voice* asserted, with *Dare To Be Surprised,* "Barlow and Davis show a way out of the indie trap in which charisma must be simultaneously denied and flaunted. Against the album's endless store of casual-seeming but maddeningly catchy looped rhythms, their twinned voices emerge as if from a kid singing a DJ's dance floor exhortations to himself in the backseat on a long night's car trip.... Folk Implosion reject a dull charade for one they can enjoy, making music over which personal emotions slide like water off a duck's back."

The two also made peace with their ambivalence over the success of "Natural One," which took some getting used to by these otherwise opponents of the popular music industry. As Davis wrote for the Folk Implosion's website, "hearing it [the hit] pop up in such unlikely places as Karaoke bars, fashion runways, and Yankee Stadium did a lot to lighten our mood." In addition to spending time in the studio during 1995 and 1996, Barlow recorded *Harmacy* with Sebadoh, while Davis worked on a solo project, *Blue Mountains,* in February and June of 1996. In order to promote *Harmacy,* Barlow embarked on a short tour in the United States and Europe with his other group in late 1996 and into early 1997. During the same time, Davis toured in support of his solo album, playing dates on the West coast with the Double U and opening for Sebadoh for their East coast shows. The Folk Implosion made time, though, during the spring and summer of 1997, to tour North America and Europe supporting *Dare To Be Surprised.*

In early 1998, Barlow bid farewell to his hometown of Boston. He and wife Kathleen bought a home in the town of Silver Lake in the Los Angeles area. When asked why he decided to move, Barlow answered "Because it's cheaper," as quoted by Jim Sullivan of the *Boston Globe*. "All the places I'd want to live in Boston are extremely expensive. Plus, I need a place to play that's also my house. I've been living in my cave, trying desperately not to bug anybody." He also added that although he would miss the security and loyal fans of Boston, he felt that the change of lifestyle—living in the suburbs near the world's center of entertainment—might help to further his musical development.

While Barlow admitted that he would miss his hometown, he nevertheless felt glad to say farewell to 1997, despite the success enjoyed by both the Folk Implosion and Sebadoh. He revealed, "It's been the most frustrating year for me, musically, ever," as quoted by Sullivan. "The records I spent time promoting [*Dare To Be Surprised* with the Folk Implosion and *Harmacy* with Sebadoh] were made in '96, and with Sebadoh, we were winding down and getting a new drummer. We had to acclimate ourselves, spend time hanging out and not pushing ourselves.... It was a nonmusical year, a non-creative juggling of facts and figures, which I found enervating. I feel I'm in the midst of an amazing writer's block, even though I'm not."

Barlow also realized the disadvantages of remaining on an independent label, as neither of the albums sold as well as anticipated. While Sebadoh would remain with Sub Pop for future releases, Barlow and the group opted to distribute through Sire/Warner Brothers. Likewise, the Folk Implosion signed with Interscope Records in early 1998 for forthcoming releases. In addition to developing songs for Sebadoh's next release, Barlow started recording new tracks for the Folk Implosion during 1998 and 1999 with Davis at his new house in California, and the geographic change proved to be the cure for his lacking creativity.

In the fall of 1999, the Folk Implosion released their fourth album, *One Part Lullaby*, which also won critical approval. Here, Barlow and Davis "leave lo-fi jinks behind in favor of sleek, lushly textured pop, the kind of infectious drone they brilliantly captured with 'Natural One,'" concluded Edna Gunderson of *USA Today*. "Without losing their bite, the two abandon trademark gloom and mute sarcasm to let optimism and cheer percolate to the surface... In such highlights as the gorgeous 'Back to the Sunrise,' arresting 'Mechanical Man' and atmospheric 'Easy L.A.,' Folk Implosion devises ingenious mutations that fuse electro chops to retro-pop."

Selected discography

Take a Look Inside the Folk Implosion, Communion, 1994.
The Folk Implosion, Communion, 1996.
Dare to Be Surprised, Communion, 1997.
One Part Lullaby, Interscope, 1999.

Sources

Books

MusicHound Rock: The Essential Album Guide, Visible Ink Press, 1999.

Periodicals

Billboard, October 23, 1999.
Boston Globe, April 4, 1997; January 2, 1998; March 18, 1999.
Magnet, October/November 1999, p. 77.
Melody Maker, December 5, 1998.
Rolling Stone, August 5, 1999.
Village Voice, May 6, 1997.
USA Today, September 14, 1999.

Online

Folk Implosion at Interscope Records, http://www.folkimplosion.com (January 10, 2000).
Folk Implosion at the Communion label, http://www.midheaven.com (January 10, 2000).
Rolling Stone.com, http://www.rollingstone.tunes.com (January 10, 2000).

—*Laura Hightower*

Kenny Garrett

Alto saxophone

Photograph by Jack Vartoogian. Reproduced by permission. ©

Low-keyed and soft-spoken, Kenny Garrett lets his music do the talking, and he communicates clearly through his post-bop saxophone styles, exuding easy listening from his alto horn. After years of apprenticeship with legendary jazz bands including the Jazz Messengers and the Woody Shaw Quintet, Garrett came to prominence during the 1980s as Miles Davis's sideman. After Davis died, Garrett moved into his own spotlight as the bandleader of the Kenny Garrett Quartet. In addition to his various album releases during the 1990s, he contributed to dozens of works by his fellow jazz musicians. He is an incessant philosopher, an innovator, a composer, and a musical arranger.

Garrett was born in Detroit, Michigan, on October 9, 1960. He was the second of four siblings. Musically, his parents were heterodyne; his mother enjoyed rhythm and blues, while his father listened to jazz. Garrett's father was a professional saxophone player, and as a result, Garrett developed an early interest in music. His father taught him the scales, and Garrett started to play his own saxophone at the age of nine or ten. He enjoyed the instrument and brought it with him to school, playing whenever he found the opportunity. Garrett got his original groove in his hometown of Detroit, where he worked with Marcus Belgrave. Belgrave, well known for his community spirit, mentored Garrett for a time.

In high school, Garrett played gigs around town on the weekends, and predictably each Monday morning he stumbled tardily into the classroom. Despite his youth, he had matured into an old-school jazzman by the time he graduated, maintaining a reserved and skeptical cynicism for academia. In 1978 he gained acceptance to the famous Berklee School of Music. Coincidentally, he received an invitation to join Mercer Ellington on tour. Garrett subsequently chose not to attend Berklee and elected instead to tour with the Duke Ellington Orchestra. Garrett avowed repeatedly that he never regretted the decision to forego school because his experience with the orchestra proved invaluable and contributed to his development as a uniquely skilled musician. From the Ellington Orchestra, Garrett's career led him to stints with Freddie Hubbard's band and with Woody Shaw.

After many months on the road, Garrett moved to New York City in 1980. There he played with a band called Out of the Blue. He cut his debut album on the Criss Cross label as a bandleader with the Kenny Garrett Quintet. The album, released in 1984, was called *Introducing Kenny Garrett.* Around that same time, Garrett joined with Art Blakey's Jazz Messengers. In 1986, still with Blakey, Garrett earned a spot as sideman for Miles Davis. He worked with Davis for five years and developed a singular musical rapport with Davis. Additionally,

For the Record . . .

Born on October 9, 1960, in Detroit, MI.

Member of Duke Ellington Orchestra, 1978; played with Art Blakey's Jazz Messengers, Woody Shaw, Freddie Hubbard, and Miles Davis, 1986-91; Kenny Garrett Quartet, 1995—; with Atlantic Records, late 1980s; with Warner Brothers Records, 1991—.

Awards: Album of the Year, *Down Beat,* 1997; Alto Saxophonist of the Year, *Down Beat,* 1997.

Addresses: *Record company*—Warner Bros. Records Inc., 3300 Warner Boulevard, Burbank, CA 91505-4694.

Garrett continued as a bandleader, recording for the Atlantic Jazz label. He released *Prisoner of Love* in 1989 and *African Exchange Student* in 1990. When Davis passed away in 1981, Garrett stepped full speed into the bandleader's shoes, having apprenticed for nearly 20 years and having worked with the great jazz players of history.

For the duration of the decade, Garrett settled into a quartet with Nat Reeves on bass, drummer Jeff "Tain" Watts, and Kenny Kirkland on piano. Garrett recorded a handful of albums on the Warner Brothers label during the remainder of the 1990s, including *Black Hope* in 1992, *Trilogy* in 1995, and *Pursuance: The Music of John Coltrane* in 1996. His next two albums—*Songbook* in 1997 and *Simply Said* in 1999—were written almost exclusively by Garrett himself. In July of 1997 he and his band spent three days in the Netherlands at the North Sea Jazz Festival at The Hague, and in June of 1998 they performed on the Symphony Space concert ticket at the JVC Jazz Festival along with jazz violinist Regina Carter. Following Kirkland's untimely death late in 1998, the Kenny Garrett Quartet regrouped to include former Toni Braxton drummer Christopher Dave, bassist Nat Reeves, and Shedrick Mitchell on piano. Pianists Nick Smith and Mulgrew Miller also contributed guest performances.

Garrett paid homage openly and often to his predecessors and heroes in American jazz. His 1996 remembrance of John Coltrane, called *Pursuance: The Music of John Coltrane,* featured Pat Metheny on guitar, drummer Brian Blade, and Rodney Whitaker on bass. The recording earned recognition as the Jazz Album of the Year, according to a readers' poll from *Down Beat.* Garrett himself was named Alto Saxophone Player of the year in the same poll. His self-produced 1999 release, called *Simply Said,* reflects the influence of his half-decade stint with Miles Davis.

It is Garrett's philosophical attitude that rules his music. He is a paradoxical purist in the juxtaposed arena of jazz and subscribes to an idealistic school of thought and lets the truth resound from his horn. He is a "righteously devoted musician working toward a purpose somewhat higher than mere entertainment," *Down Beat's* Howard Mandel said of Garret. "His horn's cries are honest...." Despite his traditional, "hard-knocks" approach to performing jazz, Garrett refuses to discount the validity of other music styles and encourages musicians to experiment with popular music as well as jazz, in a quest for new and stimulating arrangements. "Young musicians shouldn't be afraid to take the opportunity to play popular music.... It doesn't mean you have to stay there," he confided to Martin Johnson of *Down Beat.* Garrett's own compositions often surprise his listeners because his music adheres closely to rhythm and form, in apparent opposition to Garrett's impressive improvisational style and reputation. *Billboard's* Steve Graybow said that Garrett is "one of the music's most dynamic and adventurous players...." yet he has composed "songs that he hopes will nurture the next generation of jazz musicians." On *Songbook,* his 1997 Warner Brothers release, Garrett revealed what he called his "softer side," according to Mandel. "I'm trying to tell a story in a different way with the same jazz language my heroes employed.... That's why I try to mix my music up [and] play something for everybody," Garrett said.

Evolution is the paradigm that rules Garrett's art. In adherence to his belief that to do is to learn and to further his quest for stimulating new styles, Garrett spent time beyond his years of band apprenticeship working at times with artists from schools of music foreign to modern American jazz. On tour with Sting for Amnesty International, Garrett traveled to Africa, Greece, and Indonesia. While in Indonesia he spent some weeks working with a local saxophone player named Ibu (Ebu) from whom Garrett learned Polynesian rhythms and the Balinese scale. Additionally, he spent time working with vocalist Jano Okiko of Japan and learning Japanese scales. Garrett also plays both the flute and the soprano sax at various times. He has worked with vibraphonist Bobby Hutchinson on *Skyline* in 1999 and appeared with the Kenny Garrett Quartet at the Montreaux Jazz festival in Switzerland. Also in 1999, Garrett joined Mulgrew Miller and others in contributing to the *Urban Dreams* album produced by saxophonist Ron Brown's Mankind Records. The non-profit project helped to sponsor a community-based arts program for children in Austin, Texas.

Selected discography

Introducing Kenny Garrett, Criss Cross, 1984.
African Exchange Student, Atlantic Jazz, 1990.
Black Hope, Warner Brothers, 1992.
Pursuance: The Music of John Coltrane, Warner Brothers, 1996
Trilogy, Warner Brothers, 1995.
Songbook, Warner Brothers, 1997.
Simply Said, Warner Brothers, 1999.
Urban Dreams (contributor), Mankind Records, 1999.

Sources

Periodicals

Billboard, June 12, 1999, p. 32.
Down Beat, September 1995, p. 16; September 1997, p. 16; December 1997, p. 38; September 1999, p. 14; December 1999, p. 58.

Online

"Kenny Garrett," *AMG All Music Guide,* http://allmusic.com/ (February 5, 2000).
"My Conversation with Kenny Garrett,"interview with Fred Jung, June 1999, http://visionx.com/jazz/iviews/Garrett.htm (March 14, 2000).

—Gloria Cooksey

The Go-Betweens

Rock group

The Go-Betweens, established and led by longtime friends Robert Forster and Grant McLennan, became one of the most consistent songwriting teams to emerge from Australia. Rendering melodic songs about love and loneliness throughout the 1980s that earned the adoration of critics, the Go-Betweens, driven by the influences of 1960s folk and 1970s punk, nevertheless only managed to capture a limited following of fans. Although they were always expected to cross over into the mainstream, the Go-Betweens continually went unnoticed, an unfortunate outcome that the band eventually came to accept. "Oh that doesn't worry us unduly," McLennan, referring to the group's lack of success in the pop business, told Stuart Maconie of *New Musical Express* (*NME*) in August of 1988. "We no longer expect our records to be massive hits. Within the pages of the music press there exists a kind of willful pursuit of the new and whilst that can be exciting, over the last couple of years it's meant a celebration of the ephemeral, music as supermarket trash. And we are not part of it. I'm into writing classic songs that will last forever...."

Forming as a somewhat Bob Dylan-inspired duo in Brisbane, Australia, in late 1977 (some sources say January of 1978), the Go-Betweens initially involved Brisbane University students Forster on vocals and guitar, and McLennan on bass and vocals, with no permanent drummer. From the beginning, Forster intended to eschew universal songwriting themes in favor of more personal revelations, such as "my feelings in the bedroom, Brisbane, driving my car and anything from overheard conversations," as quoted by Andrew Mosley in the *Rough Guide to Rock.* Early on, the Go-Betweens' output centered mainly around Forster's frank songwriting and at times out-of-tune singing. Later, however, McLennan's influences would come into the picture, as he began to discover his own compositional and stylistic voice. Together, the duo would develop complementary songwriting and singing styles—McLennan's extroverted minstrels balanced by Forster's poetic odes. While both men embraced different ways to express themselves, they nonetheless wrote about similar subjects, namely strange people, strange situations, and love, loading their gentle, yet moody melodies with intense emotion.

The pair, along with various guests on drums, recorded a few singles in Brisbane before traveling to England for the first time in early 1980. Here, with Steven Daly taking on drumming duties, the Go-Betweens recorded a single called "I Need Two Heads" for the Scottish record company Postcard Records, as well as the Dylan-sounding songs "Lee Remick" and "Karen," both released on the Abe label. Around the same time, the Go-Betweens recorded the keyboard-dominated single "People Say," one of Forster's personal favorites. Soon thereafter, they returned to Brisbane and enlisted drummer Lindy Morrison, who brought more variation to the band's music, as a permanent member. With their introspective lyrics and music resonant of the Velvet Underground, the Cure, the classic 1960s rock of the Byrds, and the folk-rock leanings of Dylan, the Go-Betweens quickly found a loyal, though cult-sized following in their homeland.

Augmented by Morrison, the Go-Betweens recorded their debut album, 1981's *Send Me a Lullabye,* toured throughout Australia, and in 1982 moved to London, where they signed a contract with Rough Trade Records. In 1983, the Go-Betweens released their second album, *Before Hollywood,* marking the emergence of McLennan as an important songwriting force. Two songs penned by McLennan for the record included the haunting "Cattle and Cane" and the tear-jerking "Dusty In Here." That same year, after recording *Before Hollywood,* the Go-Betweens introduced bass player Robert Vickers into the lineup, allowing McLennan to serve as a second guitarist. The addition of Vickers also coincided with the band's 1983 signing with Sire Records.

In 1984, the Go-Betweens released the acclaimed album *Spring Hill Fair,* which included praiseworthy songs like "Bachelor Kisses" and the bitter "Draining the Pool for You." Despite the critical acceptance of *Spring Hill Fair,*

For the Record . . .

Members include **Amanda Brown** (joined band in 1986), violin, oboe, vocals; **Robert Forster** (born on June 29, 1957, in Brisbane, Australia), vocals, guitar; **Grant McLennan** (born on February 12, 1958, in Rock Hampton, Australia), vocals, guitar, bass; **Lindy Morrison** (born on November 2, 1951, in Australia; joined band in 1980), drums; **Robert Vickers** (joined band in 1983; left band in 1988), bass; **John Willsteed** (joined band in 1988), bass.

Forster and McLennan formed band, 1977; released debut album *Send Me a Lullabye,* 1981; released the acclaimed *Spring Hill Fair,* 1984; released the now-classic *16 Lovers Lane,* 1988; disbanded, 1989. Both McLennan and Forster pursued solo careers.

Addresses: *Record company*—Beggars Banquet, 580 Broadway, Ste. 1004, New York, NY 10012, phone: (212) 343-7010, fax: (212) 343-7030, email: beggars@beggars.com. *Website*—The Robert Forster Homepage, http://www.go-betweens.com/frontpag.html

new fans in Europe and North America, and successful tours, the band's label, Sire, fired the Go-Betweens because of low record sales. Subsequently, in 1985, the group signed with True Tone in Australia and with Elektra in Europe and in the United States, but never recorded anything for these two companies. Instead, they signed a new contract in January of 1986, this time with the Beggars Banquet label. Three months later, the Go-Betweens hired a fifth band member, a classically trained musician named Amanda Brown. For the Go-Betweens, Brown played violin, oboe, and keyboards and sang back-up vocals.

Prior to the addition of Brown, the other band members had already recorded their next album,1986's *Liberty Belle and the Black Diamond Express.* One song from the project, a breezy pop tune entitled "Spring Rain," earned radio airplay and brought the Go-Betweens to the brink of chart success. However, the follow-up singles "Right Here" and "Bye Bye Pride," failed to initiate a major sales breakthrough. It appeared as though popular notoriety would continue to elude the Go-Betweens. Rumors circulated that the group, feeling disillusioned, was thinking of splitting up. The group's next single, "Streets of Your Town," a sunny-sounding song that condemned domestic violence and appeared on the band's subsequent effort, also received airplay, but again the Go-Betweens failed to make the pop charts.

In early 1988, Vickers left group to move to New York City, hoping to form a new band. He cited "geographical differences as opposed to the time-honoured 'musical' ones," as quoted by *NME* in February of 1988, as his reason for leaving band. A new bassist named John Willsteed, who also occasionally played organ and piano, stepped in as Vickers' replacement, and the band recorded their next album, *16 Lovers Lane* in Australia. As before, the 1988 release won stellar reviews. Bob Remstein and Daniel Durchholz of *MusicHound Rock,* for example, named the work a "mini-classic," while Mosley described *16 Lovers Lane* as "a polished affair with effortless driving pop like 'Love Is A Sign' and 'Dive For Your Memory.'"

After playing together for more than a decade and writing some of the highest quality pop music, Forster and McLennan disbanded the Go-Betweens in the fall of 1989 (some sources say early 1990) following a United States tour with Lloyd Cole. "We started as teenagers in '78," McLennan told *Boston Globe* writer Jim Sullivan at a "reunion" performance with Forster in June of 1999 to support the release of two Go-Betweens compilation albums that year. "Twelve years together is a long time—even the Beatles didn't last that long. We hit our 30s and, though it's a bit American to say this, we grew up and it was time to experiment, time to be an adult. You can't be in a gang all your life. That's why bands are so good when they're young—they have that fire and dignity."

Following the demise of the Go-Betweens, both McLennan and Forster pursued solo careers, though McLennan received the greater acclaim. Forster settled in southern Germany and recorded *Danger in the Past,* released in 1990, in Berlin at Hansa Studio with several members of Nick Cave's group The Bad Seeds. His other solo projects included the country-influenced *Calling From a Country,* released in 1993, and an album of covers entitled *I Had a New York Girlfriend,* released in 1994. McLennan made his home in Brisbane and recorded two experimental/collaborative albums with Steve Kilbey of the Church as Jack Frost: 1991's *Jack Frost* and 1996's *Snow Job.* Under his own name, McLennan released the albums *Watershed* in 1991, *Fireboy* in 1993, and the impressive *Horsebreaker Star* in 1995.

In 1996, Beggars Banquet re-issued all of the Go-Betweens' albums. Although the group separated over a decade ago, the Go-Betweens remained a critical favorite and McLennan and Forster performed together from time to time. "Hiding their hooks in arrangements and lyrics as often as they brandished them in tunes," recalled Robert Christgau in the December 31, 1996, issue of the *Village Voice,* "they were modest, affectionate, funny, cheerful, never too oblique or ironic pop for the ages if anything is."

Selected discography

Go-Betweens

Send Me a Lullabye, Rough Trade, 1982.
Before Hollywood, Rough Trade, 1983.
Spring Hill Fair, Sire, 1984.
Metals and Shells, PVC, 1985.
Liberty Belle and the Black Diamond Express, Big Time/RCA, 1986.
Tallulah, Beggars Banquet, 1987.
16 Lovers Lane, Beggars Banquet/Capitol, 1988.
1978-1990, Capitol, 1990.
'78-'79/The Lost Album, Jetset, 1999.
Bellavista Terrace—The Best of the Go-Betweens, Beggars Banquet, 1999.

Robert Forster

Danger in the Past, 1990.
Calling From a Country, 1993.
I Had a New York Girlfriend, 1994.

Grant McLennan

(With Jack Frost) *Jack Frost,* Arista, 1991.
Watershed, Beggars Banquet/RCA, 1991.
Fireboy, (U.K.) Beggars Banquet, 1993; Beggars Banquet, 1994.
Horsebreaker Star, Beggars Banquet/Atlantic, 1995.
(With Jack Frost) *Snow Job,* (U.K.) Beggars Banquet, 1996.

Sources

Books

MusicHound Rock: The Essential Album Guide, Visible Ink Press, 1999.
Nichols, David, *The Go-Betweens,* Puncture Publications, 1997.

Periodicals

Billboard, December 10, 1988; January 21, 1995; February 3, 1996
Boston Globe, October 25, 1996; June 25, 1999.
Fortune, July 19, 1999.
Magnet, April/May 1999, p. 12.
Melody Maker, October 15, 1988; June 23, 1990; October 27, 1990.
New Musical Express (*NME*), August 6, 1988; February 27, 1988.
Rolling Stone, February 23, 1995.
Stereo Review's Sound & Vision, June 1999.
Village Voice, January 28, 1992; December 31, 1996; June 22, 1999.
Washington Post, June 18, 1999; June 26, 1999.

Online

"Bonniers Rocklexikon, 1993," http://www.users.dircon.co.uk/~jturner/gb/gbbonnie.htm (March 5, 2000).
"The Go-Betweens," *Rough Guide to Rock,* http://www.roughguides.com/rock/entries/entries-g/GO-BETWEENS.html (March 5, 2000).
The Robert Forster Homepage, http://www.go-betweens.com/frontpag.html (March 5, 2000).
Rolling Stone.com, http://www.rollingstone.tunes.com (March 5, 2000).

—Laura Hightower

Gogi Grant

Singer

AP/Wide World Photos. Reproduced by permission.

Gogi Grant, one of the premier vocalists of the 1950s and 1960s, is known for her crystal clear voice, perfect pitch, and a strong vocal range. She was born Myrtle Audrey Arinsberg on September 20, 1924, in Philadelphia, Pennsylvania, to Alexander and Rose Jacobsen Arinsberg, first generation Americans whose parents had come from England and Germany. Toward the end of the depression, her parents packed everything they owned into an automobile and, with their four children, drove to California knowing no one there and possessing only the hope of finding a better job opportunity. Her father found work as a jewelry salesman and later sold some of the first Wilcox-Gay home recording devices. Two additional siblings were later born in California.

She began singing as a child but never considered it as a career or received any formal vocal lessons because her parents could not afford them. She took typing and shorthand in high school and thought of becoming a commercial artist or a school teacher. With the urging of friends, she entered a weekly talent contest at the famous Macambo nightclub on the Sunset Strip in Los Angeles. Grant remarked, "Many of the night clubs of the early 1950s were losing business because of a little box they called television that kept people in their homes. So contests were held to try and bring the people out." An orchestra leader at the club directed her to a vocal coach, who worked with her for a very short time. This led to an interview with MCA, a top talent agency based in Los Angeles. When she was asked if she had musical arrangement material and the necessary gowns and other clothing necessities to perform, she told an MCA official that she could not afford it at this time but wished to be considered at a later date if these things became more affordable to her at a later time. Unknowingly, she had been interviewed in another executive's office at MCA and had accidentally left behind a sample recording of her demonstration record, "I'm Yours." When the executive returned from a vacation in Tahiti and heard the recording, he was so impressed that he immediately contacted her and signed her to a contract with MCA.

In the early 1950s, she began her career singing under the name Audrey Brown, her married name at the time. With the advice of her manager it was changed to Audrey Grant because he claimed he was a friend of the actor, Cary Grant and it would be good luck. In 1952 she was later signed by RCA Records and Dave Kapp, an executive there, changed it once again to Gogi Grant. He claimed the name came to him in a dream but many who knew Kapp recalled that he frequently dined at a Manhattan restaurant called "Gogi's La Rue." At RCA her first release was "Where's There's Smoke, There's Fire" and it failed to chart as well as subsequent recordings.

For the Record . . .

Born Myrtle Audrey Arinsberg, September 20, 1924, in Philadelphia, PA; daughter of Alexander, a salesman and Rose, nee Jacobsen, the eldest of six children; married and divorced twice; children: Jeri, born 1943, and Joshua, born 1965.

Recorded first under the name of Audrey Brown and later Audrey Grant before adopting the stage name "Gogi Grant" given to her by record executive Dave Kapp; entertained US armed forces personnel in Europe and North Africa, 1953-54; first hit recording on the ERA label "Suddenly There's a Valley," 1955; recorded "The Wayward Wind", 1957; moved to RCA and recorded the soundtrack to *The Helen Morgan Story*, 1957; returned to performing in nightclubs all across the U.S. in 1989, after a 20 year layoff.

Awards: Most Popular Vocalist Award, *Billboard* magazine, 1956; Most Popular Vocalist Award, *Cashbox* magazine, 1956.

Addresses: *Home*—Gogi Grant, 10323 Almayo Avenue, Los Angeles, CA 90064

During this time she sang and entertained in and around Pennsylvania and New York on the Borscht Belt nightclub circuit.

In 1955, she moved to Herb Newman's ERA record label, where she recorded "Suddenly There's a Valley." It rose to number nine on the charts. Grant recalled, "There were so many cover versions of "Suddenly There's A Valley" that if I hadn't gone on a 28 city promotional tour in 30 days, I would have probably lost the record." It was written by composer Biff Jones and pianist Chuck Meyer in 1955 to convey the thought that while we crave the excitement of the mountain top, the heights are filled with disappointments, and it's in the serene, settled valleys that earth and man are at peace. They had originally wrote it to be sung by a man, but Grant persuaded ERA to let her record it. Over one million copies were sold despite the fact that such famous recording artists as Jo Stafford and Julius LaRosa also had favorable sales of their recordings and they had been also covered by all the major labels.

In 1956, Newman pulled out his manuscript of the song that he and Stan Lebousky had written while they were students at UCLA many years earlier. It was brown with age and had been written in the first person. Newman knowing Grant could not read music asked her to sing the lyric as he hummed it. Grant explained, "There was something special about the song" and she proceeded to change the lyrics to sing from a woman's point of view in the third person. She also mentioned, "There was a country or western trend sound to it and that it would seem attractive to listeners." "Wayward Wind" was recorded in only fifteen minutes in two takes of studio time and five weeks later on June 16, 1956, it knocked Elvis Presley's "Don't Be Cruel" out of the number one chart position. It remained number one until July 28, 1956, when Presley's "I Want You, I Need You, I Love You" replaced it. It also charted at number nine in the United Kingdom. *The All Music Book of Hit Singles* written by Dave McAleer compiled a list of the top singles of the last fifty years using a formula point system, which took in consideration the record's weekly top 20 position, its peak position and the number of weeks it remained in the top ten and the top 20. "The Wayward Wind" ranks number 36 over tens of thousands of recordings for five decades and it sold over two million records.

In 1957, Gogi was selected for the singing role in the musical motion picture "The Helen Morgan Story". Although the leading actress Ann Blythe had a lovely voice, it was operatic in nature and musical director Ray Heindorf wanted an original torch type. Grant was heard on the radio and Heindorf hired her on the telephone without an audition over sixty other singers had applied and been heard. Her voice was used to dub over Blythe's and this biographical film of singer Helen Morgan also starred Paul Newman. Her film career also included appearing in musical shorts with country singer Eddy Arnold for Universal Studios.

She frequented the nightclub circuit for many years appearing at the Palmer House in Chicago, Ambassador Hotel, the Coconut Grove in Los Angeles and various clubs in Reno, Las Vegas, and other cities both in the United States and overseas.

From 1956 through 1970, Grant made fifteen long playing (LP) vinyl albums on the Charter, ERA, Liberty, Pete, and RCA labels and has appeared on dozens of others. In addition, her singles recordings were made on the Charter, ERA, Liberty, Monument, Pete, RCA and Twentieth Century Fox labels. Grant performed songs by Richard Rodgers, Oscar Hammerstein II, George Gershwin, Noel Coward, Ray Henderson, Irving Berlin, Lorenz Hart, Harry Warren, Johnny Burke, Jimmy Van Heusen, Gus Kahn, Jimmy McHugh, Leo Robin, Ralph Rainger, Ted Koehler, Ray Noble, Duke Ellington, Irving Mills, Stanley Lebousky, Isham Jones, Gerald Marks, Henry

Nemo, Seymour Simons, John Redmond, Duke Ellington, Jerome Kern, Johnny Burke, Irving Mills, John Golden and others. She has also appeared three times as a guest vocalist performing solos for the Academy Award presentations

After a 15-year career from 1952 to 1967, Grant took a 20- year absence to raise her two children but returned with rave reviews by the Los Angeles Times and Los Angeles Examiner reflecting that her layoff had no diminished effect on her performance. She has remained an elegant performer. In addition to appearing in sold out shows in and around the Los Angeles area, Grant performs in nightclubs and music halls around the United States including nightclubs in Palm Springs, California. She remains deeply devoted to her children and family.

Selected discography

The Wayward Wind, ERA EL106.
Welcome to My Heart, RCA LPM 1717.
60 Years of Show Tunes, RCA PR100.
Granted It's Gogi, RCA LSP 2000.
Gigi, RCA LPM 1716.
Showboat, RCA LSO 1505.
Helen Morgan Story, RCA LOC 1030.
Gogi Grant, Pete S-1101.
City Girl in the Country, CRC CLM 107.
If You Want to Go to Heaven, Shout, Liberty LRP 3144.
The Best of Gogi Grant, K-Tel.
Torch Time, RCA 43213-86292-7.
The Wayward Wind, the Best of Gogi Grant, ERA 22775-5011-2.
Welcome to My Heart, RCA 74321421262.

Singles

"Suddenly There's a Valley"
"Love Is"
"Who Are We"
"We Believe in Love"
"The Wayward Wind"
"No More than Forever"
"You're in Love"
"When the Tide Is High"
"The Golden Ladder"
"All of Me"
"I Gave You My Heart"
"I Don't Want to Walk Without You"

Sources

Books

Bronson, Fred, *The Billboard Book of Number One Hits*, Billboard Books, 1992.
Lax, Roger and Frederick Smith, *The Great Song Thesaurus,* Oxford University Press, 1989.
Maltin, Leonard, *Movie and Video Guide 1995,* Penguin Books Ltd., 1994.
McAleer, Dave, *The All Music Book of Hit Singles From 1954 to the Present Day*, Miller Freeman Books, 1994.
Osborne, Jerry, *Rockin Records,* Osborne Publications, 1999.
Reader's Digest How Great Thou Art, Liner Notes, 1979.

Periodicals

Los Angeles Herald Examiner, 1989.
Los Angeles Times, 1989.

Online

"Gogi Grant," *All Music Guide Books*, http://www.allmusic.com/cg/x.dll, (January 2000).
"Gogi Grant," *Greg Purcott Productions, Inc.*, http://www.gpproductions.com/acts/grant.htm (January 2000).

Additional information was obtained through interviews with Gogi Grant on September 27, 1998, and March 15, 1999.

—Francis D. McKinley

Tom Harrell

Trumpet

When he is lost in his music while entertaining, sometimes electrifying listeners, Tom Harrell is in his element. Ever since he first picked up a trumpet at the age of eight, Harrell was enthralled by a music that did not seem to have any rules—jazz. Throughout his childhood and adolescence, Harrell was listening to Duke Ellington and Louis Armstrong when others his age were consumed by the burgeoning world of rock and roll. The world at large might not easily have recognized his name. To those knowledgeable fans of the big band sounds and jazz, none surpassed his talent.

According to Michael Bloom, writing for *Down Beat* in December of 1996, when Harrell was named at the top of the magazine's readers' and critics' polls alike, some of his more current renown surged when the RCA Victor label caught wind of his playing on other independent labels including Criss Cross, Contemoprary and Chesky. Having a big name like RCA behind him went a long way to make Harrell's music available to a wider audience. From 1977 on, Harrell took *Down Beat*'s critics' and readers' poll for trumpet every year, and for composer in

Photograph by Jack Vartoogian. Reproduced by permission. ©

For the Record . . .

Born on June 16, 1946, in Urbana, IL; son of a psychologist (father); married: wife Angela. *Education*: Graduate of Stanford University, Palo Alto, CA.

Started playing professionally at age 13; played with big bands of Stan Kenton and Woody Herman, 1969-70; began leading own bands, 1989.

Awards: "Jazz Trumpeter of the Year," *Down Beat*, 1977-99.

Addresses: *Record company*—RCA, 1540 Broadway, New York City, NY 10036, (212) 930-4000. *Website*—Tom Harrell website: www.earthlink.net/~tomharrell.

1995. In 1999, he took the magazine's top prize again in their 64th Annual Readers Poll. Other prizes throughout the years have included *JazzTimes*' critics' choice for his albums, *Visions, Passages* and *Upswing*; the Prix Oscar for *Form*, awarded by the French Academy of Jazz; and a nomination for the 1995 Danish JazzPar prize. In biographical notes from his website, Harrell confirmed that while the prizes and recognition are an honor, the reward comes from deep inside him. "Every time I play, I feel that if I'm a good vehicle, I'll be rewarded by being able to experience beauty," Harrell said.

Harrell was born in Urbana, Illinois, on June 16, 1946. When he was six, his family moved to Los Altos, California, down the peninsula from San Francisco. His father was a business psychologist and had accepted a faculty post at Stanford University, at nearby Palo Alto. By the fifth grade, only a couple of years after he first started playing the trumpet with a flair that belied his age, Harrell began to compose. He had already tried transcribing music, with his early efforts including Charlie Parker's "Relaxing at Camarillo." By the time he was in seventh grade, he was studying from Russell Garcia's text on arranging. Harrell began to play professionally by the time he was 13. He played both trumpet and piano with groups all over the San Francisco Bay area, and sat in on jam sessions that included saxophonist Dewey Redman and trumpeter Eddie Henderson. Harrell noted that he chose the trumpet because he "liked the sound." "Lee Konitz got me to transcribe Louis Armstrong solos. I could see parallels between Louis' playing and Miles [Davis]. The way they phrased, using short phrases, was unbelievably similar," Harrell said in comments available at his website.

Crisis came at the time Harrell was beginning studies at Stanford University in 1963. A half-hearted suicide attempt was the first step in a diagnosis that determined he was a borderline schizophrenic. Harrell talked about his illness with Gene Santoro of *Nation* in February of 1995. "I had feelings of unreality and obsessive thoughts when I was a teenager. I started drinking in high school, then I stopped. I started therapy in the sixties, and that's when I started takingmedicine for paranoia." It was after the suicide attempt that he starting taking medicine and began to have control over his life, especially his music. "It also helped me get started writing again–until I got medicine, I stopped being able to write." Santoro also noted that "Harrell's medication–the only thing that keeps him from being institutionalized–helps depress his illness' symptoms.... He talks in a low near-monotone, and rarely faces you, although he turns his face toward you regularly and fixes you with his bright, glistening eyes—windows so suggestively open you can scan both his intelligence and his vulnerability at a glance."

But if his medication keeps him quiet and calm in social situations, the musician onstage portrays an entirely different personality. "When he walks onstage," said Santoro, "he looks like a human question mark: his head, with its slicked-back hair, bent almost perpendicular to his body, eyes on the floor, arms stiff at his sides. Then suddenly, when it's time for him to blow, he straightens to his full, thin, six-foot-two inch height, puts the horn to his mouth and proceeds to carve the splendid sounds that have made him such a reputation among his fellow musicians and among critics and fans." Despite all, Harrell got his bachelor's degree from Stanford University in 1969.

From 1969 through 1970, Harrell captured his first love by touring with the big bands of Stan Kenton and Woody Herman. He then returned to the San Francisco area, which is where, while still a student, he got together with a small jazz group in Berkeley every Saturday morning. Harrell explored new venues when he was a charter member of the Latin/jazz group Azteca, and also played with Malo, a Latin/jazz/rock band led by Jorge Santana, Carlos' brother. Beginning in 1973 he played for five years with Horace Silver's band, and recorded five albums with the group, including *Silver 'n Brass.* Working with Silver, Harrell said, "helped my rhythmic awareness because he's a master of rhythm."

By the time Harrell left Silver's band, he was settled in New York City, where he still lives with his wife, Angela, in their small upper west side apartment. In 1977, the year he left Silver, he co-led a big band with the bassist Sam Jones and worked with Gerry Mulligan, Bill Evans, the Mel Lewis Orchestra, Charlie Haden's Liberation Music Orchestra and Lee Konitz' nonet. After he joined Phil Woods' quintet in 1983 he recorded albums with the group that included *Bouquet* and *Bop Stew* on the Concord Jazz label. When he left Woods in 1989, he began leading his own bands. As well as recording with various groups and musicians, Harrell debuted his first solo album in the late 1970s, *Moon Alley,* on the independent Criss Cross label. Other solo albums have included *Form, Stories, Sail Away* and *Visions*, all for Contemporary; and *Passages* and *Upswing* for Chesky.

If his talent has become legendary, so have the sometimes odd, sometimes magical moments that have happened to those around him who have experienced the personality quirks that come with Harrell's disease. According to James Hale, writing for *Down Beat* in December of 1998, fellow musicians have told many stories. "In an airport, if the hustle and bustle become too much for him, he might wander off to a quiet spot in a parking garage and blow his trumpet until the noises in his head hush. Sometimes he will hear a chord in the hum of the refrigerator or the engine of a passing jet and work the rest of the day writing a composition based on what he has heard," noted Hale. It is his wife Angela who keeps him grounded and helps keep the symptoms of his illness in check. She travels with him and even does his sound check before his performance, whether he is on tour or playing at home in New York.

His need for quiet before as how keeps him at home or in his hotel room until performance time. Hale also related a story of the time when Harrell's medicine caused a toxic reaction, nearly killing him. When he stopped taking it, the outcome was "fascinating and frightening. His moods changed more quickly and furiously than ever, from happy to sad, confident to insecure ... he became something close to affable. He would buy groceries and leave them in front of his neighbors' doors as anonymous gifts. On the bandstand, when his turn came to solo, he would stun his audiences by scat singing in falsetto. His emergent personality was wonderful, and it was terrifying."

After over 30 years of playing for the public, Harrell defies his challenges every day and smooths them away with his 17-piece orchestra—a feat for someone without the distress his illness can bring. From the time he listened to his father's whistling around the house and became hooked on the sounds that brought America out of a devastating war, big bands have been his true love. Following a performance at Los Angeles' area Jazz Bakery in December of 1999, *Los Angeles Times* critic Don Heckman noted that "many of the pieces were either arranged or composed decades ago." "Chasin the Bird," was orchesrated in 1964; "Dream," 1968; and "Times Mirror," in 1993. "Yet there was a consistency of style and manner stretching across the entire program of pieces, convincing evidence of the persistent survival powers of Harrell's extraordinary creativity."

By 2000, it had been nearly 50 years since Harrell first picked up a trumpet to play. What has kept him going can best be described in his own words to Hale: "you merge with the infinite and transcend your ego. Sometimes it seems to flow without any conscious effort." As a child he might have been precocious. As a veteran adult musician, he has proven that he has a true genius that audiences cherish.

Selected discography

Moon Alley, 1977.
Stories, late 1970s, reissued on RCA, 1988.
Sail Away, late 1970s, reissued on RCA, 1989.
Form, late 1970s, reissued on RCA, 1990.
Visions, late 1970s, reissued on RCA, 1992.
Passages, late 1970s, reissued on RCA, 1992.
Upswing, late 1970s, reissued on RCA, 1993.
Labyrinth, RCA, 1996.
Art of Rhythm, RCA, 1998.
Time's Mirror, RCA, 1999.

Sources

Books

Gerard, Charley, editor, *Straight-Ahead Jazz Fake Book,* Gerard & Sarzin, 1993.
Harrell, Tom, *Tom Harrell Solos,* Jamey Aebersold Jazz.
Harrell, Tom, *Volume 63: Tom Harrell Jazz Originals*, Play-A-Long Book/Recording Set, Jamey Aebersold Jazz.
The New Real Jazz Fakebook, Sher Music Co.

Periodicals

Chicago Tribune, Oct. 14, 1999.
Down Beat, Feb. 1992; Feb. 1994; July 1996; Dec, 1996; Dec. 1998; Nov. 1999; Dec. 1999.
Los Angeles Times, Nov. 5, 1995; Aug. 4, 1996; Nov. 4, 1998; Nov. 7, 1999; Nov. 26, 1999; Dec. 4, 1999.
Nation, Feb. 13, 1995.

Online

"Time's Mirror," *All About Jazz,* http://www.allaboutjazz.com (April 2000).
"Tom Harrell biography" *Tom Harrell website*, http://www.home.earthlink.net/~tomharrell (April 2000).

—Jane Spear

Penelope Houston

Singer, songwriter

AP/Wide World Photos. Reproduced by permission.

Genre-crossing vocalist and songwriter Penelope Houston is known as one of the most shocking reincarnations from the original punk era. The lead singer of the legendary and influential 1970s San Francisco Bay area punk band the Avengers, Houston eventually transformed into a folk-rock singer/songwriter, to the surprise of those who remembered her work with the Avengers, with alternative rock sensibilities. Her solo material, including the acclaimed 1993 album *The Whole World,* through her 1999 mainstream-sounding effort *Tongue,* emphasized acoustic textures, haunting melodies, and Houston's gentle soprano voice. While not an overly polished vocalist, fans and critics say that her voice has an appealing quality that makes one want to keep listening. Some of Houston's admirers include Suzanne Vega, Shawn Colvin, and Christine Lavin. A popular entertainer in the Bay area and in Europe, especially Germany, Houston has a substantial cult following in cities across the United States, but has found difficulties reaching mainstream audiences.

Houston, born around 1958 in Los Angeles, California, and raised in Seattle, Washington, spent her childhood surrounded by music, albeit of the more classical persuasion. Her mother held a doctorate degree in choral conducting, while her sister studied cello and her brother played violin. In spite of her influences at home, Houston sought something new and different, and in late December of 1976 moved to San Francisco, California, to prepare to attend the San Francisco Art Institute, where she intended to study painting and printmaking.

Soon after she settled into her studies in January of 1977, 19-year-old Houston found herself in an environment where art, culture, and music collided. Early punk bands were also gaining ground in the United States, persuading the young student to take her first step into the music world as the lead singer and songwriter for a short-lived, yet highly influential, pre-hardcore punk band called the Avengers. "I was there [San Francisco] when that whole punk thing started coming up. Rock 'n' roll had become this boring, prog-rock thing," she recalled to *St. Louis Post-Dispatch* writer Chris Dickinson in 1996. "The idea of punk was that it was going to turn that on its head. It was a cultural explosion, but not just in rock. Every aspect of the arts was being affected, and that was really exciting."

Inspired by the music of the Rolling Stones, the Sex Pistols, and the Stooges, the Avengers formed in 1977 in San Francisco and became the undisputed leaders of the city's punk movement, but disbanded in 1979 after only two years together. Along with Houston, the group's other members included guitarist Greg Westermark, who

For the Record . . .

Born c. 1958 in Los Angeles, CA; married guitarist/mandolinist Meletios ("Mel") Peppas; *Education*: Attended the San Francisco Art Institute.

Lead singer for the Avengers, 1977-79; released acclaimed acoustic/folk-rock solo album *The Whole World,* 1993; released major-label debut *Cut You,* 1996; released mainstream album *Tongue,* 1999.

Addresses: *Record company*—Reprise Records, 3300 Warner Blvd., Burbank, CA 91505, (818) 846-9090. *Management*—Victor Ratto. *Websites*—Official Penelope Houston Site: http://www.penelope.net; Penelope Houston at Reprise Records, http://www.RepriseRec.com

played with the band from 1977-78, bassist James Calvin Wilsey, drummer Danny Furious, and guitarist Brad Kent, who replaced Westermark in 1979. Adhering to punk's progressive and radical social stances, Houston called attention to her intelligence, biting social criticism, sharp attitude, and edgy voice, rather than to her gorgeous looks to define the band. Consequently, her revolutionary refusal to play the sex-role gender game of the popular music culture helped blaze the trail for women in rock musicfor years to come. No longer did a woman fronting a rock band earn her reputation on the basis of physical characteristics alone. She could also win acceptance for her thoughts and musical accomplishments.

Houston's band mates, likewise, in comparison to the pop music of the time, played in an unorthodox style. As a whole, the Avengers reveled in breaking and ignoring handed down music rules in glorious, remarkable fashion. However, without a cemented record contract, the Avengers' funds ran low, and the band was forced to split up after only two years. They left behind two indie records, one three-song single, and a four-song twelve-inch record, produced by the Sex Pistols' Steve Jones and released around the same time the Avengers called it quits. They met Jones when they opened for the Sex Pistols' final show at San Francisco's Winterland in January of 1978. In addition to appearing with established acts such as the Sex Pistols, the Avengers also headlined dates with other up-and-coming bands like the Go-Go's, X, and the Dead Kennedys.

Four years after their demise, in 1983 Go! Records released a retrospective album entitled *The Avengers,* featuring standout songs such as "The American in Me," "We Are the One," "Car Crash," "Corpus Christi," and a searing cover of the Rolling Stones' "Paint it Black." Produced by the Avengers and David Fergusson, the LP compiled the band's seven released songs and six unreleased songs from demo tapes and was widely regarded as the finest United States pre-hardcore punk album the West Coast produced. Lookout! Records issued another Avengers collection, *Died for Your Sins,* in 1999. Combining studio outtakes, bootleg-quality live tapes, and three new "reunion" recordings, this album, according to most reviewers, was more of a fans-only souvenir. Although the Avengers only recorded a handful of songs, the band and their music lived on to inspire such acts as the Dead Kennedys, Bikini Kill, Jawbox, and Cold Cold Heart. "It's strange," Houston admitted to Dickinson, when asked how it felt later to have been involved with a band often referred to as "seminal" years later. "At the time, we knew it was this really exciting corner that pop culture was taking ... but we didn't look at it in any long-term way," she continued. "We didn't think of ourselves as musicians. We just thought of ourselves as punks."

Following her contribution to the Avengers, Houston left music for a while to explore other creative outlets, moving first to Los Angeles to work in film and video. In the mid-1980s, she emerged from her post-punk hiatus, relocating to England to work on projects with Howard Devoto, the founder of the now defunct group Magazine. Around the same time, Houston's feelings about the punk scene started to change. She believed early 1980s punk had taken on a more narrow definition. "In '77, it was more fun," she explained to Dickinson. "There were more women, people dressing weird, film, lots of different things going on. By '81, '82, it turned into bands like Black Flag, the Circle Jerks. It turned into teen-age guys stage-diving. It became something more like heavy metal, a right of passage for boys, a group grope for guys." Thus, collaborating with Devoto and Alex Gibson, Houston abandoned her punk days and released her first recording since the Avengers, a minimal single under the name -30-. That record's two tracks appeared on Houston's debut solo outing, *Birdboys,* released on the Subterranean label in1987. A melodic and spirited album, *Birdboys* nevertheless failed to impress critics. And, in retrospect, Houston came to the same conclusion; it later appeared that the singer/songwriter lacked the skills and command at the time to work in a softer context.

After spending time overseas, Houston eventually returned to San Francisco, where she began listening to artists such as Tom Waits and the Violent Femmes, who stirred in Houston the possibility of approaching her own songs from a more acoustic point of reference. In the early 1990s, with a new approach in mind,

Houston formed her own acoustic band, a folk-styled combo comprised of guitarist/mandolin player Meletios ("Mel") Peppas (Houston's husband), bassist Steven Strauss, guitarist Eliot Nemzer, and drummer Kevin Mummey. After a six-year absence from the recording studio and stage, the singer released 1993's *The Whole World.* According to critics, the years between her debut and second offering spent writing, traveling, and discovering alternate musical directions paid off. "Houston's phrasing is controlled and masterful, the songs are witty, well sketched and tinged with bittersweet urgency," concluded Jason Cohen in the *Trouser Press Guide to '90s Rock.* "A virtually perfect record, with one of the best displays of pure vocal gifts the 'alternative' universe will ever hear."

Touring the United States as well as Europe, Houston soon found herself at the center of the neo-folk movement. *The Whole World* enjoyed its warmest reception overseas, where reviewers dubbed Houston the "Queen of New Folk" in several languages. Her substantial following in Europe allowed her to record new material for Germany's Normal label. Houston's only formal album issued abroad, *Karmal Apple,* while not so captivating as *The Whole World,* nevertheless garnered favorable reviews and further endeared the performer's European audience.

In 1996, after signing a contract with Reprise Records, Houston released her major-label debut entitled *Cut You.* With eight songs taken from her earlier studio albums (including the defiant, though beautiful "Sweetheart" and the brilliant "Qualities of Mercy from *The Whole World*) plus six new tracks, *Cut You,* the singer said, was intended as a sort of reintroduction to her music and revealed both her upbeat and darker sides. "There are a lot of levels in each of the songs," Houston told *Boston Globe* writer Jim Sullivan in 1996. "I like the complexity of humans. Communication and emotion."

Like her prior recordings, the album won praise from numerous mainstream publications, including *Newsweek, Rolling Stone,* and *Billboard,* but after recording *Cut You* and touring across Europe and the United States, Houston, who now claimed influences as diverse as Patti Smith, Dusty Springfield, Leonard Cohen, and Burt Bacharach, felt driven to explore new territory when she returned to her home in Oakland, California.

"I was burned out and a little frustrated," the singer recalled to *Billboard* magazine's Jim Bessman. Despite *Cut You*'s critical reception, the album failed to sell as well as expected in the United States, and Houston's father was in the midst of recovering from a stroke. Subsequently, when Houston began working on the album *Tongue* (released in January 1999 on Reprise), she stepped outside the framework of her band's organic sound for the first time, giving her the freedom to place her lyrics at the center of each song. Another major change in her musicinvolved programmed beats designed by Jaime Lemoine for half the album's tracks; Steve Bowman, a former member of the Counting Crowes, and Tim Mooney of American Music Club shared drumming duties for the remainder of the songs. The resulting 14-song collection, recorded at Fantasy Studios in Berkeley, California, stretched beyond her folk/acoustic dimension to include rock ("Worm," "Crushing," and the blues-based "Hundertwasser 576"), electronica ("Subway"), pop ("Grand Prix"), and ballads ("My Angel Lost Her Wings"). The opening track, "Grand Prix," was written with Pat Johnson, a longtime friend of Houston whose songwriting credits include work with Sid Griffith and the Coal Porters.

Collaborating on the song with Johnson "was the turning point for my new sound," Houston revealed on her official website. The album's title track, as well as the seductive song "Things," was written with two other close friends, Charlotte Caffey and Jane Wiedlin of the Go-Go's. Other highlights included "Scum," a digging song that referred to an unnamed person in the music industry, the acoustic "Frankenstein Heart," and "The Ballad of Happy Friday and Tiger Woods," set against the backdrop of a string arrangement. *Tongue* also included the bonus track "New Day," featuring Green Day's Billie Joe Armstrong on guitar. Other performers appearing on the album included bassist Joel Reader of the band Mr. T. Experience, guitarist Chuck Prophet, and Caffey and Wiedlin, who performed for the title track. The album won critical praise, and "Scum" received airplay on modern rock/adult alternative radio stations. With this, Houston hoped to strengthen her hold in the United States. "I've been so spoiled by Europe, because audiences there know all the songs, and the clubs treat you great," she told Bessman. "Someone even put my initials and birthday on his license plate."

Selected discography

Solo

Birdboys, Subterranean, 1987.
The Whole World, Heyday, 1993.
(With Pat Johnson) *Crazy Baby,* (Germany) Return to Sender/Normal, 1994.
Silk Purse (From a Sow's Ear), (Germany) Return to Sender/Normal, 1994.
Karmal Apple, (Germany) Normal, 1995.
Cut You, Reprise, 1995.
Tongue, Reprise, 1999.

With the Avengers

The Avengers, Go! Records, 1983.
Died for Your Sins, Lookout!, 1999.

Sources

Books

MusicHound Rock: The Essential Album Guide, Visible Ink Press, 1999.

Robbins, Ira A., editor, *Trouser Press Guide to '90s Rock,* Fireside/Simon and Schuster, 1997.

Periodicals

Billboard, March 16, 1996; February 7, 1998; March 27, 1999.

Boston Globe, February 8, 1996; May 19, 1996; July 14, 1999.

Los Angeles Times, April 28, 1996.

Melody Maker, April 24, 1999.

Rolling Stone, April 4, 1996.

St. Louis Post-Dispatch, April 4, 1996, p. 08; May 16, 1996, p. 07.

Stereo Review, August 1993.

Stereo Review's Sound & Vision, May 1999.

Village Voice, June 29, 1999; September 28, 1999.

Washington Post, May 26, 1996.

Washington Times, May 8, 1999, p. D4.

Online

Ectophiles' Guide—Penelope Houston, http://www.smoe.org/ectoguide/guide.cgi?artists/houston.penelope (February 12, 2000).

Official Penelope Houston Site, http://www.penelope.net (February 12, 2000).

Reprise Records, http://www.RepriseRec.com (February 12, 2000).

—Laura Hightower

Jay-Z

Rap/hip-hop artist

AP/Wide World Photos. Reproduced by permission.

In early December of 1999 when rapper Jay-Z was arrested for the stabbing of record executive Lance "Un" Rivera, at a Times Square nightclub, the news came at the wrong time. His much-awaited new CD, *Volume 3: The Life & Times of S. Carter*, was due to be released right after Christmas. With parents hesitant enough to allow their teens to buy music they don't understand in the first place, the question was asked whether this latest incident would hurt sales due to the negative publicity. For a guy who grew up on the mean streets of Brooklyn, New York, this was just another one of the "hard knocks" that has formed his voice in rap.

Jay-Z was born Shawn Carter on December 4, 1970, in Brooklyn, New York, the youngest of four children. He grew up in the well-known Marcy Projects, where the J and Z subway trains run. He has gained his fans despite of, or maybe because of his life as a cocaine dealer before he joined the world of rap. Jay-Z rose to fame with his 1996 gold-certified single, a duet with Foxy Brown. The controversy started immediately. Its title, "Ain't No N-G-A" (Like the One I Got) was not the language that even the most daring disc jockeys wanted to play.

According to Janine McAdams of *Billboard* in June of 1996, "For now, 'Ain't No N-G-A' has radio production rooms working overtime. None of the stations contacted for this story advocate the use of the n-word over the air, but their solutions are varied: Some edit the word out; others substitute 'brother' or 'player.'" Still, radio stations pointed out that, however reluctant they were to broadcast that and other offensive words, the public knew when it was cut out anyway. In some cases, the change altered the content enough to lose its intended impact and appeal. Yet it was Jay-Z who also began to transform the hip-hop scene from its hardcore "gangsta rap" to something that bears a more refined style—that of "Armani suits, alligator boots, Rolex watches, expensive cars, broads and Cristel," noted Shawnee Smith of *Billboard,* in November of 1999.

Jay-Z's drug days and the hustling that went with them was a theme that would permeate all of his music. When an article in the *Village Voice* appeared in August in of 1996 at the beginning of his career, Jay-Z said his philosophy was very much an important piece of understanding his music. The other subject of the article was fellow rapper, Nas, and the contrast between the two of them was highlighted. "Nas is a radical philosopher in the tradition of Rakim and Nietzsche.... Jay-Z is strictly business, with visions of expansion ('Dabbled in crazy weight/ ...I'm still spending money from '88'). Nas is a pensive poet with a vast vocabulary. Jay-Z is a sharp conversationalist with impeccable timing," the reporters noted. "Mostly," they said, "Nas and Jay-Z were born to rhyme."

For the Record . . .

Born Shawn Carter on December 4, 1970, in Brooklyn, New York.

Rap artist, performing pop-rap, crossover rap, harcore rap, East Coast rap, urban, hip-hop for Def Jam, Priority, Roc-A-Fella/Def Jam, BMG International labels; released debut album, *Reasonable Doubt,* Freeze/Rock-A-Fella, 1996; *In My Lifetime, Vol. I,* Rock-A-Fella/Def Jam, 1997; released *Vol.2: Hard Nock Life*, Rock-A-Fella/Def Jam, 1998; released *Vol. 3: The Life and Times of Shawn Carter*, Def Jam, 1999.

Awards: Grammy Award, Best Rap Album of 1998, for *Vol. 2: Hard Knock Life*, 1998 .

Addresses: *Record company*—Def Jam Records, 160 Varick St., 12th Floor, New York City, NY 10013, phone: (212) 229-5200, fax: (212) 229-5299.

At the end of 1996, Havelock Nelson reflected on the year in rap for *Bilboard.* Nelson summarized the movement Jay-Z had made when he said that he, "masterfully reinvented himself after receiving battle scars from his previous rhyme life." Jay-Z indicated his interest in the corporate side of the business, too. Since 1994, Jay-Z had been producing records for other artists as chief of operations for the Roc-A-Fella label. The same handle he had for money in the drug business translated well into the music industry. He talked about his future at that time;"Although my album has already gone gold, it will be my last one. From this point, it's all about the business." Obviously, Jay-Z could not stay away from performing any more than he could make a bad business decision. He came back in 1997, with his album, *In My Lifetime*, and in 1998 his bestselling, *Vol. 2: Hard Knock Life,* won him a Grammy as best rap album.

On December 27, 1999, Steve Jones of *USA Today* talked about the artist Jay-Z. When Jones sat in on a session with Jay-Z and rapper Beanie Sigel, he noticed that Jay-Z never writes down a lyric. "I don't write songs. I just sit there and listen to the track, and I come up with the words. It's a gift. A gift from God." Jay-Z also had big anticipation for his upcoming album, *Vol 3: The Life & Times of Shawn Carter.* He talked about how his life had changed in the few short years of his success. "With five million records out there, there are all kinds of things that you have to deal with," he said. "Even though it's just been a year, people think that things change with you and start treating you differently. Street people start thinking that maybe you've gone soft. But I'm the same dude. That's why I did the song, 'Come and Get Me.' I'm still holding firm in my position."

When *Vol 3...* came out, reviews were mixed. Soren Baker wrote in *The Los Angeles Times,* on December 31, 1999, the week the new release came out, "For a man who rode to commercial prominence with the help of up-tempo, dance-ready tracks, Jay-Z is sounding pretty laid-back." According to Baker, the album fell behind his Grammy-winning *Vol. 2,* out last year. It was from a calmer, even less-clever and humorous Jay-Z, in that reviewer's opinion.

In the weeks between the stabbing incident in New York, and the release of his new album, Jon Caramanica talked about Jay-Z's difficult week in early December of 1999. Jay-Z has denied his guilt and made a plea of "not guilty" when he went to court on January 31, 2000. The case is still pending. "After the breakout success of last year's *Vol. 2: Hard Knock Life,* the expectations on Jay-Z were greater than ever," Caramanica wrote. "In fact, it's been speculated that the entire stabbing incident was part of some large marketing conspiracy to guarantee strong buzz and sales. In hip-hop, where crime is often flipped as a marketing tool, having your artist splashed across the cover of the *Daily News* may well work financial wonders, but that option seems absurd for a man in Jay's position. Still, the very existence of such a theory hints at an underlying belief that Jay, of all rappers, is too smart to go out like this. Business, never personal." A Mariah Carey special recorded prior to the incident that included Jay-Z as a featured guest star was not edited to exclude him for the January broadcast.

Jay-Z has worked with some of the biggest stars of the rap and hip-hop scene, including, Lil' Kim, Jermaine Dupri, Busta Rhymes, Kelly Price, Doug Wilson, Sean "Puffy" Combs, Nasheim Myrick, Kid Capri, Mase, Deric Angelettie, Too $hort, Joe Quinde, Sauce Money, Stephen Dent, Big Jaz, and Stevie J.

Whatever the reviews on his *Life and Times of Shawn Carter* said or did not say about him, Jay-Z showed no signs of retiring. The album was an instant platinum success, emphasizing what a number one seller he still was in the genre he has helped to define. For this man who was "born to rhyme" Jay-Z did not seem to be running out of words any time soon.

Selected discography

Singles

"In My Lifetime," Ffrr, 1995.
"Can't Knock the Hustle," Priority 1996.
"Feelin'," It, Roc-A-Fella/Priority, 1997.
"This City Is Mine," Def Jam, 1998.
"Can I Get a Rush Hour," BMG International, 1999.
"Hard Knock Life," Def Jam, 1999.
"Do It Again," Def Jam, 1999; released on Polygram International, 2000.
"Things That U Do," Def Jam, 2000.
"Anything," Def Jam, 2000.

Albums

Reasonable Doubt, 1996.
In My Lifetime, Vol. 1, 1997.
Vol. 2: Hard Knock Life, 1998
Vol. 3: The Life and Times of Shawn Carter, 1999.

Sources

Periodicals

Billboard, June 29, 1996; Nov. 23, 1996; Dec. 28, 1996.
Los Angeles Times, Dec. 27, 1999; Dec. 31, 1999.
Newsweek, Dec. 13, 1999.
New York Times, Dec. 26, 1999; Dec. 30, 1999; Jan. 1, 2000.
Rolling Stone, Oct. 14, 1999.
USA Today, Dec. 27, 1999; Jan. 3, 2000.
Village Voice, Aug. 13, 1996; Dec. 14, 1999.
Washington Post, Dec. 14, 1999; Jan. 2, 2000.

Online

"Jay-Z discography," *All Music Guide*, http://www.allmusic.com (April 2000).
MTV Online, http://www.mtv.com (April 2000).

—Jane Spear

Eyvind Kang

Composer, bandleader, violin

Since 1994, Seattle/New York-based composer and violinist Eyvind Kang has become one of the hottest new faces in jazz. Along with straight-ahead and improvisational jazz, Kang has also worked in genres as diverse as experimental rock, the avant-garde, folk, Renaissance dance music, World music, and modern classical. "He's got this absolutely wide-open curiosity," guitarist Bill Frisell told Paul de Barros of *Down Beat* in October of 1999. "Even though he's young, he has this sort of wisdom about him, this kind of inner calm." By the end of 1999, Kang had composed music for and released three albums as a bandleader, including his acclaimed NADEs series: *7 Nades* and *Theater of Mineral NADEs*, in addition to *The Sweetness of Sickness.* Just five years into his career, Kang had already collaborated with several musicians from an eclectic array of concentrations, from jazz greats like Wayne Horvitz to alternative rock Beck. "I play with countless groups," said Kang, who refused to adhere to the music industry's fixation on more permanent collaborations. "I'm interested in creating my own life outside the capitalistic grid of the music industry. Music can exist—does exist, will exist—without that. Like, I saw in the Himalayans they found a 10,000-year-old frozen body. The guy had a flute and a bag of pot."

Born around 1972 in Seattle, Washington, to parents of Asian and Icelandic descent, Kang spent his formative years in a region known for its creative spirit. Although during the late 1980s and into the following decade, Seattle was more widely recognized for its coffee brewers, software developers, and grunge rock bands, the Northwest city was at the same time quietly developing and delivering several of America's first-rate jazz players. Like other musicians from the Seattle area who emerged on the jazz scene in the 1990s such as trumpeter Dave Douglas, drummer Mike Sarin (who worked in the Dave Douglas String Group and Myra Melfords's The Same River, Twice), guitarist Brad Shepik, reedman Chris Speed, and drummer Jim Black, Kang had the good fortune of growing up in a city with a healthy jazz infrastructure: strong school music programs, inspiring teachers and role models, and opportunities to hear great players at a multitude of venues. "It maybe even goes as far back as the music programs in elementary school," offered Shepik, who grew up in the suburbs east of Seattle, where he met Speed and Black, as quoted by de Barros in the August 1999 issue of *Down Beat.* "Everybody in that area had the opportunity to play in bands in school."

Taking advantage of such opportunities, Kang learned to play violin beginning at the age of six, and along the way picked up a slew of other instruments, including guitar, bass, keyboards, mandolin, tuba, recorders, and drums. In 1991, Kang enrolled at the Cornish College for the Arts, a school with a curriculum embracing free-improvisation and open form, as well as other jazz traditions. Here, Kang met his definitive influence, faculty member and violinist Michael White of the legendary John Handy Quintet. Other prominent faculty members at Cornish College have included drummer Jerry Granelli, trombonist Julian Priester, tenor saxophonist and flutist Hadley Caliman, female vocalist Jay Clayton, and double bassist Gary Peacock. While studying with White, Kang met keyboardist Wayne Horvitz, who, in turn, introduced the young musician to John Zorn. Following in the path of other promising young jazz musicians, Kang by this timehad settled on a part-time basis in New York City, splitting his time between the East Coast and his hometown. In spite of Seattle's opportunities, most top players discover that only the downtown New York jazz scene offers steady work and a large, stimulating pool of like-minded players. "COBRA (Zorn's group-improv game piece) was being done every week at the old Knitting Factory," Kang recalled to de Barros in *Down Beat*'s October 1999 issue. "I went there to hear it, and [Zorn] invited me to play. Then he invited me on the tour."

Since 1992, COBRA, Zorn's best-known musical game show, had been played at least once a month at the legendary Knitting Factory jazz club. The musicians, usually numbering 12, are separated into various teams and prompted with flash cards and hand signals. COBRA, named after a military game, "is like a cross

For the Record . . .

Born c. 1972 in Seattle, WA; son of parents of Icelandic and Asian descent. *Education*: Attended Cornish College for the Arts; studied with violinist Michael White and classical Indian violinist Dr. N. Rajam in Bombay, India.

Joined John Zorn's COBRA group, 1994; joined guitarist Bill Frisell's quartet, 1995; released debut album *7 Nades* as a bandleader on Zorn's Tzadik label, 1996; released *Theater of Mineral NADEs,* 1998; toured with Frisell's band the Willies, 1999; toured Japan with alternative musician Beck, 2000.

Awards: Artist Support Program grant from the Jack Straw Foundation, 1994.

Addresses: *Record company*—Tzadik Records, email: tzadik@tzadik.com; website: http://www.tzadik.com.

between an exhibition sports match and a board game," wrote *Down Beat*'s John Corbett in June of 1994. "Its rules guide musicians into and out of musical roles and relationships, wherein they must use their improvising skills to negotiate." More often than not, therefore, the success of each show weighs heavily on the musicians who play in the game, rather than with the structures and regulations created by Zorn. When Kang joined COBRA that night at the Knitting Factory in the spring of 1994, Zorn had decided to take his exhibition on the road. The opportunity seemed perfect for Kang, who wanted to take a new, less restrained direction in his career. According to critics, Kang displayed superb improvisational skills and an ability to interact with his comrades, despite his young age. At one COBRA performance in Chicago at the Vic Theater, "Kang was a vertiginous delight, working wonderfully with [cellist] Erik Friedlander and putting forward a lovely Middle Eastern mode, at one point," declared Corbett.

Also in 1994, Kang received an Artist Support Program grant from the Jack Straw Foundation and used the funds to record the first seven of his series of musical compositions entitled *7 Nades* (released in 1996 on Zorn's label, Tzadik). The astonishing, eccentric album, named after a play on the word "serenades," earned critical accolades and appeared on several "Best 10" lists in 1996. Zorn hailed the work as "One of the quirkiest and most indescribable of sound sculptures from a new generation of experimentalists. A composition that will bring new revelations with each listening," as quoted on the Tzadik website. By this point in his young career, Kang had already performed with and/or recorded with the likes of Zorn, the Sun City Girls, Wayne Horvitz and Motel 6 (and later his 4 + 1 ensemble), Joe McPhee, Deformation, and others.

Meanwhile, Kang in 1995 was approached by guitarist Bill Frisell (who, incidentally, moved from New York City to Seattle in the mid-1980s) to play on the soundtrack for a television special on Gary Larson's *Far Side* cartoon series. Later that year, Kang joined Frisell's new quartet. "I'm so excited about this guy," an enthused Frisell told Fred Bouchard of *Down Beat* in April of 1995. "He's classically trained in Suzuki method and can play bebop, Stravinsky's Soldier's Tale or hip-hop." Not only did Kang play violin on Frisell's acclaimed *Americana, Quartet* (released in 1996 on Elektra/Nonesuch), he also revealed his proficiency on the tuba. The enterprising album, in terms of instrumentation, also featured a number of the compositions written for the Larson *Far Side* special. In addition to playing with Frisell and releasing his debut as a bandleader and composer in 1996, Kang also played violin on Doghead's self-titled release and Karen Pernick's album entitled *Apartment 12.* The following year saw Kang lending his skills as a violinist to We's *As Is* and Gabriela's *Detra's del Sol;* he also served as arranger and multi-instrumentalist for the album *Great Jewish Music: Serge Gainsbour.*

In 1998, Kang continued to compose, record, and further his interests in World music, spending four months that year in Bombay, India, studying classical Indian violin with Dr. N. Rajam. That year also saw the release of another installment of the NADEs series, the epic *Theater of Mineral NADEs,* which was destined to become one of the year's most talked about jazz albums, as well as a multi-genre effort entitled *The Sweetness of Sickness,* released on the Rabid God Inoculator label. Another project showcasing Kang's diversity, the album featured free-jazz, experimental noise, folk, World music, Renaissance dance music, and modern classical sounds that hit the listener at sometimes dizzying speeds. He also formed a group called Dying Ground, a dark, apocalyptic trio that also included drummer G. Calvin Weston and bassist Kato Hideki; the trio released their self-titled debut album in 1998. Kang's other appearances in 1998 included playing violin for Andrew Drury's *Polish Theater Posters* and Horvitz's *4 + 1 Ensemble.*

The following year, an album with clarinetist François Houle and drummer Dylan VanDerSchyff entitled *Pieces of Time* was released on Canada's Spool label, and Kang guested on both violin and viola for Mister Bungle's *California* and Arto Lindsay's *Prize.* Also in 1999, Kang performed gigs in Seattle and later across Europe with Frisell's new group called the Willies, a bluegrass-inspired quartet that included banjo player Danny Barnes. Later that year, in addition to working on a new project for Tzadik, Kang recorded on a new album by Motorbison, a Seattle grunge/jazz band, scheduled for release in early 2000. In the spring of 2000, Kang took his talents to the alternative rock scene, joining renowned musician Beck on a three-week tour of Japan.

Selected discography

(With the Bill Frisell Quartet) *Americana Quartet,* Elektra/Nonesuch, 1996.
7 Nades, Tzadik, 1996.
(With Dying Ground) *Dying Ground,* 1998.
The Sweetness of Sickness, Rabid God Inoculator, 1998.
Theater of Mineral NADEs, Tzadik, 1998.
(With Houle and VanDerSchyff) *Pieces of Time,* 1999.

Sources

Books

Cook, Richard and Brian Morton, *Penguin Guide to Jazz on Compact Disc,* Penguin Books, 1998.

Periodicals

Billboard, April 13, 1996.
Boston Globe, February 6, 1998.
Down Beat, June 1994; April 1995; April 1996; August 1996; October 1997; August 1999; October 1999, p. 54.
Village Voice, January 26, 1999.

Online

All Music Guide, http://www.allmusic.com (February 9, 2000).
Tzadik Records, http://www.tzadik.com (February 9, 2000).

—Laura Hightower

Stacey Kent

Jazz singer

Photograph by Jim Cooper. AP/Wide World Photos. Reproduced by permission.

American-born vocalist Stacey Kent became one of the most popular jazz singers in Great Britain during the late 1990s. Known for her optimistic, uncluttered singing style, Kent's repertoire includes the standard songs of the "Great American Songbook," which included jazz, big band, and swing. "What I love about the genre is that it is so natural," the singer revealed to *United Press International* reporter Ken Franckling. "This music is so infectious. I'm just me up on the stage. I like that." And despite her age, Kent believes that the songs of days past remain applicable to more modern times. "I'm living in today's world singing songs that are still relevant and performing them the way that we do and the way we are" she revealed to John McDonough in *Downbeat*. "That makes them fresh." Although not so renowned in the United States, Kent has earned numerous honors from critics throughout Europe, and has become the toast of the jazz scene in her adopted home of Great Britain. Kent received her first recognition when she was voted 1998's Vocalist of the Year at the 1999 British Jazz Awards, and her three albums all became top-selling jazz collections in the United Kingdom.

Kent was born in 1969 just outside of New York City, New York, where she spent her childhood. Her father, an architect, and mother, a magazine editor, exposed their daughter to music early on. Kent's favorite performers include Frank Sinatra, Nat King Cole, Benny Goodman, Fred Astaire, Doris Day, Ella Fitzgerald, and other legends of the "Great American Songbook" whose songs would become standards. In addition to singing the music of popular entertainers, Kent also enjoyed the tenor solos of Paul Gonsalves from the Duke Ellington band. Although she never studied singing in the formal sense, she did sing in her high school's chorus and recalled that she always sang around the family home. "There was always music in the house when I was growing up, and I suppose it was obvious that I had a certain ability," she told Steve Graybow in a 1999 interview with *Billboard* magazine. She further added that taking piano lessons inadvertently allowed her to develop her singing skills. "I guess that I had sort of run my own ear-training course. I would hear a song or theme in a movie or on television and hurry to the piano to figure it out. I ended up with much more of a trained ear than I realized."

Nonetheless, Kent never considered a career as a professional singer. Instead, her love for speaking and studying foreign languages led her to attend Sarah Lawrence College in New York after graduating from high school. Here, she graduated with a bachelor's degree in comparative literature and intended to one day earn a master's degree. Already fluent in both Italian and French, Kent took some upper level courses, earning

For the Record . . .

Born in 1969 near New York City, NY; daughter of an architect (father) and a magazine editor (mother); married tenor saxophonist Jim Tomlinson. *Education*: Graduated from Sarah Lawrence College in NY with a bachelor's degree in comparative literature; attended Guildhall School of Music and Drama in London, England.

Appeared as the singer in opening scene of film Richard III, 1995; signed with Candid Record's, 1996; released debut album *Close Your Eyes*, 1997; released *The Tender Trap*, toured the U.S. East Coast, 1998; featured in documentary profile on *CBS Sunday Morning*, released album *Let Yourself Go*, a tribute to Fred Astaire, 1999.

Awards: 1998 Vocalist of the Year, 1999 British Jazz Awards.

Addresses: *Record company*—Candid Productions Ltd., 16 Castlenau, London SW13 9RU England, phone: (44) 0181 741 3608, fax: (44) 0181 563 0013, email: CandidRecords@compuserve.com, website: http://www.candidrecords.com; U.S. record sales and information, Artists Only! Records, 580 Broadway, Ste. 910, New York City, NY 10012, phone: (212) 941-9100, website: http://www.artistsonly.com. *Booking and management*—Mark Butcher, email: MarkButcher@compuserve.com. Stacey Kent Appreciation Society—David Mitchell, email: sk.as@virgin.net. *Email*—StaceyKent@aol.com. *Website*—http:www.members.aol.com/staceykent.

enough credit hours to complete half of those needed for her graduate studies. However, fate intervened when Kent took some time off before further pursuing graduate work to travel in Europe. She first traveled to Munich, hoping to improve her command of the German language. Then, during one of her stops in 1991, she visited some friends who were students at Oxford University in England and by chance met some musicians on their way to London to audition for a one-year, postgraduate jazz course at the Guildhall School of Music and Drama. On a whim, Kent decided to join them to audition, and despite her lack of training, won acceptance. Most of her classmates were music majors and well-versed in technical vocabulary. Thus, they reacted with amazement at Kent's talent.

Subsequently, music, rather than academics, began to shape Kent's future. In addition to realizing her natural aptitude for singing while attending Guildhall, Kent also met English tenor saxophonist Jim Tomlinson, a philosophy graduate and another student without a music degree, as well as guitarist Colin Oxley. Kent, Tomlinson, and Oxley discovered that they shared the same ideas musically and soon started playing together as a trio at parties. As Kent's career progressed, both Tomlinson and Oxley would appear on records and on the stage with the singer on a regular basis. Moreover, Kent credited Tomlinson, whom she eventually married and settled with in North London, as the person who most encouraged her to pursue a career as a jazz singer.

Other important opportunities arose from her studies as well. Because Kent's jazz course held close ties to the London music scene, she soon received unanticipated offers to work as a vocalist. Her first singing job was with a 1930s-style big band called the Vile Bodies Swing Orchestra, the resident band for dinner dances at the Ritz Hotel in London. Following this, she started earning dates at major jazz clubs in London and across Great Britain. Like her childhood inspirations, Kent also found herself performing with a big band before establishing a solo career. "Suddenly, I found myself in the position of having a career as a singer, which I never expected," Kent revealed to Graybow. "I sang with a 14-piece big band [at the Ritz]. I sang at Ronnie Scott's club. I met and performed with lots of up-and-coming musicians. It all cumulated in my record deal with Candid Records. At that point, of course, there was no turning back."

Meanwhile, Kent received more exposure when she appeared as the big band vocalist in the opening scene of a 1995 film version of playwright William Shakespeare's *Richard III,* starring Ian Mckellen. The role, as well as Kent's performance on the film's opening track, led critics in both Britain and the United States to take notice. Since that time, Kent has continued to play with big bands across Europe, including the British Broadcasting Company (BBC) Big Band. One of her greatest and most fulfilling endeavors with the BBC Big Band occurred a few years later in 1998, when she participated in a broadcast at the Queen Elizabeth Hall for a show entitled *Big Band Legends in Concert,* with Les Brown, Billy May, and Ray Anthony.

Two years earlier, in 1996, Kent signed with London's Candid Records. The label would issue her recorded work throughout the world, except in the United States, where Chiaroscuro and Artists Only! provided distribution. Her debut album, *Close Your Eyes,* a collection of standard love ballads as well as swing numbers, appeared in May of 1997 to rave reviews. *Jazzwise* magazine called her debut "CD of the Month," and numerous critics, including writers for the American publication *Jazziz* and Britain's own *Jazz Journal,* placed the album on their top ten lists for 1997. One critic, Bill Protzman of the *St. Paul Pioneer Press,* asserted, "This is such a marvelous debut that it immediately places Stacey Kent among today's finest jazz singers.... She has a voice that is distinctive and captivating, with an appealing vibrato that gives her singing a girlish sweetness a la Ella Fitzgerald." Recorded with a five-piece band, which included Tomlinson on saxophone, Steve Brown on drums, and David Newton on piano, *Close Your Eyes* received extensive airplay in England and became one of the best-selling jazz albums across Europe in 1997.

In June of 1998, Kent released her second album, *The Tender Trap,* to European audiences, prompting *Mojo* to declare the project "Jazz Album of the Month" in the magazine's August1998 issue. A collection of 12 songs from the "Great American Songbook," *The Tender Trap* became one of Britain's top-selling jazz albums that year as well. Towards the end of 1998 and into 1999, Kent embarked on an extensive tour throughout the world, including stops in Scandinavia and the American East Coast, where she performed at major venues such as New York City's Birdland and the Blue Note. And following a February 14, 1999, feature profile of the singer which aired on the American television program *CBS Sunday Morning,* Kent's popularity in the United States skyrocketed. The Tender Trap (released on February 9, 1999 in the United States entered the Billboard charts at number 15 on March 27 of that year, and reached number one in sales for numerous internet sites including Amazon.com, Music Boulevard, and CDnow. As a result, Candid went into second and third pressings to keep up with the unexpected demands. By the end of the year, The Tender Trap had sold over 20,000 units in the United States, and the young singer was named 1998's vocalist of the year at the 1999 British Jazz Awards.

Europe saw the release of Kent's third album, *Let Yourself Go,* in October of 1999. The record hit the American market in the spring of 2000. This time, Kent chose to celebrate another favorite entertainer, Fred Astaire, in a 13-song collection that included songs such as "Isn't This a Lovely Day?" "One For My Baby," "A Fine Romance," and "S'Wonderful," all of which were composed by some of America's most legendary songwriters. Her backing band included Tomlinson, Newton, and Oxley, as well as a rhythm team consisting of Simon Thorpe and Steve Brown. Another successful album, *Let Yourself Go* hit number one on the Tower Europe jazz chart and earned stellar reviews; Andrew Vine in the *Yorkshire Post* called the album "faultless and exhilarating," as well as "by far the best thing she has yet recorded." In addition to recording *Let Yourself Go,* Kent also sang on Tomlinson's solo project *Only Trust Your Heart,* guested several times that year with the Humphrey Lyttelton Band, and appeared in the weekly BBC radio series *Live From London,* hosted by Simon Fanshawe.

Selected discography

Close Your Eyes, Candid, 1997.
The Tender Trap, Candid, 1998.
Let Yourself Go, Candid, 1999.

Sources

Periodicals

Arizona Republic, February 4, 1999, p. 38.
Associated Press, June 3, 1999.
Billboard, November 1, 1997; January 30, 1999.
Downbeat, September 1999, p. 29.
Jazz Journal, October 1998; October 1999.
Jazz Rag, November 1999.
Jazz Review, October 1999.
Jazz Times, May 1999.
Jazz UK, July/August 1997.
Jazzwise, June 1997.
Mojo, August 1998.
Repertoire, March 1999.
St. Paul Pioneer Press, October 12, 1997.
Tablet, October 1999.
Times (London), July 21, 1998; September 21, 1999.
United Press International, May 4, 1999.
USA Today, September 19, 1997.
Variety, April 19, 1999.
Yorkshire Press, November 24, 1999.

Online

Artists Only! Records, http://www.artistsonly.com/stacey.htm (January 20, 2000).
Candid Records, http://www.candidrecords.com/staceykent.htm (January 20, 2000).
Stacey Kent, http://members.aol.com/staceykent (January 20, 2000).

—*Laura Hightower*

Lambert, Hendricks and Ross

Vocal group

Lambert, Hendricks and Ross were one of the most respected, popular, and innovative vocal groups of the jazz era. They developed a singing style, known as "vocalese," to a level of complexity previously unknown and revolutionized jazz singing in the process. They influenced a wide range of vocalists from vocal groups of the seventies and eighties, such as Manhattan Transfer and the Pointer Sisters, to individual singers like Joni Mitchell and Bette Midler. No one, however, has matched their brilliance or imagination. Almost 40 years after the group broke up, Jon Hendricks commented to Lloyd Sachs of the *Chicago Sun Times*, "We were so new, so far ahead of our time. The entertainment world has not caught up to us yet."

Born a minister's son in Toledo, Ohio, Jon Hendricks started singing when he was seven years old in the church choir run by his mother. By the time he was a teenager, he was singing professionally under the name Little Johnny Hendricks, and was exposed to cutting-edge jazz at an early age. The big bands called on his parents whenever they came through Toledo. More

Photograph by Ken Franckling. Corbis. Reproduced by permission.

For the Record . . .

Members include **Jon Hendricks** (born in 1921 in Toledo, OH; married, wife, Judith; daughters, Michelle and Aria; son Eric), vocals; **Dave Lambert** (born 1917, died 1966), vocals; **Annie Ross** (born 1930; one daughter), vocals.

Lambert teamed with Buddy Stewart resulting in hit "What's This?" mid-1940s; Hendricks teamed with Lambert to record for Avalon Records, early 1950s; Ross wrote and recorded "Twisted" for Prestige Records, mid-1950s; Lambert, Hendricks, & Ross record *Sing A Song Of Basie* for ABC Paramount, 1957; Lambert, Hendricks, & Ross signed with Columbia Records, 1959; Ross left group and was replaced first with Annie Moss, then with Yolande Bavan, 1962; Hendricks left group, 1964; Lambert died in car crash, 1966; Hendricks and Ross reunited briefly with Bruce Scott, 1985; Hendricks and Ross reunited as a duo, 1999.

Addresses: *Record company*—Columbia Records, 2100 Colorado Avenue, Santa Monica, CA 90404.

significantly, when he was 14, Hendricks began singing regularly with another resident of Toledo, piano great Art Tatum. Because of that experience, "modern harmony was no problem for me...," Hendricks told Bob Blumenthal of the *Boston Globe*. "When I first sat in with Bird, he said, 'Where'd you learn those changes?' "

Hendricks began writing his own lyrics early on, mostly R&B songs in the style of Louis Jordan. He experienced two epiphanies after World War II: the first was hearing the recordings of Buddy Stewart and Dave Lambert on Keynote Records, work that took scat singing into the bebop era. The second ear-opener was hearing King Pleasure's recording of "Moody's Mood for Love." The song was an early example of vocalese, in which words were written for an instrumental solo recorded by another artist. King Pleasure's song, for example, put words to a solo previously recorded by James Moody. So impressed was Hendricks, he stopped writing R&B and took to writing his own vocalese numbers, beginning with the solos from Woody Herman's "Four Brothers." When Avalon Records offered him a contract and asked who he wanted to record with, Hendricks never hesitated: Dave Lambert.

Dave Lambert was a Boston native, who did a bewildering variety of jobs before becoming a professional singer, including tree surgeon and parachute jumper. In the mid-1940s, he sang with Gene Krupa's band where he met his first recording partner Buddy Stewart. The two had a hit with "What's This?" one of the first bop vocal records. Hendricks' lyrics impressed Lambert, and they decided to work together right away. Their recording of "Four Brothers" for Avalon was not a hit, but it got them noticed by Decca Records, one of the majors labels of the day. They re-recorded the song, and again it seemed to flop. But the flip side, "Cloudburst," based on a saxophone solo by Wardell Gray, became a number one hit in England. Creed Taylor, a producer at ABC-Paramount was interested in the project, the group's vocalese versions of Count Basie tunes. Hendricks wrote lyrics to four songs and Lambert arranged them for a large group of singers. When they got the singers into the studio, Lambert and Hendricks discovered they had a problem: the singers could sing but they couldn't swing; they couldn't reproduce the special feelof Basie's band. Only one singer seemed to have it, a Scottish singer-actress named Annie Ross.

Ross had lived in Los Angeles since she was four, had performed in some early Our Gang comedies, and had sung on occasion with Paul Whiteman's Orchestra. She knew her jazz as well. "The first record I was given was Ella Fitzgerald's 'A-Tisket, A-Tasket,' " Ross told Blumenthal, "and the rhythm was just so incredible. I didn't know what the style was called; I just knew that was the way I wanted to sing. My aunt was Ella Logan, a vocalist who veered toward modern jazz, so it didn't seem that complicated to me." As an adult, she sang in Lionel Hampton's band, and in the fifties moved to Europe where she worked with musicians like James Moody and Kenny Clarke. "They would play chords for me and say, 'OK, sing the chords down.'" she told Don Heckman of the *Los Angeles Times*. "I always had a good ear, but they introduced me to different chord changes that were going on at the time that just opened up a whole new world for me." In the early 1950s she began writing her own vocalese lyrics and recording the results for Prestige. One of them was "Twisted," the story of a self-minded crazy woman sane enough to outfox her psychiatrist, which was based on a Wardell Gray solo.

Lambert and Hendricks had found Ross, but it looked like their Basie project was in big trouble. They had spent $1,250 on a chorale group that couldn't sing jazz, were in the studio with nothing to show for it, and were convinced they had gotten their producer fired. At the last minute, Lambert came up with what then sounded like a crazy idea. The three of them used overdubbing to sing *all* the vocal parts themselves. Taylor thought the plan was insane, but agreed to sneak them into the studio late in the evening when no one was around. In one session, between midnight and six in the morning, they recorded all the tracks for the album *Sing A Song Of Basie*. From the first playback of the record they knew they pulled off something remarkable. The record was an instant hit, and within months Lambert, Hendricks and Ross were the most popular singing group in jazz. There was a magical chemistry between the three singers: "I couldn't believe anybody could be as quintessentially hip as Annie," Hendricks told Blumenthal. "I'd give her a solo, she'd go off in a corner and learn it within 30 minutes. And Dave could arrange faster than anyone I've ever met. We were all like-minded.... I'm convinced that we were not put together by man. We were ordained."

All three wrote lyrics for the group, but most were done by Hendricks. He explained the process of composing vocalese to Marc Fisher of the *Washington Post*: "It's like translating a novel. You listen to the notes again and again and find the words that make the closest sounds in English. And then you find a story to link the words. The title of the song gives you the subject matter and then each horn becomes a character, commenting on his place in the drama." Brilliant songs like "Cottontail"—the Peter Rabbit story set to a Duke Ellington arrangement—and "Charleston Alley" show how preternaturally gifted Hendricks was as a vocalese writer.

They recorded three LPs for smaller labels in the latter half of the 1950s. In 1959, they were signed by Columbia, and their first Columbia record was their masterpiece. It was so good that when Columbia re-released it, unchanged, in the 1970s, they called it simply *Lambert, Hendricks and Ross' Greatest Hits*. It includes showstoppers like "Charleston Alley," "Gimme That Wine," "Everybody's Boppin'," and "Summertime," along with re-recorded versions of their pre-Lamber, Hendricks and Ross hits "Cloudburst" and "Twisted." They recorded two more albums forColumbia, *Lambert, Hendricks and Ross Sing Ellington*, and *High Flying*.

In 1962, Annie Ross left the group because of health and personal problems. Lambert and Hendricks attempted to carry on with other singers, first with Annie Moss, then with Yolande Bavan. But the reconstituted group didn't click, at least not for Hendricks. In 1964, he left. "I walked away because I became very disenchanted," Hendricks told John S. Wilson of the *New York Times*. "I had been with Dave and Annie when they were at their peak. When you work with someone like Annie and you write a part for her and she sings it right back to you and it's tremendous, you didn't have to worry about how it was going to sound. It was just extraordinary. But after Annie left, I found it was hard to get the sound that I wanted. I guess everybody got tired. There wasn't the fire that I felt ought to be in it."

Dave Lambert died in an automobile accident in 1966. Jon Hendricks pursued a solo career and Annie Ross went back to acting. They reunited for a short time in 1985, with Bruce Scott singing Dave Lambert's parts. Critics liked the group, but Hendricks and Ross didn't. They both felt it was disrespectful to Lambert's memory to have another singer singing for him. When they reunited again in 1999, it was as a duo, with Hendricks' guitarist Paul Meyers playing the third part when Hendricks or Ross couldn't cover it themselves. Age had affected both voices, reducing their range and slowing down the old rapid fire performance style. But the savoir faire and swing was there in full measure, ready to influence a new generation of vocalists.

Selected discography

Sing A Song Of Basie, ABC, 1957.
Sing Along With Basie, Roulette, 1958.
The Swingers, Pacific Jazz, 1959.
The Hottest New Group in Jazz, Columbia, 1959.
Lambert, Hendricks and Ross Sing Ellington, Columbia.
High Flying with Lambert, Hendricks and Ross, Columbia.
Twisted: The Best Of, Sony/Rhino.
The Hottest New Group In Jazz, Columbia, 1996 (includes all three Columbia LPs).
Lambert, Hendricks and Ross, Giants of Jazz, 1998.

Sources

Boston Globe, January 8, 1999.
Chicago Sun-Times, February 3, 1999.
Christian Science Monitor, September 9, 1985.
Los Angeles Times, July 23, 1998; November 4, 1999.
New York Times, April 2, 1982.
Washington Post, January 14, 2000.

—*Gerald E. Brennan*

Fred Lane

Bible Belt Surrealist

In 1988, a mysterious album appeared in record stores. At first glance, *Car Radio Jerome* was full of silly nonsense with songs like "Upper Lip Of A Nostril Man," "The Man With The Foldback Ears," and "Hittite Hot Shot." Listening to it though, one discovered darker undertones in songs like "White Woman," which became downright ominous in "Car Radio Jerome." By the time the album wrapped up, the "French Toast Man" was selling kids tasty goodies so rank that rats dragged it out of garbage pails and keeled over dead. In the last cut, a clinically depressed relative of Elvis croons his weepy ballad of woe "Pneumatic Eyes"—and blows himself up. The records ends with a hand grenade going off. Whether one loved, loathed or *feared* it, everyone had more or less the same question: What kind of human being had perpetrated *Car Radio Jerome?* It was attributed to Fred Lane and the Hittite Hot Shots. But who were they? No one had ever heard of the group. They never toured, never made videos, never once appeared on Johnny Carson.

In fact, the Reverend Fred Lane did make public appearances, though not many and none outside of Tuscaloosa, Alabama. He first appeared at the *Raudelunas Pataphysical Revue* in 1975, a show mounted by Raudelunas, a group of artists in Tuscaloosa. The origins of their name is as obscure as those of Lane. According to Ron 'Pate, the leader of the band the Debonairs which accompanied Lane at the Revue, "it was an Armenian family name meaning 'moonlight' or 'worship of the moon as a deity.' "

Fred Lane was called upon to emcee the *Pataphysical Revue,* which was a stage show held on the opening night of an exhibit of Raudelunas art at the University of Alabama. He took the stage in a form that would soon be familiar to a few friends and aficionados, if not the country at large: a snap-brim fedora, sunglasses, cut-away tux, boxer shorts, pink socks, and wing-tip brogues, all accented by a few Band-Aids on his face. Lane, backed by Ron 'Pate and the Debonairs, opened the show with a swinging cover of "My Kind of Town (Chicago Is)." After performances by the Blue Denim Deals Without the Sleeves, the Nubis Oxis Quarum doing the music of ancient Rome, the Captains of Industry all-appliance orchestra, and the world premier of Anne LeBaron's "Concerto for Active Frogs," Lane sang "Volare" to close the show.

A recording of the show, entitled *Raudelunas Pataphysical Revue,* was released on the local Say Day Bew label. Despite an original pressing of only 500 copies, the disc had a remarkably wide impact. It was picked up eventually by Recommended Records in England; their catalog read "Nothing I've ever heard is remotely like this." As a result *Raudelunas Pataphysical Revue* sold more in Europe than the United States. Ironically, most orders were from American customers. In 1998, *The Wire,* an English music magazine, named the *Pataphysical Revue* one of the "100 records that set the world on fire." The record has never been completely out-of-print—some 20 copies were still available in the summer of 1999—and tentative plans are afoot for a CD re-release.

The following year, in November of 1976, looking to outdo the *Pataphysical Revue*, the Raudelunatics staged *From The One That Cut You*, a show written by Fred Lane. Lane described it as "a more formal vaudeville of short comedy blackouts and congenial psychotic big band numbers." The inspiration for the show—"And this is actually true as opposed to some other things," Lane said—was a note a friend found that read in part "I hope the pain is through. This is the one that cut you." It was written on paper torn from a garbage bag, wrapped around a hunting knife and stashed under a 1950 Dodge panel truck.

The show featured nearly 20 sketches, which frequently concluded with a death. The Four Dons, a musical group, would then come on stage, put the body into a box and carry it away. A special guest appearance was made by Bill Yeast in a coma. An apparently lifeless body was set on stage and introduced by Lane: "Ladies and gentlemen, let's welcome Bill Yeast! In a coma!" Yeast was

For the Record . . .

Members of Ron 'Pate and the Debonairs include **Omar Bhag-dad-a**, piano, organ; Abdul Ben Camel, acoustic bass; **Doc "Bob" Cashion**, trombone; **Cyd Cherise**, guitar, plataphone, clarinet; **Bill The Kid Dap**, drums, marimba; **Shep Estms** drums, bongos; **Johnny Fent-Lister**, saxophone; **Dick Foote**, saxophone; **Asa Gaston**, drums; **Jane Hathaway** flute, vocals; **Motor Hobson**, saxophone; **Dimples LaCroix**, vocals; **Rev. Dr. Fred Lane**, vocals; **Rip McBoutie**, violin; **Ron Pate**, trombone, guitar; **Danny Pla**, saxophone; **E. Baxter Put**, bass, percussion; **Dean Norman** Scheidt, marimba; **Don "Pretty Boy" Smith**, piano, viola, cornet; **Bill Starsh**, engineering; **Whitey Stencil**, clarinet.

Emceed and performed at *Raudelunas Pataphysical Revue*, 1975; wrote *From The One That Cut You* and *I Talk To My Haircut*, 1975-76; released *From The One That Cut You* on Day Bew Records, 1983; recorded *Car Radio Jerome,* 1985; *Car Radio Jerome* released on Shimmy Disc 1988; *From The One That Cut You*, released on Shimmy Disc 1989.

Addresses: *Record company*—Shimmy Disc, c/o Knitting Factory, 74 Leonard Street, New York, NY 10013.

left to lie on the stage "two minutes probably," `Pate recalled, "but that seemed like a long time!" Later in the show Yeast was brought back onstage as the Debonairs played "Open Up Them Pearly Gates."

Lane composed four original songs for *From The One That Cut You.* The title tune was a demented country-western number. "Oatmeal" was a proto-sea shanty sung during a puppet show. "Danger Is My Beer" was a garage band instrumental led by the Debonairs inimitable guitarist, Cyd Charisse. At the end of the show, Lane encounters 'Pate on a street corner, begging and selling gum balls. The good Reverend beats him up and takes his gum balls. But when he turns his back, 'Pate shoots him. The Debonairs break into the finale, "Fun In The Fundus," one of Lane's "congenial, psychotic big band numbers," Fred sings, and the curtain falls.

Fred Lane wrote another play around the same time, *I Talk To My Haircut.* It was never staged but the songs Lane wrote were released along with those from the earlier show in 1983 on a Day Bew album, *From The One That Cut You.* The story of *I Talk To My Haircut*—what folks remembered of it more than 20 years later—took place in a hotel and involved the bellhop in the title song. That song and "Rubber Room" are two of the most remarkable big band arrangements on vinyl. The first features a brilliant Dick Foote solo, described by 'Pate as "the sound of a tenor sax being strangled." "Rubber Room," a Lane masterpiece, opens with the Reverend crooning over a lounge piano, before he starts to swing: "I'm sick of my job/I'm sick of my wife/I'm sick of your face/I'm sick of this life/Gonna go to the store/Buy me some hardware, my dear." Lane sings of his plans for the hardware while 'Pate and the Debonairs vamp like an asylum orchestra. For a moment one hears people laughing, glasses tinkling, like there's a party going on. Lane doesn't notice it; he's too busy singing off the contents of his shopping bag, or his mind, who knows which. The Debs slide down a few ragged glissandi and Lane wraps up it up: "I'm a happy, sappy son-of-a-gun/ Living in a rubber room!" The Debonairs bray out one final blast.

Lane's last record, *Car Radio Jerome,* was recorded in December of 1985, using the core of the Debonairs, including Cyd Charisse, Don "Pretty Boy" Smith, and Dick Foote, performing as the Hittite Hot Shots. There was no show, no art exhibition behind the album. "We were just trying to get a record company to sign us up," Lane said. It must have worked. Shimmy Disc released it in 1988 and followed it up with the re-release of *From The One That Cut You* the next year. *Car Radio Jerome* was a catalog of styles: big band, country, kid songs, free jazz, spaghetti western, and a little *musique concréte.*

In the summer of 1999, Lane had laid his own basic tracks for a new album to be called *Ice Pick To The Moon.* He had finished about 12 songs for the record, including a gospel number entitled "I'm Gonna Go To Hell When I Die," and he writes new pieces regularly. Asked what his message would be to the youth of America, Lane thought for a moment. "I guess it's like the French Toast Man said," he answered, "evacuate your bowels, eat a hot lunch, and don't be late for school."

Selected discography

Raudelunas Pataphysical Revue, Say Day Bew Records, 1975.

From the One That Cut You, Day Bew Records, 1983, reissued on Shimmy Disc, 1989.

Car Radio Jerome, Shimmy Disc, 1988.

Sources

Telephone interviews with Ron 'Pate and Fred Lane, July-August 1999.

—Gerald E. Brennan

Lyle Lovett

Singer, songwriter, guitar

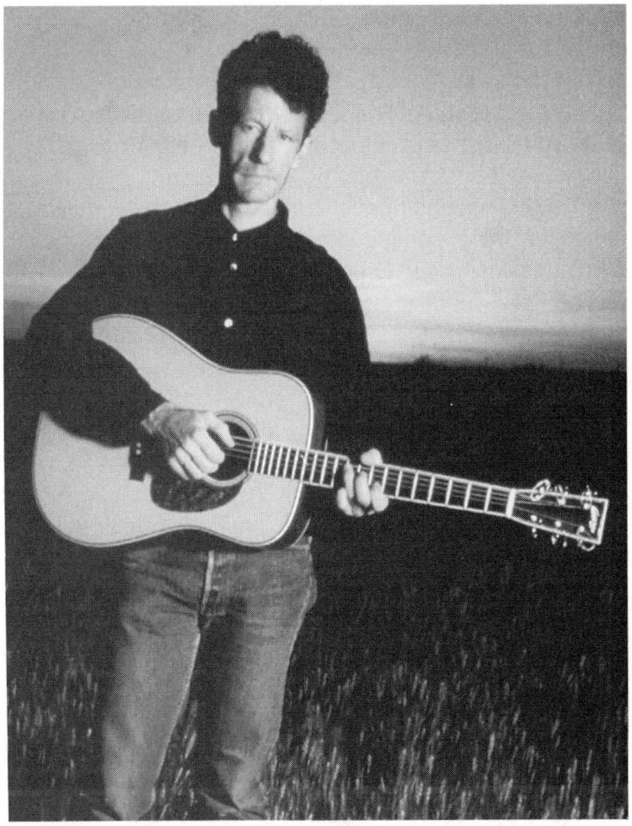

Photography by Will Van Overbeer. Corbis. Reproduced by permission.

Classifying the type of music Lyle Lovett writes and plays is often difficult, if not impossible. Although his music is generally called country, Lovett incorporates jazz, blues, pop, and big band sound into his music to express the stories he tells through his songs. Sam Hurwitt writes in *Salon,* "Lyle Lovett has for the last decade had the dubious honor of being a country singer for people who hate country music." Hurwitt adds that Lovett's music is "a simpler, down-home kind [of country music], with educated forays into jazz and gospel and talking blues."

Lovett's style has little in common with mainstream country music. He has more in common with singers and songwriters of the seventies, such as Guy Clark, Jesse Winchester, Randy Newman, and Townes Van Zandt. These artists, along with Lovett, have the ability of "combining a talent for incisive, witty lyrical detail with an eclectic array or music...." says Stephen Thomas Erlewine in the *All Music Guide.*

Besides the inability to categorize Lyle Lovett into a category or type of music, he is also infamous as one of the few artists who creates all his own material, both melodies and lyrics. Apart from the 1998 release of *Step Inside This House,* Lovett's albums are comprised almost solely of his own original material.

Lovett's First Love

Lovett was born in Klein, Texas, a town located just outside of Houston. He was an only child and was raised on his family's horse ranch. Growing up as an only child on the family's horse farm, Lovett had ample time to pursue his two passions—riding his motorcycle and playing the guitar.

All through high school, Lovett worked at the Cycle Shack in his home town. He competed in local competitions and got his father interested in motorcycling as well. In *Canadian Biker,* Lovett tells Maurine Karagianis, "My dad got involved when I got my first bike and he started riding because I was interested in it. And we still ride together today." Lovett still loves motorcycling and still races from time to time.

Lovett did not consider a musical career until he began writing songs while attending Texas A&M in the late seventies. While studying journalism and German, Lovett performed covers and original songs at local folk festivals, coffee shops, and clubs. As a graduate student in Germany, Lovett continued to write and perform in Europe. He met country musician Buffalo Wayne while in Europe in 1979, who booked Lovett for a show he was

For the Record . . .

Born November 1, 1957, in Klein, TX; son of William and Bernell Lovett. *Education:* graduated from Texas A&M, located in College Station, TX, with a B.A. in journalism and German.

During college, started performing folk music festivals, coffee shops, and clubs; continued to write and perform while a graduate student in Europe; signed with MCA Records, released debut self-titled album, 1986; released defining, acclaimed album *Pontiac,* 1988; released *Lyle Lovett and His Large Band,* 1989; released *Joshua Judges Ruth,* an album embraced by pop and adult alternative audiences, 1990; released country-flavored *The Road to Ensenada,* 1996; released tribute album to Texas singers and songwriters entitled *Step Inside This House,* 1998 all on MCA.

Awards: Grammy Awards for best male country vocal performance for *Lyle Lovett and His Large Band*, 1989; best country album for *Road to Ensenada*, 1996.

Addresses: *Record company*—MCA/Curb Records, 70 Universal City Plaza, Universal City, CA 91608.

organizing in Luxenbourg in 1983. At that time, Lovett was introduced to keyboardist Matt Rollings and guitarist Ray Herndon, both of whom played a central role on some of his later albums. Also, while in Europe, Lovett played with J. David Sloan and the Rogues. Lovett developed a friendship with the Rogues, who he later recruited for his sessions after signing with MCA Records.

Career Beginnings

Lovett did not pursue a musical career in earnest until he returned to the United States in 1983 when he landed a spot in the Mickey Rooney television movie *Bill: On His Own.* The following year, Nanci Griffith, who Lovett had interviewed for a school paper while attending Texas A&M, covered his song "If I were the Woman You Wanted" on her *Once in a Very Blue Moon* album. Lovett also sang on the album as well as her next, *Last of the True Believers.*

Also in 1984, fellow Texas songwriter/singer Guy Clark heard Lovett's demo tape. Liking what he heard, Clark directed the recording to Tony Brown of MCA Records. Brown signed Lovett in 1986 and produced his first three albums.

Later that same year, Lovett released his debut album entitled *Lyle Lovett* which was an immediate hit. Although the album lacked traditional Nashville sounds and included undercurrents of folk, rock, and jazz, five of the album's singles reached the country top 40, including "Cowboy Man" which reached the top ten. Erlrwine wrote, "Despite his strong showing on the country charts, it was clear from the outset that Lovett's musical tastes didn't rely on country, though the genre provided the foundation of his sound." Overall *Lyle Lovett* was a "spectacular debut" stated Daniel Durchholz of *MusicHound Rock.*

Crossed Boundaries

Lovett followed his debut with *Pontiac*, released early in 1988, which truely defined Lovett's ability to reach across the defined boundaries of country and pop/rock music. Although only two of the singles reached the country charts' top 30, Lovett gained "enough new fans in the pop mainstream to guarantee him a strong cult following," reported Erlewine. The bluesy sound of *Pontiac* confirmed that Lovett "was one of country's more offbeat performers," said Hugh Gregory in *The Rough Guide to Rock.*

This reputation was even more defined with the 1989 release of *Lyle Lovett and His Large Band* which won him a Grammy for best male country vocal performance. The album included the additions of guitars, a cellist, a pianist, horns, and gospel-trained backup singer, Francine Reed. Most critics "drooled over Lyle's eclecticism and sense of humor" Gregory recalled. However, his cover of Tammy Wynette's "Stand By Your Man" received a great deal of attention and some criticism from Nashville. The song was later used in the 1993 movie, *The Crying Game.*

In 1990, Lovett moved to Los Angeles where he recorded his next album, *Joshua Judges Ruth.* Although the album was ignored by country radio as a whole, pop audiences embraced the record. Lovett received wide air play on adult alternative radio and the VH-1 cable television network. *Joshua Judges Ruth* reached number 57 on the album charts and went gold.

Lovett reached new-found super stardom in 1993 when he married Julia Roberts, whom he met while making the Robert Altman film, *The Players*, where he made his acting debut. Lovett reached a level of fame he had never experienced before and became a regular in the tabloids and celebrity magazines. Also in 1993, Lovett appeared in another Altman film entitled *Short Cuts*.

Lovett's next album, *I Love Everyboby*, released in 1994, failed to reach gold status. Many critics felt it was not Lovett's best work. For example, Durchholz described the release as "Lovett's only recording made during his brief tenure as Mr. Julia Roberts has its moments of wry humor, but it mostly consists of stale leftovers and trifles...." Other critics received the album with warm reviews, although they admitted it had its problems. One critic in *Fireside* wrote, "The full complement of the eighteen tunes is a little overlong, but as a curio it serves its purpose well." Lovett and Roberts divorced in the spring of 1995, allowing Lovett to retreat from the spotlight to some extent. He spent the remainder of the year touring and writing.

Took a New Road

In 1996, Lovett released *The Road to Ensenada*, his first album since *Pontiac* with a dominant country flavor. Not only did the album peak at 24 on the pop charts, but *The Road to Ensenada* also entered at number four on the country charts. Tha album also won Lovett a Grammy for Best Country Album.

Step Inside This House, released in 1998, marked a significant difference from all of Lovett's previous albums. In the two-disc set, Lovett stepped away from the roll of songwriter to pay homage to fellow Texas singers/songwriters. The collection of songs pays tribute to the artists Lovett feels are among his strongest influences including Townes Van Zant, Michael Martin Murphy, Walter Hyatt, Stephen Fromholtz, and Guy Clark. Although Lovett had considered devoting an album to songs by Texas-based singer/songwriters since he took part in the Nanci Griffith album *Other Voices, Other Rooms*, he was not spurred on to doing the album until the deaths of two of his biggest influences, Townes Van Zandt, who died New Year's Eve 1996 and Walter Hyatt, who died suddenly in the ValuJet airliner crash in Florida in 1996. "That sort of determined the theme of the album really," said Lovett to Michael McCall of *LAUNCH Music*. "It was a difficult year in a lot of ways, and this seemed like the most appropriate way to deal with it."

Although Lovett did not write the songs on the album, he sang them with the same intensity of his own songs. Michael Evans of the *Oregonian* commented, "Equipped with a dry vocal delivery (and a sense of humor), Lovett not only paid ample tribute to such idols as Townes Van Zandt and Guy Clark, but also sang their personal and often provocative story songs as if they were his own." Lovett himself admits he chose songs that had a great influence on him. "It's really a personal list of songs for me," Lovett told Michael McCall. "There was such a long list of songs that I could've done once I started compiling all the Texas songs that mean a lot to me. I lest some witers out that I love, but every one of these songs were favorites of mine long before I ever went to Nashville."

Lovett continued to strive for change with the release of *Live in Texas*, his first live performance which was recorded in San Antonio, Texas. For the recording, Lovett was again joined by his acclaimed large band. Critics raved at Lovett's versitility and ability to record a live album. "Lyle Lovett is one of those rare performers who pretty much sounds exactly the same live in concert as he does in the studio," wrote Mary Jo DiLonardo of *CNN Interactive*. "Because of his stark, unmistakable vocal style, he doesn't require the magic of studio enhancements to make his voice richer or more resonant."

Overall, Lovett continues to have a story to tell. "My music is all about communication," Lovett told Karagianis. "There's always one person that would understand a song better than anybody else ... the songs I write are directed specifically at somebody. So it's really a way to talk to somebody—and I think songs have the added emotional impact of the music to go with what the words are saying, which can be a very powerful thing."

Selected discography

Lyle Lovett, MCA, 1985.
Pontiac, MCA, 1988.
Lyle Lovett and His Large Band, MCA, 1989.
Joshua Judges Ruth, MCA, 1992.
I Love Everybody, Curb, 1994.
The Road to Ensenada, MCA, 1996.
Step Inside This House, MCA, 1998.
Live In Texas, MCA, 1999.

Sources

Books

Graff, Gary and Daniel Durchholz, editors, *MusicHound Rock: The Essential Album Guide,* Visible Ink Press, 1999.

Gregory, Hugh, editor, *The Rough Guide to Rock,* Penguin Books, 1996.

Robbins, Ira A., *Trouser Press Guide to '90s Rock,* Fireside/Simon and Schuster, 1997.

Periodicals

Esquire, May 1994
Oregonian, October 8, 1998.
Washington Post, September 5, 1996.

Online

All Music Guide, wysiwyg://13/http://allmusic.com/c...?UID=10:46:49IAM&p=amg&sql=B4798~C (January 20, 2000).

"Lyle Lovett," *iMusic,Country Showcase*, http://imusic.com/showcase/country/lylelovett.html (December 29, 1999).

"Lyle Lovett," *LAUNCH Music,* http://www.launch.com/music/artist/ArtistContainer/0,2498,true_1016251_Bio_,00.html, 1999 (January 3, 2000).

"Lyle Lovett," *Rolling Stone Press,* http://rollingstone.tunes.com/sections/artists/text/artistgen/asp?afl=ses&LookUpString=949, 1995 (January 3, 2000).

"Lyle Lovett: His First Love Was Motorcycling," *Canadian Biker,* http:www.canadianbiker.com/lyl.html (December 29, 1999).

"Lyle Lovett: Live in Texas," MCA Records, http://www.mcarecords.com/artists/artist.asp?artistid=46 (December 29, 1999).

"Lyle Lovett: Step Inside This House," *LAUNCH Music,* http://www.launch.com/Promotional/lyle_lovett_ft.html (December 29, 1999).

"Review: Lyle Lovett live and large," *CNN.com,* http://www.cnn.com/SHOWBIZ/Music/9906/22/review.lylelovett/, Tuesday, June 22, 1999 (January 3, 2000).

"Thank God, He's a Country Boy," *Salon,* http://www.salon.com/weekly/music960624.html (January 3, 2000)

—Julie Sweet

The Magnetic Fields

Pop band

Essentially, the Magnetic Fields represented the creative output of songwriter, singer, producer, and multi-instrumentalist Stephin Merritt, who, along with various band members, guest musicians on cello, tuba, percussion, vocals, and various other instruments, became the quintessential pop eccentric of the 1990s. In the studio, the Magnetic Fields were almost solely the result of Merritt's efforts, dispatching universally touching albums beginning with 1991's *Distant Plastic Trees* through 1999's *69 Love Songs,* one of the best-reviewed albums that year. In addition to recording, the band also became a popular live act. On the road, Merritt assembled a performance group that usually consisted of himself as lead vocalist and guitarist, as well as a second guitarist, a cellist, and a drummer. As a writer and producer, Merritt concocted through his group "a sort of indie-pop synth-rock," described contributor Richie Unterberger in the *All Music Guide.* While reminiscent of the synthesized sounds of ABBA, Roxy Music, and Joy Division and at first pointed toward the alternative rock enthusiast, Merritt's music nonetheless revealed a warmer, more pop-oriented tone than his predecessors that was in the same breath often compared to the likes of Brian Wilson of the Beach Boys and Phil Spector.

According to Merritt, his life began on a houseboat in St. Thomas, where he was conceived by "barefoot hippies," as quoted by *Village Voice* writer Rob Tannenbaum. Suffering from epilepsy as a baby, he was raised by his mother, an English teacher. Throughout his upbringing and as an adult, Merritt enjoyed a close relationship with his mother. However, he never met his father, an obscure folk singer named Scott Fagan who recorded during the 1960s for RCA and Atlantic Records. Like many single parents, Merritt's mother and her son often had little money. A native of Boston, Massachusetts, Merritt lived in 33 homes in his first 23 years, primarily in the Northeast, as well as in West Berlin, Germany, when his mother was married for a brief time to an Army officer.

Growing up, Merritt was drawn to classic love/pop songs, like those penned and/or recorded by Phil Spector, the Beach Boys, and Burt Bacharach. He was also encouraged by the electronic textures of vintage acts such as the Smiths, Joy Division, ABBA, Kraftwerk, Roxy Music, Brian Eno, and Gary Newman. Borrowing from these styles, Merritt began recording songs with a guitar and synthesizer on his own four-track tape deck from the age of 14. An outcast at school and acknowledged introvert who preferred music and reading to socializing with his classmates, Merritt was threatened with violence on a regular basis in the public schools. To avoid the bullying, as well as the mandatory participation in sports, Merritt enrolled at the Cambridge School of Weston, a preparatory school for bohemian children located near Boston. For the first time, the musically-inclined Merritt felt a sense of belonging. Moreover, his new school's curriculum was heavily influenced by the arts. Thus, Merritt took advantage of the music program, studying theory augmented by a tutor from Boston's Berklee College of Music. "I'm a professional musician because that's what I've had the most success in," he told Tannenbaum, hinting that he was a child prodigy of sorts. "I was told I had promise in several other areas: poetry, acting, science."

Around the same time, Merritt, after watching a television program about tracking junk mail, started devising different spellings of his given first name, Stephen, to reflect the various aspects of his life. The name "Stephin" defined his musical side, and eventually this spelling stuck. During his school years, Merritt also discovered that he was a homosexual. The openly gay musician who at the same time kept his emotions surrounding his sexuality closeted said that he never had to officially come out, however, because all of his friends and his mother knew and told him that he wasn't straight.

After graduating from prep school, Merritt attended college, but his education, he said, was interrupted by a bout with a fatigue virus. An itinerant student, he spent some time at New York University (NYU) Film School, attended art school briefly in Boston, and took courses

For the Record . . .

Members include **Susan Anway** (left band in 1992; former member of the early-1980s Boston, MA, punk band V), vocals; **Johnny Blood**, tuba; **Sam Davol** (a Chinese American legal aid lawyer), cello, flute; **Claudia Gonson** (Harvard College graduate; Ph.D. from City University in New York), drums, percussion, keyboards, ukulele, vocals, band manager; **Stephin Merritt** (born Stephen Merritt in Boston, MA; son of an English teacher and folk singer Scott Fagan; attended NYU and Harvard Extension School), vocals, guitar, songwriter; **John Woo** (a Korean American graphic designer), guitar.

Merritt formed band in 1989 in Boston, MA; released debut album *Distant Trees,* 1991; signed with Merge Records, 1993; released breakthrough album *69 Love Songs,* 1999.

Addresses: *Record company*—Merge Records, P.O. Box 1235, Chapel Hill, NC 27514.

for several years at Harvard Extension School, where he studied film and the history of the built environment, a discipline that applies semiotic theories to industrialized cultures. However, Merritt never earned his degree in that field, falling short of just one exam in statistics in order to graduate.

Although Merritt had recorded songs on his own since his early teens, he would not complete his first album until the emergence of the Magnetic Fields. By that time, he was well into his twenties. Merritt initiated his musical career first in New York City, where he was involved with the still developing club-kid scene. From there, he returned to his birthplace, founding what would become the Magnetic Fields in 1989. Over the years, Merritt's outfit would also include vocalist Susan Anway; drummer, percussionist, keyboardist, and longtime band manager Claudia Gonson; Gonson's college mate Sam Davol; another of Gonson's college mates guitarist John Woo; and tuba player Johnny Blood.

Merritt's first two albums with the Magnetic Fields, 1991's *Distant Plastic Trees*—which yielded the band's first college radio sensation "100,000 Fireflies," a song later covered by several groups including Superchunk—and 1992's *The Wayward Bus* featured Anway on vocals; Merritt, who called himself a terrible singer in his early recording days, had not yet felt secure enough about his own singing. Wendy Smith, a cover artist for Weekend, an early-1980s alternative band that recorded for the Rough Trade label, designed the album art for both releases. For the first record, Merritt disclosed his tales of lost or unconsummated love through songs about lust ("Railroad Boy") and self-loathing ("Falling in Love With the Wolfboy"). The songwriter also utilized pop structures from the classics he held so dear for tracks such as "Smoke Signals." At first issued only in Britain on Red Flame Records and in Japan on RCA Victor, *Distant Plastic Trees* was included on *The Wayward Bus* on the band's own label, PoPuP. In 1995, both albums, minus one track, were reissued as an official co-billed twofer by Merge Records.

After Anway left the Magnetic Fields to relocate to Arizona, Merritt, singing in a "splendid baritone croon," remarked David Sprague in the *Trouser Press Guide to '90s Rock,* took over the vocal duties for 1993's *The House of Tomorrow,* a seven-inch EP issued on the Feel Good All Over label. This release led reviewers to compare his voice to that of Morrissey (formerly of the Smiths), particularly for the song "Love Goes Home to Paris in the Spring." The band followed this in 1994 with the low-key effort *Holiday* CD, also on Feel Good All Over. Highlights from this album, which balanced innocence with decadence included "Deep Sea Driving Suit," "Desert Island," "Take Ecstasy With Me," and "Strange Powers."

Signing with Merge in the fall of 1993, the Magnetic Fields in 1994 also released an ill-advised, country-flavored album entitled *The Charm of the Highway Strip.* Fortunately, Merritt returned to his pop roots for 1995's *Get Lost,* an intricately layered effort that added new instrumentation such as ukulele (played by Gonson), banjo, and bass guitar. Here, Merritt revealed his new-wave sensibilities with "The Desperate Things You Made Me Do" and "You and Me and the Moon," as well as his feelings of cynicism in "Why I Cry" and "The Dreaming Moon." That same year, Merritt released the album *Wasp's Nest* with one of his numerous side projects called the 6ths. Other members of this outfit, performing songs written by Merritt, included Sebadoh's Lou Barlow, Unrest frontman Mark Robinson, Amelia Fletcher of the band Heavenly, Yo La Tengo's Georgia Hubley, Robert Scott of the Bats, and Helium's Mary Timony. In 1996, the Magnetic Fields on Feel Good All Over released the album *The House of Tomorrow,* which included songs from the like-titled EP. Merge reissued this CD, packaged along with *Holiday,* in 1999.

That same year, the Magnetic Fields returned with their breakthrough album, *69 Love Songs,* released as both a trio of separate CDs and as a limited-edition three-disc box set. According to Merritt, no one believed he would be able to write 69 good love songs. "It was clear they were humoring me," he said to Tannenbaum. Determined to complete such a daunting task, Merritt spent a full year developing the songs, "working whenever I was awake," he added. "I had no life. I sat around all day writing songs. Which is often what I do all day long, anyway." Some of those songs included primal accounts of lust ("Underwear"), romance ("The Luckiest Guy on the Lower East Side"), and heartbreak ("I Don't Want to Get Over You"). *69 Love Songs* earned stellar reviews in 1999; *Spin* magazine, for example, listed the effort as one of the best albums of the year. After the success of Merritt's *69 Love Songs,* the songwriter began work on his next project: writing a musical with novelist Daniel Handler.

Selected discography

Distant Plastic Trees, (U.K) Red Flame, (Japan) RCA Victor, 1991; reissued, Merge, 1995.
The Wayward Bus, PoPuP, 1992; reissued, Merge, 1995.
The House of Tomorrow, (seven-inch EP), Feel Good All Over, 1993.
The Charm of the Highway Strip, Merge, 1994.
Holiday, Feel Good All Over, 1994.
Get Lost, Merge, 1995.
(With the 6ths) *Wasp's Nest,* London, 1995.
The House of Tomorrow, (CD), Feel Good All Over, 1996.
69 Love Songs, Merge, 1999.
The House of Tomorrow and *Holiday,* Merge, 1999.

Sources

Books

Robbins, Ira A., editor, *Trouser Press Guide to '90s Rock,* Fireside/Simon and Schuster, 1997.

Periodicals

Boston Globe, December 31, 1999.
Los Angeles Times, December 12, 1999; December 26, 1999.
Magnet, April/May 1999.
Melody Maker, February 20, 1999.
New York Times, October 22, 1999; January 5, 2000.
Rolling Stone, October 14, 1999; November 25, 1999.
USA Today, November 26, 1999.
Village Voice, September 14, 1999; December 7, 1999.
Washington Post, October 10, 1999.

Online

All Music Guide, http://www.allmusic.com (February 27, 2000).
"The Magnetic Fields," *Merge Records Band Bios,* http://merge,catalogue.com/biomag.html (February 27, 2000).

—Laura Hightower

Johnny Mandel

Composer, arranger, conductor, producer

Corbis. Reproduced by permission.

Musicians within bands have often developed into important arrangers, and Johnny Mandel is a classic example as he played trombone and bass trumpet, eventually leading him to arrange for Artie Shaw and many other top band leaders. Mandel's parents, Alfred and Hannah Mandel, migrated from their native Chicago to New York in 1920 because his mother was an aspiring opera singer and his father a garment manufacturer. When the Depression came, the family moved to California but returned to New York City after the death of Mandel's father in 1937.

When the Mandel family returned to New York City, they temporarily moved into the Essex House Hotel. It was there Johnny met Marshall Robbins, son of music publisher Jack Robbins. It was the height of the swing era. Mandel recounted, "There were bands in all the hotels, theaters and night clubs, and they were good ones. At night, Jack would take us around to hear all the big bands. It was the treat of all times, the ultimate Disneyland for me." After listening to big band music as well as the jazz music his mother regularly aired on her radio in their home, 12-year-old Mandel decided he wanted to become a music arranger and at the same time advance his musical career by playing a wind instrument he excelled at.

He began his career in 1943 playing trumpet in Joe Venuti's Orchestra in New York City. In 1944 he joined Billie Rogers' band and toured with a number of popular bands including the big bands of Jimmy Dorsey, Georgie Auld, Henry Jerome, and Alvino Rey as a trombonist. In the early 1940s, renown band leader Alvino Rey utilized the arrangements of Mandel and other future stars describing his band as "the best band I ever had." In 1944, big band leader Boyd Raeburn enlisted Mandel to make new arrangements and contribute new scores. Another New York area band leader, Henry Jerome, became displeased with his arrangements and the quality of his band. He hired several new musicians and singers along with 19-year-old Johnny Mandel to write new scores at Child's Paramount Restaurant in Times Square in New York City. Two of Mandel's band mates were tenor saxophonists Alan Greenspan, who currently heads the United States Federal Reserve, and Leonard Garment, a key lawyer for President Richard Nixon. Mandel said, "We were always paid on time because Alan handled the payroll." Jerome felt it was his finest orchestra.

Mandel also played trombone in Buddy Rich's first band in the mid-1940s and was considered one of the finest sidemen of that period. Subsequent stints with Rich occurred in 1947 and 1948. In 1948 he wrote the big band composition "Not Really the Blues" for Woody Herman, and it became his first important arrangement. In the late

For the Record . . .

Born John Alfred Mandel, November 23, 1925, in New York, NY; son of a garment manufacturer, Alfred, and Hannah (Hart-Rubin) Mandel, an aspiring opera singer; married Martha Blaner, 1970; children: Marrisa, born 1976. *Education:* Attended the New York Military Academy on a band scholarship, where he formed a small jazz band; attended Manhattan School of Music and Juilliard School of Music, New York City, where he studied symphonic forms and writing for a symphony orchestra; also studied with Stefan Wolpe and Ben Alexander.

Arranged musical scores for many motion pictures and television productions including Sid Caesar's *Your Show of Shows*, *Markham*, *General Electric Theater*, Andy Williams' NBC variety show, and *Evita Peron*; crafted musical arrangements for such singing stars as Gogi Grant, Michael Jackson, Frank Sinatra, Peggy Lee, Diana Krall, Natalie Cole, Barbra Streisand, Ray Charles, Michael Bolton, Barry Manilow, Manhattan Transfer, Tony Bennett, Dick Haymes, Nancy Wilson, Vic Damone, and Andy Williams; well-known songs include "Emily," "Close Enough for Love," Hershey Bar," "Suicide Is Painless (theme from *M*A*S*H*)," and "A Time For Love."

Awards: Academy Award, *The Shadow of Your Smile*; five Grammy Awards; American Society of Composers, Authors and Publishers Henry Mancini Award, 1997.

Addresses: *Home*—Johnny Mandel, 28946 Cliffside Dr., Malibu, CA 90265.

1940s he joined the music department at radio station WMGM where he wrote arrangements for the staff orchestra and then joined band leader Elliot Lawrence because he was considered one of the finest young songwriters and one of the best jazz arrangers in the country. Mandel remained with Lawrence through 1953, supplying many arrangements. Between June and November of 1953 he traveled with Count Basie's band. He said working with Count Basie was one of the most enjoyable experiences of his life and commented, "I couldn't wait to get to work every night." He then joined Zoot Sim's band in Los Angeles playing the bass trumpet at the Haig. He also worked in Las Vegas writing dance sections working with Gordon Jenkins at the Tropicana Hotel and others.

Having moved to Hollywood, in 1957 Mandel composed part of the score for the Dean Martin and Jerry Lewis motion picture *You're Never Too Young*. This was followed a year later by his musical film score for the Susan Heyward blockbuster motion picture *I Want to Live,* marking the first time that jazz had been successfully integrated into a musical score. Mandel's reputation as an arranger continued to soar as a result of his contribution to this film. He has provided music for more than 30 films including *M*A*S*H, The Russians Are Coming! The Russians Are Coming!*, and Academy Award-winning music for *The Sandpiper.*

In the late 1950s, Frank Sinatra left Capitol Records and opened his own recording company. In 1961 Sinatra's Reprise label was born during a period when the entertainer had been moving more and more in the direction of a jazz oriented style. Mandel was considered brilliant by many jazz musicians and enthusiasts and was one of several arrangers and conductors who had gained a highly respected reputation during an era of what was then called "The West Coast Jazz." For Sinatra's first Reprise album release, *Ring a Ding Ding!,* Mandel was chosen as the arranger. Wide respect by singers, orchestra leaders, and even Paul Weston—one of the finest arrangers of popular music of the twentieth century—helped Mandel secure the job of arranger and producer for Jo Stafford's album *Jo + Jazz.*

Mandel was commissioned to write the score for the 1965 motion picture *The Sandpiper,* starring Elizabeth Taylor and Richard Burton. When Mandel played the melody for Johnny Mercer with the intention of Mercer writing the lyric for the film's major song, Mercer felt the composition sounded too much like Hoagy Carmichael's "New Orleans" and turned Mandel down. Mandel then co-authored the song with Paul Francis Webster, an already accomplished award winning lyricist. Their collaboration resulted in the 1966 Academy Award and Grammy Award-winning song "The Shadow of Your Smile," performed by Tony Bennett. Before the Academy Award ceremonies, Mercer expressed his regret that he had not worked on Mandel's melody, and every time he saw Mandel later, he would remark how foolish he had been for turning him down. Mandel said, "Carmichael once commented that when he heard the song that he never associated it with his composition." Bennett later went on to record two more Mandel and Webster compositions—"A Time for Love," which was also nominated for an Academy Award, and "A Lonely Place."

In 1965, Mandel mailed a copy of a melody he had written for the motion picture *The Russians Are Coming! The Russians Are Coming!* to renowned vocalist and lyricist Peggy Lee. After the picture was assembled, Mandel took Lee to the Director's Guild for a preview. Their song,

"The Shining Sea," had been interpolated into the movie, and her lyric described the film of a young couple walking on the beach as though Lee intuitively had known the film's script. It fit the scene with such accurate detail, Lee was amazed at the finished product.

The *Theme for M*A*S*H (Suicide is Painless)* wasn't intended to be the theme of the motion picture. It was written in 1970 for the "Last Supper" scene and was actually intended to be played by one of the actors. It had to be written before the movie was actually shot. Director Robert Altman hired Mandel to write the music and indicated he wanted something that was funny and kind of stupid to accompany this particular scene. After several days, Altman came back and said "I can't write anything that ridiculous but all is not lost." His 14-year-old son, Mike Altman, was enlisted and wrote the lyrics in five minutes to which Mandel later added the melody. Later when the movie was being edited, Mandel heard the song being played over the film's title in the helicopter scene and protested, saying, "It was the stupidest thing I have ever seen" and angrily walked out insisting it didn't fit. The studio ignored his protest. The song was not only heard all over the world in the award-winning comedy television series, but it brought Mandel his highest copyright revenues. He later remarked, "I'm glad I lost that battle."

Since 1989, Mandel has actively served on the Board of Directors of the American Society of Composers, Authors and Publishers (ASCAP), an organization he has been a member of since 1956. Since 1944, Mandel has made musical contributions as an arranger, producer, orchestra leader, and musician for many singing notables in the entertainment business from Nat King Cole to Michael Jackson. He remains active, continuing to provide musical compositions that help him satisfy the ambitions he has had since he was a 12-year-old boy.

Selected discography

Film scores

You're Never Too Young, 1957.
I Want to Live, 1958.
The Third Voice, 1959.
The Americanization of Emily, 1964.
The Sandpiper, 1965.
The Russians Are Coming!, The Russians Are Coming!, 1966.
An American Dream, 1966.
Point Blank, 1967.
*M*A*S*H,* 1970.
The Last Detail, 1973.
Freaky Friday, 1976.
Agatha Being There, 1979.
The Baltimore Bullet, 1980.
Deathtrap, 1982.
The Verdict, 1982.
Caddy Shack, 1988.
Prince of Tides, 1991.

As Arranger/Producer

The Artistry of Tony Bennett, Forty Years, Columbia 46886.
Natalie Cole-Unforgettable-Special Edition, Elektra, 61243.
Four Freshman, Still Fresh, Gold Label 80052.
Diana Krall, When I Look in Your Eyes, Verve 03042.
Peggy Lee, The Peggy Lee Songbook-There'll Be Another Spring, Musicmasters 60249.
Peggy Lee, Cross Country Blues, Blue Note 20088.
Barry Manilow, Manilow Sings Sinatra, Arista 19033.
Frank Sinatra, Complete Reprise, Reprise 47045.
Jo Stafford, Jo + Jazz, Corinthian 180.
Andy Williams, Greatest Hits, Columbia 9979.

Sources

Books

Bennett, Tony, *The Good Life,* Pocket Books, 1998.
Feather, Leonard, *The Encyclopedia of Jazz*, Horizon Press, 1960.
Gammond, Peter, *The Oxford Companion to Popular Music,* Oxford University Press, 1993.
Kaplan, Mike, *Variety, Who's Who in Show Business*, Garland Publishing Co., 1983.
Lax, Roger and Frederick Smith, *The Great Song Thesaurus,* Oxford University Press, 1989.
Maltin, Leonard, *Movie and Video Guide 1995,* Penguin Books Ltd., 1994.
Musiker, Reuben and Naomi Musiker, *Conductors and Composers of Popular Orchestral Music*, Greenwood Press, 1998.
Shaw, Arnold, *Sinatra: 20th Century Romantic*, Holt, Rhinehart and Winston, Inc., 1968.
Simon, George T., *The Big Bands*, The Macmillan Co., 1967.

Online

"Johnny Mandel," *All Music Guide*, http://www.allmusic.com (January 2000).
"Johnny Mandel," *American Society of Composers, Authors and Publishers*, http://www.ascap.com (January 2000).

Additional information was obtained through an interview with Johnny Mandel on October 13, 1999.

—*Francis D. McKinley*

Mercury Rev

Experimental pop band

Photograph by Rune Hellestad. Corbis. Reproduced by permission.

Although the members of Mercury Rev initially came together to record soundtracks for experimental student films and to make tapes for friends, the band from rural upstate New York would become one of America's most successful experimental groups. Mercury Rev's 1991 debut became a favorite in Great Britain. Many established publications in Britain, including *Melody Maker* and the *Independent,* hailed the album as one of the year's best. Although personal conflicts plagued the band from the onset, Mercury Rev survived the odds, recording a list of acclaimed albums throughout the 1990s, including 1998's *Deserter's Songs,* the group's best-selling effort.

"We've always tried to achieve something that's timeless with our music," Mercury Rev's lead singer and guitarist Jonathan Donahue told Jud Cost in a 1999 interview with *Magnet* magazine. "Where if you hear it, you would say, 'I have no idea when that record was made. It doesn't sound like something from 1998.'" More than this, however, *Deserter's Songs* was a triumph of will, a comeback of sorts for a band that was at one time virtually defunct because of substance abuse, staggering debt, and emotional warfare. "Because of the state we were in," guitarist Sean "Grasshopper" Mackiowiak revealed in 1999 to *Rolling Stone* writer David Fricke, "we wanted the album to be emotional, to have that longing and hopefulness, but also catch the desperation."

Mercury Rev formed in 1989 in Buffalo, New York, as a wildly chaotic, avant-pop sextet. Originally, the psychedelically-inclined group consisted of vocalist David Baker; vocalist, guitarist, and primary songwriter Jonathan Donahue; guitarist and clarinetist Grasshopper (born Sean Mackiowiak); flutist Suzanne Thorpe (who also played other woodwind instruments); bassist Dave Fridmann; and drummer Jimmy Chambers. Personality conflicts plagued the group in the beginning, and unlike most young bands, the members interacted with one another as little as necessary. Fridmann, who stopped touring with the band in 1994 but stayed on as a studio member, engineer, and producer, held doubts immediately. "I felt it was never a good thing for the band to tour," he admitted to Cost. "Most bands get together because they're friends. We just weren't that group of people. Being together weeks on end wasn't good for us. It made us not like each other."

Doors Opened for Mercury Rev

Thus, never intending early on to spend the next decade making music together, Mercury Rev's first recordings evolved simply as a means of creating soundtracks for their individual student films and to occasionally make

For the Record . . .

Members include **David Baker** (left band in 1993), vocals; **Jimmy Chambers**, drums; **Jonathan Donahue**, vocals, guitar; **Dave Fridmann**, bass, producer, engineer; **Grasshopper** (born Sean Mackiowiak), guitar, clarinet; **Jeff Mercel**, drums; **Jayson Russo**, guitar; **Justin Russo**, keyboards; **Adam Snyder**, organ; **Suzanne Thorpe**, flute, woodwind instruments.

Formed band in 1989 in Buffalo, NY; debuted with *Yerself Is Steam,* 1991; released *Boces,* toured with Lollapalooza, 1993; released "comeback" album *Deserter's Songs,* 1998.

Addresses: *Record company*—V2 Records (BMG) 14 E. 4th St., New York City, NY 10012, phone: (212) 320-8500, fax: (212) 320-8600, website: http://www.V2music.com. *Website*—Mercury Rev official website: http://www.mercuryrev.net.

tapes for friends. However, encouraged to expand their musical pursuits by academic mentor Tony Conrad, a fabled minimalist composer and multimedia artist who had performed with John Cale, LaMonte Young, and Faust, Mercury Rev started to take shape. Baker, Grasshopper, and Thorpe had all taken classes with Conrad at the University of Buffalo. "The most important thing we learned from him was that anything counts," Grasshopper recalled, as quoted in a 1993 *Rolling Stone* feature by Glenn Kenny. The article appeared after the band was removed mid-performance from the Lollapalooza tour in Denver, Colorado, for playing too loud.

Meanwhile, Fridmann was enrolled in the musical engineering program at SUNY-Fredonia, some 50 miles to the southwest of Buffalo, giving him free access to the college's studio from midnight until six in the morning. Here, the band recorded their first demo tape as Mercury Rev. "Every time Jon [Donahue] would come into the studio, whatever name was on the track sheet the last time was scratched out and some other name would be there instead," Fridmann told Cost, revealing how the group came up with an official name. "Eventually 'Mercury Rev' appeared—I'm not even sure that name came from us—and it kept staying." Later on, according to the band's website, the name was attributed to various sources, from an imaginary Russian ballet dancer to a sharp rise in temperature, to a revved-up automobile engine.

At the same time Mercury Rev began recording, Donahue worked as a local concert promoter. Following a scheduled Butthole Surfers gig, he befriended the supporting act, a band called the Flaming Lips from Oklahoma. Initiating a working relationship with the band, Donahue soon joined the Flaming Lips tour as a guitar technician and soundman. Ultimately, under the alias "Dingus," Donahue worked his way up to lead guitarist for the Flaming Lips and recorded with the band on 1990's *In a Priest Driven Ambulance,* an album co-produced by Fridmann. Fridmann went on to produce other albums for the Flaming Lips, including *Hit to Death in the Future Head* in 1992, and the four-CD set *Zaireeka* in 1997.

Debuted with *Yerself Is Steam*

Although the future of Mercury Rev, with members scattered across the country and involved in various other projects, appeared uncertain, an early demo tape came into the hands of officials at the Rough Trade label in Britain, who approached Baker about signing the band. After securing the record deal, Mercury Rev entered the studio to record their debut album, *Yerself Is Steam,* at the same time Fridmann and Donahue continued to work with the Flaming Lips. First released in 1991, *Yerself Is Steam* was largely overlooked in the United States, but became a hit in the United Kingdom. Several British publications cited the debut as one of the year's best records; *Melody Maker,* for one, named *Yerself Is Steam* one of the top four albums of 1991. Examples of the most compelling songs from Mercury Rev's first outing, which *Rough Guide to Rock* contributor Chris Tighe hailed an "essential," included the aggressively challenging "Sweet Oddysee of a Cancer Cell T' Th' Center of Yer Heart," "Chasing a Bee," and "Coney Island Cyclone."

However, Mercury Rev would again experience uncertainty when, within weeks of the LP's release, the American branch of Rough Trade filed for bankruptcy, halting any hope of proper promotion and distribution. Nevertheless, the band fulfilled a prior obligation to tour Britain, though not without incident. These early live shows, performed without practice sessions or predetermined set lists, saw Mercury Rev on the verge of disintegration. On stage, the band was at once fascinating, volatile, and unpredictable. Baker frequently left the stage in the middle of songs to grab a drink, and reports circulated that the band was banned from air travel after Donahue and Grasshopper had a brawl during a flight. Following the *Yerself Is Steam* tour, the members of Mercury Rev went their separate ways until Columbia Records, a Sony subsidiary, picked up the band and re-issued their first release.

Amid the internal strife, Mercury Rev entered a makeshift studio in a barn to record a second album, 1993's *Boces,* which included samples taken from sites such as New York's Times Square and NASA's Cape Canaveral. The unexpected record, which took its name from an upstate New York program designed to train the unskilled labor force for the future, again astounded critics with its acute sense of melody. However, tension within the band continued to persist. Mercury Rev toured in support of the album with the same results; concert security removed the band during the Lollapalooza 1993 stop in Denver, and Baker, because of his soured relations with his bandmates, was traveling to gigs apart from Mercury Rev. In late 1993, Baker departed from the band after months of conflict. While some sources called his departure a mutual agreement, others claimed Baker was, in fact, dismissed from the band. Rebounding from his departure under the name Shady, Baker released a well-received solo album in 1994 entitled *World,* a project recorded with guest musicians from the Boo Radleys, Rollerskate Skinny (the band's former guitarist Jimi Shields), and St. Johnny (Bill Whitten).

Continuing to record as a quintet, Mercury Rev defied speculations again with the release of 1995's *See You on the Other Side,* an album marking Donahue's role as an unchallenged leader. More accessible than prior efforts, the album featured echoes of the Beach Boys' *Pet Sounds,* New Orleans brass band sounds, and acid jazz. A huge leap for the band and an exhilarating success, *See You on the Other Side* was "a record of high-wire wit and elegantly twisted poignancy," concluded David Fricke in *Rolling Stone* in 1995. Notable tracks from the album included the brass-lined "Sudden Ray of Hope," the bliss-pop tune "Young Man's Stride," and the darker closing song "Peaceful Night." Also in 1995, Mercury Rev released an album as their alter ego, the Harmony Rockets, entitled *Paralyzed Mind of the Archangel Void.* The pseudonym enabled them to digress from their Mercury Rev formula, and the recording consisted of a single 45-minute ambient/noise piece that recalled late 1960s trance-rock meditations.

Touring again posed problems within the band, in spite of Baker's departure and Mercury Rev's 1995 successes. During the *See You on the Other Side* tour, drummer Chambers quit the band several times. At one point, Grasshopper physically removed Chambers from a train in an attempt to talk him out of leaving. Upon returning to New York, Donahue took refuge at his house in the Catskills, while Grasshopper retreated to a Jesuit monastery near Saratoga for several weeks. When Donahue and Grasshopper reconvened at their homes in Kingston, New York, in 1997 to record a new Mercury Rev album, they called upon their two famous neighbors Levon Helm and Garth Hudson (both lived in nearby Woodstock) of the legendary group the Band to perform on some songs. Chambers and Thorpe also returned for studio work but did not participate in subsequent touring.

Comeback Album

The resulting *Deserter's Song,* released in 1998 on the group's new label V2, captured the pain and yearning of the past, evidenced in songs such as "Holes," "Tonite It Shows," and "The Funny Bird." "There's a lot of emotions tied up in the record," said Donahue to Steve Appleford in a 1999 interview for the *Los Angeles Times.* "We went through a few tough years. It's just a very genuine, honest record. You can't buy that or fake it in the studio. I think that's what people pick up on, the sincerity there." The album, another critical achievement, also earned substantial sales as well. It went gold in England and Ireland, and as of the fall of 1999, had sold over 250,000 copies.

For touring purposes, Mercury Rev revealed a new lineup to support *Deserter's Songs.* The most recent performance version of the band consisted of, in addition to Donahue and Grasshopper, guitarist Jayson Russo, his keyboardist brother Justin Russo, organist Adam Snyder, and drummer Jeff Mercel. During 1998 and 1999, Mercury Rev headlined dates in Australia, New Zealand, and Britain. The band also supported the Jesus & Mary Chain for their United States tour, as well as Bob Mould's farewell tour of the United Kingdom. In the United States, Mercury Rev opened for acts such as Buffalo Tom and R.E.M. Back in Britain, they played at the V99 music festival in Staffordshire, England, along with bands like the Cardigans, Gomez, Cast, (London) Suede, Gay Dad, Massive Attack, and Orbital. From his studio in Cassadaga, New York, a small Lake Erie town close to Buffalo and his home in Fredonia, Fridmann continued to record with and produce for Mercury Rev and for other groups, including Jane's Addiction, the Flaming Lips, Mogwai, and Elf Power.

Selected discography

Yerself Is Steam, Rough Trade, 1991; reissued, Columbia, 1992.
The Hum Is Coming From Her, (EP), Columbia, 1993.
Boces, Columbia, 1993.
Something for Joey, (EP), Columbia, 1993.
Everlasting Arm, (EP), Big Cat, 1994.
(As the Harmony Rockets) *Paralyzed Mind of the Archangel Void,* Big Cat, 1995.
See You on the Other Side, Work, 1995.
Deserter's Songs, V2, 1998.

Sources

Books

MusicHound Rock: The Essential Album Guide, Visible Ink Press, 1999.

Periodicals

Boston Globe, December 31, 1999.
Guitar Player, April 1993.
Los Angeles Times, November 17, 1995; August 8, 1999.
Magnet, January/February 1999, pp. 33-35; August/September 1999, p. 104.
Melody Maker, June 8, 1991; August 24, 1991; March 28, 1992; February 12, 1994; August 28, 1999; September 18, 1999.
Rolling Stone, September 2, 1993; December 28, 1995; August 19, 1999; September 2, 1999.

Online

Mercury Rev, http://www.mercuryrev.net (March 6, 2000).
"Mercury Rev," *Rough Guide to Rock*, http://www.roughguides.com/rock/entries/entries-m/MERCURY_REV.html (March 6, 2000).
Music365, http://www.music365.com/autocontent/news_010423.htm (March 6, 2000).

—Laura Hightower

Monks of Doom

Rock group

The Monks of Doom were one of the smartest, hippest, heaviest bands of the 1980s and 1990s. As their name suggests, the band was a hermetic group which dedicated itself to producing rock and roll music of high quality while outside the Dark Ages of arena rock, grunge and mega-labels raged. Like the monks of the Middle Ages, the band labored in obscurity. Although they were enjoyed by a small group of enthusiasts, the Monks' records went largely unnoticed by the larger music public. When the band broke up in 1993, it left behind five rocking albums that wait to be discovered by some future rock renaissance.

The Monks of Doom were formed in 1986 by four members of the band Camper Van Beethoven: bassist Victor Krummenacher, guitarists Greg Lisher and Chris Molla, and drummer Chris Pedersen. The Monks represented an opportunity to go beyond Camper's brand of folk-rock and sixties pop and into the type of music played by Henry Cow, Snakefinger, King Crimson, Richard Thompson and Fred Frith, artists who commanded as fierce and loyal a cult following as the Monks later would. "We were interested in doing slightly more outside music," Krummenacher said in a phone interview with *Contemporary Musicians*. "Music that that had, for lack of a better word, 'progressive' tendencies. It was an outside expansion, a chance to go wherever our imagination took us."

During their first couple years, the Monks existed primarily as a side project to Camper Van Beethoven, and Krummenacher discounted claims that the Monks caused Camper's break-up. "I think it actually prolonged Camper in the long run," he said. "There was not a lot of Monks work done while Camper was active, although I think we were always hoping that there would be more. But Camper was so busy at the time and that was really the focus of our lives for the most part, doing the Camper stuff." Still the new band exacerbated existing tensions in Camper. David Lowery, Camper's leader, dissed the Monks regularly in print after Camper's break up.

Most of the Monks' distinctive characteristics are revealed on their first album, the 1987 release *Soundtrack to the Film "Breakfast on the Beach of Deception."* These characteristics included ironic, distanced lyrics combined with impassioned playing that sometimes threatened to spin out of control; pseudo-ethnic electric folk tunes; enigmatic titles; and Krummenacher's virile yet measured vocals. Instrumentals comprised most of the record, which may account for why it is called a "soundtrack." "The first record was a free-form freak out," Krummenacher recounted. "We had a few extra dollars sitting around and decided to go into the studio. I don't think we really had a clue about what we wanted to do—we just went for it and did it. We didn't really have any idea we were making a record until we actually made the record."

The Monks' next record, *The Cosmodemonic Telegraph Company*, was made in early 1989, at the same time Camper was making its last record. Though they never gave up writing instrumentals—indeed every Monk record included one or more, and about fifty percent of their live sets were always instrumental—the second album saw the band opting to do more non-instrumental songs. They also extended their two-guitar attack, greatly abetted by the addition of David Immergluck of the Ophelias, who replaced Molla at the end of 1986. Together Immergluck and Lisher created an intricate, composed sound that managed to be tough and elemental at the same time. The sonic assault of instruments combined with Krummenacher's intelligent lyrics, which were more like literature than rock, produced a chemistry unlike most other rock bands.

The band worked creatively as a cooperative. The music on every album, with the exception of a few cover songs, was credited to the band as a unit. Krummenacher wrote most of the lyrics, but everything after that was worked out in the crucible of the rehearsal room. Krummenacher described the creative process: "The typical pattern was: Set up in the rehearsal studio. Turn on the tape deck. Play. Listen back. Think that's cool and work it out.

For the Record . . .

Members include **David Immergluck**, guitar, vocals; **Victor Krummenacher**, bass, vocals; **Greg Lisher**, guitar; **Chris Molla** (with the group during its first six months), guitar; **Chris Pedersen**, drums.

Camper Van Beethoven rhythm section formed Monks of Doom, Chris Molla left band, David Immergluck replaced Molla, 1986; first album, *Soundtrack to the Film "Breakfast on the Beach of Deception"* released, 1987; Camper Van Beethoven breaks up, Monks begin grueling three years of touring, 1990; *Meridian* released, 1991; signed by IRS, 1992; David Immergluck leaves Monks to join Counting Crows, remaining members disband, 1993.

Addresses: *Record company*—Magnetic Records, P.O. Box 460816, San Francisco, CA 94146-0816; website: Magnetic Records, http://www.sirius.com/~magnetic; email: magnetic@netcom.com.

We did hours and hours and hours and hours of jamming. When we were writing, we were basically improving twenty hours a week or more."

For Krummenacher, *Cosmodemonic* represented an "experimental time between the first idea of the Monks and the second idea of the Monks." That second idea is represented by *Meridian*, the band's third album and their undisputed masterpiece. "On the third record we figured out that we were this really unique blend of post-punk and prog rock. That's where we blend the folkier and the weirder stuff, bring together the Neil Young and Captain Beefheart and King Crimson and the Fall and Richard Thompson and all these odd influences, and get away with it." *Meridian* is a mood piece, in which the vocals, lyrics and instruments contribute unerringly to an atmosphere pervaded by mystery, dread, and loss. It culminates in the freak show horror of "Circassian Beauty," one of the heaviest rock songs ever committed to tape, and surely one of the most fearful, especially at the end as the singer devolves into pre-vocal babble. *Meridian* was also the beginning of a year of intense music making by the Monks. Between July 1991 and June 1992, the group cut three CDs—*Meridian*, the EP *The Insect God*, and *Forgery*—for three different labels. *Insect God* is basically a holding action on which the Monks played a short but powerful set of music. Two of the five pieces were covers—Frank Zappa's "Who Are The Brain Police?" and Syd Barrett's "Let's Split;"one is an instrumental. The highpoint of the CD is its title track, a deliciously sardonic, decidedly politically incorrect adaptation of an Edward Gorey story of alien abduction.

Three months after completing *Insect God*, the Monks were back in the studio again to make *Forgery*, which turned out to be their final record. *Forgery* bears the distinct sound of the Monks. But the group seemed to have given up their hard edge on the album in favor of a dreamier sound, one strangely appropriate to songs like "Virtual Lover" or "Cigarette Man (Cast of Characters)." The record was a disappointment to some fans. Krummenacher agrees, explaining the Monks tried to do too much in too little time. "We made three records in a year, and it was just too much work," he said. "I think that's why *Forgery* is as hit and miss as it was. I think *Forgery* had some good moments, and I think we were going in some good directions. We were touching on a lot of Peter Green's Fleetwood Mac stuff, which is great as a guitar influence. But it really wasn't going where it could have gone had we held onto some of the stuff that we did on Insect God and written some more and taken our time. Then we would have and a better record and a better response."

Forgery was the Monks' major label debut. The president of IRS wanted to sign Camper in 1986 but the band refused, Krummenacher explained. "He signed the Monks because it was the closest he could get." Unfortunately the band's sales had been in a downward spiral since their first record. *Beach of Deception*, on the band's own Pitch-A-Tent label, sold a respectable 20,000 copies and was the Monks' best-selling record. *Forgery*, even with IRS' national distribution, only sold about 7,000 CDs.

In 1993, after *Forgery*'s release, the Counting Crows approached Immergluck about working with them. The prospect of giving up the endless Monks tours—they had been going on virtually unabated for three years—and earning decent money from music persuaded him to accept. At first, Krummenacher, the nominal leader of the group, intended to bring a new guitarist in and carry on. IRS, however, was unhappy with *Forgery*'s poor sales and unwilling to produce the second CD it had contracted for. Immergluck's departure gave the label a way out of its contract, and it dropped the Monks without exercising its option for the second record. Without a record contract, the Monks decided to cut their losses and disband.

After the Monks, David Immergluck established himself as a sought-after studio guitarist, who continues to play with the Counting Crows, John Hiatt, and Papa's Culture. Victor Krummenacher pursued a variety of solo projects that included the bands Fifth Business and A Great Laugh.

His two solo albums, *Out in the Heat* and *St. John's Mercy* are available from Magnetic Records. As 2000 began, Krummenacher was preparing for tours with Cracker and Eugene Chadbourne, and had a third album, tentatively titled *Bittersweet*, in the works. Greg Lisher has played guitar with A Great Laugh. His first solo project was expected to be released on Magnetic in early 2000.

Five years after the Monks broke up, drummer Chris Pedersen announced plans to move to Australia and the band decided to perform one last time together before he left. Twenty hours of rehearsals got them back in form and they took the stage in San Francisco. "I felt really good about the show, it capped the band off well," Krummenacher said. "We went out and did all our hotshot licks, showed off a little bit, sold the club out, and had a really good time. And I mean it, it was a really good time. But we've all moved on." That may not have been the final Monks project, however. Krummenacher hopes to have the time and money at some point in the future to put out a live record by the Monks.

Selected discography

Soundtrack to the Film "Breakfast on the Beach of Deception," Pitch-A-Tent Records, 1987; reissue IRS Records, 1992.
The Cosmodemonic Telegraph Company, Pitch-A-Tent Records, 1989; reissue IRS Records, 1992.
Meridian, Moist/Baited Breath, 1991.
The Insect God, (EP), C/Z Records, 1992.
Forgery, IRS Records, 1992.

Sources

Magnetic Records website, http://www.sirius.com/~magnetic (January 31, 2000).

Additional information was obtained through a telephone interview with Victor H. Krummenacher on January 28, 2000.

—Gerald E. Brennan

Dave Murray

Avant-garde jazz musician

Photograph by Jack Vartoogian. Reproduced by permission. ©

Among the most recorded jazz musicians in history and arguably one of the genre's greatest tenor saxophonists, Dave Murray dominated jazz in the 1980s as thoroughly as Charlie Parker dominated the genre in the 1940s. Murray, considered a giant of the avant-garde style, nonetheless played all forms of jazz, from straight-ahead to free improvisational to post-bop. He was devoted to saxophonists as conservative as Paul Gonsalves and as radical as Albert Ayler. His name, however, has not become as legendary as Parker's during his earlier years, primarily because few people paid close attention to the progressive, free-jazz movement of the 1980s, an era distracted by other forms such as commercial fusion and hard-bop nostalgia. Meanwhile, Murray refused to let the times discourage his ambitions, and from behind the scenes, he developed a distinct and powerful personal voice on both the tenor saxophone and clarinet. By the 1990s, many regarded Murray as the most proficient synthesizer since Charles Mingus (another of Murray's influences). Regardless of his well-deserved recognition, Murray never broke from the downtown scene and refused to let the jazz culture assign him to a single category. Composing enchanting melodies that flowed with ease into far-reaching abstraction before returning back to the music's roots in blues and gospel, Murray is also known for his trademark playing technique of sudden leaps into the upper register of his instrument, and his ability to draw a rich, expansive sound from his horn on both ballads and upbeat numbers.

In addition to Mingus, Parker, Gonsalves and Ayler, Murray also held jazz greats such as Bobby Bradford, Arthur Blythe, Archie Shepp, Sonny Rollins, Ben Webster, Coleman Hawkins, Duke Ellington, and others in high esteem, though his main mission as a jazz artist has been the continuation of work initiated by John Coltrane. Murray believed that following Coltrane's death in 1967, there were still new territories to explore in pushing improvisation to its limit by playing long, complex solos without reverting to favorite licks and phrases. A renowned bandleader from the onset of his career, Murray organized free-wheeling quartets and trios, a big band, and an acclaimed octet. He is also known for his work with the World Saxophone Quartet, a group that endured over 20 years, yet allowed members to pursue their individual careers.

Peers Recognized Talent

Born David Keith Murray on February 19, 1955, in Berkeley, California, the future legend, whose mother was a church pianist, started off playing alto saxophone at the age of nine, then played tenor saxophone in a soul group he lead as a teenager. After high school, Murray

For the Record . . .

Born David Keith Murray on February 19, 1955, in Berkeley, CA; son of a church pianist; married and divorced Ming. *Education*: Attended Ponoma College.

Started playing alto saxophone at the age of nine, then played tenor saxophone in a soul group he lead as a teenager; moved to New York City and began his recording career, 1975; debuted with album *Last of the Hipman,* 1976; released three breakthrough albums in 1980; has recorded over 220 albums during his career; formed acclaimed octet, several combos, and a big band, 1980s; returned to gospel influences and African roots, 1990s; member of the World Saxophone Quartet and founder of the group Fo Deuk Revue.

Awards: Danish Jazzpar prize, 1991.

Addresses: *Record company*—Columbia Records, 550 Madison Ave., New York, NY 10022-3211, (212) 833-8000.

moved to Southern California to attend Ponoma College, located near Los Angeles. Here, he often played with critic, drummer, and teacher Stanley Crouch, cornetist Lawrence "Butch" Morris, clarinetist John Carter, Bobby Bradford, and saxophonist Arthur Blythe. In 1975, Murray relocated to New York City, hoping to establish himself on the jazz scene. He easily achieved his goal, given the fact that by the time Murray arrived in New York, he was already a brash and accomplished horn player. Upon his entrance into the city's jazz culture, Murray started to gravitate toward the experimental scene led by Sam Rivers and Sunny Murray and invigorated bygroups like Air and the Art Ensemble of Chicago. Within no time, Murray's peers acknowledged the young musician's presence.

Soon after he arrived in New York, Murray commenced his recording career as a bandleader, releasing a string of impressive records through the remainder of the decade. In 1976, Murray released three albums, teaming with Morris for *Last of the Hipman;* Crouch and Air bassist Fred Hopkins for *Live at the Peace Church;* and Morris, Hopkins, Crouch, and pianist Don Pullen, who played with Charles Mingus's band, for *Flowers for Albert.* Hopkins, drummer Phillip Wilson, and Art Ensemble of Chicago trumpeter Lester Bowie joined Murray for 1978's *Live at the Lower Manhattan Ocean Club, Vols. 1 & 2,* while Cecil Taylor, drummer Andrew Cyrille, and bassist Johnny Dyani appeared for 1980's *3D Family.* On these earlier recordings, although Murray revealed his strong, original voice, he still needed to further develop the shape of his sound.

Murray accomplished this with a breakthrough in 1980; he had discovered how to combine the intensity of his instrument with the gospel-rooted melody that so inspired him in his youth, within just five years on the New York scene. Forming a new and later acclaimed octet comprised of the core group of Morris, Air drummer Steve McCall, and saxophonist Henry Threadgill, Murray released three albums that year: *Ming* (named after his wife at the time), *Home,* and *Murray's Steps.* All three were ranked among the decade's very best jazz records. Over the years, the octet, which included various personnel to compliment Murray, remained his most effective vehicle. Some of his most majestic recordings with this group included *New Life* and *Hope Scope* (both released in 1987), as well as 1993's *Picasso.*

Leader of the Band

Although Murray excelled with his octet, he had always dreamed of leading a big band. While he only managed to pull together a jazz orchestra a few times, the result was a band with all the sturdiness of his octet that produced a more expansive sound, beginning with 1985's *Live at Sweet Basil, Vol. 1* and the following year's *Live at Sweet Basil, Vol. 2.* Representative of his most successful endeavors as a big band leader included 1992's *David Murray Big Band Conducted by Lawrence "Butch" Morris* and 1995's *South of the Border.*

During the 1980s, Murray also led a number of small combos. Critics named *Morning Son* (released in 1984) and *Ming's Samba* (released in 1989 and his first album issued on an American label) as two of his best. Both recordings featured New Orleans, Louisiana, jazz drummer Ed Blackwell, who brought his regional influences to the fore. Another favorite pick of the 1980s, a trio session entitled *The Hill* (released in 1988), included compositions by Duke Ellington and Billy Strayhorn. The album also led many to start defining Murray a neotraditionalist for his blend of harmony and melody with swing and post-bop.

The close of the decade and the early1990s also saw Murray further exploring his gospel roots—influences he gained from his mother's work as a church pianist. Along with pianist Dave Burell and assorted rhythm sections, he recorded such reflections of his childhood as 1989's *Deep River,* 1990's *Spirituals,* and 1991's *Remembrances,* all evoking the African American church tradition through hymns and new spiritual compositions.

Other like offerings followed with Pullen, who Murray convinced to play organ for 1991's *Shakill's Warrior* and 1994's *Shakill's II.* In 1999, *Wall Street Journal* writer Jim Fusilli named the former one of the best albums of the 1990s. "Murray's playing is phenomenal, full of melody and adventure," Fusilli wrote. Also during the time he explored his spiritual side, Murray also recorded a series of well-received duo albums with pianists John Hicks, Burell, Randy Weston, George Arvanitas, Aki Takase, and Donal Fox. The most noteworthy of these included *The Healers* (recorded with Weston and released in 1987) and *Brother to Brother* (recorded with Burrell and released in 1993). In 1991, Murray received the prestigious Danish Jazzpar prize for his work in jazz.

Explored Other Styles

Murray continued his explorative nature in the mid 1990s, forming an eight-piece jazz-funk band anchored by keyboardist Robert Irving III, who played with Miles Davis's band. In 1996, the band released *Dark Star: The Music of the Grateful Dead.* Murray, who grew up in the San Francisco Bay area listening to the Dead in the 1960s and played with them on several occasions in the 1990s, had been a longtime fan of the band. According to Jason Fine of *Rolling Stone*, "*Dark Star* is a revelation for Deadheads who never thought jazz could rock so hard and for jazz snobs who never imagined so much life could be squeezed from the Dead." Also in the mid 1990s, Murray moved on a part time basis to Paris, France, and created a new ensemble, the Fo Deuk Revue. In Paris, music such as Afro-pop, hip-hop, and jazz inspired him to form the group, which uses Senegalese musicians, singers, rappers, and syncopation much like Bradford Marsalis's Buckshot LeFonque group and draws a different kind of audience. Poet, writer, and critic Amiri Baraka also worked with the group.

In the 1990s, Murray also recorded rhythm and blues-influenced originals such as 1994's *The Tip* and 1995's *Jug-a-Lug,* reunited with an old friend from California for 1996's *The David Murray/James Newton Quintet,* and continued to play and record with the World Saxophone Quartet. The group, which recorded more than a dozen albums together, consisted of Murray, Oliver Lake, Hamiet Bluiett, founder Blythe, John Stubblefield, and Eric Person. After the loss of the quartet's founder, John Purcell joined in 1996 as a multi-reedist producer and saxophone consultant. Murray continued to record into the later part of the decade, releasing *Long Goodbye: A Tribute to Don Pullen* in 1998 and *Creole,* an album of regional-inspired music, in 1999.

He also started work on a musical about Satchel Paige with the Grateful Dead's Bob Weir and bluesman Taj Mahal, toured in 1999 with a 45-piece big band paying tribute to Duke Ellington, and toured the same year with Fo Deuk Revue, which means "Where do you come from?" in the African Wolof language. Murray made his home in both Brooklyn, New York, and Paris and often visited Africa. However, he tried not to hold any illusions about the continent and only studied its history an music. Scoffing at American blacks who adopt African dress and rejecting the notion that the story of slavery was black and white, Murray felt that many African Americans "get too caught up in the Afrocentric thing," he told *Washington Post* writer Marc Fisher in 1998. "Fo Duek Revue is my way of addressing my relationship with Africa without going out and shouting slogans or dressing like them," he continued. "I just get to the meat of it."

Selected discography

Last of the Hipman, Red, 1976.
Live at the Peace Church, Danola, 1976.
Flowers for Albert, India Navigation, 1976; reissued, 1997.
Penthouse Jazz, Circle, 1977.
(With James Newton) *Solomon's Son,* Circle, 1977.
Conceptual Saxophone, Cadillac, 1978.
Holy Seige on the Intrigue, Circle, 1978.
Interboogieology, Black Saint, 1978.
Let the Music Take You, EPM Musique, 1978; reissued, 1993.
Live at the Lower Manhattan Ocean Club, Vols. 1 & 2, India Navigation, 1978; reissued, 1989.
Low Class Conspiracy, Adelphi, 1978.
Organic Saxophone, Palm, 1978.
Sur-Real Saxophone, Horo, 1978.
The London Concert, Cadillac, 1979.
The People's Choice, Cecma, 1979.
3D Family, Hat Hut, 1980; reissued, 1989.
Ming, Black Saint, 1980.
Solo Live, Vol. 1, Cecma, 1980.
Solo Live, Vol. 2, Cecma, 1980.
Sweet Lovely, Black Saint, 1980.
Home, Black Saint, 1982.
Murray's Steps, Black Saint, 1982.
Morning Song, Black Saint, 1984.
Children, Black Saint, 1985.
Live at Sweet Basil, Vol. 1, Black Saint, 1985.
I Want to Talk About You, Black Saint, 1986.
Live at Sweet Basil, Vol. 2, Black Saint, 1986.
N.Y.C., 1986, DIW, 1986; reissued, 1993.
(With Randy Weston) *The Healers,* Black Saint, 1987.
Hope Scope, Black Saint, 1987.
New Life, Black Saint, 1987.
The Hill, Black Saint, 1988.

(With Jack DeJonette) *In Our Style,* DIW, 1988.
Lovers, DIW, 1988.
Deep River, DIW, 1989.
Ming's Samba, Portrait, 1989.
Ballads, DIW, 1990.
(With Dave Burrell) *Daybreak,* Gazell, 1990.
(With Kahil El'Zabar) *Golden Sea,* Sound Aspects, 1990.
(With John Hicks) *Sketches of Tokyo,* DIW, 1990.
Spirituals, DIW, 1990.
(With the Bobby Battle Quartet), *The Offering,* Mapleshade, 1991.
Remembrances, DIW, 1991.
(With the Bob Thiele Collective) *Sunrise, Sunset,* Red Baron, 1991.
(With George Arvanitas) *Tea for Two,* Fresh Sounds, 1991.
Black & Black, Red Baron, 1992.
David Murray Big Band Conducted by Lawrence "Butch" Morris, DIW, 1992.
Death of a Sideman, DIW, 1992.
(With Dave Burrell) *In Concert,* Victo, 1992.
MX, Red Baron, 1992.
(With Milford Graves) *Real Deal,* DIW, 1992.
A Sanctuary Within, Black Saint, 1992.
Shakill's Warrior, DIW, 1992.
Special Quartet, DIW, 1992.
Ballads for Bass Clarinet, DIW, 1993.
Body & Soul, Black Saint, 1993.
(With Dave Burrell) *Brother to Brother,* Gazell, 1993.
Fast Life, DIW, 1993.
Jazzosaurus Rex, Red Baron, 1993.
(With Pierre Dørge's New Jungle Orchestra) *Jazzpar Prize,* Enja, 1993.
Lucky Four, Tutu, 1993.
Picasso, DIW, 1993.
(With Aki Takase) *Blue Monk,* Enja, 1994.
Live '93 Acoustic Octofunk, Sound Hills, 1994.
Saxmen, Red Baron, 1994.
Shakill's II, DIW, 1994.
The Tip, DIW, 1994.
Tenors, DIW, 1994.
For Aunt Louise, DIW, 1995.
Jug-a-Lug, DIW, 1995.
South of the Border, DIW, 1995.
(With Donal Fox) *Ugly Beauty,* Evidence, 1995.
Dark Star: The Music of the Grateful Dead, Astor Place, 1996.
Fo Deuk Revue, Justin Time, 1996.
The David Murray/James Newton Quintet, DIW, 1996.
Creole, Justin Time, 1998.
Long Goodbye: A Tribute to Don Pullen, DIW, 1998.
Lovers, FTC, 1999.
Seasons, Pow Wow, 1999.
Speaking in Tongues, Justin Time, 1999.

Sources

Books

Swenson, John, editor, *Rolling Stone Jazz & Blues Album Guide,* Random House, 1999.

Periodicals

Down Beat, September 1996; July 1998; November 1999; December 1999.
Los Angeles Times, September 27, 1996; July 4, 1999.
Rolling Stone, September 5, 1996.
Stereo Review, September 1996; December 1996.
Village Voice, January 12, 1999.
Washington Post, August 1, 1998; June 8, 1999.

Online

All Music Guide, http://www.allmusic.com (February 24, 2000).

—*Laura Hightower*

Neurosis

Heavy metal band

Throughout the late 1980s, heavy metal bands owned the pop music charts. From Poison and Bon Jovi to Ratt and Ozzy Osbourne, music fans wrapped themselves in the reverb of electric guitars. However, by the early 1990s, a new style of music from the Pacific Northwest called grunge—led by Nirvana, Pearl Jam, and others—tossed metal into the scrap pile. Most heavy metal acts, unable to adapt to this change, disbanded. But Neurosis found a way to survive by "developing a style that blended industrial, heavy metal, and alternative rock with often spiritually focused lyrics," according to Steve Huey of *All Music Guide*, in comments available at the CDNOW website. The attention focused by the public on grunge did little to thwart Neurosis' mission for taking chances. However, exploring new sounds was nothing new for the band; in fact, with each subsequent album since their debut in 1987, Neurosis has been evolving and maturing. By adapting to the ever-changing styles of music, Neurosis is "a shining example," stated *Guitar Player*, "of what traditional metal can become when it takes the road less traveled."

Neurosis began its trip down the road less traveled in 1986. Formed in Oakland, California, by vocalist/guitarist Scott Kelly, bassist Dave Edwardson, and drummer Jason Roeder, Neurosis released their debut album, *Pain of Mind,* as a trio in 1987. Issued on the independent Alchemy label, *Pain of Mind*, as stated in an AOL online biography, was "discontented hardcore fury." In 1990, with the addition of vocalist and guitarist Steve Von Till, Neurosis released *The Word as Law.* With this album, according to the group's website, Neurosis "began to experiment with constructing music of varied textures." The band's second release marked other artistic changes. With the release of their second effort, Neurosis began incorporating visual elements into their act, building a devoted underground following.

In 1992, Neurosis continued down a more familiar path by signing with San Francisco's legendary Alternative Tentacles label to release their next two albums: *Souls at Zero* and *Enemy of the Sun. Souls at Zero* with its "mammoth sound" as *Reflex* reviewed, "challenge[d] the boundaries of the recording studio and their own minds." Yet, according to their website, Neurosis not only wanted to challenge themselves, but also their listeners "who dare listen to tap into the undeniable strength that they emanate—to act on the depravity that surrounds them, and join their uncompromising musical vision." These two albums also saw Neurosis incorporating more intense percussion into their music.

Neurosis implemented visual imagery, in addition to their musical intensity, to reveal the group's musical vision—imagery that articulated the band's suspicions concerning a modern consumerist society. Neurosis believed that music alone failed to fully reveal the band's outlook. Rather, they needed art and images as supplements to describe their concept. According to Neurosis, as quoted by Yahoo! Music, "The words are just one part, it takes pictures and moving pictures and sound to create the whole."

Neurosis's blend of art, words, and sound has been inspired by a variety of cultures. Unlike many rock bands, Neurosis refused to limit themselves to the influences of Western societies. Guitarist/vocalist Scott Kelly told the online magazine Loop.com, "we've been inspired by all the native cultures ... the North American Indians, Odinism, and Druidism." Yet, Kelly continued, "we're just really kind of inspired by the idea that all people were sharing the same thoughts without having any sort of mass form of communication back in those times."

In 1996, after three years of hard work, Neurosis released *Through Silver in Blood,* the band's most recognized work in terms of popular and critical attention. This album, as described in an AOL online biography is "their most prophetic warning" and "furthers the scope of their vision, and wraps its black wings around the consciousness like a dire warning." The album also, as further described by AOL, is a "call to arms for the angry multitudes to either act on the atrocities around them, or

For the Record . . .

Members include **Dave Edwardson,** bass; **Scott Kelly**, vocals, guitar; **Jason Roeder**, drums; **Simon**, keyboards; **Steve Von Til** (joined band 1990), guitar, vocals.

Kelly, Edwardson, and Roeder formed band, 1986; released 1990's *The Word as Law* album; signed with Alternative Tentacles, released *Souls at Zero*, 1992; released *Enemy of the Sun,* 1993; returned two years later in 1995 with the re-release of *Pain of Mind*; signed with Relapse Records and released *Through Silver in Blood,* 1996; released *Times of Grace* and recorded as an expansion group called Tribes of Neurot, 1999.

Addresses: *Record company*—Relapse Records, P.O. Box 2060, Upper Darby, PA 19082, (610) 734-1000; email: www.relapse.com. *Website*—The Official Site of Neurosis and Tribes of Neurot: http://www.neurosis.com.

simply spiral down the waiting coil of futility." However, guitarist Scott Kelly pointed out to *Guitar Player* that the goal for the album was to "create atmosphere with the music ... to use all of the instruments to create one massive sound." This album led Neurosis down two more roads less traveled: a personal invitation to tour with the legendary metal band Pantera for OZFEST, as well as a professional formation of an experimental band called Tribes of Neurot.

In 1996, Tribes of Neurot released *Silver Blood Transmission* which was described on their website as "soundscape-laden [and] experimental." Yet, with the success of *Through Silver in Blood*, why would Neurosis form this side project? "We formed the Tribes of Neurot," the band explained in a *Corridor of Cells* interview, "because we realized that the ideas and philosophies that we were dealing with as Neurosis actually require to be expressed in many different ways."

Neurosis continued down their less traveled road in 1999 by releasing *Times of Grace* with producer Steve Albini. With this album, *CMJ New Music Magazine* praised, "the band has expanded its reach considerably, interspersing the wall of pain with a few genteel ballads...." *CMJ New Music Report* offered their take on the album by comparing it to a famous writer: "*Times of Grace* is a lot like the plot of Edgar Allen Poe's *The Cask of Amontillado.* Each epic song is like a brick, laid to erect a tower of sound that wraps itself around its listeners and seals them in, offering no escape." Yet, it is not only the sound that seals in listeners, but also the lyrics. The band told an AOL online interviewer, "we have kind of our own mythology or folklore in which we bring our lyrics from." The band further commented that the lyrics are "like a pallet of colors in which we draw... [with no] central theme.... Each song kind of speaks for itself." Thus, it seems as if Neurosis has no specific message, or as the band told *Corridor of Cells*, "we try to avoid giving people specific messages ... we don't want to tell people how to experience things... [only] capture the tone and the emotions behind situations."

At the beginning of a new millennium, Neurosis, along with other metal-centered groups such as Type O Negative and 16 Volt, has successfully adapted to music's ever-changing world and saved itself from heavy metal's scrap pile. Through their aural and visual albums, Neurosis, as stated on their website, "isn't a music group, it's a state of mind. A state of frustration. A state of turmoil and confusion. A state of furied aggression. A state of ominous, death tranquility—the portent of storm on the horizon of musical perception."

Selected discography

As Neurosis

Pain of Mind, Alchemy/Alternative Tentacles, 1987.
The Word As Law, Lookout!, 1989.
Souls at Zero, Alternative Tentacles, 1992.
Enemy of the Sun, Alternative Tentacles, 1993.
Through Silver in Blood, Relapse, 1996.
Times of Grace, Relapse, 1999.

As Tribes of Neurot

Silver Blood Transmission, Relapse, 1996.

Sources

Periodicals

CMJ New Music Magazine, November, 1999.
CMJ New Music Report, November, 1999.
Guitar Player, March 01, 1997.
Reflex, November 10, 1992

Online

"Neurosis," *America Online*, http://www.members.aol.com/_ht_a/earthad43 (November 15, 1999).

CDNOW, http://www.cdnow.com (November 15, 1999).
Loop.com, http://www.loop.com (November 15, 1999).
Official Site of Neurosis and Tribes of Neurot, http://www.neurosis.com (November 15, 1999).
Yahoo! Music Finder, http://www.musicfinder.yahoo.com (November 15, 1999).

—Ann M. Schwalboski

NOFX

Punk rock band

Punk rock evolved from the authentic angst of the 1980s Southern California hardcore scene to bratty skate punk, idealistic peace punk, and even mainstream pop punk in the 1990s. A few outstanding punk rock bands have played through the evolution to emerge as dominant forces. NOFX was considered royalty in the underground punk rock scene with a career that spanned over 15 years. The band rotated members many times, toured relentlessly, and developed their sound in continual efforts of improve, all the while releasing albums and EPs through independent record companies and avoiding MTV, commercial radio, and interviews. Following their Bad Religion influence of straight forward warp speed rhythms, high volume sonic attacks and buzzing harmonies in their early years, provided a basis for growth into ska and reggae sounds from groups such as Operation Ivy, Misfits, and Bad Brains. Mixing the political cynicism of Bad Religion, dark, sarcastic observations of their time and place, and abundant tongue-in-cheek humor made NOFX's music appeal to a wide range within the punk audience. The group's later albums contained lyrics which would entertain most any teenage boy and others who enjoy Southern California punk. Often offensive, their song lyrics exhibited a pissed-off attitude of social injustice, always contained plenty of sexual innuendo, and usually celebrated some sort of juvenile behavior.

NOFX was formed in Los Angeles in 1983 by a few friends who attended Fairfax High School. Punk was a raging scene during the 1980s in Southern California, so there was ample interest in pulling together a band. Vocalist and bassist Fat Mike played in a group called False Alarm and was a huge Misfits fan. Drummer Smelly knew Fat Mike from skateboarding and was invited to join him and guitarist and vocalist Eric Melvin. A fourth person did not show, so the band started as a three-piece unit. Those three members started with the group and were in the band for their last release in 1999. El Hefe, on guitar, trumpet, and vocals, joined about mid way into NOFX's career. During the time that the group started playing together, three of the members were into the straight-edge punk movement. However, Fat Mike was not attracted to that style, and the group claimed they were never a straight-edge band. They wanted to differentiate themselves from excessive use of gimmicks employed by many bands of the mid to late 1980s and thus called their group NOFX. The group wanted to avoid facades and maintain an open, accessible style of music.

Hit the Road

The group's live performances began in Hollywood, California, where Minor Threat, Black Flag, and Social Distortion had played. A club called Cathay de Grande hosted NOFX's first gig of four songs with another band's equipment. The trio believed that touring would make their name and music familiar to people and generate a following which would allow them to grow as a band. A demo tape was recorded with the guidance of Dan Bolles of the Germs and was made available to fans if they mailed a self-addressed, stamped envelope with a cassette. Songs were recorded on the tape and sent back to the interested fan. NOFX's first tour was in 1985 and covered cities in the Pacific Northwest. A band member's parent made the family station wagon available, and the group played in Reno, Nevada; Boise, Idaho; Portland, Oregon; and Ashland, Oregon. Friends made at the shows usually provided a place to crash for the night, while food and gas were stretched as thin as possible. Boise's gig was a house party and pay off was promised to be $200. Not surprising to the band, the promoter only gave them the $50 he had collected and apologized for not having the remainder of the money because he was broke.

Several changes in the lineup occurred over the following year. Smelly left for Santa Barbara, California, and two different drummers filled in the rhythm section. Dave Allen joined as vocalist, and the band headed out on another tour during the winter of 1985 to the Southwest United States. Fat Mike moved to San Francisco, California, to attend San Francisco State University after the Southwest tour. Unfortunately, Allen, the recently

For the Record . . .

Members include **El Hefe** (born Aaron Abeyta), guitar, trumpet; **Fat Mike** (born Mike Burkett), vocals, bass; **Eric Melvin**, guitar, vocals; **Smelly** (born Erik Sandin), drums; other members.

Formed in Los Angeles, CA, 1983; first U.S. tour, 1985; released first EP, *The P.M.R.C. Can Suck on This*, on Fat Mike's Fat Wreck Chords label, 1987; debut album, *S&M Airlines*, released on Epitaph, 1989; released *Ribbed*, 1991; released *The Longest Line*, 1992, and *Punk in Drublic*, 1994; released *The Decline* EP, 1999; band played in the 1998 Warped Tour.

Addresses: *Record company*—Epitaph Records, 2798 Sunset Blvd., Los Angeles, CA 90026, phone: (323) 413-7353, fax: (323) 413-9678, website: http://www.epitaph.com; Fat Wreck Chords, P.O. Box 193690, San Francisco, CA 94119, phone: (415) 284-1790, fax: (415) 284-1791, email: mailbag@fatwreck.com, website: http://www.fatwreck.com. *Website*—NOFX Official Website: http://www.nofxofficialwebsite.com.

added vocalist, died in an automobile accident. Smelly was convinced to join the band again, and Melvin moved to Santa Barbara to attend city college. Dave Casillas of Rat Pack joined as a second guitar player and participated in two United States tours and a European tour despite a head injury due to a diving accident. He played on NOFX's first three releases.

NOFX released their first EP, *The P.M.R.C. Can Suck on This,* in 1987 on Fat Wreck Chords, Fat Mike's recording label. It was an outcry against the 1980s conservative ideals. In 1988, an LP, *Liberal Animation*, was released on Fat Wreck Chords, with production credits to Brett Gurewitz of Bad Religion and Epitaph Records. The album included straight forward punk with some reggae mixed into the grooves. *Liberal Animation* was reissued on Epitaph in 1991.

Spread the News

The withdrawal of the Adolescents from a European tour created an opportunity for NOFX to expand their listening audience. A German booking agent had organized a tour for a German band called the Drowning Roses along with an American group. A van, equipment, and gigs were ready, and NOFX, who replaced the Adolescents, played overseas. Shortly after returning, Casillas was replaced by another guitar player. *S&M Airlines* was released in 1989 on Epitaph as their debut album. NOFX kept the pace speedy and added more guitar solos along with a ska groove while poking fun at American society. A tour of Canada and the United States was initiated before the *S&M Airlines* release, then another six weeks was spent in Europe promoting the album.

NOFX adjusted their sound for their 1991 Epitaph release, *Ribbed.* Epitaph invested heavily in NOFX, spending much time honing the vocals. Vocal harmonies reminiscent of Bad Religion found their way into the album which had cover art featuring a picture of a condom. In addition, NOFX released their first ballad on the innuendo-laden project. A song was even written about societies' false portrayals and facades throughout Southern California titled "New Boobs?" The group had achieved big-time punk status by this time and ventured once again to Europe along with The Leaving Train, Bad Religion, and Mudhoney. After the tour, an audition was held for a new guitar player because the previous guitarist departed for fear of falling into addictive druguse. Aaron Abeyta was so impressive on the guitar and trumpet that he was chosen as the new addition and given the name El Hefe, as he was the most skilled musician of the bunch.

Meanwhile, Fat Mike was working on his record company, Fat Wreck Chords, which gave NOFX total artistic freedom to pen lyrics which may be offensive. Not surprisingly, Fat Mike had been criticized for sidestepping political correctness. In a 1991 interview with *Maximum Rock and Roll,* available at the NOFX website, Fat Mike stated that he thought morals were important but that "most of society's mores are total bullshit...," especially those associated with conservatism. However, he stated that it is important for people to take a stand according to each issue, not just automatically fall in line with conservative or liberal concepts. This belief was exhibited in Fat Mike's opinion about rating albums similarly to how movies are rated. He expressed that "'Artists have to be just as responsible as other people."

Attitude and Humor

El Hefe's musicianship was the largest influence on 1992's Fat Wreck Chords release, *The Longest Line.* His driving guitar and skillful trumpet added a new dimension to NOFX's sound. The band continued to use a humorous approach to cover issues such as racism, as well as

American middle-class plight with a reggae vocal twist. Epitaph released another tongue-in-cheek titled album in 1992 called *White Trash, Two Heebs, and a Bean.* The album was softer than previous releases with more pop melodies, but still full of attitude and humor, even including a track poking fun at a lesbian relationship. Yet another testament to NOFX's disgust with commercial radio, "Please Play This Song on the Radio," began as a catchy melodic tune only to disintegrate into a stream of obscenities.

Punk in Drublic, released in 1994, included pop punk melodies similar to those found in Green Day and Offspring material. Otherwise, it was much the same as previous work, humorous and fast. A live project was issued in 1995 titled, *I Heard They Suck Live,* which was recorded at a Hollywood club and contained straightforward live versions from earlier albums. Sexual innuendo reached its climax with the release of 1996's *Heavy Petting Zoo,* which portrayed a suggestive scene with a male and a sheep on the album cover and was promoted with blow up sheep dolls for record stores.

NOFX sold out concerts in 1997 with huge popularity. Nevertheless, they avoided the hype. Fat Mike told *Flipside* in a 1997 interview about why the band stayed away from interviews, MTV, and commercial radio. He stated they were not looking for publicity and by not interviewing, they could live their lives without having someone twist their words into fiction. As far as NOFX was concerned, according to Fat Mike, all his band wanted was to play music and have fun making records. *So Long and Thanks for All the Shoes,* released in 1997, remained true to their desire by coming out true hardcore, fast and intense. *The Decline,* an EP released on Fat Wreck Chords in 1999, was one track where songs blended together without title. It targeted NOFX's problems with government and society.

Selected discography

The P.M.R.C. Can Suck on This, (EP), Fat Wreck Chords, 1987.
Liberal Animation, Fat Wreck Chords, 1988, reissued, Epitaph, 1991.
S&M Airlines, Epitaph, 1989.
Ribbed, Epitaph, 1991.
The Longest Line, (EP), Fat Wreck Chords, 1992.
White Trash, Two Heebs, and a Bean, Epitaph, 1992.
Punk in Drublic, Epitaph, 1994.
I Heard They Suck Live, Fat Wreck Chords, 1995.
Heavy Petting Zoo, Epitaph, 1996.
So Long and Thanks for All the Shoes, Epitaph, 1997.
The Decline EP, Fat Wreck Chords, 1999.

Sources

Books

MusicHound Rock: The Essential Album Guide, Visible Ink Press, 1999.
Robbins, Ira A., editor, *The Trouser Press Guide to '90s Rock,* Fireside/Simon and Schuster, 1997.

Online

Epitaph Records.com, http://epitaph.com/ (January 31, 2000).
Fat Wreck Chords.com, http://fatwreck.com/ (January 31, 2000).
NOFX Official Website, http://nofxofficialwebsite.com/ (January 31, 2000).
RollingStone.com, http://rollingstone.tunes.com/ (January 31, 2000).
Spin.com, http://www.spin.com/ (January 31, 2000).

—Nathan Sweet

Olivia Tremor Control

Rock band

The community of Athens, Georgia, earned distinction for having a credible local music scene first in the early 1980s, when bands like R.E.M., the B-52's, Pylon, and many others put the college town—home to the University of Georgia—on the map. While many speculated that Athens' new-found infamy was only temporary, bands such as Olivia Tremor Control proved them wrong, upholding the tradition well into the 1990s. "I think it's better than ever," said David Barbe, the former leader of the 1980s group Mercyland who co-owned and produced records at Chase Park Transduction, a studio that served as a popular stop for the new generation of acts from Athens. "Granted, there was some excitement in the early '80s. It was a new thing, and it will never happen again," he continued, as quoted by *Atlanta Journal-Constitution* writer Steve Dollar in 1999, the same year R.E.M. invited Olivia Tremor Control and another Athens band, Elf Power, to open a show during their three-night stand at Chastain Park Amphitheatre in Atlanta. "But the quality and quantity of bands coming out of here is at an all-time high. The really good stuff, what's really good about it is it's all unique. And it's unique in a really melodic way."

Creating music that is often described as a cross between the 1960s pop stylings of Brian Wilson and the Beach Boys and the spaced-out tendencies of Brian Eno, Olivia Tremor Control earned acclaim for layering psychedelic touches over irresistible pop melodies. Notwithstanding, the band never limited their work to these specific categories, occasionally dabbling in ambient textures, punk, the avant-garde, experimental noises, and various other hard to pin down sounds. As Vickie Gilmer of the *Minneapolis Star Tribune* explained, "OTC [Olivia Tremor Control] is the bastard child of [Brian] Wilson, able to manipulate sound, pop melodies, off-kilter rhythms and loops into a fantastical whole." However, the inability of critics and fans to neatly categorize the group's music suits Olivia Tremor Control just fine. "As soon as you give music a name, you pigeonhole it," Bill Doss, who sings and plays guitar, in addition to numerous other instruments, for the band, told Catherine Mantione Holmes of the *Atlanta Journal-Constitution* in 1988. "It takes away from the imagination of the listener." And although Olivia Control illustrated through their music an abundance of influences, Doss cited minimalist musician John Cage as one of his own greatest sources of inspiration. "It's not so much Cage's music as the way he goes about it. Letting things happen as they happen," he said to Holmes.

Because of the group's innovative and diverse, yet pop-sounding music, Olivia Tremor Control became the most visible and accessible members of a loose collective of like-minded indie outfits called the Elephant 6 Recording Company. "We can't describe [Elephant 6]," Olivia Tremor Control guitarist and vocalist William Cullen Hart revealed to *Billboard* magazine's Chris Morris. "People have described it as a group of friends that make music. We don't try to define it. I don't think we need to release some kind of manifesto." Other prominent Elephant 6 bands included the Apples (in Stereo), Neutral Milk Hotel, Elf Power, and Secret Square. Although Olivia Tremor Control drifted together gradually in Athens where they started work on their first album in 1993, most of the band had roots in the isolated town of Ruston, Louisiana. The band's primary songwriters and co-frontmen, singers/songwriters/multi-instrumentalists Hart and Bill Doss, both grew up in Ruston, along with friends Robert Schneider and Jeff Mangum, who went on to form the Apples and Neutral Milk Hotel, respectively.

Throughout high school, the four aspiring musicians shared similar influences, namely the Beatles, the Beach Boys, the Zombies, Pink Floyd, and Sonic Youth, and regularly exchanged home recordings and participated in one another's bands. After graduating from high school, Hart and Doss attended Louisiana Tech University together, where they worked as deejays for the school's college radio station. Often visited by pals Schneider and Mangum, Hart and Doss spent most of their free time at the station, further building their musical education and ambitions. It was also during the time spent at Louisiana Tech that the four developed a common

For the Record . . .

Members include **Bill Doss**, guitar, vocals; **Peter Erchick** (joined band in 1996), keyboards; **John Fernandes**, bass; **Eric Harris**, drums; **William Cullen Hart**, guitar, vocals.

Formed band in 1993 in Athens, GA; released debut album *Music from the Unrealized Film Script "Dusk at Cubist Castle,"* 1996; released *Black Foliage: Animation Music by the Olivia Tremor Control,* 1999. Also recorded as the Black Swan Network, and were part of a loose collective called the Elephant 6 Recording Company.

Awards: Athens Music Award for best album cover for *Black Foliage: Animation Music by the Olivia Tremor Control,* 1999.

Addresses: *Record company*—Flydaddy Records, Newport, RI. *Management*—Autotonic, Memphis, TN. *Booking*—c/o Jim Romeo, Legends of the 21st Century, New York City, NY. *Websites*—Flydaddy Records: http://www.flydaddy.com, Olivia Web: http://www.home.clara.net/hamlin/index.htm.

aesthetic that joined the formalistic experimentation of psychedelia with the unrestrained ethic of punk.

In 1990, Hart, Doss, and Mangum moved to Athens, forming a group together called Cranberry Life Cycle. The band was short-lived, however, because Mangum left the band shortly after it got underway. Nonetheless, Hart and Doss wanted to continue making music together, so they enlisted bassist/multi-instrumentalist John Fernandes and changed their name to Synthetic Flying Machine. Soon thereafter, Moss defected for a short period to the group Chocolate USA, and upon his return to Synthetic Flying Machine, the band mutated into the Olivia Tremor Control. Meanwhile, Schneider and Mangum relocated to Denver, Colorado, to form their own bands.

According to Doss, the group's name refers to the legend of Jacqueline and Olivia, two friends separated during the California earthquake of 1906. Since that time, as the story goes, they continued to search for each other across different dimensions of time and space. But according to Eric Harris, who joined the band for their debut EP and subsequent albums on drums and as "technical advisor," Olivia Tremor Control's name holds no specific meaning. "It's supposed to be evocative of whatever comes to mind," Harris told Holmes. "It doesn't have any special meaning outside of that." Likewise, Olivia Tremor Control experienced trouble in naming which instruments each member played. "We all play everything," said Doss. Because the band's songs feature theremin, violin, clarinet, saxophone, xylophone, flute, and keyboards, the matter of exchanging instruments is more complicated than simply switching a guitar for a bass. "But during a live show, on the straight pop songs, we play the instruments we play best," Doss added.

In 1995, Olivia Tremor Control, now consisting of Doss, Hart, Harris, and Fernandes (keyboardist Peter Erchick joined the band in 1996), debuted with the EP *California Demise,* the first installment of concept recordings built around a surreal, imaginary film conceived by Hart and Doss. Following the release of the vinyl-only EP *Giant Day,* Olivia Tremor Control released the 1996 double LP *Music from the Unrealized Film Script "Dusk at Cubist Castle."* The first few thousand copies sold also included a companion disc of ambient sequences entitled *Explanation to: Instrumental Themes and Dream Sequences.* Produced by Schneider and utilizing material first recorded as far back as 1989, the band's debut album, issued by Newport, Rhode Island-based Flydaddy Records, won stellar reviews. Robert Levine, for instance, in *MusicHound:Rock* hailed the creation a "masterpiece" of both psychedelic weirdness and Beatles-era pop. With their debut, Olivia Tremor Control's popularity started to extend beyond the Athens area as listener-supported stations and modern-rock radio picked up on the band'smusic. And as the band toured to more remote areas and appeared in larger venues, they sealed their reputation as an exciting live act, incorporating film features and abstract images into their shows.

The following year saw Olivia Tremor Control debuting the dreamy, ambient-leaning sounds of their alter ego, which they named the Black Swan Network. In 1997, they released a 20-minute EP entitled *Olivia Tremor Control vs. the Black Swan Network,* which featured both their ambient and pop sides, followed by the album *The Late Music.* For this release, the members of the band asked fans to send recorded description of their dreams, and the Black Swan Network layered the accounts over ambient music.

Two years later, in 1999, Olivia Tremor Control arrived with their second full-length album, *Black Foliage: Animation Music by the Olivia Tremor Control.* Again, critics applauded the band's ability to explore both pop and experimental music simultaneously. With tracks ranging from eleven seconds to eleven minutes, the songs of *Black Foliage,* as stated by Brett Milano in *Stereo Review's Sound & Vision,* "are sunny and bubbly, full of innocent sentiments and vintage pop harmonies—but they're segued, and sometimes interrupted, by wildly abstract tape collages." Furthermore, Milano went on to call the release "one of the more elaborately produced albums in recent memory."

In the spring of 1999, Olivia Tremor Control toured the East Coast, the Midwest, the Mid-South, and Canada, planning to perform in Europe as well as Japan during the summer months. That same year, the band received their first honor at the Athens Music Awards for best album cover for *Black Foliage: Animation Music by the Olivia Tremor Control.* In addition to music, all the band members were involved in the visual arts. Their record company, Flydaddy, reported that some of their work would soon be made available for sale.

Selected discography

California Demise, (EP), 1995.
Explanation to: Instrumental Themes and Dream Sequences, Flydaddy, 1996.
Giant Day, (vinyl-only EP), Drug Racer, 1996.
Music from the Unrealized Film Script "Dusk at Cubist Castle," Flydaddy, 1996.
(Black Swan Network) *The Late Music,* Camera Obscura, 1997.
(Olivia Tremor Control and Black Swan Network) *Olivia Tremor Control vs. the Black Swan Network,* (EP), Flydaddy, 1997.
Black Foliage: Animation Music by the Olivia Tremor Control, Flydaddy, 1999.

Sources

Books

MusicHound Rock: The Essential Album Guide, Visible Ink Press, 1999.

Periodicals

Atlanta Journal-Constitution, March 27, 1998, p. P03; April 15, 1999; June 25, 1999; August 29, 1999.
Billboard, March 13, 1999; May 15, 1999.
Boston Globe, April 5, 1999.
Chicago Tribune, March 29, 1999.
Los Angeles Times, November 23, 1999.
Melody Maker, April 3, 1999.
Minneapolis Star Tribune, March 26, 1999, p. 03E.
New York Times, February 9, 1999.
Stereo Review's Sound & Vision, April 1999.
Village Voice, April 13, 1999.
Washington Post, April 2, 1999; April 9, 1999.

Online

All Music Guide, http://www.allmusic.com (February 14, 2000).
Flydaddy Records, http://www.flydaddy.com (February 14, 2000).
Olivia Web, http://www.home.clara.net/hamlin/index.htm (February 14, 2000).

—Laura Hightower

Evan Parker

Saxophone

Evan Parker's love affair with the saxophone began when he was still a teenager. He started playing at age 14, and soon found a group of musicians who were as interested in West Coast jazz as he was. His hero was Paul Desmond, a member of the Dave Brubeck quartet. Had he been a California boy, Parker's love of West Coast jazz might not have been very noteworthy. But he was living in Bristol, England, far away from any major music scenes of that design. For observers–critics and fans alike–what has made Parker a standout in the world of improvisational jazz is not only his skill and creativity, but also his energy and passion.

In his *Down Beat* review of Parker's release, "Waterloo 1985," in October of 1999, Jim Macnie said that, "the saxophonists' playing is hallmarked by potency." In December of 1993, another *Down Beat* reviewer, John Corbett, talked about Parker on his release, *Conic Sections*. He commented that, "Anyone who thinks they know about contemporary saxophone music but hasn't heard the solo-soprano work of Brit Evan Parker is gravely mistaken. Taking the most extreme elements of late Coltrane [John Coltrane, American saxophonist who died in 1967]–overblowing, multiphonics, biting and slap-tonguing hte reed, cross-patterned fingering–Parker has combined these with seamless circular-breathing and rolled them into a one-man sonic adventure, certain to dumbfound you on first exposure." If Paul Desmond was his first love, Parker discovered the music of John Coltrane and Eric Dolphy shortly after that. According to Paul Keegan for *Down Beat* in July of 1994, Parker said that after he discovered Coltrane and Dolphy, "I started to depend less on ideas coming from my peer group and to formulate my own ideas. Coltraine and Dolphy became the absolute dominating forces in my life."

Perhaps Parker's greatest luck was being born to a father who was a pilot for British Airways. He was born on April 5, 1944 in Bristol, England, during the last year of World War II. By the time he was 18, his father arranged to send him on a two-week trip to New York. His interest in jazz had clearly become more than a youthful obsession by that time. That trip was the first of several he would be able to take thanks to his flight privileges. Parker talked about his first trip to Keegan, telling him that, "I saw Dolphy play at Birdland, and I was astonished at how easy it was to see him. Just walk in and there he is. It was like being in the presence of God." When he was 22, Parker was invited by drummer John Stevens to sit in at a club Stevens ran. There he met the players who would be a key to his future, including, Derek Bailey, Kenny Wheeler, Barry Guy, Dave Holland, Paul Rutherford and Trevor Wats. These were the people doing what interested Parker the most: innovative improvisation.

Parker's first step as a professional was with the Spontaneous Music Ensemble. Along with guitarist Derek Bailey, trumpeter Kenny Wheeler, bassist Dave Holland, and drummer John Stevens, Parker had already made a name for himself by 1970. His first recording with that group in 1968 was *Karyobin*. He joined Wheeler for two albums for ECM, *Around 6* and *Music for Large and Small Ensembles*. By the mid-1970s, Parker played with many American free improvisers, including Steve Lacy, Anthony Braxton and George Lewis.

The influence John Coltrane had on Parker would be unmistakable throughout his career. In a biography of Parker, for *All About Jazz*, Robert Spencer noted that, "his tone sounds a great deal like Coltrane's, and his phrasing recalls some of the last words from the master: the twilight pyrotechnics of *Interstellar Space* and *Expression*. No one, however, would ever hear Evan Parker playing either tenor or soprano [saxophone] and mistake the player for John Coltrane. Or anyone else!"

In his introduction for an interview he did with Parker in 1995, for the *San Francisco Bay Guardian*, John Shiurba said that, "There once was a time when jazz was jazz, and then came Evan Parker. Although the British saxophonist humbly explains his ground-breaking ventures into 'free improvisation' in the late 1960s as simply following in the tradition of John Coltrane and Eric Dolphy, the truth is that he and his associates literally

For the Record . . .

Born on April 5, 1944, in Bristol, England; son of a pilot.

Debuted as a member of the Spontaneous Music Ensemble with *Kaeyobin,* 1968; broke ground in free improvisation, late-1960s; other releases include *Two Octobers* (with Paul Lytton), 1972-75; *Saxophone Solos*, 1976; *Monocerso*, 1978; *Incision*, 1981; *Tracks*, 1983; *Chicago Solo*, 1997; *Most Materiall*, 1998; *Unity Variations*, 1999. "Evan Parker Festival" held in New York, 1994.

Addresses: *Email*—evanparker@musicnow.co.uk.

brought the walls down, creating a music so exciting and different that it virtually defied categorization."

Parker has done more than 140 albums since that first recording in 1968, 49 during the 1990s alone. Most of the recordings were done in limited pressings, and therefore very few are still available for listeners. The long list of recordings includes work he has done solo, as well as his many collaborations with others. John Corbett interviewed Parker and German saxophonist Peter Brotzmann, who met in 1968 when Parker went from London to Bremen, Germany. While their work has taken them in various directions, and they no longer find themselves on stage together as often, they still shared common beliefs regarding their music. According to Corbett, these saxophonists are, "The two most influential voices in improvised reed music from Europe." One of those beliefs they share has to do with the spirit of jazz and improvisation, and the importance of a group doing the improvising together. When Corbett asked Parker if the "idea of living music" still implied the core of the social activity from which it emerges, he answered, "I would say that you have to have something to *bring* to the group, and a great way of finding what you have to bring to the group is to work alone. Not just practicing, but finding what ideas you can sustain in performance. You must have material that you can bring, rather than coming every time ready to be blown by whatever current crops up but without any ability to steer or create a current yourself. You have to be able to push as well as pull, to supply food as well as eat. It's not enough to come to the table hungry; you've got to bring food."

Parker seemed to follow his own advice–playing both alone and with other similarly directed and gifted musicians, still a relatively small pool of a couple of hundred jazz artists for whom improvisation was the focus. Two recordings made in the spring of 1998 and reviewed by Corbett for *Down Beat* in April reflected how much Parker was continually willing to stretch to new dimensions. The first of these recordings, *Monkey Puzzle*, was a duet with New York reed player Ned Rothenberg, who joins Parker's soprano and tenor saxophones with his bass clarinet and alto saxophone. Corbet noted that the collaboration was a, "hugely exciting encounter that should utterly floor fellow saxophonists, this disc offers yet more evidence of the seriousness, openness and collaborative spirit of Mr. Parker." The other recording, *Most Materiall*, paired Parker with percussionist Eddie Prevost. About one of the selections, "Rejecting Simple Enumeration," Corbett said that it combined "Prevost's bowed and stroked cymbals with relatively static, long-tone matching sax," while another song, "Chastise Me, But Listen," was a free-jazz hit for tenor and kit, Parker's tensile tenor coiling up and springing like a venomous snake."

Parker's music was the subject "The Evan Parker Festival" in New York in the late summer of 1994.Crowds were packed into the three concerts he gave during the week of music and interviews. Kevin Whitehead said in *Down Beat* that "his music's really about fluidity, about continuity in change." Much of Parker's success has to do with his participation in the group effort, with whomever he might be playing. He has never seen himself as being the center of the music, only as a part of it.

In a September 1999 review for *Down Beat*, reviewer Jon Andrews talked about Parker's most recent recording, *Unity Variations*, which was a 1998 improvisational concert duet with pianist Georg Grawe. "It's never easy with Evan Parker," wrote Andrews. "No one demands more of audiences and fellow musicians than this uncompromising saxophonist does." Parker intends it that way. "The whole philosophy of why we improvise is to maximally involve the listener," he told Shiurba. "You always get more of people's attention if they think they're witnessing something they may never see again."

Well into his fourth decade of performing, Parker showed no signs of slowing down, or softening the work his audience must do when listening to him–on recordings or in live appearances. When he was interviewed in 1987, he reflected on his 20 years of playing and talked about his future. "With luck, I may have another 20 to go–after all, it's a fairly physical music. It's still the same instrument with the same buttons on it," he said with a smile. "It's just a different imagination. Different music from a different time." In the years following that interview, it seemed as if Parker was more active than he had ever been. Despite the physical demands of the music, Parker's imagination was still fertile.

Selected discography

Karyobin, Island, 1968.
Two Octobers (with Paul Lytton), 1972-75.
Saxophone Solos, Chronoscope (U.K.), 1976.
Monoceros, Incus (U.K.), 1978.
Incision, FMP (Germany), 1981.
Tracks, Incus (U.K.), 1983
Conic Sections, 1993.
Darn It! (with Paul Haines, et al.), 1994.
Breaths and Heartbeats (with Barry Guy and Paul Lytton Trio), 1995.
Three Blokes (with Steve Lacy and Lol Coxhill), 1996.
Chicago Solo, Okka Disk, 1997.
Natives and Aliens (with Barry Guy, Paul Lytton and Marilyn Crispell), 1998.
Monkey Puzzle (with Ned Rothenberg), 1998.
Most Materiall (with Eddie Prevost), 1998.
Unity Variations (withGeorg Grawe), 1999.
Waterloo 1985 (with Paul Lytton, Paul Rutherford and Hans Schneider), 1999.

Sources

Periodicals

All About Jazz, October 1998. Available at:
Chicago Tribune, January 11, 1999.
Down Beat, Jan. 1992; Dec. 1993; July 1994; Sept. 1994; Nov. 1994; Oct. 1995; Nov. 1995; Dec. 1995; Feb. 1996; June 1996; April 1998; May 1998; Sept. 1999; Oct. 1999; Jan. 2000.
Rolling Stone, New York, May 14, 1998.
San Francisco Bay Guardian, June 21, 1995.
Village Voice, New York, October 8, 1996.

Online

CDDB Online, http://www.cddb.com/xm/cd/misc./46e63cbe214b5025 (April 2000).
"Evan Parker biography," *All About Jazz*, www.allaboutjazz.com (April 2000).

–Jane Spear

The Promise Ring

Punk band

The Milwaukee-based alternative punk band the Promise Ring, whose members include lead vocalist and guitarist Davey Von Bohlen, drummer Daniel (Dan) Didier, guitarist Jason Gnewikow, and bassist Scott Schoenbeck became one of the leading "emocore" outfits of the late 1990s. The term emocore, which is short for "emotional hardcore," arose as a way to label a sub-genre of hard-core punk music popular in the Midwest and Washington, D.C., that combined the speed and music of the punk sound with more thoughtful, less angry words. Along with other emotionally-driven punk acts such as Rainer Maria (named for a 19th-century German poet), Dismemberment Plan, Jets to Brazil, and Jimmy Eats World, the Promise Ring was influenced by Washington, D.C., groups like Jawbox, Fugazi, and the Rites of Spring. However, such a label sometimes brings with it negative assumptions. "The minute you know what to call a scene you're in a museum with a tag around you," J. Robbins, the former leader of Jawbox, told Jeff Salamon in a 1999 interview for *Spin* magazine. "Maybe the problem is that 'emocore' isn't a cool sounding name. It doesn't feel cool." Nonetheless, the Promise Ring took the emocore label in stride, and became one of the few bands to remain on an independent label and gain mainstream media attention. By the time they released their second album, 1997's *Nothing Feels Good*, the Promise Ring had realized that they had more to offer, beyond their speed-punk signature, with more thought-provoking lyrics.

All of the members of the Promise Ring grew up playing in various hard-core punk bands that favored loudness and speed above all else. Davey Von Bohlen once played guitar for Cap'n Jazz, a Chicago-based alternative punk band. The other members of the group included lyricist Tim Kinsella and his brother, drummer Mike Kinsella. Although Cap'n Jazz stood apart from their counterparts in the Midwest for their unique brand of hyper-driven suburbia punk, Von Bohlen started to contemplate a side project. In early 1995, he started rehearsing with drummer Dan Didier, guitarist Jason Gnewikow, and original bassist Scott Beschta (later replaced by Tim Burton, who was replaced by Scott Schoenbeck) in Milwaukee, Wisconsin, as the Promise Ring, though he remained uncertain at the time if he really wanted to take much time away from his current group. Likewise, his collaborators were busy with other punk acts. However, when Cap'n Jazz disintegrated shortly thereafter, Von Bohlen found time to dedicate to his new band, and Didier, Gnewikow, and Beschta decided to join full-time as well. After the Cap'n Jazz split in 1995, the Kinsella brothers formed Joan of Arc, for whom Gnewikow does graphic work. Both Joan of Arc and the Promise Ring later became label mates on Jade Tree Records, and in 1998 Jade Tree, based in Wilmington, Delaware, released a comprehensive, two-disc collection of Cap'n Jazz songs entitled *Analphabepolotho,* a compilation that became a sacred text of the Midwest alternative punk scene.

Soon after officially forming in 1995, the Promise Ring recorded their first seven-inch single, which was issued by Foresight Records and later went out of print. The single, along with their reputation for performing, came to the attention of Jade Tree Records, and the small, independent label signed the Promise Ring in late 1995. Early in 1996, the group released their first seven-inch single for Jade Tree entitled "Falsetto Keeps Time," which became an instant localhit. Next, they joined another group, Texas Is the Reason, to release a seven-inch split record with that band. During the summer of 1996, the Promise Ring spent time touring, and while in Chicago recorded their first full-length album, *30 Degrees Everywhere,* which sold around 12,000 copies. The band rounded out 1996 with *The Horse Latitudes* EP, a CD-only singles compilation that included their single for Foresight, as well as their split with Texas is the Reason, "Falsetto Keeps Time," and two new songs. With these releases, the Promise Ring quickly became a favorite with college audiences, and their first two seven-inch singles sold in excess of 8,000 units. In addition, the group earned a spot performing at the *CMJ* (*College Music Journal*) Music Festival, a showcase of new, rising talent held in New York. The band also enjoyed widespread "fanzine" coverage, appearing in both *Alternative Press* and *Raygun.*

For the Record . . .

Members include **Scott Beschta** (left band c. 1998), bass; **Tim Burton** (joined and left band c. 1998), bass; **Daniel Didier**, drums; **Jason Gnewikow** (born c. 1974), guitar; **Scott Schoenbeck** (joined band c. 1999), bass; **Davey Von Bohlen** (former member of Cap'n Jazz), vocals, guitar.

Formed band, 1995; signed with Jade Tree Records, released debut album *30 Degrees Everywhere*, 1996; released *Nothing Feels Good*, 1997; released *Very Emergency*, 1999.

Awards: SESAC award for *Very Emergency*, 1999.

Addresses: *Home*—The Promise Ring, 2016 N. Booth, Milwaukee, WI 53212. *Record company*—Jade Tree Records, 2310 Kennwynn Rd., Wilmington, DE 19810, (302) 656-5856.

Now an underground sensation, the Promise Ring returned in October of 1997 with their second full-length album, *Nothing Feels Good,* and started breaking through into mainstream publications with mention in music magazines such as *Spin.* Recorded in June 1997 under the guidance of producer J. Robbins (leader of the Burning Airlines, the now defunct group Jawbox) and mixing engineers Stuart Sikes, Doug Easley, and David McCain, the album generated considerable attention. Full of fast-paced, intense rock and roll, as well as a wry sense of humor in terms of lyrical content, *Nothing Feels Good* showcased the band's confident sound. For the record, the group experimented with more radio-friendly songs as well with the tracks "Red & Blue Jeans," "Forget Me," and "Is This Thing On?" These songs, wrote Jon M. Gilbertson for *Let's Go Online/Milwaukee Journal Sentinel,* "ride straightforward, beautiful pop melodies as von Bohlen's desperate voice conveys the album's central theme of vagueness and confusion."

Von Bohlen further explained the basic premise behind the album. "The basic idea is that you think you know things, but really you never know," he told Gilbertson. "'Nothing Feels Good' means that life is really bizarre, but at the same time, it feels totally good not to feel as if you know things." Guitarist Gnewikow also discussed the group's decision to add a sense of feeling to the traditional punk ethic. "When we started this band we were getting older," he recalled to Salamon in *Spin.* "We were trying to figure out what we wanted to do," added Von Bohlen. "It was the end of this tight-knit Madison-Milwaukee punk scene and a lot of people were moving away or growing up." Upon the success of *Nothing Feels Good,* one of the act's fans, video director Darren Doane, known for his work for Blink 182, MxPx, and the Descendents, directed two videos for the song "Why Did Ever We Meet" from the album. He shot one of the videos free of charge as a concept project.

Although major record labels continued to call, the Promise Ring opted to stay with Jade Tree, selling approximately 30,000 units per album. In 1999, the band released their third album, *Very Emergency,* which earned favorable reviews and greater mainstream attention and firmly established Promise Ring as the day's most prominent of "emocore" bands. The lyrics of *Very Emergency* told stories of lost love and nostalgic memories set to catchy punk music, exemplified in the opening track "Happiness Is All the Rage," where Von Bohlen sings, "I've got my body and my mind on the same page/And, honey, now happiness is all the rage." Greg Kot of the *Chicago Tribune* described the opening song as "a perfect pop moment that somehow also feels like the antithesis of pop: private, confessional, awkward." Other highlights, such as "Happy Hour" and "Skips A Beat," were sure to make *Very Emergency* another college chart favorite. The release earned industry recognition as well, and in November of 1999 the Promise Ring won an SESAC (a performing rights organization) award in the alternative rock category for *Very Emergency.*

Selected discography

"Falsetto Keeps Time," (single), Jade Tree, 1996.
The Horse Latitudes, (EP), Jade Tree, 1996.
30 Degrees Everywhere, Jade Tree, 1996.
Nothing Feels Good, Jade Tree, 1997.
Very Emergency, Jade Tree, 1999.

Sources

Periodicals

Advocate, September 28, 1999.
Billboard, November 29, 1997; November 20, 1999.
Chicago Tribune, November 26, 1999.
Magnet, October/November 1999, p. 88.
Spin, November 1999, pp. 145-148.
Village Voice, July 21, 1998.

Online

Let's Go Online/Milwaukee Journal Sentinel, http://www.jsonline.com/daily/0918promisering.stm (January 18, 2000).

MTV Online, http://www.mtv.com (January 18, 2000).

The Promise Ring at Jade Tree Records, http://www.jadetree.com (January 18, 2000).

Rolling Stone.com, http://www.rollingstone.tunes.com (January 18, 2000).

—Laura Hightower

Roswell Rudd

Jazz trombone

Photograph by Jack Vartoogian. Reproduced by permission. ©

As a part of the growing jazz scene in New York in the 1950s, Roswell Rudd was in consort with some of the best jazz innovators the world has known. Sun Ra, John Coltrane, Carla Bley, Thelonious Monk, Herbie Nichols and others were all a part of a new direction in American music. New York's Greenwich Village was home to the Beat movement of the literary world and the avant-garde movement in jazz. To all whose image of jazz comes from those days, Rudd was a key player with sounds that blasted into dimensions unimagined–even if he has often been overlooked.

"You blow in this end of the trombone, and sound comes out the other end and disrupts the cosmos," Rudd told *Willamette Week*'s Bill Smith who did a preview of the trombonist's show in Portland, Oregon, in January of 1999. Smith noted that "in the last 40 years, no one has taken the instrument further, from Dixieland to the outer edges of the avant-garde, often at the same time. His playing evokes city life–both Uptown and the Bowery, black tie and tails and the same suit you've slept in for days. His trombone sounds like a species all its own. Nat Hentoff has said that Rudd's sound goes 'back to New Orleans and further ahead than anyone has yet reached.' His trombone is alive."

Roswell Rudd was born on November 17, 1935, in the small town of Sharon, Connecticut. As a kid he was interested in music and started playing the French horn. He studied music at Yale University, and moved to New York not long after that. From 1954, while still in college, and until 1959, he was deep into Dixieland music and toured with a group known as Eli's Chosen Six. The band appears in the 1958 Newport, Rhode Island, documentary "Jazz on a Summer's Day." Until the 1970s, Newport, Rhode Island, was home to one of the world's best known festivals every summer, The Newport Jazz Festival, that eventually moved to New York City in order to accommodate the crowds that increased annually. By 1960, Rudd's direction shifted to the free jazz that Cecil Taylor was playing, and the two began playing together. He went on to play with the Steve Lacy Quartet, Bill Dixon, Archie Shepp, Albert Ayler, and a few others included in New York's Composers Guild that assembled in 1964 and created a revolution in jazz.

Rudd counts his two major influences as Thelonious Monk and Herbie Nichols. He told Smith that "There was a great influx of music that came into my life when I first got to New York in the late 1950s and discovered these two." While he was in Steve Lacy's group, he had the chance to meet Monk. Lacy had played with him, and they would go watch him live. Rudd had a feel for Monk's music from the first time he heard him. He was able to

For the Record . . .

Born on November 17, 1935, in Sharon, CT. *Education:* Attended Yale University; graduated 1958.

Has played with Herbie Nichols, Thelonius Monk, Archie Shepp, Cecil Taylor, Albert Ayler, Steve Lacy Quartet, New York Art Quartet, Carla Bley, John Tchicai, and others who composed the New York Jazz Composers Guild of the 1960s; taught music at Bard College and the University of Maine.

Addresses: *Record company*—Knitting Factory Works, 4 Leonard Street, New York, NY 10013, phone: (212) 219-3006, fax: (212) 219-3401; website: http://www.knittingfactory.com.

listen to Monk, then play exactly the same way. Herbie Nichols entered Rudd's life just as he was nearing the end of his. Nichols died of leukemia at the age of 44. He had only gotten a chance to record 30 of his 170 compositions, and died without the appreciation Rudd believed he deserved. "He needed adventurous younger guys who had the drive to learn new music, and that was definitely me," Rudd remembered. They shared another bond, too. Nichols played in a swing/Dixieland band in order to pay the rent while he worked on his own more innovative music.

Rudd fell into obscurity for several years, resurfacing once in awhile to play, mostly in New York. He taught at Bard College, up the Hudson River from New York City, as well as at the University of Maine. For several years he spent his time in the Catskills, where he got his first professional break working with the Dixieland band at resorts. In an interview with *Cadence* magazine in the early 1990s, Rudd said that he "had been living around there, doing landscaping and being a clerk and doing delivery work," according to Lynn Darroch in the *Oregonian*, talking about Rudd's West Coast tour in 1999 that took him to 13 cities in Washington, Oregon, and California.

On the tour, Rudd worked with a new quartet that included Portland saxophonist Rob Scheps, who fell in love with Rudd's trombone playing the first time he heard it. At his various stops along the way, Rudd reunited with former colleagues: John Tchicai, who joined the group in Oakland, and bassist Chuck Israels, who sat in when the tour stopped in Bellingham, Washington. Rudd told Smith that the tour was "a wonderful adventure–I can hear it in my music already."

In the fall of 1998, Bob Blumenthal of the *Boston Globe* welcomed Rudd to that city for his performance at the Green Street Grill. In a phone interview prior to his arrival in Boston, Rudd talked about his present and his past with Blumenthal. He mentioned that he was working on his ongoing project of getting Herbie Nichols' music heard, putting together CDs of his unpublished music. Another project, one he called "Mystery of Light," included varying sorts of singers, songs, dances, visual effects, and dialogue. Rudd said that "when it's fully realized, it will have its own band featuring 'bone and African percussion." He also offered Blumenthal his perspective on the notoriety that practically passed him by, without leaving him any bitterness. "It's been a long struggle, but there are those moments—sometimes just a flash—that make you go on. There may have been five times when I was lucky enough to be in situations where the chemistry was just right. The New York Art Quartet was one, meeting Herbie Nichols was another.... You have to put your shoulders to the wheel, even when you feel you're running out of juice, and then that flash comes and you're stronger than before."

When Rudd joined with alto saxophonist John Tchicai, drummer Milford Graves and bassist Lewis Worrell to form the New York Art Quartet in 1964, he was establishing himself as a true jazz artist. The ensemble stayed together only about two years. None of them became common names even among most jazz lovers. When they played together for a jazz festival at the Seaport Atrium, they shared a bill with rock group Sonic Youth. Previewing the show in the *New York Times* on June 13, 1999, Francis Davis noted that this presentation was not an "act of charity by Thurston Moore, Sonic Youth's founder and guitarist, and an ardent devotee of '60s free jazz," he said. "The show might be one of the Bell Atlantic Jazz Festival's hottest tickets even without Sonic Youth as the opening act, such is the anticipation about the reunion of Mr. Rudd and Mr. Tchicai, who have not played together since the New York Art Quartet's breakup in February 1966 and who perform in New York individually only once in a blue moon...."

One of Rudd's earliest recordings emerged under new auspices in 1994. In March of 1963, Steve Lacy, Rudd, and the rest of the quartet recorded some Thelonius Monk tunes on a borrowed tape recorder in a New York City coffeehouse. "School Days" was the only one of those recordings that survived for this historical release.

Jon Andrews reviewed it in *Down Beat* in September of 1994 saying that "both Lacy and Rudd impress with their ability to range far from the theme while perfectly maintaining the rhythm and feel of the composition." Andrews noted that while the sound was less than perfect, "the performances make up for it." Throughout the years, Rudd has recorded with the Carla Bley Band. Bley was also one of the originals in the Jazz Composers' Guild of the 1960s, Elton Dean, Cecil Taylor, Paul Haines and Archie Shepp. Some of the earlier recordings from the 1960s have become available in reissue since the 1990s.

Rudd is known for his "extroverted style," as Scott Yanow noted in the *All Music Guide* in 1996. And his music has been that, but his life has been spent in and out of the public eye. When renowned musicologist, filmmaker and painter Harry Smith died in 1991, he left a legacy that was translated into the Harry Smith Archives. At a benefit performance for the archives in November of 1999, Rudd caught the ears and eyes of Ben Ratliff, music critic for the *New York Times.* He noted that "one of Smith's lifelong preoccupations was the idea of alchemy, and the evening's great trick of transubstantiation was pulled off by the trombonist Roswell Rudd, who performed "Dry Bones" with Sonic Youth. Mr. Rudd placed shouting, New Orleans-funeral style trombone improvisations over a rock 'n' roll drone and it worked; then he hollered fragments of the song's lyrics, stretching out words. From a former Dixieland jazz player in his mid-60s with a lumberjack shirt, swept-back white mane and beard–-he looked like something between a country doctor and Moses...."

If Rudd has survived the fame he never quite had, he has "disrupted the cosmos" enough to keep himself in an obscurity that defies the status quo and lets him linger on with his music when others have burned out at much younger ages. "All who come will get an earful and are definitely going to be changed," Rudd promised Smith on that West Coast tour. That is what Rudd has been doing for more than 40 years, and music has been permanently altered because of him.

Selected discography

School Days, with Steve Lacy Quartet, 1963; reissued 1994.
Roswell Rudd, 1965.
Everywhere, 1966.
Mixed, with Cecil Taylor, 1966; reissued 1998.
Jazz Composer's Orchestra Plays Numatik Swing Band, 1973.
Flexible Flyer, 1974.
Maxine, 1976.
Inside Job, 1976.
The Definitive, 1979.
Regeneration, 1982.
The Unheard Herbie Nichols, Vol. 1, 1996.
Broad Strokes, Knitting Factory Works, 2000.

Sources

Books

Yanow, Scott, editor, *All Music Guide*, 2nd edition, Miller Freeman Books, 1996.

Periodicals

Atlantic, Sept. 1992.
Boston Globe, Sept. 25, 1998; June 11, 1999.
Chicago Tribune, Dec. 5, 1997.
Down Beat, June 1993; Sept. 1994; Nov. 1994; March 1996; Oct. 1997; Mar. 1999; Nov 1999.
New York Times, June 13, 1999; June 15, 1999; Aug. 7, 1999; Nov. 17, 1999.
Village Voice, June 22, 1999.
Willamette Week (Oregon), January 27, 1999.

Online

"A Roswell Rudd renaissance," *Oregon Live*, http://oregonlive.com/ent/music/99/01 (April 2000).
"Roswell Rudd discography," *Rolling Stone.com*, http://www.rollingstone.com (April 2000).

—Jane Spear

Saint Etienne

Pop band

Photograph by Steve Double. Corbis. Reproduced by permission.

A highly conceptualized group established by two longtime friends, England's Saint Etienne set out with the idea to blend the sounds of 1960s pop with modern-day, dance-club rhythms, although co-founder Bob Stanely at one time declared, "We're a pop group. We're not a dance group," as quoted by *Magnet* magazine's Fred Mills in 1998. Nevertheless, Saint Etienne, a trio that also included pal Pete Wiggs and vocalist Sarah Cracknell, helped establish a brand of music known as indie-dance as a viable genre within Great Britain. Creating music born out of an eclectic array of influences, including the songs of Glen Campbell, George McCrae, the Fall, and the Beach Boys, Saint Etienne perfected the art of combining pure pop with both alternative and avant-garde elements. A popular act and a major attraction in their homeland, Saint Etienne gradually continued to win over American fans throughout the 1990s. After nearly a decade recording together and performing throughout Europe, Saint Etienne initiated their first "proper" tour of the United States in support of the 1998 album *Good Humor.*

The origins of Saint Etienne date back to the early 1980s with the childhood friendship of Bob Stanley and Pete Wiggs, both natives of Croydon, Surrey, England. Early on, the two never planned on forming a band, preferring record collecting and fiddling with tape recorders to actually learning how to play instruments. Some of the pals' favorite records included albums by the Fall and the Beach Boys, as well as 1970s soul and early-1980s electronic productions. However, it didn't take long for Stanley and Wiggs, like their idols, to begin dreaming of their own pop songs, concert performances, and television appearances with their names prominently emblazoned on the bass drum. By the time they reached their teens, the boys began making party tapes together, often adding film dialog into their diverse mix of music, and also started contributing to fan magazines.

After high school, Stanley and Wiggs put their musical ambitions aside to enter the work force, though Stanley fulfilled to some extent his personal interests as a music journalist, writing for such publications as Britain's music press weekly *Melody Maker.* Disillusioned by the state of pop records at the time, Stanley teamed up with Wiggs again in 1988 (some sources say 1989), hoping that the two could show the rest of the world how to improve upon the current output of popular music. Adopting the group's name, Saint Etienne, from a French football team, Stanley and Wiggs intended to incorporate the uplifting feelings expressed in pop classics from the 1960s and 1970s into songs that sounded current.

Moving to the town of Camden, the duo resumed the pastime that had brought them together as children and

For the Record . . .

Members include **Sarah Cracknell** (born on April 12, 1967, in Chelmsford, Essex, England; former member of LoveCut dB and Prime Time; joined group in 1991), vocals; **Bob Stanley** (born on December 25, 1964, in Croydon, Surrey, England; former music journalist), keyboards, programming; **Pete Wiggs** (born May 15, 1966, in Croydon, Surrey, England), keyboards, programming.

Released debut hit single "Only Love Can Break Your Heart," 1990; released debut LP *Fox Base Alpha,* 1991; nominated for the U.K.'s inaugural Mercury Music Prize for *Fox Base Alpha,* 1992; released *Tiger Bay,* 1994; had first U.K. top ten hit with "He's on the Phone," 1995; signed with Sup Pop and released *Good Humor,* 1998; toured worldwide, including perfromances for the first time in the U.S., 1998-99.

Addresses: *Record company*—Sub Pop, 1932 1st. Ave., Ste. 1103, Seattle, WA, 98101, phone: (206) 441-8441, fax: (206) 441-8245, e-mail: hello@subpop.com, website: http:www,subpop.com. *Websites*—Saint Etienne: http://www.saint.etienne.net; Saint Etienne at Sub Pop Records: http://www.subpop.com/bands/stetienne.

started recording songs and sending out tapes. In early 1990, Saint Etienne signed a contract with a small label, Heavenly, and released their first single a few months later in the spring of that year. The song, an upbeat cover of Neil Young's "Only Love Can Break You Heart" recorded with Faith Over Reason's Moira Lambert on vocals, was an instant success; not only did it become a British dance floor anthem, but "Only Love Can Break Your Heart" also edged into the top 100 in the United States. In late-1990, the pair followed with another dance floor/ underground hit single, "Kiss and Make Up," a cover of a song by an indie-pop groupcalled the Field Mice. This time, St. Etienne enlisted Donna Savage of the New Zealand band Dead Famous People to take on vocal duties.

In need of a permanent female vocalist, Stanley and Wiggs expanded the lineup to include a glamorous blonde singer named Sarah Cracknell, a veteran member at the time of the dance group LoveCut dB, a former member of Prime Time, and "blessed with a set of pipes that would make Dusty Springfield's mother blush," asserted Mills. Cracknell, raised in Windsor, England, spent her early years at a convent school in Ascot and briefly attended stage school. "Rather than auditioning, which is a bit embarrassing for everybody," Cracknell recalled of her joining Saint Etienne, "it was just, 'Let's go in and do "Nothing Can Stop Us" and see how that works.' I think we just got on so well and are sort of like-minded that they thought they might as well keep me." Soon thereafter, the group released the self-penned "Nothing Can Stop Us Now" in 1991. The addition of Cracknell helped Saint Etienne develop a unique sound that was at once sweet and unsettling. While Cracknell joined as a full-time member, Saint Etienne would continue to bring in guest vocalists from time to time, including rap artist Q-Tee, Tim Burgess of the Charlatans, Stephen Duffy, Shara Nelson (a former member of Massive Attack), and French pop singer Etienne Daho.

In October of 1991, Saint Etienne released their debut album, *Fox Base Alpha,* which made the British charts and in 1992 earned the band a nomination for the United Kingdom's inaugural Mercury Music Prize. With striking tracks such as the previously released singles "Nothing Can Stop Us" and "Only Love Can Break Your Heart," as well as "London Belongs to Me" and "Like the Swallow," the band's debut won favorable press. "It's worth remembering," noted *Rough Guide to Rock* contributor Justin Lewis in an appraisal of the debut, "that Saint Etienne were trying to reinvent Britpop three years before most of their contemporaries—and with a great deal more imagination."

Subsequently, Saint Etienne gained a strong following in England and throughout the rest of Europe. A cult following in the United States also discovered Saint Etienne.1992 gave way to a series of singles, including "Join Our Club," "People Get Real," and "Avenue," that further cemented the band's popularity. In March of 1993, the trio released a second album for Heavenly in the United Kingdom entitled *So Tough* (Warner Brothers issued the record in the United States) that included the songs "Avenue," "Mario's Café," and "Calico." That same year in November, the band returned with a collection of B-sides called *You Need a Mess of Help to Stand Alone.* Again, both efforts earned favorable reviews and maintained the group's dedicated fanbase. Saint Etienne concluded the year with *Xmas '93,* a holiday EP featuring the exuberant "I Was Born on Christmas Day" and a cover of Billy Fury's "My Christmas Prayer."

Another full-length album, *Tiger Bay* (released in the United States by Warner Brothers), appeared in February of 1994. Although largely overlooked by the American market, the release contained notable songs such as "Hug My Soul" and "Former Lover." Taking a hiatus from writing and recording new songs, in 1995 Saint Etienne released a complete singles compilation entitled *To Young to Die: The Singles* that illustrated the group's development in both style and content. The album also included a new song, "He's on the Phone," that finally gave the trio their first British top ten hit at the end of 1995. *Casino Classics,* a collection of Saint Etienne remixesby the Chemical Brothers, David Holmes, Andrew Weatherall, Underworld, and Aphex Twin, appeared in October of 1996.

In 1998, after signing with Sub Pop, an independent label based in Seattle, Washington, Saint Etienne arrived to rave reviews with a new full-length LP entitled *Good Humor.* With this effort, the group abandoned the use of sampling altogether; instead, Saint Etienne opted for session-musicianship and a clean, sleek sound. However, at the same time they managed to maintain their unmistakable pop sound—maturing without losing their sense of fun. Highlights from *Good Humor* included the disco-sounding "Sylvie," the Burt Bacharach-styled "Bad Photographer," and the Beach Boys-inspired "Mr. Donut." A well-received EP, *Places to Visit,* followed in 1999.

After returning from their four-year absence, Saint Etienne toured worldwide in support of *Good Humor.* They had never played in the United States, except for a single music–industry performance in New York City that the band considered a disaster. "We were always keen [on touring in America], but nobody ever asked us." Cracknell told *Los Angeles Times* writer Mark Boehm in June of 1999. Warner Brothers, the band's United States label through the early1990s, "never seemed to think [touring] was a good idea," and repeatedly declined to front the band the money needed to play in the United States, according to the singer. The major label believed that Saint Etienne, a pop and dance outfit rather than a grunge or new punk act, wouldn't attract large enough audiences in American to make a tour worthwhile. Unlike Warner Brothers, Sub Pop felt differently and allowed the band to plan dates in several cities in the United States.

In addition to writing music and recording with Saint Etienne, Stanley, Wiggs, and Cracknell participated in other projects. Stanley and Wiggs became active producers, songwriters, and remixers for other artists as well. In 1989, Stanley founded Caff Records, a label that released singles for bands such as Pulp and the Manic Street Preachers. In 1991 (some sources say 1992), Wiggs teamed with Stanley to found the Ice Rink record label, home to Oval, Earl Brutus, Golden, and for a brief time Shampoo. Meanwhile, Cracknell guested on David Holmes' 1995 album *This Film's Crap Let's Slash the Seats,* and in May of 1997 released a well-reviewed solo album entitled *Lipside* (issued on the Total label). A single from the LP, "Anymore," reached number 39 in August of 1996 on the United Kingdom charts. Because of problems with Cracknell's ailing record company, *Lipside* was not issued in the United States and Canada until February of 2000.

Selected discography

Foxbase Alpha, (U.K.) Heavenly, 1991; Warner Brothers, 1992.
So Tough, (U.K.) Heavenly, 1993; Warner Brothers, 1993.
You Need a Mess of Help to Stand Alone, (U.K.) Heavenly, 1993.
Xmas '93, (EP), (U.K.) Heavenly, 1993.
Tiger Bay, (U.K.) Heavenly, 1994; Warner Brothers, 1994.
To Young to Die: The Singles, (U.K.) Heavenly, 1995.
Cassino Classics, (U.K.) Heavenly/Creation, 1996.
Good Humor, (U.K.) Heavenly, 1998; Sub Pop, 1998.
Places to Visit, (EP), Sub Pop, 1999.

Sources

Books

MusicHound Rock: The Essential Album Guide, Visible Ink Press, 1999.

Periodicals

Boston Globe, December 10, 1998.
Chicago Tribune, December 14, 1998.
Los Angeles Times, June 1, 1999; June 7, 1999.
Magnet, November/December 1998, pp. 57-59.
Melody Maker, May 11, 1991; April 25, 1992; May 1, 1993; September 5, 1993; October 23, 1993; November 27, 1993; December 11, 1993; December 24, 1994; October 28, 1995; November 11, 1995; November 15, 1997; August 21, 1999.
Rolling Stone, August 5, 1993.
Village Voice, August 3, 1999.
Washington Post, May 21, 1999.

Online

"Saint Etienne," *All Music Guide,* http://www.allmusic.com (March 8, 2000).
Rolling Stone.com, http://www.rollingstone.tunes.com (March 8, 2000).
Saint Etienne, http://www.saint.etienne.net (March 8, 2000).
Saint Etienne at Sub Pop Records, http://www.subpop.com/bands/stetienne (March 8, 2000).
"Saint Etienne," *Rough Guide to Rock,* http://www.roughguides.com/rock/entries/entries-s/SAINT_ETIENNE.html (March 8, 2000).
Sarah Cracknell info. page, http://www.members.tripod.com/~GlamourpussSpice/scadata.html (March 8, 2000).

—*Laura Hightower*

David Sanborn

Saxophone, composer, bandleader

Photograph by Jack Vartoogian. Reproduced by permission. ©

Two-time Grammy Award winner David Sanborn, a highly visible and often emulated entertainer in America since the mid-1970s, has influenced saxophone players from an array of styles, especially popular music. Arguably possessing the most distinctive alto saxophone sound in the pop spectrum, Sanborn has contributed to the world of music his own passionate technique—complete with crying and squealing high notes. His emotional interpretations of melodies have always uplifted any recording or live performance, regardless of the specific genre. Although most of Sanborn's own recordings take on rhythm and blues, dance music, pop, and rock and roll, he is also an accomplished jazz player. However, Sanborn has remained quick to contend that "I'm not a jazz musician," as quoted by *Down Beat* contributor Howard Mandel in 1993, and "I sometimes get looped with jazz musicians because I play sax and improvise," he told *Los Angeles Times* writer Bill Kohlhaase in 1996. "Not that I'm offended by the description," he further explained to Mandel, "but I think the rhythmic orientation of what I do is not really jazz. Where I came from, the kind of musical context I grew up in, the kind of playing I did when I was a young player, and the way my playing formed was in more of a rhythm and blues context. The music that really made me want to become a musician was by Ray Charles. David Newman and Hank Crawford were the guys. They combined the sophistication, some of the harmonic sensibility, certainly the hipness, and the rhythmic undercurrent of jazz with the emotional directness of gospel and the structural elements of r&b."

Although the majority of Sanborn's output as a bandleader and soloist is indistinguishable from one album to the next, according to music critics, his sound never seems to wear thin. He has achieved longevity with his consistent technique by shining as a soloist, assembling top sidemen for his projects, and developing first-rate arrangements. His own brand of jazz fusion has always avoided the usual clichés, and he never plays down to the listener. Essentially a groove player, Sanborn has remained enjoyable over his 25-year recording history primarily because he is one of the few saxophonists of his generation who understands how to translate a soul singer's sense of time and line to jazz. Whether performing soul, funk, pop, rock, or occasionally improvised jazz, Sanborn plays solid with each subsequent effort. During his musical career, Sanborn has led several of his own groups and participated in an eclectic number of others, including John Scofield's Electric Outlet, Steely Dan, and Rickie Lee Jones' band. He has also hosted and co-produced the NBC radio program *The Jazz Show,* hosted his own syndicated television series called *Night Music* to bring rarely seen players (like Sonny Rollins, Sun Ra, and James Taylor) to the public eye, and

For the Record . . .

Born David William Sanborn on July 30, 1945, in Tampa, FL; raised in St. Louis, MO. *Education*: Studied at Northwestern University.

Began playing in rhythm and blues bands as a teenager, including time with Albert King and Little Milton; joined Paul Butterfield Blues Band, 1976; worked with numerous other artists, among them Stevie Wonder, 1970-72; established solo career, 1975; scored music for films such as *Soul Man*; hosted radio program *The Jazz Show* and the television series *Night Music*; has appeared regularly on *The Late Show with David Letterman*.

Awards: Grammy Awards for best rhythm and blues instrumental performance for 1981's *Voyeur*, 1982; with collaborator Bob James for *Double Vision*, 1987; and for best pop instrumental for 1988's *Close-Up*, 1989.

Addresses: *Record company*—Elektra Records, 345 N. Maple Dr., Ste. 123, Beverly Hills, CA 90210, phone: (310) 288-3800. *Booking information*—ICM, 8942 Wilshire Blvd., Beverly Hills, CA 90211, phone: (310) 550-4000, fax: (310) 550-4100. *Website*—David Sanborn at Elektra Records, http://www.wlwktra.com/jazz_club/sanborn/sanborn.html.

appeared on a regular basis with Paul Schaeffer's band on CBS television's *The Late Show with David Letterman* (previously known as *Late Night with David Letterman* on NBC).

Born on July 30, 1945, in Tampa, Florida, and raised in St. Louis, Missouri, David William Sanborn started playing the saxophone as therapy for a case of polio he suffered with as a youngster. Sanborn gravitated toward the blues tradition, he believed, because at the time that was the context he found himself in. "What was available to me in St. Louis was rhythm & blues bands," he remarked in a 1994 interview with Ed Enright of *Down Beat.* "I also think thatemotionally I went there because of the directness of the music." He began playing in rhythm and blues bands in St. Louis, including time with jazz greats Albert King and Little Milton while still a teenager, and also studied music at Northwestern University—one of the few schools with a saxophone department at the time—under Fred Hemke. While at Northwestern, located near Chicago, Illinois, Sanborn developed an interest in the city's rich blues tradition, a form that would help shape his work as a composer and solo recording artist. Playing with King, as well as with Gil Evans and his orchestra, in jazz and blues clubs around St. Louis taught the aspiring saxophonist to play with conviction and emotion all the time. Along with Evans, King, and his primary influence, Crawford, Sanborn also cited Lou Donaldson, Jackie McLean, and Charlie Parker as important figures in his own development.

By the late 1960s and early 1970s, Sanborn had become a much sought-after sideman and session musician. In this capacity, he participated with an array of artists from across the musical spectrum. Not only did Sanborn further explore his rhythm and blues roots during his days as a sideman, but he also extended his talents to rock, soul, funk, and pop. Some of his most significant connections early on included stints with Paul Butterfield (aside from recording several albums with the bandleader, whose band he joined in 1967, Sanborn also performed with the Paul Butterfield Blues Band at the original Woodstock), the Gil Evans Orchestra, Stevie Wonder (1972's *Talking Book*), James Brown, David Bowie (the 1975 soul classic *Young Americans*), Paul Simon, B.B. King, the Becker Brothers, the Eagles, and numerous others.

As a solo artist and bandleader, Sanborn accumulated a long list of popular successes. His debut solo outing arrived in 1975 with *Taking Off,* which included the memorable wah-wah pedal track "Butterfat" and helped spur major-label record company interest in fusion music. After recording his 1976 self-titled effort, Sanborn returned in 1978 with the acclaimed *Heart to Heart.* Here, Sanborn made changes and took chances, such as augmenting the usual pop-fusion rhythm section with horns (courtesy of the Gil Evans Orchestra) that earned him critical praise. His fourth effort, the breakthrough rhythm and blues album *Hideaway* released in 1980 placed Sanborn at the forefront, establishing him as one of pop's premier saxophonists and cementing his mainstream appeal. With this release, Sanborn garnered the first of his several Grammy Award nominations.

In 1982, Sanborn took home his first Grammy for best rhythm and blues instrumental performance for his gold-selling album *Voyeur* (released in 1981). His next album, 1982's *As We Speak,* brought Sanborn further acclaim for his chance-taking and musical experimentation. Rather than focus solely on alto saxophone, *As We Speak* saw the composer switching from alto to soprano for several numbers. Continuing to investigate a myriad of styles throughout the remainder of the decade, in 1984 Sanborn released one of his greatest critical achievements, *Straight to the Heart,* which used a live studio strategy to add extra fire to the instrumental interplay. In 1987, Sanborn, along with collaborator Bob James, earned another Grammy for the platinum-selling *Double Vision,* and in 1989, Sanborn earned a third Grammy, this time for best pop instrumental for 1988's *Close-Up.*

Sanborn maintained his popularity throughout the 1990s as well. In all, Sanborn boasted album sales exceeding the six million mark, netting one platinum and six gold albums, including the urban funk album *Upfront* released in 1992. Occasionally, he surprised the music industry with non-pop ventures such as the acclaimed *Another Hand* released in 1991. A complete departure that earned critical overwhelming approval, the album matched Sanborn with an eclectic mix of new-jazz artists such as guitarists Bill Frisell and Marc Ribot, as well as traditional jazz heavyweights like bassist Charlie Haden and drummer Jack DeJohnette. Likewise, Sanborn guested on a 1993 album entitled *Diminutive Mysteries,* recorded with avant-garde alto saxophonist Tim Berne. A tribute to Berne's teacher and main influence, Julius Hemphill, *Mysteries* collected seven Hemphill compositions, plus one Berne piece, played by a group fronted by Berne on alto and baritone saxophone and Sanborn on alto and soprano saxophone. In 1995, Sanborn revealed another side of his musicianship with *Pearls,* for which he was accompanied by a string orchestra arranged by Johnny Mandel.

Returning to traditional rhythm and blues textures and urban music influences in 1996, Sanborn released *Songs from the Night Before,* his fourteenth solo outing. "I'm lucky enough to really love what I do," said Sanborn, as quoted on his website at Elektra Records. "I get to do an album every 12 to 18 months, and it always seems to be a reflection of where I'm at musically at that particular point. I've been listening to more R&B pop recently ... like D'Angelo for example. It's interesting how some of it goes back to some of the `70s stuff I grew up around. The production is different, but the vibe is there."

In 1999, Sanborn returned with *Inside,* and also performed at Madison Square Garden in New York with a concert billed as "Eric Clapton and Friends." The show, which also featured Bob Dylan, Sheryl Crow, and Mary J. Blige and aired on television's VH1, raised over $5 million for Clapton's Crossroads Centre, a drug and alcohol treatment facility that the legendary guitarist/ songwriter founded on the island of Antigua in 1997.

Selected discography

Taking Off, Warner Brothers, 1975.
David Sanborn, Warner Brothers, 1976.
Heart to Heart, Warner Brothers, 1978.
Hideaway, Warner Brothers, 1979.
Voyeur, Warner Brothers, 1981.
As We Speak, Warner Brothers, 1982.
Backstreet, Warner Brothers, 1983.
Straight to the Heart, Warner Brothers 1984.
A Change of Heart, Warner Brothers, 1987.
Close-Up, Reprise 1988.
Another Hand, Elektra, 1991.
Upfront, Elektra, 1992.
The Best of David Sanborn, Warner Brothers, 1994.
Hearsay, Warner Brothers, 1994.
Pearls, Elektra, 1995.
Songs from the Night Before, Elektra, 1996.
Inside, Elektra/Asylum, 1999.

Sources

Books

Contemporary Musicians, Vol. 1, Gale Research, 1989.
Swenson, John, editor, *Rolling Stone Jazz & Blues Album Guide,* Random House, 1999.

Periodicals

Boston Globe, July 2, 1999.
Down Beat, February 1993; October 1994; March 1998.
Los Angeles Times, June 19, 1996; July 11, 1998; August 23, 1999; October 4, 1999.
People, December 18, 1989.
Washington Post, June 2, 1999.

Online

All Music Guide, http://www.allmusic.com (March 9, 2000).
"David Sanborn," *Centerstage Media,* http://www.centerstage.net/chicago/music/whoswho/DavidSanborn.html (March 9, 2000).
David Sanborn at Elektra Records, http://www.wlwktra.com/jazz_club/sanborn/sanborn.html (March 9, 2000).
PRA Presents David Sanborn, http://www.prarecords.com/artists/sanborn/ (March 9, 2000).

—Laura Hightower

Pharoah Sanders

Saxophone

Photograph by Jack Vartoogian. Reproduced by permission. ©

Although largely a tenor saxophonist, the always spiritually-connected jazz great Pharoah Sanders has the ability to blow alto and soprano with equal power, resonating a blues-based sound that has become his signature. "The unvarnished, rough-edged sound that Sanders coaxes from his horn, in fact, is one of the most appealing facets of his work. Other tenorists—young and old—may strive for a sleek evenness of timbre from one register of the instrument to the next, but Sanders' ideal is quite different: a tough, acidic, rough-edged sound that speaks of direct emotional expression," wrote *Chicago Tribune* arts critic Howard Reich in 1997. An influential improvisational player who helped establish the avant-garde style during the 1960s and 1970s, Sanders repertoire gave him a new audience in the 1990s; art rockers and free-music fans alike embraced Sanders' unbridled, all-inclusive style.

Born Farrell Sanders on October 13, 1940, in Little Rock, Arkansas, Sanders—who, like many great jazzmen, picked up an aristocratic nickname later on—grew up surrounded by musical influences. His grandfather, a school teacher, taught both mathematics and music, while his mother and sisters sang in clubs and gave piano lessons. Sanders himself started out playing drums with his high school band, but soon learned to play tuba, baritone horn, clarinet, and flute as well. In 1959, still a member of his school's band, Sanders picked up tenor saxophone, and the instrument resonated a sound that instantly captivated him. At first, Sanders focused mostly on rhythm and blues melodies—eventually backing Bobby Bland at a local club and touring for a short time with a band called the Thrillers—until his school band teacher and one of his major influences, Jimmy Cannon, introduced him to the jazz style. Aside from idol John Coltrane, Sanders cited Little Rock during the 1950s as a source of significant influence. "There were also a lot of guys [in addition to Cannon] who came down from Memphis to work and get paid in the clubs there," he recalled to Martin Johnson of *Down Beat* in a 1995 interview. "I was only in high school, but I would dress up—put on a suit, put a little thing here [pointing at his lip] like I had a mustache and some dark shades, and sneak into the club. I had to walk a little different and talk a little different, but I met some good players like Gilbert Capers. It was a good scene until they closed it down."

But despite his dedication to and love for music, Sanders envisioned a career in commercial art rather than in jazz. Thus, upon graduating from high school, Sanders left Arkansas, moving to California in 1959 to study at Oakland Junior College. Playing in rhythm and blues clubs in Oakland and San Francisco while attending college, Sanders soon realized that music was his true calling. It was in Oakland that Sanders met Coltrane

For the Record . . .

Born Farrell Sanders on October 13, 1940, in Little Rock, AR; married Thembi (divorced) and Shukuru. *Education*: Studied music with Jimmy Cannon, mid-1950s; attended Oakland Community College, Oakland, CA, late 1950s.

Played with Sun Ra Arkestra, early 1960s; recorded and performed with John Coltrane, 1965-67; signed with Impulse! and released a string of acclaimed albums, late 1969-74; recorded softer albums for India Navigation, Arista, and Theresa labels, late 1970s-80s; signed with Evidence and returned to experimental jazz, 1992; collaborated with Maleem Mahmoud Ghania on *The Trance of Seven Colors,* 1994; signed with Verve Records, c. 1996; released *Save Our Children,* 1998.

Addresses: *Record company*—Verve Music Group (distributes Vereve, GRP, and Impulse!), 555 W. 57th St., New York City, NY 10019, phone: (212) 333-8000 or (212) 603-7919.

briefly for the first time, and the two men spent time together touring local pawn shops for horns and mouthpieces. Meanwhile, Sanders was developing an interest in the burgeoning jazz scene of the early-1960s, a particularly exciting period for the form marked by ventures into more sonically adventurous territory. Saxophone innovators like Coltrane, Sonny Rollins, Eric Dolphy, Ornette Coleman, and others presented new possibilities for the genre. Such influences led Sanders to begin expanding his own technique.

Driven to take part in the new movement, Sanders left Oakland in 1962 to move to New York City, where he played jazz and blues and took odd jobs to make ends meet. During this time, New York welcomed an influx of young jazz players, and as American jazz was entering a troubled yet exciting new phase, Sanders was one of many voices—alongside others such as Archie Shepp, John Tchicai, and Albert Ayler—who wanted to make waves. By now, Sanders had developed his own unique sound, and like-minded players such as Coleman, Don Cherry, Sun Ra, and other notables began calling. "I would go everyday to rehearse with them [Sun Ra's Arkestra]," Sanders told Johnson. "If we weren't rehearsing, the Sun would talk to us about different things, because he was very knowledgeable about things I hadn't even thought about. I was amazed by how much he knew about history." Although working steadily with Sun Ra's group during the early 1960s, Sanders nonetheless found himself living in poverty, and the hardships multiplied when the saxman struck out on his own. "At the time, I didn't have my own place, so when I left [the Arkestra], I was out on the street," Sanders continued. "I met quite a few other musicians on the streets. It was hard times. Everyone who stayed in New York City struggled till daylight came. I used to give blood to make five dollars. Since a slice of pizza was only 15 cents and a candy bar cost only a nickel, if I had a dollar, that would take care of you and me all day long!"

When Sanders first arrived in New York, he had hoped to contact Coltrane, but found that his phone number had changed. Finally, he found the tenor saxophonist playing at the Half Note club in 1963. "I was outside. I couldn't go in because I was dirty and all, but John saw me and let me in," Sanders recalled to Johnson. Playing together that night and exchanging numbers, the two men, both devout Muslims, kept in touch and became friends. Two years later, in 1965, Sanders joined Coltrane's band, a position for which he would always be remembered. During the two years spent with Coltrane's final group before the master saxophonist's death in 1967, Sanders, serving as the second tenor and the innovator's unofficial number-one son of the group, stood at the older musician's elbow, helping to tear down the few remaining walls that surrounded free-jazz improvisation. Whereas Coltrane stood as the patron saint of the jazz vanguard, the younger Sanders "was like his mischievous sidekick, a strange, cathartic noisemaker whose flights of sonic uproar seemed even more outlandish than those of Coltrane himself," wrote Richard Cook for the *New Statesman* in 1998. "Where Coltrane was all steely majesty, Sanders sprayed notes and sounds everywhere, drawing multiphonic sounds from his saxophone which the leader seemed to be bewitched by." On challenging, dissonant albums with Coltrane such as *Ascension, Meditations,* and *Live at the Village Vanguard Again,* Sanders made his first mark on the world of experimental jazz.

Although Sanders had recorded two solo albums prior to Coltrane's death—1964's *First Album* and 1966's *Tauhid*—the young musician seemed unsure of what to do next. After death martyred Coltrane, critical interest in the avant-garde also faded. Moreover, the birth of rock music started to steal attention from the jazz scene, and many musicians, unable to compete with the new sound of the electric guitar, fell by the wayside. In spite of such obstacles, Sanders persisted, emerging from his mentor's shadow to define his own artistic personality. His own pursuits between 1969 and 1974, during which time he recorded a series of albums for the Impulse! label, often reflected his interest in non-Western idioms, free-form soloing, and highly charged atmospheres. Throughout this period, Sanders "managed to distill the spiritual concerns ofColtrane's later work into simple motifs that would rise into conflagrations of sound but would then subside into trance-like meditations," noted *Washington Post* writer Geoffrey Himes in 1998. Key efforts from the saxophonist's early years as a soloist included 1969's *Jewels of Thought,* 1971's *Thembi,* and 1974's *Love in Us All.* Another album from these years, 1969's *Karma,* included Sanders' best-known composition, a mesmerizing, 32-minute piece entitled "The Creator Has a Master Plan."

Featuring musicians like pianist Lonnie Liston Smith, bassist Cecil McBee, drummer Roy Haynes, violinist Michael White, and vocalist/songwriter Leon Thomas, the above-mentioned recordings exemplified Sanders at his toughest, at the peak of his career. "Those guys seemed to understand the way I played," Sanders fondly recalled to Himes. "They understood right away that I wasn't confining them to [chord] changes, that I didn't want them to be so intellectual, that I wanted them to play whatever they felt.... we listened to each other. No matter what we were doing, we always listened to what everyone else was doing. Some musicians play with lots of energy and play well, but they're more like show musicians than spiritual types. They don't come to give, and when the ego is involved, everyone can feel it.... But the band I had back then, those were spiritual musicians, and they came to give."

During the late 1970s and 1980s, most critics, expecting further experimentation, attacked Sanders for softening his style, with the exception of 1982's *The Heart Is a Melody,* which included the long saxophone piece "Olé." But Sanders himself stood by his work, refusing to let others dictate his musical direction. "I have never said I was a jazz player; I'm just a player. I get jobs with whoever calls me, you know, and I perform in whatever the situation may be," he said to Johnson. "I am most certainly not a jazz player," Sanders emphasized.

However, Sanders revisited his earlier work—full of foreign influences such as African percussion, Indian harmonies, and Islamic tonalities—throughout the 1990s. In 1994, after paying tribute to Coltrane with the acclaimed *Crescent of Love* and contributing a track to the *Red Hot + Cool* AIDS benefit album, Sanders recorded *The Trance of Seven Colors* with a group of Gnawan musicians—all descendants of slaves from West Africa—led by Maleem Mahmoud Ghania in Morocco. Released later that year, *The Trance of Seven Colors* remained one of Sanders' fondest projects. "It was very exciting," he recalled to Johnson about the recording session. "They build on the music, add things in layers; everybody gets involved." One piece for the album entitled "Peace in Essaouira" was written by Sanders himself to eulogize friend and guitarist Sonny Sharrock, with whom Sanders had record in the 1970s and early 1990s, after he passed away shortly before recording sessions took place.

In 1998, Sanders recorded the album *Save Our Children,* which included an 11-minute piece showing the musician at his best called "The Ancient Sounds." Released by the Verve label later that year and recapturing the spiritual feel of his Impulse! years, the well-received *Save Our Children* was produced by Bill Laswell, who worked with Sanders previously for *The Trance of Seven Colors* and 1996's *Message From Home.* Again, with *Save Our Children* Sanders called upon musical elements from across the globe. "When I was living in Oakland, I played with some Moroccan musicians there, because I felt we both were more into a spiritual kind of thing," he said to Himes. "Instead of looking at music as notes, they were looking at it as a feeling theywere trying to project through the notes. I hear that in a lot of music around the world—in India, in Japan, in Africa."

Now in his sixties, Sanders continues to record, explore music from different cultures, give performances with his band, and participate in jazz festivals. Regardless of his activities, no matter where his travels take him or what style of music he plays, Sanders never strays far from his blues roots back in Arkansas. "When I was learning to play the blues," he explained to Himes, "I had to practice all keys, because all the guitarists played in such weird keys. The guys in the South had a different way of playing the blues, a certain way of attacking the note I don't hear anymore. And they would try anything. There was a drummer called Candy Man who could play a Maxwell House coffee can and make it sound like Miles Davis's trumpet. All those experiences showed me that no limits should be put on music. When I play today, every note is like the blues, because I put the same feeling into whatever I play. You can't just jump out there and start playing; you have to have some feeling behind it. I just open up and blow from the spirit."

Selected discography

With John Coltrane

Ascension, Impulse!, 1965.
Meditations, Impulse!, 1966.
Expression, Impulse!, 1967.

Solo

First Album, ESP, 1964.
Tauhid, Impulse!, 1966, reissued, 1993.
Izipho Zam, Impulse!, 1969.
Karma, Impulse!, 1969, reissued, 1995.
Jewels of Thought, Impulse!, 1969, reissued, 1998.
Thembi, Impulse!, 1971, reissued, 1998.
Black Unity, Impulse!, 1971, reissued, 1997.
Live at the East, Impulse!, 1971.
Summun Bukmun Umyun, Impulse!, 1972, reissued 1998.
Wisdom Through Music, Impulse!, 1972.
Village of the Pharoahs, Impulse!, 1972.
Elevation, Impulse!, 1973.
Love Is in Us All, Impulse!, 1974.
Harvest Times, India Navigation, 1976.
Love Will Find a Way, Arista, 1977.
Pharoah Sanders, India Navigation, 1977, reissued 1996.
Journey to the One, Theresa, 1980, reissued, Evidence, 1994.
Rejoice, Theresa, 1981, reissued, Evidence, 1992.
The Heart Is a Melody, Theresa, 1982, reissued Evidence 1993.
Live, Theresa, 1982.
Shukuru, 1987, reissued, Evidence 1992.
Oh Lord, Let Me Do No Wrong, Dr. Jazz, 1987.
Prayer Before Dawn, 1988, reissued, Evidence, 1993.
Welcome to Love, Timeless, 1991, reissued, Evidence, 1996.
Ed Kelly & Pharoah Sanders, Evidence, 1993.
Crescent with Love, Evidence, 1994.
(Contributor) "This Is Madness," *Stolen Moments: Red Hot + Cool,* 1994.
(With Maleem Mahoud Ghania) *The Trance of Seven Colors,* Axiom, 1994.
Message From Home, Verve, 1996.
Priceless Jazz, GRP, 1997.
Save Our Children, Verve, 1998.

Sources

Books

Contemporary Musicians, volume 16, Gale Research, 1996.
Swenson, John, editor, *Rolling Stone Jazz & Blues Album Guide,* Random House, 1999.

Periodicals

Audio, December 1994; June 1996.
Chicago Tribune, September 27, 1997.
Down Beat, March 1995; April 1995; August 1996; July 1998; August 1999.
Los Angeles Times, February 24, 1995; March 12, 1995; June 20, 1997; January 31, 1999; February 26, 1999.
New Statesman (London), August 14, 1998.
New York Times, February 10, 1999.
Washington Post, April 24, 1998.

—*Laura Hightower*

Mongo Santamaria

Percussionist

Photograph by Frank Diggs. Archive Photos. Reproduced by permission.

Afro-Cuban percussionist and bandleader Mongo Santamaria is one of the most influential players of his generation. A popular performer since 1963, the year the Herbie Hancock-penned "Watermelon Man" reached the pop charts in the United States, Santamaria has explored his own Cuban musical roots throughout his career and has blended elements of jazz, rhythm and blues, rock, and popular music with the traditional sounds of his homeland. A "mesmerizing spectacle for both eyes and ears" in concert, the master percussionist "creates an incantory spell rooted in Cuban religious rituals, quietly seating himself before his congas and soloing with total command over the rhythmic spaces between the beats while his band pumps out an endless vamp," asserted *All Music Guide* contributor Richard S. Ginell. In addition to his ability to captivate an audience (evidenced on the hypnotic "Mazacote" from his 1972 *African Roots* album), Santamaria has proven himself a powerful bandleader as well. Many future notables have passed through Santamaria's ranks or collaborated with the conga player, from Nat Adderly and Jimmy Cobb, through Chick Corea, Hubert Laws, and Bob James. According to music historians, no Cuban percussionist, with the exception of Santana's Armando Peraza (and not counting Desi Arnaz), has reached as many listeners as Santamaria.

Touring and recording songs well into his late seventies, Santamaria in his later years has expressed his annoyance over the name given to his generation's music by critics and the press when several entertainers revived Cuban-influenced music during the 1990s. "What they call 'salsa' is the Afro-Cuban music that we did 50 years ago," he told Aaron Cohen of *Down Beat* in November of 1999. "I don't see calling it a new thing. We used to call it mambo, guaracha, guanco, and every other name. Today they take everything and just call it salsa. It's an economical thing—with the Cuban Revolution, they tried to forget the music had anything to do with Cuba."

Ramon "Mongo" Santamaria was born on April 7, 1922, in Havana, Cuba. Raised in the city's Jesus Maria district, Santamaria was exposed to all kinds of Afro-Cuban rhythms—rumbas and Santeria rituals were everywhere. During his childhood, Santamaria first played the violin, but eventually switched to drums, dropping out of school in his teens to become a professional musician. In spite of his youth, he played in some of the city's most famous pre-Castro clubs, especially the Tropicana. By the early 1940s, Santamaria had established himself as one of Havana's leading percussionists, participating in an array of bands that drove the city's flourishing nightlife. One such group, the Orquestra Casino de la Playa, counted another famous Cuban, Perez Prado, among its members. When Prado took his

For the Record . . .

Born Ramon "Mongo" Santamaria on April 7, 1922, in Havana, Cuba; raised in the city's Jesus Maria district.

Played at famous Havana clubs as a teen such as the Tropicana; moved to Mexico with Perez Prado and his orchestra, 1948; moved to New York City and made his American debut with Prado, 1950; played with Tito Puente's orchestra, c. 1950-56; played with vibraphonist Cal Tjader's group, 1957-60; released debut album as a bandleader entitled *Yambu,* 1958; released *Go, Mongo!,* which included the Latin jazz standard "Afro Blue," 1962; returned to the Fantasy label, 1995; performed with various artists, including Willie Bobo, Chick Corea, and Dizzy Gillespie.

Addresses: *Office*—c/o Hook, 78-08 223rd St., Flushing, NY 11364-3637.

own band to Mexico City in 1948, he took young Santamaria with him.

In 1950, Santamaria moved to New York City, where he made his American debut with Prado. After spending a total of three years on the road with Prado's orchestra, he left the ensemble to work with Tito Puente and his band. During the six years spent as a percussionist for Puente's orchestra, Santamaria eventually became well-known throughout California, earning him a position in 1957 with a pioneering Latin-American jazz band in San Francisco led by vibraphonist Cal Tjader that also featured bassist Al McKibbon, pianist Vince Guaraldi, and a percussion section consisting of Willie Bobo, Louis Kant, and Santamaria's cousin Armando Peraza.

It was during his tenure with the Tjader group (which lasted until 1960) that Santamaria penned the piece "Afro Blue," a springboard for the formation of his own ensemble, a traditional Latin charanga band billed as Mongo Santamaria y Sus Ritmos Afro-Cubanos. With this group, Santamaria as a bandleader made an impressive debut for the Fantasy label in December of 1958 entitled *Yambu,* a collection of percussion songs, including the musical highlight "Timbales y Bongo," reflecting religious thought and music in the African tradition. The conga drummer returned in 1959 with a second Fantasy album entitled *Mongo,* which contained Santamaria's "Afro Blue" composition. The song immediately became a Latin jazz standard taken up by trumpeters John Coltrane, Dizzy Gillespie, and others. Afro-Cubanos soon evolved into the Mongo Santamaria Afro-Latin Group, which included the likes of saxophonist Pat Patrick, who had worked with Sun Ra, and a promising young keyboard player named Armando "Chick" Corea. This group's first album, *Go, Mongo!* (first released in 1962 and later packaged with the band's final Riverside album as *Skins* in 1976), further cemented Santamaria's reputation and included his own standout composition "Carmela."

Although by now an important figure in both Latin and jazz circles, Santamaria would break through into the mass market in a moment of consequence—the result of a bad night at a Cuban nightclub in the Bronx, New York, in 1962. When only three people showed in the audience for a scheduled gig, the musicians held a bull session, and when a substitute pianist named Herbie Hancock performed a new tune of his entitled "Watermelon Man," all of the band members gradually joined in. Santamaria, for his part, brought his own Afro-Latin rhythmic flourishes to Hancock's design. Eventually, Hancock's song became a regular part of Santamaria's repertoire, and after record producer Orrin Keepnews heard the composition, he immediately pulled the musicians into the studio to record a single. Released in 1963, "Watermelon Man" rose to number ten on the pop charts, and more importantly, pointed to the development of funk music in the 1970s, helping to broaden the fusion of pop and Latin influences.

Upon the success of "Watermelon Man," Santamaria went on to become one of the most prolific composers and recording artists of his generation, producing a lengthy catalog of staggering variety and musical depth that was considered the definitive textbook on Afro-Cuban styles. An essential introduction to anyone wishing to explore the performer's history can be found in 1972's *Afro Roots,* a two-record set that contains tracks recorded between 1958 and 1959. After recording several acclaimed albums for the Riverside label and its subsidiaries, Santamaria signed a high-profile contract with Columbia Records. His association with this label resulted in a wave of danceable albums between 1965 and 1970 that often covered hits of the day. Although these records offered a brighter, brassy sound, aided by trumpeter Marty Shelley, Santamaria never completely let go of his roots and continued to mix genres into the early 1970s.

Subsequently, Santamaria focused on the Afro-Cuban tradition for much of the remainder of his career. In 1987, he released *Soy Yo,* which found Santamaria bridging the gap between contemporary black pop and Afro-

Cuban music, while 1988's *Soca Me Nice* explored the soca,or soul calypso genre. Despite his successes in the studio, however, Santamaria favored producing live records, using this type of recording opportunity to advance his multicultural musical agenda. Some of his most recognized live outtakes include 1963's *Mongo at the Village Gate;* 1981's *Summertime,* a live gig with Gillespie and Toots Thielemans recorded in 1980; 1990's *Live at Jazz Alley*; and 1994's *At the Black Hawk,* a CD compilation of two 1962 live releases, *Mighty Mongo* and *Viva Mongo,* both recorded at the legendary Black Hawk club in San Francisco.

In 1995, he returned to the Fantasy label, via its subsidiary Milestone, with the release of *Mongo Santamaria: Mongo Returns.* A two-disc compilation, *Skin on Skin: The Mongo Santamaria Anthology, 1958-1995* arrived in 1999 on the Rhino label. By the late 1990s, Santamaria was unable to tour because of health problems. He continued to live in the same apartment that he moved into back in 1964 on New York's Upper West Side. "I'm not a hero, but I did my best to make everybody happy," the percussionist told Cohen. "Everything I did, I did it with con mucho amor."

Selected discography

Yambu, Fantasy, 1958; reissued Original Jazz Classics, 1987.
Afro Roots, Prestige, 1972; reissued, 1989.
Our Man in Havana, Fantasy, 1960; reissued 1993.
Mongo at the Village Gate, 1963; reissued, Original Jazz Classics, 1990.
Mongo Introduces La Lupe, Fantasy, 1963; reissued, Milestone, 1993.
Sabroso, 1959; reissued, Original Jazz Classics, 1993.
Skins, Milestone, 1976.
Summertime, 1981; reissued, Original Jazz Classics, 1991.
Mongo y Su Charanga, Fantasy, 1987.
Soy Yo, Concord Picante, 1987.
Soca Me Nice, Concord Picante, 1988.
Olé Ola, Concord Picante, 1989.
Live at Jazz Alley, Concord Picante, 1990.
At the Black Hawk, Fantasy, 1994.
Mongo's Greatest Hits, Fantasy, 1995.
Mongo Santamaria: Mongo Returns, Fantasy, 1995.
Skin on Skin: The Mongo Santamaria Anthology, 1958-1995, Rhino, 1999.

Sources

Books

Complete Marquis Who's Who, Marquis Who's Who, 1999.
Swenson, John, editor, *Rolling Stone Jazz and Blues Album Guide,* Random House, 1999.

Periodicals

Atlanta Journal-Constitution, December 3, 1999.
Down Beat, March 1996, p. 57; March 1998; November 1999, p. 52.
Fortune, May 24, 1999.
Hispanic, September 1999.
Los Angeles Times, May 27, 1997; October 27, 1997; November 22, 1999; December 17, 1999.
Rolling Stone, May 13, 1999.
Washington Post, December 17, 1997; July 12, 1998; May 14, 1999.

Online

All Music Guide, http://www.allmusic.com (March 10, 2000).
"Mongo Homepage," *AO! Records*, http://www.artistsonly.com/mongo.htm (March 10, 2000).
Mongo Santamaria Home Page, http://www.onlinetalent.com/Mongo_Santamaria_homepage.html (March 10, 2000).

—Laura Hightower

Randy Scruggs

Singer, songwriter, producer, guitar

Photograph by Christopher Berkey. AP/Wide World Photos. Reproduced by permission.

Although Randy Scruggs has spent most of his time behind the scenes, appearing on and/or producing a multitude of country albums, his influence on country music has been significant. As an award-winning songwriter, producer, guitarist and vocalist, Randy Scruggs, who began his musical career in the 1970s, continued to break new ground in music into the 1990s. Scruggs "has firmly established his own imprint on contemporary country music," said Janet E. Williams in *The Encyclopedia of Country Music.*

Born in the heart of Nashville, Tennessee, to legendary banjo great Earl Scruggs of Flatt & Scruggs, Randy Scruggs was immersed in country and bluegrass music. Mother Maybelle Carter introduced Scruggs to the autoharp when he was just six years old. His fascination with the instrument led him to learn many of the songs of the Carter Family and other traditional artists. Impromptu jam sessions at the Scruggs home were a regular event. Guests included the Carter Family, the Byrds, Ravi Shankar, Johnny Cash, Linda Ronstadt, and Neil Young.

Although Scruggs' earlier influences were the sounds of Flatt & Scruggs, the Carter Family and Doc Watson, he also incorporated the sounds of Muddy Waters, Duane Allman, Michael Bloomfield, and Eric Clapton into his later music. The XPN website said that "while raised in country, Randy has had a successful and prolific career bringing together all genres of roots music." Overall, Scruggs admitted that his biggest influence has always been his father. "I see that passion when he picks up an instrument," Scruggs told Michael Gray in comments available on the *Country* website. "I see it, too, in the faces of people that hear him play. It's reflective. The passion he puts into the music becomes a part of those people who are exposed to it. I hope that my music is reflective in that way, that it goes beyond just being a personal statement and affects people in a positive way."

After he learned to play the autoharp, Scruggs continued to develop skills with other instruments and in various areas of music. From his early years and into adulthood, Scruggs never slowed down and has been playing music ever since. At nine years old, Scruggs made his first guest appearance on his father's syndicated television program *Flatt & Scruggs.* Two years later, Scruggs' interest in the acoustic guitar began to grow, and, at age 13, he played on his first recording. Soon after, his guitar work became a regular feature on recordings by Flatt & Scruggs, and he played on other artists' albums as well. Scruggs' Reprise Records biography said, "He fondly remembers being pulled out of middle school so he could record an album with country-great Waylon Jennings, a mentor who taught him an early lesson about individualistic expression...."

For the Record . . .

Born August 3, 1953 in Nashville, TN; son of banjo player Earl Scruggs.

Made first recording at the age of 13; has worked with artists such as Linda Ronstadt, Johnny Cash, Ricky Scaggs, Waylon Jennings, the Nitty Gritty Dirt Band; named one of the nation's top guitarist by *Guitar Player*, 1980; has produced albums for artists including Moe Bandy, Bobby Bare, Carl Perkins, Patty Loveless, and Wilco; released solo debut album, *Crown of Jewels*, 1998.

Awards: CMA Award, Producer of the Year, for the Nitty Gritty Dirt Band's *Will the Circle Be Unbroken, Volume 2*, 1989; Grammy Award, Best Country Instrumental, for "Amazing Grace" in 1989, and for "A Soldier's Joy" (with Vince Gill), 1998; CMA Award, Producer of the Year, for Alison Krauss & Union Station's "When You Say Nothing at All," 1995.

Addresses: *Record company*—Reprise Nashville, c/o Reprise Records/Warner Brothers, 75 Rockefeller Plz., New York City, NY 10019, phone: (212) 275-4500; website: http://www.wbr.com.

In 1969, Scruggs teamed up with his brother Gary to form The Scruggs Brothers. Under this name the duo released two albums on Vanguard Records. Shortly after, the two were joined by younger brother Steven and father Earl to form the Earl Scruggs Revue. Although Scruggs had a good singing voice, his focus in the Revue was acoustic guitar. "I think I the way the Revue was originally set up, my concentrations really were on guitar. And Gary's was as a vocalist and, ofcourse, he played bass," Scruggs told Rich Kienzle in *Country Music*. "I didn't feel the urge to be a vocalist at that time, but also I think through the years my voice has matured and that there's more character to it now. I feel like I can bring more to it than when I was younger."

While part of the Revue, Scruggs continued to be a highly requested session player and worked with artist such as Linda Ronstadt, Johnny Cash, Ricky Skaggs, Waylon Jennings, and The Nitty Gritty Dirt Band. He became one of the industry's most respected and sought after session players, and was named one of the nation's top guitarist by *Guitar Player* in 1980. Also in 1980, Scruggs opened his own production company and produced records by Moe Bandy, Bobby Bare, Earl Thomas Conley, Dean Dillon, Skip Ewing, Steve Forbert, Waylon Jennings, Sawyer Brown, Steve Wariner, and others. Most notably, Scruggs earned a CMA Award as producer for the 1989 Album of the Year, *Will the Circle Be Unbroken, Volume 2*, by the Nitty Gritty Dirt Band. The same year he also won a Grammy Award for Best Country Instrumental for his recording of "Amazing Grace."

His production of *Red Hot and Country* illustrated that Scruggs' talent and dedication extended beyond the musical sound to social issues. The compilation, a benefit album for AIDS research and awareness, found Scruggs producing Johnny Cash, Carl Perkins, Patty Loveless, Wilco, and Crosby, Stills and Nash, to name a few. In 1995, another of Scruggs' productions helped bridge the gap between the country and pop genres. *Keith Whitley: A Tribute Album* featured Alison Krauss & Union Station singing "When You Say Nothing At All." The single not only won Scruggs a CMA award for Single of the Year, but also proved that his skills were applicable to other styles besides country. A substantial country radio hit, the song also received significant play on pop and top 40 radio stations.

In addition to his accomplishments as a producer, Scruggs also lent his songwriting talents to more than 100 songs that were recorded by major artist, including Patty Loveless, Trisha Yearwood, Ricky Skaggs, Sawyer Brown, Steve Wariner, John Anderson, Waylon Jennings, Earl Thomas Conley, and Deana Carter. It was not until 1998 that he released his first album. For the first time, Scruggs stood in the spotlight rather than behind the scenes. He did not exactly come to the front as a solo performer, however. Scruggs was joined by several special guests including Rosanne Cash, Vince Gill, Mary Chapin Carpenter, John Prine, Bruce Hornsby, Joan Osborne, Emmylou Harris, Travis Tritt, Trisha Yearwood, Sam Bush, Kenny Aronoff, Roger McGuinn, Delbert McClinton, John Hiatt, and his father, Earl Scruggs. Scruggs' 17-year-old daughter, Lindsey, also contributed to the album. Scruggs had produced and written songs for many of the artists previously mentioned, and all involved felt excited to be a part of the new album. "His expertise as a writer, producer and player has helped shape the works of countless musicians and singers, many of whom returned the favor with their participation on *Crown of Jewels*," said Gray.

Crown of Jewels was a career summary, tracing the path Scruggs had taken from the beginning of his autoharp playing days until the release of the album. "This has been a lifetime in the making as far as how deep it goes back from the roots until now," Scruggs told Reno Kling in the *Main Event*. He later added, "From all the experience I've had as a producer, writer and musician, I'm able to put all those elements together. It's all added to the depth and the qualityof the project. *Crown of Jewels* is a reflection of my musical lifetime. I'm thrilled now to go inside and look at myself and find out what it is that wants me to wake up and pick up a guitar and be inspired. This album is what dreams are made of."

Scruggs did not forget his influences while choosing the songs for the album. "Wild Flower," performed by Emmylou Harris and Iris DeMent, incorporated the old time sound of The Carter Family and Mother Maybelle and brought them into the present. "I first started playing the autoharp when I was six, and it was [Mother Maybelle's] and [The Carter Family's] music. And then a little bit later, I started playing the guitar, and 'Wild Flower' was one of the earliest songs I ever learned through her style," Scruggs told Kienzle. "Including it on *Crown of Jewels* was special for me, not only because of The Carter Family influence, but also with Emmylou and Iris DeMent." Scruggs remembered his greatest influence in his cover of his father's classic instrumental hit, "Lonesome Ruben." For the song, Scruggs was joined by his father and Jerry Douglas. He was excited to have the opportunity to record with his father on his own album. He recalled to Kienzle, "I was ecstatic about [the recording]. Dad and I have played together all throughout my life at home and in the studio. It's a very relaxed feeling to record with him."

Although Scruggs did cover some of his old favorites, he also included new material, writing or co-writing five of the songs on the album. Scruggs penned "Passin' Thru" with Johnny Cash. While working as producer and artist in the past, this was the first time the two had written a song together. "It felt great to do something with him on a writing level," said Scruggs told Gray, "because it's such an intimate process— perhaps the most intimate element of making an album. The key to writing meaningful songs is to be able to get at your deepest emotions— remove the veil and expose it all." Performed as a duet, Scruggs' vocals were joined by pop artist Joan Osborne who was able to blend her voice and contemporary style with his own bluegrass/country heritage.

The title track, "Crown of Jewels," was written especially for the project by Bruce Hornsby at the request of Scruggs. The song also featured Hornsby on vocals and piano. Although Scruggs did not sing every song, he continued to play the roles of guitarist and producer. "Scruggs is the glue to each tune, and his gentle and heartfelt touch is the reason all these folks came to play," said James Bickers in the *Courier-Journal*. "The only potential problem with *Crown of Jewels* is the impossibly high standard it sets for the rest of the country-music business. After such an accomplishment, the calculated hit-making that passes for much of country songwriting surely feels like a bitter pill."

Crown of Jewels gave Randy Scruggs the opportunity to be in the spotlight. "It's about time that Randy Scruggs got some of the credit due him," the *Twangzine* website concluded. "He's been in the background long enough. His dynamic picking has graced a lot of hit records. He's been behind the producer's glass on a lot more. But now it's his time to shine....This disc is a collection of Jewels. It's a crown he can wear proudly."

Selected discography

Solo

Crown of Jewels, Reprise Records, 1998.

With Gary Scruggs

The Scruggs Brothers, Vanguard, 1972.
All the Way Home, Vanguard, 1994.

Sources

Books

Kingsbury, Paul, editor, *The Encyclopedia of Country Music,* Oxford University Press, 1998.

Periodicals

Country Music, November 1, 1998, pp. 48-49.
Courier-Journal (Louisville, KY), August 22, 1998.

Online

"Cat Paws," *The Folk Sampler Cat Paw Music Review,* http://www.folksampler.com/reviews/1998/october/scruggs.htm (Feburary 13, 2000).
"Randy Scruggs," *All Music Guide,* http://allmusic.com/cg/x.dll (February 13, 2000).
"Randy Scruggs," *Reprise Records,* http://www.wbr.com/nashville/randyscruggs/cmp/rsbio.html (February 13, 2000).
"Randy Scruggs," *www.country.com,* http://www.country.com/gen/music/artist/randy-scruggs.html (February 13, 2000).
"Randy Scruggs, Crown of Jewels," *Main Event,* http://www.gibson.com/magazines/amplifier/1998/7/mainevent.html (February 13, 2000).

"Randy Scruggs-Crown of Jewels," *Twangzine,* http://www.klondyke.net/whome/rev/rev-scruggs.html (February 13, 2000).
"Randy Scruggs, Crown of Jewels," *XPN's Featured Album,* http://www.xpn.org/sections/featured_album_past/featured_album_072098.html (Feburary 13, 2000).
"Randy Scruggs Has Set A Musical Gem In His *Crown of Jewels," Randy Scruggs Feature,* http://www.country.com/article/mus-news-new/randy-scruggs-feature.html (Feburary 13, 2000).
"Sharps & Flats," *Salon,* http://www.salon.com/ent/music/reviews/1998/08/19review.html (Feburary 13, 2000).

—Julie Sweet

George Shearing

Composer, arranger, piano

AP/Wide World Photos. Reproduced by permission.

A prominent composer and arranger for over five decades, British musician George Shearing always regarded himself as a pianist who happened to play jazz. During the 1950s and 1960s, he led one of the world's most popular jazz quintets, playing in a style he called "locked hands" and inventing a unique quintet sound derived from the combination of piano, vibraphone, electric guitar, bass, and drums. Along with the success of his quintet, Shearing made other great contributions throughout these years, including leading several small, Afro-Cuban jazz combos in the 1950s. Vibraphonist/percussionist Cal Tjader, along with esteemed congueros like Mongo Santamaria, Willie Bobo, and Armando Peraza, all played with Shearing's Latin-influenced bands. Throughout his career as a soloist, fellow pianists admired his light, refined touch, and though he developed his own unique style, Shearing claimed both the great boogie-woogie pianists and classical players as prominent influences. A prolific composer, Shearing wrote over 300 pieces over the course of his lifetime, including the classic "Lullaby of Birdland," which became a jazz standard.

George Albert Shearing was born on August 13, 1919, in the Battersea district of Southwest London, England. Blind since the time of his birth, Shearing was one of nine children of a coal worker. Although his parents "read very little beyond the headlines of a newspaper," as Shearing recalled in an online interview with Steve Capra, they never discouraged the youngster in his musical development, although they never encouraged their son either. Nonetheless, by the time Shearing was three years old, he had already started playing piano and displayed an acute ear for music.

Receiving some training in his teens at the Linden School for the Blind, Shearing, excluding these four years at school, trained very little in the formal sense. During his school years, he also started picking up stylistic cues from a variety of sources, namely jazz influences from Teddy Wilson and Fats Waller records. When the young pianist reached the age of 16, his instructor at school had all but given up on trying to teach his student classical lessons, telling Shearing's parents, "You know, further study of classical music for this young man would be a total waste of time," as quoted by Capra. "It is obvious to me that he's gonna become a jazz pianist." Despite this prediction, however, Shearing would later play the music of classical composers such as Bach, Mozart, Debussy, and Stravinsky (some of Shearing's personal influences) for his own enjoyment, as well as with orchestras throughout the world.

Upon completing school, Shearing earned several scholarship offers from a number of universities, but turned

For the Record . . .

Born George Albert Shearing on August 13, 1919, in the Battersea district of Southwest London, England; son of a coal worker.

Made first recording in England, 1937; emigrated to New York City, 1947; formed first and most famous quintet, 1949; settled into lucrative recording associations with MGM (1950-55) and Capitol Records (1955-69); recorded with singers like Nancy Wilson, Peggy Lee, and Nat King Cole while signed to Capitol; disbanded quintet, 1978; signed with Concord, reinvigorating his career during the 1980s; signed to the Telarc label, 1992; invited to play before three U.S. presidents: Gerald Ford, Jimmy Carter, and Ronald Reagan; performed at a Royal Command Performance for Queen Elizabeth II and Prince Philip; member of the Friars Club and Lotos Club in New York, as well as the Bohemian Club in San Francisco, CA.

Awards: Horatio Alger Award for Distinguished Americans, 1978; Grammy Awards with Mel Tormé for best jazz vocal performance for *An Evening with Mel Tormé & George Shearing,* 1982, and for *Top Drawer,* 1983; Ivor Novello Award for Lifetime Achievement, May 1993; invested an Officer of the Order of the British Empire, November 26, 1996; received the first American Music Award by the National Arts Club in New York City, March 1998.

Addresses: *Record company*—Telarc International, 23307 Commerce Park Rd., Cleveland, OH 44122, (216) 464-2313, website: http://www.telarc.com.

them down in order to pursue a more financially productive endeavor—playing piano in a neighborhood pub. In the 1930s, he joined an all-blind band (the Ambrose dance band) and developed a friendship with the a noted British jazz critic and author named Leonard Feather, who encouraged Shearing to make his first recording in 1937 and helped him land his first appearance on BBC (British Broadcasting Company) radio. From there, Shearing became a star in his homeland, performing on a regular basis for the BBC, playing a role in the London-based groups of French violinist Stéphane Grappelli (1908-1997) in the1940s, and winning several *Melody Maker* polls.

At the prompting of Feather, Shearing emigrated to New York City in 1947, hoping to extend his fame to the United States. He quickly absorbed the popular bebop style of the time (his early recordings in England focused mainly on the swing genre), joining the Oscar Pettiford Trio as Erroll Gardner's replacement and leading a quartet with Buddy DeFranco. With his unique sound commanding national attention, in 1949 Shearing formed his first and most famous quintet, comprised of Marjorie Hyams on vibes, Chuck Wayne on guitar, John Levy on bass, and Denzil Best on drums. An instant success on the national level since the quintet's debut, Shearing began performing at the most respected venues of the era, including the legendary Birdland jazz club in New York, and became one of the most popular recording artists in the United States.

Shearing recorded briefly for the Discovery label before settling into lucrative association with MGM (from 1950 to 1955) and Capitol Records (from 1955 to 1969). During his years with Capitol, Shearing recorded albums with such singers as Nancy Wilson, Peggy Lee, and Nat King Cole, and released a lone album for the Jazzland label with the Montgomery Brothers in 1961. In addition to working in jazz and even more pop-oriented fare, the pianist around this time also started playing concerts with symphony orchestras.

Leaving Capitol in 1969, Shearing slowly started to phase out his work with the quintet, which he felt had become too predictable, and finally disbanded the unit for good in 1978. "I couldn't wait to get rid of it," he told *Los Angeles Times* writer Zan Stewart in 1995. "I felt I'd put myself in a box. I could go on autopilot and play" the band's repertoire, "so I went to the duo" for piano and bass. Before breaking up the quintet, Shearing started his own label called Sheba, and the company lasted a few years into the early-1970s. From there, he moved briefly to MPS in the later part of the decade, recording some trio efforts for the label. Nevertheless, Shearing's profile had lessened in the 1970s by comparison to his stature during the MGM and Capitol years.

However, in the 1980s Shearing found the perfect home at Concord, signing with the label in 1979. He recorded five acclaimed albums with Mel Tormé, including *An Evening with Mel Tormé & George Shearing,* a 1982 Grammy Award winner for best jazz vocal performance. The duo earned a second Grammy the following year, with Tormé garnering the award for their Concord album *Top Drawer.* Other notable projects included collaborations with bassists Brian Torff (*Blues Alley Jazz* and *On a Clear Day*) and Don Thompson (*Live at the Café Carlyle*), pianists Hank Hones (*The Spirit of 176*) and Marian McPartland (*Alone Together*), guitarist Jim Hall

(*First Edition*), and vocalist Carmen McRae (*Two for the Road*). The decade also saw Shearing recording the solo *Grand Piano* sessions, sets for which the pianist's full palette comes into play.

Shearing continued to be a vital force well into the 1990s, signing with the Telarc label in 1992. *I Hear a Rhapsody: Live at the Blue Note* (1992) and *Walkin': Live at the Blue Note* (1995) both were taken from a live engagement (with bassist Neil Swanson and drummer Grady Tate) at the New York club and won stellar reviews. For *That Shearing Sound* (1994), the pianist returned to his quintet format, and in 1997, he released a solo album entitled *Favorite Things.* Penning over 300 compositions in his lifetime, Shearing enjoyed one of the most prolific and longest recordingcareers in jazz history.

A recipient of numerous honors and awards, Shearing earned an honorary Doctorate of Music degree from Westminster College in Salt Lake City, Utah, in May of 1975, as well as an honorary doctorate in music by Hamilton College in upstate New York in May of 1994. In 1978, he received the prestigious Horatio Alger Award for Distinguished Americans. That same year, a community recreational facility in Battersea, South London, was the named the George Shearing Centre in his honor. In May of 1993, Shearing was presented with the Ivor Novello Award for Lifetime Achievement—the British equivalent of the Grammy honor. On November, 26, 1996, the pianist was invested by Queen Elizabeth II at Buckingham Palace as an Officer of the Order of the British Empire for his musicianship and service in promoting British/American relations. In March of 1998, Shearing received the first American Music Award by the National Arts Club in New York City. In addition to these and other awards, Shearing was invited to play before three U.S. presidents, Gerald Ford, Jimmy Carter, and Ronald Reagan, and performed at a Royal Command Performance for Queen Elizabeth II and Prince Philip. His organizational memberships include the Friars Club and Lotos Club in New York, as well as the Bohemian Club in San Francisco.

All of these honors, said Shearing, represented a collective highlight of his career. When asked what his favorite moment as a pianist was, he replied: "I think it would be the idea of knowing that I can appear in Carnegie Hall with Dizzy [Gillespie] in 1948 ... and knowing that I've played for three presidents ... knowing I've played command performance for Queen Elizabeth ... knowing that I played with a number of symphony orchestras throughout the country," as quoted by Capra. "And all this from a little blind kid born on the wrong side of the tracks ... whose parents were quick to say 'Oh, we don't get those kind of jobs, son. They're for the nobs, you know.'"

During the late 1990s, Shearing continued to perform in select music halls on occasion. He and his wife, Ellie, divided time between homes in New York and abroad in Cotswold, in the English countryside. Even in his later years, Shearing remained, according to *Stereo Review*'s Chris Albertson, "a remarkable artist who's creativity remains undiminished."

Selected discography

So Rare, Savoy, 1947.
Piano Solo, Savoy, 1947.
George Shearing Quintet, Discovery, 1949.
Lullaby of Birdland, Verve, 1949.
You're Hearing the George Shearing Quartet, MGM, 1950.
Touch of Genius, MGM, 1951.
The Shearing Spell, Capitol, 1955.
Shearing Caravan, MGM, 1955.
Shearing in Hi Fi, MGM, 1955.
White Satin & Black Satin, Capitol, 1956.
Black Satin, Capitol, 1956.
Latin Escapade, Capitol, 1956.
Shearing Piano, Capitol, 1956.
Shearing on Stage, Capitol, 1957.
In the Night, Capitol, 1957.
Latin Affair, Capitol, 1958.
Burnished Brass, Capitol, 1958.
Blue Chiffon, Capitol, 1958.
On the Sunny Side of the Strip, Capitol, 1959.
White Satin, Capitol, 1960.
San Francisco Scene, Capitol, 1960.
The Swingin's Mutual, Capitol, 1960.
Mood Latino, Capitol, 1961.
Satin Affair, Capitol, 1961.
George Shearing and the Montgomery Brothers, Jazzland, 1961; reissued, Original Jazz Classics, 1989.
Jazz Moments, Capitol, 1962; reissued, *Blue Note,* 1995.
Nat "King" Cole Sings/George Shearing Plays, Capitol, 1962; reissued, Capitol, 1991.
Shearing Bossa Nova, Capitol, 1962.
Soft and Silky, MGM, 1962.
Latin Rendezvous, Capitol, 1963.
Out of the Woods, Capitol, 1964.
That Fresh Feeling, Capitol, 1966.
Out of This World, Sheba, 1970.
The George Shearing Quartet, Sheba, 1972.
The George Shearing Trio, Vol. 1, Sheba, 1973.
Light Airy and Swinging, MPS, 1974.
Live, Concord Jazz, 1979.
Blues Alley Jazz, Concord Jazz, 1980.
Two for the Road, Concord, 1980.
Alone Together, Concord Jazz, 1981.
An Evening with George Shearing and Mel Tormé, Concord Jazz, 1982.
First Edition, Concord Jazz, 1982.

Live at the Cafe Carlyle, Concord Jazz, 1984.
Grand Piano, Concord Jazz, 1985.
George Shearing and Barry Tuckwell Play the Music of Cole Porter, Concord Concerto, 1986.
Breakin' Out, Concord Jazz, 1987.
In Dixieland, Concord Jazz, 1989.
The Spirit of 176, Concord Jazz, 1989.
Piano, Concord Jazz, 1990.
(With Mel Tormé) *Mel and George "Do" World War II,* Concord Jazz, 1991.
I Hear a Rhapsody: Live at the Blue Note, Telarc, 1992.
Midnight on Cloud 69, Savoy, 1993.
My Ship, Verve, 1994.
That Shearing Sound, Telarc, 1994.
Walkin': Live at the Blue Note, Telarc, 1995.
The Best of George Shearing, Capitol, 1995.
The Best of George Shearing, Vol. 2, Capitol, 1997.
Favorite Things, Telarc, 1997.

Sources

Books

Swenson, John, editor, *Rolling Stone Jazz & Blues Album Guide,* Random House, 1999.

Periodicals

Audio, January 1995.
Billboard, April 10, 1999; June 19, 1999; November 20, 1999.
Chicago Tribune, February 13, 1997.
Down Beat, November 1992; August 1993; October 1994.
Fortune, May 26, 1997.
Los Angeles Times, July 28, 1995; August 4, 1995; October 28, 1996; December 2, 1997; January 23, 1998.
New York Times, December 3, 1999.
People, June 21, 1999.
Stereo Review, April 1995.

Online

All Music Guide, http://www.allmusic.com (March 19, 2000).
CD Review: George Shearing Biography, http://www.allaboutjaz.com/bios/gsbio.htm (March 19, 2000).
The Jazz Corner—George Shearing, http://www.thejazzcorner.com/performers/performer_shearing.htm (March 19, 2000).
Steve Capra's Interview with George Shearing, http://www.xlnt-arts.com/stevecapra/intervie/shearing.htm (March 19, 2000).

—Laura Hightower

Sloan

Alternative rock band

The Halifax, Nova Scotia, power-pop band Sloan became one of Canada's most popular rock acts of the 1990s, but their success proved both a curse as well as a blessing. From the same remote maritime city previously marked as the town that pop musician Sarah McLachlan left, Sloan, whose Beatlesque music became a radio staple on Canadian radio, was a band the young people of their homeland knew well. Despite their presence in Canada, however, Sloan experienced difficulty breaking into the American market, especially after their record label DGC (David Geffen Company) refused to market Sloan's hooky pop tunes in the wake of grunge rock. After years fighting to be heard outside Canada and nearly dissolving the group, Sloan, angered because DGC would not promote their records in the United States, finally left the label in 1994. Although rumors circulated of an eminent breakup, to the surprise of many Sloan returned in 1996 with *One Chord to Another,* an album that became an instant sensation across Canada and a critical favorite in the United States upon its 1997 American release.

Through their records, their involvement with the Canadian indie label Murderecords, and their stylistic influence on other bands from the frozen north, Sloan not only elevated pop bands and records originating in the Northeast, but also helped bridge the gap between Canadian and American rock, bringing music from both countries into greater synch with one another. Thanks in large part to the success of Sloan, Halifax became regarded as "Canada's Seattle," leading to the signing of several local bands to major record deals. Some of the Halifax-based groups benefiting from Sloan's exposure included Eric's Trip, Thrush Hermit, the Hardship Post, and Jale.

Influenced by an array of musical styles from the Beatles to Sonic Youth, drummer Andrew Scott, bassist/vocalist Chris Murphy, guitarist/vocalist Patrick Pentland, and guitarist/vocalist Jay Ferguson formed Sloan in Halifax, Nova Scotia, in 1990. They derived the band's name from an unlikely and not so referential source. "It's the nickname of this pot-smoking musician we knew in Halifax," Scott revealed to Jud Cost in a 1998 interview for *Magnet* magazine. "He worked in a restaurant as a busboy and used to be known as 'the slow one.'" All of the members held prior interests in art and/or music, and all participate in songwriting and musical arrangement for Sloan. Ferguson and Murphy were former members of a local band called Kearney Lake Rd, a group inspired by underground American acts like R.E.M. and the Minutemen, while Scott and Pentland played in various local bands as well. The four men eventually coalesced when Murphy and Scott met each other while studying at the Nova Scotia School of Art and Design, and after only a short time of playing local clubs—their first performance was held in the spring of 1991—Sloan had amassed a small, yet supportive following for their feedback-laden live shows.

In early 1992, Sloan arrived with their first record, a six-song EP entitled *Peppermint.* Recorded quickly and casually at co-producer Terry Pulliam's Halifax home and released on the band's own Murderecords label, *Peppermint* demonstrated the quartet's best attributes in raw form: thick, noisy guitar energy; alluring and melodic vocals (with guest help from Jennifer Pierce of Jale); and clever, self-effacing lyrics. The first single from the EP in particular, "Underwhelmed,"struck an instant nerve with young Canadians, helping to establish Halifax as a hotbed for alternative rock activity. The song also appeared on the local Halifax compilation album *Hear and Now.*

Sloan's profile continued to escalate, and by the summer of 1992, they had signed with the major label DGC. In October of 1992 in Canada and in January of 1993 in the United States, the group released their debut album, *Smeared,* which included three songs cleaned up by producer David Ogilvie from the *Peppermint* EP—"Underwhelmed," "Marcus Said," and "Sugartune"—as well as nine other cuts including "I Am the Cancer" and "500 Up." When Ogilvie finished remixing songs for the debut, Sloan's songs had transformed from inexperienced punk enthusiasm into sublimely balanced punk/power-pop music that revealed the multiplicity of the foursome's

For the Record . . .

Members include **Jay Ferguson,** guitar, vocals; **Chris Murphy**, bass vocals; **Patrick Pentland**, guitar, vocals; **Andrew Scott**, drums.

Formed in Halifax, Nova Scotia, Canada, in 1990; played first gig as a band, spring of 1991; released debut album *Smeared,* 1992; contemplated breaking up, 1994-95; released "comeback" album *One Chord to Another,* 1996; called upon 1970s rock influences for *Navy Blues,* 1998. All members share in songwriting and arranging duties.

Awards: Juno Award, best alternative album for *One Chord to Another,* 1997.

Addresses: *Record company*—Murderecords, P.O. Box 68510, 360A Bloor St. West, Toronto, Ontario, M5S 1X1, Canada; website: http://www.murderecords.com, e-mail: murderecords@hotmail.com. *Website*—Sloan: the official site, http://sloan.a-d-n.com.

influences. Often referred to as Sonic Youth meets the Beatles, *Smeared* blended the sounds of My Bloody Valentine, Nirvana, Dinosaur Jr, the Velvet Underground, Cheap Trick, and others, showing the diversity that comes with having four competent songwriters in one band. The album earned stellar reviews worldwide as well as in Canada, where it eventually went gold, but also led critics to pigeonhole Sloan as a "retro band," a label the band has fought ever since. Although they freely admitted that *Smeared* shared much in common with the music of My Bloody Valentine, "That's what we loved in 1992," Pentland explained to Cost. "And I think that's okay for a band's first record, but by the fourth one, you should be somewhere else."

Despite positive press in the United States, as well as tours in the states with the Lemonheads and fIRE-HOUSE, Sloan's debut failed to sell outside of Canada. Nevertheless, Sloan forged ahead, releasing their second album, *Twice Removed,* in 1994. Recorded two and a half years after *Smeared* and produced with Jim Rondinelli, *Twice Removed* marked a more mature, pensive, and eclectic change in Sloan's style. Rather than concentrating on the distorted rock sound of their prior work, the band instead progressed to carefully intertwined and spaciously electric arrangements, 1960s-styled melodies and harmonies, and more complex rhythms exemplified in songs such as "Penpals," "Bells On," and "Snowsuit Sound." However, DGC, who wanted a noisier product, failed to promote the bright and melodic album, especially for the American market, though the album received rave reviews and earned substantial Canadian sales. Trying to compensate for the lack of support, Sloan toured relentlessly to promote the album with little success. All the while, *Twice Removed* was named "The Best Canadian Album of All Time" in a readers' poll by *Chart!* magazine and the American publication *Spin* dubbed the effort one of the "Ten Best Albums You Didn't Hear."

The lack of recognition in terms of sales figures caused Sloan to lose its center, and in late 1994, DGC dropped the group amid rumors of a breakup. Canceling shows for the new year, the members of Sloan contemplated their future. To their fans' amazement, however, the band re-emerged in the summer of 1995, playing a handful of concerts and releasing a new single called "Same Old Flame" on Murderecords. During the time apart, the members of Sloan pursued other interests. Scott formed the group Maker's Mark and played with the Sadies, Murphy drummed for the Super Friendz, and Pentland penned a handful of songs. Ferguson focused his energies at Murderecords, where he managed the Inbreds and co-produced a record by the Local Rabbits. He also spent time working with Thrush Hermit, Jale, the Super Friendz, and Eric's Trip. "I'd recommend it to any band who has a good beginning," Ferguson said to Cost aboutSloan's hiatus. "Take a break to get your feet on the ground and realize what you want to do. Tons of bands get signed, make a record and then break up. But we've had our own label to fall back on. It's exciting to make your own records and run your own career. Rather than jumping from one label to another, I feel like we're in the driver's seat."

Deciding to reunite on a permanent basis in the late summer of 1995, Sloan shrugged off retirement and entered the studio in the winter of that year to record *One Chord to Another.* Expanding the power-pop approach of *Twice Removed,* with nods to the Beach Boys as well as the Beatles, Sloan's "comeback" album was recorded in Halifax at Idea of East Recording for two-thirds the cost of their prior effort. Another instant hit upon its June 1996 Canadian release, *One Chord to Another* reached certified gold sales in Canada, won the best alternative album Juno Award for 1997, and earned positive reviews. Following months of negotiating with distributors, *One Chord to Another* was finally made available in the United States in the spring of 1997 by the fledging EMI subsidiary the Enclave.

After touring to support *One Chord to Another,* the band entered the Chemical Sound Studios in Toronto, Canada, in the winter of 1997 and early-1998 to record their fourth album, 1998's *Navy Blues,* a record again produced by the band with help from engineer Daryl Smith. In addition to playing their regular instruments and further expanding their pop sensibilities, Sloan added organ, piano, strings, horns, and cello to the lineup. "We've had horns and piano on our records before," said Ferguson in an interview with the iMusic.com website, "but there's more of it on this record. Andrew plays a lot of piano. I wrote both my songs on piano and I'd never done anything like that before." In addition to earning acclaim for its expanded instrumentation, the album also received comparisons to 1970s rock bands like AC/DC and Thin Lizzy, though the band preferred to think of *Navy Blues* as simply rock and roll. "We get these people telling us, 'You guys are a '60s band and this new one sounds like the '70s' " Murphy said to Cost. "'What's next, an '80s record?' " Notable tracks from the diverse album included "Sinking Ships," "On the Horizon," "Money City Maniacs," and "Iggy and Angus." Another Canadian hit, *Navy Blues*, gave Sloan another gold album in their homeland.

By late 1998, after the relocation of Pentland, all of the members of Sloan were living in Toronto, the first time in six years that the foursome had lived in the same city. Sloan hoped that basing the band in Toronto would finally give their music access to a larger market. In 1999, Sloan released a double live album entitled *Four Nights at the Palais Royale,* followed by their fifth studio effort, *Between the Bridges,* recorded again at Toronto's Chemical Sound Studios in April of that year and co-produced with engineer Brendan McGuire. "I'm really glad it's worked out like this for us," Murphy told Cost. "I think we've been through our problems, and now we're here for the long haul—with a lot of longevity in front of us. We're my own favorite band."

Selected discography

Peppermint, (EP), (Canada) Murderecords, 1992
Smeared, DGC, 1992; reissued, Murderecords, 1998.
Twice Removed, DGC, 1994; reissued, Murderecords, 1998.
One Chord to Another, (Canada) Murderecords, 1996; Enclave, 1997.
Navy Blues, Murderecords, 1998.
Four Nights at the Palais Royale, (double live album), Murderecords, 1999.
Between the Bridges, Murderecords, 1999.

Sources

Books

Canadian Encyclopedia, McClelland & Stewart, 1998.
Robbins, Ira A., editor, *Trouser Press Guide to '90s Rock,* Fireside/Simon and Schuster, 1997.

Periodicals

Magnet, November/December 1998, pp. 41-42.

Online

Rolling Stone.com, http://www.rollingstone.tunes.com (March 21, 2000).
"Sloan," *iMusic Modern Showcase,* http://www.imusic.com/showcase/modern/sloan.html (March 21, 2000).
Sloan: the official site, http://sloan.a-d-n.com (March 21, 2000).
Sloan ONLINE, http://www.cgo.wave.ca/~tarslan/main.html (March 21, 2000).
UBL.COM, http://www.ubl.com (March 21, 2000).

—Laura Hightower

Elliott Smith

Singer, songwriter, guitar

An indie-rock musician who seemingly overnight went from an underground hero to a popularly recognized songwriter, Elliott Smith established his place in music by writing beautiful songs about the pains of life. Penning tunes that often drew comparisons to Nick Drake, Bob Dylan, and the Beatles—his favorite band—Smith was cast in the roll of tunesmith to the downtrodden alternative-rock crowd. "The press at home really like to call me a 'folk hero,'" Smith shrugged in a 1998 *Melody Maker* interview with Neil Mason. "For me, that's a serious fellow who makes grand pronouncements about what's wrong with the world. I'm not quite sure what I'm doing... but it's smaller than that." Music critics, as well as listeners, tend to argue with Smith's humble view of his own music. As *Boston Globe* correspondent Joan Anderman asserted in a feature story following the release of Smith's fourth album, 1999's *XO,* "His records are filled with unflinching, emotionally raw portraits of drug addicts and alcoholics, and spare, poetic sketches of self-loathing and decayed love. Gorgeously tragic words are melded to melodies that are as simultaneously lush and forthright, and as inevitable-sounding, as those created

AP/Wide World Photos. Reproduced by permission.

For the Record . . .

Born on August 6, c. 1969, in Nebraska; son of a singer (mother) and a former preacher (father) who served as a United States Air Force pilot in Vietnam and later became a psychiatrist. *Education*: Graduated from Hampshire College, where he studied political science and philosophy.

Starrted to write own songs at age 13; member of the punk band Heatmiser, 1992-97; released first solo album, *Roman Candle,* 1994; "Miss Misery" from the *Good Will Hunting* soundtrack received an Acadamy Award nomination for best original song, signed with DreamWorks, released *XO,* 1998; released *Figure 8,* 2000.

Addresses: *Record company*—DreamWorks Records, 9268 W. 3rd St., Beverly Hills, CA 90210, phone: (310) 234-7700, fax: (310) 234-7750. *Management*—Girlie Action Media, Felice Ecker, phone: (212) 334-3200 ext. 110, fax: (212) 334-4413, e-mail: felice@girlie.com.

by Smith's great inspiration, the Beatles." In addition to the Beatles, Smith's other musical heroes included the Clash, Hank Williams, the Kinks, and Elvis Costello.

Because Smith's lyrics feel so intimate, many listeners assume that his life is an open book. However, as writer Chris Mundy explained in a 1998 *Rolling Stone* feature, "Smith's songs have always been less confession than collage—beautifully rendered glimpses of ugly realities, pieced together with little more than voice and guitar." Likewise, Smith himself offered a similar description of his songwriting: "I don't really have any goals as a songwriter, other than to show what it's like to be a person—just like everybody else who's ever played music does," he told *Los Angeles Times* writer Richard Cromelin in 1998. "I don't feel like my songs are particularly fragile or revealing.... They're songs. It's not like a diary, and they're not intended to be any sort of super intimate confessional singer-songwriterish thing. I like the Beatles. Dylan. The Saints and the Clash. All the good things about what they did or do is probably the same things that I'm trying to do."

While Smith reveals an openness in singing about life's darkest details, he often hesitates when asked to provide the specifics of his own childhood. Born in Nebraska on August 6, around 1969, Smith spent most of his childhood just outside Dallas, Texas, living with his mother, stepfather, and his stepfather's children. His own parents divorced when Smith was only a year old, and his mother, a singer herself, later remarried when he was four year of age. "There were family problems," Smith, who added that most of his other childhood friends also came from broken families, recalled to Mundy. "It wasn't a good situation." And problems persisted outside the home as well; often picked on by his peers because of his small size—Smith was also extremely thin as a young adult—he spent much of his time getting into fights in spite of his frailty. Known as a soft-spoken performer, Smith believed that all of the fighting, evidenced by scars and a nose broken several times over, impacted his demeanor later on. "It's probably pretty easy to put together why somebody who grew up in Texas getting into fights a lot would not want to get up on stage and start belting out songs at the top of their lungs. I've had enough of people yelling."

At the age of 14, Smith finally left his oppressive life in Texas behind, moving to Portland, Oregon, to live with his biological father, with whom he had remained close, and his new family. A former preacher who served as a United States Air Force pilot in Vietnam and later became a psychiatrist, Smith's father bought his son his first nylon string guitar at the age of 12. Before long, at the age of 13, Smith started to write his own songs. Displaying a talent for music early in life, back in Texas Smith studied piano beginning at the age of ten, playing Debussy and Rachmaninoff pieces until his mother and stepfather abruptly pulled him out of lessons a year later.

Although he had always dreamed of becoming a musician, Smith, lacking the confidence, instead enrolled at Hampshire College, an ultra-liberal school in Massachusetts, where he studied political science and philosophy. Upon graduating, however, Smith "was on this big kick that there's no point occupying a spot because it would be better occupied by someone else," he told Mundy, and at the time seriously contemplated training to become a fireman. Moving back to Portland, he went through a period marked by a series of failed relationships, serious drinking, and bouts of depression. His friend and fellow songwriter Neil Gust stepped in, reminding Smith about his true calling: music.

Giving in to Gust's prodding, Smith joined his friend to form the band Heatmiser in 1992. A punk quartet that featured the melodic-abrasive formula popular in the Northwest, the Portland-based band, taking cues from groups like Fugazi, Hüsker Dü, and Helmet, signed with the small Frontier label and released their first album, *Dead Air,* in 1993, followed by the *Yellow No. 5* EP in 1994. Although Smith enjoyed the success of Heatmiser, he nevertheless started to feel smothered amid the noise of the punk-inspired act. "We would play shows, and afterward he would cordon himself off with an acoustic guitar and start practicing," Smith's former band mate, Sam Coomes, said to Mundy. "That was the first time I'd ever heard him play stuff like that. He was trying to evolve away from the stuff he was playing [with Heatmiser]."

Thus, while still a member of Heatmiser, Smith began to branch out on his own, performing solo at Portland clubs and recording tapes in friends' basements. Taking a stylistic departure from the thrash of his band, Smith instead focused on acoustic songs. By now a minor hipster sensation in Portland recognized for his artistic sensibilities, the singer caught the interest of a local label called Cavity Search. For that indie label, Smith released his first work, an eight-track mini-album entitled *Roman Candle*, in 1994. Recorded on a home four-track machine, the folksy, acoustic effort earned critical praise for its brittle, brooding, and consistent set of songs. Some highlights included "No Name #1," "Condor Ave.," and "No Name #3." In the meantime, Smith continued to participate in Heatmiser, and the band released a second album entitled *Cop and Speeder* in 1994. According to reviewers, Smith's solo activities only strengthened the group's music, giving Heatmiser a powerful sense of mood in songs such as "Flame!," "Antonio Carlos Jobim," and the honest confessional "Busted Lip."

In 1995, Smith changed to a new label, Kill Rock Stars, based in Olympia, Washington, for the release of his second solo project, that year's self-titled album. Progressing to an eight-track machine, yet remaining in local basements for *Elliott Smith,* the songwriter saw his style fall into place. Although many early critics inaccurately placed Smith's music in the folk genre becauseof his acoustic tendencies, his songs covered much more territory; echoes of the Clash, the Beatles, the Saints, and, most of all, American pop icon Alex Chilton resonated throughout. "The eponymous second album was a dark, disquieting work," noted *Rough Guide to Rock* contributor Duncan Cooper, "by turns furious ('Southern Belle'), and desperate ('The Biggest Lie')."

Around the same time Smith's solo career was gaining ground—including the signing of a major-label recording deal with Virgin Records—Heatmiser was in the process of dissolving. The band's final album, *Mic City Sons,* was released in 1996. Consequently, he spent time honing his craft, practicing guitar in his living room while watching countless hours of television re-runs. Unhappy with his relationship with Virgin, however, Smith disentangled himself from the company when he started work on a third album. As before, Smith abandoned the idea of recording in a studio in favor of homes and basements and arrived in February of 1997 with the acclaimed album *Either/Or* for Kill Rock Stars. Offering expanded instrumentation, as well as glimpses of urban life and intense, telling emotional vignettes, the album earned favorable responses, but remained for the most part unheard of outside the Pacific Northwest.

In the spring of 1997, Heatmiser officially disbanded, and Smith moved to Brooklyn, New York, hoping that the move from Portland would renew his anonymity. But despite his intentions, this did not happen. Soon after leaving Oregon, Smith was approached by film maker Gus Van Sant, who was gathering music for a film called *Good Will Hunting.* Smith and Van Sant, both sharing mutual friends, had met while both men lived in Portland. When the soundtrack for the film appeared, it featured four songs from *Either/Or,* one from *Roman Candle,* and a new original called "Miss Misery," a song that Smith had been working on when Van Sant first contacted him. When he played the work in progress for the director, Van Sant was instantly impressed. "Miss Misery," an impressionistic song about making mistakes and searching for redemption, to Smith's surprise, earned an Academy Award nomination for best original song, along with songs performed by the likes of pop diva Celine Dion and country star Trisha Yearwood. "I had fully armored myself against having to be crushed by the presence of Celine Dion," Smith admitted to Mundy. "But she was the nicest person I've met in a while." Although he did not take home the Oscar, Smith performed his song for the event telecast on February 10, 1998, giving the musician instant exposure.

By now, Smith had signed with a major label, DreamWorks, for the release of his forthcoming album. With a larger budget, Smith strayed from recording in homes and basements, and instead recorded 1998's *XO* at Sunset Sound studios in Los Angeles, California. Insisting that the decision was his and not that of DreamWorks or co-producers Tom Rothrock or Ron Schnapf (who had previously worked with Beck, the Foo Fighters, and Mary Lou Lord), Smith explained to *Washington Post* writer Mark Jenkins in 1999, "I wanted to have more things, more instruments. Nobody wants to make the same record over and over. It was something that was new for me to do." Such stepped-up production concerned many fans, who worried that lush instrumentation would overshadow Smith's songs. However, fears subsided when the album arrived; the instruments used simply served to accent rather than drown out Smith's minimalist tendencies. He added horns to retro-rock song "A Question Mark," discreet strings for "Oh Well, Okay," and rolling piano to the single cut "Waltz #2." *XO* appeared on several top ten lists for 1998.

In the August of 1999, after a tour with his two-person band to support his album, Smith moved to Los Angeles and started work on the follow-up to *XO,* a record he hoped would utilize more piano. Since his successes of 1998, Smith grew more comfortable with his rising career fortunes. Adding to his upbeat outlook, he reconciled with his girlfriend and also started to mend relationships with family members. Nevertheless, an element of sadness was always evident in his songwriting. As far as his future as a musician, Smith commented, "I don't have any particular [musical] path," as quoted by *Boston Globe* writer Jim Sullivan in 1998. "I mean, I don't want to make the same record more than once, but ... as long as I can do something different—or something that feels different to me—I'll be pretty satisfied with that."

On April 18, 2000, Smith released his second album for DreamWorks entitled *Figure 8.* Working again with co-producers Rothrock and Schnapf, Smith recorded the project at Abbey Road, Capitol, Sunset Sound, and Sonora studios. A collection of 16 flawless songs, *Figure 8,* like Smith's prior albums, earned stellar reviews. Following in the paths of the Beatles' Paul McCartney and John Lennon, as well as Chilton, Smith proved again why he is perhaps the greatest pop songwriter of his generation.

Selected discography

Solo

Roman Candle, Cavity Search, 1994.
Elliott Smith, Kill Rock Stars, 1995.
Either/Or, Kill Rock Stars, 1997.
XO, DreamWorks, 1998.
Figure 8, DreamWorks, 2000.

With Heatmiser

The Music of Heatmiser, (tape), 1992.
Dead Air, Frontier, 1993.
Yellow No. 5, (EP), Frontier, 1994.
Cop and Speeder, Frontier, 1994.
Mic City Sons, Frontier, 1996.

Sources

Books

Robbins, Ira A., editor, *Trouser Press Guide to '90s Rock,* Fireside/Simon and Schuster, 1997.

Periodicals

Billboard, August 1, 1998; August 22, 1998.
Boston Globe, March 12, 1998; March 26, 1999; March 31, 1999.
Chicago Tribune, October 9, 1998.
Esquire, January 1998.
Los Angeles Times, April 19, 1998; June 13, 1999; February 19, 2000.
Melody Maker, June 27, 1998; July 11, 1998; August 8, 1998; January 2, 1999; May 8, 1999; May 15, 1999.
Rolling Stone, September 3, 1998.
Village Voice, April 15, 1997.
Washington Post, March 19, 1999; March 25, 1999; February 22, 2000.

Online

"Elliott Smith," *Rough Guide to Rock,* http://www.roughguides.com/rock/entries/entries-s/SMITH(ELLIOTT.html (March 20, 2000).
"Elliott Smith: XO," *Ink Blot Magazine,* http://www.inkblotmagazine.com/rev-archive/Elliott(Smith(XO.htm (March 20, 2000).

Additional information provided by DreamWorks Records.

—*Laura Hightower*

Tommy Smith

Composer, bandleader, tenor saxophone

Photography by Ken Franckling. Corbis. Reproduced by permission.

When tenor saxophonist Tommy Smith returned to his native Scotland at the age of 20 after studying music in the United States, the young musician made it his mission to establish an elevated awareness of jazz in his country throughout the 1990s. By creating more opportunities for musicians to tour, arranging higher quality performances, and encouraging a younger generation to study the genre, Smith, who played both straight-ahead jazz and fusion, accomplished his desire to lessen the gap between classical music and jazz for audiences and artists across Scotland. One of Smith's most significant contributions occurred in 1995 with his founding of the Scottish National Jazz Orchestra, as well as an offshoot called the Scottish Composers Jazz Ensemble. "I use the best players in the country and bring in special guests as needed," Smith told *Downbeat* magazine's Ken Franckling in October of 1999, following a spring series of Duke Ellington centennial concerts and another set of dates that featured Gil Evans and Miles Davis orchestral music.

For these performances, Smith's ensembles played selected music from Davis's *Sketches of Spain*, released in 1960, and *Porgy and Bess*, released in 1958. "I have never worked harder on a gig [just conducting]," said the jazz talent told Franckling, who funds his orchestras through grants and money earned at performances. "I'm always trying to find compositions to challenge the musicians. Musicians are inherently lazy in Scotland. Nobody has the time or patience. For the first two years, I did it for no money at all. Now we're getting some remuneration at last."

Smith was born on April 27, 1967, in Edinburgh, Scotland, and started playing tenor saxophone while attending a school on a Scottish housing estate near the town of his birth. Recognizing Smith's unique talent, his teachers encouraged him to develop his skills, and by the age of 15, Smith had advanced his technique enough to win acceptance to the prestigious Berklee College of Music in Boston, Massachusetts. However, Smith's family remained unable to fund a trip to the United States at the time. Nonetheless, after the local community initiated a massive fund-raising effort that spread to other nearby settlements, Smith accepted a position at Berklee the following year in 1984.

While attending Berklee, 18-year-old Smith took a position in a band led by master vibraphonist Gary Burton in 1986. Burton hired Smith, who was already recognized as a bold and unabashed young talent, upon the recommendation of pianist and keyboard prodigy Chick Corea, best known as one of the first to popularize jazz-rock fusion. After completing his studies at Berklee around 1988, Smith, at age 20, moved back to Scotland

For the Record . . .

Born April 27, 1967, in Edinburgh, Scotland. *Education*: Graduated from Berklee College of Music in Boston, MA, c. 1988.

Began attending Berklee, 1984; accepted position in band led by vibraphonist Gary Burton at age 18, 1986; signed with New York's Blue Note label, 1989; released the acclaimed album *Paris* for Blue Note, 1992; signed with Glasgow, Scotland's Linn Records, 1993; released *Misty Morning and No Time*, which contained pieces inspired by the poetry of Norman Craig, founded the Scottish National Jazz Orchestra and the Scottish Composers Jazz Ensemble, 1995; released *Azure* (inspired by artwork of Joan Miro) and *Beasts of Scotland* (inspired by poetry of Edwin Morgan), founded and acted as director for Scotland's first National Jazz Institute as part of Strathclyde University in Glasgow, 1996; released *The Sound of Love*, a tribute to ballads of Duke Ellington and Billy Strayhorn, 1998; released *Gymnopedie*, which revealed Smith's classical side, and the jazz/blues album *Blue Smith*; became Edinburgh's Heriot-Watt University's youngest honorary "Doctor of the University," 1999.

Awards: Arts Foundation/Barclays Private Banking Jazz Composition Fellowship, c. 1996.

Addresses: *Record company*—Linn Records, Glasgow, Scotland. *Website*—Tommy Smith at Linn Records, http://www.linnrecords.com.

from Boston with plans of establishing himself in the British jazz scene.

In 1989, Smith signed a multi-album contract with New York's Blue Note record label, for which he recorded his first major albums: 1990's Burton-produced fusion/post-bop album, *Peeping Tom*, and 1991's straight-ahead jazz record, *Standards*. During the early 1990s, Smith also released a series of jazz programs for the British Broadcasting Company (BBC) which featured Corea, Burton, accompanying pianist Tommy Flanagan, double bassist Arild Andersen,alto saxophonist Bobby Watson, and the BBC Scottish Symphony Orchestra. In addition, Smith released an album entitled *Paris*, issued in 1992, often referred to as Smith's best project for Blue Note, and accepted commissions from the Scottish Ensemble to write his first saxophone concerto in 1990, as well as a suite for saxophone and strings in 1991.

But despite Smith's mature, highly individual sound, Blue Note decided against extending the promising saxophonist's contract. According to the *Penguin Guide to Jazz on Compact Disc,* Blue Note found it difficult to market a British jazz artist in North America. Therefore, in 1993 Smith signed with Linn Records, headquartered in Glasgow, Scotland, and released a steady flow of work for the label throughout the remainder of the 1990s. Smith's first album for Linn, 1993's *Reminiscence,* showed Smith's ambition, evolving technique, and enthusiasm for playing with his new band, a trio composed of artists from northern lands such as Norway and his native Scotland, known as Forward Motion. Produced by the band, whose members also included bassist Terje Gewelt and drummer Ian Froman (both of whom Smith met while studying at Berklee), *Reminiscence* earned favorable reviews and critics believed that Smith was on the verge of taking his music in a new direction. That same year, Smith, at the time the composer in residence at the Glasgow International Jazz Festival, composed work, including his *Sonata No. 1* for saxophone and piano, for the Strathclyde Youth Jazz Orchestra. The composition was performed by pianist Murray McLachlan and published by London's Camden Music.

The following year, Smith recorded his second album, *Misty Morning and No Time,* written for a sextet and considered his most ambitious project in terms of composition up to this point. Gewelt and Froman again provided the rhythm section, while Scottish pianist Steve Hamilton (also a graduate of Berklee), British trumpeter Guy Barker, and British saxophonist Julian Arguëlles completed the band. All of the 14 works showcased in *Misty Morning and No Time,* including four wholly composed ensemble pieces, were inspired by the poetry of Norman Craig, one of Scotland's most distinguished contemporary poets. Using Craig's words to bring forth his musical ideas, Smith shed his former label of "teenage prodigy" with pieces such as "Memorial," an emotional tribute to Craig's deceased daughter, and "Estuary," a theme which opens with gentle saxophones intertwined with Barker's monette (a cross between a trumpet and a flugelhorn) and slowly builds to a striking climax.

In 1995, Smith received another major commission, this time from the Orchestra of St. John's Smith Square for a work entitled "Hiroshima," which premiered in the fall of 1996. Also in 1995, Smith embarked on a European tour, performing ten new compositions inspired by one of the century's most celebrated Surrealists, the Catalan painter, graphic artist, and sculptor Joan Miro. Smith, interested in innovative, modern art since his childhood, once considered a career in painting before he learned to play the saxophone. Released under the title *Azure* by Linn in

1996, the album (and concert series) was a collaborative effort that also featured Kenny Wheeler on trumpet and flugelhorn, Lars Danielsson (also a well-known keyboardist) on bass, and Jon Christensen on drums. Compositions such as the opening "The Gold of the Azure" and "The Calculation" led critics to suggest that had the above mentioned quartet stayed together long term, the *Azure* lineup would have become legendary.

Around the same time, Smith acquired the Arts Foundation/Barclays Private Banking Jazz Composition Fellowship and used the grant to compose new works. In 1996, Smith undertook another project with the hopes of bringing jazz further into the Scottish culture by opening his country's first National Jazz Institute as part of Strathclyde University in Glasgow. Serving as the institute's director of music, Smith developed a course that included formal education in jazz harmony, jazz ear training, jazz history, jazz piano, and technology and ensembles. And by the spring of that year, the National Jazz Institute offered its first "Berklee on the Road in the U.K." course, an intensive, one-week workshop that focused on the study of the African American jazz tradition.

For Smith's next recorded work, a suite of music commissioned by the Glasgow International Jazz Festival, the musician returned to representing poetry through music by teaming with one of Scotland's most respected modern poets, Edwin Morgan. Born in Glasgow in 1920, Morgan also held the post of professor of English at Glasgow University until his retirement in 1980. The resulting collaboration, the playfully conceived yet inventive *Beats of Scotland,* was recorded by Smith's sextet and released in May of 1996 by Linn. His sidemen included Barker on trumpet, flumpet, and flugelhorn; Hamilton on piano and synthesizer; Andy Panayi on flute and alto saxophone; Alec Dankworth on bass; and Tom Gordon on drums and percussion. Smith concluded the year with a reunion tour in October with Burton and accompanying musicians Christensen and Danielsson.

Resuming his tireless work schedule in 1997, Smith received commissions from the Royal Scottish National Orchestra, the Paragon Ensemble, and the Traverse Theatre to compose new music. His next release, *The Sound of Love,* a passionate and introspective tribute to the ballads of Ellington and pianist, composer, and arranger Billy Strayhorn, arrived in 1998 and earned rave reviews. Smith assembled an American band for this album, which consisted of pianist Kenny Barron, bassist Peter Washington, and drummer Billy Drummond. "Knowing I couldn't play a ballad properly, I went back to really work on the lyrics and phrasing," Smith admitted to Franckling. "I think I mostly matured because I started playing with people who really swung."

Two more albums, both of which showcased Smith's aptitude in other musical genres, were released in 1999. *Gymnopedie*, released in May of 1999, revealed Smith's classical side with arrangements of works by Satie, Grieg, and Bartók, as well as his own sonatas for saxophone and piano. His second album that year, *Blue Smith,* which combined elements of both jazz and the blues, was released in October and featured pianist Dave Kikoski, guitarist John Scofield, bassist James Genus, and drummer Greg Hutchinson. In addition to his continued work in the studio, as well as with the Scottish National Jazz Orchestra in 1999, Smith was named Heriot-Watt University's (located in Edinburgh, Scotland) youngest honorary "Doctor of the University" at the age of 32.

Selected discography

Peeping Tom, Blue Note, 1990.
Standards, Blue Note, 1991.
Paris, Blue Note, 1992.
Reminiscence, Linn, 1993.
Misty Morning and No Time, Linn, 1994.
Azure, Linn, 1996.
Beasts of Scotland, Linn, 1996.
The Sound of Love, Linn, 1998.
Blue Smith, Linn, 1999.
Gymnopedie, Linn, 1999.

Sources

Books

Cook, Richard and Brian Morton, editors, *Penguin Guide to Jazz on Compact Disc,* Penguin Books, 1998.

Periodicals

Downbeat, October 1999, p. 52.

Online

All Music Guide, http://www.allmusic.com (January 4, 2000).
Linn Records, http://www.linnrecords.com (January 4, 2000).

—*Laura Hightower*

Smog

Singer, songwriter, guitar, keyboards

With a rotating lineup of backing musicians, though most of his early releases were one-man efforts, Bill Callahan has released work since the late 1980s under the Smog name. A pioneer of the lo-fi movement, the eclectic songwriter and minimalist musician combined elements of rock, blues, country, and experimental sounds that usually revealed a dark and hopeless view of the world. His words are largely intimate self-revelations: melancholy, often bitter pessimisms that veer between painful candor and self-parody. His low-end production style has said to have been an influence on such bands as Pavement and Guided by Voices. Throughout the 1990s, and especially since the issue of *The Doctor Came at Dawn* in 1996, Callahan amassed a loyal cult following, primarily in the United States and Great Britain. One of his most vocal supporters includes Lou Barlow, the indie rock guru and leader of Sebadoh and Folk Implosion.

Despite comparisons to diverse styles and other musicians, such as Neil Young and the Replacements, Callahan always hesitated to align himself with one particular genre. "It's hard to wake up in the morning and say, 'I'm a country musician today,'" Callahan explained to Corey duBrowa in *Magnet* magazine. "Or, 'I'll be a rock musician now'—(those) jackets don't really fit. You can't look at yourself in the mirror and say those things. If there's a rock element in a song, if anything, I'll put an opposite element in there just to balance it." And when asked about how he feels about the music press placing him in the lo-fi category, Callahan replied, "It never meant anything to me, and I never really understood it," as quoted by Marlene Goldman from a February, 1999, interview with the Rolling Stone.com website. "I don't believe in these sorts of movements in music. I don't even think they exist.... it's just music, and has been since music started."

Callahan was born in Maryland in 1966. Shortly after his birth, his family moved to England, where he lived until the age of three. The family then returned to the United States, remaining in America for the next four years. At the age of seven, Callahan returned to Knaresborough in North Yorkshire, England, for another five years, before going back to the United States at age 12. Despite his frequent moves between the two countries during his early childhood, Callahan, as an adult, regarded himself as 100 percent American. Nevertheless, the songwriter admitted that he has always felt he never really fit in anywhere he lived. During his adult life, Callahan called several cities home, including Prosperity, South Carolina, San Francisco and Sacramento, California, and Chicago, where he has lived since around 1999.

Callahan, who realized in his early twenties that he would never enjoy working in an office and wanted to maintain his freedom, began his recording career releasing a series of self-made cassette tapes on his own Disaster label under the name Smog. The first of these tapes, *Macramé Gunplay,* arrived in 1988, while his second cassette, *Cow,* was released in 1989. 1990 saw the release of three more tapes: the enigmatic, minimalist *A Table Setting, Tired Tape Machine,* and the primitive yet promising *Sewn to the Sky. Sewn to the Sky* caught the attention of Chicago's Drag City label, echoed the Residents and Captain Beefheart. And as the vague, atmospheric title and the name Smog suggest, Callahan's repetitive guitar riffs, complemented by his occasional and deeply subdued vocals, formed the bleak soundscapes of notable tracks such as "Garb" and "Fruit Bats."

After signing with Drag City, Callahan released his first EP, *Floating,* in 1991. Smog's debut full-length album for Drag City, *Forgotten Foundation,* arrived in 1992. Though still purposefully crude in terms of musical development and production, *Forgotten Foundation* nonetheless showed Callahan's song-oriented side for some tracks with more traditional arrangements, additional vocals, and more fully developed melodies, paving the way for Smog's follow-up, *Julius Caesar.* Released in 1991 and recorded with musicians Cynthia Dall and Jim O'Rourke, the spare, folk-inspired *Julius Caesar* was Smog's first release to earn critical acclaim. Here, Callahan incorporated cello, violin, acoustic guitar, and banjo into the mix

For the Record . . .

Born in 1966 in Maryland.

Released series of self-made cassettes on own Disaster label, beginning with *Macramé Gunplay* in 1988; signed with Chicago's Drag City label, released EP *Floating*, 1991; released debut album for Drag City, *Forgotten Foundation*, 1992; released acclaimed album *Julius Caesar*, 1993; released *The Couple Came at Dawn*, 1996; released the more optimistic *Knock Knock*, 1999.

Addresses: *Record company*—Drag City, P.O. Box 476867, Chicago, IL 60647, (312) 455-1015.

and established himself as a focused songwriter. He composed tracks that revealed both elation, as in "When You Walk," and more commonly depression, as in "Your Wedding." Highlights from the album included the upbeat "I Am Star Wars!," the instrumental cello piece "One Less Star," and the immortal "37 Push Ups."

Smog released the six-song EP *Burning Kingdom*, which found Callahan further breaking with his lo-fi tendencies, in 1994. For the song "My Shell," for example, Callahan's words of alienation are complemented by electric guitar, cello, and drums. Other notable tracks included "My Family," a low-key, relentless psychodrama, and "The Desert," which tells the story of crawling through the desert without water to the accompaniment of a funeral-like organ. In 1995, Smog released another more fully-produced album entitled *Wild Love*, which found Callahan for the most part abandoning hopefulness—excluding the brilliant "Prince Alone in the Studio," a metaphor for an artist's lonely existence—in favor of a relentless, often bitter pessimism that some critics found hard to take seriously. Throughout the album, Callahan tells stories of an unhappy childhood, failed romances, and life's disappointments in general.

In 1996, Smog released the *Kicking a Couple Around* EP, which opened with a solo acoustic performance of the song "Your New Friend" from a British Broadcasting Company (BBC) broadcast and also included three tracks recorded and produced in Chicago with Steve Albini. Overall, Callahan again focused on introspection, gloom, and feelings of displacement, such as in "The Orange Glow of a Stranger's Living Room" and "I Break Horses," a song "which can reduce strong men and women ... to heaps of quivering gelatin," according to Ben Thompson of Independent on Sunday. That same year, Callahan followed with the groundbreaking album *The Doctor Came at Dawn,* comprised of quiet, acoustic songs of reflection. However, Callahan admitted that unanticipated events led him to concentrate on his acoustic side for his 1996 records. "I'm really haphazard how I work. I like to work around difficulties and not really plan things," he said to Goldman. "Like, I had a keyboard that got stolen [on tour in Barcelona]—the keyboard I used on the *Wild Love* album. The I made *Kicking a Couple Around,* which is just with acoustic guitar. It was my reaction to having my keyboard stolen."

Callahan returned in 1997 with another mostly acoustic effort, *Red Apple Falls,* a country-informed album with unexpected dashes of French horns and steel guitar that bore similarities to the songs of Neil Young. *Red Apple Falls* took just five days to record, but included songs that reveal concepts that could take years to understand, exemplified in the tracks "Inspirational" and "I Was a Stranger." His subsequent release, *Knock Knock,* appeared in 1999 and was co-produced by O'Rourke. Considered Smog's most diverse release, *Knock Knock* featured orchestral qualities and members of the Chicago Children's Choir for the chorus in tracks like "No Dancing," as well as acoustic numbers like "Left Only With Love." Unlike his prior work, which overwhelmingly centered around a doomed and pessimistic view of life, *Knock Knock* provided a more optimistic view of the world. "It's more forward-thinking. I guess I had some realizations about not letting things crush you," Callahan explained to duBrowa. "The fact that you can always move... you don't have to stay in a bad place."

Selected discography

Macramé Gunplay, (Cassette), Disaster, 1988.
Cow, (Cassette), Disaster, 1989.
A Table Setting, (Cassette), Disaster, 1990.
Tired Tape Machine, (Cassette), Disaster, 1990.
Sewn to the Sky, Disaster, 1990, reissued by Drag City, 1995.
Floating, (EP), Drag City, 1991.
Forgotten Foundation, Drag City, 1992.
Julius Caesar, Drag City, 1993.
Burning Kingdom, (EP), Drag City, 1994.
Wild Love, Drag City, 1995.
Kicking a Couple Around, (EP), Drag City, 1996.
The Couple Came at Dawn, Drag City, 1996.
Red Apple Falls, Drag City, 1997.
Knock Knock, Drag City, 1999.

Sources

Books

Robbins, Ira A., editor, *Trouser Press Guide to '90s Rock*, Fireside/Simon and Schuster, 1997.

Periodicals

Chicago Tribune, December 12, 1997; January 29, 1999.
Guitar Player, May 1997.
Independent, April 19, 1996, pp. 8-9; October 22, 1997, p. 4; February 12, 1999, p. 12; May 18, 1999, p. 9.
Independent on Sunday, May 11, 1997, p. 18
Magnet, April/May 1999, p. 25.
Washington Post, February 26, 1999.

Online

"Quiet Knocking," *Rolling Stone.com,* http://www.rollingstone.tunes.com (January 14, 2000).

—*Laura Hightower*

Britney Spears

Pop singer

AP/Wide World Photos. Reproduced by permission.

Britney Spears was barely 16 years old when her first album, *... Baby One More Time,* appeared at number one on album charts in 1999. Simultaneously, the album's title song also debuted at number one on the singles charts. A former Mouseketeer on the Disney Channel's *Mickey Mouse Club*, with bright-eyes and wavy blond hair, she came to symbolize the peppiest and perkiest of the shifting currents of the popular music culture at the threshold of the twenty-first century. Spears reflected an image in direct contradiction to the trends of the times; she posed instead a wholesome and non-threatening image to counteract the sinister gangsta' rap and sullen gothic subcultures that permeated the recording industry in the 1990s. Her innocent appeal extended beyond the teenage throngs that traditionally controlled the realm of popular music. Young girls emulated her appearance, and young boys harbored secret crushes, while parents nodded overwhelming. Spears's name became a household word, and she earned over $1 million by the age of 17. Her popularity soared to such heights that a contingency of her fans reportedly camped outside in the wintry January weather of Charleston, Virginia, for days in order to get tickets for one of her concerts.

Spears was born in 1982 in the small town of Kentwood, not far from New Orleans, Louisiana. She was the second of three children—and the oldest daughter—of Jamie Spears, a building contractor; and Lynne Spears, a second-grade teacher. Spears was a mere toddler, two years of age, when she first tried to sing. She mimicked popular crooners such as Whitney Houston and even donned makeup to complete the fantasy. As soon as she was able, Spears, who was raised a Baptist, sang with church choirs. Additionally, she danced and performed in talent showcases.

Spears was eight years old when she first auditioned to be a Mouseketeer on the Disney Channel's *Mickey Mouse Club* show, a reprise of the original *Mickey Mouse Club* program from the 1950s. The producers, impressed with the talented youngster, referred Spears instead to the Professional Performing Arts School and the Off-Broadway Dance Center in New York City, because she was too young to conform to the format of the Disney show. With assistance and support from her family, the budding superstar availed herself of the opportunity to develop her talent. In 1991, at age nine, she moved along with her mother and younger sister to New York City. There Spears enrolled at the professional school, and before long, she began performing in live theater presentations and in television commercials. Later, in 1992, she returned to Disney studios to audition a second time for the *Mickey Mouse Club.* Spears by then was eleven years old and a show

For the Record . . .

Born on December 2, 1982, in Kentwood, LA; daughter of Lynne and Jamie Spears; second of three siblings. *Education*: Off-Broadway Dance Center, New York City; Professional Performing Arts School.

Mouseketeer on the Disney Channel's *Mickey Mouse Club*, 1992-94; Jive Records recording artist, 1997—; debut LP, *...Baby One More Time*, 1999.

Awards: American Music Award, favorite new pop-rock artist, 2000.

Addresses: *Record company*—BMG Entertainment International, 1540 Broadway, New York, NY 10036. *Website*—Britney Spears website, www.britneyspears.com.

business veteran, and she easily secured a position as one of the Mouseketeers.

Britney Spears performed with the Mouseketeers for two years, during which time she worked with another soon-to-be diva, Christina Aguilera, as well as with Keri Russell (television's Felicity), and 'N Sync's JC Chasez and Justin Timberlake. Following the cancellation of *Mickey Mouse Club*, her friendship with Chasez and Timberlake led to a meeting between Spears and 'N Sync manager Johnny Wright, an acquaintance that set her on the path to superstardom. Subsequently she moved into a regular spot as the opening act for 'N Sync. She developed a hugefollowing of fans in very little time and distinguished herself quickly as a solo act on her own merits, which led her mother to send a demonstration tape to the New York-based manager Larry Rudolph. Rudolph, an entertainment lawyer, secured a contract with Jive Records for the 15-year-old Spears, and in 1999 Jive released Spears's first album along with a single release of the CD's title song, "... Baby One More Time."

Phenomenally, both the album and the single debuted on the music charts at number one. Spears became an overnight sensation. Her first album went "diamond" and sold 8.4 million copies by the end of the calendar year to rate as the second highest selling album that year. Early in 2000 she won the American Music Award for favorite new pop-rock artist. Additionally, she received two Grammy Award nominations from the National Academy of Recording Arts and Sciences for her debut album, which by then had sold over ten million copies.

When a dislocated knee limited her movement and kept her from the dance floor in 1999, Spears bounced back seemingly without missing a beat. Although she canceled her scheduled appearance at the American Music Awards ceremony in Los Angeles, wherein she was to perform a routine combining her three hit songs "... Baby One More Time," "(You Drive Me) Crazy," and "Sometimes," she performed ably at the Grammy Award ceremonies in 2000.

Spears admittedly takes criticism from reviewers because of her spun-sugar-candy adolescent image. Regardless, her popularity on the record charts is proof of her talent. Her name, according to Searchterms.Com, is among the most frequently searched keywords on the Internet. The various Britney Spears Internet sites rank among the top ten of the most commonly sought locations on the World Wide Web. Her Internet appeal was so high that with her mother's assistance, Spears undertook the construction of her own personal website. The site includes pictures of Spears—for which she wrote clever captions—videos, and fan photos taken at her concerts and other personal appearances. Also online, Spears participated in chats with the Disney Corporation and with America Online.

Spears's appearances in the number one slot of the *Billboard* charts keep her consistently in the public spotlight. Her music video, "Time Out With Britney Spears," rose to number one on *Billboard*'s music video sales for January 13, 2000, with her second album scheduled for release in May of 2000. Her hectic performance schedule for the first year of the millenium included an appearance at the Baltimore Arena in March, and at Miami, Florida's American Airlines Arena. Spears has also contracted to appear at Boston's Tweeter Center, Chicago's New World Music Theatre, Houston's Cynthia Woods Mitchell Pavilion, and the Hollywood Bowl and the Glen Helen Blockbuster Pavilion in Los Angeles, California. Additionally, she aspires to act and appeared in a guest role on television's *Touched by an Angel*.

Even in the midst of her superstardom, Spears remains focused on maintaining her sensibilities. At her family home in Louisiana, she retains responsibility for humdrum household chores, and in between her exotic touring commitments and her assignments as the celebrity model for designer Tommy Hilfiger, she continues her high school studies. Additionally, when school, chores, dance and recording sessions, and "Tommy" fail to usurp all of her time, Spears honors contracts to pose for posters and miscellaneous endorsements. As her career flourished, she transferred from her private high school in McComb, Mississippi to a home schooling program from the University of Nebraska, all the while retaining the "bubble-gum teeny-bopper" image that suited her lifestyle so adeptly. Indeed, *Time* called her first album "cuddly."

Her admitted indulgences in life include fast food, sunshades, vanilla body lotion, and fantasizing about movie heartthrobs, especially Brad Pitt. Spears professed further to enjoying television, especially the sitcom *Friends,* and *Felicity*; *Steal Magnolias* and *Beaches* are among her favorite movies. With respect to other musicians, Spears's taste in music remains within the limits of the same genre that she performs. She enjoys Lauryn Hill, Brandy, and TLC. Despite her superstar income, expensive clothes do not hold particular appeal for the young woman who professed, in fact, that she loves to shop at thrift stores. Within the confines of a brimming adolescent schedule, Spears, for relaxation, gads around the highways in a Mercedes SL500 convertible that she purchased for herself since earning her driver's license. Her dislikes include body piercing and hard/gothic rock music.

As with any popular ingenue, Britney Spears's social life is a topic of great media interest. According to widespread reports, she established a pen pal correspondence with England's Prince William after meeting him and his family. The two "made a date" for Valentine's Day in 2000, it was reported further. To help fuel gossip, an agent revealed that Spears started house hunting in the Bohemian-style nineteenth-century community of Primrose Hill in north London, where her dream home might cost over $3 million. Her public relations contingency meanwhile persisted in reinforcing her youthful image with a host of innocent merchandise and other paraphernalia geared squarely at children of elementary age and younger. Among the Britney Spears merchandise: a doll, and a flashing Britney Spears wristwatch.

Media fascinations notwithstanding, Spears maintains a level head for matters on the serious vein. She started the Britney Spears Fund in conjunction with the Giving Back Fund to provide summer camp opportunities for underprivileged children who aspire to the performing arts. The camp, for children ten to twelve years old, in Berkshire Hills in Massachusetts, was scheduled to open in the summer of 2000.

Selected discography

Singles

"... Baby One More Time," Jive, 1999.
"Sometimes," Jive, 1999.
"From the Bottom of My Broken Heart," Jive 2000.

Albums

... Baby One More Time, Jive, 1999.

Sources

Periodicals

Courier-Mail (Brisbane, Australia), January 19, 2000, p. 4.
Daily Telegraph (Sydney, Australia), January 25, 2000, p. 34.
Entertainment, September 17, 1999, p. 7; December 24, 1999, p. 28; January 14, 2000, p. 86.
Newsweek, March 1, 1999, p.64.
People, February 15, 1999, p. 71; May 10, 1999, p. 114.
Record, (Bergen County, NJ), January 4, 2000, p. A-2.
St. Louis Post-Dispatch, January 15, 2000, p. 24.
Sunday Telegraph, January 23, 2000.
Teen, August 1999, p. 60-62.
Time, December 28, 1998, p. 186; March 1, 1999, p. 71.
Toronto Sun, January 14, 2000, p. 15; January 19, 2000, p. 49.

Online

"Britney Spears," *AMG All Music Guide,* wysiwyg://5/http://allmusic.com/cg/x.dll (February 4, 2000).

—Gloria Cooksey

Ronnie Spector

Singer

Photograph by Lynn Goldsmith. Corbis. Reproduced by permission.

As the effervescent lead singer of the Ronettes, one of the most popular "girl groups" of the 1960s, Ronnie Spector enlivened the group with her powerful voice and distinctive, sultry vibrato. Under the watchful genius of her record producer, Bronx-born Phil Spector, Ronnie Spector, along with her sister, Estelle Bennett, and their cousin, Nedra Talley Ross, left an indelible mark in the annals of rock and roll through their recordings and performances as the Fabulous Ronettes.

Veronica "Ronnie" Spector was born Veronica Bennett in New York City on August 10, 1943. She grew up along with her sister, Estelle, on 151st Street in the Spanish Harlem district of New York City. Their father left the family when Spector was still in grade school, yet despite the painful loss she bore little ill will. Most of her elementary school career was spent at PS 92, and she later attended George Washington High School. Her father, Louis Bennett, was Irish, and her mother, Beatrice Bennett, was African American and Cherokee, which resulted in identity confusion for Spector as a child. Although she turned briefly—and with little success—to tanning lotion in her attempt to resolve the adolescent crisis, she ultimately learned to appreciate her unique heritage and exotic appearance. Indeed her facial features and coloring combined to enhance her media appeal, and her affinity for flashy clothes and exotic hairdos, reminiscent of the street life in Spanish Harlem, evoked a bad-girl image that served her well as "Ronnie Ronette," the lead singer of the Fabulous Ronettes.

As a young child, Spector loved to perform for her family. Little Frankie Lymon was her idol, and she strove to imitate his girlish falsetto, singing "Why Do Fools Fall in Love" persistently. By early adolescence she had taken to re-arranging the family's living room furniture into an imaginary auditorium and standing on the coffee table for a stage, after school and whenever else she had the opportunity to be at home by herself. She sang in a group with her sister, Estelle Bennett, and various cousins. For a time they called themselves Ronnie and the Relatives, until eventually she established a routine with her sister Estelle and cousin Nedra Talley Ross as the Rondettes—a combination of all three girls' names. They played amateur shows at the Apollo Theater and as teenagers showed promise. They worked with a singing coach and by 1961 the three girls were singing locally at social functions and elsewhere. The trio renamed themselves the Ronettes and signed with Colpix Records that year. The Ronettes first release was a double-sided single, "I Want a Boy"/"What's So Sweet about Sweet Sixteen." A second double-sided single released that same year was called "I'm Gonna Quit While I'm Ahead"/"My Guiding Light." Several singles followed in 1962, including an old favorite, "Silhouettes."

For the Record . . .

Born Veronica Bennett on August 10, 1943, in New York, NY; daughter of Louis and Beatrice Bennett; married Phil Spector, 1966; three sons; divorced, 1974; married Jonathan Greenfield, January 16, 1982; two sons: Austin, born 1981, Jason, born 1983.

Formed the Darling Sisters with sister Estelle and cousin Nedra Taylor, 1959; signed with Colpix Records, 1961; made first records, including "Be My Baby," as the Ronettes on Phil Spector's Philles label, 1963; group broke up, 1966; Spector signed with Apple Records, 1970; Buddha Records, 1974; Columbia Records, 1987-90; published autobiography, *Be My Baby: How I Survived Mascara, Miniskirts, and Madness,* 1990; released *She Talks to Rainbows*, Kill Rock Stars Records, 1999.

Addresses: *Record company*—Kill Rock Stars Records, 120 N.E. State Ave., #418, Olympia, WA 98501, (360) 357-9732. *Website*—www.killrockstars.com. *Email*—krs@killrockstars.com.

In addition to recording for Colpix, the Ronettes continued to work locally. Eventually, through a case of mistaken identity combined with pluck, the girls secured a regular stint as dancers at New York City's popular Peppermint Lounge. Although they were underage, they stuffed their brassieres with tissue in an attempt to look older and maneuvered their way discretely through the 46th Street club. Through a chance meeting with a popular New York disc jockey, Murray the K, they secured a job performing with his weekly rock and roll revue at the Brooklyn FoxTheater, and they appeared every evening after school on a local radio show.

"Ronnie Ronette"

The early Ronettes recorded for Colpix with little success through 1962. By early 1963 the group determined to find another producer and called Phil Spector "cold," without introduction. Phil Spector, who produced many of the greatest rock and roll hits of the 1960s, agreed to audition the Ronettes at Mirasound Studios. Already familiar with the girls' dancing, he wanted to see and hear more.

Phil Spector recognized immediately that Ronnie Spector's voice was a good match for his recording technique, called the "wall of sound," an immensely popular special effect involving the vocal overdubbing of orchestral recordings. Wall of sound involved multiple voices singing in harmony and "exploding" through the elaborate orchestral track. Phil Spector employed the wall of sound to create some of the greatest hit records of the 1960s, including "Unchained Melody" and "Ebb Tide" by the Righteous Brothers. Upon hearing the Ronettes, he set to work and wrote songs explicitly for the trio to sing, and by the fall of 1963, the Ronettes' signature hit, "Be My Baby," was written, recorded, and released on Philles Records. Dick Clark picked up the song on his perennial *American Bandstand,* and he introduced the song as the "record of the century." The song was immensely popular; the Ronettes became a sensation overnight, and their lifestyle approached fantasy level. The girls traveled to England early in 1964 and performed on *Sunday Night at the Palladium* with the Beatles. Another band, called the Rolling Stones, who were unknown at the time, opened for the Ronettes; and the late Beatle, John Lennon, developed an infatuation for Ronnie Spector.

The Ronettes, and Spector in particular, developed a close personal bond with the two English groups, and the musicians all visited back and forth whenever their touring engagements brought them to the same city. Phil Spector continued to write hit songs for the Ronettes, and the group cultivated a street-wise image that evoked its Spanish Harlem roots. The girls teased their hair and painted heavy black mascara on their eyes in emulation of the exotic women of the streets. They shortened and tightened their skirts until they could go neither shorter nor tighter and then added a slit for movement and more sex appeal. As the classic 1960 "girl group" soared to fame, a romance bloomed between Spector and the masterful young producer of her records. Ironically, Spector and her singing partners retained a wholesome quality off stage, as Beatrice Bennet kept a watchful eye over the girls and their activities. Spector remained naïve and failed to succumb to the shallow and tawdry lure of show business, even as she traveled the world as a major rock and roll star at a time when rock and roll reigned supreme.

Dark Days

The Ronettes recorded 28 songs with Philles Records prior to Phil Spector's unofficial retirement in 1966, after which the popular singing group faded into rock and roll history. The pace of Spector's life slowed. Many of the Ronettes' later recordings were never released; and otherswere released but inexplicably credited to other girl groups. On April 14, 1968, "Ronnie Ronette" unassumingly married Phil Spector, and within hours, her life plunged into an abyss of loneliness that she endured for nearly ten years. Both she and her husband turned increasingly to alcohol and drugs as a means of coping with daily life, and by the age of 25 she had become for practical purposes a has-been and a drunk.

The Spectors, unable to conceive a child, adopted a baby named Donté, born March 23, 1969. Spector, who saw the bi-racial child on television, felt a kinship with the infant because of her own mixed heritage. Additionally, Spector in her naivete hoped that her fractured marriage would improve with the presence of a child, but the situation worsened. In 1969, still fraught with depression and overwhelmed by chronic drug use, she inadvertently drove her car to the edge of a cliff, where it teetered ominously. She was rescued in an unconscious state. Overwhelmed and frightened by the thought of the near disaster that she escaped so narrowly, Spector sought professional help for her depression and substance abuse.

In 1970 she signed with Apple Records, at the request of the Beatles who presented her with a song written by George Harrison. The song, released in 1971, was called, "Try Some, Buy Some" but failed to revive her waning career. Upon her return to the United States, she immediately resumed her self-abusive lifestyle, suffered a seizure, and underwent detoxification treatment at St. Francis Hospital. Ironically, Spector found comfort in the atmosphere at the hospital, and for months thereafter she subjected herself to bouts of drug abuse for the purpose of returning to the hospital as an escape from the overbearing lifestyle forced upon her by her husband. In 1971, a desperate Phil Spector coerced his wife into adopting six-year-old twins, in attempt to revive the marriage. The ruse failed, and in 1972 Ronnie Spector joined Alcoholics Anonymous and summoned the courage to leave her husband permanently. In her desperation she left behind all of her personal belongings in the couple's 23-room mansion, and although she tried at a later time to recover her possessions, she met with no success.

Ronnie Spector filed for and secured a divorce. The settlement awarded her partial custody of her son, Donté. She set out to revive her shattered career, and the music world was receptive. In 1973 she worked with Alice Cooper and spent some time on tour as a solo act. After she settled her divorce in 1974, she returned to New York City and successfully revived the Ronettes with new backup singers. Her following grew, and her colleagues in the music world—including disc jockey, Murray the K, and popular teen host, Dick Clark—presented her with opportunities to gain exposure. She played at Madison Square Garden, and in 1974, Buddha Records signed her to a short-lived recording contract. Her prospects improved steadily until a series of mishaps instigated by her ex-husband—including a telephoned death threat—that caused Ronnie Spector to retreat once more from the public spotlight. With encouragement from Steven Van Zandt, she maintained a limited performance calendar, and in 1975 released a single, "You'd Be Good for Me," with Tom Cat Records. She toured for over a year with Johnny and the Asbury Jukes as the opening act for Bruce Springsteen & the E Street Band, and in 1977 Van Zandt produced her recording of "Say Goodbye to Hollywood." Her efforts met with little success.

New Beginning

As her reprised career slumped, she focused her attention on gaining full custody of her son. Around that same time, in 1978, she became acquainted with a theater worker named Jonathan Greenfield at Hurrah disco in New York City. Greenfield, a long-time admirer of Spector and the Ronettes, proved to be a positive influence and a highly supportive friend. Spector and Greenfield married on June 16, 1982. The couple has two sons, Austin and Jason. With her confidence restored, Spector published her autobiography, *Be My Baby,* with Harmony Books of New York in 1990.

Career-wise, Greenfield successfully arranged for Spector to fill a headline bill at the prestigious Bottom Line nightclub in 1981, and she resumed her professional singing career for a third time. In 1986 Spector accepted an offer from Eddie Money to sing on "Take Me Home Tonight," a hit single of 1986. The record led to a recording contract with Columbia Records and resulted in her subsequent release of *Unfinished Business* in 1987. In 1999, Spector performed on *Born Again Savage,* on Van Zandt's label, Renegade Nation. She released a second album that year, a Kill Rock Stars production called *She Talks to Rainbows.* The album features one of Spector's own songs, "I Wish I Never Saw the Sunshine," and "Don't Worry Baby" written by Beach Boy Brian Wilson for Spector two decades earlier. She made personal appearances and was on the bill to perform with the new Ronettes at a national, White House backed economic summit in Denver in June of 1997. In July of 1998 she joined with approximately 300 musicians in the Intel New York Music Festival, hosted on the Internet across 20 locations in New York City. She appeared with Tommy James in the CBS Oldies Concert on the Central Park Summer Stage in June of 1999. She also performed in the *Columbia Media Journal* (*CMJ*) Music Marathon, along with Willie Nelson, the Foo Fighters, and other popular stars. When cable television network VH1 aired "VH1 100 Women of Rock and Roll," Ronnie Spector appeared at number 67 on the list.

During the late 1990s, in a well-publicized court action in the State Supreme Court of Manhattan, Ronnie Spector brought suit against her ex-husband for millions of dollars in past due royalties from the sale and other use of the Ronettes recordings. Her sister and her cousin joined her in the lawsuit alleging that Phil Spector employed coercive tactics to withhold royalties from the singers, since 1964. The members of the Ronettes revealed in court that they received a collective total of $14,000 following the release of "Be My Baby," and received no further payment for subsequent recordings and royalties. The Ronettes maintained their right to the royalties and disputed the ownership of the master tapes of their recordings in an involved court battle.

Selected discography

Singles

"Try Some, Buy Some," Apple Records, 1971.
"You'd Be Good for Me," Tom Cat Records, 1975.
"Say Goodbye to Hollywood" (with E-Street Band), 1977.
"Take Me Home Tonight" (with Eddie Money), Columbia, 1986.

Albums

Unfinished Business, Columbia, 1987.
She Talks to Rainbows (includes "I Wish I Never Saw the Sunshine," and "Don't Worry Baby"), 1999.

With the Ronettes

"Sweet Sixteen," Colpix, 1961.
"Silhouettes," May 1962.
"Be My Baby," Philles Records, 1963.
A Christmas Gift for You (with others), Philles Records, 1963.
"Baby I Love You," Philles Records, 1963.
Presenting the Fabulous Ronettes, Philles Records, 1963.
"The Best Part of Breakin' Up," Philles Records, 1964.
The Ronettes Sing Their Greatest Hits, Vol. II, Philles Records, 1965.
"Walkin' in the Rain."

Sources

Books

Spector, Ronnie, *Be My Baby: How I Survived Mascara, Miniskirts, and Madness,* Harmony Books, 1990.

Periodicals

Entertainment, September 17, 1999, p. 80.
Independent, June 27, 1989, p. 1-2; December 12, 1998, p. 12.
Magnet, October/November 1999, p. 26.
Newsday, September 20, 1999, p. B9.
Rolling Stone, October 28, 1999, p. 104.
USA Today, July 16, 1999, p. 5E.

—Gloria Cooksey

Sunny Day Real Estate

Rock band

The re-formation of Sunny Day Real Estate in 1997 was regarded as one of the most unlikely reunions in the history of modern rock. After a furious split in late 1994, the band's bass guitarist Nate Mendel and drummer William Goldsmith joined the Foo Fighters, lead vocalist and guitarist Jeremy Enigk (who left Sunny Day Real Estate for religious beliefs) released a solo album, and guitarist Dan Hoerner left the recording industry all together. However, when Goldsmith left the Foo Fighters in 1997, Enigk and Hoerner, who had already made peace, persuaded the drummer to help resurrect Sunny Day Real Estate. Although Mendel chose to stay with the Foo Fighters, the remaining members, with bassist Jeff Palmer replacing Mendel, recorded their third and most highly anticipated album, *How It Feels to Be Something On,* in 1998.

Sunny Day Real Estate began to take shape around 1992 in Seattle, Washington, when Hoerner (also the group's initial lead singer), Goldsmith, and Mendel decided to form a melodic, punk-metal band. The group changed its name frequently, once dubbing themselves Chewbacca

Photograph by Karen Mason Blair. Corbis. Reproduced by permission.

For the Record . . .

Members include **Jeremy Enigk** (joined band, 1993), vocals, guitar; **William Goldsmith** (joined Foo Fighters in 1995, left Foo Fighters in 1997 to reunite with Sunny Day Real Estate), drums; **Dan Hoerner,** guitar; **Nate Mendel** (joined Foo Fighters in 1995), bass; **Jeff Palmer** (joined band in 1997 to replace Mendel), bass.

Goldsmith, Hoerner, and Mendel formed band in Seattle, WA, 1992; band enlisted lead vocalist Enigk, 1993; signed with Sub Pop Records, released debut album, Diary, 1994; group disbanded, late 1994; Sunny Day Real Estate reunited (minus Mendel), 1997; released *How It Feels to Be Something On,* 1998.

Addresses: *Record company*—Sub Pop Records, 1932 1st Ave, Ste. 1103, Seattle, WA 98101, phone (206) 441-8441, fax (206) 441-8245. *Website*—Sunny Day Real Estate Official Website, http://www.sunnydayrealestate.com

Kaboom as well as Thief, Steal Me a Peach, then finally Sunny Day Real Estate. In 1992, the trio released their first seven-inch single, "Flatland Spider," on their own label called One Day I Stopped Breathing Records. Two of the record's songs, "Flatland Spider" and "The Onlies," included driving guitars and tortured vocals set to turbulent drumming. While the precise drums and guitars brought forth the sound that the band desired, Hoerner's vocals failed to provide Sunny Day Real Estate with an appropriate balance. Thus, the band enlisted a young, yet talented 18-year-old musician named Jeremy Enigk to soften the group's edges with his introspective and distinctive vocalization. Critics compared Enigk's mystic voice and guitar technique to that of the legendary Van Morrison, as well as an emotive cross between Paul McCartney and Shannon Hoon of Blind Melon. Though not considered as skilled as Morrison, Enigk nonetheless paid tribute to the latter musician's phrasing and repetition of key couplets.

With a new singer, Sunny Day Real Estate released a second seven-inch single in 1993 entitled "Thief Steal Me a Peach," which the band's official website dubbed "a masterpiece of post-hardcore melodic adventure." The eye-catching record cover, designed by Hoerner, featured a scene of ant-like humanoids standing on the brink of disaster, and the package included prints by Seattle artist Christopher Thompson to enhance a poem written by Hoerner called "A Non-Musical Accompaniment." Subsequently, Sunny Day Real Estate caught the attention of local audiences and the influential Sub Pop Records, also home to Nirvana and Mudhoney.

After signing with Sub Pop, Sunny Day Real Estate released their first full-length album, *Diary,* in 1994, which fared well in sales and included guitar-driven anthems such as "Seven" and "In Circles." Years later, the aforementioned singles remained two of the most popular audience requests during Sunny Day Real Estate concerts. Another highlight included "Grendel," while tracks such as "Song About an Angel" drew attention to Enigk's growing interest in spirituality.

Considering the band's acclaimed debut, their affiliation with Sub Pop, and Sunny Day Real Estate's rising popularity, commercial success seemed unavoidable. However, just as the quartet were on the verge of breaking through, Sunny Day Real Estate came to an end. The sudden success, combined with extensive touring, internal conflict, and Enigk's new devotion to Christianity led to a fallout among band members. In late winter, 1994, following a long, exhausting tour with Shudder to Think and Soul Coughing, Sunny Day Real Estate thought it best to dissolve the band.

Just weeks earlier, Enigk had completely devoted his life to Christ, believing that religion would help relieve his personal conflicts and the band's inner turmoil. "I watched myself slowly shrivel up into a hopeless, bitter and lonely person," he wrote in a letter sent by e-mail to close friends in December, as quoted by *Magnet* magazine's David Daley. "I could not take it anymore, so I took a shot on calling upon God. He answered me. All the hope that was squeezed out of me was replaced 10 times." Moreover, Enigk wanted the other members of the band to find the same sense of hope in religion he had. However, Hoerner, Goldsmith, and Mendel failed to understand, and Enigk opted to sacrifice his band for his beliefs. Gradually, communication almost ceased to exist within the band and on their small tour bus, as Enigk's band mates harbored feelings of betrayal and shattered dreams.

The strained relationships of Sunny Day Real Estate came to a boiling point during a show at the Black Cat club in Washington, D.C., shortly before the breakup. Everyone but the audience realized that this cold winter night would most likely mark Sunny Day Real Estate's last performance. (Michael) Doughty, Enigk started quietly praying. "This was exactly the big ... huge rift that made everybody feel so uncomfortable," Doughty told Daley. "Nate just threw his hands up, put his bass down and left the stage. Dan just started drowning everything in feedback. The club got so hot they'd opened a door behind the stage, and Willie, who had worked so hard during the show—as the cold air poured in, steam is pouring off his body. He was so pissed off, just venting this incredible rage, staring at Jeremy, the steam exploding off him." Despite the group's stormy ending, the members of Sunny Day Real Estate agreed to finish their self-titled second LP, unofficially known as *The Pink Album* because of the color of the album cover. Issued in 1995 by Sub Pop, the record turned out to be a poorly-produced, miscellaneous collection of B-sides and demos for new songs. Although fans welcomed another release from Sunny Day Real Estate, *The Pink Album* made less of an impact on critics. David Sprague and Ira A. Robbins in the *Trouser Press Guide to '90s Rock* described the record as "vexing for a band this dramatically inclined."

Shortly after Sunny Day Real Estate disbanded, Mendel and Goldsmith joined one of the most successful rock and roll bands of the 1990s, the Foo Fighters, led by former Nirvana drummer David Grohl. However, during the recording of the Foo Fighters' second album, 1997's *The Colour and the Shape,* in 1997. Goldsmith discovered that Grohl had recorded new drum lines without consulting him first. Irritated by the situation, Goldsmith decided to quit drumming for the Foo Fighters. "He [Goldsmith] got all his drum tracks recorded over after he worked his ass off to put them down," Hoerner revealed to Kevin Murphy in the *Arizona Republic.* "He made the choice and walked away from it and I am extremely grateful." Also during the three years Sunny Day Real Estate were apart, Hoerner left the music business all together, fleeing to his farm in eastern Washington state with his wife, while Enigk pursued a solo career. On his own, Enigk recorded one album, the ornate Return of the Frog Queen (issued in 1996 by Sub Pop), a collection of songs he composed which earned critical praise. His songs, according to Stephen Thompson of the *Wisconsin State Journal,* "have a stately, classical quality that somehow complements his passionate, strained-but-gorgeous vocals." And despite his transition into a born-again Christian, Enigk, backed by a 21-piece orchestra, revealed few insights into his personal beliefs with *Return of the Frog Queen.*

Around 1997, Enigk and Hoerner began to mend their friendship and collaborate together. Because of Goldsmith's departure from the Foo Fighters, rumors circulated that the members of Sunny Day Real Estate were contemplating a reunion. At first, the band agreed to come together to record another odds and ends and B-sides album. However, driven by their fans' desire for a complete reunion, Sunny Day Real Estate resolved their differences and announced that they would officially regroup in August of 1997. "When we played, it felt like this weight being lifted off my shoulders," Goldsmith, who retreated back to Washington state and started playing with various friends since leaving Grohl's band, admitted to Daley. "That's when I knew this is where I belong." According to Hoerner, Mendel also wished to play with Sunny Day Real Estate again, but ultimately decided to stay with the Foo Fighters. As Mendel commented to Daley, "That was an extremely difficult choice for me.... I didn't know if the band would last. I really do love playing in the Foo Fighters. I think we're making great music, and I love the people involved."

Enigk, Hoerner, and Goldsmith recruited Jeff Palmer, a former member of San Francisco's Mommyheads, to play bass in Mendel's place. In March of 1998, the new lineup recorded an album entitled How It Feels to Be Something On, released in September of the same year. Daley described the album as "a beautiful, sprawling, life-affirming mess of power and prog rock that should make more than a few top-10 lists this year." Other reviewers commented on the group's evident maturity with tracks like the R.E.M.- influenced "Roses in Water" and the Beatles-inspired "Two Promises."

Because of Sunny Day Real Estate's unstable past, many fans as well as the music press questioned whether or not the reunion would endure. But Sunny Day Real Estate insisted that the collaboration was permanent. "We're totally going for it," Hoerner said to Murphy with enthusiasm. "We just really want to make music. I think we're all looking forward to getting into the studio and making the next record."

Selected discography

Diary, Sub Pop, 1994.

Sunny Day Real Estate, (unofficially known as *The Pink Album*), Sub Pop, 1995.

How It Feels to Be Something On, Sub Pop, 1998.

Sources

Books

Robbins, Ira A., editor, *Trouser Press Guide to '90s Rock,* Fireside/Simon and Schuster, 1997.

Periodicals

Arizona Republic, November 19, 1998, p. 39.
Dallas Morning News, November 13, 1998, p. 67.
Magnet, November/December 1998, pp. 49-91.
Wisconsin State Journal, March 13, 1997, p. 10.

Online

Sunny Day Real Estate Official Website, http://www.sunnydayrealestate.com (December 24, 1999).

—Laura Hightower

Super Furry Animals

Pop band

Corbis. Reproduced by permission.

Throughout the early to mid-1990s, in the wake of the popular success of Oasis, a slew of English bands emerged to revive and/or reinterpret the classic melodies of the Beatles, the Kinks, and other precedent-setting groups from the United Kingdom. Towards the end of the decade, however, one of the most innovative scenes in Great Britain centered around a handful of bands from Wales—including Gorky's Zygotic Mynci, 60 Ft. Dolls, and Catatonia, as well as the Super Furry Animals—dubbed by the rock press as the imminent "Welsh invasion." But while the music press often categorizes bands based on their members' country of origin, the Super Furry Animals, said frontman Gruff Rhys, would rather earn recognition for their music. "Music isn't a sport, you know," Rhys said in a 1999 interview with *Magnet* magazine's Corey Dubrowa. "We don't 'play our country.' The power of music is that it brings people together, whereas sports divide people. Some fans come to our gigs and start waving Welsh flags around, which is ludicrous. When I go to see Neil Young, the last thing that crosses my mind is to break out the Maple Leaf." Focusing on Wales was "obviously media-driven," Rhys continued. "There's always been good bands about and loads of crap bands around too. It's probably just coincidental that a lot of great young Welsh bands were signed at the same time by well-known companies and then exposed to the media ... Even now (in Wales), there's still a really strong underground scene."

And although all of the above-mentioned groups rising from the Welsh club scene received considerable coverage in the United States, most failed to resonate with American audiences with exception of the Super Furry Animals. Apprenticing by playing clubs in the small yet vibrant Welsh club circuit, occasionally gigging in England, appearing in cultural festivals across Celtic Europe, and eventually becoming fixtures on the alternative scene in Germany, the Super Furry Animals, by the time they reached the legal voting age, were regulars on British television, making music videos, and releasing their own records. According to the band's record company website, the Super Furry Animals' appeal is simple: "they cover all the bases from the cathartic three-minute guitar thrash, to the headspinning techno anthem and all points in between. They make you jump about and they make you think." And as Daniel Booth explained in the October 25, 1997, issue of *Melody Maker*, the Super Furry Animals "sculpt the most arresting melodies the same innocuous way we, mere talentless mortals, may comb our hair."

Consisting of vocalist/guitarist Rhys, keyboardist Clan Ciaran, bassist Guto Pryce, guitarist Huw "Bunf" Bunford, and drummer Dafydd "Daf" Ieuan, the Super Furry

For the Record . . .

Members include **Huw "Bunf" Bunford**, guitar; **Clan Ciaran**, keyboards; **Dafydd "Daf" Ieuan**, drums; **Guto Pryce**, bass; **Gruff Rhys**, vocals, guitar.

Formed Super Furry Animals as a techno quartet around 1993; released debut album *Fuzzy Logic*, 1996; moved away from Britpop with *Radiator*, 1997; released gold-selling *Guerrilla*, 1998.

Awards: *NME* Brat Award for best new band, 1997.

Addresses: *Record company*—Creation Records, 109X Regents Park Rd., London, England NW1 8UR, phone: 44-171-722-8866, fax: 44-171-722-3443, website: http://www.creation.co.uk. *Website*—The Official Super Furry Animals website: http://www.superfurry.com.

Animals began as a techno quartet around 1993, and all of the members had already played in proper bands since their teens. Prior to forming the Super Furry Animals, Rhys and Ieuan played with a group called Ffa Coffi, Cian for the band WWZZ, and Pryce and Bunford with the band U Thant. Joining forces, according to the band, was not a hasty decision, as they had considered getting together for nearly two years and had already recorded a few singles together with the band Ankst. Leuan, for one, felt certain that the Super Furry Animals would sign a contract within no time, and his confidence helped fuel the determination of the other members.

Billed as the Super "Fury" Animals for their first show in March of 1994, the band made an instant impression. After only their fourth appearance on stage together, the British weekly *New Musical Express* (*NME*) featured the Super Furry Animals on its cover with an accompanying review, a statement that made the band a hot prospect for record labels. Soon thereafter, an executive from Creation Records, Alan McGee, attended a show at the Camden Monarch club in England. Afterwards, he told the band they could become stars if they would simply include more English language songs in their set, obviously unaware that the Super Furry Animals, unlike most of their usual gigs, had not sung a word of Welsh all night. "Welsh is our first language—what we grew up speaking—and it's what we speak around each other, so it's natural for us to sing in it as well," explained Rhys to Dubrowa.

After sparking Creation's interest, in spite of their heavy accents, the Super Furry Animals showed the label a list of 45 songs they had already written, requested a decent recording studio and their own producer (Gorwel Owen), and asked for a horn and strings section. Creation immediately obliged, and by early-1995, the Super Furry Animals had signed a contract. Their first album, *Fuzzy Logic,* arrived in May of 1996 (distributed by Epic in the United States) and marked the first time that Rhys recorded entirely in English. "It sounds like I'm singing in about 10 different accents," he admitted, as quoted by the band's record label. Nonetheless, the group's debut won rave reviews, with the *Independent* running a front-page story that named *Fuzzy Logic* one of the ten best British albums of all times. Two singles from the album, "Something 4 the Weekend" and "If You Don't Want Me to Destroy You," reached the British top 20.

However, the lumping of the Super Furry Animals in with the Britpop phenomenon by the rock press, to a certain extent, rubbed the group the wrong way. "We've definitely been exposed to [British pop] music, but we don't listen exclusively to it. You can hear a lot of our influences in the records, and we fully acknowledge anyone you might care to name," Rhys said to Dubrowa, responding to comparisons to British acts like XTC, the Jam, and Small Faces, among others. "But we also used to listen to (American bands like) the Butthole Surfers, Dead Kennedys, Beach Boys—these are pretty obvious names, sure, but things like Love ... we're huge Love fans."

Feeling somewhat disillusioned after "speeding on this pop conveyer belt, playing the game without knowing what the rules were," Rhys said, as quoted by Creation Records, the Super Furry Animals retired to North Wales in January of 1997 to record their follow-up to *Fuzzy Logic.* Although Ieuan suffered a broken ankle soon after sessions commenced, the band's spirits were nonetheless elevated after they received an NME Brat Award for best new band.

In August of 1997, the Super Furry Animals released their second full-length record entitled *Radiator,* which hit the American market later in March of 1999 on the Flydaddy label. A more fully-rounded album with greater emotional potency than their debut, *Radiator* stimulated critics and fans with cuts such as the ornate horn piece "Demons," the folk-rock "Down a Different River," and the surreal "Chupacabras." Victoria Segal concluded in the December 20-27, 1997, issue of *Melody Maker* that Radiator "is a thing of great beauty, a shaken-and-stirring cocktail of Stevie Wonder and Pavement, ELO and Supergrass, Aerosmith and Nick Drake, ranging in subject matter from goat-eating bats to Einstein, class war to astroturf." Four singles were released from the album, including "Hermann Loves Pauline," "International Language of Screaming," and "Play It Cool," and "Demons."

After releasing an album of rarities and b-sides entitled *Out Spaced* in November of 1998, the Super Furry Animals continued to determine their own musical direction, releasing their third studio album entitled *Guerrilla* in June of 1998 (issued on Flydaddy in the United States the following year). The highly anticipated release, recorded at Real World Studios, was the group's first self-produced album and contained some of the Super Furry Animals' most sophisticated songs to date. According to Dubrowa, Rhys described *Guerrilla* to his native country's press as "a declaration of war against mainstream music," a statement backed up by songs like the engaging "Something Comes From Nothing," the psychedelic "Night Vision," and the Brian Wilson-inspired "Fire In My Heart." The album went on to reach gold-level sales in the United Kingdom and sold well across Europe and America as well.

Pushing the envelope even further, the band recorded their first entirely Welsh language album, *Mwng,* early in 2000. Set for release in Britain in May 2000 on the Super Furry Animals own Placid Casual label, Rhys called the effort "the simplest record we've made," as quoted for the group's official website. An almost entirely live recording, *Mwng* saw the Super Furry Animals extending their sound to include saxophones and more complex harmonies, with lyrics visiting subjects such as the death of rural communities and friction among people. Most assuredly, the Super Furry Animals were poised once again to mesmerize critics and fans alike through their ever-evolving inventiveness.

Selected discography

Fuzzy Logic, Creation (U.K.), 1996; Epic, 1996.
Radiator, Creation (U.K.), 1997; Flydaddy, 1999.
Out Spaced, Creation (U.K.), 1998.
Guerrilla, Creation (U.K.), 1998; Flydaddy, 1999.
Mwng, Placid Casual (U.K.), 2000.

Sources

Periodicals

Billboard, November 2, 1996.
Magnet, August/September 1999, pp. 41-43.
Melody Maker, October 25, 1997; November 29, 1997; December 20-27, 1997; May 1, 1999; July 3, 1999; October 9, 1999; October 27-November 2, 1999; November 10-16, 1999.
Rolling Stone, October 17, 1996.
Washington Post, March 28, 1999; April 2, 1999.

Online

Creation Records, http://www.creation.co.uk (March 30, 2000).
Flydaddy Records, http://www.flydaddy.com (March 30, 2000).
The Official Super Furry Animals website, http://www.superfurry.com (March 30, 2000).

—Laura Hightower

Teri Thornton

Singer, composer, piano

Photograph by Janet Sommer. Archive Photos. Reproduced by permission.

Hailed by the legendary Cannonball Adderly in the 1960s as "the greatest voice since Ella Fitzgerald," as quoted in *People* magazine, singer and pianist Teri Thornton appeared destined to become a star. Likewise, in the liner notes for her debut album *Devil May Care,* Riverside Records producer Orrin Keepnews wrote, "This girl has got to make it. If she doesn't, something's very wrong. If Teri doesn't quickly soar to the top, it will surely be only because of some external, unlooked-for, and unfair twist of fate." And unfortunately, various external factors—namely alcohol problems, trying to raise a family, marital difficulties, a self-imposed exile to California, and physical illness—did arise and contributed to her disappearance. Thornton soon fell out of popular sight just as her career took off. In the late 1980s, however, Thornton decided to attempt a professional career for a second time, and in 1997 recorded her first album in nearly three decades. After defeating cancer to take first prize at the Thelonius Monk International Jazz Competition in 1998, Thornton signed a contract with Verve Records, which released *I'll Be Easy* in 1999.

Thornton has worked with such jazz luminaries as Clark Terry, Johnny Griffin, Cannonball Adderly, and Duke Ellington. Her singing style bears similarities to legendary jazz singers such as Ella Fitzgerald, Sarah Vaughan, and Carmen McRae, but Thornton herself insisted that the voices of her idols could never be replaced. "You don't fill those places, like you don't fill Babe Ruth's place," she cautioned, as quoted by *Boston Globe* correspondent Bob Blumenthal in February 2000. "Someone else will come along with a new talent—but it will be new. And I'll just keep doing what I do."

Teri Thornton was born and raised in Detroit, Michigan, the same city that produced the late Betty Carter and Aretha Franklin; later on, both singers became huge fans of Thornton. Throughout her childhood, Thornton was surrounded by music, especially gospel, jazz, and the blues. Her grandmother was an evangelist at the local Methodist Episcopal Church, while Thornton's mother served as a choir director, performed with a local opera company, and even hosted her own radio show. "I heard a great deal of music in the house and in church," Thornton said, as quoted by the Jazzchool website. "My mother made sure that I was exposed to music right away, taking me to shows in town. I used to pick out songs on the piano from the time that I was three. I tried to play boogie-woogie even though my hands did not reach very far at the time!"

A mostly self-taught player who loved listening to bebop pianist Barry Harris and Tommy Flanagan (a Detroit native who became famous for accompanying Tony Bennett and Ella Fitzgerald) when they performed near

For the Record . . .

Born c. 1934 in Detroit, MI; daughter of a choir director, opera singer, and radio host; three children.

Started playing piano and singing at age three; won amateur contests in Detroit during teens; moved to New York City, 1960; released debut album *Devil May Care,* 1961; signed with Columbia Records and released *Open Highway,* 1963; released first album in over 30 years, *I'll Be Easy to Find,* 1999.

Awards: Winner of the 12th Annual Thelonius Monk International Jazz Competition, 1998.

Addresses: *Record company*—Verve Records, 825 8th Ave., 26th Fl., New York City, NY 10019, (212) 333-8184.

her home, Thornton always preferred developing her own interpretations of songs rather than playing straight classical music. By the time Thornton reached her teens, she was already gaining attention for her singing and musicianship. "Someone in the neighborhood discovered I could sing and called me up onstage one day. My knees shook but I sang a couple of songs my mother liked. Then it was just going to Monday night jam sessions and entering amateur contests," recalled Thornton to Blumenthal.

Embarked on Professional Career

Soon after she started entertaining live audiences, Thornton "got lucky" and won a couple of amateur shows, prompting her decision to try and sing professionally. In 1956, she landed a job performing at the Ebony Club in Cleveland, Ohio, where she honed her skills, before moving to Chicago, Illinois in the late 1950s. It was in Chicago where jazz saxophone legends Cannonball Adderly and Johnny Griffin heard her singing at a club. Recognizing Thornton's talent, Griffin immediately took Thornton under his wing. "I worked with Johnny a couple of years in Chicago and then he preceded me to New York, paving the way for me," she noted for Jazzchool. "I moved to New York in 1960 because it was the best place for me to get the energy and feedback I needed in order to grow musically. Johnny and Cannonball Adderly were soon responsible for my first record deal with Riverside Records."

Upon Thornton's arrival in New York City, Griffin and Adderly convinced Orrin Keepnews of the now-hallowed Riverside recording label to sign the promising new singer for her first album, 1961's *Devil May Care.* Earning considerable praise and seemingly destined to become a star, Thornton returned in 1962 with her second album entitled *Somewhere in the Night* for the now-defunct Dauntless label. An instant success, the album included Thornton's first number one hit, the title track "Somewhere in the Night," the theme song for the television show *Naked City* that later became a jazz standard. She also reprised the song for her 1998 return release *I'll Be Easy to Find.*

During this time, Thornton's career skyrocketed. She headlined at the top venues of the era, including the Birdland, the Apollo, and the Basin Street East in New York, as well as the Flamingo in Las Vegas, Nevada. She also toured Australia, Europe, and Japan, and appeared on several television variety shows, including *The Tonight Show.* A dynamic entertainer with a clear, interpretive strength, Thornton captivated audiences wherever she performed. "Yet I suffered from stage fright for many years," she confessed to Blumenthal. "I think it was genetic, just like my singing ability, because my mother who was a singer on the radio and in opera productions, needed smelling salts before she would go on. But you can develop confidence from sheer desire, and from wanting to be different."

With her rising notoriety, Thornton signed with the larger label Columbia Records and recorded and released her third album, *Open Highway,* in 1963. The title cut became the theme song for *Route 66,* and singer Tony Bennett wrote rave liner notes, but because Columbia marketed Thornton as a pop singer, as opposed to a performer open to the influences of jazz, rhythm and blues, and even rock and roll, *Open Highway* failed to sell as well as anticipated. Following another recording for Riverside in 1964 that went unnoticed, in part because a new generation of record buyers began to favor rock and soul over jazz, Thornton disappeared from the mainstream music business, retiring and settling in Los Angeles, California, to raise her family. She had three children, the last of which was born in 1968.

Left the Music Industry

"It basically involved my domestic scene, and a custody battle with my husband over my third child," she told Blumenthal. (According to other sources, Thornton was also battling alcohol problems.) "Not to mention that I was living in California by then, and there was not much jazz going on out there. I gigged where I could, and the fact that I knew standards kept me working far more than would have been the case if I had been doing jazz tunes exclusively. Composing became my primary outlet when I couldn't find places to sing, trying to come up with a tune that might sneak into the Top 10."

In 1987, with her children grown, Thornton returned to New York, hoping to renew her recording career. Although she performed on a regular basis, major label interest continued to elude the once-promising star. In the 1990s, however, Thornton finally started generating attention again. In November of 1995, after Thornton had returned from a concert in Berlin, Germany, sponsored by the Jazz Foundation of America, she was approached by manager/producer Suzi Reynolds, a longtime fan of the singer, after a performance at the Blue Note Jazz Club in New York. Reynolds offered to help and hooked Thornton up with jazz giants such as flutist/saxophonist Jerome Richardson and cornetist/tuba player/clarinetist/saxophonist Howard Johnson, who both played on Thornton's earlier albums. Along with Richardson, Johnson, and notable others, Thornton independently recorded her comeback effort entitled *I'll Be Easy to Find* in June of 1997 .

However, circumstances intervened in Thornton's career again in October of 1997 when doctors diagnosed the singer with bladder cancer. Thus, with her health in decline, her first studio album in over 30 years was put on hold for release, and Thornton underwent cancer surgery at the Englewood Hospital in New Jersey. "I remember walking into her hospital room and seeing Teri with tubes down her throat, having lost 50 pounds," Reynolds informed Jason Koransky of *Down Beat.* "I had to give her something to get better for, so I entered her in the competition." That event was the 12th Annual Thelonius Monk International Jazz Competition, dedicated to vocals, that was held in December of 1998 at the Smithsonian Institution's Baird Auditorium in Washington, D.C. Driven by her manager's proposal, Thornton felt well enough by April of 1998 to travel to Switzerland to sing with the all-female big band, Diva, at the Bern Jazz Festival. Although she returned to the hospital after the trip because of exhaustion, Thornton was free of cancer by June of 1998.

In past years, Thornton would not have been eligible to participate at the Monk International Jazz Competition, which formerly limited the age of singer to 33. "Vocalists often develop their voices later in their careers, so we felt we had to drop the age limit," Shelby Fischer, the executive producer of the Monk Institute, informed Koransky. Viewing the event as a chance to put on a show for the crowd as well as to impress a distinguished panel of judges, comprised of Joe Williams, Dianne Reeves, Nnenna Freelon, Dee Dee Bridgewater, and Diana Krall, Thornton "turned the three songs she performed into a theatrical vignette tracing the course of a love affair, from first blush to final longing, displaying an alternately warm, lively and sassy voice," wrote Mike Joyce for the *Washington Post.* Utilizing her skills as a pianist to complement her vocal talent, Thornton won the first-prize scholarship of $20,000. "I knew she was real," said host Thelonius Monk, Jr., after her performance, as quoted by Joyce. "And tonight she came out and proved it."

Returned to the Spotlight

In October of 1999, Thornton's 1997 recording was released on Verve Records. *I'll Be Easy to Find* featured 12 songs, including swing numbers, rarely chosen ballads, and seven blues-inspired originals, and won considerable praise. Bob McCullough of the *Boston Globe*, in February of 2000, called Thornton "an old-fashioned jazz diva in the best sense of the word, using her husky, sultry contralto to grab a tune by the throat and make it her own, and the arrangements are first-class from start to finish."

Tours across the country, including a performance in Brooklyn, New York, in front of a 70-piece orchestra led by Skitch Henderson, followed Thornton's studio comeback, and she looked toward more successes in the future and making up for lost time. "There are many people who I would love to record with," she told Jazzchool, "particularly having Herbie Hancock play behind me and recording a few songs with the Basie band.... I'd like to work on jingles, compose some movie themes and sing on some movie soundtracks. I also look forward to recording more in the future. Through public performances and recordings I want to be in contact with as many people as I can. My main goal is that they leave happier after hearing me than when they came in."

Selected discography

Devil May Care, Riverside, 1961; reissued, Fantasy/Original Jazz Classics, 1999.
Somewhere in the Night, Dauntless, 1962.
Open Highway, Columbia, 1963.
I'll Be Easy to Find, Uni/Verve, 1999.

Sources

Periodicals

Billboard, September 25, 1999.
Boston Globe, February 17, 2000; February 18, 2000.

Down Beat, December 1998, pp. 18-19; March 1999; December 1999, p. 65.
New York Times, October 6, 1998; January 20, 2000.
People, December 20, 1999, p. 43.
Washington Post, September 28, 1998.

Online

Amazon.com, http://www.amazon.com (March 15, 2000).
Jazzchool Artists, http://www.jazzchool.com/newartist/left.cfm?contact_num=1040&session_num=48 (March 15, 2000).
Verve Music Group, http://www.verveinteractive.com (March 15, 2000).

—Laura Hightower

Trick Daddy

Rap artist

Although a style of hip-hop known as Southern rap or "booty music"—a combination of high-energy dance with often explicit rap vocals—crossed over with 95 South's 1993 hit "Whoot, There It Is," it appeared unlikely that songs by other Southern rappers, most hailing from Georgia, Florida, and Louisiana (dubbed "The Dirty South"), would follow suit. But after the new form of hip-hop started receiving airplay, Southern rap became a national craze. In Miami, Florida, rap artist Trick Daddy helped revitalize his hometown's rap recording industry. A former convict who later focused his energies penning rhymes that told the stories about his life as a "thug" and the experiences of growing up in the projects, Trick refused to categorize himself with rappers who invent tales of street life in order to sell records. "When Trick raps about bustin' rounds and gun play, sexual escapades, serving time, welfare, auto theft, jugglin' weight, living in the projects, food stamps, street killings, baby-momma-drama, kickin' with the homies, contract hits, smokin' out, flossin', trafficking dope, probation etc., he's lived it!" as quoted by Trick's website.

In order to understand Trick Daddy's music and the subject matter of his rhymes, one should first examine and consider his background. One of 20 children (many were half brothers and sisters, and his mother had 12 children by different fathers), Trick was born Maurice Young around 1976 in Miami, Florida, and raised in the city's Liberty Square Housing Development—known as the "Pork 'N' Beans Projects" to locals. "Growing up, that shit was never nothing nice," he recalled later from his Miami Lakes condominium, as quoted by Charisse Nikole in a 1999 interview with *Blaze* magazine. "You watch mamas and step-daddies and half-brothers getting in fights and see how you come out. We see people getting shot and killed every day." As a young adult, Trick readily admitted that many of his problems stemmed from childhood issues, which he continued to deal with.

Because he came from such a large family and lived in a dangerous environment, Trick learned early on to push and fight his way to the front of the line, behaviors which often got him into trouble. His first outburst occurred when he was just eleven year old; angered after a teacher embarrassed him in front of his grade school class, according to Trick, he retaliated by hitting her in the head with a lead pipe. For this act of violence, he found himself at one of the Miami/Dade County schools for problem children. Apparently, the school did little to help rehabilitate the youngster, as just a few years later, in May of 1991, Trick was sentenced to a four-year prison term at the Apalachee Correctional Institution for armed trafficking with the intent to distribute cocaine. Although released on probation after serving a year of the sentence, Trick was locked up again for violating the terms of his release, as well as attempted murder, and subsequently spent two more years behind bars. Meanwhile, during Trick's incarceration, five of his close friends and his brother, nicknamed Hollywood, had all been killed by firearms.

Determined to start anew, and as a way to cope with the death of his brother, Trick left jail and started writing candid rap songs that documented the life he had led up to that point. His first break into the music business came when a Miami rap artist named Luke saw Trick performingat a local club and approached him. Later, Luke invited him to join as one of the lead rappers for the song "Scarred." The hip-hop dance track, which introduced Trick's unique flow and booming voice, appeared on Luke's 1996 album *Uncle Luke.* The song became a hit and immediately caught the attention of fans and record producers alike. Later, Trick credited Luke as the person who helped make his recording career possible.

Upon the success of "Scarred," former concert promoter Ted Lucas signed Trick to his newly-formed Slip-N-Slide Records under the alias Trick Daddy Dollars. (Trick has since dropped "Dollars" from his name.) "Trick is remarkably talented, confident and eager to work," Lucas said of the rising rap star, as quoted by the iMusic Urban Showcase website. "All of his boasting is backed up by what he lays down in the studio."

For the Record . . .

Born Maurice Young c.1976 in Miami, FL.

Started writing raps and performing in local clubs after serving jail time; appeared on Luke's 1996 album *Uncle Luke* for the hit song "Scarred;" debuted as a solo artist with *Based on a True Story*, 1997; single from 1998's *www.thug.com* entitled "Nann" became a national hit, 1999.

Addresses: *Record company*—Atlantic Records, 1290 Avenue of the Americas, New York, NY 10104, (212) 707-2144. *Website*—Trick Daddy, http://www.thug.com.

Trick, who had already been developing songs for some time, released his solo debut, *Based on a True Story*, in October of 1997 (before Los Angeles rapper Mack 10 released an album of the same title). Many of the 17 songs on Trick's first record, dedicated to the memory of Hollywood, contained dark, volatile, and introspective lyrics, illustrating the rapper's own predicament: coping with life and loss. "For everything I do positive, it counteracts with something I've suffered for," he explained to Nikole, referring to his transformation from an ex-convict into an established rap artist. Selling moderately and surpassing 200,000 copies, *Based on a True Story* contained club favorites such as "They Don't Live Long," "Bout a Lotta Thangs," performed with fellow Slip-N-Slide rapper Buddy Roe, and "Gone with Your Bad Self," with the quick-verse rap artist Verb, who also shared rhyming duties with Trick for "Scarred."

In 1998, Trick returned with his sophomore effort, *www.thug.com*, another street-credible album that picked up on his life's story where *Based on a True Story* left off. According to Trick's website, "Fans and 'thugs' alike can feel his pain, understand his philosophies, comprehend his actions, and relate to his turbulent experiences...." The second single from the album, "Nann," a Southern term meaning "no one else," became a popular success, although the song took some time to catch on. Initially released in December of 1998 by Slip-N-Slide, "Nann" (an edited version of the explicit original album cut "Nann Nigga" that became a street hit) finally gained national attention the following year when radio stations started playing it. Although he had to wait awhile, Trick assured Launch.com writer Billy Johnson, Jr., that he remained hopeful that the song would earn recognition. "Sooner or later you got to come on in," he said. "I felt really confident about it." The confrontational "Nann" paired Trick with Miami's Trina, with whom he exchanged sexually charged lyrics. "The song is one where men and women connect because it gives both sides something they can relate to," Trina, whose own career was sparked by the single's popularity, told Nikole.

After "Nann" received airplay outside of Miami, *www.thug.com* was picked up for major distribution by Atlantic Records. Extensive video play of "Nann" followed on MTV (Music Television), the Box, and BET (Black Entertainment Television), and Trick's second album went on to earn gold sales status, approaching platinum sales. With the success of *www.thug.com*, Trick became the first rap artist from Miami since Luke Campbell and 2 Live Crew entered the scene in the mid-1980s to generate national attention. He was featured in such publications as *Murder Dog*, *XXL*, the *Source*, and *Rap Pages* magazine, while several well-known rap/hip-hop artists like Cappadonna of the Wu-Tang Clan, Mase, and C-Low expressed interest in working with the newcomer.

In February of 2000, Trick furthered the cause of Miami hip-hop with the release of *Book of Thugs: Chapter AK, Verse 47*, which debuted on the *Billboard* charts at number 26 and featured guest rappers such as Mystikal, Twista, and Trina. Although the album included notable songs such as the brassy "Shut Up," the jamming "SNS (Get on Up)," and the thoughtful "Amerika," where Trick details the struggles of blacks from all backgrounds, *Book of Thugs: Chapter AK, Verse 47* overall earned mediocre reviews for its lower production quality. Nevertheless, Trick continued to draw in fans nationwide with his stories about running the streets. "To me it's personal; I got to know that you feeling me some type-of-way," Trick stated on his website. "When you have people to question you [about a particular song] and ask you, 'did that really happen to you'?, then you know they really got deep into that song."

Selected discography

Based on a True Story, Slip-N-Slide, 1997.
www.thug.com, Slip-N-Slide/Warlock, 1998.
(With various artists) *South Park: Bigger, Longer & Uncut—Music From and Inspired by the Motion Picture*, Atlantic, 1999.
Book of Thugs, Atlantic, 2000.

Sources

Periodicals

Billboard, June 19, 1999; August 14, 1999; September 11, 1999; October 16, 1999; January 29, 2000.

Blaze, August 1999, pp. 64-66.
Jet, February 21, 2000.
Los Angeles Times, February 12, 2000; February 24, 2000.
Rolling Stone, June 10, 1999; December 16-23, 1999
USA Today, February 29, 2000.
Village Voice, February 8, 2000.
Washington Post, August 1, 1999.

Online

Launch: Discover New Music, http://www.launch.com (March 14, 2000).
MTV News Gallery, http://www.mtv.com/news/gallery/t/trickdaddy000217.html (March 14, 2000).
Trick Daddy, http://www.thug.com (March 14, 2000).
"Trick Daddy," *iMusic Urban Showcase,*http://www.imusic.com/showcase/urban/trickdaddy.html (March 14, 2000).
"Trick Daddy," *ThrottleBox Arena,* http://www.throttlebox.com/Content/signed/788.html (March 14, 2000).

—Laura Hightower

Ken Vandermark

Multi-reedman

Photograph by Todd Ambrosini. Reproduced by permission.

Ken Vandermark is one of the brightest lights on the contemporary music scene. By the time he reached the age of 35, he had played tenor, clarinet and bass clarinet on a prodigious number of recordings, 60 or more, including collaborations and guest appearances. He's been part of more than 18 different ongoing performing groups. Not only is he extremely active, he is a musical democrat, playing in musical styles ranging from free jazz, to soul, to funk, to avant-punk. He has performed with the elder statesmen of new jazz such as Joe McPhee, Fred Anderson, Sun Ra, drummer Robert Barry, and Peter Brötzmann. "Ken is constantly looking to find new sides of his talent," saxophonist Mars Williams told Lloyd Sachs of the *Chicago Sun-Times*, "There is no on who is more open-minded to different styles of music." All these attributes have made him one of the key forces energizing the Chicago music scene and turning it into one of the most vibrant and successful in the country.

Ken Vandermark was born in 1964 in Warwick, Rhode Island, and raised in the Boston area. He started playing tenor sax in high school, switching from trumpet which he'd been studying since elementary scool. Growing up, Ken heard a steady stream of music on the family stereo. "I grew up in a family where my parents, particularly my father, were listening to jazz all the time," Vandermark told *Downbeat*'s John Corbett. "My father never categorized things at all. We'd listen to Stravinsky, then Duke Ellington, then Monk, then Sly and the Family Stone. It was all music, just music in the house. That made me hear Ellington and Stravinsky on the same level, not to listen to Ellington as a 'jazz' musician and somehow, subconsciously, look down on him."

That may explain why Vandermark's music frequently blurs the lines that divide musical genres and makes him slippery when it come to categorizing what he does. For example, he calls himself a jazz musician but acknowledges that a lot of jazz purists—for whom history ended in the early sixties—hate his music. Young rock fans often make up the lion's share of the crowds at his live shows. The bands he's played with have been just as unclassifiable: He described the Waste Kings, one of his early Chicago groups, to Chum's Dan Kelly as "a garage rock band" that transmogrified itself into "a soul/R&B instrumental group." Carbon 14 noted "an almost metal/hardcore level of intensity" in Utility Hitter, by Vandermark's Barrage Double Trio. And more than one critic has noted how the Vandermark 5 seamlessly integrate rock vocabulary into the language of jazz.

All Vandermark's musical activity has one thing in common though: he's blowing free, improvising. His personal involvement in free music dates back to when

For the Record . . .

Born on September 22, 1964, in Warwick, R.I. *Education:* attended McGill University, Montreal, Quebec, Canada; studied saxophone with George Garzone, Boston, MA.

Led group Fourth Stream, Montreal, Canada, 1983-1986; led group Lombard Street in Boston MA, began studying bass clarinet, 1986-89; moved to Chicago, fall 1989; formed Ken Vandermark Quarter, added Bb clarinet to instrumental arsenal, 1992; performed with Caffeine, Steelwool Trio, Waste Kings, Flying Luttenbachers, 1992-1994; forms DKV Trio, 1994; forms Vandermark 5, 1996; Empty Bottle performance series, co-organized by Vandermark and John Corbett began, 1996; performed with Joe McPhee, 1996; formed Steam, 1997; the Vandermark 5 selected for inclusion in the sound aspect of exhibition *Art In Chicago: 1945-1995*, the Museum of Contemporary Art, Chicago, IL, Nov. 16, 1996 - Mar. 23, 1997; first recorded with Fred Anderson, 1997; receiveed MacArthur Grant, 1999.

Awards: Named one of "Chicagoans of the Year in the Arts: 1994" by the Chicago Tribune, January 1995; Vandermark and John Corbet named Best Underground Music Promoters by New City, Chicago, IL September 1997. Named one of "25 For The Future", Downbeat, 1998. MacArthur Grant, 1999.

Addresses: *Home*—Chicago, Illinois, phone & fax: (773)549-8132; *e-mail*—ambu@flash.net; *U.S. Booking*—Billions Corporation, phone (312)997-9999, fax (312)997-2287, boche@billions.com; *European booking*—khessling1@aol.com; *Record company*—Atavistic Worldwide, P.O. Box 578266 Chicago, IL 60657.

he was a teenager. One day his father put an album on, saying "You gotta hear this." It was Joe McPhee's Tenor, an album's worth of free improv on the tenor sax. His ears were opened to free playing for the first time. "I'd heard some free stuff and it sounded to me like people just squonking around," he told Option's John Corbett. "Here's McPhee, making just as much noise, but all the concept of melody and structure was totally there. It was like: 'That's it! That's what I want to do!' It totally floored me." McPhee's musical example continues to guide Vandermark approach to music-making. In 1993 he met McPhee for the first time and in 1997 the two cut a CD together, Meeting in Chicago.

Vandermark went off to McGill University in Montreal to study film, but eventually changed his mind. "By the time I graduated I'd decided that I wanted to devote myself to music," he told Brian Marley of Avant. "In the United States the options are to have a day job and play at night, or try to become a professional musician, which means you do weddings and things like that which really didn't interest me at all. So I worked at a convenience store and a hardware store in Boston." Back home he played for a while in the Lombard Street Trio, but frustrated with the limited opportunities Boston offered jazz musicians, he pulled up stakes and headed for Chicago in 1989.

The first couple years in the Windy City were difficult. Despite its history as a center for musical innovation—think only of the Art Ensemble of Chicago, Anthony Braxton and Sun Ra—he connected with few musicians in the city's cliquish scene. By 1992 he was ready to pack it in. "It's hard to essentially—for two years—sit in a room and practice and compose and have that be the gist of everything that you're doing," he told Chum's Dan Kelly. "I'm not really a solo artist. If you don't have people to play with, you just hear stuff in your head, and that's it. That was incredibly frustrating."

Drummer Michael Zerang persuaded Vandermark to stick it out for another year. He did, and almost immediately things started happening. Without his knowing it things had already started turning around for him. He had started his own band, the Ken Vandermark Quartet, with Zerang on percussion, Kent Kessler on bass, and Todd Colburn on guitar. The following year the Quartet released a critically well-received CD, Big Head Eddie, a record described by Downbeat's Aaron Cohen as a "seamless blend of exploratory jazz tones, driving rock beats, and high-octane funk." Soon he was performing regularly in a plethora of bands around town, including Caffeine, a trio with keyboardist Jim Baker and drummer Steve Hunt; the Flying Luttenbachers, a "punk-jazz trio" with saxist Chad Organ and pecussionist Weasel Walter; the Waste Kings; and, the NRG Ensemble, a free-improv group led by local jazz doyen, Hal Russell.

Vandermark was sometimes criticized for his involvement in so many musical groups and styles during much of the 1990s. His musical interests were broad though—and anyway who could blame him for diving in head-first after a two year performance drought? "I happen to play with a lot of people," he admitted to Dan Kelly, "But I see all these different groups as representing different sides of myself, and different sides of my music that are really interesting; I want to participate in that. I want to be involved in that. Not to control it and decide what happens to it, but to participate in this really interesting stuff that's happening, and interact with it. It's hard for me to understand approaching it any other way."

As the 1990s rolled on however the pace got to be a little stressful even for Vandermark, whom Kelly tagged "The Hardest Working Man in Chicago." Not surprisingly either. Besides playing in all his various bands, the business side of things usually landed on Vandermark's shoulders as well—organizing rehearsals, finding gigs, and the like. In the latter half of the 1990s, he cut back and eventually concentrated on two new groups, the DVK Trio with Vandermark stalwart Kent Kessler on bass and percussionist/drummer Hamid Drake, and the Vandermark 5, originally comprised of Vandermark on reeds, Kessler, Mars Williams on sax, Jeb Bishop on trombone and guitar, and Tim Mulvenna on drums.

Both groups are well-represented on CD. The DKV Trio released *Baraka* in 1997 and *Live in Wels & Chicago, 1998* in 1999 both on Okkadisk. The first Vandermark 5 line-up released two CDs on Atavistic, *Single Piece Flow*, in 1997 and *Target or Flag* in 1998. Mars Williams left the group after the second CD was recorded, and was replaced by alto player Dave Rempis. The new group's Atavistic release, Simpatico, was one of the most acclaimed jazz releases of 1999. The quintet is a perfect setting for Vandermark, both as a performer and as a composer. "Ideally the Vandermark 5 is the closest I've come to having a group that can do all the kinds of things I like to do—at least musically," he told Wire's Jon Morgan. "Some bands are better at doing certain kinds of things, and so if you want to do a wide variety of music it's hard to come up with a band that can do them all."

By 1999 he had added important priorities to his musical life. "I am putting greater emphasis on playing with older musicians," he told Bob Blumenthal of the Boston Globe. "You learn so much from people like Fred Anderson and [ex-Sun Ra drummer] Robert Barry, guys who were the experimenters in Chicago 40 years ago. Guys like that, who have been committed to the music for decades show me how it's possible to find new things to do every day." For one thing, playing with older musicians puts Vandermark in touch with jazz traditions that differ from the ones he is used to. "Fred has a much more methodical sense of exposition. In most of the groups I play with there's a lot of radical shifting and changing. Almost on a constant basis. We're like really wired, coffee-drinking musicians," Vandermark told Lazaro Vega of Blue Lake Public Radio. "Fred Anderson's playing really comes out of Sonny Rollins and John Coltrane. When I'm playing with Fred, he takes, say, a 12 minute solo on one of his tunes. That's longer than some of the songs I play in their entirety.... If he plays a great solo that lasts for 12 minutes and he plays all the tenor saxophone that you can on a tune, I follow that and it makes me radically rethink how I'm going to approach this." The DKV Trio and Anderson made a record together on Okkadisk. Vandermark has also been performing regularly with Robert Barry, who played drums in Sun Ra's Arkestra, and his old hero, Joe McPhee.

Like many other American jazz musicians, money has been a frustrating issue for Vandermark. And like others he sometimes looked with longing across the Atlantic at Europe where musicians have it better. "The money has been so pitifully bad," he told *Carbon 14*. "That's the biggest problem in the US; people want you to play, but they want you to play for next to free. In Europe there's a lot more, mostly government, support, so a lot of clubs can bring people in." That changed in a big way in summer 1999. The MacArthur Foundation selected Vandermark for one of their multi-year "genius award" grants, an award worth $265,000. He was the youngest musician ever selected for the grant, which the MacArthur Foundation gave with an unusually enlightened view that he was going to do even greater work in the future. "I hope to invest half the grant in ongoing projects," he told Bob Blumenthal, "and use the other half for things that would otherwise be impossible. For example, I'm a member of Peter Brötzmann's Tentet, which is playing the Vancouver Jazz Festival next June [2000], and the MacArthur funds might make it possible to tour elsewhere in North America.... I'd also like to get musicians like Paul Lovens over to the US and pay them better, give them a motel room to sleep in rather than just the floor of my apartment."

Receiving a "genius grant" is the kind of thing sure to go straight to some musicians' heads. But Vandermark was strikingly modest about it. "I try not to think about the MacArthur in terms of who else has won," he told Blumenthal. "I can't seriously say that it puts me on the same level as Cecil Taylor or Steve Lacy or George Russell. I can say that it will assist me in my efforts to reach that level." But it's hard to imagine a musician who deserves such an award any more than Ken Vandermark. He persevered through the tough early days in Chicago, and his dedication to music helped build the Chicago music scene and to build bridges between the different musicians there. But through the time of the day job to support there was never any question of altering his music to make it more commercially viable. He always worked at attracting an audience on his own terms. "That's the process that I have to figure out," he explained to Dan Kelly. "How do you get them into the room? That's business that has nothing to do with art. The 'art' is when you get 'em in the room, then you do you do. You should never compromise that."

What's also unusual for some jazz musicians, Vandermark has nearly complete confidence his audience; he trusts them to get what he's doing. And he's gratified that so many who attend his shows are open-minded music lovers who let themselves feel his music, let it move them. He reciprocates by giving his all every time he performs. "One of the best things I heard is what drummer Han Bennink said in an Eric Dolphy documentary," Vandermark told John Corbett. "They asked him what it was like to play, and he said, 'Every time I play I feel like I got my back against the wall, 'cause I don't know if it's gonna be the last time.' That's the whole thing! When you step onstage to play in front of people, why be there if you're not going to play your ass off?"

Selected discography

(With Vandermark Quartet) *Big Head Eddie*, Platypus, 1993.
(With NRG Ensemble) *Calling All Mothers*, Quinnah, 1994.
Caffeine, Okkadisk, 1994.
(With Steelwool Trio) *International Front*, Okkadisk, 1995.
(With Barrage Double Trio) *Utility Hitter*, Quinnah, 1996.
(With NRG Ensemble) *This Is My House*, Delmark, 1996.
(With Vandermark 5) *Single Piece Flow*, Atavistic, 1997.
Fred Anderson/DKV Trio, Okkadisk, 1997.
DKV Trio: Baraka, Okkadisk, 1997.
Steam, Real Time, Eighth Day, 1997.
Joe McPhee/Ken Vandermark, A Meeting in Chicago, Eighth Day, 1997; reissued on Okkadisk, 1998.
(With Vandermark 5) *Target or Flag*, Atavistic, 1998.
(With NRG Ensemble) *Bejazzo Gets a Facelift*, Atavistic, 1998.
AALY Trio + Ken Vandermark, Hidden in the Stomach, Silkheart, 1998.
Peter Brötzmann, The Chicago Octet/Tentet, Okkadisk, 1998.
DKV Trio: Live in Wels & Chicago, 1998, Okkadisk, 1999.
(With Vandermark 5) *Simpatico, Atavistic*, 1999.
The Joe Harriott Project, Atavistic, 1999.

Sources

Periodicals

Avant #8, Summer 1998.
Boston Globe, August 6, 1999.
Carbon 14, #11.
Chicago Sun-Times, May 11, 1997.
Chum #2, 1995.
Downbeat, April 1994; January 1999.
Option, September/October 1993.
Wire, July 1998.

Online

"Ken Vandermark: Interview," *OkkaDisk*, http://www.okkadisk.com, (January 19, 2000).

—Gerald E. Brennan

Caetano Veloso

Singer, songwriter

Since the 1960s, Caetano Veloso has been a dominant force in contemporary Brazilian music, helping to shape his nation's popular music. A pop musician whose stature is on par with or has exceeded that of Bob Dylan, Bob Marley, John Lennon, and Paul McCartney, Veloso matured during the 1980s and 1990s into a Brazilian renaissance man: a poet, writer, and painter as well as a revered musician.

"One might theorize that Caetano is the great pop singer America never had," explained Ben Ratliff in *Spin* magazine in June of 1999. "Who in our country combines actual poetry, rigorous with wordplay and fantastic imagery, with a responsible accounting of natural history? (Not Bruce Springsteen.) Who puts sensual pleasure within an intellectual framework? (Not Madonna.) Who maintains a public complexity on issues of race and sexuality but remains engaged with the press and his fans? (Not the Artist Formerly Known as Prince.) Who's a middle-age pop musician routinely interviewed on highbrow television programs, quoted by his country's current president during his nomination-acceptance

Photograph by David Atlas. Reproduced by permission. ©

For the Record . . .

Born in 1942 in Santo Amaro da Purificação in Brazil's Bahia region; married and divorced first wife Dede, with whom he had son Moreno, born in November, 1972; married second wife and manager Paula Lavigne, with whom he had son Zeca, born c. 1992. *Education*: Studied philosophy at the Federal University of Bahia.

Founded the Tropicalismo movement with Gilberto Gil and others, 1967; exiled to London, England, 1969; returned to Brazil, 1972; continued to record throughout the 1970s, 1980s, and 1990s with Gil and other musicians and as a solo artist; published memoir entitled *Verdade Tropical,* 1999.

Addresses: *Record company*—Nonesuch Records, c/o Debbie Ferraro, 75 Rockefeller Plz., New York, NY 10019, phone: (212) 275-4917, fax: (212) 315-1124, e-mail: Debbie.Ferraro@warnermusic.com.

speech, and studied by academics? (Not Garth Brooks.) Who's an avant-gardist, a political maverick, a sex symbol, a singer fully convincing with a full band or just alone with a guitar? (Not Bob Dylan, Paul Simon, or Puffy.) Who's a national hero—not just for specific racial, generational, and economic subsets, but for *everyone*? In our nation, sadly, Caetano has no equal."

Born in 1942 in Santo Amaro da Purificação in Brazil's Bahia region, Veloso absorbed a rich Bahian musical heritage that was influenced by Caribbean, African, and North American pop music. Nevertheless, it was the cool, seductive bossa nova sound of Joao Gilberto, a Brazilian superstar in the 1950s, that would later serve as the foundation for Veloso's own intense, eclectic pop. In 1960, he moved from his hometown to Salvador in order to attend high school, and in 1963, Veloso entered the Federal University of Bahia as a philosophy student. During this time, Brazil experienced a cultural explosion in art, political thought, and music. Bossa nova, a revolutionary new musical style that combined thoughtful lyricism with subtle rhythm, became an important aspect of Brazilian modernism.

Inspired like many young Brazilians by the movement, Veloso started writing criticism for the local newspaper, acting in avant-garde theater, and singing bossa nova in bars. Following his sister Maria Bethânia—a very successful singer in her own right—to Rio de Janeiro so she could act in a stage play in the mid-1960s, the 23-year-old Veloso initiated his own career by winning a lyric writing contest with his song "Um Dia" and was quickly signed to the Phillips label. His music career began in earnest in 1965 when he started recording in Rio, and by 1966, he was competing in televised music festivals with great success.

Soon, Veloso, along with other Brazilian stars such as Gal Costa and Gilberto Gil (a longtime friend and artistic collaborator whom Veloso had met in Salvador in 1963) represented the new wave of Música Popular Brasileira (or MPB), the all-purpose term used by Brazilians to describe their pop music. Intelligent, ambitious, creative, and given to an unapologetic leftist politicaloutlook, Veloso would soon become a controversial figure in Brazilian pop. By 1967, he had aligned himself with Brazil's burgeoning hippie movement, and, along with Gil, created a new form of pop music dubbed by artist Helio Oiticica as Tropicalismo. That same year, Veloso released his first album, *Domingo,* recorded with Costa in 1966. Arty and eclectic, Tropicalismo retained a bossa nova influence, but added elements of folk-rock and art-rock to a mixture of loud electric guitars, poetic spoken-word sections, and jazz-like dissonance.

Although not well-received at first by traditional pop-loving Brazilians—both Veloso and Gil faced the wrath of former fans—Tropicalismo was nonetheless a breathtaking stylistic synthesis that signaled a new generation of daring, provocative, and politically outspoken musicians who would remake the face of MPB. "We were fascinated by advances in technology," Veloso declared, as quoted by Ratliff, "and we were also interested in the death of sexual hypocrisy, not a usual aim of leftist movements. We put new rock'n'roll together with tango from Argentina, music from the brothels in Brazil, and very raw music from the Northeast, the backlands. We could be ambiguous sexually. Communists never liked gays much. But we did."

However, such a cultural shift also entailed considerable dangers. Since 1964, Brazil had been ruled by a military dictatorship, a government that would continue to hold power for 20 years, that did not look kindly upon such radical music made by such radical musicians. Almost immediately, those in power initiated government-sanctioned attempts to circumscribe the recordings and live performances of many Tropicalistas. Censorship of song lyrics, not to mention radio and television play lists (Veloso had become a television performer on Brazilian variety shows) occurred on a regular basis. Moreover, officials set out to persecute performers who criticized the government, and Veloso and Gil topped the dictatorship's hit list. Both men spent two months in prison for "anti-government activity" and another four months under house arrest. After a defiant 1968 performance together, Veloso and Gil were forced into exile in London in 1969. "Although it did not feel good to leave Brazil, London was a very interesting place to be in 1969," he recalled to Don Heckman of *Rhythm* in 1999. Veloso continued to record abroad and write songs for other Tropicalismo stars, but he would not receive permission to return to Brazil permanently until 1972.

Although his commitment to politicized art never wavered, Veloso, over the next 20 years, transformed from being a very popular Brazilian singer/songwriter to standing at the center of Brazilian pop. He maintained a grueling pace of recording, producing, and performing. In the mid-1970s, Veloso added writing to his resume, publishing a book of articles, poems and song lyrics covering a period from 1965 to 1976 entitled *Algeria, Algeria*—also the title of his first noted hit song. In the 1980s, Veloso's popularity began to spread beyond the borders of Brazil. He toured in Africa, Paris, and Israel; interviewed the Rolling Stones' Mick Jagger for Brazilian television; and in 1983, playing in the United States for the first time at the age of 41, sold out three nights at the Public Theater in New York City, performances that earned stellar reviews from *New York Times* pop critic Robert Palmer. This steady increase in popularity occurred despite the fact that Veloso's records were extremely hard to find in American record stores.

However, Veloso never seemed bothered by his low profile outside of Brazil. His work over the years, even after he became a more well-known international pop figure, remained challengingand intriguing, and Veloso refused to modify his style to suit other cultural (including American) tastes—he sang in English (most of his recorded work was performed in the Portuguese language) only when he felt like it, not because he wanted sell more records to American listeners. And while Veloso gained recognition in the years following his exile throughout the world, he nevertheless opted to focus on his own country. "I've always thought that what I do could only interest Brazilians," he humbly explained to Ratliff. "For two reasons: because of the words, and because of the knowledge of our history and our problems. Outside of that, I couldn't see any appeal in my work." Likewise, Veloso developed relationships with several trend-setting New York musicians, such as Brazilian native Arto Lindsay and David Byrne, but he never made a big deal about it. Rather, Veloso stood as one of the rare musicians who, despite his superstar status and substantial record sales (at least in Brazil), did not become self-aggrandizing, narcissistic, or overly concerned with his hipness.

In his later years, Veloso showed no signs of slowing down. After his 1989 recording *Estrangeiro*, produced by Arto Lindsay of the Ambitious Lovers and Peter Scherer, became his first non-import release in America, Veloso's profile in the United States increased significantly. He continued to attract American listeners with the release of 1993's *Tropicalia 2*. Recorded with Gil, the album was considered brilliant by the music press and made numerous American "ten-best" lists that year. Another effort, 1994's Spanish-language album *Fina Estampa*, won considerable praise as well. The 15-song compilation contained "Latin American songs that I like very much, that I had known since childhood," Veloso told John Lannert of *Billboard* magazine.

Other non-import albums, including 1992's *Circulado* and 1997's *Circulado Vivo*—which included versions of Michael Jackson's "Black and White" and Dylan's "Jokerman"—also fared well in the United States, leading the pop star, in the summer of 1997, to embark on his largest American tour up to that time. In 1999, Veloso returned with *Livro*, originally released in Europe in late 1998, which was selected by critics for both the *New York Times* and the *Village Voice* as one of the best albums of the year. Peter Watrous of the *New York Times*, for example, described the record as "wildly intelligent and sensual, and perfectly produced, moving from orchestral works to minimalist ballads and Brazilian drum workouts."

That same year, Veloso completed a memoir of his involvement in the Tropicalismo movement of the 1960s, as well as Brazilian music and culture, entitled *Verdade Tropical*, which was published in the United States by Alfred A. Knopf. In 1999 at the age of 56, Veloso continued to live in Brazil with his second wife and manager, Paula Lavigne, and their son Zeca.

Selected discography

Caetano Veloso, Nonesuch, 1986.
Estrangeiro, Nonesuch, 1989.
Circulado, Nonesuch, 1992.
Fina Estampa, PolyGram, 1994.
(With Gilberto Gil) *Tropicália 2*, Nonesuch, 1994.
Livro, Nonesuch, 1999.

Sources

Periodicals

Billboard, October 8, 1994, p. 59; May 1, 1999, p. 20; October 30, 1999, p. 43.
Down Beat, November 1, 1999.

New York Times, January 29, 1999.
Newsweek, July 12, 1999, p. 67.
Rhythm, June 1999, p. 33.
Spin, June 1999, pp. 106-112.

Online

"Caetano Veloso," *Europe Jazz Network Musicians,* http://www.ejn.it/mus/veloso.htm (June 16, 1999).

Additional information provided by Nonesuch Records.

—*Laura Hightower*

Velvet Crush

Pop band

A melodic power-pop trio in the same vein as Matthew Sweet, the Smithereens, and the Replacements, the Velvet Crush draw from the soft and strong embellishments of the Byrds, Moby Grape, and the Beach Boys of the 1960s, yet they have also developed their own distinct sound. "Most guitar-based pop bands are really safe," the group's drummer, Ric Menck, told *Rolling Stone* magazine in December of 1992. "We didn't want to be that, because we all grew up listening to punk rock and the Beatles and Big Star." Critics as well recognized the distinction between Velvet Crush and their predecessors. "Obviously, Velvet Crush is composed of devout, old-school power poppers who have done their homework and have exquisite taste in influences," noted *Stereo Review* writer Parker Puterbaugh in a review for the band's acclaimed 1994 album *Teenage Symphonies to God.* "At the same time they bring something fresh to the formula, and their enthusiasm shines through in track after delectable track."

Before joining forces for Velvet Crush, founders Ric Menck on drums, and Paul Chastain on vocals and bass, pursued the pop formula separately in different parts of Illinois. Menck, regarded as one of pop's truest believers and a devoted follower of Brian Wilson, Alex Chilton, Roger McGuinn, Ray Davies, Pete Townsend, Phil Spector, and other legends of the two-minute single, followed the path of his idols not with a piano or guitar as do most songwriters, but from behind a small drum kit, making his keen insight into the pop style all the more intriguing. Although the Illinois native could play both guitar and sing, he rarely did so in public. Menck first served as one-half of a band called the Reverbs with vocalist John Brabeck. The duo released one album in 1984, the seven-track, power-pop effort *The Happy Forest,* which made little impact due to poor production and Brabeck's colorless vocals. Meanwhile, Chastain worked on a career of his own around. His first venture was as a soloist, arriving with a 12-inch vinyl EP in 1985. Although a brief effort, the six-track record and original song entitled *Halo* earned favorable attention for its brushes with R.E.M. and the Beatles, as well as for Chastain's singing ability.

Declining to continue on with the Reverbs, Menck worked under the name Pop the Balloons with future solo artist Adam Schmitt for a brief time, then the trio Choo Choo Train with Chastain and guitarist Darren Cooper in the late 1980s. In 1988, the group released the EPs *Briar Rose* and *High,* both compiled for the eleven-song *Briar High* in 1992, in spite of Menck's strong objections. Although Menck and Chastain had moved on to Velvet Crush, *Briar High* documented the duo's early Anglo-pop obsessions with light, yet well-informed tunes such as "Flower Field," "When Sunday Comes (She Sighs)," and "My Best Friend." Songwriter Jeff Murphy, vocalist and guitarist of the Illinois band Shoes, guested for the song "Every Little Knight," while Menck made a rare appearance singing lead on "Big Blue Buzz" and "Wishing on a Star."

Moving to Providence, Rhode Island, in 1990, Menck and Chastain concurrently retired Choo Choo Train to form a more serious group with guitarist Jeffrey Borchardt, a Wisconsin native who had played in the White Sisters and later led the group Honeybunch. As the Velvet Crush,the trio debuted in 1991 with two EPs, *Ash and Earth* and *The Soul Crusher e.p.*, followed by their first full-length album, *In the Presence of Greatness,* produced and recorded on an eight-track machine with friend and fellow pop musician Matthew Sweet in his living room. A critical and college listener favorite, the trio's introduction saw Velvet Crush embracing pop music as a living ideal, not as a convenience, a religion, or for nostalgic refuge. As Ira Robbins noted in the March 5, 1992, issue of *Rolling Stone,* the trio's spirit "is wholly current, an informal sense of pop tradition unpolluted by nostalgia." And in December of that year, the same magazine named *In the Presence of Greatness* "the year's most addictive masterpiece—equal parts perfect harmonies and hopelessly ragged innovation." Revealing a steady flow of top-notch pop, Velvet Crush's debut album included highlights such as "Drive Me Down, "Ash and Earth," "Window to the World," "White Soul," and "Blind Faith."

For the Record . . .

Members include **Jeffrey Borchardt** (born in Wisconsin; former member of White Sisters and leader of Honeybunch; left band in 1998), guitar; **Paul Chastain** (born in Illinois; former member of Choo Choo Train; recorded as a solo artist; played in Matthew Sweet's band), vocals, bass; **Ric Menck** (born in Illinois; former member of the Reverbs and Choo Choo Train; played in Matthew Sweet's band), drums, occasional guitar and vocals.

Formed band in Providence, RI, in 1990; released debut album, *In the Presence of Greatness,* 1991; released *Free Expression* without a record company contract in 1999.

Addresses: *Record company*—Bobsled Records, P.O. Box 6407, Aurora, IL 60598.

The Velvet Crush borrowed the phrase "Teenage Symphonies to God," coined by Brian Wilson to describe his inspired work with the Beach Boys in the mid-1960s, in naming their next album. However, 1994's *Teenage Symphonies to God* more followed the guitar-based pop of the Byrds, the Raspberries, and Big Star, as well as the country-rock influence of Gram Parsons. For the album, the Velvet Crush covered former Byrd Gene Clark's "Why Not Your Baby," performed a song written by Sweet entitled "Something's Got to Give," co-wrote a convincing country-soul song called "Faster Days" with Stephen Duffy, and crafted other original pop and country-inspired numbers such as the romantic folk-rock song "Weird Summer" and the spiraling guitar piece "Atmosphere."

Co-produced by Mitch Easter—who also performed with Velvet Crush as a second guitarist on the road, replacing Dave Gibbs of the Gigolo Aunts and preceding Tommy Keene and other guests—*Teenage Symphonies to God* also received a warm reception. On tour to promote the album, audiences were surprised to find that the group's live performances veered away from the typical, low-key pop show. "Velvet Crush is much harder live than on disc," *Boston Globe* staff writer Michael Saunders reported in 1995 after a gig at a Boston area venue, "far more intense and committed to hammering away at a song until the tune wilts from exhaustion."

Despite critical successes and a growing fanbase, especially in the college/indie markets, the Velvet Crush retreated for a few years, but returned in 1998 with *Heavy Changes,* their first record since 1994. Adopting a harder-edge rock approach and tossing aside their Byrds/Big Star influences, the Velvet Crush disappointed many fans. Similarly, *Heavy Changes* hadn't gone over well with the band's former label, Creation Records, either, and the company refused to release the record shortly after its completion. Although eventually picked up and issued by Cooking Vinyl, the trio's third effort won less than admirable reviews. "The Velvet Crush have attempted to spruce themselves up for a cruise down racket road at 180 mph," wrote one critic for the *New Musical Express* (*NME*) website, "but they've gotten so caught up in the momentum of their journey that they've left the tunes behind."

Also in 1998, Menck and Chastain were further shaken when longtime guitarist Borchardt announced his resignation from the Velvet Crush. Thus, the duo decided to record their next album on their own terms, setting up at Sweet's home studio in Los Angeles, California, free from the pressures and hassles of the music business. "It was fun again," Menck told Dan Epstein in an interview for Launch.com. "We weren't signed to Creation, so we didn't have to submit our songs for approval; we paid for it ourselves and did it like we did in the old days—just set up the equipment in a room and press the 'record' button."

The result, 1999's *Free Expression*, marked a return to the Velvet Crush's sixties roots and re-established their reputation with critics. Co-produced by Sweet, who also served as an ad hoc band member co-writing songs and contributing some guitars and keyboards, the album revealed an uncluttered, low-key production quality with songs that touched upon country, folk, and 1960s pop. Highlights from the effort included "Roman Candle," "Gentle Breeze," "Melody #7," and "Between the Lines."

In addition to playing in the Velvet Crush, both Menck and Chastain were regular mainstay's in Sweet's band, and Menck also worked with singer/songwriter Liz Phair. Although Menck freely admitted to using touches from his pop inspirations in the Velvet Crush's own recordings, he nonetheless stressed that the band never sought to recreate the past. "I have such a hard time talking to Velvet Crush fans," he laughed, as quoted by Epstein, "because they want to talk about the Raspberries, while I'd much rather talk about the new Madonna single, which I think is a pop classic. The essence of rock 'n' roll is the cross-pollination of it all—pop, soul, country, blues, whatever. And that's really where Velvet Crush is coming from."

Selected discography

Velvet Crush

Ash and Earth, (EP7), Bus Stop, 1991.
The Soul Crusher e.p., (EP7), (Australia) Summershine, 1991.
In the Presence of Greatness, Ringers Lactate, 1991
The Post-Greatness e.p., (EP), (U.K.) Creation, 1992.
Teenage Symphonies to God, Creation/550 Music/Epic, 1994.
Heavy Changes, Cooking Vinyl, 1998.
Free Expression, Bobsled, 1999.

Reverbs

The Happy Forest, Metro-America/Enigma, 1984.

Paul Chastain

Halo, (EP), Pet Sounds, 1985.

Choo Choo Train

Briar Rose, (EP), (U.K.) Subway Organisation, 1988.
High, (EP), Subway Organisation, 1988.
Briar High (Singles 1988), Subway Organisation, 1992.

Honeybunch

Time Trails, Summershine, 1996.

Sources

Books

Robbins, Ira A., editor, *Trouser Press Guide to '90s Rock,* Fireside/Simon and Schuster, 1997.

Periodicals

Audio, December 1994.
Boston Globe, January 9, 1995; October 8, 1998; November 11, 1999.
Los Angeles Times, August 27, 1999.
Melody Maker, May 9, 1992.
People, August 15, 1994.
Rolling Stone, March 5, 1992; December 10, 1992; December 1, 1994.
Stereo Review, January 1995.
Stereo Review's Sound and Vision, November 1999.

Online

Launch.com, http://www.launch.com (March 15, 2000).
NME.com, http://www.nme.com (March 15, 2000).

—Laura Hightower

Arcadi Volodos

Concert pianist

When he made his debut in New York in 1991, the Russian-born pianist Arcadi Volodos was unknown in the United States. By the time he made his Carnegie Recital Hall debut in the autumn of 1998, the fame he achieved through successful concert tours and recordings was more than a pleasant surprise. Volodos was considered one of the most gifted young artists that vied to fill the void left by the legendary Vladimir Horowitz after his death in 1989. The album produced from the Carnegie Hall concert won Volodos the prestigious Gramophone award at London's Royal Festival Hall on October 18, 1999, as Best Instrumental Recording of the year. For someone who did not take piano seriously until he was 16, Volodos plays with the wizardry of one who was a child prodigy. In less than ten years he has earned a presence on stages the world over, stunning audiences with his virtuoso.

Arcadi Volodos was born in St. Petersburg, Russia, in 1972. His parents were both singers, a direction in the music profession he intended to follow. Volodos also studied conducting. On the advice of his teacher he decided, at age 16, to give piano another try, having only played it early when he was not interested in it for career purposes. In an interview with German newspaper *Suddeutsche Zeitung*, when he made his Munich debut in March of 1998, Volodos said that, "It is not too late at 16 [to learn piano]. In the end it depends on how you deal with the music. I have never practiced scales and I always got bad marks for technique." For the young artist who critics have crowned as the artist most likely to have filled the Horowitz tradition, Volodos seemed to have a gift for making music. He began his studies at the St. Petersburg Conservatory, went on to the Moscow Conservatory to study with Galina Egiazarova, to Paris with Jacques Rouvier, and to Madrid for study with Dimitri Bashkirov at the Escuela Superior de Musica Reina Sofia.

The praise for Volodos has been filled with superlatives. In January of 1998, *Stereo Review* noted that, "Volodos seems to have a gift for preserving the intrinsic character of each individual piece–and its musical values.... He brings his own personality to the music while preserving the character Horowitz created for it.... It's all a great show, truly musical in every bar, very vividly recorded, and provided with valuable annotation." Tim Parry, writing for *Gramophone* in March of 1998, commented on Volodos' Classic CD: "Here is a disc of visceral excitement and unashamed virtuosity, blending refined poetry with an exploitation of colour and sonority, Volodos' magical control of pedaling and finger-weighting demonstrating a rare feel for melodic and inter-voicing. Few recent discs have served the art of transcription so well."

With all of the mention of Horowitz, *Suddeutsche Zeitung* also asked Volodos if he saw himself as the "inheritor of the virtuoso tradition in the style of Liszt and Horowitz." Volodos answered that, "Yes, this is often mentioned in the press. However, I do not regard myself as a virtuoso. I do find these pieces at all difficult. Many people think, only because there are really a lot of notes that the pieces have to be difficult. That is basically not the case. The only difficulty lies in the musical form–it is really about achieving the correct sound image. Once you have this, you just have to play it back. And this is good fun. The technical side should not be separated from the music–this is important. I was never really so interested in Horowitz as a pianist but rather as acomposer."

Volodos enjoys the improvisation that comes with performance. His career itself has been somewhat of an improvisation as well. He did not follow the usual agenda for a budding young pianist. He never entered a single competition. Luck came when he was staying at a friend's house in the south of France at the same time as a manager from Sony. He offered Volodos a contract on the spot, and they produced a CD very soon afterwards. That CD won Volodos the German Record Prize. Featured were transcriptions of works by Rachmaninoff, Schubert, Bach, Mozart, Bizet, Tchaikovsky and other composers, including some by Volodos himself. In addition to the German prize, the CD was also awarded *Gramophone*'s Editor's Choice, Classic CD's Disc of the Year, and the French Choc du Monde de la Musique.

For the Record . . .

Born in 1972 in St. Petersburg, Russia. *Education*: Studied piano at the St. Petersburg Conservatory; Moscow Conservatory with Galina Egiazarova; in Paris with Jacques Rouvier; in Madrid with Dimitri Bashkirov at Escuela Superior de Musica Reina Sofia.

Awards: *Gramophone*'s Editor's Choice; Classic CD's Disc of the Year; German Record Critics' Award; the French Choc du Monde de la Musique; and a Gramophone Award for the Best Instrumental Recording of the Year, 1999.

Addresses: *Website*—Arcadi Volodos website: http://www.volodos.com.

Volodos has performed all over the world with many of the most renowned orchestras, including the Berlin Philharmonic Orchestra, the Israel Philharmonic Orchestra, the Philharmonia Orchestra, the Rotterdam (Netherlands) Philharmonic Orchestra, the Royal Concertgebouw Orchestra, the Royal Philharmonic Orchestra, the Tonhalle Orchestra, the Boston Symphony Orchestra, the Chicago Symphony Orchestra and the San Francisco Symphony Orchestra. Conductors with whom he has played include Vladimir Ashkenazy, Riccardo Chailly, Valery Gergiev, James Levine, Zubin Mehta and Seiji Ozawa. Plans for 2000 included appearances with the San Francisco Symphony and Michael Tilson Thomas, the Los Angeles Philharmonic and Lawrence Foster, the Philadelphia Orchestra and David Zinman, the Philharmonia Orchestra led by Lorin Maazel, and the Orchestra di Santa Cecilia conducted by Myung-Whun Chung. Repeat performances at New York's Carnegie Hall, the Berlin Philharmonie and London's Royal Festival Hall were also scheduled.

Writing for *Classic CD* in April of 1998, the year Volodos was named Keyboard CD of the Year by that publication, Jeremy Nicholas described Volodos' playing as being full of "peerless articulation and enormous power that captivate; it's the beautiful, richly-rounded tone he produces throughout, with a range of colour and long-breathed phrasing, especially in the more reflective numbers, that proclaim him as a musician of the first rank."

Volodos does not see himself as fitting easily into an image his early praise garnered. He did not want to be seen as a virtuoso on the rise. Instead, his interests are broader than simply the romantic piano music for which he was getting so well known. "It really does not matter to me which image the journalists have worked out for me. I cannot then be labelled forever from this one record. I also play Bach and Schubert at concerts and this is not about virtuosity," he told *Suddeutsche Zeitung* in 1998. For Volodos, it is about creating the music anew every time he plays, with new intonations, new understandings. The key for him was "the listening, not the playing," Volodos said. "Taking everything into consideration, I believe that the singing, conducting and individual composing were the best means for my development. If you look at a piece you have to develop a sound image in your mind and then try to project this onto the keys. That's all."

What the future would bring for this pianist with such a flair was full of the promise of his genius. His transcriptions have been the object of awe, whether with Tchaikovsky or Brahms orothers. His allure captured by his own inventiveness was sure to take him to the stage for decades to come and to make the audience excited each and every time he did.

Selected discography

Volodos, Sony, 1997.
Live at Carnegie Hall, Sony, 1999.
Russian Music and Revolution, 1999.
The Triumph of the Piano, 2000.

Sources

Periodicals

New York Times, Jan. 4, 1998; Oct. 18, 1998; Oct. 23, 1998.
Suddeutsche Zeitung, March 20, 1998.

Online

"Arcadi Volodos," *Sony Classical*, http://www.sonyclassical.com/artists/volodos/adhome.html (March 6, 2000).
Arcadi Volodos website, http://www.volodos.com (March 6, 2000).

—Jane Spear

Joe Louis Walker

Guitar

Photograph by Jack Vartoogian. Reproduced by permission. ©

Guitarist Joe Louis Walker interprets not only the blues but also a bevy of diverse musical genres, tempered with aspects of contemporary jazz. Diversity of style is the hallmark of his talent, and critics praise his bent for improvisation and his boundless adaptability for performing jazzy styles and themes. Walker's trademark is a wellspring of extraordinary energy that explodes into melody and permeates his performance. The core of his genius lies in his ability to channel his energy into a remarkable juxtaposition of musical styles and musical instruments. His performance on assorted instruments, including the dobro, acoustic guitar, electric guitar, and harmonica is rivaled and surpassed only by his extensive collaborative efforts with a spectrum of musicians who stand each at the forefront of his or her own respected discipline within the music world.

Walker was steeped in jazz and blues as a child. His parents were migrant farm workers from Arkansas. When they moved to California they transported an extensive collection of 78 rpm blues recordings. Walker, who was born in San Francisco, California on Christmas Day in 1949, grew up listening to the treasured music. He revered the old record collection and learned to appreciate all music in general. As a result of his intensely religious upbringing, gospel music, according to Walker, fused the substance of his being. He sang gospel at his grandmother's church as a child and again professionally in his early career. He never let go of the gospel beat and maintained that gospel serves as the underlying theme for all of his music.

In grade school Walker amused himself by checking out the various instruments from the school music department. Everything musical appealed to him—violins, accordions—every instrument captured his imagination. He brought each home and played with it. At around 12 years of age he bought an inexpensive guitar and learned to play. He took lessons when he was 14 and also learned techniques from his cousins, who by that time had formed a band. In short time Walker joined the band, stepping in as a performing member when one of the cousins went alone on tour. Walker and his cousins played at dances, Elks Clubs, even at San Francisco's Fillmore Community Center Auditorium. Additionally, as he matured he developed an appreciation of the soul music recordings that his brothers and sisters enjoyed.

Walker, still in his early teens, performed in nightclubs around town, where he had to supply false identification because he was underage. In time his obsession with music led him to ignore his schoolwork. His studies suffered desperately, until he stopped attending school altogether, a situation that led his father to issue an ultimatum and confront him with the option of returning

For the Record . . .

Born on December 25, 1949, in San Francisco, CA.

Signed with High Tone Records, 1986; released *Cold Is the Night*, 1986; *The Gift*, 1988; *Blue Soul*, 1988; *Live at Slim's Volume 1*, 1991; *Live at Slim's Volume 2*, 1992; signed with Verve Records, 1992; released *Blues Survivor*, 1992; *JLW*, with James Cotton, 1994; *Blues of the Month Club*, 1995; *Great Guitars*, 1997; *Silvertone Blues*, Blue Thumb, 1999.

Awards: Contemporary Blues Artist of the Year, W. C. Handy Award, 1988-90.

Addresses: *Record company*—Blue Thumb Records, The Verve Music Group, 555 West 57th St., 10th Floor, New York, NY 10019.

to school or leaving home. Walker accepted the challenge and set out on his own at age 16. He took up residence in San Francisco's artsy Haight Ashbury district and survived by answering want ads for guitar players. He drifted between bands, frequently as a stand-in for a regular member, and quickly developed a flexibility of style that he retained even as a solo performer.

Before long Walker fostered a friendship with session guitarist and Paul Butterfield Blues Band cohort, Mike Bloomfield. Walker and Bloomfield became roommates and frequented a popular club called the Matrix where they performed as the opening act for stars like Muddy Waters. Opportunities unfolded easily for the talented Walker as he made the acquaintances of prominent professional bluesmen, including Lightnin' Hopkins, Freddie King, and John Lee Hooker.

Walker experimented briefly with psychedelic rock and spent time jamming with the Grateful Dead and the late Jimi Hendrix during the 1960s, until a brief bout with substance abuse led Walker to reevaluate himself and his career. He expanded his repertoire in the 1970s and joined the Spiritual Corinthians, a performing gospel quartet, in 1975. With Walker singing tenor, the Spiritual Corinthians cut several records including their 1980 release, "God Will Provide." Gospel, Walker asserted repeatedly, was the substance of his music always. When the quartet disbanded in 1985, Walker toured Europe with the Mississippi Delta Blues band. That same year he found himself enervated by the New Orleans Jazz & Heritage Festival and, as a result, immersed himself increasingly into modern blues styles throughout the remainder of the decade. He made three albums for High Tone in the late 1980s, and spent time developing his skill on the electric guitar.

Walker emerged with renewed energy in the early 1990s. He signed with Verve Records in 1992, and his first album with that label, *Blues Survivor,* featured two tracks with his former colleagues, the Spriritual Corinthians. By mid-decade he had formed an ensemble with Tom Rose on guitar, Mike Eppley on keyboard, Tony Saunders on bass, and Curtis Nutall on drums. Together the five versatile musicians performed live, frequently as a back-up band, at venues in the San Francisco Bay Area. Their repertoire extended from R&B to blues and funk.

In 1994, Walker recorded *JLW* with the distinguished harp (harmonica) master, James Cotton, and reciprocated the favor in 1996 by contributing to Cotton's *Deep in the Blues,* a Grammy-award winning album. Also heard on *JLW,* were jazz saxophone player Brandon Marsalis, and pianist Terry Adams. Walker's next album, *Blues of the Month Club,* released on Verve Records in 1995 featured the Memphis Horns and the guitar styles of the album's co-producer, Steve Cropper. Cropper was heard again, not surprisingly, on Walker's *Great Guitars* in 1997. Walker personally orchestrated the 1997 album with many of his own compositions, embellished by an impressive assortment of great guitarists from all genres and eras; Ike Turner, Bonnie Raitt, Otis Rush, Taj Mahal, and "Gatemouth" Brown among others contributed to the disc. The notion of *Great Guitars* was not unanticipated because throughout his career Walker made a tradition of sharing his spotlight with a wide spectrum of collaborating musicians, including blueswoman Debbie Davies, and vocalist Angela Strehli.

By 1999, with the release of *Silvertone Blues, Down Beat* tabbed Joe Louis Walker as a hands-down winner. "If Joe Louis Walker were a stock car racer, he'd be the clear favorite who laps the field again and again," the publication noted of Walker and went on to praise his "killer slide guitar," on an "album [that] has no weak spots." Walker played both electric and acoustic guitar, along with dobro, harmonica, and piano on *Silvertone Blues*; he also sang and played Hawaiian (slide) style guitar. The album features guest performances by Alvin Youngblood Hart on guitar and vocals, and by James Cotton on harmonica. Kenny Wayne contributed his piano styles; Joe Thomas added acoustic bass; and Chris Sandoval is heard on drums.

For three consecutive years, in 1988, 1989, and 1990, Walker received the W.C. Handy Award as Contemporary Blues Artist of the Year. He performed at the Pocono Blues Festival on July 27, 1997 and played at the Waterfront Blues Festival in Portland, Oregon on July 5, 1999. Additionally he participated at B. B. King's Blues Summit. Throughout his musical adventures, Walker habitually collected posters from all over the world, and he displays the scores of souvenirs with pride as decoration on the walls of his music room.

In the year 2000, Walker contributed to the soundtrack of *Hellhounds on My Trail: The Afterlife of Robert Johnson,* a Robert Mugge film. For that project Walker assisted Robert Santelli with the musical direction. Also featured in that work were Billy Hector, Alvin Youngblood Hart, and [the new] Roy Rogers. *Hellhounds* is a quasi-documentary that portrays the story of an obscure depression-era bluesman from Mississippi. The film includes concert footage and explores the mystique of a poor and humble blues artist who, unlike Walker, lived and died with little fanfare.

Walker maintains an extensive guitar collection that serves to reflect and to emphasize the versatility of his talent as well as his love for music. The assortment includes an array of name brands and models; some are acoustic, and some are electric. In all Walker stands commended for his talents as a guitarist and songwriter, as a bandleader, and for his production skills.

Selected discography

Cold Is the Night, High Tone, 1986.
The Gift, High Tone, 1988.
Blue Soul, High Tone, 1988.
Live at Slim's Volume 1, High Tone, 1991.
Live at Slim's Volume 2, High Tone, 1992.
Blues Survivor, Verve, 1993.
JLW (with James Cotton), Verve, 1994.
Blues of the Month Club, Verve, 1995.
Great Guitars, Verve, 1997.
The Preacher and the President, 1998.
Silvertone Blues, Blue Thumb, 1999.

Sources

Periodicals

Down Beat, December 1999.
Record (Bergen County, NJ), January 1, 2000.

Online

"Caught in the Act," *Jazz Online,* http://www.gibson.com/magazines/amplifier/12-95/caught/ (January 25, 2000).
"Joe Louis Walker," *AMG All Music Guide*", http://allmusic.com/cg/.dll (February 9, 2000).
"Joe Loius Walker," *Mai's Interview of the Month,* http://www.realblues.com/interv11.html (January 25, 2000).
"Joe Louis Walker," *Russian River Blues Fest,* http://russianriverbluesfest.com/artists/joewalker.html (January 25, 2000).
"Joe Louis Walker," *Verve Music Group,* http://www.bluethumb.com/bfeatures/joe_walker/main.html (February 9, 2000).
"Joe Louis Walker," *Waterfront Blues Festival,* http://www.waterfrontlbuesfest.com/jlwalker.htm (January 25, 2000).

—Gloria Cooksey

The Wedding Present

Indie rock group

Corbis. Reproduced by permission.

Since the late-1980s, the British pop band the Wedding Present, with its ever-shifting lineup, has been primarily the creative outlet for singer/songwriter/guitarist David Gedge, known for his idiosyncratic vocal style and lovelorn, conversation-like lyrics. "Love songs are the ideal pop form," Gedge, who grew up a fan of the Beatles in Yorkshire, England, told Brendan Farrington of the *Patriot Ledger* in 1996. "I've tried to write about other stuff, like science fiction, and I always come back to love songs.... It's my forte." In addition to the Beatles, Gedge also claimed the Monkees and the Velvet Underground as early influences, although musically, the latter of the two bands had the most profound effect on the songwriter's own creations. But while Gedge's tunes relied on a heavy-guitar sound ranging from almost-punk to gritty pop, they nonetheless revealed the musician's penchant for writing lyrics about break-ups, unreciprocated love, unfaithful relationships, and at times the pure joy of falling in love.

Similar to the Smiths, the Jam, the Beatles, Joy Division, and other imaginative bands who preceded them, the Wedding Present became a part of England, an outfit that resonated a renewed sense of musical nationalism in addition to popular tunes. Despite fame in their homeland and charting numerous singles in the United Kingdom, the Wedding Present remained under-appreciated in the United States, kept alive stateside mainly by college radio listeners even without significant airplay. Nevertheless, Gedge felt appreciative of the band's American following, regardless of its small size. "We're like a cult band over here," Gedge said to Farrington. "(Fans) are very loyal as well. There are loads of people that have every record that you ever made, and they travel around to see you." Likewise, Gedge took the Wedding Present's membership changes in stride. "Actually, I'm glad about all the changes. Change is good," he revealed in an interview with Pieter Hoffmann of *Drop-D* magazine in 1996. "We've had a lot of good players come through the band and that keeps the sound fresh, I believe. With all that diversity, we tend not to put out the same old album every time."

Along with original band members Peter Solowka on guitar, Keith Gregory on bass, and Shaun Charman on drums, Dave Gedge founded the Wedding Present (later dubbed the Weddoes by faithful fans) in 1985 in Leeds, England. Emerging around the same time the Smiths, the U.K.'s most successful indie-pop band of the 1980s, disbanded, the Wedding Present was conveniently poised to take over and fill the cultural void. They became an immediate success, especially among university students, thanks to numerous live shows. The foursome's catchy, offhand songs, and the patronage of influential DJ John Peel, who cut the Wedding Present's first radio

For the Record . . .

Members include **Darren Belk** (joined band in 1993; left band in 1996), bass, guitar; **Shaun Charman** (left band in 1988), drums; **Simon Cleave** (joined band in 1996), guitar; **Paul Dorrington** (joined band in 1991; left band in 1995), guitar; **David Gedge** (formed side project called Cinerama c. 1998), vocals, guitar; **Keith Gregory** (left band in 1993), bass; **Hugh Kelly** (joined band in 1995; left band in 1996), drums; **Jayne Lockley** (joined band in 1995), bass, vocals; **Simon Smith** (joined band in 1988), drums; **Peter Solowka** (left band in 1991 to form the Ukrainians), guitar.

Founded band in 1985 in Leeds, England; released debut album on own label entitled *George Best,* 1987; released collection of Ukrainian folk songs inspired by Solowka's father called *Ukrainski Vistupi v Johna Peela,* 1989; released 12 charting singles, one each month, 1992; released *Saturnialia,* 1996.

Addresses: *Record company*—Cooking Vinyl Records, P.O. Box 311, Port Washington, NY 11050, phone: (516) 484-2863, fax: (516) 484-6179.

session in February of 1986 contributed to the group's popularity. With their blistering rhythm guitars, a refreshing disregard for fine-tuned production, and Gedge's agonized songs about unrequited love backed by upbeat instrumentation, the Wedding Present became the new darlings of the British press.

Named for iconoclastic soccer star George Best (both Gedge and Solowka were raised near Manchester, England, for whose team Best played), the Wedding Present's remarkable debut album arrived in 1987 on their own Reception label to instant critical acclaim. On songs such as"Everyone Thinks He Looks Daft," "It's What You Want that Matters," and "My Favourite Dress," Solowka played as though "his hands were on fire," noted Ira Robbins in the *Trouser Press Guide to '90s Rock,* keeping pace with Gedge's off-kilter vignettes. The Wedding Present appeared to be just the type of sound Britain was looking for at the time. "Things were different then," noted *Melody Maker* writer Jade Gordon, looking back on the era in 1997. "There was no 'Drugs Don't Work' at Number One, no Oasis to frighten George Michael. But there was a haven for non-corporate music, a breeding ground bustling with youth, ideas, idealism and freedom. It was called the Independent Chart and it gave a profile to genuinely independent (i.e. not bankrolled by a major) bands, and we will never see its like again."

After the Wedding Present established themselves with *George Best* on the British indie charts, the band put together a hasty compilation of early singles, cover songs, and radio broadcasts entitled *Tommy.* Released in 1988 with the hopes of capitalizing on the group's overnight success, the effort earned less than favorable reviews. However, the band returned for more sessions with Peel, resulting in a complete departure for 1989's *Ukrainski Vistupi v Johna Peela,* issued on RCA Records. A detour into traditional Ukrainian folk songs inspired by Solowka's father and featuring guest vocals by Len Liggins, the credible effort made an unusual and successful attempt to cross elements of rock and world music. In addition to the usual rock instruments, *Ukrainski Vistupi v Johna Peela* made use of traditional instruments like mandolin and balalaika as well. The recording also introduced a new drummer, Simon Smith, who stepped in to replace Charman after he left the Wedding Present to form the Popguns; Charman played for half of the tracks, while Smith served on drums for the remainder.

The Wedding Present continued to stray from formulaic indie-pop with 1989's *Bizarro,* a more conventional rock album with four songs produced by American noise-rock, hardcore guru Steve Albini. While some critics referred to the record as uneventful, and even the band admitted that "all the songs sound the same," as quoted by *Rough Guide to Rock* contributor Huw Bucknell, *Bizarro* nonetheless indicated the Wedding Present's musical growth. Two tracks from the album, "Brassneck" and "Kennedy," fared well with fans as they became live favorites, with the latter reaching the British top 40 when it was submitted as a single prior to the album's release. Around the same time, the group showed their lighter side, releasing hit singles such as "Corduroy" and a cover of Steve Harley & Cockney Rebel's "Make Me Smile (Come Up and See Me)."

Hiring Albini to produce a whole album, the Wedding Present returned with *Seamonsters* in 1991. Receiving mixed criticism, the album revealed "dense and expressionistic layers of guitar noise" that "underpinned a sharper, more aggressive lyrical edge," noted Bucknell. *Seamonsters* also marked another lineup change; this time, Solowka resigned in order to further explore his world music roots in the group the Ukrainians, a side project he initiated after the Wedding Present recorded *Ukrainski Vistupi v Johna Peela.* Replaced by guitarist Paul Dorrington, Solowka went on to release three albums and one EP (a hysterical collection of translated Smiths covers) with his new group.

The following year, the Wedding Present opted not to record a new album, but instead released a new single every month throughout 1992. Hitting the British singles chart with each new song,the Wedding Present's experiment won them entry into the *Guinness Book of Records.* Both sides of all 12 singles were later released on *Hit Parade 1* and *Hit Parade 2,* arriving in 1992 and 1993 respectively. Each consisted of six original songs and six covers, including remakes of the Monkees' "Pleasant Valley Sunday," Neil Young's "Don't Cry No Tears," Isaac Hayes' "Theme from Shaft," Bow Wow Wow's "Go Wild in the Country," and Julee Cruise's "Falling" (the theme from *Twin Peaks*).

Taking time off in 1993 to recuperate from a frenzied year, the Wedding Present saw Gregory leave the group to found Cha Cha Cohen, leaving Gedge the only original band member. Replacing Gregory with bassist Darren Belk, the Wedding Present moved from RCA to Island Records for 1994's *Watsui.* Produced by Steve Fisk, a prominent figure on the American love-rock indie scene from Olympia, Washington, and featuring Beat Happening vocalist Heather Lewis for two tracks, the effort earned positive criticism for its musical variety but suffered from underexposure. "This is the kind of excellent record the Wedding Present should have made years ago," wrote Robbins.

In 1995, another lineup change occurred when Belk quit the band, and Gedge to some extent felt responsible for the Wedding Present's inability to maintain members. "I guess I'm a bit of a social defect. I'm all-consumed by the band," he said to Hoffmann. "I think that's why Darren left. The Wedding Present means everything to me. Many of the people that have come through the band think it's great being with the band and making all these records. But we tour all the time and, myself, I think Wedding Present twenty-four hours a day. A lot of people can't take the schedule." Thus, with Belk's departure, Gedge brought in bassist Jayne Lockley, who he said "adds another dimension to the sound that allows for, dare I say, a more optimistic sounding Wedding Present. It's like having a new string on the bow."

In 1996, the Wedding Present returned with a significant amount of new material. After releasing the *Mini* EP and *Mini Plus* (the EP and added tracks), the group arrived at the end of the year with the full-length album *Saturnalia,* recorded in the summer at the Cocteau Twins' studio and co-produced by Cenzo Townshend. A compilation of later songs was issued in 1999 in the United Kingdom under the title *The Wedding Present Singles 95-97* on Cooking Vinyl.

In addition to leading the Wedding Present, Gedge worked on a side project with Sally Murrell called Cinerama, an outlet for his acoustic, more introspective songs. Cinerama debuted in 1998 with the album *Va Va Voom,* which earned rave reviews for its unrestrained, joyous pop quality. "If there's anything I hate about music right now," Gedge told Everett True of *Melody Maker* in 1998, "it's all these successful bands who seem to be making a career out of being miserable. This last year, there's been this epic rock Oh-No-I've-Got-So-Much-Money miserablism. If you want to get anywhere, it seems like you have to have these dour chords and wallow in desolation."

Selected discography

George Best, (U.K.) Reception, 1987.
Tommy, (U.K.) Reception, 1988.
Ukrainski Vistupi v Johna Peela, (U.K.) RCA, 1989.
Janice Long Evening Show, (EP), (U.K.) Nighttracks/Strange Fruit, 1988.
The BBC Sessions, Strange Fruit/Dutch East India Trading, 1988.
Bizarro, (U.K.) RCA, 1989; RCA, 1990; reissued, Manifesto, 1996.
Brassneck, (EP), (U.K.) RCA, 1990.
Seamonsters, (U.K.) RCA, 1991; First Warning, 1992; reissued, Bizarre/Planet, 1994; reissued, Manifesto, 1996.
Hit Parade 1, First Warning, 1992; reissued Bizarre/Planet, 1994; reissued, Manifesto, 1996.
Hit Parade 2, (U.K.) BMG, 1993; Bizarre/Planet, 1994; reissued, Manifesto, 1996.
John Peel Sessions 1987-90, Strange Fruit/Dutch East India Trading, 1993.
Watsui, Island, 1994.
Mini, (EP), (U.K.) Cooking Vinyl, 1996.
Mini Plus, Cooking Vinyl, 1996.
Saturnalia, Cooking Vinyl, 1996.
The Wedding Present Singles 95-97, (U.K.) Cooking Vinyl, 1999.

Sources

Books

MusicHound Rock: The Essential Album Guide, Visible Ink Press, 1999.
Robbins, Ira A., editor, *Trouser Press Guide to '90s Rock,* Fireside/Simon and Schuster, 1997.

Periodicals

Billboard, January 9, 1993; February 24, 1996.
Edmonton Journal, February 4, 1996.
Melody Maker, January 11, 1992; October 25, 1997; July 11, 1998; August 1, 1998; August 15, 1998; September 25, 1999.

Patriot Ledger (Quincy, Massachusetts), March 15, 1996.
Rolling Stone, December 12, 1996.

Online

All Music Guide, http://www.allmusic.com (March 18, 2000).
"His Only Constant is Change," *Drop-D Magazine*, http://www.dropd.com/issue/28/WeddingPresent/index.html (March 18, 2000).
Rolling Stone.com, http://www.rollingstone.tunes.com (March 18, 2000).
"The Wedding Present," *Rough Guide to Rock*, http://www.roughguides.com/rock/entries/entries-w/WEDDING_PRESENT.html (March 18, 2000).

—Laura Hightower

Margaret Whiting

Singer

Photograph by Jack Vartoogian. Reproduced by permission. ©

The daughter of famed songwriter Richard Whiting, vocalist and actress Margaret Whiting was surrounded by legendary song writers including such notables as Harold Arlen, Johnny Mercer, Frank Loesser, Jule Styne, Jerome Kern, Leo Robin, and the Gershwin Brothers. Her father had been a contributor to popular music including such classics as "Ain't We Got Fun," "Sleepy Time Gal," "Beyond the Blue Horizon," "Breezin' Along with the Breeze," "Too Marvelous for Words," "She's Funny that Way," "Hooray for Hollywood," and many more popular songs of the 1920s and 1930s. It was not unusual to find Johnny Mercer in one room with Harold Arlen, and Judy Garland and Mel Torme singing together in another. Mercer had always been a close friend of her father and soon became her chief mentor, helping to coach and guide her as her career developed as a teen. The first piece of advice he gave Margaret was to "grow up and learn to sing." Mercer helped her learn to sing, and Whiting was also coached by the great song writer Harold Arlen, as well as other notable composers and friends of her father.

When popular songwriter Johnny Mercer co-founded Capitol Records in 1942, 16-year-old Whiting was one of the first artists he signed to the new label. She had appeared on the Lucky Strike sponsored *Your Hit Parade* the previous year but was fired by the owner of the company because he said he couldn't dance to her songs. Her first major hit in 1942 was Mercer's and Arlen's "That Old Black Magic" with Freddie Slack and his orchestra. The song was recorded on the Capitol Records label one week after Whiting's eighteenth birthday. In 1943 Margaret recorded her late father's 1930s song "My Ideal," with lyrics by Leo Robin. It also was the precursor to a long list of hits she made for Capitol and the first of over a dozen records that sold over a million copies.

In 1944, Mercer heard a song written by two unknown songwriters, Johnny Blackburn and Karl Suessdorf, entitled "Moonlight in Vermont." He felt it was perfect for Margaret and when Mercer approached her about singing it, she replied, "I don't know what to sing about in this song. I've never been to Vermont. How can I sing a song about a place I've never been to? What is the significance of pennies in a stream? What will I do with the lyric? What are ski tows?" Mercer replied, "I don't know. I'm from Savannah. We'll use our imagination." Mercer talked to the songwriters about the use of the words "ski tows" and they accommodated him by changing the words to "ski trails." It is one of the few popular songs ever written without a rhyme in the entire lyric, and it became her signature song, complemented by Billy Butterfield and his orchestra, and selling millions of records and copies of sheet music. Incidentally, it was many years later before she ever visited Vermont.

For the Record . . .

Born on July 22, 1924, in Detroit, MI; daughter of songwriter Richard "Dick" Whiting and Eleanore (Young), a homemaker and manager of singers including Margaret Young and Sophie Tucker; eldest of two daughters; married CBS business executive Hubbell Robinson; married Lou Busch, Capitol Records music director and a pianist (aka Joe "Fingers Carr) and Richard Moore, the inventor of Panavision; married Jack Wrangler, 1987. All four marriages ended in divorce; children: Deborah, born 1950, with husband Lou Busch. *Education*: Attended El Rodeo School, Marymount Preparatory School, Los Angeles, CA; Taught to sing by aunt, Margaret Young, Alison Ryan's Dancing School; studied with Lillian Goodman for eleven years and with Harriet Lee.

Signed with Capitol Records, 1942; first major hit, "That Old Black Magic," 1942; released signature song, "Moonlight in Vermont," 1944; performed a series of duets with country singer Jimmy Wakely, 1949; host television show, *The Whiting Girls,* with sister Barbara, 1950s; remained with Capitol Records for 17 years until 1958, then moved to Dot Records; switched to Verve Records, 1960; returned to Capitol in the early 1960s, then joined London Records,1966; has recorded over 500 popular songs; film and Broadway actress.

Awards: Songwriters' Hall of Fame; 12 gold records.

Addresses: *Home*—Margaret Whiting, 41 West 58th Street, Apt. 5A, New York, NY 10019.

In the 1940s, composer Walter Gross wrote a beautiful melody and entitled it "Walter's Melody." He wrote it for Margaret Whiting when they were dating, and it remained unpublished. When Margaret Whiting heard the song, she felt it was beautiful and introduced Gross to lyricist Jack Lawrence, who added a set of lyrics. Lawrence also changed the title, and it became the all-time classic standard, "Tenderly." It was one of the most widely recorded songs of the twentieth century. Oddly, it was never recorded by Whiting, though she was directly responsible for itscreation.

In the summer of 1948, Whiting's recording of Englishman Billy Reid's "A Tree in the Meadow" sold over a million copies and became Reid's first of several winning gold discs, rising to number one on the Hit Parade. That same year Whiting recorded "Now is the Hour" and "Far Away Places," which were also enormous hits. She collaborated with orchestra leader Paul Weston and recorded Richard Rodgers' and Oscar Hammerstein II "It Might As Well Be Spring." The song became a big hit for Whiting and Dick Haymes who starred in the motion picture musical *State Fair.* In 1949, she performed a series of duets with country singer Jimmy Wakely and their rendition of "Slippin Around" reached number one on the charts. She remained with Capitol Records for 17 years until 1958 and then moved to Dot Records. In 1960, Whiting switched to Verve Records and recorded a number of albums including one with vocalist Mel Torme. She returned to Capitol in the early sixties and then joined London Records in 1966 and recorded two additional charting pop singles. Whiting has recorded more than 500 popular songs.

In the interim, Whiting appeared in a number of Broadway productions including *Gypsy, Pal Joey,* and *Call Me Madam*, as well as an off-Broadway play, *Taking My Turn* in 1983. Her activities also included appearing in cabarets and joining three other 1940s and1950s singers Kay Starr, Rosemary Clooney, and Helen O'Connell, and comediennes Rosemarie, Martha Raye, and Kaye Ballard in a rotating singer/comedienne act called *4 Girls 4.* They toured for 12 years together, each performing their own songs and concluding the performance with a joint finale. In addition, Whiting has appeared in many motion picture films as an actress and vocalist. She worked on television on the *Bob Hope Show* as a resident vocalist and regularly appeared on the *Jack Smith Show* as a twice a week regular as well as guest appearances on many major television shows. In the 1950s, Whiting and her sister, Barbara, hosted their own television series, *The Whiting Girls*, a sitcom about two sisters striving for a career in show business.

Whiting is a board member of the Songwriters Hall of Fame, the Society of Singers, Grammy Awards, The Manhattan Association of Cabarets and Clubs, and is a master teacher at the Eugene O'Neill Foundation's Cabaret Symposium located in Waterford, Connecticut. In addition, she can be found entertaining aboard cruise ships, and at music halls and night clubs from New York to California. In 1997, she appeared in the Broadway salute to Johnny Mercer entitled *Dream* that ran from April 3, 1997, through July 6, 1997, with a total of 133 performances. Whiting went on nostalgic big band tours with Freddy Martin and his orchestra in the 1970s accompanied by Frankie Carle and Bob Crosby. In addition, she sang with the St. Louis Symphony. Since that time Whiting has appeared in a number of films and television productions, and has performed in cabarets, music halls and as late as 1999 performed on the television show *Larry King Live* on the CNN cable television network.

Over a career that spans six decades, Whiting has performed songs by Johnny Mercer, Cole Porter, Richard Rodgers, Jerome Kern, Oscar Hammerstein II, Arthur Schwartz, Otto Harbach, George Gershwin, Jule Styne, Harold Arlen, Dorothy Fields, Richard Whiting, and many other prominent popular songwriters of the twentieth century. During her tenure, Whiting has worked with vocalists and songwriters such as Cole Porter, Mel Torme, Johnny Mercer, Hoagy Carmichael, Jimmy Wakely, Gerry Mulligan, Lex Baxter, Paul Weston, and Bing Crosby, toname but a few. One of her most remarkable traits is her willingness to share her time to be supportive of new and young talent as well as other experienced professional singers. She is also chairperson of the Johnny Mercer Charitable Foundation.

Selected discography

Albums

Goin' Places, Dot DLP 3072.
Jerome Kern Song Book, Verve V6-4038.
Just a Dream, Dot DLP 25337.
Love Songs by Margaret Whiting, Capitol T410.
Margaret, Dot DLP 3113.
Past Midnight, MGM SE 4006.
Ten Top Hits, Dot DLP 25235.
Margaret Whiting Sings for the Starry Eyed, Capitol T-685.
Margaret Whiting Sings Rodgers and Hart, Capitol H 209.
The Wheel of Hurt, London LL3497.

CDs

Capitol Collector Series, 93194.
Come a Little Closer, Audiophile 173.
Greatest Hits, CEMA 9404.
The Lady's in Love With You, Audiophile 207.
Maggie's Back in Town, Pair 1224.
One and Only, Jasmine 343.
Spotlight on Margaret Whiting, Capitol 29395.
Margaret Whiting, Then and Now, Cabaret 21471-1403-2.
Then and Now, DRG 91403.
Too Marvelous for Words, Audiophile 152.

Films

Showtime, 1955.
Fresh From Paris, 1955; aka *Paris Follies of 1956.*
Underworld Informers, 1965; aka *The Informers.*
The Counterfeit Constable, 1966.
The Old Curiosity Shop, 1975; aka *Mr. Quilp.*
Sinbad and the Eye of the Tiger, 1977.
Taking My Turn-A Musical Celebration, 1983.
Trespasser, 1985.
The Secret Garden, (Television), 1987.

Sources

Books

Balliett, Whitney, *American Singers 27 Portraits in Song,* Oxford University Press, 1988.
Bennett, Tony, *The Good Life,* Pocket Books, 1998.
Gammond, Peter, *The Oxford Companion to Popular Music,* Oxford University Press, 1993.
Jablonski, Edward, *Harold Arlen, Rhythm, Rainbows and Blues,* Northeastern University Press, 1996.
Lax, Roger and Frederick Smith, *The Great Song Thesaurus,* Oxford University Press, 1989.
Maltin, Leonard, *Movie and Video Guide 1995,* Penguin Books Ltd., 1994.
Osborne, Jerry, *Rockin Records,* Osborne Publications, 1999.
Simon, William L., *Parade of Popular Hits,* The Reader's Digest Association Inc., 1989.
Simon, William L., *Readers' Digest Treasury of Best Loved Songs,* The Reader's Digest Association Inc., 1987.
White, Mark, *You Must Remember This,* Charles Scribner's Sons, 1985.
Whiting, Margaret and Will Holt, *It Might as Well Be Spring,* William Morrow & Co., 1987.

Periodicals

People, May 4, 1987.

Online

All Music Guide, http://www.allmusic.com/cg/x.dll (January 2000).
City Cabaret, http://www.citycabaret.com (October 1999).
Elibrary, www.elibrary.com (January 2000).
Johnny Mercer website, http://www.johnnymercer.com (January 2000).

Additional information was obtained through an interview with Margaret Whiting on July 1, 1999.

—Francis D. McKinley

Willem Breuker Kollektief

Jazz ensemble

The Willem Breuker Kollektief is a musical snake that can shed its skin at the drop of a hat. The group moves effortlessly from swing rhythms reminiscent of Stan Kenton, to tributes to spaghetti western composer Ennio Morricone, to stately tangos by Kurt Weill, to Philip Glass-style minimalist pieces, to arrangements worthy of 1930s musicals sung by Breuker himself, into honkin' free jazz improvisations. And all on a single album, *Bob's Gallery*! All the Kollektief's records are full of such musical surprises. But throughout its explorations, the group maintains its own musical personality. Part of that personality is its sense of humor. You never know when a solemn Glass ostinato will be interrupted by the burp of a tuba or an aria by a gargling diva.

Tenor saxophonist Willem Breuker was born in Amsterdam, Holland on November 4, 1944, during the last days of the Second World War. As a school boy he took up the clarinet, then the soprano sax, and in the early 1960s fell under the spell of Ornette Coleman's music. He achieved a small measure of notoriety in the Netherlands in 1966 while he was leading a 23 piece ensemble at the Loosdrecht Jazz Competition. During the performance he pointedly dedicated one of his compositions to a student who had been killed not long before in a demonstration. The gesture came at a time when lines were being drawn increasingly between old and young, and between conservative, liberal and radical. It was also shocking because until then, no Dutch musician had overtly aligned his art with politics.

Social upheaval was sweeping Europe like the rest of the world. At the same time a remarkable flowering was occurring in European jazz. Among the musicians getting started then were saxist Evan Parker and guitarist Derek Bailey in Britain, saxist Peter Brötzmann and pianist Alex von Schlippenbach in Germany, drummer Han Bennink in Holland. And the music was often fierce, in your face jazz, like nothing ever heard before, fired on by the student protests sweeping the continent, that reached a high point when Brötzmann's earth-shattering improv LP *Machine Gun* was recorded in the revolutionary month of May 1968.

Willem Breuker was a member of the all-star ensemble that played on *Machine Gun*, and he composed one of the three pieces that appeared on the album. Although he proved himself a formidable improviser, Breuker soon began moving away from free jazz to concentrate on composing and playing in a more structured accessible framework. Not that he ever gave up improvisational playing; but henceforth his outpourings would take place against the backdrop of carefully arranged charts written for the Kollektief.

Breuker met Han Bennink in 1966 and together with pianist Misha Mengelberg, they formed the Instant Composer's Pool (ICP). It was with the ICP that Breuker's ideas about doing music collectively began. The ICP fell apart in 1973 following disagreements between members. Breuker left and formed the Kollektief. "It's pretty anachronistic ," Breuker told Mike Zwerin of the *International Herald Tribune*, "a holdover from my socialist days in Amsterdam in the '60s and '70s." Whatever its roots, the Kollektief served a number of purposes. For one thing it suited Breuker's style of composition. As he developed, he found his music becoming more complex than the average jazz combo could handle. "I write too many notes," Breuker explained to Greg Baise of the *Metro Times*, "I cannot play my music with three or four musicians. I need more musicians."

Being a collective also helped minimize personal problems that have destroyed many a band. Most importantly it helped prevent destructive competition from developing between the players. "There is no hierarchy, no stars," Breuker told *New City*, "Everybody earns the same and has equal say in how band money is spent. I am 54 but the newest, youngest member gets paid the same I do." The atmosphere created by the group also drew the players closer together too. Zwerin. "We are not employees, we are members," he told Zwerin, "to make music with close friends—well, that is our own good luck."

Being a collective also enabled the group to cut the costs of operating a large performing ensemble. On tour, the

For the Record . . .

Members include **Andy Altenfelder**, (born June 7) trumpet; **Willem Breuker**, (born Novem ber 4, 1944, Amsterdam, The Netherlands), sax, clarinet, recorder, vocals; **Alex Coke**, (born November 13) sax, flute, piccolo, kazoo, whistle, vocals; **Hermine Deurloo**, (born March 8), sax, harmonica; **Arjen Gorter**, (born January 2) bass; **Bermard Hunnekink**, (born Nobvember 1), trombone; **Henk de Jonge**, (born December 14), piano, synthesizer; **Nico Nijholt**, (born May 2), trombone; **Boy Raaymakers**, (born August 20), trumpet, ukele, vocals; **Lorre Lynn Trytten**, (born December 25) violin, musical saw; **Rob Verdurmen**, (born March 20), drums, percussion; numerous other musicians over the years.

Formd Instant Composer's Pool (ICP) with Han Bennink and Misha Mengelberg, 1966; performed on Peter Brötzmann's *Machine Gun*, 1968; ICP disbanded, 1973; Breuker formed Willem Breuker Kollektief, 1974; Kollektief celebrated 25th anniversary, 1999.

Addresses: *Record company*—BVHAAST Records, 99 Prinseneiland, 1013 LN Amsterdam, Holland, phone: 020-6239799, e-mail: wbk@xs4all.nl.

Kollektief musicians do everything themselves, from unloading their bus, to setting up and tearing down. The group does not have to employ any roadies; the only employee who tours with them is their bus driver. The idea worked. By the 1980s the Kollektief was successful enough to afford its own touring bus, and a rehearsal hall and offices in Amsterdam, and even its own record company, BVHaast. The name translates to Haste Inc.—Willem Breuker is not a man who likes to waste time.

But the collective identity extends only as far as music-making is concerned. The members of the Kollektief live in their own homes, not communally, and when they are on the road together each has her or his own room. Breuker has even admitted he has never even seen where some of his musicians live. But some distance is necessary considering the group is on the road together for 100 or more gigs a year. The Kollektief arrangements must work—twenty five years later a number of its founding members were still playing with the group.

And then there is the music, the often indescribably music the Kollektief plays. It's usually called "jazz" and when their records can be found in record stores, they are somewhere between Anthony Braxton and Dave Brubeck. But their jazz is a European variant that owes as much to Stravinsky as Duke Ellington. One of their records, for example. features a ballet by Erik Satie, "Parade," arranged by Breuker for the Kollektief. The 1999 CD *Hunger* features an aria from Rossini's *Barber of Seville* that eventually veers into Monty Python territory alongside powerful jazz solos by various Kollektief members and a version of "Yes We Have No Bananas" straight out of vaudeville. In truth, the Kollektief is an ensemble that refuses to be hemmed in by narrow categories like jazz, pop, or classical music. "I don't believe in music that comes out of a book," Breuker told Zwerin. "I don't believe in music made for musicians. My music is for old people, young people, city people farmers, for every social class—music accessible to everybody." Breuker himself labeled his music "Human Being Music— music made by and for humans—and once said he thought it was probably good for one's health.

The Kollektief's closet musical relative, in spirit if not style, may be Sun Ra and his Arkestra. Like Sun Ra's band, the Kollektief is made up of talented improvisers who at the same time are highly disciplined ensemble players who have mastered a wide range of musical styles. Like Sun Ra, the Kollektief's leader Breuker is a brilliant composer and arranger as well as a talented instrumentalist. Both groups have built careers on deflating expectations. And, of course, Arkestra members *did* live communally.

The sense of humor present in the Kollektief's work, especially live, sets it apart from many other jazz groups. It might express itself as subtly as the oom-pah of a tube gently intruding on Philip Glass or as broadly as a Rossini aria, sung in rather low sounding Dutch and punctuated by a sneeze from the singer. Some critics complain about the Kollektief's shenanigans, especially in 1999 when the trombonist took to falling to his knees in concert and barking like a dog. But deadly serious jazz can be heard in clubs and festivals the world over. "We have always incorporated theatrics as our distinctive style," Breuker told *Coda*'s Bill Besecker. I think we are independent from styles or directions or fashion. We just do what we can do.... I don't want to copy people."

The Kollektief has toured steadily for the better part of two decades. In 1990, Breuker said he believed it was the last band in Europe that tours constantly. To highlight the fact, the publicity photo on the occasion of the Kollektief's 25th anniversary showed them standing in front of their bus. And Breuker is proud of the fact that

that the group can—and has—played in all kinds of circumstances. "I can play anywhere in the world," he told Baise, "We've played in small cellars for 16 people. But we've also played in the street for 35,000 people, like in Italy and Montreal and Toronto. I don't care at all. We just play. And we're a band that can come to a pace and [be ready to] play in ten minutes."

As the year 2000 started, the Kollektief had eleven members, two of whom were American—tenor player Alex Coke and violinist Lorre Lynn Trytten. Coming off their 25th anniversary year, they were still mourning the death of member Peter Barkema at the end of 1998, but moving into the future in best Breuker style, touring the United States for the tenth time.

Selected discography

Baal Brecht Breuker Handke, (BVHAAST CD 9006)
De Onderste Steen, (Entr'acte 2)
To Remain, (BVHAAST CD 8904)
Bob's Gallery, (BVHAAST CD 8801)
Metropolis, (BVHAAST CD 8903)
Parade, (BVHAAST CD 9101)
The Parrot, (BVHAAST CD 9601)
Kurt Weill, (BVHAAST CD 9808)
Pakkepapèn, (BVHAAST CD 9807)
Hunger, (BVHAAST CD 9916)
Celebrating 25 Years, BVHAAST

Sources

Periodicals

Coda, March 1990.
International Herald Tribune, September 26-27, 1992
Metro Times, October 6-12, 1999.
New City

Other

Hunger liner notes. Some material graciously provided by the Willem Breuker Kollektief.

—*Gerald E. Brennan*

John Williams

Composer, conductor

Photograph by David Strick. Archive Photos. Reproduced by permission.

Not since Henry Mancini of the 1960s has a composer attained the popular recognition of John Williams, who created music for some of Hollywood's most successful motion pictures of all time; *Star Wars, E.T. the Extra Terrestrial, Jurassic Park,* and *Schindler's List* represent a small sampling of the musician's extensive list of credits. Undoubtedly the most dominant force in film music since the 1970s, the era in which he initiated the first of several collaborations with filmmakers Steven Spielberg and George Lucas, Williams realized the importance of music as it relates to the silver screen and possessed a unique ability to capture the emotional core of a film, to articulate through music what the audience sees. "Film conspires with your imagination to remove you from your present reality and take you on a free-wheeling trip through your unconsciousness," composer Elmer Bernstein once said about the power of film music, as quoted by Timothy E. Sheurer in *Popular Music and Society.* "What better companion for such a medium than music? Music is, quite possibly, the most removed from reality. Of all the arts, music makes the most direct appeal to the emotions. It is a non-plastic, non-intellectual communication between sound vibration and spirit. The listener not generally burdened with a need to ask what it means. The listener assesses how the music made him feel."

Whether scoring music for comedies, musicals, disaster and adventure films, or blockbusters, the award-winning musician enhanced each new project with his original scores, writing music that was not just mere accompaniment, but could stand on its own merit as well. Over the years, Williams saw his soundtracks sell well into the millions, earning him numerous gold and platinum records. An accomplished musician beyond the world of Hollywood film as well, Williams has written several concert pieces, including two symphonies, and served as conductor and director for the Boston Pops, one of the world's most recognized orchestras. "When writing music away from the film world, I felt I could be more experimental. I felt I could test myself and try not to be daunted by the great masters of the past," he explained to *Los Angeles Times* writer Chris Pasles in 1997.

Born on February 8, 1932, in Flushing, New York, John Williams was himself the son of a movie studio musician who had also worked as a CBS radio orchestra percussionist. Taking cue from his father, Williams started playing piano at the age of six, picking up the bassoon, cello, clarinet, trombone, and trumpet as well by the time he entered grade school. Eventually, Williams formed a small band at school, though he soon discovered that instruments like the piano and clarinet could not be played from the same sheet of music. Hence, he taught himself how to transpose music, spending hours in the

For the Record . . .

Born John Towner Williams, February 8, 1932, in Flushing, NY; son of John (a percussionist) and Esther Williams; married Barbara Ruick, c. 1956 (died, 1974); married Samantha Winslow (a photographer), 1980; children: (first marriage) Jennifer, Mark, Joe. *Education:* Attended University of California, Los Angeles; studied orchestra with Robert van Epps at Los Angeles City College; studied composition with Mario Castelnuovo-Tedesco, c. 1950-52; studied piano with Rosina Lhevinne at Julliard School of Music, 1954-55.

Worked as jazz pianist in New York City night clubs, c. 1954-55; pianist in Hollywood film studios such as Columbia Pictures and Twentieth Century Fox, beginning in 1956; contracted by Revue Studios to pen television themes, beginning in the late-1950s; wrote first film score for *Daddy-O,* 1959; teamed with Steven Spielberg for the first time for *Sugarland Express,* 1974; collaborated with George Lucas for the first time for *Star Wars,* 1977; conductor and music director for the Boston Pops Orchestra, 1980-93; artist-in-residence at Tanglewood Music Center in MA, 1993—; frequent guest conductor with the London Symphony Orchestra, the Los Angeles Philharmonic, and others.

Selected awards: Seventh Annual Career Achievement Award, Society for the Preservation of Film Music, 1991; Richard Kirk Award for outstanding career achievement, BMI Film and Television, 1999; Academy Awards for best adaptation and original song score for the following: *Fiddler on the Roof,* 1971; best original score for *Jaws,* 1975; best original score for *Star Wars,* 1977; best original score for *E.T. The Extra Terrestrial,* 1982; best original score for *Schindler's List,* 1993; 17 Grammy Awards, four British Academy Awards, three Golden Globe Awards; two Emmy Awards; honorary doctorate degrees in music from several American universities, including Boston University, New England Conservatory of Music, Tufts University, the University of Southern California; numerous gold and platinum records.

Addresses: *Agent*—Michael Gorfaine, The Gorfaine/Schwartz Agency, Inc., 3301 Barham Blvd., No. 201, Los Angeles, CA 90068. *Website*—The John Williams Pages: http://www.johnwilliams.org.

basement of his home pouring over orchestration books. "I applied the principles of Rimsky-Korsakov to the pop tunes of 1940 and 1941," he told Richard Dyer in *Ovation,* as quoted by Rob Nagel in *Contemporary Musicians, Volume 9,* "and by the time our band was in high school, we were already quite sophisticated." Although Williams was still in his teens, he had nevertheless already discovered his calling as a composer and conductor.

Moving with his family in 1948 to Los Angeles, California, Williams decided to focus on a professional career in music after completing high school. Around 1950 Williams enrolled at UCLA, where he took courses in orchestration and also studied compositions privately with Italian composer Mario Castelnuovo-Tedesco. Around 1952, Williams joined the United States Air Force, serving for two years during the Korean War, before returning to New York in 1954 to enroll at the Julliard School of Music. While living in New York, he studied piano with Madame Rosina Lhevinne and worked as a jazz pianist in night clubs and on recordings.

After completing his apprenticeship at Julliard and concluding his brief stint as a jazz club player, Williams returned to Los Angeles in 1956 and soon landed jobs on a regular basis as a pianist in the Hollywood film studios. However, Williams' greater talents lay in composition and orchestration, and established film scorers such as Bernard Herrmann, Alfred Newman, and Franz Waxman soon took notice, inviting Williams to orchestrate cues for their material. The veteran composers also encouraged Williams to focus on his own writing, and while he was able to score some low budget films, his first big break arrived during the late1950s, when studios suddenly needed a vast amount of music specifically for television.

Honed Skills on Television

Some of Williams' first television jobs included performances, such as playing the famous riff in Henry Mancini's theme to *Peter Gunn* and appearing in the detective series *Johnny Staccato.* However, he soon focused his energies on composition, mostly working for Revue Studios, the television production arm of Universal Studios. Under contract with Revue to pen as many as 39 scores a year—writing 20 to 25 minutes of music each week—Williams gained invaluable experience in spite of the pressures, writing music for such shows as *Playhouse 90, Checkmate, Kraft Playhouse,* and many others. "Dramatic anthologies are a thing of the past on television now, but they provided the greatest possible training ground for me," he recalled to critic Leonard Feather in the April 1969 issue of *International Musician,* as quoted in the John Williams Web Pages. "I had never learned about movie or television writing in a formal way, but I gained a great deal of knowledge simply by being around people like Franz Waxman and Alfred Newman; I observed their methods closely and intimately while I was playing piano in the studio orchestras. The good luck of being in physical proximity with so many of the masters provided me with the technique I needed by the time I got to television." And just as observing his predecessors prepared the composer for television work, his hands-on training in that realm, for which Williams had to learn to adapt music to a wide range of settings, in turn helped pave the way for his forthcoming ventures into film.

In 1959, Williams took his first leap into the motion picture format with his score for *Daddy-O,* spending the first half of the 1960s composing an occasional film score—primarily for lighter comedic fare such as *Gidget Goes to Rome* and *Bachelor Flat*—amid his busy television schedule. Meanwhile, Williams somehow managed to find time to write "serious" compositions, such as the ensemble work *Prelude and Fugue,* as well as to accept session work as a pianist, arranger, and conductor. By the middle part of the decade, Williams was receiving more offers to work in the motion picture format, scoring music for films like *The Killers* and *The Plainsman,* and less often writing themes for television series like *Gilligan's Island* and *Lost in Space.* In the late 1960s and into the 1970s, Williams wrote music for television movies, including 1968s *Heidi,* 1970s *Jane Eyre,* and 1972's *The Screaming Woman.*

Concentrated on Film

However, Williams would dedicate the remainder of his career primarily to film. Williams' first major success arrived in 1968, when he earned his first of many Academy Award nominations for his work in *Valley of the Dolls.* Nominations for both *The Reivers* and *Goodbye, Mr. Chips* followed in 1970, and in 1972, he finally won the honor for *Fiddler on the Roof.* More nominations, not to mention popular recognition, followed in the 1970s for features such as *The Poseidon Adventure, Images, Tom Sawyer,* and *The Towering Inferno.*

Another turning point in Williams' career resulted in 1974, when he teamed for the first time with a young filmmaker named Steven Spielberg for *Sugarland Express.* Jennings Lane, then the vice president of Universal, told Williams after assigning Spielberg to his first feature film that he ought to meet with the aspiring director. "So I had lunch with Steven in Beverly Hills. I was 40 and he was 23, and I felt like a kind of Dutch uncle, especially because he looked as if he were all of 16," Williams recalled of his first encounter with Spielberg, as quoted by Dyer in a 1997 *Boston Globe* interview. "He was beardless then, and so polite, sweet, and bright. He also had an astonishing accumulation of information. He knew more about the film composer Bernard Herrmann than I did—and Benny was my friend! Steven told me he could sing all the themes from movies I had scored, like *The Cowboys* and *The Reivers*—and he could!"

After *Sugarland Express,* Williams continued to team with Spielberg with often astounding results. Some of their pairings included *Jaws, Close Encounters of the Third Kind, Raiders of the Lost Ark, E.T., Jurassic Park, Schindler's List, Amistad,* and *Saving Private Ryan,* with *Jaws, E.T.,* and *Schindler's List* all winning Academy Awards in 1975, 1982, and 1993 respectively for best original score. "I guess you could say that Steven has been a very pivotal figure in my life!," Williams said to Dyer of his relationship with Spielberg, who also introduced the composer to his friend and fellow filmmaker George Lucas.

Lucas would become Williams' other most frequent collaborator, beginning in 1977 with *Star Wars,* a film that earned the musician yet another Academy Award for best original score. Williams admitted later that he, as well as Spielberg and Lucas, had all underestimated the success of the film. "I thought it would be a successful Saturday-afternoon movie; that is the category I had put it in," he told Dyer in the *Boston Globe.* "What I didn't realize was that all aspects of the public would be entranced by it." Also not realizing that *Star Wars* was to be a trilogy, Williams joined Lucas again for 1980s *The Empire Strikes Back* and 1983's *Return of the Jedi.* And when Lucas asked Williams to score music for his new trilogy, a prequel to *Star Wars,* the composer agreed. The first installment of the new series arrived in 1999 with *Star Wars: Episode 1: The Phantom Menace,* another popular success, and Williams started work on the two forthcoming film scores.

In total, Williams penned music for more than 75 films; examples of other noted scores include 1979s *Superman,* 1987's *The Witches of Eastwick,* 1988's *The Accidental Tourist,* 1989's *Born on the Fourth of July,* 1991's *JFK,* 1995's *Nixon,* 1996's *Sleepers,* and 1999's *Angela's Ashes,* adapted from Frank McCourt's acclaimed memoir. By the end of the 1990s, Williams had received 35 Academy Award nominations, taking home a total of five Oscars, four British Academy Awards, 16 Grammy Awards, and three Golden Globe Awards.

Beyond the Silver Screen

Although he earned mainstream attention for his film and television work, Williams pursued other interests as well. His other compositions include two symphonies; a bassoon concerto premiered by the New York Philharmonic in 1995; a cello concerto premiered by Yo-Yo Ma and the Boston Symphony Orchestra in 1994; concertos for flute and violin recorded by the London Symphony Orchestra; concertos for clarinet and tuba; and a trumpet concerto premiered by the Cleveland Symphony Orchestra in 1996. In addition, Williams composed the NBC News theme "The Mission," a piece entitled "Liberty Fanfare" for the rededication of the Statue of Liberty, "We're Lookin' Good!" for the Special Olympics for the organization's 1987 International Summer Games, as well as the themes for the 1984, 1988, and 1996 Summer Olympic Games.

In 1980, Williams replaced the late Arthur Fiedler as conductor of the Boston Pops, a post he held until his retirement in December of 1993. During his tenure, he recorded several acclaimed albums with the orchestra and led the Pops on United States tours in 1985, 1989, and 1992, as well as on three tours of Japan in 1987, 1990, and 1993. Other major orchestras for which he served as a guest conductor included the London Symphony Orchestra, the Cleveland Orchestra, the Chicago Symphony Orchestra, the Philadelphia Orchestra, the Pittsburgh Symphony, the Denver Symphony, the San Francisco Symphony, the Dallas Symphony, the Indianapolis Symphony, and the Los Angeles Philharmonic. Widely acknowledged for his concert compositions, Williams earned honorary doctorate degrees in music from fourteen American universities and in 1993, became an artist-in-residence at the Tanglewood Music Center in Massachusetts.

Williams realized that his connections to both the concert and film world are somewhat out of the ordinary. "The two areas of activity are so vastly different, as are the requirements of the composer, both technically and temperamentally. You haven't seen film composers become successful as concert composers. The reverse is also true," he told Pasles. "Thirty or 40 years ago, serious conservatory students wouldn't deign to even aspire to written for film. That's not true any more. I've met many young composers—very, very gifted ones—who are very interested in films. It really is the popular art medium of our era."

Selected discography

Film scores

Because They're Young, Columbia, 1960.
Gidget Goes to Rome, Columbia, 1963.
Valley of the Dolls, Columbia, 1967.
Goodbye Mr. Chips, MGM, 1969.
Fiddler on the Roof, United Artists, 1971.
Jane Eyre, British Lion, 1971.
The Poseidon Adventure, Twentieth Century Fox, 1972.
Cinderella Liberty, Twentieth Century Fox, 1973.
Earthquake, Universal, 1974.
The Towering Inferno, Twentieth Century Fox/Warner Bros., 1974.
Jaws, Universal, 1975.
Star Wars, Twentieth Century Fox, 1977.
Close Encounters of the Third Kind, Columbia 1977.
Superman, Warner Bros., 1978.
Dracula, Twentieth Century Fox, 1979.
The Empire Strikes Back, Twentieth Century Fox, 1980; reissued Varèse Sarabande, 1992.
Raiders of the Lost Ark, Paramount, 1981.
E.T. The Extra-Terrestrial, Universal, 1982.
Return of the Jedi, Twentieth Century Fox, 1983.
Indiana Jones and the Temple of Doom, Paramount, 1984.
Empire of the Sun, Warner Brothers, 1987.
The Witches of Eastwick, Warner Bros., 1987.
The Accidental Tourist, Warner Bros., 1988.
Born on the Fourth of July, Universal, 1989.
Indiana Jones and the Last Crusade, Paramount, 1989.
Presumed Innocent, Warner Bros., 1990.
Home Alone, Twentieth Century Fox, 1990.
JFK, Warner Bros., 1990.
Far and Away, Imagine Entertainment, 1992.
Home Alone 2: Lost in New York, Arista, 1992.
Jurassic Park, Sony Classical, 1993.
Schindler's List, Sony Classical, 1993.
Sabrina, A&M, 1995.
Nixon, Hollywood, 1995.
Sleepers, Philips, 1996.
Rosewood, Sony Classical, 1997.
The Lost World, MCA, 1997.
Seven Years in Tibet, Mandalay/Sony, 1997.
Amistad, Dream Works, 1997.
Saving Private Ryan, Dream Works, 1998.
Stepmom, Sony Classical, 1998.
The Phantom Menace, Sony Classical, 1999.
Angela's Ashes, Sony Classical, 1999.

Concert music

Prelude and Fugue, (LP) Capitol, (CD) EMD/Blue Note.
Sinfonietta for Wind Ensemble, Deutsche Grammophon.
Flute Concerto, Varèse Sarabande.
Thomas and the King, (LP) That's Entertainment Records, (CD) Jay Records.
Violin Concerto, Varèse Sarabande.
America, the Dream Goes On, Philips.
Olympic Fanfare and Theme, (LP) Columbia, (CD) Philips; reissued, (CD) Sony Classical.

Liberty Fanfare, Philips.
A Hymn to New England, BMG/RCA Victor.
Olympic Spirit, Arista; reissued, Sony Classical.
Summon the Heroes, Sony Classical.
The Five Sacred Trees, Sony Classical, 1997.
Film Music, Silva, 1999.

With the Boston Pops

Pops in Space, Philips, 1981.
Pops on the March, Philips, 1981.
We Wish You a Merry Christmas, Philips, 1981.
Pops Around the World, Philips, 1982.
On Stage, Philips, 1984.
(With James Ingram) *America, the Dream Goes On,* Philips, 1985.
(With Dudley Moore) *Prokofiev—Peter and the Wolf,* Philips, 1985.
Swing, Swing, Swing, Philips, 1986.
Pops in Love, Philips, 1987.
Holst—The Planets, Philips, 1988.
Pops Brittania, Philips, 1989.
Music of the Night: Pops on Broadway, Sony Classical, 1990.
I Love a Parade, Sony Classical, 1991.
The Spielberg/Williams Collaboration, Sony Classical, 1991.
The Green Album, Sony Classical, 1992.
Iberia, Sony Classical, 1992.
Kid Stuff, PolyGram, 1992.
Joy to the World, Sony.
Night Before Christmas.
Summon the Heroes, Sony Classical, 1996.

Sources

Books

Contemporary Musicians, Vol. 9, Gale Research, 1993.

Periodicals

Atlanta Journal-Constitution, February 25, 1999.
Billboard, June 5, 1999.
Boston Globe, June 4, 1997; January 28, 2000.
Los Angeles Times, December 19, 1997.
Popular Music and Society, Spring 1997.

Online

"John Williams," *All Music Guide*, http://www.allmusic.com (March 22, 2000).
"John Williams," *Hollywood Composers*, http://www.hollywoodcomposers.com (March 22, 2000).
The John Williams Pages, http://www.johnwilliams.org (March 22, 2000).

—Laura Hightower

Nancy Wilson

Singer, actress

Photograph by Jack Vartoogian. Reproduced by permission. ©

African American jazz singer Nancy Wilson, known for her old-fashioned glamour and timeless, sultry voice, has become a legendary entertainer and enjoyed a career that has endured over 40 years. However, Wilson defied and resisted labels that many used to describe her style. Not only has she been a renowned jazz singer and balladeer, but she has also performed cabaret, sophisticated pop, and rhythm and blues. Placing her music in any one or all of such categories denies what Wilson felt her songs represented. "I'm a song-stylist—although I have been pigeonholed as a jazz singer," Wilson asserted in a 1994 cover story by Robert E. Johnson published in *Jet* magazine. And *Essence* magazine writer Audrey Edwards, in May of 1992, described the singer as "an artist of such enduring talent, class and elegance that she doesn't just defy the labels, she transcends them." Moreover, Wilson believed that her music cut across class and race. "I didn't know I was a 'Black artist' until I was nominated for a Grammy in a Black category," she told continued. The music, rather than racial categories is "what people identify me with." With 60 albums to her name, beginning with her 1960 debut *Like in Love* through her 1997 release *If I Had My Way,* Wilson and her music have surpassed the longevity of most, garnering fans of all races and ages.

The oldest in a family of six children, Nancy Wilson was born on February 20, 1937, in the small southern Ohio town of Chillicothe, where she spent many of her formative years and where she attended Burnside Heights Elementary School. Wilson's parents, Olden and Lillian (Ryan) Wilson, were hard-working and raised their children in a close-knit environment. Her mother labored as a domestic, while her father worked in an iron foundry. Throughout her childhood, Wilson, along with her brothers Anthony and Michael and sisters Rita, Brenda, and Karen, often spent summers in the company of their grandmother at her home on Whiskey Run Road just outside of Columbus, Ohio. It was during these extended family get-togethers that Wilson first delighted audiences with her singing. A vocalist who never took part in formal voice training and often referred to her ability as a gift, Wilson realized at the tender age of four that her goal was to sing professionally.

In her hometown of Chillicothe and later in Columbus, where her family moved when Wilson reached her teens, she developed her skills singing in church choirs and emulating the styles of a variety of post-war American music. Some of her favorite musical legends included Nat King Cole, Billy Eckstine, LaVern Baker, Louis Jordan, Dinah Washington, Ruth Brown, and her self-proclaimed greatest influence, "Little" Jimmy Scott. Wilson's own career began to take shape at the age of 15 after she won a local talent contest in Columbus and was

For the Record . . .

Born February 20, 1937, in Chillicothe, OH; daughter of Olden and Lillian (Ryan) Wilson; married Kenneth C. Dennis (a drummer; divorced, 1970); married Wiley Burton (a minister), 1974; children: (first marriage) Kenneth "Kacy;" (second marriage) Samantha, Sheryl. *Education*: Attended Central State College in Wilberforce, OH, 1955. Memberships include Presidential Council for Minority Business Enterprises; National Association for the Advancement of Colored People (NAACP); Southern Christian Leadership Conference; Operation PUSH (chairperson); United Negro College Fund; and Committee for the Kennedy Center for the Performing Arts.

Sang in church choirs and clubs, Columbus, OH, early 1950s; star of local television show, *Skyline Melodies*, Columbus, OH, 1952-54; member of Rusty Bryant's Carolyn Club Big Band, 1956-58; released first album, *Like in Love*, for Capitol Records, 1959; hosted *The Nancy Wilson Show*, 1967-68; released sixtieth album, *If I Had My Way*, 1997. Made numerous appearances on variety shows, including *The Ed Sullivan Show, The Flip Wilson Show, The Merv Griffin Show, The Tonight Show, and The Arsenio Hall Show*; guest starred on numerous television series; had roles in the films *The Big Score* and *Meteor Man*. Cofounder, Nancy Wilson Foundation, which introduces inner-city youth to rural settings.

Awards: Grammy Award, 1964, for *How Glad I Am*; Emmy Award, 1975, for *The Nancy Wilson Show*; winner, Tokyo Song Festival, 1983; Global Entertainer of the Year, World Conference of Mayors, 1986; Image Award, NAACP, 1986; star, Hollywood Walk of Fame, 1990; Essence Award, *Essence* magazine, 1992; Whitney Young Jr. Award, Urban League, 1992; Martin Luther King Center for Social Change Award, 1993; Turner Broadcasting Trumpet Award for Outstanding Achievement, 1994.

Addresses: *Record company*—Columbia Records, 2100 Colorado Ave., Santa Monica, CA 90404, (310) 449-2100 *Management*—c/o Devra Enterprises, 361 W. California Ave. 8, Glendale, CA 91203.

awarded her own television series, *Skyline Melodies*, for a local station. The show, which was also broadcast on local radio, featured Wilson singing phoned-in requests. Even then, her repertoire included a wide range of musical styles, from jazz and big band to the pop, ballad, and torch song categories. In addition to performing on her television/radio show, Wilson started singing live shows everywhere she could at local clubs in and around Columbus.

Although continuing as an entertainer remained Wilson's primary goal, she decided to play itsafe when she graduated in 1955 from West High School in Columbus, entering college in order to obtain her teaching credentials. However, after only one year as an education major at Ohio's Central State College, the singer dropped out in order to follow her original dreams, auditioning for and subsequently joining Rusty Bryant's Carolyn Club Big Band in 1956. As the ensemble's female vocalist, Wilson spent much of the next three years touring the United States and Canada with the Carolyn Club Big Band. Her association with Bryant also produced her first, and now rare, recording for Dot Records.

In the meantime, while performing in Columbus, Wilson made another important connection that helped to build her career when she had the opportunity to sit in with jazz saxophonist Cannonball Adderley, who immediately sensed her enormous potential. Adderley, who would prove a major influence on Wilson's future in the recording business, convinced the talented singer to move away from the pop performance style and emphasize the more sophisticated jazz and ballad material. Taking Adderley's advice, the pair started performing together from time to time and later recorded an album together, 1962's *Nancy Wilson/Cannonball Adderley*, which was recorded with Adderley's quintet and became a jazz classic.

Solo Career

Following her stint with Bryant's band, Wilson decided in 1959 to relocate to New York City, hoping to establish herself as a solo entertainer. Upon her arrival, she accepted a job as a secretary at the New York Institute of Technology, where she worked days in order to support herself until she got a break, and also started singing at clubs at night. More than anything, Wilson desperately wanted to record for one of the most respected labels of the day, Capitol Records, though she realized the possibility of waiting months or even years to earn such an offer. However, with only four weeks under her belt in New York, Wilson received her first important assignment: to fill in for singer Irene Reid at an established nightclub. That evening, Wilson gave such a stellar performance that the club owner wanted to book the singer on a permanent basis. Still holding on to her secretarial job to supplement her income, Wilson sang four nights a week at the nightclub, and the public, as well as record producers and agents, quickly took notice. One night, John Levy, a well-known figure in the music business and manager to Adderley, came to the club to hear her sing. Because of her friendship with Adderley, not to mention her undeniable talent, Levy offered his help and set about arranging a session to record a demonstration tape. He would continue to manage Wilson's affairs throughout her entertainment career.

At the scheduled session, Wilson recorded the songs "Guess Who I Saw Today" and "Sometimes I'm Happy." Within a week after Levy sent the tapes to Capitol Records, Wilson had signed a contract with the label. Capitol, known for its outstanding roster of singers who performed the standard ballad repertoire, proved a fortunate first home for Wilson. Suddenly, she found herself in the company of world-renowned stars like Cole, Frank Sinatra, and Peggy Lee, in addition to some of the industry's most cherished lyricists and composers. Her first album for Capitol, *Like in Love,* arrived in April of 1960, and she scored her first hit with a rhythm and blues song recorded with Adderley entitled "Save Your Love for Me" in 1962.

Also that year, Capitol released her second album, *Something Wonderful,* which included one of the songs used on her demo tape "Guess Who I Saw Today." Although only a moderate hit at the time of its release, "Guess Who I Saw Today," a song about infidelity, remained her most requested number well into the late 1990s and became her signature song. "It is one of those experiences everybody can relate to," she explained to Stewart Weiner in a 1999 interview for *Palm Springs Life* magazine. Wilson's audience further broadened the following year with the song "Tell Me the Truth," and between April of 1960 and July of 1962, Capitol issued five of the singer's albums. These early accomplishments set a frenetic pace for Wilson and her first husband, drummer Kenny Dennis, who married in 1960. Before long, Wilson found herself performing more than 40 weeks out of the year, at times giving two shows a night at top clubs such as the Coconut Grove in Los Angeles and the Sahara Hotel in Las Vegas, Nevada.

Top-selling Singer

By the mid-1960s, Wilson was one of her label's best-selling artist, second only to the Beatles. An uninhibited performer who included jazz-styled pop in her repertoire and proudly displayed her glamorous good looks, she even surpassed established entertainers such as Cole, Lee, and the popular West Coast rock and roll group the Beach Boys in sales. In 1964, she won a Grammy Award for best rhythm and blues recording for the album *How Glad I Am.* Four other Grammy nominations since followed this honor, including a nomination for *Gentle Is My Love* in 1965. As 1966 approached, Wilson was earning a generous income in excess of $1 million per year, and her rise in popularity showed no sign of slowing down. In addition to enjoying stardom in the United States, she had also established a significant fanbase overseas, especially in Japan, where she would remain a favorite for years to come.

As a result of her recognized depth and diverse talent, Wilson saw other opportunities within the entertainment industry arise. From the mid-1960s and 1970s, the singer headlined shows in Las Vegas that had been booked two years in advance, performed at the most sophisticated supper clubs, and received offers for television work. During the 1967-68 season, she hosted her own top-rated television program on NBC called *The Nancy Wilson Show,* for which she won an Emmy Award. All the while, Wilson maintained a seamless string of hit records, repeatedly garnering top honors for both *Billboard* and *Playboy* magazine's music polls.

Despite her efforts to juggle a family, constant touring and recording, and a television career, Wilson's busy schedule took a toll on her personal life. In 1970, Wilson divorced her first husband, with whom she had one son, Kenneth (Kacy) Dennis, Jr., in 1963, and that same year married Reverend Wiley Burton. Wilson had two more children with her second husband, daughters Samantha Burton, born in 1975, and Sheryl Burton, born in 1976. Learning from past experiences, Wilson curtailed her professional engagements somewhat after marrying Burton. In 1973, for example, she opted not to perform in supper clubs, although she did perform concert dates in South America and Japan. Nonetheless, her decision to focus on her family made little if any impact on her stardom. In fact, Wilson herself believed that performing less actually improved her shows, noting that not playing in the same venue for two to four weeks straight gave a freshness and excitement to her singing. In the mid-1970s, Wilson and Burton bought a home—which grew to occupy over 17,000 square feet by late 1999—140 miles away from Los Angeles in the California high desert. Wilson moved to the rural location Pioneertown, made famous as the background landscape for the Roy Rogers television series, to raise her children.

Resisted Electronic Age

As the next decade approached, many record companies, especially those involved with pop and rhythm and blues artists, started using technical enhancements for album production. Wilson, who preferred to record her songs live, resisted such innovations that might alter the sound of her voice and never wanted to release a record that she was unable to perform before an audience. Therefore, since most labels in the United States declined to meet her standards, Wilson spent the 1980s primarily recording for Japanese labels. "They've allowed me to sing so that I can sing," she told *Jet* magazine in 1986. "I can't sing for a splice in the middle. I say 'We'll do it from the top until you get what you want.' The day the music died, is the day... when they stopped recording live, they started doing things you can't reproduce live." She expressed a similar, though somewhat more resigned, sentiment later in 1999. "When we were recording those Capitol albums, all of the musicians were in the same room playing," she recalled to Weiner. "Now, you record all by yourself with headphones on." Without losing her fans in the United States, Wilson further endeared herself to legions of Japanese jazz enthusiasts during these years. In 1983, she was declared the winner of the annual Tokyo Song Festival and released a total of five acclaimed albums for Japanese labels. Back in the United States, Wilson started recording for Columbia Records as well, beginning in 1984 with a collaborative effort, *The Two of Us,* that also featured pianist/keyboardist Ramsey Lewis.

With her children grown, Wilson found more time to devote to her career during the 1990s. In addition to maintaining a busy touring and recording schedule and expanding her acting interests, she was honored in 1990 with a star on the Hollywood Walk of Fame. Around the same time, she worked on a landmark album of previously unpublished lyrics by legendary songwriter Johnny Mercer set to the music of co-producer Barry Manilow. The Mercer tribute album, *With My Lover Beside Me,* was released in 1991. Several other albums followed, including her fifty-fourth full-length recording, a collection of love songs entitled *Love, Nancy*, released in 1994, as well as her sixtieth album, *If I Had My Way*, released in 1997. In 1998, Wilson received a *Playboy* readers poll award for best female jazz vocalist and resumed her radio career by hosting the National Public Radio (NPR) *Jazz Profiles* series. That same year, Wilson suffered the loss of both her parents, who both died in November of 1998. Wilson continued to work steadily through this time, which she referred to as the most difficult year of her life. The following year, Wilson honored one of jazz music's most legendary singers, Ella Fitzgerald, when she hosted a biography television special entitled *Forever Ella,* which aired on the A & E cable television network.

Television, Film, and Charitable Work

Wilson took advantage of other opportunities in both television and film. Her film roles includedRobert Townsend's *Meteor Man* and *The Big Score,* with Fred Williamson and Richard Roundtree. She appeared on *The Sinbad Show* and in a recurring role in the number one-rated series *The Cosby Show.* Her other work in television series included guest roles for *I Spy, Room 222, Police Story, O'Hara: U.S. Treasury, The F.B.I.,* and *Hawaii Five-O.* Some of her other television appearances included performances for *The Tonight Show, The Merv Griffin Show, The Today Show, The Sammy Davis Jr. Show, The Flip Wilson Show, The Andy Wilson Show,* and *The Carol Burnett Show.* Her own television special, *Nancy Wilson in Concert,* aired in 1989, and the singer made frequent appearances on both *The Lou Rawls Parade of Stars* and the *March of Dimes Telethon.*

Throughout her years as an entertainer, Wilson devoted considerable time and money to numerous charitable causes, such as the Martin Luther King Center for Social Change, the Cancer Society, the Minority Aids Project, the National Urban Coalition, and the Warwick Foundation. Organizations that honored Wilson for her dedication included the United Negro College Fund, the Urban League, and the National Association for the Advancement of Colored People (NAACP). Her family also established the Nancy Wilson Foundation to enable inner-city children to visit the country and experience alternate lifestyles. She earned an honorary degree from the Berklee College of Music in Boston, Massachusetts, for her contributions to music, and although she never finished college, Central State College presented her with an honorary degree, an accolade that reflects the teacher that she really was in her song and compassionate nature. In 1992, the Urban League presented Wilson with the Whitney Young Jr. Award, while *Essence* magazine rated the singer as one of jazz music's current "grand divas."

During her prolific and enduring career as an entertainer, Wilson witnessed the dramatic changes within the music industry. "It's now a record industry—whereas the business before emphasized nightclub performing, concerts, television appearances as well as recording records," she said to Edwards, recalling the entertainment industry of times past. Although she misses the era that gave birth to what many call the "real singers," like Joyce Bryant, Lena Horne, and Wilson herself, she insisted that the modern times have produced talent as well. "I love Oleta Adams," Wilson continued. "And Regina Belle, Anita Baker, Phyllis Hyman. These women have a lot of power and are doing some meaty material. The music is good." In addition, Wilson's daughters have introduced their mother to hip-hop artists such as Mary J. Blige, who she also came to admire. Nonetheless, Wilson looked back on her days with Capitol with a sense of nostalgia. "It was the wonder years there," she told Weiner. "Look at the artists who were recording for Capitol: Nat King Cole, Dakota Stanton, Peggy Lee, Dean Martin… And, of course, Frank Sinatra!" When asked what made the label so different, Wilson replied, "It was owned by Johnny Mercer," she explained. "And there was such a feeling of family." However, Wilson adapted with her usual grace and eased into the 1990s and beyond, bringing her stylish music to a whole new generation. Now entering into her fifth decade as a professional singer, Wilson planned to record and perform for many years to come, singing songs that have stood the test of time.

Selected discography

Like in Love, Capitol, 1960.
Something Wonderful, 1960.
The Swingin's Mutual, 1961.
Nancy Wilson/Cannonball Adderley, Capitol, 1962.
Hello Young Lovers, 1962.
Broadway—My Way, 1963.
Hollywood—My Way, 1963.
Yesterday's Love Songs, Today's Blues, 1963.
Today, Tomorrow, Forever, 1964.
How Glad I Am, 1964.
The Nancy Wilson Show at the Coconut Grove, 1965.
Nancy Wilson Today—My Way, 1965.
Gentle Is My Love, 1965.
From Broadway With Love, 1966.
A Touch of Love Today, 1966.
Tender Loving Care, 1966.
Nancy—Naturally, 1966.
Just for Now, 1967.
Lush Life, 1967.
Welcome to My Love, 1968.
Easy, 1968.
The Best of Nancy Wilson, 1968.
Sound of Nancy Wilson, 1968.
Nancy, 1969.
Son of a Preacher Man, 1969.
Close Up, 1969.
Hurt So Bad, 1969.
Can't Take My Eyes Off You, 1970.
Now I'm a Woman, 1970.
Double Play, 1971.
Right to Love, 1971.
I Know I Love Him, 1973.
All in Love Is Fair, 1974.
Come Get to This, 1975.
This Mother's Daughter, Capitol, 1976.
I've Never Been to Me, 1977.
Music on My Mind, 1978.
Life, Love and Harmony, 1979.
Take My Love, 1980.
At My Best, ASI Records, 1981.
Echoes of an Era, Elektra, 1982.
What's New, EMI Japan, 1982.
I'll Be a Song, Interface, 1984.
(With Ramsey Lewis) *The Two of Us,* Columbia, 1986.
Keep You Satisfied, Columbia, 1986.
Forbidden Lover, Epic/Sony, 1987.
Nancy Now!, Epic/Sony, 1990.
With My Lover Beside Me, *Columbia, 1991.*
The Best of Nancy Wilson, Epic/Sony, 1992.
(With Grover Washington) *Next Exit,* 1992.
Color and Light, 1994.
(With the Boston Pops Orchestra) *It Don't Mean a Thing,* Sony Classical, 1994.
Joyful Christmas, Columbia, 1994.
Love, Nancy, Columbia, 1994.
(With Quincy Jones and others) *Jook Joint,* 1995.
Spotlight on Nancy Wilson, Capitol, 1995.
Ballads, Blues and Big Bands, (Box set), Capitol, 1996.
If I Had My Way, Columbia, 1997.

Sources

Books

Contemporary Black Biography, Volume 10, Gale Research, 1995.
Notable Black American Women, Book 1, Gale Research, 1992.
Pavletich, Aida, *Rock-A-Bye, Baby,* Doubleday, 1980.
Who's Who Among African Americans, 12th edition, Gale Group, 1999.

Periodicals

American Visions, June/July 1997, pp. 28-32.
Billboard, April 26, 1997, pp. 30-32.
Ebony, July 1994, p. 24.
Essence, May 1992, pp. 65-72.
Jet, July 28, 1986; June 27, 1994, pp. 58-61; March 10, 1997, p.36; December 21, 1998, p. 63.
Palm Springs Life, December 1999, pp. 56-59.

Online

Nancy Wilson, http://www.missnancywilson.com (February 4, 2000).

—Laura Hightower

Cumulative Indexes

Cumulative Subject Index

Volume numbers appear in **bold.**

A cappella
Brightman, Sarah **20**
Bulgarian State Female Vocal Choir, The **10**
Golden Gate Quartet **25**
Nylons, The **6**
Sweet Honey In The Rock **26**
Earlier sketch in CM **1**
Take 6 **6**
Zap Mama **14**

Accordion
Buckwheat Zydeco **6**
Chenier, C. J. **15**
Chenier, Clifton **6**
Queen Ida **9**
Richard, Zachary **9**
Rockin' Dopsie **10**
Simien, Terrance **12**
Sonnier, Jo-El **10**
Yankovic, "Weird Al" **7**

Ambient/Rave/Techno
2 Unlimited **18**
Aphex Twin **14**
Chemical Brothers **20**
Deep Forest **18**
Front Line Assembly **20**
Gus Gus **26**
KMFDM **18**
Kraftwerk **9**
Lords of Acid **20**
Man or Astroman? **21**
Orb, The **18**
Propellerheads **26**
Shadow, DJ **19**
Sheep on Drugs **27**
Underworld **26**

Bandoneon
Piazzolla, Astor **18**
Saluzzi, Dino **23**

Banjo
Boggs, Dock **25**
Bromberg, David **18**
Clark, Roy **1**
Crowe, J.D. **5**
Fleck, Bela **8**
Also see New Grass Revival, The
Hartford, John **1**
McCoury, Del **15**
Piazzolla, Astor **18**
Scruggs, Earl **3**
Seeger, Pete **4**
Also see Weavers, The
Skaggs, Ricky **5**
Stanley, Ralph **5**
Watson, Doc **2**

Bass
Brown, Ray **21**
Carter, Ron **14**
Chambers, Paul **18**
Clarke, Stanley **3**
Collins, Bootsy **8**
Dixon, Willie **10**
Fender, Leo **10**
Haden, Charlie **12**
Holland, Dave **27**
Kaye, Carol **22**
Laswell, Bill **14**
Love, Laura **20**
Mann, Aimee **22**
McBride, Christian **17**
McCartney, Paul **4**
Also see Beatles, The
Mingus, Charles **9**
Ndegéocello, Me'Shell **18**
Sting **19**
Earlier sketch in CM **2**
Sweet, Matthew **9**
Was, Don **21**
Also see Was (Not Was)
Watt, Mike **22**
Whitaker, Rodney **20**

Big Band/Swing
Andrews Sisters, The **9**
Arnaz, Desi **8**
Atomic Fireballs, The **27**
Bailey, Pearl **5**
Basie, Count **2**
Beiderbecke, Bix **16**
Bennett, Tony **16**
Earlier sketch in CM **2**
Berrigan, Bunny **2**
Blakey, Art **11**
Brown, Lawrence **23**
Calloway, Cab **6**
Carter, Benny **3**
Chenille Sisters, The **16**
Cherry Poppin' Daddies **24**
Clooney, Rosemary **9**
Como, Perry **14**
Cugat, Xavier **23**
Dorsey Brothers, The **8**
Eckstine, Billy **1**
Eldridge, Roy **9**
Ellington, Duke **2**
Ferguson, Maynard **7**
Fitzgerald, Ella **1**
Fountain, Pete **7**
Getz, Stan **12**
Gillespie, Dizzy **6**
Goodman, Benny **4**
Henderson, Fletcher **16**
Herman, Woody **12**
Hines, Earl "Fatha" **12**
Jacquet, Illinois **17**
James, Harry **11**
Jones, Spike **5**
Jordan, Louis **11**
Krupa, Gene **13**
Lee, Peggy **8**
Madness **27**
McGuire Sisters, The **27**
McKinney's Cotton Pickers **16**
Miller, Glenn **6**
Norvo, Red **12**
Parker, Charlie **5**
Prima, Louis **18**
Puente, Tito **14**
Ray Condo and His Ricochets **26**
Rich, Buddy **13**
Rodney, Red **14**
Roomful of Blues **7**
Scott, Jimmy **14**
Severinsen, Doc **1**
Shaw, Artie **8**
Sinatra, Frank **23**
Earlier sketch in CM **1**
Squirrel Nut Zippers **20**
Stafford, Jo **24**
Strayhorn, Billy **13**
Teagarden, Jack **10**
Torme, Mel **4**
Vaughan, Sarah **2**
Welk, Lawrence **13**
Whiteman, Paul **17**

Bluegrass
Auldridge, Mike **4**
Bluegrass Patriots **22**
Clements, Vassar **18**
Country Gentlemen, The **7**
Crowe, J.D. **5**
Flatt, Lester **3**
Fleck, Bela **8**
Also see New Grass Revival, The
Gill, Vince **7**
Grisman, David **17**
Hartford, John **1**
Krauss, Alison **10**
Louvin Brothers, The **12**
Martin, Jimmy **5**
Also see Osborne Brothers, The
McCoury, Del **15**
McReynolds, Jim and Jesse **12**
Monroe, Bill **1**
Nashville Bluegrass Band **14**
New Grass Revival, The **4**
Northern Lights **19**
O'Connor, Mark **1**
Osborne Brothers, The **8**
Parsons, Gram **7**
Also see Byrds, The
Reverend Horton Heat **19**
Scruggs, Earl **3**
Seldom Scene, The **4**
Skaggs, Ricky **5**
Stanley Brothers, The **17**
Stanley, Ralph **5**
Stuart, Marty **9**
Watson, Doc **2**
Wiseman, Mac **19**

Blues
Allison, Luther **21**
Ayler, Albert **19**
Bailey, Pearl **5**
Baker, Ginger **16**
Also see Cream
Ball, Marcia **15**
Barnes, Roosevelt, "Booba" **23**
Berry, Chuck **1**
Bill Wyman & the Rhythm Kings **26**
Bland, Bobby "Blue" **12**
Block, Rory **18**
Blood, Sweat and Tears **7**
Blues Brothers, The **3**
Boggs, Dock **25**
Broonzy, Big Bill **13**
Brown, Clarence "Gatemouth" **11**
Brown, Ruth **13**
Burdon, Eric **14**
Also see War
Also see Animals
Cale, J. J. **16**
Charles, Ray **24**
Earlier sketch in CM **1**
Clapton, Eric **11**
Earlier sketch in CM **1**
Also see Cream
Also see Yardbirds, The
Collins, Albert **4**
Cray, Robert **8**
Davis, Reverend Gary **18**
Diddley, Bo **3**
Dixon, Willie **10**
Dr. John **7**
Dupree, Champion Jack **12**
Earl, Ronnie **5**
Also see Roomful of Blues
Estes, John **25**
Everlast **27**
Fabulous Thunderbirds, The **1**
Fuller, Blind Boy **20**
Fulson, Lowell **20**
Gatton, Danny **16**
Guy, Buddy **4**
Handy, W. C. **7**
Hart, Alvin Youngblood **27**
Hawkins, Screamin' Jay **8**
Healey, Jeff **4**
Holiday, Billie **6**
Hooker, John Lee **26**
Earlier sketch in CM **1**
Hopkins, Lightnin' **13**
House, Son **11**
Howlin' Wolf **6**
James, Elmore **8**
James, Etta **6**
Jefferson, Blind Lemon **18**
Johnson, Blind Willie **26**
Johnson, Lonnie **17**
Johnson, Robert **6**
Jon Spencer Blues Explosion **18**
Joplin, Janis **3**
King, Albert **2**
King, B. B. **24**
Earlier sketch in CM **1**
King, Freddy **17**
Lang, Jonny **27**
Leadbelly **6**
Led Zeppelin **1**
Lewis, Furry **26**
Little Feat **4**
Little Walter **14**
Lockwood, Robert, Jr. **10**
Mayall, John **7**
McClennan, Tommy **25**
McClinton, Delbert **14**
McDowell, Mississippi Fred **16**
McLean, Dave **24**
McTell, Blind Willie **17**
Memphis Jug Band **25**
Memphis Minnie **25**
Montgomery, Little Brother **26**
Muldaur, Maria **18**
Patton, Charley **11**
Plant, Robert **2**
Also see Led Zeppelin
Professor Longhair **6**
Raitt, Bonnie **23**
Earlier sketch in CM **3**
Redding, Otis **5**
Reed, Jimmy **15**
Rich, Charlie **3**
Robertson, Robbie **2**
Robillard, Duke **2**
Roomful of Blues **7**
Rush, Otis **12**
Sanborn, David **28**
Earlier sketch in CM **1**
Santamaria, Mongo **28**
Shaffer, Paul **13**
Shines, Johnny **14**
Smith, Bessie **3**
Snow, Phoebe **4**
Spann, Otis **18**
Sunnyland Slim **16**
Sykes, Roosevelt **20**
Taj Mahal **6**
Tampa Red **25**
Taylor, Koko **10**
Thornton, Big Mama **18**
Toure, Ali Farka **18**
Turner, Big Joe **13**
Ulmer, James Blood **13**
Van Zandt, Townes **13**
Vaughan, Jimmie **24**
Vaughan, Stevie Ray **1**
Waits, Tom **27**
Earlier sketch in CM **12**
Earlier sketch in CM **1**
Walker, Joe Louis **28**
Walker, T-Bone **5**
Wallace, Sippie **6**
Washington, Dinah **5**
Waters, Ethel **11**
Waters, Muddy **24**
Earlier sketch in CM **4**
Wells, Junior **17**
Weston, Randy **15**
Whitfield, Mark **18**
Whitley, Chris **16**
Whittaker, Hudson **20**
Williams, Joe **11**
Williamson, Sonny Boy **9**
Wilson, Gerald **19**
Winter, Johnny **5**
Witherspoon, Jimmy **19**
ZZ Top **2**

Cajun/Zydeco
Ball, Marcia **15**
Brown, Clarence "Gatemouth" **11**
Buckwheat Zydeco **6**
Chenier, C. J. **15**
Chenier, Clifton **6**
Doucet, Michael **8**
Landreth, Sonny **16**
Queen Ida **9**
Richard, Zachary **9**
Rockin' Dopsie **10**
Simien, Terrance **12**
Sonnier, Jo-El **10**

Cello
Casals, Pablo **9**
DuPré, Jacqueline **26**
Harrell, Lynn **3**
Holland, Dave **27**
Ma, Yo Yo **24**
Earlier sketch in CM **2**
Rasputina **26**
Rostropovich, Mstislav **17**

Children's Music
Bartels, Joanie **13**
Cappelli, Frank **14**
Chapin, Tom **11**
Chenille Sisters, The **16**
Harley, Bill **7**
Lehrer, Tom **7**
Nagler, Eric **8**
Penner, Fred **10**
Raffi **8**
Rosenshontz **9**
Sharon, Lois & Bram **6**

Christian Music
4Him **23**
Anointed **21**
Ashton, Susan **17**
Audio Adrenaline **22**
Avalon **26**
Champion, Eric **21**
Chapman, Steven Curtis **15**
dc Talk **18**
Duncan, Bryan **19**
Eskelin, Ian **19**
Grant, Amy **7**
Jars of Clay **20**
Joy Electric **26**
Keaggy, Phil **26**
King's X **7**
Newsboys, The **24**
Paris, Twila **16**
Patti, Sandi **7**
Petra **3**
Point of Grace **21**
Rice, Chris **25**
Sixpence None the Richer **26**
Smith, Michael W. **11**
St. James, Rebecca **26**
Stryper **2**
Taylor, Steve **26**
Waters, Ethel **11**

Clarinet
Adams, John **8**
Bechet, Sidney **17**
Braxton, Anthony **12**
Brötzmann, Peter **26**
Byron, Don **22**
Fountain, Pete **7**
Goodman, Benny **4**
Herman, Woody **12**
Russell, Pee Wee **25**
Shaw, Artie **8**
Stoltzman, Richard **24**
Vandermark, Ken **28**

Classical
Ameling, Elly **24**
Anderson, June **27**
Anderson, Marian **8**

Argerich, Martha **27**
Arrau, Claudio **1**
Austral, Florence **26**
Baker, Janet **14**
Beecham, Thomas **27**
Beltrán, Tito **28**
Bernstein, Leonard **2**
Boulez, Pierre **26**
Boyd, Liona **7**
Bream, Julian **9**
Britten, Benjamin **15**
Bronfman, Yefim **6**
Canadian Brass, The **4**
Carter, Ron **14**
Casals, Pablo **9**
Chang, Sarah **7**
Church, Charlotte **28**
Clayderman, Richard **1**
Cliburn, Van **13**
Copland, Aaron **2**
Davis, Anthony **17**
Davis, Chip **4**
Davis, Colin **27**
DuPré, Jacqueline **26**
Dvorak, Antonin **25**
Fiedler, Arthur **6**
Fleming, Renee **24**
Galway, James **3**
Gardiner, John Eliot **26**
Gingold, Josef **6**
Gould, Glenn **9**
Gould, Morton **16**
Hampson, Thomas **12**
Harrell, Lynn **3**
Hayes, Roland **13**
Hendricks, Barbara **10**
Herrmann, Bernard **14**
Hinderas, Natalie **12**
Horne, Marilyn **9**
Horowitz, Vladimir **1**
Jarrett, Keith **1**
Kennedy, Nigel **8**
Kissin, Evgeny **6**
Kronos Quartet **5**
Kunzel, Erich **17**
Lemper, Ute **14**
Levine, James **8**
Liberace **9**
Ma, Yo Yo **24**
Earlier sketch in CM **2**
Marsalis, Wynton **6**
Mascagni, Pietro **25**
Masur, Kurt **11**
McNair, Sylvia **15**
McPartland, Marian **15**
Mehta, Zubin **11**
Menuhin, Yehudi **11**
Midori **7**
Mutter, Anne-Sophie **23**
Nyman, Michael **15**
Ott, David **2**
Parkening, Christopher **7**
Pavarotti, Luciano **20**
Earlier sketch in CM **1**
Perahia, Murray **10**
Perlman, Itzhak **2**
Phillips, Harvey **3**
Pires, Maria João **26**
Quasthoff, Thomas **26**
Rampal, Jean-Pierre **6**
Rangell, Andrew **24**
Rieu, André **26**
Rostropovich, Mstislav **17**
Rota, Nino **13**
Rubinstein, Arthur **11**
Salerno-Sonnenberg, Nadja **3**
Salonen, Esa-Pekka **16**
Schickele, Peter **5**
Schuman, William **10**
Segovia, Andres **6**
Shankar, Ravi **9**
Solti, Georg **13**
Stern, Isaac **7**
Stoltzman, Richard **24**
Sutherland, Joan **13**
Takemitsu, Toru **6**
Temirkanov, Yuri **26**
Thibaudet, Jean-Yves **24**
Tilson Thomas, Michael **24**
Toscanini, Arturo **14**
Upshaw, Dawn **9**
Vanessa-Mae **26**
Vienna Choir Boys **23**
Volodos, Arcadi **28**
von Karajan, Herbert **1**
Weill, Kurt **12**
Wilson, Ransom **5**
Yamashita, Kazuhito **4**
York, Andrew **15**
Zukerman, Pinchas **4**

Composers

Adams, John **8**
Adamson, Barry **28**
Allen, Geri **10**
Alpert, Herb **11**
Anderson, Wessell **23**
Anka, Paul **2**
Arlen, Harold **27**
Atkins, Chet **5**
Bacharach, Burt **20**
Earlier sketch in CM **1**
Badalamenti, Angelo **17**
Beiderbecke, Bix **16**
Benson, George **9**
Berlin, Irving **8**
Bernstein, Leonard **2**
Blackman, Cindy **15**
Blegvad, Peter **28**
Bley, Carla **8**
Bley, Paul **14**
Boulez, Pierre **26**
Braxton, Anthony **12**
Brickman, Jim **22**
Britten, Benjamin **15**
Brubeck, Dave **8**
Burrell, Kenny **11**
Byrne, David **8**
Also see Talking Heads
Byron, Don **22**
Cage, John **8**
Cale, John **9**
Casals, Pablo **9**
Clarke, Stanley **3**
Coleman, Ornette **5**
Cooder, Ry **2**
Cooney, Rory **6**
Copeland, Stewart **14**
Also see Police, The **20**
Copland, Aaron **2**
Crouch, Andraé **9**
Curtis, King **17**
Davis, Anthony **17**
Davis, Chip **4**
Davis, Miles **1**
de Grassi, Alex **6**
Dorsey, Thomas A. **11**
Dvorak, Antonin **25**
Elfman, Danny **9**
Ellington, Duke **2**
Eno, Brian **8**
Enya **6**
Esquivel, Juan **17**
Evans, Bill **17**
Evans, Gil **17**
Fahey, John **17**
Foster, David **13**
Frisell, Bill **15**
Frith, Fred **19**
Galás, Diamanda **16**
Garner, Erroll **25**
Gillespie, Dizzy **6**
Glass, Philip **1**
Golson, Benny **21**
Gould, Glenn **9**
Gould, Morton **16**
Green, Benny **17**
Grusin, Dave **7**
Guaraldi, Vince **3**
Hamlisch, Marvin **1**
Hammer, Jan **21**
Hancock, Herbie **25**
Earlier sketch in CM **8**
Handy, W. C. **7**
Hargrove, Roy **15**
Harris, Eddie **15**
Hartke, Stephen **5**
Henderson, Fletcher **16**
Herrmann, Bernard **14**
Hunter, Alberta **7**
Ibrahim, Abdullah **24**
Isham, Mark **14**
Jacquet, Illinois **17**
Jarre, Jean-Michel **2**
Jarrett, Keith **1**
Johnson, James P. **16**
Jones, Hank **15**
Jones, Howard **26**
Jones, Quincy **20**
Earlier sketch in CM **2**
Joplin, Scott **10**
Jordan, Stanley **1**
Kang, Eyvind **28**
Kenny G **14**
Kenton, Stan **21**
Kern, Jerome **13**
Kitaro **1**
Kottke, Leo **13**
Lacy, Steve **23**
Lateef, Yusef **16**
Lee, Peggy **8**
Legg, Adrian **17**
Lewis, Ramsey **14**
Lincoln, Abbey **9**
Lloyd, Charles **22**
Lloyd Webber, Andrew **6**
Loesser, Frank **19**
Mancini, Henry **20**
Earlier sketch in CM **1**
Mandel, Johnny **28**
Marsalis, Branford **10**
Marsalis, Ellis **13**
Martino, Pat **17**
Mascagni, Pietro **25**
Masekela, Hugh **7**
McBride, Christian **17**
McPartland, Marian **15**
Menken, Alan **10**
Metheny, Pat **26**
Earlier sketch in CM **2**
Miles, Ron **22**
Mingus, Charles **9**

Moby **27**
Earlier sketch in CM **17**
Monk, Meredith **1**
Monk, Thelonious **6**
Montenegro, Hugo **18**
Morricone, Ennio **15**
Morton, Jelly Roll **7**
Mulligan, Gerry **16**
Nascimento, Milton **6**
Newman, Randy **4**
Nyman, Michael **15**
Oldfield, Mike **18**
Orff, Carl **21**
Osby, Greg **21**
Ott, David **2**
Palmieri, Eddie **15**
Parker, Charlie **5**
Parks, Van Dyke **17**
Perez, Danilo **25**
Peterson, Oscar **11**
Piazzolla, Astor **18**
Ponty, Jean-Luc **8**
Porter, Cole **10**
Post, Mike **21**
Previn, André **15**
Puente, Tito **14**
Pullen, Don **16**
Reich, Steve **8**
Reinhardt, Django **7**
Ritenour, Lee **7**
Roach, Max **12**
Rollins, Sonny **7**
Rota, Nino **13**
Sakamoto, Ryuichi **19**
Salonen, Esa-Pekka **16**
Sanders, Pharoah **16**
Satie, Erik **25**
Satriani, Joe **4**
Schickele, Peter **5**
Schuman, William **10**
Shankar, Ravi **9**
Shaw, Artie **8**
Shearing, George **28**
Shorter, Wayne **5**
Silver, Horace **19**
Smith, Tommy **28**
Solal, Martial **4**
Sondheim, Stephen **8**
Sousa, John Philip **10**
Story, Liz **2**
Strauss, Richard **25**
Stravinsky, Igor **21**
Strayhorn, Billy **13**
Styne, Jule **21**
Summers, Andy **3**
Also see Police, The
Sun Ra **27**
Earlier sketch in CM **5**
Sylvian, David **27**
Takemitsu, Toru **6**
Talbot, John Michael **6**
Tatum, Art **17**
Taylor, Billy **13**
Taylor, Cecil **9**
Tesh, John **20**
Thielemans, Toots **13**
Threadgill, Henry **9**
Tilson Thomas, Michael **24**
Towner, Ralph **22**
Tyner, McCoy **7**
Vangelis **21**
Wakeman, Rick **27**
Also see Yes
Was, Don **21**
Also see Was (Not Was)
Washington, Grover, Jr. **5**
Weill, Kurt **12**
Weston, Randy **15**
Whelan, Bill **20**
Whiteman, Paul **17**
Williams, John **28**
Earlier sketch in CM **9**
Wilson, Cassandra **26**
Earlier sketch in CM **12**
Winston, George **9**
Winter, Paul **10**
Worrell, Bernie **11**
Yanni **11**
Yeston, Maury **22**
York, Andrew **15**
Young, La Monte **16**
Zappa, Frank **17**
Earlier sketch in CM **1**
Zimmerman, Udo **5**
Zorn, John **15**

Conductors

Bacharach, Burt **20**
Earlier sketch CM **1**
Beecham, Thomas **27**
Bernstein, Leonard **2**
Boulez, Pierre **26**
Britten, Benjamin **15**
Casals, Pablo **9**
Copland, Aaron **2**
Davies, Dennis Russell **24**
Davis, Colin **27**
Domingo, Placido **20**
Earlier sketch in CM **1**
Evans, Gil **17**
Fiedler, Arthur **6**
Gardiner, John Eliot **26**
Gould, Morton **16**
Herrmann, Bernard **14**
Ibrahim, Abdullah **24**
Jarrett, Keith **1**
Jones, Hank **15**
Kunzel, Erich **17**
Levine, James **8**
Mancini, Henry **20**
Earlier sketch in CM **1**
Mandel, Johnny **28**
Marriner, Neville **7**
Mascagni, Pietro **25**
Masur, Kurt **11**
Mehta, Zubin **11**
Menuhin, Yehudi **11**
Nero, Peter **19**
Previn, André **15**
Rampal, Jean-Pierre **6**
Rieu, André **26**
Rostropovich, Mstislav **17**
Salonen, Esa-Pekka **16**
Schickele, Peter **5**
Solti, Georg **13**
Strauss, Richard
Temirkanov, Yuri **26**
Tilson Thomas, Michael **24**
Toscanini, Arturo **14**
Valdes, Chuco **25**
von Karajan, Herbert **1**
Welk, Lawrence **13**
Williams, John **28**
Earlier sketch in CM **9**
Zukerman, Pinchas **4**

Contemporary Dance Music

Abdul, Paula **3**
Aphex Twin **14**
Bee Gees, The **3**
B-52's, The **4**
Brown, Bobby **4**
Brown, James **2**
C + C Music Factory **16**
Cherry, Neneh **4**
Clinton, George **7**
Craig, Carl **19**
Deee-lite **9**
De La Soul **7**
Depeche Mode **5**
Earth, Wind and Fire **12**
English Beat, The **9**
En Vogue **10**
Erasure **11**
Eurythmics **6**
Exposé **4**
Fox, Samantha **3**
Fun Lovin' Criminals **20**
Gang of Four **8**
Hammer, M.C. **5**
Harry, Deborah **4**
Also see Blondie
Ice-T **7**
Idol, Billy **3**
Jackson, Janet **16**
Earlier sketch in CM **3**
Jackson, Michael **17**
Earlier sketch in CM **1**
Also see Jacksons, The
James, Rick **2**
Jones, Grace **9**
Madonna **16**
Earlier sketch in CM **4**
Massive Attack **17**
Moby **27**
Earlier sketch in CM **17**
M People **15**
New Order **11**
Orbital **20**
Peniston, CeCe **15**
Pet Shop Boys **5**
Pizzicato Five **18**
Portishead **22**
Prince **14**
Earlier sketch in CM **1**
Queen Latifah **24**
Earlier sketch in CM **6**
Rodgers, Nile **8**
Salt-N-Pepa **6**
Shadow, DJ **19**
Shamen, The **23**
Simmons, Russell **7**
Soul II Soul **17**
Sugar Ray **22**
Summer, Donna **12**
Technotronic **5**
TLC **15**
Tricky **18**
2 Unlimited **18**
Vasquez, Junior **16**
Village People, The **7**
Was (Not Was) **6**
Waters, Crystal **15**
Young M.C. **4**

Contemporary Instrumental/New Age

Ackerman, Will **3**
Arkenstone, David **20**
Clinton, George **7**
Collins, Bootsy **8**
Davis, Chip **4**
De Gaia, Banco **27**
de Grassi, Alex **6**

Enigma **14**
Enya **6**
Esquivel, Juan **17**
Hedges, Michael **3**
Isham, Mark **14**
Jarre, Jean-Michel **2**
Kitaro **1**
Kronos Quartet **5**
Legg, Adrian **17**
Mogwai **27**
Roth, Gabrielle **26**
Sete, Bola **26**
Story, Liz **2**
Summers, Andy **3**
Also see Police, The
Tangerine Dream **12**
Tesh, John **20**
Winston, George **9**
Winter, Paul **10**
Yanni **11**

Cornet

Armstrong, Louis **4**
Beiderbecke, Bix **16**
Cherry, Don **10**
Handy, W. C. **7**
Oliver, King **15**
Vaché, Jr., Warren **22**

Country

Acuff, Roy **2**
Akins, Rhett **22**
Alabama **21**
Earlier sketch in CM **1**
Anderson, John **5**
Arnold, Eddy **10**
Asleep at the Wheel **5**
Atkins, Chet **26**
Atkins, Chet **5**
Auldridge, Mike **4**
Autry, Gene **25**
Earlier sketch in CM **12**
Barnett, Mandy **26**
Bellamy Brothers, The **13**
Berg, Matraca **16**
Berry, John **17**
Black, Clint **5**
BlackHawk **21**
Blue Rodeo **18**
Boggs, Dock **25**
Bogguss, Suzy **11**
Bonamy, James **21**
Bond, Johnny **28**
Boone, Pat **13**
Boy Howdy **21**
Brandt, Paul **22**
Brannon, Kippi **20**
Brooks & Dunn **25**
Earlier sketch in CM **12**
Brooks, Garth **25**
Earlier sketch in CM **8**
Brown, Junior **15**
Brown, Marty **14**
Brown, Tony **14**
Buffett, Jimmy **4**
Byrds, The **8**
Cale, J. J. **16**
Campbell, Glen **2**
Carter, Carlene **8**
Carter, Deana **25**
Carter Family, The **3**
Cash, Johnny **17**
Earlier sketch in CM **1**
Cash, June Carter **6**
Cash, Rosanne **2**
Chapin Carpenter, Mary **25**
Earlier sketch in CM **6**
Chesney, Kenny **20**
Chesnutt, Mark **13**
Clark, Guy **17**
Clark, Roy **1**
Clark, Terri **19**
Clements, Vassar **18**
Cline, Patsy **5**
Coe, David Allan **4**
Collie, Mark **15**
Confederate Railroad **23**
Cooder, Ry **2**
Cowboy Junkies, The **4**
Crawford, Randy **25**
Crowe, J. D. **5**
Crowell, Rodney **8**
Cyrus, Billy Ray **11**
Daniels, Charlie **6**
Davis, Linda **21**
Davis, Skeeter **15**
Dean, Billy **19**
DeMent, Iris **13**
Denver, John **22**
Earlier sketch in CM **1**
Desert Rose Band, The **4**
Diamond Rio **11**
Dickens, Little Jimmy **7**
Diffie, Joe **27**
Earlier sketch CM **10**
Dixie Chicks **26**
Dylan, Bob **21**
Earlier sketch in CM **3**
Earle, Steve **16**
Estes, John **25**
Evans, Sara **27**
Flatt, Lester **3**
Flores, Rosie **16**
Ford, Tennessee Ernie **3**
Foster, Radney **16**
Frizzell, Lefty **10**
Gayle, Crystal **1**
Germano, Lisa **18**
Gill, Vince **7**
Gilley, Mickey **7**
Gilmore, Jimmie Dale **11**
Gordy, Jr., Emory **17**
Greenwood, Lee **12**
Griffith, Nanci **3**
Haggard, Merle **2**
Hall, Tom T. **26**
Earlier sketch in CM **4**
Harris, Emmylou **4**
Hartford, John **1**
Hay, George D. **3**
Herndon, Ty **20**
Hiatt, John **8**
Highway 101 **4**
Hill, Faith **18**
Hinojosa, Tish **13**
Howard, Harlan **15**
Jackson, Alan **25**
Earlier sketch in CM **7**
Jennings, Waylon **4**
Jones, George **4**
Judds, The **2**
Keith, Toby **17**
Kentucky Headhunters, The **5**
Kershaw, Sammy **15**
Ketchum, Hal **14**
Kristofferson, Kris **4**
Lamb, Barbara **19**
Lane, Fred **28**
Lang, kd **25**
Earlier sketch in CM **4**
Lawrence, Tracy **11**
LeDoux, Chris **12**
Lee, Brenda **5**
Little Feat **4**
Little Texas **14**
Lonestar **27**
Louvin Brothers, The **12**
Loveless, Patty **21**
Earlier sketch in CM **5**
Lovett, Lyle **28**
Earlier sketch in CM **5**
Lynn, Loretta **2**
Lynne, Shelby **5**
Mandrell, Barbara **4**
Mattea, Kathy **5**
Mavericks, The **15**
McBride, Martina **14**
McCann, Lila **26**
McClinton, Delbert **14**
McCoy, Neal **15**
McCready, Mindy **22**
McEntire, Reba **11**
McGraw, Tim **17**
Messina, Jo Dee **26**
Miller, Roger **4**
Milsap, Ronnie **2**
Moffatt, Katy **18**
Monroe, Bill **1**
Montgomery, John Michael **14**
Morgan, Lorrie **10**
Murphey, Michael Martin **9**
Murray, Anne **4**
Nelson, Willie **11**
Earlier sketch in CM **1**
Newton-John, Olivia **8**
Nitty Gritty Dirt Band, The **6**
O'Connor, Mark **1**
Oak Ridge Boys, The **7**
Oslin, K. T. **3**
Owens, Buck **2**
Parnell, Lee Roy **15**
Parsons, Gram **7**
Also see Byrds, The
Parton, Dolly **24**
Earlier sketch in CM **2**
Pearl, Minnie **3**
Pierce, Webb **15**
Price, Ray **11**
Pride, Charley **4**
Rabbitt, Eddie **24**
Earlier sketch in CM **5**
Raitt, Bonnie **3**
Ray Condo and His Ricochets **26**
Raye, Collin **16**
Reeves, Jim **10**
Restless Heart **12**
Rich, Charlie **3**
Richey, Kim **20**
Ricochet **23**
Rimes, LeAnn **19**
Robbins, Marty **9**
Rodgers, Jimmie **3**
Rogers, Kenny **1**
Rogers, Roy **24**
Earlier sketch in CM **9**
Sawyer Brown **27**
Earlier sketch in CM **13**
Scruggs, Earl **3**
Scud Mountain Boys **21**
Seals, Dan **9**
Shenandoah **17**
Skaggs, Ricky **5**

Sonnier, Jo-El **10**
Statler Brothers, The **8**
Stevens, Ray **7**
Stone, Doug **10**
Strait, George **5**
Stuart, Marty **9**
Sweethearts of the Rodeo **12**
Texas Tornados, The **8**
Tillis, Mel **7**
Tillis, Pam **25**
  Earlier sketch in CM **8**
Tippin, Aaron **12**
Travis, Merle **14**
Travis, Randy **9**
Tritt, Travis **7**
Tubb, Ernest **4**
Tucker, Tanya **3**
Twain, Shania **17**
Twitty, Conway **6**
Van Shelton, Ricky **5**
Van Zandt, Townes **13**
Wagoner, Porter **13**
Walker, Clay **20**
Walker, Jerry Jeff **13**
Wariner, Steve **18**
Watson, Doc **2**
Wells, Kitty **6**
West, Dottie **8**
White, Lari **15**
Whitley, Keith **7**
Williams, Don **4**
Williams, Hank, Jr. **1**
Williams, Hank, Sr. **4**
Williams, Lucinda **24**
  Earlier sketch in CM **10**
Willis, Kelly **12**
Wills, Bob **6**
Wills, Mark **27**
Wynette, Tammy **24**
  Earlier sketch in CM **2**
Wynonna **11**
  Also see Judds, The
Yearwood, Trisha **25**
  Earlier sketch in CM **10**
Yoakam, Dwight **21**
  Earlier sketch in CM **1**
Young, Faron **7**

Dobro
Auldridge, Mike **4**
  Also see Country Gentlemen, The
  Also see Seldom Scene, The
Knopfler, Mark **25**
  Earlier sketch in CM **3**
  Also see Dire Straits
Whitley, Chris **16**

Drums
Aronoff, Kenny **21**
  See **Percussion**
Colaiuta, Vinnie **23**
Parker, Leon **27**
Starr, Ringo **24**

Dulcimer
Ritchie, Jean **4**

Fiddle
MacIsaac, Ashley **21**
  See **Violin**

Film Scores
Anka, Paul **2**
Arlen, Harold **27**
Bacharach, Burt **20**
  Earlier sketch in CM **1**
Badalamenti, Angelo **17**
Berlin, Irving **8**
Bernstein, Leonard **2**
Blanchard, Terence **13**
Britten, Benjamin **15**
Byrne, David **8**
  Also see Talking Heads
Cahn, Sammy **11**
Cliff, Jimmy **8**
Copeland, Stewart **14**
  Also see Police, The
Copland, Aaron **2**
Crouch, Andraé **9**
Dibango, Manu **14**
Dolby, Thomas **10**
Donovan **9**
Eddy, Duane **9**
Elfman, Danny **9**
Ellington, Duke **2**
Ferguson, Maynard **7**
Froom, Mitchell **15**
Gabriel, Peter **16**
  Earlier sketch in CM **2**
  Also see Genesis
Galás, Diamanda **16**
Gershwin, George and Ira **11**
Gould, Glenn **9**
Grusin, Dave **7**
Guaraldi, Vince **3**
Hamlisch, Marvin **1**
Hancock, Herbie **25**
  Earlier sketch in CM **8**
Harrison, George **2**
Hayes, Isaac **10**
Hedges, Michael **3**
Herrmann, Bernard **14**
Isham, Mark **14**
Jones, Quincy **20**
  Earlier sketch in CM **2**
Knopfler, Mark **25**
  Earlier sketch in CM **3**
  Also see Dire Straits
Lennon, John **9**
  Also see Beatles, The
Lerner and Loewe **13**
Loesser, Frank **19**
Mancini, Henry **20**
  Earlier sketch in CM **1**
Marsalis, Branford **10**
Mayfield, Curtis **8**
McCartney, Paul **4**
  Also see Beatles, The
Menken, Alan **10**
Mercer, Johnny **13**
Metheny, Pat **26**
  Earlier sketch in CM **2**
Montenegro, Hugo **18**
Morricone, Ennio **15**
Nascimento, Milton **6**
Newman, Randy **27**
  Earlier sketch in CM **4**
Nilsson **10**
Nyman, Michael **15**
Parks, Van Dyke **17**
Peterson, Oscar **11**
Porter, Cole **10**
Previn, André **15**
Reznor, Trent **13**
Richie, Lionel **2**
Robertson, Robbie **2**
Rollins, Sonny **7**
Rota, Nino **13**
Sager, Carole Bayer **5**
Sakamoto, Ryuichi **18**
Schickele, Peter **5**
Shankar, Ravi **9**
Taj Mahal **6**
Waits, Tom **27**
  Earlier sketch in CM **12**
  Earlier sketch in CM **1**
Weill, Kurt **12**
Williams, John **28**
  Earlier sketch in CM **9**
Williams, Paul **26**
Williams, Paul **5**
Willner, Hal **10**
Young, Neil **15**
  Earlier sketch in CM **2**

Flugelhorn
Sandoval, Arturo **15**
Mangione, Chuck **23**

Flute
Galway, James **3**
Jethro Tull **8**
Lateef, Yusef **16**
Mangione, Chuck **23**
Mann, Herbie **16**
Najee **21**
Nakai, R. Carlos **24**
Rampal, Jean-Pierre **6**
Ulmer, James Blood **13**
Wilson, Ransom **5**

Folk/Traditional
Altan **18**
America **16**
Anonymous 4 **23**
Arnaz, Desi **8**
Axton, Hoyt **28**
Baez, Joan **1**
Belafonte, Harry **8**
Belle and Sebastian **28**
Black, Mary **15**
Blades, Ruben **2**
Bloom, Luka **14**
Blue Rodeo **18**
Boggs, Dock **25**
Brady, Paul **8**
Bragg, Billy **7**
Bromberg, David **18**
Buckley, Tim **14**
Buffalo Springfield **24**
Bulgarian State Female Vocal Choir, The **10**
Byrds, The **8**
Campbell, Sarah Elizabeth **23**
Caravan **24**
Carter Family, The **3**
Chandra, Sheila **16**
Chapin, Harry **6**
Chapman, Tracy **20**
  Earlier sketch in CM **4**
Chenille Sisters, The **16**
Cherry, Don **10**
Chesnutt, Vic **28**
Chieftains, The **7**
Childs, Toni **2**
Clannad **23**
Clegg, Johnny **8**
Cockburn, Bruce **8**
Cohen, Leonard **3**
Collins, Judy **4**
Colvin, Shawn **11**
Cotten, Elizabeth **16**
Crosby, David **3**
  Also see Byrds, The

Cruz, Celia **22**
Earlier sketch in CM **10**
de Lucia, Paco **1**
DeMent, Iris **13**
Donovan **9**
Dr. John **7**
Drake, Nick **17**
Driftwood, Jimmy **25**
Dylan, Bob **21**
Earlier sketch in CM **3**
Elliot, Cass **5**
Enya **6**
Estefan, Gloria **15**
Earlier sketch in CM **2**
Fahey, John **17**
Fairport Convention **22**
Feliciano, José **10**
Galway, James **3**
Germano, Lisa **18**
Gibson, Bob **23**
Gilmore, Jimmie Dale **11**
Gipsy Kings, The **8**
Gorka, John **18**
Griffin, Patty **24**
Griffith, Nanci **3**
Grisman, David **17**
Guthrie, Arlo **6**
Guthrie, Woody **2**
Hakmoun, Hassan **15**
Hardin, Tim **18**
Harding, John Wesley **6**
Hartford, John **1**
Havens, Richie **11**
Henry, Joe **18**
Hinojosa, Tish **13**
Ian and Sylvia **18**
Ian, Janis **24**
Earlier sketch in CM **5**
Iglesias, Julio **20**
Earlier sketch in CM **2**
Incredible String Band **23**
Indigo Girls **20**
Earlier sketch in CM **3**
Ives, Burl **12**
Khan, Nusrat Fateh Ali **13**
Kingston Trio, The **9**
Klezmatics, The **18**
Kottke, Leo **13**
Kuti, Fela **7**
Ladysmith Black Mambazo **1**
Larkin, Patty **9**
Lavin, Christine **6**
Leadbelly **6**
Lightfoot, Gordon **3**
Los Lobos **2**
Makeba, Miriam **8**
Mamas and the Papas **21**
Masekela, Hugh **7**
McKennitt, Loreena **24**
McLean, Don **7**
Melanie **12**
Mitchell, Joni **17**
Earlier sketch in CM **2**
Moffatt, Katy **18**
Morrison, Van **24**
Earlier sketch in CM **3**
Morrissey, Bill **12**
N'Dour, Youssou **6**
Nascimento, Milton **6**
Near, Holly **1**
O'Connor, Sinead **3**
Ochs, Phil **7**
Odetta **7**
Parsons, Gram **7**
Also see Byrds, The
Paxton, Tom **5**
Pentangle **18**
Peter, Paul & Mary **4**
Pogues, The **6**
Prine, John **7**
Proclaimers, The **13**
Rankins, The **24**
Redpath, Jean **1**
Ritchie, Jean, **4**
Roches, The **18**
Rodgers, Jimmie **3**
Russell, Tom **26**
Sainte-Marie, Buffy **11**
Santana, Carlos **19**
Earlier sketch in CM **1**
Seeger, Peggy **25**
Seeger, Pete **4**
Also see Weavers, The
Selena **16**
Shankar, Ravi **9**
Simon and Garfunkel **24**
Simon, Paul **16**
Earlier sketch in CM **1**
Also see Simon and Garfunkel
Snow, Pheobe **4**
Steeleye Span **19**
Story, The **13**
Sweet Honey in the Rock **26**
Earlier sketch in CM **1**
Taj Mahal **6**
Thompson, Richard **7**
Tikaram, Tanita **9**
Toure, Ali Farka **18**
Van Ronk, Dave **12**
Van Zandt, Townes **13**
Vega, Suzanne **3**
Wainwright III, Loudon **11**
Walker, Jerry Jeff **13**
Waterboys, The **27**
Watson, Doc **2**
Weavers, The **8**
Whitman, Slim **19**

Funk
Avery, Teodross **23**
Bambaataa, Afrika **13**
Brand New Heavies, The **14**
Brown, James **2**
Burdon, Eric **14**
Also see War
Also see Animals
Citizen King **27**
Clinton, George **7**
Collins, Bootsy **8**
Fishbone **7**
Front 242 **19**
Gang of Four **8**
Jackson, Janet **16**
Earlier sketch in CM **3**
Jamiroquai **21**
Joy Electric **26**
Khan, Chaka **19**
Earlier sketch in CM **9**
Mayfield, Curtis **8**
Meters, The **14**
Ohio Players **16**
Parker, Maceo **7**
Prince **14**
Earlier sketch in CM **1**
Red Hot Chili Peppers, The **7**
Sly and the Family Stone **24**
Stone, Sly **8**
Also see Sly and the Family Stone
Toussaint, Allen **11**
Worrell, Bernie **11**
Wu-Tang Clan **19**

Fusion
Anderson, Ray **7**
Avery, Teodross **23**
Beck, Jeff **4**
Also see Yardbirds, The
Clarke, Stanley **3**
Coleman, Ornette **5**
Corea, Chick **6**
Davis, Miles **1**
Fishbone **7**
Hancock, Herbie **25**
Earlier sketch in CM **8**
Harris, Eddie **15**
Johnson, Eric **19**
Lewis, Ramsey **14**
Mahavishnu Orchestra **19**
McLaughlin, John **12**
Metheny, Pat **26**
Earlier sketch in CM **2**
O'Connor, Mark **1**
Ponty, Jean-Luc **8**
Reid, Vernon **2**
Ritenour, Lee **7**
Shorter, Wayne **5**
Summers, Andy **3**
Also see Police, The
Washington, Grover, Jr. **5**

Gospel
4Him **23**
Anderson, Marian **8**
Armstrong, Vanessa Bell **24**
Baylor, Helen **20**
Boone, Pat **13**
Brown, James **2**
Caesar, Shirley **17**
Carter Family, The **3**
Charles, Ray **24**
Earlier sketch in CM **1**
Cleveland, James **1**
Cooke, Sam **1**
Also see Soul Stirrers, The
Crouch, Andraé **9**
Dorsey, Thomas A. **11**
Five Blind Boys of Alabama **12**
Ford, Tennessee Ernie **3**
Franklin, Aretha **17**
Earlier sketch in CM **2**
Franklin, Kirk **22**
Golden Gate Quartet **25**
Greater Vision **26**
Green, Al **9**
Hawkins, Tramaine **17**
Houston, Cissy **26**
Earlier sketch in CM **6**
Jackson, Mahalia **8**
Johnson, Blind Willie **26**
Kee, John P. **15**
Knight, Gladys **1**
Little Richard **1**
Louvin Brothers, The **12**
Mighty Clouds of Joy, The **17**
Oak Ridge Boys, The **7**
Oakland Interfaith Gospel Choir **26**
Paris, Twila **16**
Pickett, Wilson **10**
Presley, Elvis **1**
Redding, Otis **5**

Reese, Della **13**
Robbins, Marty **9**
Smith, Michael W. **11**
Soul Stirrers, The **11**
Sounds of Blackness **13**
Staples, Mavis **13**
Staples, Pops **11**
Sweet Honey In The Rock **26**
Earlier sketch in CM **1**
Take 6 **6**
Waters, Ethel **11**
Watson, Doc **2**
Williams, Deniece **1**
Williams, Marion **15**
Winans, The **12**
Womack, Bobby **5**

Guitar
Abercrombie, John **25**
Ackerman, Will **3**
Adamson, Barry **28**
Adé, King Sunny **18**
Allen, Daevid **28**
Allison, Luther **21**
Alvin, Dave **17**
Atkins, Chet **26**
Earlier sketch in CM **5**
Autry, Gene **25**
Earlier sketch in CM **12**
Axton, Hoyt **28**
Barnes, Roosevelt "Booba" **23**
Beck **18**
Beck, Jeff **4**
Also see Yardbirds, The
Belew, Adrian **5**
Benson, George **9**
Berry, Chuck **1**
Berry, John **17**
Bishop, Jeb **28**
Blegvad, Peter **28**
Block, Rory **18**
Bloom, Luka **14**
Bond, Johnny **28**
Boyd, Liona **7**
Bream, Julian **9**
Bromberg, David **18**
Brooks, Garth **25**
Earlier sketch in CM **8**
Brötzmann, Caspar **27**
Brown, Junior **15**
Buckingham, Lindsey **8**
Also see Fleetwood Mac
Burrell, Kenny **11**
Campbell, Glen **2**
Carter, Deana **25**
Chapin-Carpenter, Mary **25**
Earlier sketch in CM **6**
Chaquico, Craig **23**
Chesney, Kenny **20**
Chesnutt, Mark **13**
Chesnutt, Vic **28**
Christian, Charlie **11**
Clapton, Eric **11**
Earlier sketch in CM **1**
Also see Cream
Also see Yardbirds, The
Clark, Roy **1**
Cockburn, Bruce **8**
Collie, Mark **15**
Collins, Albert **19**
Earlier sketch in CM **4**
Cooder, Ry **2**
Cotten, Elizabeth **16**
Cray, Robert **8**
Cropper, Steve **12**
Dahl, Jeff **28**
Dale, Dick **13**
Daniels, Charlie **6**
Dave, Edmunds **28**
Davis, Reverend Gary **18**
de Grassi, Alex **6**
de Lucia, Paco **1**
Del Rubio Triplets **21**
Denver, John **22**
Earlier sketch in CM **1**
Di Meola, Al **12**
Dickens, Little Jimmy **7**
Diddley, Bo **3**
DiFranco, Ani **17**
Drake, Nick **17**
Earl, Ronnie **5**
Also see Roomful of Blues
Eddy, Duane **9**
Ellis, Herb **18**
Emmanuel, Tommy **21**
Etheridge, Melissa **16**
Earlier sketch in CM **4**
Fahey, John **17**
Fankhauser,, Merrell **24**
Feliciano, José **10**
Fender, Leo **10**
Flatt, Lester **3**
Flores, Rosie **16**
Ford, Lita **9**
Frampton, Peter **3**
Fripp, Robert **9**
Frisell, Bill **15**
Frith, Fred **19**
Fuller, Blind Boy **20**
Fulson, Lowell **20**
Garcia, Jerry **4**
Also see Grateful Dead, The
Gatton, Danny **16**
Gibson, Bob **23**
Gil, Gilberto **26**
Gill, Vince **7**
Gorka, John **18**
Green, Grant **14**
Guy, Buddy **4**
Hackett, Bobby **21**
Haley, Bill **6**
Hall, Tom T. **26**
Hardin, Tim **18**
Harper, Ben **17**
Harrison, George **2**
Hart, Alvin Youngblood **27**
Hatfield, Juliana **12**
Also see Lemonheads, The
Havens, Richie **11**
Healey, Jeff **4**
Hedges, Michael **3**
Hendrix, Jimi **2**
Hepcat, Harry **23**
Hitchcock, Robyn **9**
Holly, Buddy **1**
Hooker, John Lee **26**
Earlier sketch in CM **1**
Hopkins, Lightnin' **13**
Howlin' Wolf **6**
Hunter, Charlie **24**
Ives, Burl **12**
Jackson, Alan **25**
Earlier sketch in CM **7**
James, Elmore **8**
James, Skip **24**
Jean, Wyclef **22**
Jefferson, Blind Lemon **18**
Jewel **25**
Jobim, Antonio Carlos **19**
Johnson, Blind Willie **26**
Johnson, Eric **19**
Johnson, Lonnie **17**
Johnson, Robert **6**
Jordan, Stanley **1**
Keaggy, Phil **26**
Keith, Toby **17**
King, Albert **2**
King, B.B. **24**
Earlier sketch in CM **1**
King, Freddy **17**
Klugh, Earl **10**
Knopfler, Mark **25**
Earlier sketch in CM **3**
Also see Dire Straits
Kottke, Leo **13**
Landreth, Sonny **16**
Lang, Jonny **27**
Larkin, Patty **9**
Leadbelly **6**
Legg, Adrian **17**
Lennon, John **9**
Also see Beatles, The
Lindley, David **2**
Lockwood, Robert, Jr. **10**
Loeb, Lisa **19**
Lofgren, Nils **25**
Lovett, Lyle **28**
Earlier sketch in CM **5**
Malmsteen, Yngwie **24**
Malone, Russell **27**
Martino, Pat **17**
Matthews, Eric **22**
Mayfield, Curtis **8**
McClinton, Delbert **14**
McCoury, Del **15**
McDowell, Mississippi Fred **16**
McLachlan, Sarah **12**
McLaughlin, John **12**
McLean, Dave **24**
McLennan, Grant **21**
McTell, Blind Willie **17**
Metheny, Pat **26**
Earlier sketch in CM **2**
Mitchell, Joni **17**
Earlier sketch in CM **2**
Mo', Keb' **21**
Montgomery, Wes **3**
Morrissey, Bill **12**
Muldaur, Maria **18**
Nugent, Ted **2**
Oldfield, Mike **18**
Owens, Buck **2**
Page, Jimmy **4**
Also see Led Zeppelin
Also see Yardbirds, The
Parkening, Christopher **7**
Parnell, Lee Roy **15**
Pass, Joe **15**
Patton, Charley **11**
Perkins, Carl **9**
Petty, Tom **9**
Also see Tom Petty and the Heartbreakers
Phair, Liz **14**
Phillips, Sam **12**
Powell, Baden, **23**
Prince **14**
Earlier sketch in CM **1**
Raitt, Bonnie **23**
Earlier sketch in CM **1**
Redbone, Leon **19**
Reed, Jimmy **15**
Reid, Vernon **2**
Also see Living Colour

Reinhardt, Django **7**
Richards, Keith **11**
Also see Rolling Stones, The
Richman, Jonathan **12**
Ritenour, Lee **7**
Robbins, Marty **9**
Robertson, Robbie **2**
Robillard, Duke **2**
Rodgers, Nile **8**
Rush, Otis **12**
Sambora, Richie **24**
Also see Bon Jovi
Santana, Carlos **19**
Earlier sketch in CM **1**
Satriani, Joe **4**
Scofield, John **7**
Scruggs, Randy **28**
Segovia, Andres **6**
Sete, Bola **26**
Sexsmith, Ron **27**
Sharrock, Sonny **15**
Shepherd, Kenny Wayne **22**
Shines, Johnny **14**
Simon, Paul **16**
Earlier sketch in CM **1**
Also see Simon and Garfunkel
Skaggs, Ricky **5**
Smith, Elliott **28**
Smog **28**
Springsteen, Bruce **25**
Earlier sketch in CM **6**
Stills, Stephen **5**
Stuart, Marty **9**
Summers, Andy **3**
Also see Police, The
Tampa Red **25**
Thielemans, Toots **13**
Thompson, Richard **7**
Tippin, Aaron **12**
Toure, Ali Farka **18**
Towner, Ralph **22**
Townshend, Pete **1**
Travis, Merle **14**
Trynin, Jen **21**
Tubb, Ernest **4**
Ulmer, James Blood **13**
Vai, Steve **5**
Van Ronk, Dave **12**
Vaughan, Jimmie **24**
Also see Fabulous Thunderbirds, The
Vaughan, Stevie Ray **1**
Wachtel, Waddy **26**
Wagoner, Porter **13**
Waits, Tom **27**
Earlier sketch in CM **12**
Earlier sketch in CM **1**
Walker, Jerry Jeff **13**
Walker, Joe Louis **28**
Walker, T-Bone **5**
Walsh, Joe **5**
Also see Eagles, The
Wariner, Steve **18**
Waters, Muddy **24**
Earlier sketch in CM **4**
Watson, Doc **2**
Weller, Paul **14**
White, Lari **15**
Whitfield, Mark **18**
Whitley, Chris **16**
Whittaker, Hudson **20**
Wilson, Brian **24**
Also see Beach Boys, The
Winston, George **9**
Winter, Johnny **5**
Wiseman, Mac **19**
Wray, Link **17**
Yamashita, Kazuhito **4**
Yoakam, Dwight **21**
Earlier sketch in CM **1**
York, Andrew **15**
Young, Neil **15**
Earlier sketch in CM **2**
Zappa, Frank **17**
Earlier sketch in CM **1**

Harmonica

Barnes, Roosevelt, "Booba" **23**
Dylan, Bob **3**
Guthrie, Woody **2**
Horton, Walter **19**
Lewis, Huey **9**
Little Walter **14**
McClinton, Delbert **14**
Musselwhite, Charlie **13**
Reed, Jimmy **15**
Thielemans, Toots **13**
Waters, Muddy **24**
Earlier sketch in CM **4**
Wells, Junior **17**
Williamson, Sonny Boy **9**
Wonder, Stevie **17**
Earlier sketch in CM **2**
Young, Neil **15**
Earlier sketch in CM **2**

Heavy Metal

AC/DC **4**
Aerosmith **22**
Earlier sketch in CM **1**
Alice in Chains **10**
Anthrax **11**
Black Sabbath **9**
Blue Oyster Cult **16**
Cinderella **16**
Circle Jerks **17**
Danzig **7**
Deep Purple **11**
Def Leppard **3**
Dokken **16**
Faith No More **7**
Fear Factory **27**
Fishbone **7**
Flying Luttenbachers, The **28**
Ford, Lita **9**
Guns n' Roses **2**
Iron Maiden **10**
Judas Priest **10**
Kilgore **24**
King's X **7**
Kiss **25**
Earlier sketch in CM **5**
L7 **12**
Led Zeppelin **1**
Megadeth **9**
Melvins **21**
Metallica **7**
Mötley Crüe **1**
Motörhead **10**
Neurosis **28**
Nugent, Ted **2**
Osbourne, Ozzy **3**
Pantera **13**
Petra **3**
Queensryche **8**
Reid, Vernon **2**
Also see Living Colour
Reznor, Trent **13**
Roth, David Lee **1**
Also see Van Halen
Sepultura **12**
Skinny Puppy **17**
Slayer **10**
Soundgarden **6**
Spinal Tap **8**
Stryper **2**
Suicidal Tendencies **15**
Tool **21**
Type O Negative **27**
Warrant **17**
Wendy O. Williams and The Plasmatics **26**
White Zombie **17**
Whitesnake **5**

Humor

Borge, Victor **19**
Coasters, The **5**
Dr. Demento **23**
Jones, Spike **5**
Lehrer, Tom **7**
Pearl, Minnie **3**
Russell, Mark **6**
Sandler, Adam **19**
Schickele, Peter **5**
Shaffer, Paul **13**
Spinal Tap **8**
Stevens, Ray **7**
Yankovic, "Weird Al" **7**

Inventors

Fender, Leo **10**
Harris, Eddie **15**
Paul, Les **2**
Teagarden, Jack **10**
Theremin, Leon **19**

Jazz

Abercrombie, John **25**
Adderley, Cannonball **15**
Allen, Geri **10**
Allison, Mose **17**
Anderson, Ray **7**
Armstrong, Louis **4**
Art Ensemble of Chicago **23**
Avery, Teodross **23**
Bailey, Mildred **13**
Bailey, Pearl **5**
Baker, Anita **9**
Baker, Chet **13**
Baker, Ginger **16**
Also see Cream
Barbieri, Gato **22**
Basie, Count **2**
Bechet, Sidney **17**
Beiderbecke, Bix **16**
Belle, Regina **6**
Bennett, Tony **16**
Earlier sketch in CM **2**
Benson, George **9**
Berigan, Bunny **2**
Blackman, Cindy **15**
Blakey, Art **11**
Blanchard, Terence **13**
Bley, Carla **8**
Bley, Paul **14**
Blood, Sweat and Tears **7**
Brand New Heavies, The **14**
Braxton, Anthony **12**
Bridgewater, Dee Dee **18**
Brötzmann, Peter **26**
Brown, Clifford **24**
Brown, Lawrence **23**
Brown, Ray **21**
Brown, Ruth **13**

Brubeck, Dave **8**
Burrell, Kenny **11**
Burton, Gary **10**
Calloway, Cab **6**
Canadian Brass, The **4**
Carter, Benny **3**
Also see McKinney's Cotton Pickers
Carter, Betty **6**
Carter, James **18**
Carter, Regina **22**
Carter, Ron **14**
Chambers, Paul **18**
Charles, Ray **24**
Earlier sketch in CM **1**
Cherry, Don **10**
Christian, Charlie **11**
Clarke, Stanley **3**
Clements, Vassar **18**
Clooney, Rosemary **9**
Cole, Holly **18**
Cole, Nat King **3**
Coleman, Ornette **5**
Coltrane, John **4**
Connick, Harry, Jr. **4**
Corea, Chick **6**
Crawford, Randy **25**
Davis, Anthony **17**
Davis, Miles **1**
DeJohnette, Jack **7**
Di Meola, Al **12**
Dietrich, Marlene **25**
Dirty Dozen **23**
Eckstine, Billy **1**
Eldridge, Roy **9**
Also see McKinney's Cotton Pickers
Ellington, Duke **2**
Ellis, Herb **18**
Evans, Bill **17**
Evans, Gil **17**
Ferguson, Maynard **7**
Ferrell, Rachelle **17**
Fitzgerald, Ella **1**
Five Iron Frenzy **26**
Flanagan, Tommy **16**
Fleck, Bela **8**
Also see New Grass Revival, The
Flying Luttenbachers, The **28**
Fountain, Pete **7**
Frisell, Bill **15**
Galway, James **3**
Garner, Erroll **25**
Garrett, Kenny **28**
Getz, Stan **12**
Gillespie, Dizzy **6**
Goodman, Benny **4**
Gordon, Dexter **10**
Grappelli, Stephane **10**
Green, Benny **17**
Green, Grant **14**
Guaraldi, Vince **3**
Hackett, Bobby **21**
Haden, Charlie **12**
Hampton, Lionel **6**
Hancock, Herbie **25**
Earlier sketch in CM **8**
Hardcastle, Paul **20**
Hargrove, Roy **15**
Harrell, Tom **28**
Harris, Eddie **15**
Harris, Teddy **22**
Hawkins, Coleman **11**
Hawkins, Erskine **19**
Hedges, Michael **3**
Henderson, Fletcher **16**
Henderson, Joe **14**
Herman, Woody **12**
Hines, Earl "Fatha" **12**
Hirt, Al **5**
Holiday, Billie **6**
Holland, Dave **27**
Horn, Shirley **7**
Horne, Lena **11**
Humes, Helen **19**
Hunter, Alberta **7**
Hunter, Charlie **24**
Ibrahim, Abdullah **24**
Incognito **16**
Isham, Mark **14**
Israel "Cachao" Lopez **14**
Jackson, Milt **15**
Jacquet, Illinois **17**
James, Boney **21**
James, Harry **11**
Jarreau, Al **1**
Jarrett, Keith **1**
Jensen, Ingrid **22**
Jobim, Antonio Carlos **19**
Johnson, James P. **16**
Johnson, Lonnie **17**
Jones, Elvin **9**
Jones, Hank **15**
Jones, Philly Joe **16**
Jones, Quincy **20**
Earlier sketch in CM **2**
Jones, Thad **19**
Jordan, Stanley **1**
Kang, Eyvind **28**
Kennedy, Nigel **8**
Kenny G **14**
Kent, Stacey **28**
Kenton, Stan **21**
Kirk, Rahsaan Roland **6**
Kitt, Eartha **9**
Klugh, Earl **10**
Krall, Diana **27**
Kronos Quartet **5**
Krupa, Gene **13**
Laine, Cleo **10**
Lambert, Hendricks and Ross **28**
Lateef, Yusef **16**
Lee, Peggy **8**
Lewis, Ramsey **14**
Lincoln, Abbey **9**
Lloyd, Charles **22**
Lovano, Joe **13**
Mahavishnu Orchestra **19**
Mahogany, Kevin **26**
Malone, Russell **27**
Mancini, Henry **20**
Earlier sketch in CM **1**
Mangione, Chuck **23**
Manhattan Transfer, The **8**
Mann, Herbie **16**
Marsalis, Branford **10**
Marsalis, Ellis **13**
Marsalis, Wynton **20**
Earlier sketch in CM **6**
Martino, Pat **17**
Masekela, Hugh **7**
McBride, Christian **17**
McCorkle, Susannah **27**
McFerrin, Bobby **3**
McKinney's Cotton Pickers **16**
McLaughlin, John **12**
McPartland, Marian **15**
McRae, Carmen **9**
Metheny, Pat **26**
Earlier sketch in CM **2**
Mingus, Charles **9**
Monk, Thelonious **6**
Montgomery, Wes **3**
Morgan, Frank **9**
Morton, Jelly Roll **7**
Mulligan, Gerry **16**
Murray, Dave **28**
Najee **21**
Nascimento, Milton **6**
Navarro, Fats **25**
Norvo, Red **12**
O'Day, Anita **21**
Oliver, King **15**
Palmer, Jeff **20**
Palmieri, Eddie **15**
Parker, Charlie **5**
Parker, Evan **28**
Parker, Leon **27**
Parker, Maceo **7**
Pass, Joe **15**
Paul, Les **2**
Payton, Nicholas **27**
Pepper, Art **18**
Perez, Danilo **25**
Peterson, Oscar **11**
Ponty, Jean-Luc **8**
Powell, Bud **15**
Previn, André **15**
Professor Longhair **6**
Puente, Tito **14**
Pullen, Don **16**
Ralph Sharon Quartet **26**
Rampal, Jean-Pierre **6**
Redman, Joshua **25**
Earlier sketch in CM **12**
Reeves, Dianne **16**
Reid, Vernon **2**
Also see Living Colour
Reinhardt, Django **7**
Rich, Buddy **13**
Roach, Max **12**
Roberts, Marcus **6**
Robillard, Duke **2**
Rodney, Red **14**
Rollins, Sonny **7**
Russell, Pee Wee **25**
Saluzzi, Dino **23**
Sanborn, David **28**
Earlier sketch in CM **1**
Sanders, Pharoah **28**
Earlier sketch in CM **16**
Sandoval, Arturo **15**
Santamaria, Mongo **28**
Santana, Carlos **19**
Earlier sketch in CM **1**
Schuur, Diane **6**
Scofield, John **7**
Scott, Jimmy **14**
Scott-Heron, Gil **13**
Severinsen, Doc **1**
Sharrock, Sonny **15**
Shaw, Artie **8**
Shaw, Woody **27**
Shearing, George **28**
Shorter, Wayne **5**
Silver, Horace **19**
Simone, Nina **11**
Smith, Tommy **28**
Solal, Martial **4**
Strayhorn, Billy **13**
Summers, Andy **3**
Also see Police, The
Sun Ra **27**
Earlier sketch in CM **5**

Take 6 **6**
Tatum, Art **17**
Taylor, Billy **13**
Taylor, Cecil **9**
Teagarden, Jack **10**
Terry, Clark **24**
Thielemans, Toots **13**
Thornton, Teri **28**
Threadgill, Henry **9**
Torme, Mel **4**
Tucker, Sophie **12**
Turner, Big Joe **13**
Turtle Island String Quartet **9**
Tyner, McCoy **7**
Ulmer, James Blood **13**
US3 **18**
Valdes, Chuco **25**
Vandermark, Ken **28**
Vaughan, Sarah **2**
Walker, T-Bone **5**
Washington, Dinah **5**
Washington, Grover, Jr. **5**
Weather Report **19**
Webb, Chick **14**
Weston, Randy **15**
Whitaker, Rodney **20**
Whiteman, Paul **17**
Whitfield, Mark **18**
Whittaker, Rodney **19**
Willem Breuker Kollektief **28**
Williams, Joe **11**
Wilson, Cassandra **26**
  Earlier sketch in CM **12**
Wilson, Nancy **28**
  Earlier sketch in CM **14**
Winter, Paul **10**
Witherspoon, Jimmy **19**
Young, La Monte **16**
Young, Lester **14**
Zorn, John **15**

Juju
Adé, King Sunny **18**

Keyboards, Electric
Aphex Twin **14**
Bley, Paul **14**
Brown, Tony **14**
Chemical Brothers **20**
Corea, Chick **6**
Davis, Chip **4**
Dolby, Thomas **10**
Eno, Brian **8**
Foster, David **13**
Froom, Mitchell **15**
Hammer, Jan **21**
Hancock, Herbie **25**
  Earlier sketch in CM **8**
Hardcastle, Paul **20**
Jackson, Joe **22**
  Earlier sketch in CM **4**
Jarre, Jean-Michel **2**
Jones, Booker T. **8**
  Also see Booker T. & the M.G.'s
Kitaro **1**
Man or Astroman? **21**
Orbital **20**
Palmer, Jeff **20**
Sakamoto, Ryuichi **19**
Shaffer, Paul **13**
Smog **28**
Sun Ra **27**
  Earlier sketch in CM **5**
Wakeman, Rick **27**
  Also see Yes
Waller, Fats **7**
Winwood, Steve **2**
  Also see Spencer Davis Group
  Also see Traffic
Wonder, Stevie **17**
  Earlier sketch in CM **2**
Worrell, Bernie **11**
Yanni **11**

Liturgical Music
Cooney, Rory **6**
Talbot, John Michael **6**

Mandolin
Bromberg, David **18**
Grisman, David **17**
Hartford, John **1**
Lindley, David **2**
Monroe, Bill **1**
Skaggs, Ricky **5**
Stuart, Marty **9**

Musicals
Allen, Debbie **8**
Allen, Peter **11**
Andrews, Julie **4**
Andrews Sisters, The **9**
Bacharach, Burt **20**
  Earlier sketch in CM **1**
Bailey, Pearl **5**
Baker, Josephine **10**
Berlin, Irving **8**
Brightman, Sarah **20**
Brown, Ruth **13**
Buckley, Betty **16**
  Earlier sketch in CM **1**
Burnett, Carol **6**
Carter, Nell **7**
Channing, Carol **6**
Chevalier, Maurice **6**
Crawford, Michael **4**
Crosby, Bing **6**
Curry, Tim **3**
Davis, Sammy, Jr. **4**
Day, Doris **24**
  Earlier sketch in CM **7**
Garland, Judy **6**
Gershwin, George and Ira **11**
Hamlisch, Marvin **1**
Horne, Lena **11**
Johnson, James P. **16**
Jolson, Al **10**
Kern, Jerome **13**
Laine, Cleo **10**
Lerner and Loewe **13**
Lloyd Webber, Andrew **6**
LuPone, Patti **8**
Martin, Mary **27**
Masekela, Hugh **7**
Menken, Alan **10**
Mercer, Johnny **13**
Merman, Ethel **27**
Moore, Melba **7**
Patinkin, Mandy **20**
  Earlier sketch in CM **3**
Peters, Bernadette **27**
Porter, Cole **10**
Robeson, Paul **8**
Rodgers, Richard **9**
Sager, Carole Bayer **5**
Shaffer, Paul **13**
Sondheim, Stephen **8**
Styne, Jule **21**
Waters, Ethel **11**
Weill, Kurt **12**
Whiting, Margaret **28**
Yeston, Maury **22**

Oboe
Lateef, Yusef **16**

Opera
Adams, John **8**
Ameling, Elly **24**
Anderson, June **27**
Anderson, Marian **8**
Austral, Florence **26**
Baker, Janet **14**
Bartoli, Cecilia **12**
Battle, Kathleen **6**
Beltrán, Tito **28**
Blegen, Judith **23**
Bocelli, Andrea **22**
Bumbry, Grace **13**
Caballe, Monserrat **23**
Callas, Maria **11**
Carreras, José **8**
Caruso, Enrico **10**
Church, Charlotte **28**
Copeland, Stewart **14**
  Also see Police, The
Cotrubas, Ileana **1**
Davis, Anthony **17**
Domingo, Placido **20**
  Earlier sketch in CM **1**
Fleming, Renee **24**
Freni, Mirella **14**
Gershwin, George and Ira **11**
Graves, Denyce **16**
Hampson, Thomas **12**
Hendricks, Barbara **10**
Heppner, Ben **23**
Herrmann, Bernard **14**
Horne, Marilyn **9**
McNair, Sylvia **15**
Norman, Jessye **7**
Pavarotti, Luciano **20**
  Earlier sketch in CM **1**
Price, Leontyne **6**
Quasthoff, Thomas **26**
Sills, Beverly **5**
Solti, Georg **13**
Sutherland, Joan **13**
Te Kanawa, Kiri **2**
Toscanini, Arturo **14**
Upshaw, Dawn **9**
von Karajan, Herbert **1**
Weill, Kurt **12**
Zimmerman, Udo **5**

Percussion
Aronoff, Kenny **21**
Baker, Ginger **16**
  Also see Cream
Blackman, Cindy **15**
Blakey, Art **11**
Burton, Gary **10**
Collins, Phil **20**
  Earlier sketch in CM **2**
  Also see Genesis
Copeland, Stewart **14**
  Also see Police, The
DeJohnette, Jack **7**
Hampton, Lionel **6**
Henley, Don **3**
Jones, Elvin **9**
Jones, Philly Joe **16**
Jones, Spike **5**

Krupa, Gene **13**
Mo', Keb' **21**
N'Dour, Youssou **6**
Otis, Johnny **16**
Palmieri, Eddie **15**
Parker, Leon **27**
Puente, Tito **14**
Rich, Buddy **13**
Roach, Max **12**
Santamaria, Mongo **28**
Sheila E. **3**
Starr, Ringo **10**
Also see Beatles, The
Walden, Narada Michael **14**
Webb, Chick **14**

Piano
Adamson, Barry **28**
Allen, Geri **10**
Allison, Mose **17**
Amos, Tori **12**
Apple, Fiona **28**
Argerich, Martha **27**
Arrau, Claudio **1**
Axton, Hoyt **28**
Bacharach, Burt **20**
Earlier sketch in CM **1**
Ball, Marcia **15**
Basie, Count **2**
Berlin, Irving **8**
Blake, Eubie **19**
Bley, Carla **8**
Bley, Paul **14**
Borge, Victor **19**
Brendel, Alfred **23**
Brickman, Jim **22**
Britten, Benjamin **15**
Bronfman, Yefim **6**
Brubeck, Dave **8**
Bush, Kate **4**
Carpenter, Richard **24**
Also see Carpenters
Charles, Ray **24**
Earlier sketch in CM **1**
Clayderman, Richard **1**
Cleveland, James **1**
Cliburn, Van **13**
Cole, Nat King **3**
Collins, Judy **4**
Collins, Phil **20**
Earlier sketch in CM **2**
Also see Genesis
Connick, Harry, Jr. **4**
Crouch, Andraé **9**
Davies, Dennis Russell **24**
DeJohnette, Jack **7**
Domino, Fats **2**
Dr. John **7**
Dupree, Champion Jack **12**
Ellington, Duke **2**
Esquivel, Juan **17**
Evans, Bill **17**
Evans, Gil **17**
Feinstein, Michael **6**
Ferrell, Rachelle **17**
Flack, Roberta **5**
Flanagan, Tommy **16**
Frey, Glenn **3**
Galás, Diamanda **16**
Garner, Erroll **25**
Glass, Philip **1**
Gould, Glenn **9**
Green, Benny **17**
Grusin, Dave **7**
Guaraldi, Vince **3**
Hamlisch, Marvin **1**
Hancock, Herbie **25**
Earlier sketch in CM **8**
Harris, Teddy **22**
Helfgott, David **19**
Henderson, Fletcher **16**
Hinderas, Natalie **12**
Hines, Earl "Fatha" **12**
Horn, Shirley **7**
Hornsby, Bruce **25**
Earlier sketch in CM **3**
Horowitz, Vladimir **1**
Ibrahim, Abdullah **24**
Jackson, Joe **22**
Earlier sketch in CM **4**
James, Skip **24**
Jarrett, Keith **1**
Joel, Billy **12**
Earlier sketch in CM **2**
John, Elton **20**
Earlier sketch in CM **3**
Johnson, James P. **16**
Jones, Hank **15**
Jones, Howard **26**
Joplin, Scott **10**
Kenton, Stan **21**
Kissin, Evgeny **6**
Krall, Diana **27**
Levine, James **8**
Lewis, Jerry Lee **2**
Lewis, Ramsey **14**
Liberace **9**
Little Richard **1**
Manilow, Barry **2**
Marsalis, Ellis **13**
Matthews, Eric **22**
McPartland, Marian **15**
McRae, Carmen **9**
Milsap, Ronnie **2**
Mingus, Charles **9**
Monk, Thelonious **6**
Montgomery, Little Brother **26**
Morton, Jelly Roll **7**
Nero, Peter **19**
Newman, Randy **27**
Earlier sketch in CM **4**
Palmieri, Eddie **15**
Perahia, Murray **10**
Perez, Danilo **25**
Peterson, Oscar **11**
Pires, Maria João **26**
Post, Mike **21**
Powell, Bud **15**
Pratt, Awadagin **19**
Previn, André **15**
Professor Longhair **6**
Puente, Tito **14**
Pullen, Don **16**
Rangell, Andrew **24**
Rich, Charlie **3**
Roberts, Marcus **6**
Rubinstein, Arthur **11**
Russell, Mark **6**
Schickele, Peter **5**
Sedaka, Neil **4**
Shaffer, Paul **13**
Solal, Martial **4**
Solti, Georg **13**
Spann, Otis **18**
Story, Liz **2**
Strayhorn, Billy **13**
Sunnyland Slim **16**
Sykes, Roosevelt **20**
Tatum, Art **17**
Taylor, Billy **13**
Taylor, Cecil **9**
Thibaudet, Jean-Yves **24**
Thornton, Teri **28**
Tilson Thomas, Michael **24**
Tyner, McCoy **7**
Valdes, Chuco **25**
Vangelis **21**
Volodos, Arcadi **28**
Waits, Tom **27**
Earlier sketch in CM **12**
Earlier sketch in CM **1**
Waller, Fats **7**
Weston, Randy **15**
Wilson, Brian **24**
Also see Beach Boys, The
Wilson, Cassandra **26**
Earlier sketch in CM **12**
Winston, George **9**
Winwood, Steve **2**
Also see Spencer Davis Group
Also see Traffic
Wonder, Stevie **17**
Earlier sketch in CM **2**
Young, La Monte **16**

Piccolo
Galway, James **3**

Pop
10,000 Maniacs **3**
A-ha **22**
Abba **12**
Abdul, Paula **3**
Adam Ant **13**
Adams, Bryan **20**
Earlier sketch in CM **2**
Adams, Oleta **17**
Air Supply **22**
All Saints **25**
All-4-One **17**
Alpert, Herb **11**
America **16**
Amos, Tori **12**
Anderson, Laurie **25**
Earlier sketch in CM **1**
Andrews Sisters, The **9**
Arden, Jann **21**
Arena, Tina **21**
Armatrading, Joan **4**
Arnold, Eddy **10**
Artifacts **23**
Astley, Rick **5**
Atari Teenage Riot **27**
Atkins, Chet **5**
Atomic Fireballs, The **27**
Avalon, Frankie **5**
B-52's, The **4**
Bacharach, Burt **20**
Earlier sketch in CM **1**
Backstreet Boys **21**
Badu, Erykah **26**
Bailey, Pearl **5**
Baker, Arthur **23**
Bananarama **22**
Bangles **22**
Basia **5**
Bauhaus **27**
Beach Boys, The **1**
Beat Happening **28**
Beatles, The **2**
Beaver Brown Band, The **3**
Bee Gees, The **3**

Belly **16**
Bennett, Tony **16**
Earlier sketch in CM **2**
Benson, George **9**
Benton, Brook **7**
Beta Band, The **27**
Better Than Ezra **19**
Blegvad, Peter **28**
Blige, Mary J. **15**
Blink 182 **27**
Blondie **27**
Earlier sketch in CM **14**
Blood, Sweat and Tears **7**
Blue Rodeo **18**
BoDeans, The **20**
Earlier sketch in CM **3**
Bolton, Michael **4**
Boo Radleys, The **21**
Booker T. & the M.G.'s **24**
Boone, Pat **13**
Boston **11**
Bowie, David **23**
Earlier sketch in CM **1**
Boyz II Men **15**
Bragg, Billy **7**
Branigan, Laura **2**
Braxton, Toni **17**
Brickell, Edie **3**
Brooks, Garth **25**
Earlier sketch in CM **8**
Brown, Bobby **4**
Brown, Foxy **25**
Browne, Jackson **3**
Bryson, Peabo **11**
Buckingham, Lindsey **8**
Also see Fleetwood Mac
Buckley, Tim **14**
Buffett, Jimmy **4**
Burdon, Eric **14**
Also see War
Also see Animals
Burroughs, William S. **26**
Cabaret Voltaire **18**
Campbell, Glen **2**
Campbell, Tevin **13**
Captain Beefheart and the Magic Band **26**
Earlier sketch in CM **10**
Cardigans **19**
Carey, Mariah **20**
Earlier sketch in CM **6**
Carlisle, Belinda **8**
Carmichael, Hoagy **27**
Carnes, Kim **4**
Carpenter, Richard **24**
Also see Carpenters
Carpenters **13**
Carr, Vikki **28**
Case, Peter **13**
Chandra, Sheila **16**
Chapin, Harry **6**
Chapin-Carpenter, Mary **25**
Earlier sketch in CM **6**
Chapman, Tracy **20**
Earlier sketch in CM **4**
Charlatans, The **13**
Charles, Ray **24**
Earlier sketch in CM **1**
Checker, Chubby **7**
Cher **1**
Also see Sonny and Cher
Cherry, Neneh **4**
Cherry Poppin' Daddies **24**
Chicago **3**
Chilton, Alex **10**
Cibo Matto **28**
Clapton, Eric **11**
Earlier sketch in CM **1**
Also see Cream
Also see Yardbirds, The
Clayderman, Richard **1**
Clooney, Rosemary **9**
Coasters, The **5**
Cocker, Joe **4**
Cocteau Twins, The **12**
Cole, Lloyd **9**
Cole, Nat King **3**
Cole, Natalie **21**
Earlier sketch in CM **1**
Cole, Paula **20**
Collins, Judy **4**
Collins, Phil **20**
Earlier sketch in CM **2**
Also see Genesis
Color Me Badd **23**
Colvin, Shawn **11**
Commodores, The **23**
Como, Perry **14**
Connick, Harry, Jr. **4**
Cooke, Sam **1**
Also see Soul Stirrers, The
Cope, Julian **16**
Cornershop **24**
Costello, Elvis **12**
Earlier sketch in CM **2**
Cranberries, The **14**
Crash Test Dummies **14**
Crenshaw, Marshall **5**
Croce, Jim **3**
Crosby, David **3**
Also see Byrds, The
Crow, Sheryl **18**
Crowded House **12**
Cure, The **20**
Earlier sketch in CM **3**
D'Arby, Terence Trent **3**
Daltrey, Roger **3**
Also see Who, The
Darin, Bobby **4**
Dave Clark Five, The **12**
Dave, Edmunds **28**
Davies, Ray **5**
Davis, Sammy, Jr. **4**
Davis, Skeeter **15**
Day, Doris **24**
Dayne, Taylor **4**
DeBarge, El **14**
Del Amitri **18**
Del Rubio Triplets **21**
Denver, John **1**
Depeche Mode **5**
Des'ree **24**
Earlier sketch in CM **15**
Devo **13**
Diamond, Neil **1**
Dietrich, Marlene **25**
Dion **4**
Dion, Celine **25**
Earlier sketch in CM **12**
Doc Pomus **14**
Donovan **9**
Doobie Brothers, The **3**
Doors, The **4**
Droge, Pete **24**
Dubstar **22**
Duran Duran **4**
Dylan, Bob **21**
Earlier sketch in CM **3**
Eagles, The **3**
Earth, Wind and Fire **12**
Easton, Sheena **2**
Edmonds, Kenneth "Babyface" **12**
Electric Light Orchestra **7**
Elfman, Danny **9**
Elliot, Cass **5**
Also see Mamas and the Papas
En Vogue **10**
Enigma **14**
Estefan, Gloria **15**
Earlier sketch in CM **2**
Eurythmics **6**
Everly Brothers, The **2**
Everything But The Girl **15**
Exposé **4**
Fabian **5**
Fatboy Slim **22**
Feliciano, José **10**
Ferguson, Maynard **7**
Ferry, Bryan **1**
Fiedler, Arthur **6**
Fine Young Cannibals **22**
Fisher, Eddie **12**
Fitzgerald, Ella **1**
Flack, Roberta **5**
Fleetwood Mac **5**
Fogelberg, Dan **4**
Fordham, Julia **15**
Foster, David **13**
Four Tops, The **11**
Fox, Samantha **3**
Frampton, Peter **3**
Francis, Connie **10**
Franklin, Aretha **17**
Earlier sketch in CM **2**
Frey, Glenn **3**
Also see Eagles, The
Garbage **25**
Garfunkel, Art **4**
Also see Simon and Garfunkel
Gaye, Marvin **4**
Gayle, Crystal **1**
Geldof, Bob **9**
Genesis **4**
Gershwin, George and Ira **11**
Gibson, Deborah **24**
Earlier sketch in CM **1**
See Gibson, Debbie
Gift, Roland **3**
Gil, Gilberto **26**
Gin Blossoms **18**
Ginsberg, Allen **26**
Go-Go's, The **24**
Gong **24**
Goodman, Benny **4**
Gordy, Berry, Jr. **6**
Grant, Amy **7**
Grant, Gogi **28**
Grebenshikov, Boris **3**
Green, Al **9**
Guthrie, Arlo **6**
Hall & Oates **6**
Hammer, M.C. **5**
Hancock, Herbie **25**
Earlier sketch in CM **8**
Hanson **20**
Harding, John Wesley **6**
Harrison, George **2**
Also see Beatles, The
Harry, Deborah **4**
Also see Blondie
Hawkins, Sophie B. **21**
Healey, Jeff **4**
Henley, Don **3**
Also see Eagles, The

Herman's Hermits **5**
Hill, Lauryn **25**
Hitchcock, Robyn **9**
Holland-Dozier-Holland **5**
Hootie and the Blowfish **18**
Horne, Lena **11**
Hornsby, Bruce **25**
Earlier sketch in CM **3**
Houston, Cissy **26**
Earlier sketch in CM **6**
Houston, Whitney **25**
Earlier sketch in CM **8**
Human League, The **17**
Humperdinck, Engelbert **19**
Ian, Janis **24**
Earlier sketch in CM **5**
Idol, Billy **3**
Iglesias, Julio **20**
Earlier sketch in CM **2**
Imbruglia, Natalie **27**
Incubus **23**
Indigo Girls **20**
Earlier sketch in CM **3**
Ingram, James **11**
Ink Spots, The **23**
Isaak, Chris **6**
Isley Brothers, The **8**
Jackson, Janet **16**
Earlier sketch in CM **3**
Jackson, Joe **22**
Earlier sketch in CM **4**
Jackson, Michael **17**
Earlier sketch in CM **1**
Also see Jacksons, The
Jacksons, The **7**
Jam, Jimmy, and Terry Lewis **11**
James **12**
James, Harry **11**
James, Rick **2**
Jarreau, Al **1**
Jayhawks, The **15**
Jefferson Airplane **5**
Jesus Jones **23**
Jewel **25**
Jodeci **13**
Joel, Billy **12**
Earlier sketch in CM **2**
Johansen, David **7**
John, Elton **20**
Earlier sketch in CM **3**
Johnston, Freedy **20**
Jolson, Al **10**
Jones, Howard **26**
Jones, Quincy **20**
Earlier sketch in CM **2**
Jones, Rickie Lee **4**
Jones, Tom **11**
Joplin, Janis **3**
Joy Electric **26**
Kaye, Carol **22**
Keaggy, Phil **26**
Khan, Chaka **19**
Earlier sketch in CM **9**
King, Ben E. **7**
King, Carole **6**
Kiss **25**
Earlier sketch in CM **5**
Kitt, Eartha **9**
Knight, Gladys **1**
Knopfler, Mark **25**
Earlier sketch in CM **3**
Also see Dire Straits
Kool & the Gang **13**
Kraftwerk **9**
Kristofferson, Kris **4**
LaBelle, Patti **8**
Lambert, Hendricks and Ross **28**
Lane, Fred **28**
Lang, kd **25**
Earlier sketch in CM **4**
Lauper, Cyndi **11**
Lee, Brenda **5**
Leiber and Stoller **14**
Lemper, Ute **14**
Lennon, John **9**
Also see Beatles, The
Lennon, Julian **26**
Earlier sketch in CM **2**
Lennox, Annie **18**
Also see Eurythmics
Lewis, Huey **9**
Liberace **9**
Lightfoot, Gordon **3**
Lightning Seeds **21**
Lisa Lisa **23**
Loeb, Lisa **19**
Logan, Jack **27**
Loggins, Kenny **20**
Earlier sketch in CM **3**
Lovett, Lyle **28**
Earlier sketch in CM **5**
Lowe, Nick **25**
Earlier sketch in CM **6**
Lush **13**
Lynne, Jeff **5**
MacColl, Kirsty **12**
Madness **27**
Madonna **16**
Earlier sketch in CM **4**
Magnetic Fields, The **28**
Mamas and the Papas **21**
Mancini, Henry **20**
Earlier sketch in CM **1**
Manhattan Transfer, The **8**
Manilow, Barry **2**
Marley, Bob **3**
Marley, Ziggy **3**
Marsalis, Branford **10**
Marshall, Amanda **27**
Martin, Dean **1**
Martin, George **6**
Martin, Mary **27**
Martin, Ricky **26**
Marx, Richard **21**
Earlier sketch in CM **3**
Mathis, Johnny **2**
Mazzy Star **17**
McCartney, Paul **4**
Also see Beatles, The
McFerrin, Bobby **3**
McGuire Sisters, The **27**
McLachlan, Sarah **12**
McLean, Don **7**
McLennan, Grant **21**
Medley, Bill **3**
Melanie **12**
Merchant, Natalie **25**
Mercury Rev **28**
Merman, Ethel **27**
Michael, George **9**
Midler, Bette **8**
Mighty Mighty Bosstones **20**
Mike & the Mechanics **17**
Miller, Mitch **11**
Miller, Roger **4**
Milli Vanilli **4**
Mills Brothers, The **14**
Minnelli, Liza **19**
Mitchell, Joni **17**
Earlier sketch in CM **2**
Mojave 3 **26**
Money, Eddie **16**
Monica **26**
Monkees, The **7**
Montand, Yves **12**
Moore, Chante **21**
Morcheeba **25**
Morissette, Alanis **19**
Morrison, Jim **3**
Morrison, Van **24**
Earlier sketch in CM **3**
Morrissey **10**
Mouskouri, Nana **12**
Moyet, Alison **12**
Murray, Anne **4**
Myles, Alannah **4**
N Sync **25**
Neville, Aaron **5**
Also see Neville Brothers, The
Neville Brothers, The **4**
New Kids on the Block **3**
Newman, Randy **27**
Earlier sketch in CM **4**
Newton, Wayne **2**
Newton-John, Olivia **8**
Nicks, Stevie **25**
Earlier sketch in CM **2**
Also see Fleetwood Mac
Nilsson **10**
Nitty Gritty Dirt Band **6**
No Doubt **20**
Nyro, Laura **12**
O'Connor, Sinead **3**
Oak Ridge Boys, The **7**
Ocasek, Ric **5**
Ocean, Billy **4**
Odds **20**
Oldfield, Mike **18**
Orchestral Manoeuvres in the Dark **21**
Orlando, Tony **15**
Orton, Beth **26**
Osborne, Joan **19**
Osmond, Donny **3**
Page, Jimmy **4**
Also see Led Zeppelin
Also see Yardbirds, The
Page, Patti **11**
Parks, Van Dyke **17**
Parsons, Alan **12**
Parton, Dolly **2**
Pendergrass, Teddy **3**
Peniston, CeCe **15**
Penn, Michael **4**
Pet Shop Boys **5**
Peter, Paul & Mary **4**
Phillips, Sam **12**
Piaf, Edith **8**
Pizzicato Five **18**
Plant, Robert **2**
Also see Led Zeppelin
Pointer Sisters, The **9**
Porter, Cole **10**
Prefab Sprout **15**
Presley, Elvis **1**
Priest, Maxi **20**
Prince **14**
Earlier sketch in CM **1**
Proclaimers, The **13**
Prodigy **22**
Propellerheads **26**
Pulp **18**
Queen **6**

R.E.M. **25**
Earlier sketch in CM **5**
Rabbitt, Eddie **24**
Earlier sketch in CM **5**
Raitt, Bonnie **23**
Earlier sketch in CM **3**
Rea, Chris **12**
Redding, Otis **5**
Reddy, Helen **9**
Reeves, Martha **4**
Also see Martha and the Vandellas
Republica **20**
Richard, Cliff **14**
Richie, Lionel **2**
Riley, Teddy **14**
Robbins, Marty **9**
Robinson, Smokey **1**
Rogers, Kenny **1**
Rolling Stones **23**
Earlier sketch in CM **3**
Ronstadt, Linda **2**
Roots, The **27**
Ross, Diana **1**
Also see Supremes, The
Roth, David Lee **1**
Also see Van Halen
Roxette **23**
Ruffin, David **6**
RuPaul **20**
Sade **2**
Sager, Carole Bayer **5**
Saint Etienne **28**
Sainte-Marie, Buffy **11**
Sanborn, David **28**
Earlier sketch in CM **1**
Santamaria, Mongo **28**
Seal **14**
Seals & Crofts **3**
Seals, Dan **9**
Secada, Jon **13**
Sedaka, Neil **4**
Selena **16**
Shaffer, Paul **13**
Shamen, The **23**
Shearing, George **28**
Sheep on Drugs **27**
Sheila E. **3**
Shirelles, The **11**
Shonen Knife **13**
Siberry, Jane **6**
Simon, Carly **22**
Earlier sketch in CM **4**
Simon, Paul **16**
Earlier sketch in CM **1**
Also see Simon and Garfunkel
Sinatra, Frank **23**
Earlier sketch in CM **1**
Sixpence None the Richer **26**
Smith, Elliott **28**
Smiths, The **3**
Snow, Pheobe **4**
Sobule, Jill **20**
Sonny and Cher **24**
Soul Coughing **21**
Sparks **18**
Spears, Britney **28**
Spector, Phil **4**
Spector, Ronnie **28**
Spice Girls **22**
Springfield, Dusty **20**
Springfield, Rick **9**
Springsteen, Bruce **25**
Earlier sketch in CM **6**
Squeeze **5**
Stafford, Jo **24**
Stansfield, Lisa **9**
Starr, Kay **27**
Starr, Ringo **24**
Earlier sketch in CM **10**
Steely Dan **5**
Stereolab **18**
Stevens, Cat **3**
Stewart, Rod **20**
Earlier sketch in CM **2**
Also see Faces, The
Stills, Stephen **5**
Sting **19**
Earlier sketch in CM **2**
Also see Police, The
Stockwood, Kim **26**
Story, The **13**
Straw, Syd **18**
Streisand, Barbra **2**
Suede **20**
Summer, Donna **12**
Sundays, The **20**
Super Furry Animals **28**
Supremes, The **6**
Surfaris, The **23**
Sweat, Keith **13**
Sweet, Matthew **9**
SWV **14**
Sylvian, David **27**
Talk Talk **19**
Talking Heads **1**
Taylor, James **25**
Earlier sketch in CM **2**
Taylor, Steve **26**
Tears for Fears **6**
Teenage Fanclub **13**
Temptations, The **3**
Texas **27**
The The **15**
They Might Be Giants **7**
Thomas, Irma **16**
Three Dog Night **5**
Tiffany **4**
Tikaram, Tanita **9**
Timbuk 3 **3**
TLC **15**
Toad the Wet Sprocket **13**
Tony! Toni! Toné! **12**
Torme, Mel **4**
Townshend, Pete **1**
Also see Who, The
Turner, Tina **1**
Also see Ike & Tina Turner
Valli, Frankie **10**
Vandross, Luther **2**
Vanessa-Mae **26**
Vega, Suzanne **3**
Velocity Girl **23**
Veloso, Caetano **28**
Velvet Crush **28**
Vinton, Bobby **12**
Walsh, Joe **5**
Warnes, Jennifer **3**
Warwick, Dionne **2**
Was (Not Was) **6**
Washington, Dinah **5**
Waters, Crystal **15**
Watley, Jody **26**
Earlier sketch in CM **9**
Webb, Jimmy **12**
Weird Al" Yankovic **7**
Weller, Paul **14**
Whiting, Margaret **28**
Who, The **3**
Williams, Andy **2**
Williams, Dar **21**
Williams, Deniece **1**
Williams, Joe **11**
Williams, Lucinda **24**
Earlier sketch in CM **10**
Williams, Paul **26**
Earlier sketch in CM **5**
Williams, Robbie **25**
Williams, Vanessa **10**
Williams, Victoria **17**
Wilson, Brian **24**
Also see Beach Boys, The
Wilson, Jackie **3**
Wilson, Nancy **28**
Wilson Phillips **5**
Winwood, Steve **2**
Also see Spencer Davis Group
Also see Traffic
Womack, Bobby **5**
Wonder, Stevie **17**
Earlier sketch in CM **2**
Young M.C. **4**
Young, Neil **15**
Earlier sketch in CM **2**

Producers

Ackerman, Will **3**
Afanasieff, Walter **26**
Albini, Steve **15**
Alpert, Herb **11**
Austin, Dallas **16**
Baker, Anita **9**
Bass, Ralph **24**
Benitez, Jellybean **15**
Brown, Junior **15**
Brown, Tony **14**
Browne, Jackson **3**
Burnett, T Bone **13**
Cale, John **9**
Clark, Dick **25**
Earlier sketch in CM **2**
Clarke, Stanley **3**
Clinton, George **7**
Collins, Phil **2**
Also see Genesis
Combs, Sean "Puffy" **25**
Earlier sketch in CM **16**
Costello, Elvis **2**
Cropper, Steve **12**
Crowell, Rodney **8**
Dave, Edmunds **28**
Dixon, Willie **10**
Dolby, Thomas **10**
Dr. Dre **15**
Also see N.W.A.
Dupri, Jermaine **25**
Earlier sketch in CM **2**
Edmonds, Kenneth "Babyface" **12**
Enigma **14**
Eno, Brian **8**
Ertegun, Ahmet **10**
Ertegun, Nesuhi **24**
Foster, David **13**
Fripp, Robert **9**
Froom, Mitchell **15**
Gabler, Milton **25**
Gordy, Jr., Emory **17**
Gray, F. Gary **19**
Grusin, Dave **7**
Hardcastle, Paul **20**
Jackson, Millie **14**
Jam, Jimmy, and Terry Lewis **11**
Jones, Booker T. **8**
Also see Booker T. & the M.G'.s

Jones, Quincy 20
Earlier sketch in CM 2
Jordan, Montell 26
Krasnow, Bob 15
Lanois, Daniel 8
Laswell, Bill 14
Leiber and Stoller 14
Lillywhite, Steve 13
Lynne, Jeff 5
Mandel, Johnny 28
Marley, Rita 10
Martin, George 6
Master P 22
Mayfield, Curtis 8
McKnight, Brian 22
McLaren, Malcolm 23
Miller, Mitch 11
Osby, Greg 21
Parks, Van Dyke 17
Parsons, Alan 12
Post, Mike 21
Prince 14
Earlier sketch in CM 1
Queen Latifah 24
Earlier sketch in CM 6
Riley, Teddy 14
Robertson, Robbie 2
Rodgers, Nile 8
Rubin, Rick 9
Rundgren, Todd 11
Scruggs, Randy 28
Shocklee, Hank 15
Simmons, Russell 7
Skaggs, Ricky 5
Spector, Phil 4
Sure!, Al B. 13
Sweat, Keith 13
Too $hort 16
Toussaint, Allen 11
Tricky 18
Vandross, Luther 2
Vasquez, Junior 16
Vig, Butch 17
Wachtel, Waddy 26
Walden, Narada Michael 14
Was, Don 21
Watt, Mike 22
Wexler, Jerry 15
Whelan, Bill 20
Willner, Hal 10
Wilson, Brian 24
Also see Beach Boys, The
Winbush, Angela 15
Woods-Wright, Tomica 22

Promoters
Clark, Dick 25
Earlier sketch in CM 2
Geldof, Bob 9
Graham, Bill 10
Hay, George D. 3
Simmons, Russell 7

Ragtime
Johnson, James P. 16
Joplin, Scott 10

Rap
2Pac 17
Anthony, Marc 19
Arrested Development 14
Austin, Dallas 16
Bambaataa, Afrika 13
Basehead 11
Beastie Boys 25
Earlier sketch in CM 8
Biz Markie 10
Black Sheep 15
Bone Thugs-N-Harmony 18
Busta Rhymes 18
Campbell, Luther 10
Cherry, Neneh 4
Combs, Sean "Puffy" 25
Earlier sketch in CM 16
Common 23
Coolio 19
Cypress Hill 11
Das EFX 14
De La Soul 7
Digable Planets 15
Digital Underground 9
DJ Jazzy Jeff and the Fresh Prince 5
DMX 25
Dr. Dre 15
Also see N.W.A.
Dupri, Jermaine 25
Eazy-E 13
Also see N.W.A.
Eminem 28
EPMD 10
Eric B. and Rakim 9
Evans, Faith 25
Franti, Michael 16
Fugees, The 17
Gang Starr 13
Geto Boys, The 11
Goodie Mob 24
Grandmaster Flash 14
Gravediggaz 23
Hammer, M.C. 5
Heavy D 10
House of Pain 14
Ice Cube 25
Earlier sketch in CM 10
Ice-T 7
Insane Clown Posse 22
Jackson, Millie 14
Jay-Z 28
Kane, Big Daddy 7
Kid 'n Play 5
Kid Rock 27
Knight, Suge 15
Kool Moe Dee 9
Kris Kross 11
KRS-One 8
L.L. Cool J. 5
Last Poets 21
Love, G. 24
Mase 27
Master P 22
MC 900 Ft. Jesus 16
MC Breed 17
MC Eiht 27
MC Lyte 8
MC Serch 10
N.W.A. 6
Nas 19
Naughty by Nature 11
Notorious B.I.G. 20
P.M. Dawn 11
Pharcyde, The 17
Public Enemy 4
Queen Latifah 24
Earlier sketch in CM 6
Rage Against the Machine 18
Riley, Teddy 14
Rubin, Rick 9
Run-D.M.C. 25
Earlier sketch in CM 4
Salt-N-Pepa 6
Scott-Heron, Gil 13
Shaggy 19
Shanté 10
Shocklee, Hank 15
Simmons, Russell 7
Sir Mix-A-Lot 14
Slick Rick 27
Smith, Will 26
Snoop Doggy Dogg 17
Snow 23
Spearhead 19
Special Ed 16
Sure!, Al B. 13
TLC 15
Tone-Loc 3
Too $hort 16
Tribe Called Quest, A 8
Trick Daddy 28
Tricky 18
US3 18
Usher 23
Vanilla Ice 6
Wu-Tang Clan 19
Yo Yo 9
Young M.C. 4

Record Company Executives
Ackerman, Will 3
Alpert, Herb 11
Blackwell, Chris 26
Brown, Tony 14
Busby, Jheryl 9
Chess, Leonard 24
Combs, Sean "Puffy" 25
Earlier sketch in CM 16
Davis, Chip 4
Davis, Clive 14
Ertegun, Ahmet 10
Foster, David 13
Gabriel, Peter 16
Earlier sketch in CM 2
Also see Genesis
Geffen, David 8
Gordy, Berry, Jr. 6
Hammond, John 6
Harley, Bill 7
Harrell, Andre 16
Jam, Jimmy, and Terry Lewis 11
Knight, Suge 15
Koppelman, Charles 14
Krasnow, Bob 15
LiPuma, Tommy 18
Madonna 16
Earlier sketch in CM 4
Marley, Rita 10
Martin, George 6
Mayfield, Curtis 8
Mercer, Johnny 13
Miller, Mitch 11
Mingus, Charles 9
Near, Holly 1
Ostin, Mo 17
Penner, Fred 10
Phillips, Sam 5
Reznor, Trent 13
Rhone, Sylvia 13
Robinson, Smokey 1
Rubin, Rick 9
Simmons, Russell 7
Spector, Phil 4
Teller, Al 15
Too $hort 16
Wexler, Jerry 15
Woods-Wright, Tomica 22

Reggae
Bad Brains **16**
Big Mountain **23**
Black Uhuru **12**
Burning Spear **15**
Cliff, Jimmy **8**
Dube, Lucky **17**
Inner Circle **15**
Israel Vibration **21**
Marley, Bob **3**
Marley, Rita **10**
Marley, Ziggy **3**
Mystic Revealers **16**
Skatalites, The **18**
Sly and Robbie **13**
Steel Pulse **14**
Third World **13**
Tosh, Peter **3**
UB40 **4**
Wailer, Bunny **11**

Rhythm and Blues/Soul
Aaliyah **21**
Abdul, Paula **3**
Adams, Oleta **17**
Alexander, Arthur **14**
All-4-One **17**
Austin, Dallas **16**
Badu, Erykah **26**
Baker, Anita **9**
Baker, LaVern **25**
Ball, Marcia **15**
Ballard, Hank **17**
Basehead **11**
Belle, Regina **6**
Benét, Eric **27**
Berry, Chuck **1**
Blackstreet **23**
Bland, Bobby "Blue" **12**
Blessid Union of Souls **20**
Blige, Mary J. **15**
Blues Brothers, The **3**
Bolton, Michael **4**
Booker T. & the M.G.'s **24**
Boyz II Men **15**
Brandy **19**
Braxton, Toni **17**
Brown, James **16**
Earlier sketch in CM **2**
Brown, Ruth **13**
Brownstone **21**
Bryson, Peabo **11**
Burdon, Eric **14**
Also see War
Also see Animals
Busby, Jheryl **9**
C + C Music Factory **16**
Campbell, Tevin **13**
Carey, Mariah **20**
Earlier sketch in CM **6**
Carr, James **23**
Charles, Ray **24**
Earlier sketch in CM **1**
Cole, Natalie **21**
Earlier sketch in CM **1**
Color Me Badd **23**
Commodores, The **23**
Cooke, Sam **1**
Also see Soul Stirrers, The
Crawford, Randy **25**
Cropper, Steve **12**
Curtis, King **17**
D'Angelo **20**
D'Arby, Terence Trent **3**
DeBarge, El **14**
Des'ree **24**
Earlier sketch in CM **15**
Dibango, Manu **14**
Diddley, Bo **3**
Domino, Fats **2**
Dr. John **7**
Dru Hill **25**
Earth, Wind and Fire **12**
Edmonds, Kenneth "Babyface" **12**
En Vogue **10**
Evora, Cesaria **19**
Fabulous Thunderbirds, The **1**
Four Tops, The **11**
Fox, Samantha **3**
Franklin, Aretha **17**
Earlier sketch in CM **2**
Gaye, Marvin **4**
Gill, Johnny **20**
Gordy, Berry, Jr. **6**
Green, Al **9**
Guthrie, Gwen **26**
Hall & Oates **6**
Hayes, Isaac **10**
Hill, Lauryn **25**
Holland-Dozier-Holland **5**
Houston, Whitney **25**
Earlier sketch in CM **8**
Howland, Don **24**
Hurt, Mississippi John **24**
Ike and Tina Turner **24**
Incognito **16**
Ingram, James **11**
Isley Brothers, The **8**
Jackson, Freddie **3**
Jackson, Janet **3**
Jackson, Michael **17**
Earlier sketch in CM **1**
Also see Jacksons, The
Jackson, Millie **14**
Jacksons, The **7**
Jam, Jimmy, and Terry Lewis **11**
James, Etta **6**
Jodeci **13**
John, Willie **25**
Jones, Booker T. **8**
Also see Booker T. & the M.G.'s
Jones, Grace **9**
Jones, Quincy **20**
Earlier sketch CM **2**
Jordan, Louis **11**
Jordan, Montell **26**
Kelly, R. **19**
Khan, Chaka **19**
Earlier sketch CM **9**
King, B. B. **24**
Earlier sketch in CM **1**
King, Ben E. **7**
Knight, Gladys **1**
Kool & the Gang **13**
LaBelle, Patti **8**
Los Lobos **2**
Love, G. **24**
Martha and the Vandellas **25**
Maxwell **22**
Mayfield, Curtis **8**
McKnight, Brian **22**
McPhatter, Clyde **25**
Medley, Bill **3**
Meters, The **14**
Milli Vanilli **4**
Mills, Stephanie **21**
Mo', Keb' **21**
Monica **26**
Monifah **24**
Moore, Chante **21**
Moore, Melba **7**
Morrison, Van **24**
Earlier sketch in CM **3**
Ndegéocello, Me'Shell **18**
Neville, Aaron **5**
Also see Neville Brothers, The
Neville Brothers, The **4**
O'Jays, The **13**
Ocean, Billy **4**
Ohio Players **16**
Otis, Johnny **16**
Pendergrass, Teddy **3**
Peniston, CeCe **15**
Perry, Phil **24**
Pickett, Wilson **10**
Platters, The **25**
Pointer Sisters, The **9**
Price, Lloyd **25**
Priest, Maxi **20**
Prince **14**
Earlier sketch in CM **1**
Rainey, Ma **22**
Rawls, Lou **19**
Redding, Otis **5**
Reese, Della **13**
Reeves, Martha **4**
Richie, Lionel **2**
Riley, Teddy **14**
Robinson, Smokey **1**
Ross, Diana **1**
Also see Supremes, The
Ruffin, David **6**
Also see Temptations, The
Sam and Dave **8**
Scaggs, Boz **12**
Secada, Jon **13**
Shai **23**
Shanice **14**
Shirelles, The **11**
Shocklee, Hank **15**
Silk **26**
Sledge, Percy **15**
Sly & the Family Stone **24**
Soul II Soul **17**
Spinners , The **21**
Stansfield, Lisa **9**
Staples, Mavis **13**
Staples, Pops **11**
Stewart, Rod **20**
Earlier sketch in CM **2**
Also see Faces, The
Stone, Sly **8**
Subdudes, The **18**
Supremes, The **6**
Also see Ross, Diana
Sure!, Al B. **13**
Sweat, Keith **13**
SWV **14**
Temptations, The **3**
Third World **13**
Thomas, Irma **16**
Thornton, Big Mama **18**
TLC **15**
Tony! Toni! Toné! **12**
Toussaint, Allen **11**
Turner, Tina **1**
Also see Ike & Tina Turner
Vandross, Luther **24**
Earlier sketch in CM **2**
Was (Not Was) **6**
Waters, Crystal **15**
Watley, Jody **26**
Earlier sketch in CM **9**

Wexler, Jerry **15**
White, Karyn **21**
Williams, Deniece **1**
Williams, Vanessa **10**
Wilson, Jackie **3**
Wilson, Nancy **28**
Winans, The **12**
Winbush, Angela **15**
Womack, Bobby **5**
Wonder, Stevie **17**
Earlier sketch in CM **2**
Zhane **22**

Rock
10,000 Maniacs **3**
311 **20**
AC/DC **4**
Adam Ant **13**
Adams, Bryan **20**
Earlier sketch in CM **2**
Aerosmith **22**
Earlier sketch in CM **3**
Afghan Whigs **17**
Alarm **2**
Albini, Steve **15**
Alexander, Arthur **14**
Alice in Chains **10**
Alien Sex Fiend **23**
Allen, Daevid **28**
Allman Brothers, The **6**
Alvin, Dave **17**
America **16**
American Music Club **15**
Animals **22**
Anthrax **11**
Apple, Fiona **28**
Aquabats **22**
Archers of Loaf **21**
Art of Noise **22**
Audio Adrenaline **22**
Aztec Camera **22**
Babes in Toyland **16**
Bad Brains **16**
Bad Company **22**
Bad Religion **28**
Badfinger **23**
Baker, Ginger **16**
Also see Cream
Ballard, Hank **17**
Band, The **9**
Bardo Pond **28**
Barenaked Ladies **18**
Barlow, Lou **20**
Also see Sebadoh
Basehead **11**
Beach Boys, The **1**
Beastie Boys, The **25**
Earlier sketch in CM **8**
Beat Farmers, The **23**
Beatles, The **2**
Beaver Brown Band, The **3**
Beck **18**
Beck, Jeff **4**
Also see Yardbirds, The
Belew, Adrian **5**
Belle and Sebastian **28**
Belly **16**
Ben Folds Five **20**
Benatar, Pat **8**
Berry, Chuck **1**
Bettie Serveert **17**
Bevis Frond **23**
Biafra, Jello **18**
Big Audio Dynamite **18**
Big Head Todd and the Monsters **20**
Bill Wyman & the Rhythm Kings **26**
Bishop, Jeb **28**
Bjork **16**
Black Crowes, The **7**
Black Flag **22**
Black, Frank **14**
Black Sabbath **9**
Blackman, Cindy **15**
Blind Melon **21**
Blink 182 **27**
Blonde Redhead **28**
Blondie **27**
Earlier sketch in CM **14**
Blood, Sweat and Tears **7**
Blue Oyster Cult **16**
Blue Rodeo **18**
Blues Traveler **15**
Blur **17**
BoDeans, The **20**
Earlier sketch in CM **3**
Bon Jovi **10**
Boredoms, The **28**
Boston **11**
Bowie, David **23**
Earlier sketch in CM **1**
Brad **21**
Bragg, Billy **7**
Breeders **19**
Brickell, Edie **3**
Brötzmann, Caspar **27**
Browne, Jackson **3**
Buckingham, Lindsey **8**
Also see Fleetwood Mac
Buckley, Tim **14**
Buffalo Springfield **24**
Buffalo Tom **18**
Built to Spill **27**
Burdon, Eric **14**
Also see War
Also see Animals
Burnett, T Bone **13**
Bush **18**
Butthole Surfers **16**
Buzzcocks, The **9**
Byrds, The **8**
Byrne, David **8**
Also see Talking Heads
Cake **27**
Cale, J. J. **16**
Earlier sketch in CM **9**
Camel **21**
Can **28**
Captain Beefheart and the Magic Band **26**
Earlier sketch in CM **10**
Caravan **24**
Cardigans **19**
Cars, The **20**
Catherine Wheel **18**
Cave, Nick **10**
Charlatans, The **13**
Charm Farm **20**
Cheap Trick **12**
Cher **1**
Also see Sonny and Cher
Chicago **3**
Childish, Billy **28**
Christian Death **28**
Chumbawamba **21**
Church, The **14**
Cinderella **16**
Circle Jerks, The **17**
Citizen King **27**
Clapton, Eric **11**
Earlier sketch in CM **1**
Also see Cream
Also see Yardbirds, The
Clash, The **4**
Clemons, Clarence **7**
Clinton, George **7**
Coasters, The **5**
Cobra Verde **28**
Cochrane , Tom **22**
Cocker, Joe **4**
Collective Soul **16**
Collins, Phil **2**
Also see Genesis
Compulsion **23**
Congo Norvell **22**
Cooder, Ry **2**
Also see Captain Beefheart and His Magic Band
Cooke, Sam **1**
Also see Soul Stirrers, The
Cooper, Alice **8**
Cope, Julian **16**
Costello, Elvis **12**
Earlier sketch in CM **2**
Cougar, John(ny)
See Mellencamp, John
Counting Crows **18**
Cracker **12**
Cramps, The **16**
Cranberries, The **14**
Crash Test Dummies **14**
Cream **9**
Creed **28**
Creedence Clearwater Revival **16**
Crenshaw, Marshall **5**
Crosby, David **3**
Also see Byrds, The
Crosby, Stills, and Nash **24**
Crow, Sheryl **18**
Crowded House **12**
Cult, The **16**
Cure, The **20**
Earlier sketch in CM **3**
Curry, Tim **3**
Curve **13**
D Generation **26**
D.O.A. **28**
D'Arby, Terence Trent **3**
Dahl, Jeff **28**
Dale, Dick **13**
Daltrey, Roger **3**
Also see Who, The
Damon and Naomi **25**
Dandy Warhols, The
Daniels, Charlie **6**
Danzig **7**
Dave Clark Five, The **12**
Dave, Edmunds **28**
Dave Matthews Band **18**
Davies, Ray **5**
dc Talk **18**
de Burgh, Chris **22**
Dead Can Dance **16**
Dead Milkmen **22**
Death in Vegas **28**
Deep Purple **11**
Def Leppard **3**
Deftones **22**
Del Amitri **18**
Depeche Mode **5**
Devo **13**
Diddley, Bo **3**
DiFranco, Ani **17**

Dinosaur Jr. **10**
Dire Straits **22**
Doc Pomus **14**
Dog's Eye View **21**
Dokken **16**
Doobie Brothers, The **3**
Doors, The **4**
Dreamtheater **23**
Dropkick Murphys **26**
Duran Duran **4**
Dylan, Bob **3**
Eagles, The **3**
Echobelly **21**
Eddy, Duane **9**
Einstürzende Neubauten **13**
Electric Light Orchestra **7**
Elliot, Cass **5**
Emerson, Lake & Palmer/Powell **5**
Eminem **28**
Emmet Swimming **24**
English Beat, The **9**
Eno, Brian **8**
Erickson, Roky **16**
Escovedo, Alejandro **18**
Etheridge, Melissa **16**
Earlier sketch in CM **4**
Eurythmics **6**
Everclear **18**
Ex, The **28**
Extreme **10**
Faces, The **22**
Fairport Convention **22**
Faith No More **7**
Faithfull, Marianne **14**
Fall, The **12**
Fear Factory **27**
Ferry, Bryan **1**
Filter **28**
fIREHOSE **11**
Fishbone **7**
Five Iron Frenzy **26**
Flaming Lips **22**
Fleetwood Mac **5**
Flores, Rosie **16**
Flying Luttenbachers, The **28**
Fogelberg, Dan **4**
Fogerty, John **2**
Also see Creedence Clearwater Revival
Folk Implosion, The **28**
Foo Fighters **20**
Ford, Lita **9**
Foreigner **21**
Fountains of Wayne **26**
Four Seasons, The **24**
Fox, Samantha **3**
Frampton, Peter **3**
Frankie Lymon and The Teenagers **24**
Franti, Michael **16**
Frey, Glenn **3**
Also see Eagles, The
Front 242 **19**
Froom, Mitchell **15**
Fu Manchu **22**
Fuel **27**
Fugazi **13**
Gabriel, Peter **16**
Earlier sketch in CM **2**
Also see Genesis
Gang of Four **8**
Garcia, Jerry **4**
Also see Grateful Dead, The
Gatton, Danny **16**
Gene Loves Jezebel **27**
Genesis **4**
Geraldine Fibbers **21**
Ghost **24**
Gift, Roland **3**
Gin Blossoms **18**
Glitter, Gary **19**
Go-Betweens, The **28**
Goo Goo Dolls, The **16**
Graham, Bill **10**
Grant Lee Buffalo **16**
Grateful Dead **5**
Grebenshikov, Boris **3**
Green Day **16**
Griffin, Patty **24**
Guess Who **23**
Guided By Voices **18**
Guns n' Roses **2**
Gus Gus **26**
Gwar **13**
Hagar, Sammy **21**
Hagen, Nina **25**
Hall & Oates **6**
Harper, Ben **17**
Harrison, George **2**
Also see Beatles, The
Harry, Deborah **4**
Also see Blondie
Harvey, Polly Jean **11**
Hassman, Nikki **26**
Hatfield, Juliana **12**
Also see Lemonheads, The
Healey, Jeff **4**
Heart **1**
Helmet **15**
Hendrix, Jimi **2**
Henley, Don **3**
Also see Eagles, The
Henry, Joe **18**
Hiatt, John **8**
Hodgson, Roger **26**
Also see Supertramp
Hole **14**
Holland-Dozier-Holland **5**
Hooters **20**
Hootie and the Blowfish **18**
Houston, Penelope **28**
Idol, Billy **3**
Imperial Teen **26**
INXS **21**
Earlier sketch in CM **2**
Iron Maiden **10**
Isaak, Chris **6**
Jackson, Joe **22**
Earlier sketch in CM **4**
Jackyl **24**
Jagger, Mick **7**
Also see Rolling Stones, The
Jam, The **27**
Jane's Addiction **6**
Jars of Clay **20**
Jayhawks, The **15**
Jefferson Airplane **5**
Jesus and Mary Chain, The **10**
Jesus Lizard **19**
Jethro Tull **8**
Jett, Joan **3**
Jimmie's Chicken Shack **22**
Joel, Billy **12**
Earlier sketch in CM **2**
Johansen, David **7**
John, Elton **20**
Earlier sketch in CM **3**
Jon Spencer Blues Explosion **18**
Joplin, Janis **3**
Journey **21**
Joy Division **19**
Judas Priest **10**
Kennedy, Nigel **8**
Kid Rock **27**
Kidjo, Anjelique **17**
King Crimson **17**
King Missile **22**
Kinks, The **15**
Kiss **25**
Earlier sketch in CM **5**
KMFDM **18**
Knopfler, Mark **25**
Earlier sketch in CM **3**
Also see Dire Straits
Korn **20**
Kravitz, Lenny **26**
Earlier sketch in CM **5**
L7 **12**
Landreth, Sonny **16**
Led Zeppelin **1**
Lee, Ben **26**
Leiber and Stoller **14**
Lemonheads, The **12**
Lennon, John **9**
Also see Beatles, The
Lennon, Julian **26**
Earlier sketch in CM **2**
Less Than Jake **22**
Letters to Cleo **22**
Limp Bizkit **27**
Lindley, David **2**
Linkous, Mark **26**
Lit **27**
Little Feat **4**
Little Texas **14**
Live **14**
Living Colour **7**
Lofgren, Nils **25**
Logan, Jack **27**
Loggins, Kenny **20**
Earlier sketch in CM **3**
Los Lobos **2**
Love and Rockets **15**
Love Spit Love **21**
Lowe, Nick **25**
Earlier sketch in CM **6**
Luna **18**
Luscious Jackson **27**
Earlier sketch in CM **19**
Lush **13**
Lydon, John **9**
Also see Sex Pistols, The
Lynne, Jeff **5**
Lynyrd Skynyrd **9**
M People **27**
MacIsaac, Ashley **21**
Madder Rose **17**
Manic Street Preachers **27**
Marilyn Manson **18**
Martin, George **6**
Marx, Richard **3**
Matchbox 20 **27**
MC5, The **9**
McCartney, Paul **4**
Also see Beatles, The
McClinton, Delbert **14**
McKee, Maria **11**
McMurtry, James **10**
Meat Loaf **12**
Meat Puppets, The **13**
Megadeth **9**
Mekons, The **15**
Mellencamp, John **20**
Earlier sketch in CM **2**

Metallica **7**
Midnight Oil **11**
Mighty Mighty Bosstones **20**
Mike & the Mechanics **17**
Miller, Steve **2**
Ministry **10**
Moby Grape **12**
Mogwai **27**
Mojave 3 **26**
Money, Eddie **16**
Monks of Doom **28**
Moody Blues, The **18**
Morphine **16**
Morrison, Jim **3**
Also see Doors, The
Morrison, Van **24**
Earlier sketch in CM **3**
Mötley Crüe **1**
Motörhead **10**
Mould, Bob **10**
Mudhoney **16**
Muldaur, Maria **18**
Murphy, Peter **22**
Myles, Alannah **4**
Nelson, Rick **2**
Neurosis **28**
New York Dolls **20**
Newman, Randy **4**
Newsboys, The **24**
Nicks, Stevie **25**
Earlier sketch in CM **2**
Also see Fleetwood Mac
Nirvana **8**
NOFX **28**
NRBQ **12**
Nugent, Ted **2**
O'Connor, Sinead **3**
Oasis **16**
Ocasek, Ric **5**
Offspring **19**
Olivia Tremor Control **28**
Ono, Yoko **11**
Orbison, Roy **2**
Orgy **27**
Osbourne, Ozzy **3**
Our Lady Peace **22**
Page, Jimmy **4**
Also see Led Zeppelin
Also see Yardbirds, The
Palmer, Robert **2**
Pantera **13**
Parker, Graham **10**
Parker, Maceo **7**
Parsons, Alan **12**
Parsons, Gram **7**
Also see Byrds, The
Pavement **14**
Pearl Jam **12**
Pearls Before Swine **24**
Pennywise **27**
Pere Ubu **17**
Perkins, Carl **9**
Petty, Tom **9**
Also see Tom Petty and the Heartbreakers
Phillips, Sam **5**
Phish **25**
Earlier sketch in CM **13**
Pigface **19**
Pink Floyd **2**
Pixies, The **21**
Placebo **27**
Plant, Robert **2**
Also see Led Zeppelin
Pogues, The **6**
Poi Dog Pondering **17**
Poison **11**
Police, The **20**
Pop, Iggy **23**
Earlier sketch in CM **1**
Presley, Elvis **1**
Pretenders, The **8**
Pretty Things, The **26**
Primal Scream **14**
Primus **11**
Prince **14**
Earlier sketch in CM **1**
Prine, John **7**
Proclaimers, The **13**
Promise Ring, The **28**
Prong **23**
Pulp **18**
Quasi **24**
Queen **6**
Queensryche **8**
Quicksilver Messenger Service **23**
R.E.M. **25**
Earlier sketch in CM **5**
Radiohead **24**
Rage Against the Machine **18**
Raitt, Bonnie **23**
Earlier sketch in CM **3**
Rammstein **25**
Ramones, The **9**
Rasputina **26**
Red Hot Chili Peppers, The **7**
Redd Kross **20**
Reed, Lou **16**
Earlier sketch in CM **1**
Also see Velvet Underground, The
Reef **24**
Reid, Vernon **2**
Also see Living Colour
REO Speedwagon **23**
Replacements, The **7**
Residents, The **14**
Reverend Horton Heat **19**
Reznor, Trent **13**
Richards, Keith **11**
Also see Rolling Stones, The
Richman, Jonathan **12**
Robertson, Robbie **2**
Rolling Stones, The **23**
Earlier sketch in CM **3**
Rollins, Henry **11**
Roth, David Lee **1**
Also see Van Halen
Rubin, Rick **9**
Rundgren, Todd **11**
Rush **8**
Rusted Root **26**
Ryder, Mitch **11**
Sambora, Richie **24**
Also see Bon Jovi
Santana, Carlos **19**
Earlier sketch in CM **1**
Satriani, Joe **4**
Scaggs, Boz **12**
Scorpions, The **12**
Screaming Trees **19**
Scud Mountain Boys **21**
Seal **14**
Sebadoh **26**
Seger, Bob **15**
Sepultura **12**
Sex Pistols, The **5**
Shadows, The **22**
Shaffer, Paul **13**
Shannon, Del **10**
Shocked, Michelle **4**
Shonen Knife **13**
Shudder to Think **20**
Silver Apples **23**
Silverchair **20**
Simon and Garfunkel **24**
Simon, Carly **22**
Earlier sketch in CM **4**
Simon, Paul **16**
Earlier sketch in CM **1**
Also see Simon and Garfunkel
Simple Minds **21**
Siouxsie and the Banshees **8**
Skinny Puppy **17**
Skunk Anansie **27**
Slayer **10**
Sleater-Kinney **20**
Sloan **28**
Smash Mouth **27**
Smashing Pumpkins **13**
Smith, Patti **17**
Earlier sketch in CM **1**
Smithereens, The **14**
Smiths, The **3**
Smog **28**
Social Distortion **27**
Earlier sketch in CM **19**
Son Volt **21**
Sonic Youth **26**
Earlier sketch in CM **9**
Soul Asylum **10**
Soundgarden **6**
Sparks **18**
Specials, The **21**
Spector, Phil **4**
Spencer Davis Group **19**
Spin Doctors **14**
Spinal Tap **8**
Spirit **22**
Sponge **18**
Springsteen, Bruce **25**
Earlier sketch in CM **6**
Squeeze **5**
Starr, Ringo **24**
Earlier sketch in CM **10**
Also see Beatles, The
Steeleye Span **19**
Steely Dan **5**
Steppenwolf **20**
Stevens, Cat **3**
Stewart, Rod **20**
Earlier sketch in CM **2**
Also see Faces, The
Stills, Stephen **5**
Also see Buffalo Springfield
Also see Crosby, Stills and Nash
Sting **19**
Earlier sketch in CM **2**
Also see Police, The
Stone Roses, The **16**
Stone, Sly **8**
Also see Sly & the Family Stone
Stone Temple Pilots **14**
Straw, Syd **18**
Stray Cats, The **11**
Stryper **2**
Sublime **19**
Sugarcubes, The **10**
Suicidal Tendencies **15**
Summers, Andy **3**
Also see Police, The
Sunny Day Real Estate **28**
Superdrag **23**
Supertramp **25**

Surfin' Pluto **24**
T. Rex **11**
Taylor, Mick
Also see Beatles, The
Taylor, Steve **26**
Tears for Fears **6**
Teenage Fanclub **13**
Television **17**
Tesla **15**
Texas Tornados, The **8**
The The **15**
They Might Be Giants **7**
Thin Lizzy **13**
Third Eye Blind **25**
Thompson, Richard **7**
Three Dog Night **5**
Throwing Muses **15**
Timbuk 3 **3**
Toad the Wet Sprocket **13**
Tom Petty and the Heartbreakers **26**
Tool **21**
Townshend, Pete **1**
Also see Who, The
Traffic **19**
Tragically Hip, The **18**
Treadmill Trackstar **21**
Trynin, Jen **21**
Tsunami **21**
Turner, Tina **1**
Also see Ike & Tina Turner
Tuxedomoon **21**
Type O Negative **27**
U2 **12**
Earlier sketch in CM **2**
Ulmer, James Blood **13**
Underworld **26**
Unitt, Victor
Also see Beatles, The
Urge Overkill **17**
Uriah Heep **19**
Vai, Steve **5**
Valens, Ritchie **23**
Valli, Frankie **10**
Van Halen **25**
Earlier sketch in CM **8**
Vandermark, Ken **28**
Vaughan, Jimmie **24**
Vaughan, Stevie Ray **1**
Velvet Underground, The **7**
Ventures **19**
Veruca Salt **20**
Verve Pipe, The **20**
Verve, The **18**
Vincent, Gene **19**
Violent Femmes **12**
Waits, Tom **27**
Earlier sketch in CM **12**
Earlier sketch in CM **1**
Wakeman, Rick **27**
Also see Yes
Wallflowers, The **20**
Walsh, Joe **5**
Also see Eagles, The
War **14**
Warrant **17**
Waterboys, The **27**
Wedding Present, The **28**
Weezer **20**
Weller, Paul **14**
Wendy O. Williams and The Plasmatics **26**
Westerberg, Paul **26**
White Zombie **17**
Whitesnake **5**
Whitley, Chris **16**
Who, The **3**
Wilson, Brian **24**
Also see Beach Boys, The
Winter, Johnny **5**
Winwood, Steve **2**
Also see Spencer Davis Group
Also see Traffic
Wolf, Peter **25**
Wray, Link **17**
Wyatt, Robert **24**
X **11**
XTC **26**
Earlier sketch in CM **10**
Yardbirds, The **10**
Yes **8**
Yo La Tengo **24**
Young, Neil **15**
Earlier sketch in CM **2**
Zappa, Frank **17**
Earlier sketch in CM **1**
Zevon, Warren **9**
Zombies, The **23**
ZZ Top **2**

Rock and Roll Pioneers
Ballard, Hank **17**
Berry, Chuck **1**
Clark, Dick **25**
Earlier sketch in CM **2**
Darin, Bobby **4**
Diddley, Bo **3**
Dion **4**
Domino, Fats **2**
Eddy, Duane **9**
Everly Brothers, The **2**
Francis, Connie **10**
Glitter, Gary **19**
Haley, Bill **6**
Hawkins, Screamin' Jay **8**
Holly, Buddy **1**
James, Etta **6**
Jordan, Louis **11**
Lewis, Jerry Lee **2**
Little Richard **1**
Nelson, Rick **2**
Orbison, Roy **2**
Otis, Johnny **16**
Paul, Les **2**
Perkins, Carl **9**
Phillips, Sam **5**
Presley, Elvis **1**
Professor Longhair **6**
Sedaka, Neil **4**
Shannon, Del **10**
Shirelles, The **11**
Spector, Phil **4**
Twitty, Conway **6**
Valli, Frankie **10**
Wilson, Jackie **3**
Wray, Link **17**

Saxophone
Adderley, Cannonball **15**
Anderson, Wessell **23**
Ayler, Albert **19**
Barbieri, Gato **22**
Bechet, Sidney **17**
Braxton, Anthony **12**
Brötzmann, Peter **26**
Carter, Benny **3**
Also see McKinney's Cotton Pickers
Carter, James **18**
Chenier, C. J. **15**
Clemons, Clarence **7**
Coleman, Ornette **5**
Coltrane, John **4**
Curtis, King **17**
Desmond, Paul **23**
Dibango, Manu **14**
Garrett, Kenny **28**
Getz, Stan **12**
Golson, Benny **21**
Gordon, Dexter **10**
Harris, Eddie **15**
Hawkins, Coleman **11**
Henderson, Joe **14**
Herman, Woody **12**
Hodges, Johnny **24**
Jacquet, Illinois **17**
James, Boney **21**
Kenny G **14**
Kirk, Rahsaan Roland **6**
Koz, Dave **19**
Lacy, Steve **23**
Lateef, Yusef **16**
Lloyd, Charles **22**
Lopez, Israel "Cachao" **14**
Lovano, Joe **13**
Marsalis, Branford **10**
Morgan, Frank **9**
Mulligan, Gerry **16**
Murray, Dave **28**
Najee **21**
Osby, Greg **21**
Parker, Charlie **5**
Parker, Evan **28**
Parker, Maceo **7**
Pepper, Art **18**
Redman, Joshua **25**
Earlier sketch in CM **12**
Rollins, Sonny **7**
Russell, Pee Wee **25**
Sanborn, David **28**
Earlier sketch in CM **1**
Sanders, Pharoah **28**
Earlier sketch in CM **16**
Shorter, Wayne **5**
Smith, Tommy **28**
Threadgill, Henry **9**
Vandermark, Ken **28**
Washington, Grover, Jr. **5**
Winter, Paul **10**
Young, La Monte **16**
Young, Lester **14**
Zorn, John **15**

Sintir
Hakmoun, Hassan **15**

Songwriters
2Pac **17**
Acuff, Roy **2**
Adams, Bryan **20**
Earlier sketch in CM **2**
Adams, Yolanda **23**
Afanasieff, Walter **26**
Aikens, Rhett **22**
Albini, Steve **15**
Alexander, Arthur **14**
Allen, Peter **11**
Allison, Mose **17**
Alpert, Herb **11**
Alvin, Dave **17**
Amos, Tori **12**
Anderson, John **5**
Anka, Paul **2**
Apple, Fiona **28**
Armatrading, Joan **4**

Atkins, Chet **26**
Earlier sketch in CM **5**
Autry, Gene **25**
Earlier sketch in CM **12**
Bacharach, Burt **20**
Earlier sketch in CM **1**
Badu, Erykah **26**
Baez, Joan **1**
Baker, Anita **9**
Barlow, Lou **20**
Basie, Count **2**
Belew, Adrian **5**
Benét, Eric **27**
Benton, Brook **7**
Berg, Matraca **16**
Berlin, Irving **8**
Berry, Chuck **1**
Bjork **16**
Also see Sugarcubes, The
Black, Clint **5**
Black, Frank **14**
Blades, Ruben **2**
Blegvad, Peter **28**
Blige, Mary J. **15**
Bloom, Luka **14**
Bond, Johnny **28**
Brady, Paul **8**
Bragg, Billy **7**
Brandt, Paul **22**
Brickell, Edie **3**
Brokop, Lisa **22**
Brooks, Garth **25**
Earlier sketch in CM **8**
Brown, Bobby **4**
Brown, James **16**
Earlier sketch in CM **2**
Brown, Junior **15**
Brown, Marty **14**
Browne, Jackson **3**
Buckingham, Lindsey **8**
Also see Fleetwood Mac
Buckley, Jeff **22**
Buckley, Tim **14**
Buffett, Jimmy **4**
Burdon, Eric **14**
Also see War
Also see Animals
Burnett, T Bone **13**
Burning Spear **15**
Burroughs, William S. **26**
Bush, Kate **4**
Byrne, David **8**
Also see Talking Heads
Cahn, Sammy **11**
Cale, J. J. **16**
Earlier sketch in CM **9**
Also see Cale, John
Calloway, Cab **6**
Campbell, Sarah Elizabeth **23**
Captain Beefheart and His Magic Band **26**
Earlier sketch in CM **10**
Cardwell, Joi **22**
Carlisle, Bob **22**
Carmichael, Hoagy **27**
Carter, Carlene **8**
Carter, Deana **25**
Cash, Johnny **17**
Earlier sketch in CM **1**
Cash, Rosanne **2**
Chandra, Sheila **16**
Chapin, Harry **6**
Chapin-Carpenter, Mary **25**
Earlier sketch in CM **6**
Chapman, Steven Curtis **15**
Chapman, Tracy **4**
Chaquico, Craig **23**
Also see Jefferson Starship
Charles, Ray **24**
Earlier sketch in CM **1**
Chenier, C. J. **15**
Chesnutt, Vic **28**
Childish, Billy **28**
Childs, Toni **2**
Chilton, Alex **10**
Clapton, Eric **11**
Earlier sketch in CM **1**
Also see Cream
Also see Yardbirds, The
Clark, Guy **17**
Clements, Vassar **18**
Cleveland, James **1**
Clinton, George **7**
Cochrane, Tom **23**
Cockburn, Bruce **8**
Cohen, Leonard **3**
Cole, Lloyd **9**
Cole, Nat King **3**
Collie, Mark **15**
Collins, Albert **4**
Collins, Judy **4**
Collins, Phil **2**
Also see Genesis
Cooder, Ry **2**
Cooke, Sam **1**
Also see Soul Stirrers, The
Cooper, Alice **8**
Cope, Julian **16**
Costello, Elvis **12**
Earlier sketch in CM **2**
Cotten, Elizabeth **16**
Crenshaw, Marshall **5**
Croce, Jim **3**
Cropper, Steve **12**
Crosby, David **3**
Also see Byrds, The
Crow, Sheryl **18**
Crowe, J. D. **5**
Crowell, Rodney **8**
Dahl, Jeff **28**
Daniels, Charlie **6**
Davies, Ray **5**
Also see Kinks, the
de Burgh, Chris **22**
DeBarge, El **14**
DeMent, Iris **13**
Denver, John **22**
Earlier sketch in CM **1**
Des'ree **24**
Earlier sketch in CM **15**
Diamond, Neil **1**
Diddley, Bo **3**
Diffie, Joe **27**
Earlier sketch in CM **10**
Difford, Chris
See Squeeze
DiFranco, Ani **17**
Dion **4**
Dixon, Willie **10**
DMX **25**
Doc Pomus **14**
Domino, Fats **2**
Donovan **9**
Dorsey, Thomas A. **11**
Doucet, Michael **8**
Drake, Nick **17**
Dube, Lucky **17**
Dulli, Greg **17**
See Afghan Whigs, The
Dylan, Bob **21**
Earlier sketch in CM **3**
Earle, Steve **16**
Earlier sketch in CM **1**
Edmonds, Kenneth "Babyface" **12**
Elfman, Danny **9**
Ellington, Duke **2**
Emmanuel, Tommy **21**
English, Michael **23**
Enigma **14**
Erickson, Roky **16**
Ertegun, Ahmet **10**
Escovedo, Alejandro **18**
Estefan, Gloria **15**
Earlier sketch in CM **2**
Etheridge, Melissa **16**
Earlier sketch in CM **4**
Evans, Sara **27**
Everlast **27**
Faithfull, Marianne **14**
Ferry, Bryan **1**
Flack, Roberta **5**
Flatt, Lester **3**
Fogelberg, Dan **4**
Fogerty, John **2**
Also see Creedence Clearwater Revival
Fordham, Julia **15**
Foster, David **13**
Frampton, Peter **3**
Franti, Michael **16**
Frey, Glenn **3**
Also see Eagles, The
Fripp, Robert **9**
Frizzell, Lefty **10**
Gabriel, Peter **16**
Earlier sketch in CM **2**
Also see Genesis
Garcia, Jerry **4**
Also see Grateful Dead, The
Gaye, Marvin **4**
Geldof, Bob **9**
Gershwin, George and Ira **11**
Gibson, Bob **23**
Gibson, Debbie **24**
Earlier sketch in CM **1**
Also see Gibson, Deborah
Gift, Roland **3**
Gill, Vince **7**
Gilley, Mickey **7**
Goffin-King **24**
Gold, Julie **22**
Goodman, Benny **4**
Gordy, Berry, Jr. **6**
Gorka, John **18**
Grant, Amy **7**
Green, Al **9**
Greenwood, Lee **12**
Griffin, Patty **24**
Griffith, Nanci **3**
Guthrie, Arlo **6**
Guthrie, Gwen **26**
Guthrie, Woodie **2**
Guy, Buddy **4**
Hagen, Nina **25**
Haggard, Merle **2**
Hall, Tom T. **26**
Earlier sketch in CM **4**
Hamlisch, Marvin **1**
Hammer, M.C. **5**
Hancock, Herbie **25**
Earlier sketch in CM **8**
Hardin, Tim **18**
Harding, John Wesley **6**
Harley, Bill **7**

Harper, Ben **17**
Harris, Emmylou **4**
Harrison, George **2**
 Also see Beatles, The
Harry, Deborah **4**
 Also see Blondie
Hartford, John **1**
Hatfield, Juliana **12**
 Also see Lemonheads, The
Hawkins, Screamin' Jay **8**
Hayes, Isaac **10**
Healey, Jeff **4**
Hedges, Michael **3**
Hendrix, Jimi **2**
Henley, Don **3**
 Also see Eagles, The
Henry, Joe **18**
Hiatt, John **8**
Hill, Lauryn **25**
Hinojosa, Tish **13**
Hitchcock, Robyn **9**
Holly, Buddy **1**
Hornsby, Bruce **25**
 Earlier sketch in CM **3**
Houston, Penelope **28**
Howard, Harlan **15**
Ian, Janis **24**
 Earlier sketch in CM **5**
Ice Cube **25**
 Earlier sketch in CM **10**
Ice-T **7**
Idol, Billy **3**
Imbruglia, Natalie **27**
Isaak, Chris **6**
Jackson, Alan **25**
 Earlier sketch in CM **7**
Jackson, Janet **16**
 Earlier sketch in CM **3**
Jackson, Joe **22**
 Earlier sketch in CM **4**
Jackson, Michael **17**
 Earlier sketch in CM **1**
 Also see Jacksons, The
Jackson, Millie **14**
Jagger, Mick **7**
 Also see Rolling Stones, The
Jam, Jimmy, and Terry Lewis **11**
James, Rick **2**
Jarreau, Al **1**
Jennings, Waylon **4**
Jett, Joan **3**
Jewel **25**
Joel, Billy **12**
 Earlier sketch in CM **2**
Johansen, David **7**
John, Elton **20**
 Earlier sketch in CM **3**
Johnson, Lonnie **17**
Jones, George **4**
Jones, Quincy **20**
 Earlier sketch in CM **2**
Jones, Rickie Lee **4**
Joplin, Janis **3**
Jordan, Montell **26**
Kane, Big Daddy **7**
Kee, John P. **15**
Keith, Toby **17**
Kelly, R. **19**
Ketchum, Hal **14**
Khan, Chaka **19**
 Earlier sketch in CM **9**
King, Albert **2**
King, B. B. **24**
 Earlier sketch in CM **1**
King, Ben E. **7**
King, Carole **6**
King, Freddy **17**
Knopfler, Mark **25**
 Earlier sketch in CM **3**
 Also see Dire Straits
Kottke, Leo **13**
Kravitz, Lenny **26**
 Earlier sketch in CM **5**
Kristofferson, Kris **4**
L.L. Cool J **5**
Landreth, Sonny **16**
Lang, K. D. **25**
 Earlier sketch in CM **4**
Larkin, Patty **9**
Lavin, Christine **6**
LeDoux, Chris **12**
Lee, Ben **26**
Lee, Peggy **8**
Lehrer, Tom **7**
Leiber and Stoller **14**
Lennon, John **9**
 Also see Beatles, The
Lennon, Julian **26**
 Earlier sketch in CM **2**
Lewis, Huey **9**
Lightfoot, Gordon **3**
Linkous, Mark **26**
Little Richard **1**
Loeb, Lisa **23**
Logan, Jack **27**
Loggins, Kenny **20**
 Earlier sketch in CM **3**
Love, Laura **20**
Loveless, Patty **5**
Lovett, Lyle **28**
 Earlier sketch in CM **5**
Lowe, Nick **25**
 Earlier sketch in CM **6**
Lydon, John **9**
 Also see Sex Pistols, The
Lynn, Loretta **2**
Lynne, Jeff **5**
Lynne, Shelby **5**
MacColl, Kirsty **12**
Madonna **16**
 Earlier sketch in CM **4**
Manilow, Barry **2**
Mann, Aimee **22**
Mann, Billy **23**
Marley, Bob **3**
Marley, Ziggy **3**
Marshall, Amanda **27**
Marx, Richard **3**
Mattea, Kathy **5**
Mayfield, Curtis **8**
MC 900 Ft. Jesus **16**
MC Breed **17**
McCartney, Paul **4**
 Also see Beatles, The
McClinton, Delbert **14**
McCorkle, Susannah **27**
McCoury, Del **15**
McCulloch, Ian **23**
McLachlan, Sarah **12**
McLaren, Malcolm **23**
McLean, Don **7**
McLennan, Grant **21**
McMurtry, James **10**
McTell, Blind Willie **17**
Medley, Bill **3**
Melanie **12**
Mellencamp, John **20**
 Earlier sketch in CM **2**
 Also see John Cougar Mellencamp
Mercer, Johnny **13**
Merchant, Natalie **25**
 Also see 10,000 Maniacs
Messina, Jo Dee **26**
Michael, George **9**
Miller, Roger **4**
Miller, Steve **2**
Milsap, Ronnie **2**
Mitchell, Joni **17**
 Earlier sketch in CM **2**
Moffatt, Katy **18**
Morrison, Jim **3**
Morrison, Van **24**
 Earlier sketch in CM **3**
Morrissey **10**
Morrissey, Bill **12**
Morton, Jelly Roll **7**
Mould, Bob **10**
Moyet, Alison **12**
Nascimento, Milton **6**
Ndegéocello, Me'Shell **18**
Near, Holly **1**
Nelson, Rick **2**
Nelson, Willie **11**
 Earlier sketch in CM **1**
Newman, Randy **27**
 Earlier sketch in CM **4**
Nicks, Stevie **25**
 Earlier sketch in CM **2**
 Also see Fleetwood Mac
Nilsson **10**
Nugent, Ted **2**
Nyro, Laura **12**
O'Connor, Sinead **3**
Ocasek, Ric **5**
Ocean, Billy **4**
Ochs, Phil **7**
Odetta **7**
Orbison, Roy **2**
Orton, Beth **26**
Osbourne, Ozzy **3**
Oslin, K. T. **3**
Owens, Buck **2**
Page, Jimmy **4**
 Also see Led Zeppelin
 Also see Yardbirds, The
Palmer, Robert **2**
Paris, Twila **16**
Parker, Graham **10**
Parks, Van Dyke **17**
Parnell, Lee Roy **15**
Parsons, Gram **7**
 Also see Byrds, The
Parton, Dolly **24**
 Earlier sketch in CM **2**
Paul, Les **2**
Paxton, Tom **5**
Peniston, CeCe **15**
Penn, Michael **4**
Perkins, Carl **9**
Petty, Tom **9**
 Also see Tom Petty and the Heartbreakers
Phair, Liz **14**
Phillips, Sam **12**
Pickett, Wilson **10**
Plant, Robert **2**
 Also see Led Zeppelin
Pop, Iggy **23**
Porter, Cole **10**
Price, Lloyd **25**
Prince **14**
 Earlier sketch in CM **1**
Prine, John **7**
Professor Longhair **6**

Rabbitt, Eddie **24**
Earlier sketch in CM **5**
Raitt, Bonnie **23**
Earlier sketch in CM **3**
Rea, Chris **12**
Redding, Otis **5**
Reddy, Helen **9**
Reed, Lou **16**
Earlier sketch in CM **1**
Also see Velvet Underground, The
Reid, Vernon **2**
Also see Living Colour
Rice, Chris **25**
Rich, Charlie **3**
Richards, Keith **11**
Also see Rolling Stones, The
Richey, Kim **20**
Richie, Lionel **2**
Richman, Jonathan **12**
Riley, Teddy **14**
Ritchie, Jean **4**
Robbins, Marty **9**
Robertson, Robbie **2**
Robillard, Duke **2**
Robinson, Smokey **1**
Rodgers, Jimmie **3**
Rodgers, Richard **9**
Roth, David Lee **1**
Also see Van Halen
Russell, Mark **6**
Ryder, Mitch **23**
Sade **2**
Sager, Carole Bayer **5**
Sanborn, David **28**
Earlier sketch in CM **1**
Sangare, Oumou **22**
Satriani, Joe **4**
Scaggs, Boz **12**
Scott-Heron, Gil **13**
Scruggs, Earl **3**
Scruggs, Randy **28**
Seal **14**
Seals, Dan **9**
Secada, Jon **13**
Sedaka, Neil **4**
Seeger, Pete **4**
Also see Weavers, The
Seger, Bob **15**
Sexsmith, Ron **27**
Shannon, Del **10**
Sheila E. **3**
Shepherd, Kenny Wayne **22**
Shocked, Michelle **4**
Siberry, Jane **6**
Simon, Carly **22**
Earlier sketch in CM **4**
Simon, Paul **16**
Earlier sketch in CM **1**
Also see Simon and Garfunkel
Skaggs, Ricky **5**
Sledge, Percy **15**
Smith, Elliott **28**
Smith, Patti **17**
Earlier sketch in CM **1**
Smith, Will **26**
Snoop Doggy Dogg **17**
Sondheim, Stephen **8**
Spector, Phil **4**
Springsteen, Bruce **25**
Earlier sketch in CM **6**
St. James, Rebecca **26**
Stanley, Ralph **5**
Starr, Ringo **10**
Also see Beatles, The
Stevens, Cat **3**
Stevens, Ray **7**
Stewart, Rod **20**
Earlier sketch in CM **2**
Also see Faces, The
Stills, Stephen **5**
Sting **19**
Earlier sketch in CM **2**
Also see Police, The
Stockwood, Kim **26**
Strait, George **5**
Straw, Syd **18**
Streisand, Barbra **2**
Stuart, Marty **9**
Styne, Jule **21**
Summer, Donna **12**
Summers, Andy **3**
Also see Police, The
Sure!, Al B. **13**
Sweat, Keith **13**
Sweet, Matthew **9**
Taj Mahal **6**
Taupin, Bernie **22**
Taylor, James **25**
Earlier sketch in CM **2**
Taylor, Koko **10**
Taylor, Steve **26**
Thompson, Richard **7**
Thornton, Big Mama **18**
Tikaram, Tanita **9**
Tillis, Mel **7**
Tillis, Pam **25**
Earlier sketch in CM **8**
Tippin, Aaron **12**
Tone-L c **3**
Torme, Mel **4**
Tosh, Peter **3**
Toussaint, Allen **11**
Townshend, Pete **1**
Also see Who, The
Travis, Merle **14**
Travis, Randy **9**
Treadmill Trackstar **21**
Tricky **18**
Tritt, Travis **7**
Trynin, Jen **21**
Tubb, Ernest **4**
Twain, Shania **17**
Twitty, Conway **6**
Vai, Steve **5**
Also see Whitesnake
Van Ronk, Dave **12**
Van Shelton, Ricky **5**
Van Zandt, Townes **13**
Vandross, Luther **24**
Earlier sketch in CM **2**
Vega, Suzanne **3**
Wachtel, Waddy **26**
Wagoner, Porter **13**
Waits, Tom **27**
Earlier sketch in CM **12**
Earlier sketch in CM **1**
Walden, Narada Michael **14**
Walker, Jerry Jeff **13**
Walker, T-Bone **5**
Waller, Fats **7**
Walsh, Joe **5**
Also see Eagles, The
Wariner, Steve **18**
Warren, Diane **21**
Waters, Crystal **15**
Waters, Muddy **24**
Earlier sketch in CM **4**
Watley, Jody **26**
Earlier sketch in CM **9**
Watt, Mike **22**
Webb, Jimmy **12**
Weill, Kurt **12**
Weller, Paul **14**
West, Dottie **8**
Westerberg, Paul **26**
White, Karyn **21**
White, Lari **15**
Whitley, Chris **16**
Whitley, Keith **7**
Williams, Dar **21**
Williams, Deniece **1**
Williams, Don **4**
Williams, Hank, Jr. **1**
Williams, Hank, Sr. **4**
Williams, Lucinda **24**
Earlier sketch in CM **10**
Williams, Paul **26**
Earlier sketch in CM **5**
Williams, Victoria **17**
Wills, Bob **6**
Wilson, Brian **24**
Also see Beach Boys, The
Winbush, Angela **15**
Winter, Johnny **5**
Winwood, Steve **2**
Also see Spencer Davis Group
Also see Traffic
Womack, Bobby **5**
Wonder, Stevie **17**
Earlier sketch in CM **2**
Wray, Link **17**
Wyatt, Robert **24**
Wynette, Tammy **24**
Earlier sketch in CM **2**
Yearwood, Trisha **25**
Earlier sketch in CM **10**
Yoakam, Dwight **21**
Earlier sketch in CM **1**
Young, Neil **15**
Earlier sketch in CM **2**
Zappa, Frank **17**
Earlier sketch in CM **1**
Zevon, Warren **9**

Trombone
Anderson, Ray **7**
Bishop, Jeb **28**
Brown, Lawrence **23**
Mandel, Johnny **28**
Miller, Glenn **6**
Rudd, Roswell **28**
Teagarden, Jack **10**
Turre, Steve **22**

Trumpet
Alpert, Herb **11**
Armstrong, Louis **4**
Baker, Chet **13**
Berigan, Bunny **2**
Blanchard, Terence **13**
Brown, Clifford **24**
Cherry, Don **10**
Coleman, Ornette **5**
Davis, Miles **1**
Eldridge, Roy **9**
Also see McKinney's Cotton Pickers
Ferguson, Maynard **7**
Gillespie, Dizzy **6**
Hargrove, Roy **15**
Harrell, Tom **28**
Hawkins, Erskine **19**
Hirt, Al **5**
Isham, Mark **14**

James, Harry **11**
Jensen, Ingrid **22**
Jones, Quincy **20**
Earlier sketch in CM **2**
Jones, Thad **19**
Loughnane, Lee **3**
Mandel, Johnny **28**
Marsalis, Wynton **20**
Earlier sketch in CM **6**
Masekela, Hugh **7**
Matthews, Eric **22**
Mighty Mighty Bosstones **20**
Miles, Ron **22**
Navarro, Fats **25**
Oliver, King **15**
Payton, Nicholas **27**
Rodney, Red **14**
Sandoval, Arturo **15**
Severinsen, Doc **1**
Shaw, Woody **27**
Terry, Clark **24**

Tuba

Phillips, Harvey **3**

Vibraphone

Burton, Gary **10**
Hampton, Lionel **6**
Jackson, Milt **15**
Norvo, Red **12**

Viola

Menuhin, Yehudi **11**
Zukerman, Pinchas **4**

Violin

Acuff, Roy **2**
Anderson, Laurie **25**
Earlier sketch in CM **1**
Bell, Joshua **21**
Bromberg, David **18**
Carter, Regina **22**
Chang, Sarah **7**
Clements, Vassar **18**
Coleman, Ornette **5**
Cugat, Xavier **23**
Daniels, Charlie **6**
Doucet, Michael **8**
Germano, Lisa **18**
Gingold, Josef **6**
Grappelli, Stephane **10**
Hartford, John **1**
Kang, Eyvind **28**
Kennedy, Nigel **8**
Krauss, Alison **10**
Lamb, Barbara **19**
Marriner, Neville **7**
Menuhin, Yehudi **11**
Midori **7**
Mutter, Anne-Sophie **23**
O'Connor, Mark **1**
Perlman, Itzhak **2**
Ponty, Jean-Luc **8**
Rieu, André **26**
Salerno-Sonnenberg, Nadja **3**
Skaggs, Ricky **5**
Stern, Isaac **7**
Vanessa-Mae **26**
Whiteman, Paul **17**
Wills, Bob **6**
Zukerman, Pinchas **4**

Cumulative Musicians Index

Volume numbers appear in **bold**.

10,000 Maniacs **3**
2 Unlimited **18**
23, Richard
 See Front 242
2Pac **17**
 Also see Digital Underground
3-D
 See Massive Attack
311 **20**
4Him **23**
A-ha **22**
Aaliyah **21**
Abba **12**
Abbott, Jacqueline
 See Beautiful South
Abbott, Jude
 See Chumbawamba
Abbruzzese, Dave
 See Pearl Jam
Abdul, Paula **3**
Abercrombie, Jeff
 See Fuel
Abercrombie, John **25**
Abong, Fred
 See Belly
Abrahams, Mick
 See Jethro Tull
Abrams, Bryan
 See Color Me Badd
Abrantes, Fernando
 See Kraftwerk
AC/DC **4**
Ace of Base **22**
Ackerman, Will **3**
Acland, Christopher
 See Lush
Acuff, Roy **2**
Acuna, Alejandro
 See Weather Report
Adam Ant **13**
Adamendes, Elaine
 See Throwing Muses
Adams, Bryan **20**
 Earlier sketch in CM **2**
Adams, Clifford
 See Kool & the Gang
Adams, Craig
 See Cult, The
Adams, Donn
 See NRBQ
Adams, John **8**
Adams, Mark
 See Specials, The
Adams, Oleta **17**
Adams, Terry
 See NRBQ
Adams, Victoria
 See Spice Girls
Adams, Yolanda **23**
Adamson, Barry **28**
Adcock, Eddie
 See Country Gentleman, The
Adderley, Cannonball **15**
Adderly, Julian
 See Adderley, Cannonball
Adé, King Sunny **18**
Adler, Steven
 See Guns n' Roses
Aerosmith **22**
 Earlier sketch in CM **3**
Afanasieff, Walter **26**
Afghan Whigs **17**
Afonso, Marie
 See Zap Mama
AFX
 See Aphex Twin
Agnew, Rikk
 See Christian Death
Agust, Daniel
 See Gus Gus
Air Supply **22**
Aitchison, Dominic
 See Mogwai
Ajile
 See Arrested Development
Akingbola, Sola
 See Jamiroquai
Akins, Rhett **22**
Alabama **21**
 Earlier sketch in CM **1**
Alan, Skip
 See Pretty Things, The
Alarm **22**
Albarn, Damon
 See Blur
Albert, Nate
 See Mighty Mighty Bosstones
Alberti, Dorona
 See KMFDM
Albini, Steve **15**
Albuquerque, Michael de
 See Electric Light Orchestra
Alder, John
 See Gong
 Also see Pretty Things, The
Alexakis, Art
 See Everclear
Alexander, Arthur **14**
Alexander, Tim
 See Asleep at the Wheel
Alexander, Tim "Herb"
 See Primus
Ali
 See Tribe Called Quest, A
Alice in Chains **10**
Alien Sex Fiend **23**
Alkema, Jan Willem
 See Compulsion
All Saints **25**
All-4-One **17**
Allcock, Martin
 See Fairport Convention
 Also see Jethro Tull
Allen, April
 See C + C Music Factory
Allen, Chad
 See Guess Who
Allen, Daevid
 See Gong
Allen, Daevid **28**
Allen, Dave
 See Gang of Four
Allen, Debbie **8**
Allen, Duane
 See Oak Ridge Boys, The
Allen, Geri **10**
Allen, Johnny Ray
 See Subdudes, The
Allen, Papa Dee
 See War
Allen, Peter **11**
Allen, Red
 See Osborne Brothers, The
Allen, Rick
 See Def Leppard
Allen, Ross
 See Mekons, The
Allen, Wally
 See Pretty Things, The
Allison, Luther **21**
Allison, Mose **17**
Allman Brothers, The **6**
Allman, Chris
 See Greater Vision
Allman, Duane
 See Allman Brothers, The
Allman, Gregg
 See Allman Brothers, The
Allsup, Michael Rand
 See Three Dog Night
Alpert, Herb **11**
Alphonso, Roland
 See Skatalites, The
Alsing, Pelle
 See Roxette
Alston, Andy
 See Del Amitri
Alston, Shirley
 See Shirelles, The
Altan **18**
Altenfelder, Andy
 See Willem Breuker Kollektief
Alvin, Dave **17**
 Also see X
Am, Svet
 See KMFDM
Amato, Dave
 See REO Speedwagon
Amedee, Steve
 See Subdudes, The
Ameling, Elly **24**
Ament, Jeff
 See Pearl Jam
America **16**
American Music Club **15**
Amon, Robin
 See Pearls Before Swine

Amos, Tori **12**
Anastasio, Trey
See Phish
Anderson, Al
See NRBQ
Anderson, Andy
See Cure, The
Anderson, Brett
See Suede
Anderson, Cleave
See Blue Rodeo
Anderson, Emma
See Lush
Anderson, Gladstone
See Skatalites, The
Anderson, Ian
See Jethro Tull
Anderson, Jhelisa
See Shamen, The
Anderson, John **5**
Anderson, Jon
See Yes
Anderson, June **27**
Anderson, Keith
See Dirty Dozen Brass Band
Anderson, Laurie **25**
Earlier sketch in CM **1**
Anderson, Marian **8**
Anderson, Pamela
See Incognito
Anderson, Ray **7**
Anderson, Signe
See Jefferson Airplane
Anderson, Wessell **23**
Andersson, Benny
See Abba
Andes, Mark
See Spirit
Andes, Matt
See Spirit
Andes, Rachel
See Spirit
Andrews, Barry
See XTC
Andrews, Christopher
See Mojave 3
Andrews, Julie **4**
Andrews, Laverne
See Andrews Sisters, The
Andrews, Mark
See Dru Hill,
Andrews, Maxene
See Andrews Sisters, The
Andrews, Patty
See Andrews Sisters, The
Andrews, Revert
See Dirty Dozen Brass Band
Andrews Sisters, The **9**
Andy, Horace
See Massive Attack
Andy,
See Ex, The
Anger, Darol
See Turtle Island String Quartet
Angus, Colin
See Shamen, The
Animals, The **22**
Anka, Paul **2**
Anointed **21**
Anonymous 4 **23**
Anonymous, Rodney
See Dead Milkmen
Anselmo, Philip
See Pantera
Ant, Adam
See Adam Ant
Anthony, Larry
See Dru Hill
Anthony, Marc **19**
Anthony, Michael
See Massive Attack
Anthony, Michael
See Van Halen
Anthrax **11**
Anton, Alan
See Cowboy Junkies, The
Antoni, Mark De Gli
See Soul Coughing
Antunes, Michael
See Beaver Brown Band, The
Anway, Susan
See Magnetic Fields, The
Aphex Twin **14**
Appice, Vinnie
See Black Sabbath
Apple, Fiona **28**
Appleton, Natalie
See All Saints
Appleton, Nicole
See All Saints
Aqua Velvets **23**
Aquabats, The **22**
Araya, Tom
See Slayer
Archers of Loaf **21**
Arden, Jann **21**
Ardolino, Tom
See NRBQ
Arellano, Rod
See Aquabats, The
Arena, Tina **21**
Argent, Rod
See Zombies, The
Argerich, Martha **27**
Arkenstone, David **20**
Arlen, Harold **27**
Arm, Mark
See Mudhoney
Armatrading, Joan **4**
Armerding, Jake
See Northern Lights
Armerding, Taylor
See Northern Lights
Armstrong, Billie Joe
See Green Day
Armstrong, Louis **4**
Armstrong, Vanessa Bell **24**
Arnaz, Desi **8**
Arni, Stefan
See Gus Gus
Arnold, Eddy **10**
Arnold, Kristine
See Sweethearts of the Rodeo
Aronoff, Kenny **21**
Arrau, Claudio **1**
Arrested Development **14**
Art Ensemble of Chicago, The **23**
Art of Noise **22**
Arthurs, Paul
See Oasis
Artifacts **23**
Ash, Daniel
See Bauhaus
Also see Love and Rockets
Ashcroft, Richard
See Verve, The
Ashford, Rosalind
See Martha and the Vandellas
Ashley, Bob
See Guess Who
Ashton, John
See Psychedelic Furs
Ashton, Susan **17**
Asleep at the Wheel **5**
Astbury, Ian
See Cult, The
Astley, Rick **5**
Aston, Jay "J"
See Gene Loves Jezebel
Aston, Michael
See Gene Loves Jezebel
Astro
See UB40
Asuo, Kwesi
See Arrested Development
Atari Teenage Riot **27**
Atkins, Chet **26**
Earlier sketch in CM **5**
Atkins, Martin
See Pigface
Atkinson, Paul
See Zombies, The
Atkinson, Sweet Pea
See Was (Not Was)
Atomic Fireballs, The **27**
ATR
See Boredoms, The
Audio Adrenaline **22**
Auf Der Maur, Melissa
See Hole
Augustyniak, Jerry
See 10,000 Maniacs
Auldridge, Mike **4**
Also see Country Gentlemen, The
Also see Seldom Scene, The
Austin, Cuba
See McKinney's Cotton Pickers
Austin, Dallas **16**
Austral, Florence **26**
Autry, Gene **25**
Earlier sketch in CM **12**
Avalon **26**
Avalon, Frankie **5**
Avery, Eric
See Jane's Addiction
Avery, Teodross **23**
Avory, Mick
See Kinks, The
Also see Rolling Stones, The
Axton, Hoyt **28**
Ayers, Kevin
See Gong
Aykroyd, Dan
See Blues Brothers, The
Ayler, Albert **19**
Ayres, Ben
See Cornershop
Azorr, Chris
See Cherry Poppin' Daddies
Aztec Camera **22**
B, Daniel
See Front 242
B-52's, The **4**
B-Real
See Cypress Hill
Baah, Reebop Kwaku
See Can
Also see Traffic
Babatunde, Don
See Last Poets
Babes in Toyland **16**
Babjak, James
See Smithereens, The

Babyface
See Edmonds, Kenneth "Babyface"
Bacchus, Richard
See D Generation
Bacharach, Burt **20**
Earlier sketch in CM **1**
Bachman, Eric
See Archers of Loaf
Bachman, Randy
See Guess Who
Backstreet Boys **21**
Bad Brains **16**
Bad Company **22**
Bad Livers, The **19**
Bad Religion **28**
Badalamenti, Angelo **17**
Badfinger **23**
Badger, Pat
See Extreme
Badrena, Manola
See Weather Report
Badu, Erykah **26**
Baez, Joan **1**
Bailey, Keith
See Gong
Bailey, Mildred **13**
Bailey, Pearl **5**
Bailey, Phil
See Earth, Wind and Fire
Bailey, Victor
See Weather Report
Baker, Anita **9**
Baker, Arthur **23**
Baker, Bobby
See Tragically Hip, The
Baker, Brian
See Bad Religion
Baker, Chet **13**
Baker, Dale
See Sixpence None the Richer
Baker, David
See Mercury Rev
Baker, Ginger **16**
Also see Cream
Baker, Janet **14**
Baker, Jon
See Charlatans, The
Baker, Josephine **10**
Baker, LaVern **25**
Balakrishnan, David
See Turtle Island String Quartet
Balch, Bob
See Fu Manchu
Balch, Michael
See Front Line Assembly
Baldes, Kevin
See Lit
Baldursson, Sigtryggur
See Sugarcubes, The
Baldwin, Donny
See Starship
Baliardo, Diego
See Gipsy Kings, The
Baliardo, Paco
See Gipsy Kings, The
Baliardo, Tonino
See Gipsy Kings, The
Balin, Marty
See Jefferson Airplane
Ball, Marcia **15**
Ballard, Florence
See Supremes, The
Ballard, Hank **17**
Balsley, Phil
See Statler Brothers, The
Baltes, Peter
See Dokken
Balzano, Vinnie
See Less Than Jake
Bambaataa, Afrika **13**
Bamonte, Perry
See Cure, The
Bananarama **22**
Bancroft, Cyke
See Bevis Frond
Band, The **9**
Bangles, The **22**
Banks, Nick
See Pulp
Banks, Peter
See Yes
Banks, Tony
See Genesis
Baptiste, David Russell
See Meters, The
Barbarossa, Dave
See Republica
Barbata, John
See Jefferson Starship
Barber, Keith
See Soul Stirrers, The
Barbero, Lori
See Babes in Toyland
Barbieri, Gato **22**
Bardens, Peter
See Camel
Bardo Pond **28**
Barenaked Ladies **18**
Bargeld, Blixa
See Einstürzende Neubauten
Bargeron, Dave
See Blood, Sweat and Tears
Barham, Meriel
See Lush
Barile, Jo
See Ventures, The
Barker, Paul
See Ministry
Barker, Travis Landon
See Aquabats, The
Barker, Travis
See Blink 182
Barlow, Barriemore
See Jethro Tull
Barlow, Lou
See Folk Implosion, The
Barlow, Lou **20**
See Dinosaur Jr.
Also see Sebadoh
Barlow, Tommy
See Aztec Camera
Barnes, Danny
See Bad Livers, The
Barnes, Micah
See Nylons, The
Barnes, Roosevelt "Booba" **23**
Barnett, Mandy **26**
Barnwell, Duncan
See Simple Minds
Barnwell, Ysaye Maria
See Sweet Honey in the Rock
Barr, Al
See Dropkick Murphys
Barr, Ralph
See Nitty Gritty Dirt Band, The
Barre, Martin
See Jethro Tull
Barrere, Paul
See Little Feat
Barrett, (Roger) Syd
See Pink Floyd
Barrett, Dicky
See Mighty Mighty Bosstones
Barrett, Robert "T-Mo"
See Goodie Mob
Barron, Christopher
See Spin Doctors
Barrow, Geoff
See Portishead
Barson, Mike
See Madness
Bartels, Joanie **13**
Bartholomew, Simon
See Brand New Heavies, The
Bartoli, Cecilia **12**
Barton, Lou Ann
See Fabulous Thunderbirds, The
Barton, Rick
See Dropkick Murphys
Bartos, Karl
See Kraftwerk
Basehead **11**
Basher, Mick
See X
Basia **5**
Basie, Count **2**
Bass, Colin
See Camel
Bass, Lance
See 'N Sync
Bass, Ralph **24**
Batchelor, Kevin
See Big Mountain
Also Steel Pulse
Batel, Beate
See Einstürzende Neubauten
Batiste, Lionel
See Dirty Dozen Brass Band
Batoh, Masaki
See Ghost
See Pearls Before Swine
Battin, Skip
See Byrds, The
Battle, Kathleen **6**
Bauer, Judah
See Jon Spencer Blues Explosion
Bauhaus **27**
Baumann, Peter
See Tangerine Dream
Bautista, Roland
See Earth, Wind and Fire
Baxter, Adrian
See Cherry Poppin' Daddies
Baxter, Jeff
See Doobie Brothers, The
Bayer Sager, Carole
See Sager, Carole Bayer
Baylor, Helen **20**
Baynton-Power, David
See James
Bazilian, Eric
See Hooters
Beach Boys, The **1**
Beale, Michael
See Earth, Wind and Fire
Beard, Annette
See Martha and the Vandellas
Beard, Frank
See ZZ Top
Beasley, Paul
See Mighty Clouds of Joy, The
Beastie Boys **25**
Earlier sketch in CM **8**

Beat Farmers **23**
Beat Happening **28**
Beatles, The **2**
Beauford, Carter
See Dave Matthews Band
Beautiful South **19**
Beauvoir, Jean
See Wendy O. Williams and The Plasmatics
Beaver Brown Band, The **3**
Bechdel, John
See Fear Factory
Bechet, Sidney **17**
Beck **18**
Beck, Jeff **4**
Also see Yardbirds, The
Beck, William
See Ohio Players
Becker, Walter
See Steely Dan
Beckford, Theophilus
See Skatalites, The
Beckley, Gerry
See America
Bedford, Mark
See Madness
Bee Gees, The **3**
Beech, Wes
See Wendy O. Williams and The Plasmatics
Beecham, Thomas **27**
Beers, Garry Gary
See INXS
Behler, Chuck
See Megadeth
Beiderbecke, Bix **16**
Belafonte, Harry **8**
Belanger, George
See Christian Death
Belew, Adrian **5**
Also see King Crimson
Belfield, Dennis
See Three Dog Night
Belk, Darren
See Wedding Present, The
Bell, Andy
See Erasure
Bell, Brian
See Weezer
Bell, Burton C.
See Fear Factory
Bell, Carl
See Fuel
Bell, Chris
See Gene Loves Jezebel
Bell, Derek
See Chieftains, The
Bell, Eric
See Thin Lizzy
Bell, Jayn
See Sounds of Blackness
Bell, Joshua **21**
Bell, Melissa
See Soul II Soul
Bell, Robert "Kool"
See Kool & the Gang
Bell, Ronald
See Kool & the Gang
Bell, Taj
See Charm Farm
Belladonna, Joey
See Anthrax
Bellamy Brothers, The **13**
Bellamy, David
See Bellamy Brothers, The
Bellamy, Howard
See Bellamy Brothers, The
Belle and Sebastian **28**
Belle, Regina **6**
Bello, Elissa
See Go-Go's, The
Bello, Frank
See Anthrax
Belly **16**
Belove, David
See Oakland Interfaith Gospel Choir
Beltrán, Tito **28**
Belushi, John
See Blues Brothers, The
Ben Folds Five **20**
Benante, Charlie
See Anthrax
Benatar, Pat **8**
Benckert, Vicki
See Roxette
Benedict, Scott
See Pere Ubu
Benét, Eric **27**
Bengry, Peter
See Cornershop
Benitez, Jellybean **15**
Bennett, Brian
See Shadows, The
Bennett, Tony **16**
Earlier sketch in CM **2**
Bennett-Nesby, Ann
See Sounds of Blackness
Benson, George **9**
Benson, Ray
See Asleep at the Wheel
Benson, Renaldo "Obie"
See Four Tops, The
Bentley, Jay
See Circle Jerks
Bentley, Jay
See Bad Religion
Bentley, John
See Squeeze
Benton, Brook **7**
Bentyne, Cheryl
See Manhattan Transfer, The
Berenyi, Miki
See Lush
Berg, Matraca **16**
Bergeson, Ben
See Aquabats, The
Berggren, Jenny
See Ace of Base
Berggren, Jonas
See Ace of Base
Berggren, Linn
See Ace of Base
Berigan, Bunny **2**
Berkely, Anthony (Poetic the Grym Reaper)
See Gravediggaz
Berlin, Irving **8**
Berlin, Liz
See Rusted Root
Berlin, Steve
See Los Lobos
Bernal, Steve
See Poi Dog Pondering
Berndt, Jay
See Kilgore
Bernstein, Leonard **2**
Berry, Bill
See R.E.M.
Berry, Chuck **1**
Berry, John **17**
Berry, Robert
See Emerson, Lake & Palmer/Powell
Berryhill, Bob
See Surfaris, The
Bert, Bob
See Sonic Youth
Beschta, Scott
See Promise Ring, The
Bessant, Jack
See Reef
Best, Nathaniel
See O'Jays, The
Best, Pete
See Beatles, The
Beta Band, The **27**
Betha, Mason
See Mase
Bettencourt, Nuno
See Extreme
Better Than Ezra **19**
Bettie Serveert **17**
Bettini, Tom
See Jackyl
Betts, Dicky
See Allman Brothers, The
Bevan, Bev
See Black Sabbath
Also see Electric Light Orchestra
Bevis Frond **23**
Bezozi, Alan
See Dog's Eye View
Bhag-dad-a, Omar
See Lane, Fred
Biafra, Jello **18**
Big Audio Dynamite **18**
Big Head Todd and the Monsters **20**
Big Mike
See Geto Boys, The
Big Money Odis
See Digital Underground
Big Mountain **23**
Bigham, John
See Fishbone
Bill Wyman & the Rhythm Kings **26**
Bin Hassan, Umar
See Last Poets
Bingham, John
See Fishbone
Binks, Les
See Judas Priest
Biondo, George
See Steppenwolf
Birchfield, Benny
See Osborne Brothers, The
Bird
See Parker, Charlie
Birdsong, Cindy
See Supremes, The
Birdstuff
See Man or Astroman?
Biscuits, Chuck
See Circle Jerks
Also see Danzig
Also see D.O.A.
Also see Social Distortion
Bishop, Jeb **28**
Also see Flying Luttenbachers, The
Bishop, Michael
See Gwar
Biz Markie **10**
BizzyBone
See Bone Thugs-N-Harmony
Bjelland, Kat
See Babes in Toyland
Bjork, Brant
See Fu Manchu

Björk **16**
Also see Sugarcubes, The
Black, Clint **5**
Black Crowes, The **7**
Black Flag **22**
Black Francis
See Black, Frank
Black, Frank **14**
Black, Jimmy Carl "India Ink"
See Captain Beefheart and His Magic Band
Black, Mary **15**
Black Sabbath **9**
Black Sheep **15**
Black Uhuru **12**
Black, Vic
See C + C Music Factory
BlackHawk **21**
Blackman, Cindy **15**
Blackman, Tee-Wee
See Memphis Jug Band
Blackmore, Ritchie
See Deep Purple
Blackstreet **23**
Blackwell, Chris **26**
Blackwood, Sarah
See Dubstar
Bladd, Stephen Jo
See J. Geils Band
Blades, Ruben **2**
Blair, Ron
See Tom Petty and the Heartbreakers
Blake, Eubie **19**
Blake, Norman
See Teenage Fanclub
Blake, Tim
See Gong
Blakely, Paul
See Captain Beefheart and His Magic Band
Blakey, Art **11**
Blakey, Colin
See Waterboys, The
Blanchard, Terence **13**
Bland, Bobby "Blue" **12**
Blatt, Melanie
See All Saints
Blegen, Jutith **23**
Blegvad, Peter **28**
Blessid Union of Souls **20**
Bley, Carla **8**
Bley, Paul **14**
Blige, Mary J. **15**
Blind Melon **21**
Blink 182 **27**
Block, Norman
See Rasputina
Block, Rory **18**
Blonde Redhead **28**
Blondie **27**
Earlier sketch in CM **14**
Blood, Dave
See Dead Milkmen
Blood, Johnny
See Magnetic Fields, The
Blood, Sweat and Tears **7**
Bloom, Eric
See Blue Oyster Cult
Bloom, Luka **14**
Blount, Herman "Sonny"
See Sun Ra
Blue, Buddy
See Beat Farmers
Blue Oyster Cult **16**
Blue Rodeo **18**
Bluegrass Patriots **22**
Blues, "Joliet" Jake
See Blues Brothers, The
Blues Brothers, The **3**
Blues, Elwood
See Blues Brothers, The
Blues Traveler 15
Blunstone, Colin
See Zombies, The
Blunt, Martin
See Charlatans, The
Blur **17**
Bob, Tim
See Rage Against the Machine
Bocelli, Andrea **22**
BoDeans, The **20**
Earlier sketch in CM **3**
Boff, Richard
See Chumbawamba
Bogaert, Jo
See Technotronic
Bogdan, Henry
See Helmet
Boggs, Dock **25**
Bogguss, Suzy **11**
Bogle, Bob
See Ventures, The
Bohannon, Jim
See Pearls Before Swine
Bolade Casel, Nitanju
See Sweet Honey in the Rock
Bolan, Marc
See T. Rex
Bolton, Michael **4**
Bon Jovi, Jon
See Bon Jovi
Bon Jovi **10**
Bonamy, James **21**
Bond, Johnny **28**
Bone Thugs-N-Harmony **18**
Bonebrake, D. J.
See X
Bonham, John
See Led Zeppelin
Bonnecaze, Cary
See Better Than Ezra
Bonner, Leroy "Sugarfoot"
See Ohio Players
Bono
See U2
Bono, Sonny
See Sonny and Cher
Bonsall, Joe
See Oak Ridge Boys, The
Boo Radleys, The **21**
Booker T. & the M.G.'s **24**
Books
See Das EFX
Boone, Pat **13**
Booth, Tim
See James
Boquist, Dave
See Son Volt
Boquist, Jim
See Son Volt
Borchardt, Jeffrey
See Velvet Crush
Bordin, Mike
See Faith No More
Boredoms, The **28**
Borg, Bobby
See Warrant
Borge, Victor **19**
Borland, Wes
See Limp Bizkit
Borowiak, Tony
See All-4-One
Bostaph, Paul
See Slayer
Bostek, James
See Atomic Fireballs, The
Boston **11**
Boston, Mark "Rockette Morton"
See Captain Beefheart and His Magic Band
Bostrom, Derrick
See Meat Puppets, The
Bottum, Roddy
See Faith No More
Also see Imperial Teen
Bouchard, Albert
See Blue Oyster Cult
Bouchard, Joe
See Blue Oyster Cult
Bouchikhi, Chico
See Gipsy Kings, The
Boulez, Pierre **26**
Bowen, Jimmy
See Country Gentlemen, The
Bowens, Sir Harry
See Was (Not Was)
Bowie, David **23**
Earlier sketch in CM **1**
Bowie, Lester
See Art Ensemble of Chicago, The
Bowman, Steve
See Counting Crows
Box, Mick
See Uriah Heep
Boy Howdy **21**
Boyd, Brandon
See Incubus
Boyd, Eadie
See Del Rubio Triplets
Boyd, Elena
See Del Rubio Triplets
Boyd, Liona **7**
Boyd, Milly
See Del Rubio Triplets
Boyle, Doug
See Caravan
Boyz II Men **15**
Bozulich, Carla
See Geraldine Fibbers
Brad **21**
Bradbury, John
See Specials, The
Bradbury, Randy
See Pennywise
Bradfield, James Dean
See Manic Street Preachers
Bradshaw, Tim
See Dog's Eye View
Bradstreet, Rick
See Bluegrass Patriots
Brady, Paul **8**
Bragg, Billy **7**
Braithwaite, Stuart
See Mogwai
Bramah, Martin
See Fall, The
Brand New Heavies, The **14**
Brandt, Paul **22**
Brandy **19**
Branigan, Laura **2**
Brannon, Kippi **20**
Brantley, Junior
See Roomful of Blues
Braxton, Anthony **12**
Braxton, Toni **17**

Bream, Julian **9**
Breeders **19**
Brendel, Alfred **23**
Brennan, Ciaran
See Clannad
Brennan, Maire
See Clannad
Brennan, Paul
See Odds
Brennan, Pol
See Clannad
Brenner, Simon
See Talk Talk
Breuker, Willem
See Willem Breuker Kollektief
Brevette, Lloyd
See Skatalites, The
Brickell, Edie **3**
Brickman, Jim **22**
Bridgeman, Noel
See Waterboys, The
Bridgewater, Dee Dee **18**
Briggs, David
See Pearls Before Swine
Briggs, James Randall
See Aquabats, The
Briggs, Vic
See Animals, The
Bright, Garfield
See Shai
Bright, Ronnie
See Coasters, The
Brightman, Sarah **20**
Briley, Alex
See Village People, The
Brindley, Paul
See Sundays, The
Britt, Michael
See Lonestar
Britten, Benjamin **15**
Brittingham, Eric
See Cinderella
Brix
See Fall, The
Brockenborough, Dennis
See Mighty Mighty Bosstones
Brockie, Dave
See Gwar
Brokop, Lisa **22**
Bromberg, David **18**
Bronfman, Yefim **6**
Brooke, Jonatha
See Story, The
Brooker, Gary
See Bill Wyman & the Rhythm Kings
Brookes, Jon
See Charlatans, The
Brookes, Steve
See Jam, The
Brooks & Dunn **25**
Earlier sketch in CM **12**
Brooks, Baba
See Skatalites, The
Brooks, DJ
See Citizen King
Brooks, Garth **25**
Earlier sketch in CM **8**
Brooks, Leon Eric "Kix" III
See Brooks & Dunn,
Brooks, Stuart
See Pretty Things, The
Broonzy, Big Bill **13**
Brotherdale, Steve
See Joy Division
Also see Smithereens, The
Brötzmann, Caspar **27**
Brötzmann, Peter **26**
Broudie, Ian
See Lightning Seeds
Brown, Amanda
See Go-Betweens, The
Brown, Bobby **4**
Brown, Brooks
See Cherry Poppin' Daddies
Brown, Clarence "Gatemouth" **11**
Brown, Clifford **24**
Brown, Donny
See Verve Pipe, The
Brown, Duncan
See Stereolab
Brown, Foxy **25**
Brown, George
See Kool & the Gang
Brown, Greg
See Cake
Brown, Harold
See War
Brown, Heidi
See Treadmill Trackstar
Brown, Ian
See Stone Roses, The
Brown, James **16**
Earlier sketch in CM **2**
Brown, Jimmy
See UB40
Brown, Junior **15**
Brown, Lawrence **23**
Brown, Marty **14**
Brown, Melanie
See Spice Girls
Brown, Mick
See Dokken
Brown, Morris
See Pearls Before Swine
Brown, Norman
See Mills Brothers, The
Brown, Rahem
See Artifacts
Brown, Ray **21**
Brown, Ruth **13**
Brown, Selwyn "Bumbo"
See Steel Pulse
Brown, Steven
See Tuxedomoon
Brown, Tim
See Boo Radleys, The
Brown, Tony **14**
Browne, Jackson **3**
Also see Nitty Gritty Dirt Band, The
Brownstein, Carrie
See Sleater-Kinney
Brownstone **21**
Brubeck, Dave **8**
Bruce, Dustan
See Chumbawamba
Bruce, Jack
See Cream
Bruce, Joseph Frank
See Insane Clown Posse
Bruford, Bill
See King Crimson
Also see Yes
Bruno, Gioia
See Exposé
Bruster, Thomas
See Soul Stirrers, The
Bryan, David
See Bon Jovi
Bryan, Karl
See Skatalites, The
Bryan, Mark
See Hootie and the Blowfish
Bryant, Elbridge
See Temptations, The
Bryant, Jeff
See Ricochet
Bryant, Junior
See Ricochet
Bryson, Bill
See Desert Rose Band, The
Bryson, David
See Counting Crows
Bryson, Peabo **11**
Buchanan, Wallis
See Jamiroquai
Buchholz, Francis
See Scorpions, The
Buchignani, Paul
See Afghan Whigs
Buck, Mike
See Fabulous Thunderbirds, The
Buck, Peter
See R.E.M.
Buck, Robert
See 10,000 Maniacs
Buckingham, Lindsey **8**
Also see Fleetwood Mac
Buckler, Rick
See Jam, The
Buckley, Betty **16**
Earlier sketch in CM **1**
Buckley, Jeff **22**
Buckley, Tim **14**
Buckwheat Zydeco **6**
Budgie
See Siouxsie and the Banshees
Buerstatte, Phil
See White Zombie
Buffalo Springfield **24**
Buffalo Tom **18**
Buffett, Jimmy **4**
Built to Spill **27**
Bulgarian State Female Vocal Choir, The **10**
Bulgarian State Radio and Television Female Vocal Choir, The
See Bulgarian State Female Vocal Choir, The
Bulgin, Lascelle
See Israel Vibration
Bulloch, Martin
See Mogwai
Bullock, Craig "DJ Homicide"
See Sugar Ray
Bumbry, Grace **13**
Bumpus, Cornelius
See Doobie Brothers, The
Bunford, Huw "Bunf"
See Super Furry Animals
Bunker, Clive
See Jethro Tull
Bunkley, John
See Atomic Fireballs, The
Bunnell, Dewey
See America
Bunskoeke, Herman
See Bettie Serveert
Bunton, Emma
See Spice Girls
Burch, Curtis
See New Grass Revival, The
Burchill, Charlie
See Simple Minds
Burden, Ian
See Human League, The

Burdon, Eric **14**
Also see War
Also see Animals, The
Burgess, Paul
See Camel
Burgess, Tim
See Charlatans, The
Burke, Clem
See Blondie
Burkum, Tyler
See Audio Adrenaline
Burnett, Carol **6**
Burnett, T Bone **13**
Burnette, Billy
See Fleetwood Mac
Burnham, Hugo
See Gang of Four
Burning Spear **15**
Burns, Barry
See Mogwai
Burns, Bob
See Lynyrd Skynyrd
Burns, Karl
See Fall, The
Burr, Clive
See Iron Maiden
Burrell, Boz
See Bad Company
Burrell, Kenny **11**
Burrell, Raymond "Boz"
See King Crimson
Burroughs, William S. **26**
Burse, Charlie
See Memphis Jug Band
Burse, Robert
See Memphis Jug Band
Burton, Cliff
See Metallica
Burton, Gary **10**
Burton, Tim
See Promise Ring, The
Burton, Tim
See Mighty Mighty Bosstones
Busby, Jheryl **9**
Bush **18**
Bush, Dave
See Fall, The
Bush, John
See Anthrax
Bush, Kate **4**
Bush, Sam
See New Grass Revival, The
Bushwick, Bill
See Geto Boys, The
Busta Rhymes **18**
Butler, Bernard
See Suede
Butler, Richard
See Love Spit Love
Also see Psychedelic Furs
Butler, Terry "Geezer"
See Black Sabbath
Butler, Tim
See Love Spit Love
Also see Psychedelic Furs
Butterfield, Paul **23**
Butterfly
See Digable Planets
Butthole Surfers **16**
Buttrey, Kenneth
See Pearls Before Swine
Buynak, John
See Rusted Root
Buzzcocks, The **9**
Byers, Roddy
See Specials, The
Byrds, The **8**
Byrne, David **8**
Also see Talking Heads
Byrne, Dermot
See Altan
Byrom, Larry
See Steppenwolf
Byron, David
See Uriah Heep
Byron, Don **22**
Byron, Lord T.
See Lords of Acid
C + C Music Factory **16**
Caballe, Monserrat **23**
Cabaret Voltaire **18**
Cachao
See Lopez, Israel "Cachao"
Cadogan, Kevin
See Third Eye Blind
Caesar, Shirley **17**
Cafferty, John
See Beaver Brown Band, The
Caffey, Charlotte
See Go-Go's, The
Cage, John **8**
Cahn, Sammy **11**
Cain, Jonathan
See Journey
Cake **27**
Calderon, Mark
See Color Me Badd
Cale, J. J. **16**
Earlier sketch in CM **9**
Also see Velvet Underground, The
Cale, John
See Cale, J. J.
Calhoun, Will
See Living Colour
California, Randy
See Spirit
Calire, Mario
See Wallflowers, The
Callahan, Ken
See Jayhawks, The
Callahan, Ray
See Wendy O. Williams and The Plasmatics
Callas, Maria **11**
Callis, Jo
See Human League, The
Calloway, Cab **6**
Camel **21**
Camel, Abdul Ben
See Lane, Fred
Cameron, Clayton
See Ralph Sharon Quartet
Cameron, Duncan
See Sawyer Brown
Cameron, G. C.
See Spinners, The
Cameron, Matt
See Soundgarden
Cameron, Timothy
See Silk
Camp, Greg
See Smash Mouth
Campbell, Ali
See UB40
Campbell, Eddie
See Texas
Campbell, Glen **2**
Campbell, Isobel
See Belle and Sebastian
Campbell, Kerry
See War
Campbell, Luther **10**
Campbell, Martyn
See Lightning Seeds
Campbell, Mike
See Tom Petty and the Heartbreakers
Campbell, Phil
See Motörhead
Campbell, Robin
See UB40
Campbell, Sarah Elizabeth **23**
Campbell, Tevin **13**
Can **28**
Canadian Brass, The **4**
Cantrell, Jerry
See Alice in Chains
Canty, Brendan
See Fugazi
Capaldi, Jim
See Traffic
Cappelli, Frank **14**
Cappos, Andy
See Built to Spill
Captain Beefheart and the Magic Band **26**
Earlier sketch in CM **10**
Caravan **24**
Carbonara, Paul
See Blondie
Cardigans **19**
Cardwell, Joi **22**
Carey, Danny
See Tool
Carey, Mariah **20**
Earlier sketch in CM **6**
Carlisle, Belinda **8**
Also see Go-Go's, The
Carlisle, Bob **22**
Carlos, Bun E.
See Cheap Trick
Carlos, Don
See Black Uhuru
Carlson, Paulette
See Highway 101
Carmichael, Hoagy **27**
Carnes, Kim **4**
Carpenter, Bob
See Nitty Gritty Dirt Band, The
Carpenter, Karen
See Carpenters, The
Carpenter, Richard **24**
Also see Carpenters, The
Carpenter, Stephen
See Deftones
Carpenters, The **13**
Carr, Ben
See Mighty Mighty Bosstones
Carr, Eric
See Kiss
Carr, James **23**
Carr, Martin
See Boo Radleys, The
Carr, Teddy
See Ricochet
Carr, Vikki **28**
Carrack, Paul
See Mike & the Mechanics
Also see Squeeze
Carreras, José **8**
Carrigan, Andy
See Mekons, The
Carroll, Earl "Speedo"
See Coasters, The
Carruthers, John
See Siouxsie and the Banshees

Cars, The **20**
Carter, A. P.
See Carter Family, The
Carter, Anita
See Carter Family, The
Carter, Benny **3**
Also see McKinney's Cotton Pickers
Carter, Betty **6**
Carter, Carlene **8**
Carter, Deana **25**
Carter Family, The **3**
Carter, Helen
See Carter Family, The
Carter, James **18**
Carter, Janette
See Carter Family, The
Carter, Jimmy
See Five Blind Boys of Alabama
Carter, Joe
See Carter Family, The
Carter, June Cash **6**
Also see Carter Family, The
Carter, Maybell
See Carter Family, The
Carter, Nell **7**
Carter, Nick
See Backstreet Boys
Carter, Regina **22**
Carter, Ron **14**
Carter, Sara
See Carter Family, The
Carthy, Martin
See Steeleye Span
Caruso, Enrico **10**
Cary, Justin
See Sixpence None the Richer
Casady, Jack
See Jefferson Airplane
Casale, Bob
See Devo
Casale, Gerald V.
See Devo
Casals, Pablo **9**
Case, Peter **13**
Casey, Ken
See Dropkick Murphys
Cash, Johnny **17**
Earlier sketch in CM **1**
Cash, Rosanne **2**
Cashion, Doc "Bob"
See Lane, Fred
Cassidy, Ed
See Spirit
Catallo, Chris
See Surfin' Pluto
Catallo, Gene
See Surfin' Pluto
Cates, Ronny
See Petra
Catherall, Joanne
See Human League, The
Catherine Wheel **18**
Caustic Window
See Aphex Twin
Cauty, Jimmy
See Orb, The
Cavalera, Igor
See Sepultura
Cavalera, Max
See Sepultura
Cavanaugh, Frank
See Filter
Cave, Nick **10**
Cavoukian, Raffi
See Raffi
Cazares, Dino
See Fear Factory
Cease, Jeff
See Black Crowes, The
Cervenka, Exene
See X
Cetera, Peter
See Chicago
Chamberlin, Jimmy
See Smashing Pumpkins
Chambers, Guy
See Waterboys, The
Chambers, Jimmy
See Mercury Rev
Chambers, Martin
See Pretenders, The
Chambers, Paul **18**
Chambers, Terry
See XTC
Champion, Eric **21**
Chan, Spencer
See Aqua Velvets
Chance, Slim
See Cramps, The
Chancellor, Justin
See Tool
Chandler, Chas
See Animals, The
Chandra, Sheila **16**
Chaney, Jimmy
See Jimmie's Chicken Shack
Chang, Sarah **7**
Channing, Carol **6**
Chapin Carpenter, Mary **25**
Earlier sketch in CM **6**
Chapin, Harry **6**
Chapin, Tom **11**
Chapman, Steven Curtis **15**
Chapman, Tony
See Rolling Stones, The
Chapman, Tracy **20**
Earlier sketch in CM **4**
Chaquico, Craig **23**
Also see Jefferson Starship
Charlatans, The **13**
Charles, Ray **24**
Earlier sketch in CM **1**
Charles, Yolanda
See Aztec Camera
Charm Farm **20**
Charman, Shaun
See Wedding Present, The
Chasez, Joshua Scott "JC"
See 'N Sync
Chastain, Paul
See Velvet Crush
Che Colovita, Lemon
See Jimmie's Chicken Shack
Chea, Alvin "Vinnie"
See Take 6
Cheap Trick **12**
Cheatam, Aldolphus "Doc"
See McKinney's Cotton Pickers
Checker, Chubby **7**
Cheeks, Julius
See Soul Stirrers, The
Chemical Brothers **20**
Cheng, Chi
See Deftones
Chenier, C. J. **15**
Chenier, Clifton **6**
Chenille Sisters, The **16**
Cher **1**
Also see Sonny and Cher
Cherise, Cyd
See Lane, Fred
Cherone, Gary
See Extreme
Also see Van Halen
Cherry, Don **10**
Cherry, Neneh **4**
Cherry Poppin' Daddies **24**
Chesney, Kenny **20**
Chesnutt, Mark **13**
Chesnutt, Vic **28**
Chess, Leonard **24**
Chevalier, Maurice **6**
Chevron, Phillip
See Pogues, The
Chicago **3**
Chieftains, The **7**
Childish, Billy **28**
Childress, Ross
See Collective Soul
Childress Saxton, Shirley
See Sweet Honey in the Rock
Childs, Toni **2**
Chilton, Alex **10**
Chimes, Terry
See Clash, The
Chin, Tony
See Big Mountain
Chisholm, Melanie
See Spice Girls
Chopmaster J
See Digital Underground
Chrisman, Andy
See 4Him
Christ, John
See Danzig
Christian, Charlie **11**
Christian Death **28**
Christina, Fran
See Fabulous Thunderbirds, The
Also see Roomful of Blues
Chuck D
See Public Enemy
Chumbawamba **21**
Chung, Mark
See Einstürzende Neubauten
Church, Charlotte **28**
Church, Kevin
See Country Gentlemen, The
Church, The **14**
Churilla, Scott
See Reverend Horton Heat
Ciaran, Clan
See Super Furry Animals
Cibo Matto **28**
Ciccone, Don
See Four Season, The
Cieka, Rob
See Boo Radleys, The
Cinderella **16**
Cinelu, Mino
See Weather Report
Cipollina, John
See Quicksilver Messenger Service
Circle Jerks, The **17**
Cissell, Ben
See Audio Adrenaline
Citizen King **27**
Clannad **23**
Clapton, Eric **11**
Earlier sketch in CM **1**
Also see Cream
Also see Yardbirds, The
Clark, Alan
See Dire Straits

Clark, Dave
See Dave Clark Five, The
Clark, Dick **25**
Earlier sketch in CM **2**
Clark, Gene
See Byrds, The
Clark, Graham
See Gong
Clark, Guy **17**
Clark, Keith
See Circle Jerks, The
Clark, Mike
See Suicidal Tendencies
Clark, Roy **1**
Clark, Steve
See Def Leppard
Clark, Terri **19**
Clark, Tony
See Blessid Union of Souls
Clarke, "Fast" Eddie
See Motörhead
Clarke, Bernie
See Aztec Camera
Clarke, Michael
See Byrds, The
Clarke, Stanley **3**
Clarke, Vince
See Depeche Mode
Also see Erasure
Clarke, William
See Third World
Clash, The **4**
Clayderman, Richard **1**
Claypool, Les
See Primus
Clayton, Adam
See U2
Clayton, Sam
See Little Feat
Clayton-Thomas, David
See Blood, Sweat and Tears
Clean, Dean
See Dead Milkmen
Cleave, Simon
See Wedding Present, The
Cleaves, Jessica
See Earth, Wind and Fire
Clegg, Johnny **8**
Clements, Vassar **18**
Clemons, Clarence **7**
Cleveland, James **1**
Cliburn, Van **13**
Cliff, Jimmy **8**
Clifford, Douglas Ray
See Creedence Clearwater Revival
Cline, Nels
See Geraldine Fibbers
Cline, Patsy **5**
Clinton, George **7**
Clivilles, Robert
See C + C Music Factory
Clooney, Rosemary **9**
Close, Bill
See Dropkick Murphys
Cloud, Jeff
See Joy Electric
Clouser, Charlie
See Prong
Coasters, The **5**
Cobain, Kurt
See Nirvana
Cobham, Billy
See Mahavishnu Orchestra
Cobra Verde **28**
Cochran, Bobby
See Steppenwolf
Cochrane, Tom **23**
Cockburn, Bruce **8**
Cocker, Jarvis
See Pulp
Cocker, Joe **4**
Cocking, William "Willigan"
See Mystic Revealers
Coco the Electronic Monkey Wizard
See Man or Astroman?
Cocteau Twins, The **12**
Codenys, Patrick
See Front 242
Codling, Neil
See Suede
Cody, John
See Ray Condo and His Ricochets
Coe, David Allan **4**
Coffey, Jeff
See Butthole Surfers
Coffey, Jr., Don
See Superdrag
Coffie, Calton
See Inner Circle
Cohen, Jeremy
See Turtle Island String Quartet
Cohen, Leonard **3**
Cohen, Porky
See Roomful of Blues
Coke, Alex
See Willem Breuker Kollektief
Colaiuta, Vinnie **23**
Colbourn, Chris
See Buffalo Tom
Colburn, Richard
See Belle and Sebastian
Cole, David
See C + C Music Factory
Cole, Holly **18**
Cole, Lloyd **9**
Cole, Nat King **3**
Cole, Natalie **21**
Earlier sketch in CM **1**
Cole, Paula **20**
Cole, Ralph
See Nylons, The
Coleman, Helen
See Sweet Honey in the Rock
Coleman, Kevin
See Smash Mouth
Coleman, Michael
See Seldom Scene, The
Coleman, Ornette **5**
Coles, Dennis "Ghostface Killer"
See Wu-Tang Clan
Collective Soul **16**
Collen, Phil
See Def Leppard
Colletti, Dominic
See Bevis Frond
Colley, Dana
See Morphine
Collie, Mark **15**
Colligan, Michael
See Flying Luttenbachers, The
Collingwood, Chris
See Fountains of Wayne
Collins, Albert **19**
Earlier sketch in CM **4**
Collins, Allen
See Lynyrd Skynyrd
Collins, Bootsy **8**
Collins, Chris
See Dream Theater
Collins, Judy **4**
Collins, Mark
See Charlatans, The
Collins, Mel
See Camel
Also see King Crimson
Collins, Phil **20**
Earlier sketch in CM **2**
Also see Genesis
Collins, Rob
See Charlatans, The
Collins, William
See Collins, Bootsy
Colomby, Bobby
See Blood, Sweat and Tears
Color Me Badd **23**
Colt, Johnny
See Black Crowes, The
Coltrane, John **4**
Colvin, Shawn **11**
Colwell, David
See Bad Company
Combs, Sean "Puffy" **25**
Earlier sketch in CM **16**
Comess, Aaron
See Spin Doctors
Commodores, The **23**
Common **23**
Como, Perry **14**
Compulsion **23**
Condo, Ray
See Ray Condo and His Ricochets
Confederate Railroad **23**
Congo Norvell **22**
Conneff, Kevin
See Chieftains, The
Connelly, Chris
See KMFDM
Also see Pigface
Conner, Gary Lee
See Screaming Trees
Conner, Van
See Screaming Trees
Connick, Harry, Jr. **4**
Connolly, Pat
See Surfaris, The
Connors, Marc
See Nylons, The
Conti, Neil
See Prefab Sprout
Conway, Billy
See Morphine
Conway, Gerry
See Pentangle
Cooder, Ry **2**
Also see Captain Beefheart and His Magic Band
Cook, David Kyle
See Matchbox 20
Cook, Greg
See Ricochet
Cook, Jeffrey Alan
See Alabama
Cook, Paul
See Sex Pistols, The
Cook, Stuart
See Creedence Clearwater Revival
Cook, Wayne
See Steppenwolf
Cooke, Mick
See Belle and Sebastian
Cooke, Sam **1**
Also see Soul Stirrers, The
Cool, Tre
See Green Day

Cooley, Dave
See Citizen King
Coolio **19**
Coomes, Sam
See Quasi
Cooney, Rory **6**
Cooper, Alice **8**
Cooper, Jason
See Cure, The
Cooper, Martin
See Orchestral Manoeuvres in the Dark
Cooper, Michael
See Third World
Cooper, Paul
See Nylons, The
Cooper, Ralph
See Air Supply
Coore, Stephen
See Third World
Cope, Julian **16**
Copeland, Stewart **14**
Also see Police, The
Copland, Aaron **2**
Copley, Al
See Roomful of Blues
Corea, Chick **6**
Corella, Doug
See Verve Pipe, The
Corgan, Billy
See Smashing Pumpkins
Corina, Sarah
See Mekons, The
Cornelius, Robert
See Poi Dog Pondering
Cornell, Chris
See Soundgarden
Cornershop **24**
Cornick, Glenn
See Jethro Tull
Corrigan, Brianna
See Beautiful South
Cosper, Kina
See Brownstone
Costello, Elvis **12**
Earlier sketch in CM **2**
Coté, Billy
See Madder Rose
Cotoia, Robert
See Beaver Brown Band, The
Cotrubas, Ileana **1**
Cotten, Elizabeth **16**
Cotton, Caré
See Sounds of Blackness
Cotton, Jeff "Antennae Jimmy Siemens"
See Captain Beefheart and His Magic Band
Cougar, John(ny)
See Mellencamp, John
Coughlan, Richard
See Caravan
Counting Crows **18**
Country Gentlemen, The **7**
Coury, Fred
See Cinderella
Coutts, Duncan
See Our Lady Peace
Coverdale, David
See Whitesnake **5**
Cowan, John
See New Grass Revival, The
Cowboy Junkies, The **4**
Cox, Andy
See English Beat, The
Also see Fine Young Cannibals
Cox, Terry
See Pentangle
Coxon, Graham
See Blur
Coyne, Mark
See Flaming Lips
Coyne, Wayne
See Flaming Lips
Crack, Carl
See Atari Teenage Riot
Cracker **12**
Cracknell, Sarah
See Saint Etienne
Craig, Albert
See Israel Vibration
Craig, Carl **19**
Crain, S. R.
See Soul Stirrers, The
Cramps, The **16**
Cranberries, The **14**
Craney, Mark
See Jethro Tull
Crash Test Dummies **14**
Crawford, Dave Max
See Poi Dog Pondering
Crawford, Ed
See fIREHOSE
Crawford, Michael **4**
Crawford, Randy **25**
Crawford, Steve
See Anointed
Crawford-Greathouse, Da'dra
See Anointed
Cray, Robert **8**
Creach, Papa John
See Jefferson Starship
Creager, Melora
See Rasputina
Cream **9**
Creed **28**
Creedence Clearwater Revival **16**
Creegan, Andrew
See Barenaked Ladies
Creegan, Jim
See Barenaked Ladies
Crenshaw, Marshall **5**
Cretu, Michael
See Enigma
Criss, Peter
See Kiss
Crissinger, Roger
See Pearls Before Swine
Croce, Jim **3**
Crofts, Dash
See Seals & Crofts
Cronin, Kevin
See REO Speedwagon
Cropper, Steve **12**
Also see Booker T. & the M.G.'s
Crosby, Bing **6**
Crosby, David **3**
Also see Byrds, The
Also see Crosby, Stills, and Nash
Crosby, Stills, and Nash **24**
Cross, Bridget
See Velocity Girl
Cross, David
See King Crimson
Cross, Mike
See Sponge
Cross, Tim
See Sponge
Crouch, Andraé **9**
Crover, Dale
See Melvins
Crow, Sheryl **18**
Crowded House **12**
Crowe, J. D. **5**
Crowell, Rodney **8**
Crowley, Martin
See Bevis Frond
Cruikshank, Gregory
See Tuxedomoon
Cruz, Celia **22**
Earlier sketch in CM **10**
Cuddy, Jim
See Blue Rodeo
Cuffee, Ed
See McKinney's Cotton Pickers
Cugat, Xavier **23**
Culp, Dennis
See Five Iron Frenzy
Cult, The **16**
Culver, Joe
See Bardo Pond
Cumming, Graham
See Bevis Frond
Cummings, Burton
See Guess Who
Cummings, Danny
See Dire Straits
Cummings, David
See Del Amitri
Cummings, John
See Mogwai
Cunniff, Jill
See Luscious Jackson
Cunningham, Abe
See Deftones
Cunningham, Ruth
See Anonymous 4
Cuomo, Rivers
See Weezer
Cure, The **20**
Earlier sketch in CM **3**
Curl, Langston
See McKinney's Cotton Pickers
Curless, Ann
See Exposé
Curley, John
See Afghan Whigs
Curran, Ciaran
See Altan
Currie, Justin
See Del Amitri
Currie, Kevin
See Supertramp
Currie, Steve
See T. Rex
Curry, Tim **3**
Curtis, Ian
See Joy Division
Curtis, King **17**
Curve **13**
Custance, Mickey
See Big Audio Dynamite
Cuthbert, Scott
See Everclear
Cutler, Chris
See Pere Ubu
Cypress Hill **11**
Cyrus, Billy Ray **11**
Czukay, Holger
See Can
D Generation **26**
D.J. Lethal
See House of Pain
D.J. Minutemix
See P.M. Dawn
D.O.A. **28**

D'Amour, Paul
See Tool
D'Angelo **20**
D'Angelo, Greg
See Anthrax
D'Arby, Terence Trent **3**
Dachert, Peter
See Tuxedomoon
Dacus, Donnie
See Chicago
Dacus, Johnny
See Osborne Brothers, The
Daddy G
See Massive Attack
Daddy Mack
See Kris Kross
Daellenbach, Charles
See Canadian Brass, The
Dahl, Jeff **28**
Dahlheimer, Patrick
See Live
Daisley, Bob
See Black Sabbath
Dale, Dick **13**
Daley, Richard
See Third World
Dall, Bobby
See Poison
Dallin, Sarah
See Bananarama
Dalton, John
See Kinks, The
Dalton, Nic
See Lemonheads, The
Daltrey, Roger **3**
Also see Who, The
Damiani, Victor
See Cake
Dammers, Jerry
See Specials, The
Damon and Naomi **25**
Dando, Evan
See Lemonheads, The
Dandy Warhols **22**
Danell, Dennis
See Social Distortion
Daniels, Charlie **6**
Daniels, Jack
See Highway 101
Daniels, Jerry
See Ink Spots
Danko, Rick
See Band, The
Danny Boy
See House of Pain
Danzig **7**
Danzig, Glenn
See Danzig
Dap, Bill The Kid
See Lane, Fred
Darin, Bobby **4**
Darling, Eric
See Weavers, The
Darriau, Matt
See Klezmatics, The
Darvill, Benjamin
See Crash Test Dummies
Das EFX **14**
Daugherty, Jay Dee
See Church, The
Also see Waterboys, The
Daulne, Marie
See Zap Mama
Dave Clark Five, The **12**
Dave, Doggy
See Lords of Acid
Dave, Edmunds **28**
Dave Matthews Band **18**
Davenport, N'Dea
See Brand New Heavies, The
David, Stuart
See Belle and Sebastian
Davidson, Lenny
See Dave Clark Five, The
Davie, Hutch
See Pearls Before Swine
Davies, Dave
See Kinks, The
Davies, Dennis Russell **24**
Davies, James
See Jimmie's Chicken Shack
Davies, Ray **5**
Also see Kinks, The
Davies, Richard
See Supertramp
Davies, Saul
See James
Davis, Anthony **17**
Davis, Brad
See Fu Manchu
Davis, Chip **4**
Davis, Clive **14**
Davis, Colin **27**
Davis, Gregory
See Dirty Dozen Brass Band
Davis, Jody
See Newsboys, The
Davis, John
See Folk Implosion, The
Davis, John
See Superdrag
Davis, Jonathan
See Korn
Davis, Linda **21**
Davis, Michael
See MC5, The
Davis, Miles **1**
Davis, Reverend Gary **18**
Davis, Sammy, Jr. **4**
Davis, Santa
See Big Mountain
Davis, Skeeter **15**
Davis, Spencer
See Spencer Davis Group
Davis, Steve
See Mystic Revealers
Davis, Zelma
See C + C Music Factory
Davol, Sam
See Magnetic Fields, The
Dawdy, Cheryl
See Chenille Sisters, The
Dawn, Sandra
See Platters, The
Day, Doris **24**
Dayne, Taylor **4**
dc Talk **18**
de Albuquerque, Michael
See Electric Light Orchestra
de Burgh, Chris **22**
de Coster, Jean Paul
See 2 Unlimited
de Grassi, Alex **6**
de Jonge, Henk
See Willem Breuker Kollektief
de la Rocha, Zack
See Rage Against the Machine
de Lucia, Paco **1**
de Prume, Ivan
See White Zombie
de Young, Joyce
See Andrews Sisters, The
De Borg, Jerry
See Jesus Jones
De Gaia, Banco **27**
De La Luna, Shai
See Lords of Acid
De La Soul **7**
De Lisle, Paul
See Smash Mouth
De Meyer, Jean-Luc
See Front 242
De Oliveria, Laudir
See Chicago
Deacon, John
See Queen
Dead Can Dance **16**
Dead Milkmen **22**
Deakin, Paul
See Mavericks, The
Deal, Kelley
See Breeders
Deal, Kim
See Breeders
Also see Pixies, The
Dean, Billy **19**
Death in Vegas **28**
DeBarge, El **14**
Dee, Mikkey
See Dokken
Also see Motörhead
Deee-lite **9**
Deep Forest **18**
Deep Purple **11**
Def Leppard **3**
Deftones **22**
DeGarmo, Chris
See Queensryche
Deibert, Adam Warren
See Aquabats, The
Deily, Ben
See Lemonheads, The
DeJohnette, Jack **7**
Del Amitri **18**
Del Mar, Candy
See Cramps, The
Del Rubio Triplets **21**
Delaet, Nathalie
See Lords of Acid
DeLeo, Dean
See Stone Temple Pilots
DeLeo, Robert
See Stone Temple Pilots
Delonge, Tom
See Blink 182
DeLorenzo, Victor
See Violent Femmes
Delp, Brad
See Boston
DeMent, Iris **13**
Demeski, Stanley
See Luna
DeMone, Gitane
See Christian Death
Demos, Greg
See Guided By Voices
Dempsey, Michael
See Cure, The
Denison, Duane
See Jesus Lizard
Dennis, Garth
See Black Uhuru

Denny, Sandy
See Fairport Convention
Densmore, John
See Doors, The
Dent, Cedric
See Take 6
Denton, Sandy
See Salt-N-Pepa
Denver, John **22**
Earlier sketch in CM **1**
Depeche Mode **5**
Depew, Don
See Cobra Verde
Derakh, Amir
See Orgy
Derosier, Michael
See Heart
Des'ree **24**
Earlier sketch in CM **15**
Desaulniers, Stephen
See Scud Mountain Boys
Deschamps, Kim
See Blue Rodeo
Desert Rose Band, The **4**
Desjardins, Claude
See Nylons, The
Desmond, Paul **23**
Destri, Jimmy
See Blondie
Deupree, Jerome
See Morphine
Deurloo, Hermine
See Willem Breuker Kollektief
Deutrom, Mark
See Melvins
Deutsch, Stu
See Wendy O. Williams and The Plasmatics
DeVille, C. C.
See Poison
Devito, Nick
See Four Seasons, The
Devito, Tommy
See Four Seasons, The
Devo **13**
Devoto, Howard
See Buzzcocks, The
DeWitt, Lew C.
See Statler Brothers, The
Dexter X
See Man or Astroman?
di Fiore, Vince
See Cake
Di Meola, Al **12**
Di'anno, Paul
See Iron Maiden
Diagram, Andy
See James
Diamond "Dimebag" Darrell
See Pantera
Diamond, Mike "Mike D"
See Beastie Boys, The
Diamond, Neil **1**
Diamond Rio **11**
Dibango, Manu **14**
Dick, Magic
See J. Geils Band
Dickens, Little Jimmy **7**
Dickerson, B.B.
See War
Dickinson, Paul Bruce
See Iron Maiden
Dickinson, Rob
See Catherine Wheel
Diddley, Bo **3**
Didier, Daniel
See Promise Ring, The
Dietrich, Marlene **25**
Diffie, Joe **27**
Earlier sketch in CM **10**
Difford, Chris
See Squeeze
DiFranco, Ani **17**
Digable Planets **15**
Diggle, Steve
See Buzzcocks, The
Diggs, Robert "RZA" (Prince Rakeem)
See Gravediggaz
Also see Wu-Tang Clan
Digital Underground **9**
Dillon, James
See Built to Spill
Dilworth, Joe
See Stereolab
DiMant, Leor
See House of Pain
DiMucci, Dion
See Dion
DiNizo, Pat
See Smithereens, The
Dinning, Dean
See Toad the Wet Sprocket
Dinosaur Jr. **10**
Dio, Ronnie James
See Black Sabbath
Dion **4**
Dion, Celine **25**
Earlier sketch in CM **12**
Dire Straits **22**
Dirks, Michael
See Gwar
Dirnt, Mike
See Green Day
Dirty Dozen Brass Band **23**
DiSpirito, Jim
See Rusted Root
Dittrich, John
See Restless Heart
Dixie Chicks **26**
Dixon, George W.
See Spinners, The
Dixon, Jerry
See Warrant
Dixon, Willie **10**
DJ Domination
See Geto Boys, The
DJ Fuse
See Digital Underground
DJ Jazzy Jeff and the Fresh Prince **5**
DJ Muggs
See Cypress Hill
DJ Premier
See Gang Starr
DJ Ready Red
See Geto Boys, The
DJ Terminator X
See Public Enemy
DMC
See Run DMC
DMX **25**
Doc Pomus **14**
Doe, John
See X
Dog's Eye View **21**
Dogbowl
See King Missile
Doherty, Denny
See Mamas and the Papas
Dokken **16**
Dokken, Don
See Dokken
Dolby, Monica Mimi
See Brownstone
Dolby, Thomas **10**
Dolenz, Micky
See Monkees, The
Dombroski, Vinnie
See Sponge
Domingo, Placido **20**
Earlier sketch in CM **1**
Dominici, Charlie
See Dream Theater
Domino, Fats **2**
Don, Rasa
See Arrested Development
Donahue, Jerry
See Fairport Convention
Donahue, Jonathan
See Mercury Rev
Donahue, Jonathan
See Flaming Lips
Donald, Tony
See Simple Minds
Donelly, Tanya
See Belly
Also see Breeders
Also see Throwing Muses
Donohue, Tim
See Cherry Poppin' Daddies
Donovan **9**
Donovan, Bazil
See Blue Rodeo
Donovan, Jim
See Rusted Root
Doobie Brothers, The **3**
Doodlebug
See Digable Planets
Doors, The **4**
Dorge, Michel (Mitch)
See Crash Test Dummies
Dorney, Tim
See Republica
Dorough, Bob
See Pearls Before Swine
Dorough, Howie
See Backstreet Boys
Dorrington, Paul
See Wedding Present, The
Dorsey Brothers, The **8**
Dorsey, Jimmy
See Dorsey Brothers, The
Dorsey, Thomas A. **11**
Dorsey, Tommy
See Dorsey Brothers, The
Doss, Bill
See Olivia Tremor Control
Doth, Anita
See 2 Unlimited
Dott, Gerald
See Incredible String Band
Doucet, Michael **8**
Doucette, Paul John
See Matchbox 20
Doughty, M.
See Soul Coughing
Doughty, Neal
See REO Speedwagon
Douglas, Jerry
See Country Gentlemen, The
Dowd, Christopher
See Fishbone
Dowling, Dave
See Jimmie's Chicken Shack

Downes, Geoff
See Yes
Downey, Brian
See Thin Lizzy
Downie, Gordon
See Tragically Hip, The
Downing, K. K.
See Judas Priest
Doyle, Candida
See Pulp
Dozier, Lamont
See Holland-Dozier-Holland
Dr. Demento **23**
Dr. Dre **15**
Also see N.W.A.
Dr. John **7**
Dragge, Fletcher
See Pennywise
Drake, Nick **17**
Drake, Steven
See Odds
Drayton, Leslie
See Earth, Wind and Fire
Dream Theater **23**
Dreja, Chris
See Yardbirds, The
Dres
See Black Sheep
Drew, Dennis
See 10,000 Maniacs
Driftwood, Jimmy **25**
Droge, Pete **24**
Dropkick Murphys **26**
Drozd, Stephen
See Flaming Lips
Dru Hill **25**
Drumbago,
See Skatalites, The
Drumdini, Harry
See Cramps, The
Drummond, Don
See Skatalites, The
Drummond, Tom
See Better Than Ezra
Dryden, Spencer
See Jefferson Airplane
Dryer, Debroah
See Skunk Anansie
Dubbe, Berend
See Bettie Serveert
Dube, Lucky **17**
Dubstar **22**
Dudley, Anne
See Art of Noise
Duffey, John
See Country Gentlemen, The
Also see Seldom Scene, The
Duffy, Billy
See Cult, The
Duffy, Martin
See Primal Scream
Dufresne, Mark
See Confederate Railroad
Duggan, Noel
See Clannad
Duggan, Paidraig
See Clannad
Duke, John
See Pearls Before Swine
Dukowski, Chuck
See Black Flag
Dulli, Greg
See Afghan Whigs
Dumont, Tom
See No Doubt
Dunbar, Aynsley
See Jefferson Starship
Also see Journey
Also see Whitesnake
Dunbar, Sly
See Sly and Robbie
Duncan, Bryan **19**
Duncan, Gary
See Quicksilver Messenger Service
Duncan, Steve
See Desert Rose Band, The
Duncan, Stuart
See Nashville Bluegrass Band
Dunham, Nathanel "Brad"
See Five Iron Frenzy
Dunlap, Slim
See Replacements, The
Dunn, Donald "Duck"
See Booker T. & the M.G.'s
Dunn, Holly **7**
Dunn, Larry
See Earth, Wind and Fire
Dunn, Ronnie Gene
See Brooks & Dunn
Dunning, A.J.
See Verve Pipe, The
DuPré, Jacqueline **26**
Dupree, Champion Jack **12**
Dupree, Jesse James
See Jackyl
Dupri, Jermaine **25**
Duran Duran **4**
Durante, Mark
See KMFDM
Duritz, Adam
See Counting Crows
Durrill, Johnny
See Ventures, The
Durst, Fred
See Limp Bizkit
Dutt, Hank
See Kronos Quartet
Dutton, Garrett
See G. Love
Dvorak, Antonin **25**
Dyble, Judy
See Fairport Convention
Dylan, Bob **21**
Earlier sketch in CM **3**
Dylan, Jakob
See Wallflowers, The
D'Amour, Paul
See Tool
E., Sheila
See Sheila E.
Eacrett, Chris
See Our Lady Peace
Eagles, The **3**
Earl, Ronnie **5**
Also see Roomful of Blues
Earle, Steve **16**
Also see Afghan Whigs
Early, Ian
See Cherry Poppin' Daddies
Earth, Wind and Fire **12**
Easton, Elliot
See Cars, The
Easton, Sheena **2**
Eazy-E **13**
Also see N.W.A.
Echeverria, Rob
See Helmet
Echobelly **21**
Eckstine, Billy **1**
Eddy, Duane **9**
Eden, Sean
See Luna
Edge, Graeme
See Moody Blues, The
Edge, The
See U2
Edmonds, Kenneth "Babyface" **12**
Edmonton, Jerry
See Steppenwolf
Edson, Richard
See Sonic Youth
Edwards, Dennis
See Temptations, The
Edwards, Edgar
See Spinners, The
Edwards, Gordon
See Kinks, The
Also see Pretty Things, The
Edwards, John
See Spinners , The
Edwards, Johnny
See Foreigner
Edwards, Leroy "Lion"
See Mystic Revealers
Edwards, Mark
See Aztec Camera
Edwards, Michael James
See Jesus Jones
Edwards, Mike
See Electric Light Orchestra
Edwards, Nokie
See Ventures, The
Edwards, Skye
See Morcheeba
Edwardson, Dave
See Neurosis
Efrem, Towns
See Dirty Dozen Brass Band
Ehran
See Lords of Acid
Eid, Tamer
See Emmet Swimming
Einheit, F.M.
See KMFDM
Einheit
See Einstürzende Neubauten
Einstürzende Neubauten **13**
Einziger, Michael
See Incubus
Eisenstein, Michael
See Letters to Cleo
Eitzel, Mark
See American Music Club
Ekberg, Ulf
See Ace of Base
Eklund, Greg
See Everclear
El Hefe
See NOFX
El-Hadi, Sulieman
See Last Poets
Eldon, Thór
See Sugarcubes, The
Eldridge, Ben
See Seldom Scene, The
Eldridge, Roy **9**
Also see McKinney's Cotton Pickers
Electric Light Orchestra **7**
Elfman, Danny **9**
Elias, Hanin
See Atari Teenage Riot
Elias, Manny
See Tears for Fears

Ellefson, Dave
See Megadeth
Ellington, Duke **2**
Elliot, Cass **5**
Also see Mamas and the Papas
Elliott, Dennis
See Foreigner
Elliott, Doug
See Odds
Elliott, Joe
See Def Leppard
Ellis, Arti
See Pearls Before Swine
Ellis, Bobby
See Skatalites, The
Ellis, Herb **18**
Ellis, Ingrid
See Sweet Honey in the Rock
Ellis, Terry
See En Vogue
Ellison, Rahsaan
See Oakland Interfaith Gospel Choir
Elmore, Greg
See Quicksilver Messenger Service
ELO
See Electric Light Orchestra
Ely, John
See Asleep at the Wheel
Ely, Vince
See Cure, The
Also see Psychedelic Furs
Emerson, Bill
See Country Gentlemen, The
Emerson, Darren
See Underworld
Emerson, Keith
See Emerson, Lake & Palmer/Powell
Emerson, Lake & Palmer/Powell **5**
Emery, Jill
See Hole
Eminem **28**
Emmanuel, Tommy **21**
Emmet Swimming **24**
Empire, Alec
See Atari Teenage Riot
En Vogue **10**
Endo, Nic
See Atari Teenage Riot
English Beat, The **9**
English, Michael **23**
English, Richard
See Flaming Lips
Enigk, Jeremy
See Sunny Day Real Estate
Enigma **14**
Eno, Brian **8**
Enos, Bob
See Roomful of Blues
Enright, Pat
See Nashville Bluegrass Band
Entwistle, John
See Who, The
Enya **6**
Also see Clannad
EPMD **10**
Epstein, Howie
See Tom Petty and the Heartbreakers
Erasure **11**
Erchick, Peter
See Olivia Tremor Control
Eric B. and Rakim **9**
Eric B.
See Eric B. and Rakim
Erickson, Roky **16**
Erikson, Duke
See Garbage
Erlandson, Eric
See Hole
Erner, Jeff "The Shark"
See Dropkick Murphys
Errico, Greg
See Sly & the Family Stone
Also see Quicksilver Messenger Service
Erskine, Peter
See Weather Report
Ertegun, Ahmet **10**
Ertegun, Nesuhi **24**
Erwin, Emily
See Dixie Chicks
Esch, En
See KMFDM
Also see Pigface
Escovedo, Alejandro **18**
Eshe, Montsho
See Arrested Development
Eskelin, Ian **19**
Esler-Smith, Frank
See Air Supply
Esquivel, Juan **17**
Estefan, Gloria **15**
Earlier sketch in CM **2**
Estes, Sleepy John **25**
Estms, Shep
See Lane, Fred
Estrada, Roy
See Little Feat
Also see Captain Beefheart and His Magic Band
Etheridge, Melissa **16**
Earlier sketch in CM **4**
Eurythmics **6**
Evan, John
See Jethro Tull
Evans, Bill **17**
Evans, Dick
See U2
Evans, Faith **25**
Evans, Gil **17**
Evans, Mark
See AC/DC
Evans, Sara **27**
Evans, Shane
See Collective Soul
Evans, Tom
See Badfinger
Everclear **18**
Everlast **27**
Also see House of Pain
Everly Brothers, The **2**
Everly, Don
See Everly Brothers, The
Everly, Phil
See Everly Brothers, The
Everman, Jason
See Soundgarden
Everything But The Girl **15**
Evora, Cesaria **19**
Ewen, Alvin
See Steel Pulse
Ex, The **28**
Exkano, Paul
See Five Blind Boys of Alabama
Exposé **4**
Extreme **10**
Ezell, Ralph
See Shenandoah
Fabian **5**
Fabulous Thunderbirds, The **1**
Faces, The **22**
Fadden, Jimmie
See Nitty Gritty Dirt Band, The
Fagan, Don
See Steely Dan
Fahey, John **17**
Fahey, Siobhan
See Bananarama
Fairport Convention **22**
Fairs, Jim
See Pearls Before Swine
Faith No More **7**
Faithfull, Marianne **14**
Fakir, Abdul "Duke"
See Four Tops, The
Falconer, Earl
See UB40
Fall, The **12**
Fallon, David
See Chieftains, The
Fältskog, Agnetha
See Abba
Falzone, Chuck
See Flying Luttenbachers, The
Fambrough, Henry
See Spinners, The
Fame, Georgie
See Bill Wyman & the Rhythm Kings
Fankhauser, Merrell **24**
Farley, J. J.
See Soul Stirrers, The
Farndon, Pete
See Pretenders, The
Farnsworth, Ed
See Bardo Pond
Farrar, Jay
See Son Volt
Farrar, John
See Shadows, The
Farrell, Frank
See Supertramp
Farrell, Perry
See Jane's Addiction
Farris, Dionne
See Arrested Development
Farris, Tim
See Israel Vibration
Farriss, Andrew
See INXS
Farriss, Jon
See INXS
Farriss, Tim
See INXS
Fast
See Fun Lovin' Criminals
Fat Mike
See NOFX
Fatboy Slim **22**
Fatone, Joey
See 'N Sync
Fay, Bob
See Sebadoh
Fay, Johnny
See Tragically Hip, The
Fay, Martin
See Chieftains, The
Fear Factory **27**
Fearless, Richard
See Death in Vegas
Fearnley, James
See Pogues, The
Fehlmann, Thomas
See Orb, The
Feinstein, Michael **6**

Fela
See Kuti, Fela
Felber, Dean
See Hootie and the Blowfish
Felder, Don
See Eagles, The
Feldman, Eric Drew
See Pere Ubu
Also see Captain Beefheart and His Magic Band
Feliciano, José **10**
Fender, Freddy
See Texas Tornados, The
Fender, Leo **10**
Fennell, Kevin
See Guided By Voices
Fennelly, Gere
See Redd Kross
Fent-Lister, Johnny
See Lane, Fred
Fenwick, Ray
See Spencer Davis Group
Ferguson, Doug
See Camel
Ferguson, Jay
See Sloan
Ferguson, Jay
See Spirit
Ferguson, Keith
See Fabulous Thunderbirds, The
Ferguson, Maynard **7**
Ferguson, Neil
See Chumbawamba
Ferguson, Steve
See NRBQ
Fernandes, John
See Olivia Tremor Control
Ferrell, Rachelle **17**
Ferrer, Frank
See Love Spit Love
Ferry, Bryan **1**
Ficca, Billy
See Television
Fiedler, Arthur **6**
Fielder, Jim
See Blood, Sweat and Tears
Fields, Johnny
See Five Blind Boys of Alabama
Fieldy
See Korn
Fier, Anton
See Pere Ubu
Filter **28**
Finch, Jennifer
See L7
Fine Young Cannibals **22**
Finer, Jem
See Pogues, The
Finestone, Peter
See Bad Religion
Fink, Jr., Rat
See Alien Sex Fiend
Finn, Micky
See T. Rex
Finn, Neil
See Crowded House
Finn, Tim
See Crowded House
fIREHOSE **11**
Fishbone **7**
Fisher, Brandon
See Superdrag
Fisher, Eddie **12**
Fisher, Jerry
See Blood, Sweat and Tears
Fisher, John "Norwood"
See Fishbone
Fisher, Phillip "Fish"
See Fishbone
Fisher, Roger
See Heart
Fishman, Jon
See Phish
Fitzgerald, Ella **1**
Fitzgerald, Kevin
See Geraldine Fibbers
Five Blind Boys of Alabama **12**
Five Iron Frenzy **26**
Flack, Roberta **5**
Flaming Lips **22**
Flanagan, Tommy **16**
Flannery, Sean
See Cherry Poppin' Daddies
Flansburgh, John
See They Might Be Giants
Flatt, Lester **3**
Flavor Flav
See Public Enemy
Flea
See Red Hot Chili Peppers, The
Fleck, Bela **8**
Also see New Grass Revival, The
Fleetwood Mac **5**
Fleetwood, Mick
See Fleetwood Mac
Fleischmann, Robert
See Journey
Fleming, Renee **24**
Flemons, Wade
See Earth, Wind and Fire
Flesh-N-Bone
See Bone Thugs-N-Harmony
Fletcher, Andy
See Depeche Mode
Fletcher, Guy
See Dire Straits
Flint, Keith
See Prodigy
Flores, Rosie **16**
Floyd, Heather
See Point of Grace
Flür, Wolfgang
See Kraftwerk
Flying Luttenbachers, The **28**
Flynn, Pat
See New Grass Revival, The
Fogelberg, Dan **4**
Fogerty, John **2**
Also see Creedence Clearwater Revival
Fogerty, Thomas
See Creedence Clearwater Revival
Folds, Ben
See Ben Folds Five
Foley
See Arrested Development
Folk Implosion, The **28**
Foo Fighters **20**
Foote, Dick
See Lane, Fred
Forbes, Derek
See Simple Minds
Forbes, Graham
See Incredible String Band
Ford, Frankie
See Pretty Things, The
Ford, Lita **9**
Ford, Marc
See Black Crowes, The
Ford, Penny
See Soul II Soul
Ford, Robert "Peg"
See Golden Gate Quartet
Ford, Tennessee Ernie **3**
Fordham, Julia **15**
Foreigner **21**
Foreman, Chris
See Madness
Forrester, Alan
See Mojave 3
Forsi, Ken
See Surfaris, The
Forster, Robert
See Go-Betweens, The
Forte, Juan
See Oakland Interfaith Gospel Choir
Fortune, Jimmy
See Statler Brothers, The
Fortus, Richard
See Love Spit Love
Fossen, Steve
See Heart
Foster, David **13**
Foster, Malcolm
See Pretenders, The
Foster, Paul
See Soul Stirrers, The
Foster, Radney **16**
Fountain, Clarence
See Five Blind Boys of Alabama
Fountain, Pete **7**
Fountains of Wayne **26**
Four Seasons, The **24**
Four Tops, The **11**
FourHim **23**
Fowler, Bruce "Fossil Fowler"
See Captain Beefheart and His Magic Band
Fox, Lucas
See Motörhead
Fox, Oz
See Stryper
Fox, Samantha **3**
Foxton, Bruce
See Jam, The
Foxwell Baker, Iain Richard
See Jesus Jones
Foxx, Leigh
See Blondie
Frame, Roddy
See Aztec Camera
Frampton, Peter **3**
Francis, Black
See Pixies, The
Francis, Connie **10**
Francis, Mike
See Asleep at the Wheel
Franke, Chris
See Tangerine Dream
Frankenstein, Jeff
See Newsboys, The
Frankie Lymon and The Teenagers **24**
Franklin, Aretha **17**
Earlier sketch in CM **2**
Franklin, Elmo
See Mighty Clouds of Joy, The
Franklin, Kirk **22**
Franklin, Larry
See Asleep at the Wheel
Franklin, Melvin
See Temptations, The
Franti, Michael **16**
Also see Spearhead
Frantz, Chris
See Talking Heads
Fraser, Elizabeth
See Cocteau Twins, The

Frater, Shaun
See Fairport Convention
Frazier, Stan
See Sugar Ray
Fredriksson, Marie
See Roxette
Freese, Josh
See Suicidal Tendencies
Frehley, Ace
See Kiss
Freiberg, David
See Quicksilver Messenger Service
Also see Jefferson Starship
French, Frank
See Cake
French, John "Drumbo"
See Captain Beefheart and His Magic Band
French, Mark
See Blue Rodeo
Freni, Mirella **14**
Freshwater, John
See Alien Sex Fiend
Frey, Glenn **3**
Also see Eagles, The
Fricker, Sylvia
See Ian and Sylvia
Fridmann, Dave
See Mercury Rev
Friedman, Marty
See Megadeth
Friel, Tony
See Fall, The
Fripp, Robert **9**
Also see King Crimson
Frisell, Bill **15**
Frishmann, Justine
See Suede
Frith, Fred **19**
Frizzell, Lefty **10**
Froese, Edgar
See Tangerine Dream
Front 242 **19**
Front Line Assembly **20**
Froom, Mitchell **15**
Frusciante, John
See Red Hot Chili Peppers, The
Fu Manchu **22**
Fuel **27**
Fugazi **13**
Fugees, The **17**
Fulber, Rhys
See Front Line Assembly
Fuller, Blind Boy **20**
Fuller, Craig
See Little Feat
Fuller, Jim
See Surfaris, The
Fulson, Lowell **20**
Fun Lovin' Criminals **20**
Funahara, O. Chosei
See Wendy O. Williams and The Plasmatics
Fuqua, Charlie
See Ink Spots
Furay, Richie
See Buffalo Springfield
Furler, Peter
See Newsboys, The
Furr, John
See Treadmill Trackstar
Furuholmen, Magne
See A-ha
Futter, Brian
See Catherine Wheel
G. Love **24**
Gabay, Yuval
See Soul Coughing
Gabler, Milton **25**
Gabriel, Peter **16**
Earlier sketch in CM **2**
Also see Genesis
Gadler, Frank
See NRBQ
Gaffney, Eric
See Sebadoh
Gagliardi, Ed
See Foreigner
Gahan, Dave
See Depeche Mode
Gaines, Steve
See Lynyrd Skynyrd
Gaines, Timothy
See Stryper
Galás, Diamanda **16**
Gale, Melvyn
See Electric Light Orchestra
Galea, Darren
See Jamiroquai
Gallagher, Liam
See Oasis
Gallagher, Noel
See Oasis
Gallup, Simon
See Cure, The
Galore, Lady
See Lords of Acid
Galway, James **3**
Gambill, Roger
See Kingston Trio, The
Gamble, Cheryl "Coko"
See SWV
Gane, Tim
See Stereolab
Gang of Four **8**
Gang Starr **13**
Gannon, Craig
See Aztec Camera
Gano, Gordon
See Violent Femmes
Garbage **25**
Garcia, Dean
See Curve
Garcia, Jerry **4**
Also see Grateful Dead, The
Garcia, Leddie
See Poi Dog Pondering
Gardiner, John Eliot **26**
Gardner, Carl
See Coasters, The
Gardner, Suzi
See L7
Garfunkel, Art **4**
Also see Simon and Garfunkel
Garland, Judy **6**
Garner, Erroll **25**
Garnes, Sherman
See Frankie Lymon and The Teenagers
Garrett, Amos
See Pearls Before Swine
Garrett, Kenny **28**
Garrett, Peter
See Midnight Oil
Garrett, Scott
See Cult, The
Garvey, Steve
See Buzzcocks, The
Gaskill, Jerry
See King's X
Gaston, Asa
See Lane, Fred
Gates, Jimmy Jr.
See Silk
Gatton, Danny **16**
Gaudio, Bob
See Four Seasons, The
Gaudreau, Jimmy
See Country Gentlemen, The
Gaugh, "Bud" Floyd, IV
See Sublime
Gavurin, David
See Sundays, The
Gay, Marc
See Shai
Gayden, Mac
See Pearls Before Swine
Gaye, Marvin **4**
Gayle, Crystal **1**
Gaynor, Adam
See Matchbox 20
Gaynor, Mel
See Simple Minds
Gayol, Rafael "Danny"
See BoDeans
Geary, Paul
See Extreme
Geddes, Chris
See Belle and Sebastian
Gedge, David
See Wedding Present, The
Gee, Rosco
See Traffic
Gee, Rosko
See Can
Geffen, David **8**
Geils, J.
See J. Geils Band
Geldof, Bob **9**
Gene Loves Jezebel **27**
Genensky, Marsha
See Anonymous 4
Genesis **4**
Gentling, Matt
See Archers of Loaf
Gentry, Teddy Wayne
See Alabama
George, Lowell
See Little Feat
George, Rocky
See Suicidal Tendencies
Georges, Bernard
See Throwing Muses
Georgiev, Ivan
See Tuxedomoon
Geraldine Fibbers **21**
Germano, Lisa **18**
Gerrard, Lisa
See Dead Can Dance
Gershwin, George and Ira **11**
Gessle, Per
See Roxette
Geto Boys, The **11**
Getz, Stan **12**
Ghost **24**
Giammalvo, Chris
See Madder Rose
Gianni, Angelo
See Treadmill Trackstar
Gibb, Barry
See Bee Gees, The
Gibb, Maurice
See Bee Gees, The
Gibb, Robin
See Bee Gees, The
Gibbins, Mike
See Badfinger

Gibbons, Beth
See Portishead
Gibbons, Billy
See ZZ Top
Gibbons, Ian
See Kinks, The
Gibbons, John
See Bardo Pond
Gibbons, Michael
See Bardo Pond
Giblin, John
See Simple Minds
Gibson, Bob **23**
Gibson, Debbie
See Gibson, Deborah
Gibson, Deborah **24**
Earlier sketch in CM **1**
Gibson, Wilf
Gifford, Alex
See Propellerheads
Also see Electric Light Orchestra
Gifford, Katharine
See Stereolab
Gifford, Peter
See Midnight Oil
Gift, Roland **3**
Also see Fine Young Cannibals
Gil, Gilberto **26**
Gilbert, Gillian
See New Order
Gilbert, Nicole Nicci
See Brownstone
Gilbert, Ronnie
See Weavers, The
Gilbert, Simon
See Suede
Giles, Michael
See King Crimson
Gilkyson, Tony
See X
Gill, Andy
See Gang of Four
Gill, Janis
See Sweethearts of the Rodeo
Gill, Johnny **20**
Gill, Pete
See Motörhead
Gill, Vince **7**
Gillan, Ian
See Deep Purple
Also see Black Sabbath
Gillard, Doug
See Cobra Verde
Gillespie, Bobby
See Jesus and Mary Chain, The
Also see Primal Scream
Gillespie, Dizzy **6**
Gilley, Mickey **7**
Gillian, Ian
See Black Sabbath
Gillies, Ben
See Silverchair
Gillingham, Charles
See Counting Crows
Gillis, Steve
See Filter
Gilmore, Jimmie Dale **11**
Gilmour, David
See Pink Floyd
Gilvear, Marcus
See Gene Loves Jezebel
Gin Blossoms **18**
Gingold, Josef **6**
Ginn, Greg
See Black Flag
Ginsberg, Allen **26**
Gioia
See Exposé
Gipp, Cameron "Big Gipp"
See Goodie Mob
Gipsy Kings, The **8**
Giraudy, Miquitte
See Gong
Gittleman, Joe
See Mighty Mighty Bosstones
Glabicki, Michael
See Rusted Root
Glascock, John
See Jethro Tull
Glaser, Gabby
See Luscious Jackson
Glass, David
See Christian Death
Glass, Eddie
See Fu Manchu
Glass, Philip **1**
Glasscock, John
See Jethro Tull
Glenn, Gary
See Silk
Glennie, Jim
See James
Glitter, Gary **19**
Glover, Corey
See Living Colour
Glover, Roger
See Deep Purple
Gnewikow, Jason
See Promise Ring, The
Go-Betweens, The **28**
Go-Go's, The **24**
Gobel, Robert
See Kool & the Gang
Goble, Brian Roy
See D.O.A.
Godchaux, Donna
See Grateful Dead, The
Godchaux, Keith
See Grateful Dead, The
Godfrey, Paul
See Morcheeba
Godfrey, Ross
See Morcheeba
Goettel, Dwayne Rudolf
See Skinny Puppy
Goffin, Gerry
See Goffin-King
Goffin-King **24**
Gogin, Toni
See Sleater-Kinney
Goh, Rex
See Air Supply
Gold, Julie **22**
Golden Gate Quartet **25**
Golden, William Lee
See Oak Ridge Boys, The
Golding, Lynval
See Specials, The
Goldsmith, William
See Sunny Day Real Estate
Goldsmith, William
See Foo Fighters
Goldstein, Jerry
See War
Golson, Benny **21**
Gong **24**
Gonson, Claudia
See Magnetic Fields, The
Goo Goo Dolls, The **16**
Gooden, Ramone Pee Wee
See Digital Underground
Goodie Mob **24**
Goodman, Benny **4**
Goodman, Jerry
See Mahavishnu Orchestra
Goodridge, Robin
See Bush
Gordon, Dexter **10**
Gordon, Dwight
See Mighty Clouds of Joy, The
Gordon, Jay
See Orgy
Gordon, Jim
See Traffic
Gordon, Kim
See Sonic Youth
Gordon, Mike
See Phish
Gordon, Nina
See Veruca Salt
Gordy, Berry, Jr. **6**
Gordy, Emory, Jr. **17**
Gore, Martin
See Depeche Mode
Gorham, Scott
See Thin Lizzy
Gorka, John **18**
Gorman, Christopher
See Belly
Gorman, Steve
See Black Crowes, The
Gorman, Thomas
See Belly
Gorter, Arjen
See Willem Breuker Kollektief
Gosling, John
See Kinks, The
Gossard, Stone
See Brad
Also see Pearl Jam
Goswell, Rachel
See Mojave 3
Gott, Larry
See James
Goudreau, Barry
See Boston
Gould, Billy
See Faith No More
Gould, Glenn **9**
Gould, Morton **16**
Goulding, Steve
See Gene Loves Jezebel
Grable, Steve
See Pearls Before Swine
Gracey, Chad
See Live
Gradney, Ken
See Little Feat
Graffety-Smith, Toby
See Jamiroquai
Graffin, Greg
See Bad Religion
Graham, Bill **10**
Graham, Glen
See Blind Melon
Graham, Johnny
See Earth, Wind and Fire
Graham, Larry
See Sly & the Family Stone
Gramm, Lou
See Foreigner
Gramolini, Gary
See Beaver Brown Band, The

Grandmaster Flash **14**
Grant, Amy **7**
Grant, Bob
See The Bad Livers
Grant, Gogi **28**
Grant Lee Buffalo **16**
Grant, Lloyd
See Metallica
Grappelli, Stephane **10**
Grateful Dead, The **5**
Gratzer, Alan
See REO Speedwagon
Gravatt, Eric
See Weather Report
Gravediggaz **23**
Graves, Denyce **16**
Gray, David
See Spearhead
Gray, Del
See Little Texas
Gray, Ella
See Kronos Quartet
Gray, F. Gary **19**
Gray, James
See Blue Rodeo
Gray, James
See Spearhead
Gray, Luther
See Tsunami
Gray, Tom
See Country Gentlemen, The
Also see Seldom Scene, The
Gray, Walter
See Kronos Quartet
Gray, Wardell
See McKinney's Cotton Pickers
Greater Vision **26**
Grebenshikov, Boris **3**
Grech, Rick
See Traffic
Greco, Paul
See Chumbawamba
Green, Al **9**
Green, Benny **17**
Green, Carlito "Cee-lo"
See Goodie Mob
Green, Charles
See War
Green, David
See Air Supply
Green Day **16**
Green, Grant **14**
Green, James
See Dru Hill
Green, Peter
See Fleetwood Mac
Green, Susaye
See Supremes, The
Green, Willie
See Neville Brothers, The
Greene, Karl Anthony
See Herman's Hermits
Greenhalgh, Tom
See Mekons, The
Greensmith, Domenic
See Reef
Greenspoon, Jimmy
See Three Dog Night
Greentree, Richard
See Beta Band, The
Greenwood, Al
See Foreigner
Greenwood, Colin
See Radiohead
Greenwood, Gail
See Belly
Greenwood, Jonny
See Radiohead
Greenwood, Lee **12**
Greenwood,Colin
See Radiohead
Greer, Jim
See Guided By Voices
Gregg, Dave
See D.O.A.
Gregg, Paul
See Restless Heart
Gregory, Bryan
See Cramps, The
Gregory, Dave
See XTC
Gregory, Keith
See Wedding Present, The
Gregory, Troy
See Prong
Greller, Al
See Yo La Tengo
Grey, Charles Wallace
See Aquabats, The
Grice, Gary "The Genius"
See Wu-Tang Clan
Griffin, A.C. "Eddie"
See Golden Gate Quartet
Griffin, Bob
See BoDeans, The
Griffin, Kevin
See Better Than Ezra
Also see NRBQ
Griffin, Mark
See MC 900 Ft. Jesus
Griffin, Patty **24**
Griffin, Rodney
See Greater Vision
Griffith, Nanci **3**
Grigg, Chris
See Treadmill Trackstar
Grisman, David **17**
Grohl, Dave
See Nirvana
Also see Foo Fighters
Grotberg, Karen
See Jayhawks, The
Groucutt, Kelly
See Electric Light Orchestra
Grove, George
See Kingston Trio, The
Grover, Charlie
See Sponge
Grundy, Hugh
See Zombies, The
Grusin, Dave **7**
Guaraldi, Vince **3**
Guard, Dave
See Kingston Trio, The
Gudmundsdottir, Björk
See Björk
Also see Sugarcubes, The
Guerin, John
See Byrds, The
Guess Who **23**
Guest, Christopher
See Spinal Tap
Guided By Voices **18**
Gunn, Trey
See King Crimson
Guns n' Roses **2**
Gunther, Cornell
See Coasters, The
Gunther, Ric
See Bevis Frond
Gurewitz, Brett
See Bad Religion
Guru
See Gang Starr
Gus Gus **26**
Guss, Randy
See Toad the Wet Sprocket
Gustafson, Steve
See 10,000 Maniacs
Gut, Grudrun
See Einstürzende Neubauten
Guthrie, Arlo **6**
Guthrie, Gwen **26**
Guthrie, Robin
See Cocteau Twins, The
Guthrie, Woody **2**
Guy, Billy
See Coasters, The
Guy, Buddy **4**
Guyett, Jim
See Quicksilver Messenger Service
Gwar **13**
H.R.
See Bad Brains
Hacke, Alexander
See Einstürzende Neubauten
Hackett, Bobby **21**
Hackett, Steve
See Genesis
Haden, Charlie **12**
Hadjopulos, Sue
See Simple Minds
Hagar, Regan
See Brad
Hagar, Sammy **21**
Also see Van Halen
Hagen, Nina **25**
Haggard, Merle **2**
HaHa, Jimi
See Jimmie's Chicken Shack
Hakim, Omar
See Weather Report
Hakmoun, Hassan **15**
Hale, Simon
See Incognito
Haley, Bill **6**
Haley, Mark
See Kinks, The
Haley, Paige
See Orgy
Halford, Rob
See Judas Priest
Hall & Oates **6**
Hall, Bruce
See REO Speedwagon
Hall, Daryl
See Hall & Oates
Hall, John S.
See King Missile
Hall, Lance
See Inner Circle
Hall, Randall
See Lynyrd Skynyrd
Hall, Terry
See Specials, The
Hall, Tom T. **26**
Earlier sketch in CM **4**
Hall, Tony
See Neville Brothers, The
Halliday, Toni
See Curve
Halliwell, Geri
See Spice Girls

Halstead, Neil
See Mojave 3
Ham, Pete
See Badfinger
Hamer, Harry
See Chumbawamba
Hamilton, Arnold (Frukwan da Gatekeeper)
See Gravediggaz
Hamilton, Frank
See Weavers, The
Hamilton, Katie
See Treadmill Trackstar
Hamilton, Milton
See Third World
Hamilton, Page
See Helmet
Hamilton, Tom
See Aerosmith
Hamlisch, Marvin **1**
Hammer, Jan **21**
Also see Mahavishnu Orchestra
Hammer, M.C. **5**
Hammerstein, Oscar
See Rodgers, Richard
Hammett, Kirk
See Metallica
Hammon, Ron
See War
Hammond, John **6**
Hammond-Hammond, Jeffrey
See Jethro Tull
Hampson, Sharon
See Sharon, Lois & Bram
Hampson, Thomas **12**
Hampton, Lionel **6**
Hancock, Herbie **25**
Earlier sketch in CM **8**
Handley, Jerry
See Captain Beefheart and His Magic Band
Handy, W. C. **7**
Hanley, Kay
See Letters to Cleo
Hanley, Steve
See Fall, The
Hanna, Jeff
See Nitty Gritty Dirt Band, The
Hannan, Patrick
See Sundays, The
Hanneman, Jeff
See Slayer
Hannibal, Chauncey "Black"
See Blackstreet
Hannon, Frank
See Tesla
Hansen, Mary
See Stereolab
Hanson **20**
Hanson, Isaac
See Hanson
Hanson, Paul (Prince Paul A.K.A. Dr. Strange)
See Gravediggaz
Hanson, Taylor
See Hanson
Hanson, Zachary
See Hanson
Hardcastle, Paul **20**
Hardin, Eddie
See Spencer Davis Group
Hardin, Geraldine
See Sweet Honey in the Rock
Hardin, Tim **18**
Harding, John Wesley **6**
Hardson, Tre "Slimkid"
See Pharcyde, The
Hargreaves, Brad
See Third Eye Blind
Hargrove, Kornell
See Poi Dog Pondering
Hargrove, Roy **15**
Harkelroad, Bill "Zoot Horn Rollo"
See Captain Beefheart and His Magic Band
Harket, Morten
See A-ha
Harley, Bill **7**
Harley, Wayne
See Pearls Before Swine
Harms, Jesse
See REO Speedwagon
Harper, Ben **17**
Harper, Raymond
See Skatalites, The
Harrell, Andre **16**
Harrell, Lynn **3**
Harrell, Tom **28**
Harrington, Ayodele
See Sweet Honey in the Rock
Harrington, Carrie
See Sounds of Blackness
Harrington, David
See Kronos Quartet
Harris, Addie "Micki"
See Shirelles, The
Harris, Damon Otis
See Temptations, The
Harris, Eddie **15**
Harris, Emmylou **4**
Harris, Eric
See Olivia Tremor Control
Harris, Evelyn Maria
See Sweet Honey in the Rock
Harris, Gerard
See Kool & the Gang
Harris, James
See Echobelly
Harris, Jet
See Shadows, The
Harris, Joey
See Beat Farmers
Harris, Kevin
See Dirty Dozen Brass Band
Harris, Lee
See Talk Talk
Harris, Mark
See 4Him
Harris, Mary
See Spearhead
Harris, Nigel
See Jam, The
Harris, R. H.
See Soul Stirrers, The
Harris, Steve
See Iron Maiden
Harris, Teddy **22**
Harrison, George **2**
Also see Beatles, The
Harrison, Jerry
See Talking Heads
Harrison, Nigel
See Blondie
Harrison, Richard
See Stereolab
Harry, Deborah **4**
Also see Blondie
Hart, William Cullen
See Olivia Tremor Control
Hart, Alvin Youngblood **27**
Hart, Chuck
See Surfin' Pluto
Hart, Douglas
See Jesus and Mary Chain, The
Hart, Hattie
See Memphis Jug Band
Hart, Lorenz
See Rodgers, Richard
Hart, Mark
See Supertramp
Hart, Mark
See Crowded House
Hart, Mickey
See Grateful Dead, The
Hart, Robert
See Bad Company
Hart, Tim
See Steeleye Span
Hartford, John **1**
Hartke, Stephen **5**
Hartley, Matthieu
See Cure, The
Hartman, Bob
See Petra
Hartman, John
See Doobie Brothers, The
Hartnoll, Paul
See Orbital
Hartnoll, Phil
See Orbital
Harvey, Bernard "Touter"
See Inner Circle
Harvey, Philip "Daddae"
See Soul II Soul
Harvey, Polly Jean **11**
Harvie, Iain
See Del Amitri
Harwell, Steve
See Smash Mouth
Harwood, Justin
See Luna
Haseltine, Dan
See Jars of Clay
Hashian
See Boston
Haskell, Gordon
See King Crimson
Haskins, Kevin
See Bauhaus
Also see Love and Rockets
Haslinger, Paul
See Tangerine Dream
Hassan, Norman
See UB40
Hassman, Nikki
See Avalon
Hastings, Jimmy
See Caravan
Hastings, Pye
See Caravan
Hatfield, Juliana **12**
Also see Lemonheads, The
Hathaway, Jane
See Lane, Fred
Hatori, Miho
See Cibo Matto
Hauser, Tim
See Manhattan Transfer, The
Havens, Richie **11**
Hawes, Dave
See Catherine Wheel
Hawkes, Greg
See Cars, The
Hawkins, Coleman **11**
Hawkins, Erskine **19**
Hawkins, Lamont "U-God"
See Wu-Tang Clan

Hawkins, Nick
See Big Audio Dynamite
Hawkins, Richard (Dick)
See Gene Loves Jezebel
Hawkins, Roger
See Traffic
Hawkins, Screamin' Jay **8**
Hawkins, Sophie B. **21**
Hawkins, Taylor
See Foo Fighters
Hawkins, Tramaine **17**
Hawkins, Xian
See Silver Apples
Hay, George D. **3**
Hayden, Victor "The Mascara Snake"
See Captain Beefheart and His Magic Band
Hayes, Gordon
See Pearls Before Swine
Hayes, Isaac **10**
Hayes, Roland **13**
Haynes, Gibby
See Butthole Surfers
Haynes, Warren
See Allman Brothers, The
Hays, Lee
See Weavers, The
Hayward, David Justin
See Moody Blues, The
Hayward, Richard
See Little Feat
Headliner
See Arrested Development
Headon, Topper
See Clash, The
Healey, Jeff **4**
Heard, Paul
See M People
Hearn, Kevin
See Barenaked Ladies
Heart **1**
Heath, James
See Reverend Horton Heat
Heaton, Paul
See Beautiful South
Heavy D **10**
Hecker, Robert
See Redd Kross
Hedford, Eric
See Dandy Warhols
Hedges, Eddie
See Blessid Union of Souls
Hedges, Michael **3**
Heggie, Will
See Cocteau Twins, The
Heidorn, Mike
See Son Volt
Heitman, Dana
See Cherry Poppin' Daddies
Helfgott, David **19**
Hell, Richard
See Television
Hellauer, Susan
See Anonymous 4
Hellerman, Fred
See Weavers, The
Hellier, Steve
See Death in Vegas
Helliwell, John
See Supertramp
Helm, Levon
See Band, The
Also see Nitty Gritty Dirt Band, The
Helmet **15**
Hemingway, Dave
See Beautiful South
Hemmings, Paul
See Lightning Seeds
Henderson, Andy
See Echobelly
Henderson, Billy
See Spinners, The
Henderson, Fletcher **16**
Henderson, Joe **14**
Hendricks, Barbara **10**
Hendricks, Jon
See Lambert, Hendricks and Ross
Hendrix, Jimi **2**
Henley, Don **3**
Also see Eagles, The
Henrit, Bob
See Kinks, The
Henry, Bill
See Northern Lights
Henry, Joe **18**
Henry, Kent
See Steppenwolf
Henry, Nicholas "Drummie"
See Mystic Revealers
Hensley, Ken
See Uriah Heep
Hepcat, Harry **23**
Hepner, Rich
See Captain Beefheart and His Magic Band
Heppner, Ben **23**
Herdman, Bob
See Audio Adrenaline
Herman, Maureen
See Babes in Toyland
Herman, Tom
See Pere Ubu
Herman, Woody **12**
Herman's Hermits **5**
Herndon, Mark Joel
See Alabama
Herndon, Ty **20**
Heron, Mike
See Incredible String Band
Herrera, R. J.
See Suicidal Tendencies
Herrera, Raymond
See Fear Factory
Herrlin, Anders
See Roxette
Herrmann, Bernard **14**
Herron, Cindy
See En Vogue
Hersh, Kristin
See Throwing Muses
Hester, Paul
See Crowded House
Hetfield, James
See Metallica
Hetson, Greg
See Bad Religion
Hetson, Greg
See Circle Jerks, The
Heveroh, Ben
See Oakland Interfaith Gospel Choir
Hewitt, Bobby
See Orgy
Hewitt, Steve
See Placebo
Hewson, Paul
See U2
Hexum, Nick
See 311
Hiatt, John **8**
Hickey, Kenny
See Type O Negative
Hickman, Johnny
See Cracker
Hicks, Chris
See Restless Heart
Hicks, Sheree
See C + C Music Factory
Hidalgo, David
See Los Lobos
Higgins, Jimmy
See Altan
Higgins, Terence
See Dirty Dozen Brass Band
Highway 101 **4**
Hijbert, Fritz
See Kraftwerk
Hilah
See Boredoms, The
Hill, Brendan
See Blues Traveler
Hill, Dave
See Cobra Verde
Hill, Dusty
See ZZ Top
Hill, Faith **18**
Hill, Ian
See Judas Priest
Hill, Lauryn **25**
Also see Fugees, The
Hill, Scott
See Fu Manchu
Hill, Stuart
See Shudder to Think
Hillage, Steve
See Orb, The
Also see Gong
Hillier, Steve
See Dubstar
Hillman, Bones
See Midnight Oil
Hillman, Chris
See Byrds, The
Also see Desert Rose Band, The
Hinderas, Natalie **12**
Hinds, David
See Steel Pulse
Hines, Earl "Fatha" **12**
Hines, Gary
See Sounds of Blackness
Hinojosa, Tish **13**
Hirst, Rob
See Midnight Oil
Hirt, Al **5**
Hitchcock, Robyn **9**
Hitchcock, Russell
See Air Supply
Hitt, Bryan
See REO Speedwagon
Hobson, Motor
See Lane, Fred
Hodge, Alex
See Platters, The
Hodges, Johnny **24**
Hodgson, Roger **26**
Also see Supertramp
Hodo, David
See Village People, The
Hoenig, Michael
See Tangerine Dream
Hoerig, Keith
See Five Iron Frenzy
Hoerner, Dan
See Sunny Day Real Estate
Hoffman, Ellen
See Oakland Interfaith Gospel Choir

Hoffman, Guy
See BoDeans, The
Also see Violent Femmes
Hoffman, Kristian
See Congo Norvell
Hoffman, Sam
See Captain Beefheart and His Magic Band
Hoffs, Susanna
See Bangles, The
Hogan, Mike
See Cranberries, The
Hogan, Noel
See Cranberries, The
Hoke, Jim
See NRBQ
Holder, Gene
See Yo La Tengo
Hole **14**
Holiday, Billie **6**
Holland, Brian
See Holland-Dozier-Holland
Holland, Bryan "Dexter"
See Offspring
Holland, Dave
See Judas Priest
Holland, Dave **27**
Holland, Eddie
See Holland-Dozier-Holland
Holland, Julian "Jools"
See Squeeze
Holland-Dozier-Holland **5**
Hollis, Mark
See Talk Talk
Hollister, Dave
See Blackstreet
Holly, Buddy **1**
Holmes, Malcolm
See Orchestral Manoeuvres in the Dark
Holmes, Tim
See Death in Vegas
Holmstrom, Peter
See Dandy Warhols
Holt, David Lee
See Mavericks, The
Homme, Josh
See Screaming Trees
Honda, Yuka
See Cibo Matto
Honeyman, Susie
See Mekons, The
Honeyman-Scott, James
See Pretenders, The
Hood, David
See Traffic
Hook, Peter
See Joy Division
Also see New Order
Hooker, John Lee **26**
Earlier sketch in CM **1**
Hooks, Rosie Lee
See Sweet Honey in the Rock
Hoon, Shannon
See Blind Melon
Hooper, Nellee
See Soul II Soul
Also see Massive Attack
Hooters **20**
Hootie and the Blowfish **18**
Hope, Gavin
See Nylons, The
Hopkins, Doug
See Gin Blossoms
Hopkins, Lightnin' **13**
Hopkins, Nicky
See Quicksilver Messenger Service
Hoppus, Mark
See Blink 182
Hopwood, Keith
See Herman's Hermits
Horn, Shirley **7**
Horn, Trevor
See Yes
Horne, Lena **11**
Horne, Marilyn **9**
Horner, Jessica
See Less Than Jake
Hornsby, Bruce **25**
Earlier sketch in CM **3**
Horovitz, Adam "King Ad-Rock"
See Beastie Boys
Horowitz, Vladimir **1**
Horton, Jeff
See Northern Lights
Horton, Walter **19**
Hossack, Michael
See Doobie Brothers, The
Houari, Rachid
See Gong
House, Kenwyn
See Reef
House of Pain **14**
House, Son **11**
Houston, Cissy **26**
Earlier sketch in CM **6**
Houston, Penelope **28**
Houston, Whitney **25**
Earlier sketch in CM **8**
Howard, Harlan **15**
Howe, Brian
See Bad Company
Howe, Steve
See Yes
Howell, Porter
See Little Texas
Howland, Don **24**
Howlett, Liam
See Prodigy
Howlett, Mike
See Gong
Howlin' Wolf **6**
Hubbard, Gregg "Hobie"
See Sawyer Brown
Hubbard, Preston
See Fabulous Thunderbirds, The
Also see Roomful of Blues
Huber, Connie
See Chenille Sisters, The
Hubrey, Georgia
See Yo La Tengo
Hudson, Earl
See Bad Brains
Hudson, Garth
See Band, The
Hudson, Ian
See Gene Loves Jezebel
Huey
See Fun Lovin' Criminals
Huffman, Doug
See Boston
Hughes, Bruce
See Poi Dog Pondering
Hughes, Bruce
See Cracker
Hughes, Glenn
See Black Sabbath
Hughes, Glenn
See Village People, The
Hughes, Leon
See Coasters, The
Huld, Hafdis
See Gus Gus
Human League, The **17**
Humes, Helen **19**
Humperdinck, Engelbert **19**
Humphreys, Paul
See Orchestral Manoeuvres in the Dark
Hunnekink, Bermard
See Willem Breuker Kollektief
Hunt, Darryl
See Pogues, The
Hunter, Alberta **7**
Hunter, Charlie **24**
Hunter, Jason "The Rebel INS" (Inspectah Deckk)
See Wu-Tang Clan
Hunter, Mark
See James
Hunter, Shepherd "Ben"
See Soundgarden
Hurley, George
See fIREHOSE
Hurst, Ron
See Steppenwolf
Hurt, Mississippi John **24**
Hutchence, Michael
See INXS
Hutchings, Ashley
See Fairport Convention
Also see Steeleye Span
Hutchinson, Trevor
See Waterboys, The
Huth, Todd
See Primus
Hütter, Ralf
See Kraftwerk
Hutton, Danny
See Three Dog Night
Huxley, Rick
See Dave Clark Five, The
Hyatt, Aitch
See Specials, The
Hyde, Karl
See Underworld
Hyde, Michael
See Big Mountain
Hyman, Jerry
See Blood, Sweat and Tears
Hyman, Rob
See Hooters
Hynd, Richard
See Texas
Hynde, Chrissie
See Pretenders, The
Hyslop, Kenny
See Simple Minds
Ian and Sylvia **18**
Ian, Janis **24**
Earlier sketch in CM **5**
Ian, Scott
See Anthrax
Ibbotson, Jimmy
See Nitty Gritty Dirt Band, The
Ibold, Mark
See Pavement
Ibrahim, Abdullah **24**
Ice Cube **25**
Earlier sketch in CM **10**
Also see N.W.A
Ice-T **7**
Idol, Billy **3**
Iglesias, Enrique **27**
Iglesias, Julio **20**
Earlier sketch in CM **2**

Iha, James
See Smashing Pumpkins
Ike and Tina Turner **24**
Illsley, John
See Dire Straits
Imbruglia, Natalie **27**
Immergluck, David
See Monks of Doom
Imperial Teen **26**
Incognito **16**
Incredible String Band **23**
Incubus **23**
Indigo Girls **20**
Earlier sketch in CM **3**
Inez, Mike
See Alice in Chains
Infante, Frank
See Blondie
Ingber, Elliot "Winged Eel Fingerling"
See Captain Beefheart and His Magic Band
Inge, Edward
See McKinney's Cotton Pickers
Ingram, Jack
See Incredible String Band
Ingram, James **11**
Ink Spots **23**
Inner Circle **15**
Innes, Andrew
See Primal Scream
Innis, Dave
See Restless Heart
Insane Clown Posse **22**
Interior, Lux
See Cramps, The
INXS **21**
Earlier sketch in CM **2**
Iommi, Tony
See Black Sabbath
Iron Maiden **10**
Irons, Jack
See Red Hot Chili Peppers, The
Isaak, Chris **6**
Isabelle, Jeff
See Guns n' Roses
Isacsson, Jonas
See Roxette
Isham, Mark **14**
Isles, Bill
See O'Jays, The
Isley Brothers, The **8**
Isley, Ernie
See Isley Brothers, The
Isley, Marvin
See Isley Brothers, The
Isley, O'Kelly, Jr.
See Isley Brothers, The
Isley, Ronald
See Isley Brothers, The
Isley, Rudolph
See Isley Brothers, The
Israel Vibration **21**
Ives, Burl **12**
Ivey, Michael
See Basehead
Ivins, Michael
See Flaming Lips
J, David
See Bauhaus
Also see Love and Rockets
J.
See White Zombie
J. Geils Band **25**
Jabs, Matthias
See Scorpions, The
Jackson 5, The
See Jacksons, The
Jackson, Al
See Booker T. & the M.G.'s
Jackson, Alan **25**
Earlier sketch in CM **7**
Jackson, Clive
See Ray Condo and His Ricochets
Jackson, Eddie
See Queensryche
Jackson, Freddie **3**
Jackson, Jackie
See Jacksons, The
Jackson, Janet **16**
Earlier sketch in CM **3**
Jackson, Jermaine
See Jacksons, The
Jackson, Joe **22**
Earlier sketch in CM **4**
Jackson, Karen
See Supremes, The
Jackson, Mahalia **8**
Jackson, Marlon
See Jacksons, The
Jackson, Michael **17**
Earlier sketch in CM **1**
Also see Jacksons, The
Jackson, Millie **14**
Jackson, Milt **15**
Jackson, Pervis
See Spinners, The
Jackson, Quentin
See McKinney's Cotton Pickers
Jackson, Randy
See Jacksons, The
Jackson, Stevie
See Belle and Sebastian
Jackson, Tito
See Jacksons, The
Jacksons, The **7**
Jackyl **24**
Jacobs, Christian Richard
See Aquabats The
Jacobs, Jeff
See Foreigner
Jacobs, Parker
See Aquabats, The
Jacobs, Walter
See Little Walter
Jacox, Martin
See Soul Stirrers, The
Jacquet, Illinois **17**
Jade 4U
See Lords of Acid
Jaffee, Rami
See Wallflowers, The
Jagger, Mick **7**
Also see Rolling Stones, The
Jairo T.
See Sepultura
Jalal
See Last Poets
Jam, Jimmy
See Jam, Jimmy, and Terry Lewis
Jam, Jimmy, and Terry Lewis **11**
Jam, The **27**
Jam Master Jay
See Run DMC
James **12**
James, Alex
See Blur
James, Andrew "Bear"
See Midnight Oil
James, Boney **21**
James, Cheryl
See Salt-N-Pepa
James, David
See Alien Sex Fiend
James, David
See Spearhead
James, Doug
See Roomful of Blues
James, Elmore **8**
James, Etta **6**
James, Gregg
See D.O.A.
James, Harry **11**
James, Jesse
See Jackyl
James, John
See Newsboys, The
James, Onieda
See Spearhead
James, Richard
See Aphex Twin
James, Richey
See Manic Street Preachers
James, Rick **2**
James, Ruby
See Aztec Camera
James, Skip **24**
James, Sylvia
See Aztec Camera
Jamiroquai **21**
Jamison, Le Le
See Spearhead
Jane's Addiction **6**
Janovitz, Bill
See Buffalo Tom
Jansch, Bert
See Pentangle
Jardine, Al
See Beach Boys, The
Jarman, Joseph
See Art Ensemble of Chicago, The
Jarobi
See Tribe Called Quest, A
Jarre, Jean-Michel **2**
Jarreau, Al **1**
Jarrett, Irwin
See Third World
Jarrett, Keith **1**
Jars of Clay **20**
Jasper, Chris
See Isley Brothers, The
Jaworski, Al
See Jesus Jones
Jay, Miles
See Village People, The
Jay-Z **28**
Jayhawks, The **15**
Jayson, Mackie
See Bad Brains
Jazzie B
See Soul II Soul
Jean, Wyclef **22**
Also see Fugees, The
Jeanrenaud, Joan Dutcher
See Kronos Quartet
Jeczalik, Jonathan
See Art of Noise
Jefferson Airplane **5**
Jefferson, Blind Lemon **18**
Jefferson Starship
See Jefferson Airplane
Jemmott, Gerald
See Pearls Before Swine
Jenifer, Darryl
See Bad Brains

Jenkins, Barry
See Animals, The
Jenkins, Gary
See Silk
Jenkins, Stephan
See Third Eye Blind
Jennings, Greg
See Restless Heart
Jennings, Waylon **4**
Jensen, Ingrid **22**
Jensen, Ken
See D.O.A.
Jerry, Jah
See Skatalites, The
Jessee, Darren
See Ben Folds Five
Jessie, Young
See Coasters, The
Jesus and Mary Chain, The **10**
Jesus Jones **23**
Jesus Lizard **19**
Jethro Tull **8**
Jett, Joan **3**
Jewel **25**
Jimbo
See Reverend Horton Heat
Jimenez, Flaco
See Texas Tornados, The
Jimmie's Chicken Shack **22**
Joannou, Chris
See Silverchair
Jobim, Antonio Carlos **19**
Jobson, Edwin
See Jethro Tull
Jodeci **13**
Joel, Billy **12**
Earlier sketch in CM **2**
Joel, Phil
See Newsboys, The
Johansen, David
See New York Dolls
Johansen, David **7**
Johanson, Jai Johanny
See Allman Brothers, The
Johansson, Glenn
See Echobelly
Johansson, Lars-Olof
See Cardigans
John, Elton **20**
Earlier sketch in CM **3**
John, Little Willie **25**
John Spencer Blues Explosion **18**
Johns, Daniel
See Silverchair
Johnson, Alphonso
See Weather Report
Johnson, Blind Willie **26**
Johnson, Bob
See Steeleye Span
Johnson, Brian
See AC/DC
Johnson, Calvin
See Beat Happening
Johnson, Courtney
See New Grass Revival, The
Johnson, Danny
See Steppenwolf
Johnson, Daryl
See Neville Brothers, The
Johnson, David
See Can
Johnson, Eric **19**
Johnson, Eric
See Archers of Loaf
Johnson, Gene
See Diamond Rio
Johnson, Gerry
See Steel Pulse
Johnson, James P. **16**
Johnson, Jerry
See Big Mountain
Johnson, Kurt
See Flying Luttenbachers, The
Johnson, Lonnie **17**
Johnson, Matt
See The The
Johnson, Mike
See Dinosaur Jr.
Johnson, Patricia
See Sweet Honey in the Rock
Johnson, Ralph
See Earth, Wind and Fire
Johnson, Robert **6**
Johnson, Scott
See Gin Blossoms
Johnson, Shirley Childres
See Sweet Honey in the Rock
Johnson, Tamara "Taj"
See SWV
Johnson, Willie
See Golden Gate Quartet
Johnston, Bruce
See Beach Boys, The
Johnston, Freedy **20**
Johnston, Howie
See Ventures, The
Johnston, Sonnie
See Five Iron Frenzy
Johnston, Tom
See Doobie Brothers, The
JoJo
See Jodeci
Jolly, Bill
See Butthole Surfers
Jolson, Al **10**
Jon Spencer Blues Explosion **18**
Jones, Adam
See Tool
Jones, Benny
See Dirty Dozen Brass Band
Jones, Booker T. **8**
Also see Booker T. & the M.G.'s
Jones, Brian
See Rolling Stones, The
Jones, Busta
See Gang of Four
Jones, Claude
See McKinney's Cotton Pickers
Jones, Darryl
See Rolling Stones, The
Jones, Davy
See Monkees, The
Jones, Denise
See Point of Grace
Jones, Elvin **9**
Jones, Geoffrey
See Sounds of Blackness
Jones, George **4**
Jones, Grace **9**
Jones, Hank **15**
Jones, Howard **26**
Jones, Jab
See Memphis Jug Band
Jones, Jamie
See All-4-One
Jones, Jim
See Pere Ubu
Jones, John Paul
See Led Zeppelin
Jones, Kendall
See Fishbone
Jones, Kenny
See Faces, The
Jones, Kenny
See Who, The
Jones, Marshall
See Ohio Players
Jones, Maxine
See En Vogue
Jones, Mic
See Big Audio Dynamite
Also see Clash, The
Jones, Michael
See Kronos Quartet
Jones, Mick
See Clash, The
Jones, Mick
See Foreigner
Jones, Orville
See Ink Spots
Jones, Philly Joe **16**
Jones, Quincy **20**
Earlier sketch in CM **2**
Jones, Randy
See Village People, The
Jones, Rickie Lee **4**
Jones, Robert "Kuumba"
See Ohio Players
Jones, Robin
See Beta Band, The
Jones, Ronald
See Flaming Lips
Jones, Russell "Ol Dirdy Bastard"
See Wu-Tang Clan
Jones, Sandra "Puma"
See Black Uhuru
Jones, Simon
See Verve, The
Jones, Spike **5**
Jones, Stacy
See Letters to Cleo
Also see Veruca Salt
Jones, Steve
See Sex Pistols, The
Jones, Terry
See Point of Grace
Jones, Thad **19**
Jones, Tom **11**
Jones, Will "Dub"
See Coasters, The
Jonsson, Magnus
See Gus Gus
Joplin, Janis **3**
Joplin, Scott **10**
Jordan, Lonnie
See War
Jordan, Louis **11**
Jordan, Montell **26**
Jordan, Stanley **1**
Jorgenson, John
See Desert Rose Band, The
Jos
See Ex, The
Joseph, Charles
See Dirty Dozen Brass Band
Joseph, Kirk
See Dirty Dozen Brass Band
Joseph-I, Israel
See Bad Brains
Josephmary
See Compulsion
Jourgensen, Al
See Ministry

Journey **21**
Joy Division **19**
Joy Electric **26**
Joyce, Mike
See Buzzcocks, The
Also see Smiths, The
Judas Priest **10**
Judd, Naomi
See Judds, The
Judd, Wynonna
See Judds, The
Also see Wynonna
Judds, The **2**
Juhlin, Dag
See Poi Dog Pondering
Jukebox
See Geto Boys, The
Jungle DJ "Towa" Towa
See Deee-lite
Jurado, Jeanette
See Exposé
Justman, Seth
See J. Geils Band
K-Ci
See Jodeci
Kabongo, Sabine
See Zap Mama
Kahlil, Aisha
See Sweet Honey in the Rock
Kain, Gylan
See Last Poets
Kakoulli, Harry
See Squeeze
Kale, Jim
See Guess Who
Kalligan, Dick
See Blood, Sweat and Tears
Kamanski, Paul
See Beat Farmers
Kaminski, Mik
See Electric Light Orchestra
Kamomiya, Ryo
See Pizzicato Five
Kanal, Tony
See No Doubt
Kanawa, Kiri Te
See Te Kanawa, Kiri
Kand, Valor
See Christian Death
Kane, Arthur
See New York Dolls
Kane, Big Daddy **7**
Kane, Nick
See Mavericks, The
Kang, Eyvind **28**
Kannberg, Scott
See Pavement
Kantner, Paul
See Jefferson Airplane
Kaplan, Ira
See Yo La Tengo
Karajan, Herbert von
See von Karajan, Herbert
Karges, Murphy
See Sugar Ray
Karoli, Michael
See Can
Kath, Terry
See Chicago
Kato, Nash
See Urge Overkill
Katrin
See Ex, The
Katunich, Alex
See Incubus
Katz, Simon
See Jamiroquai
Katz, Steve
See Blood, Sweat and Tears
Kaukonen, Jorma
See Jefferson Airplane
Kavanagh, Chris
See Big Audio Dynamite
Kay Gee
See Naughty by Nature
Kay, Jason
See Jamiroquai
Kay, John
See Steppenwolf
Kaye, Carol **22**
Kaye, Tony
See Yes
Keaggy, Phil **26**
Kean, Martin
See Stereolab
Keane, Sean
See Chieftains, The
Kee, John P. **15**
Keelor, Greg
See Blue Rodeo
Keenan, Maynard James
See Tool
Keene, Barry
See Spirit
Keifer, Tom
See Cinderella
Keitaro
See Pizzicato Five
Keith, Jeff
See Tesla
Keith, Toby **17**
Keithley, Joey "Shithead"
See D.O.A.
Kelly, Betty
See Martha and the Vandellas
Kelly, Charlotte
See Soul II Soul
Kelly, Ed
See Oakland Interfaith Gospel Choir
Kelly, Hugh
See Wedding Present, The
Kelly, Johnny
See Type O Negative
Kelly, Kevin
See Byrds, The
Kelly, Matt
See Dropkick Murphys
Kelly, R. **19**
Kelly, Rashaan
See US3
Kelly, Scott
See Neurosis
Kelly, Sean
See Sixpence None the Richer
Kelly, Terrance
See Oakland Interfaith Gospel Choir
Kemp, Rick
See Steeleye Span
Kendrick, David
See Devo
Kendricks, Eddie
See Temptations, The
Kennedy, Delious
See All-4-One
Kennedy, Frankie
See Altan
Kennedy, Nigel **8**
Kenner, Doris
See Shirelles, The
Kenny, Bill
See Ink Spots
Kenny, Clare
See Aztec Camera
Kenny G **14**
Kenny, Herb
See Ink Spots
Kent, Julia
See Rasputina
Kent, Stacey **28**
Kenton, Stan **21**
Kentucky Headhunters, The **5**
Kern, Jerome **13**
Kerr, Jim
See Simple Minds
Kerr, Scott
See Five Iron Frenzy
Kerr, Stuart
See Texas
Kershaw, Sammy **15**
Ketchum, Hal **14**
Key, Cevin
See Skinny Puppy
Keyser, Alex
See Echobelly
Khan, Chaka **19**
Earlier sketch in CM **9**
Khan, Nusrat Fateh Ali **13**
Khan, Praga
See Lords of Acid
Kibble, Mark
See Take 6
Kibby, Walter
See Fishbone
Kick, Johnny
See Madder Rose
Kid 'n Play **5**
Kid Rock **27**
Kidjo, Anjelique **17**
Kiedis, Anthony
See Red Hot Chili Peppers, The
Kilbey, Steve
See Church, The
Kilbourn, Duncan
See Psychedelic Furs
Kilgallon, Eddie
See Ricochet
Kilgore **24**
Killian, Tim
See Kronos Quartet
Kimball, Jennifer
See Story, The
Kimball, Jim
See Jesus Lizard
Kimble, Paul
See Grant Lee Buffalo
Kinard, Tulani Jordan
See Sweet Honey in the Rock
Kincaid, Jan
See Brand New Heavies, The
Kinchla, Chan
See Blues Traveler
Kinde, Geoff
See Atomic Fireballs, The
King Ad-Rock
See Horovitz, Adam
King, Albert **2**
King, Andy
See Hooters
King, B.B. **24**
Earlier sketch in CM **1**
King, Ben E. **7**
King, Bob
See Soul Stirrers, The
King, Carole **6**
Also see Goffin-King

King Crimson **17**
King, Ed
See Lynyrd Skynyrd
King, Freddy **17**
King, Jon
See Gang of Four
King, Jr., William
See Commodores, The
King, Kerry
See Slayer
King Missile **22**
King, Philip
See Lush
King, William Jr.
See Commodores, The
King's X **7**
Kingins, Duke
See Atomic Fireballs, The
Kingston Trio, The **9**
Kinks, The **15**
Kinney, Sean
See Alice in Chains
Kirk, Rahsaan Roland **6**
Kirk, Richard H.
See Cabaret Voltaire
Kirke, Simon
See Bad Company
Kirkland, Mike
See Prong
Kirkpatrick, Chris
See 'N Sync
Kirkwood, Cris
See Meat Puppets, The
Kirkwood, Curt
See Meat Puppets, The
Kirtley, Peter
See Pentangle
Kirwan, Danny
See Fleetwood Mac
Kiss **25**
Earlier sketch in CM **5**
Kisser, Andreas
See Sepultura
Kissin, Evgeny **6**
Kitaro **1**
Kitsos, Nick
See BoDeans
Kitt, Eartha **9**
Kjartansson, Siggi
See Gus Gus
Klein, Danny
See J. Geils Band
Klein, Jon
See Siouxsie and the Banshees
Klein, Mark
See Cobra Verde
Klezmatics, The **18**
Klugh, Earl **10**
Kmatsu, Bravo
See Pizzicato Five
KMFDM **18**
Knight, Gladys **1**
Knight, Jon
See New Kids on the Block
Knight, Jordan
See New Kids on the Block
Knight, Larry
See Spirit
Knight, Peter
See Steeleye Span
Knight, Suge **15**
Knighton, Willie "Khujo"
See Goodie Mob
Knopfler, David
See Dire Straits
Knopfler, Mark **25**
Earlier sketch in CM **3**
Also see Dire Straits
Know, Dr.
See Bad Brains
Knowledge
See Digable Planets
Knox, Nick
See Cramps, The
Knox, Richard
See Dirty Dozen Brass Band
Knudsen, Keith
See Doobie Brothers, The
Konietzko, Sascha
See KMFDM
Konishi, Yasuharu
See Pizzicato Five
Konto, Skip
See Three Dog Night
Kool & the Gang **13**
Kool Moe Dee **9**
Kooper, Al
See Blood, Sweat and Tears
Koppelman, Charles **14**
Koppes, Peter
See Church, The
Korn **20**
Kottke, Leo **13**
Kotzen, Richie
See Poison
Kowalczyk, Ed
See Live
Koz, Dave **20**
Kraftwerk **9**
Krakauer, David
See Klezmatics, The
Krall, Diana **27**
Kramer, Joey
See Aerosmith
Kramer, Wayne
See MC5, The
Krasnow, Bob **15**
Krause, Bernie
See Weavers, The
Krauss, Alison **10**
Krauss, Scott
See Pere Ubu
Kravitz, Lenny **26**
Earlier sketch in CM **5**
Krawits, Michael
See Pearls Before Swine
Krayzie Bone
See Bone Thugs-N-Harmony
Krazy Drayz
See Das EFX
Kretz, Eric
See Stone Temple Pilots
Kreutzman, Bill
See Grateful Dead, The
Krieger, Robert
See Doors, The
Kriesel, Greg "Greg K."
See Offspring
Kris Kross **11**
Kristofferson, Kris **4**
Krizan, Anthony
See Spin Doctors
Kronos Quartet **5**
Kropp, Mike
See Northern Lights
KRS-One **8**
Krukowski, Damon
See Damon and Naomi
Krummenacher, Victor
See Monks of Doom
Krupa, Gene **13**
Krusen, Dave
See Pearl Jam
Kruspe, Richard
See Rammstein
Kuba,
See D.O.A.
Kulak, Eddie
See Aztec Camera
Kulick, Bruce
See Kiss
Kunkel, Bruce
See Nitty Gritty Dirt Band, The
Kunzel, Erich **17**
Kurdziel, Eddie
See Redd Kross
Kurihara, Michio
See Ghost
Kuti, Fela **7**
L.L. Cool J. **5**
L7 **12**
LaBar, Jeff
See Cinderella
LaBelle, Patti **8**
LaBrie, James
See Dream Theater
Lack, Steve
See Veruca Salt
LaCroix, Dimples
See Lane, Fred
Lacy, Steve **23**
Lady Miss Kier
See Deee-lite
Ladybug
See Digable Planets
Ladysmith Black Mambazo **1**
Lafalce, Mark
See Mekons, The
Lagerburg, Bengt
See Cardigans, The
Laine, Cleo **10**
Laine, Denny
See Moody Blues, The
Laird, Rick
See Mahavishnu Orchestra
Lake, Greg
See Emerson, Lake & Palmer/Powell
Also see King Crimson
LaKind, Bobby
See Doobie Brothers, The
Lally, Joe
See Fugazi
LaLonde, Larry "Ler"
See Primus
Lamb, Brabara **19**
Lamb, Michael
See Confederate Railroad
Lambert, Dave
See Lambert, Hendricks and Ross
Lambert, Hendricks and Ross **28**
Lamble, Martin
See Fairport Convention
Lamm, Robert
See Chicago
Lampkin, Troy
See Oakland Interfaith Gospel Choir
Lancaster, Brian
See Surfin' Pluto
Landers, Paul
See Rammstein
Landreth, Sonny **16**
Lane, Fred **28**
Lane, Jani
See Warrant

Lane, Jay
See Primus
Lane, Ronnie
See Faces, The
Lanegan, Mark
See Screaming Trees
lang, k. d. **25**
Earlier sketch in CM **4**
Lang, Jonny **27**
Langan, Gary
See Art of Noise
Langford, Jon
See Mekons, The
Langford, Willie
See Golden Gate Quartet
Langley, John
See Mekons, The
Langlois, Paul
See Tragically Hip, The
Langosch, Paul
See Ralph Sharon Quartet
Langston, Leslie
See Throwing Muses
Lanier, Allen
See Blue Oyster Cult
Lanker, Dustin
See Cherry Poppin' Daddies
Lanois, Daniel **8**
LaPread, Ronald
See Commodores, The
Larkin, Patty **9**
Larson, Chad Albert
See Aquabats, The
Larson, Nathan
See Shudder to Think
Last Poets **21**
Laswell, Bill **14**
Lataille, Rich
See Roomful of Blues
Lateef, Yusef **16**
Latimer, Andrew
See Camel
Laughner, Peter
See Pere Ubu
Lauper, Cyndi **11**
Laurence, Lynda
See Supremes, The
Lavin, Christine **6**
Lavis, Gilson
See Squeeze
Lawler, Feargal
See Cranberries, The
Lawnge
See Black Sheep
Lawrence, Tracy **11**
Lawry, John
See Petra
Laws, Roland
See Earth, Wind and Fire
Lawson, Doyle
See Country Gentlemen, The
Layzie Bone
See Bone Thugs-N-Harmony
Le Bon, Simon
See Duran Duran
Le Mystère des VoixBulgares
See Bulgarian State Female Vocal Choir, The
Leadbelly **6**
Leadon, Bernie
See Eagles, The
Also see Nitty Gritty Dirt Band, The
Lear, Graham
See REO Speedwagon
Leary, Paul
See Butthole Surfers
Leavell, Chuck
See Allman Brothers, The
LeBon, Simon
See Duran Duran
Leckenby, Derek "Lek"
See Herman's Hermits
Led Zeppelin **1**
Ledbetter, Huddie
See Leadbelly
LeDoux, Chris **12**
Lee, Ben **26**
Lee, Beverly
See Shirelles, The
Lee, Brenda **5**
Lee, Buddy
See McKinney's Cotton Pickers
Lee, Buddy
See Less Than Jake
Lee, Garret
See Compulsion
Lee, Geddy
See Rush
Lee, Peggy **8**
Lee, Pete
See Gwar
Lee, Sara
See Gang of Four
Lee, Stan
See Incredible String Band
Lee, Tommy
See Mötley Crüe
Lee, Tony
See Treadmill Trackstar
Leeb, Bill
See Front Line Assembly
Leen, Bill
See Gin Blossoms
Leese, Howard
See Heart
Legg, Adrian **17**
Legowitz, Herr
See Gus Gus
Leherer, Keith "Lucky"
See Circle Jerks
Lehrer, Tom **7**
Leiber and Stoller **14**
Leiber, Jerry
See Leiber and Stoller
LeMaistre, Malcolm
See Incredible String Band
Lemmy
See Motörhead
Lemonheads, The **12**
Lemper, Ute **14**
Lenear, Kevin
See Mighty Mighty Bosstones
Lenners, Rudy
See Scorpions, The
Lennon, John **9**
Also see Beatles, The
Lennon, Julian **26**
Earlier sketch in CM **2**
Lennox, Annie **18**
Also see Eurythmics
Leonard, Geno
See Filter
Leonard, Glenn
See Temptations, The
Lerner, Alan Jay
See Lerner and Loewe
Lerner and Loewe **13**
Lesh, Phil
See Grateful Dead, The
Leskiw, Greg
See Guess Who
Leslie, Chris
See Fairport Convention
Less Than Jake **22**
Lessard, Stefan
See Dave Matthews Band
Lethal, DJ
See Limp Bizkit
Letters to Cleo **22**
Ieuan, Dafydd "Daf"
See Super Furry Animals
Levene, Keith
See Clash, The
Levert, Eddie
See O'Jays, The
Leverton, Jim
See Caravan
Levin, Tony
See King Crimson
Levine, James **8**
Levy, Andrew
See Brand New Heavies, The
Levy, Ron
See Roomful of Blues
Lewis, Furry **26**
Lewis, Hambone
See Memphis Jug Band
Lewis, Heather
See Beat Happening
Lewis, Huey **9**
Lewis, Ian
See Inner Circle
Lewis, Jerry Lee **2**
Lewis, Marcia
See Soul II Soul
Lewis, Michael
See Quicksilver Messenger Service
Lewis, Mike
See Yo La Tengo
Lewis, Otis
See Fabulous Thunderbirds, The
Lewis, Peter
See Moby Grape
Lewis, Ramsey **14**
Lewis, Roger
See Dirty Dozen Brass Band
Also see Inner Circle
Lewis, Roy
See Kronos Quartet
Lewis, Samuel K.
See Five Blind Boys of Alabama
Lewis, Shaznay T.
See All Saints
Lewis, Terry
See Jam, Jimmy, and Terry Lewis
Lhote, Morgan
See Stereolab
Li Puma, Tommy **18**
Libbea, Gene
See Nashville Bluegrass Band
Liberace **9**
Liberty, Earl
See Circle Jerks
Licht, David
See Klezmatics, The
Liebezeit, Jaki
See Can
Liesegang, Brian
See Filter
Lifeso'n, Alex
See Rush
Lightfoot, Gordon **3**
Lightning Seeds **21**

Ligon, Willie Joe
See Mighty Clouds of Joy, The
Liles, Brent
See Social Distortion
Lilienstein, Lois
See Sharon, Lois & Bram
Lilker, Dan
See Anthrax
Lilley, John
See Hooters
Lillywhite, Steve **13**
Limp Bizkit **27**
Lincoln, Abbey **9**
Lindberg, Jim
See Pennywise
Lindemann, Till
See Rammstein
Lindes, Hal
See Dire Straits
Lindley, David **2**
Lindner, Michael
See Aqua Velvets
Linkous, Mark **26**
Linna, Miriam
See Cramps, The
Linnell, John
See They Might Be Giants
Lipsius, Fred
See Blood, Sweat and Tears
Lisa, Lisa **23**
Lisher, Greg
See Monks of Doom
Lit **27**
Little Feat **4**
Little, Keith
See Country Gentlemen, The
Little, Levi
See Blackstreet
Little Richard **1**
Little Texas **14**
Little Walter **14**
Littrell, Brian
See Backstreet Boys
Live **14**
Living Colour **7**
Llanas, Sam
See BoDeans
Llanas, Sammy
See BoDeans, The
Lloyd, Charles **22**
Lloyd, Richard
See Television
Lloyd Webber, Andrew **6**
Lo Fidelity All Stars **27**
Locke, John
See Spirit
Locking, Brian
See Shadows, The
Lockley, Jayne
See Wedding Present, The
Lockwood, Robert, Jr. **10**
Lodge, John
See Moody Blues, The
Loeb, Lisa **23**
Earlier sketch in CM **19**
Loesser, Frank **19**
Loewe, Frederick
See Lerner and Loewe
Loewenstein, Jason
See Sebadoh
Lofgren, Nils **25**
Logan, Jack **27**
Loggins, Kenny **20**
Earlier sketch in CM **3**
Lombardo, Dave
See Slayer
Lonberg-Holm, Fred
See Flying Luttenbachers, The
London, Frank
See Klezmatics, The
Lonestar **27**
Lopes, Lisa "Left Eye"
See TLC
Lopez, Israel "Cachao" **14**
Lopez, Jennifer **27**
Lord, Jon
See Deep Purple
Lords of Acid **20**
Lorenz, Flake
See Rammstein
Loria, Steve
See Spirit
Lorimer, Roddy
See Waterboys, The
Lorson, Mary
See Madder Rose
Los Lobos **2**
Los Reyes
See Gipsy Kings, The
Loughnane, Lee
See Chicago
Louison, Steve
See Massive Attack
Louris, Gary
See Jayhawks, The
Louvin Brothers, The **12**
Louvin, Charlie
See Louvin Brothers, The
Louvin, Ira
See Louvin Brothers, The
Lovano, Joe **13**
Love and Rockets **15**
Love, Courtney
See Hole
Love, Gerry
See Teenage Fanclub
Love, Laura **20**
Love, Mike
See Beach Boys, The
Love, Rollie
See Beat Farmers
Love Spit Love **21**
Loveless, Patty **21**
Earlier sketch in CM **5**
Lovering, David
See Cracker
Also see Pixies, The
Lovett, Lyle **28**
Earlier sketch in CM **5**
Lowe, Chris
See Pet Shop Boys
Lowe, Nick **25**
Earlier sketch in CM **6**
Lowe, Victoria
See Tuxedomoon
Lowell, Charlie
See Jars of Clay
Lowery, David
See Cracker
Lozano, Conrad
See Los Lobos
Luc
See Ex, The
Lucas, Gary
See Captain Beefheart and His Magic Band
Lucas, Trevor
See Fairport Convention
Luccketta, Troy
See Tesla
Lucia, Paco de
See de Lucia, Paco
Luciano, Felipe
See Last Poets
Luke
See Campbell, Luther
Lukin, Matt
See Mudhoney
Luna **18**
Lunsford, Bret
See Beat Happening
Lupo, Pat
See Beaver Brown Band, The
LuPone, Patti **8**
Luscious Jackson **27**
Earlier sketch in CM **19**
Lush **13**
Luttell, Terry
See REO Speedwagon
Lydon, John **9**
Also see Sex Pistols, The
Lyfe, DJ
See Incubus
Lymon, Frankie
See Frankie Lymon and The Teenagers
Lynch, David
See Platters, The
Lynch, Dermot
See Dog's Eye View
Lynch, George
See Dokken
Lynch, Laura
See Dixie Chicks
Lynch, Stan
See Tom Petty and the Heartbreakers
Lyngstad, Anni-Frid
See Abba
Lynn, Lonnie Rashid
See Common
Lynn, Loretta **2**
Lynne, Jeff **5**
Also see Electric Light Orchestra
Lynne, Shelby **5**
Lynott, Phil
See Thin Lizzy
Lynyrd Skynyrd **9**
Lyons, Leanne "Lelee"
See SWV
M People **27**
Earlier sketch in CM **15**
M.C. Hammer
See Hammer, M.C.
M.C. Ren
See N.W.A.
Ma, Yo-Yo **24**
Earlier sketch in CM **2**
MacColl, Kirsty **12**
MacDonald, Barbara Kooyman
See Timbuk 3
MacDonald, Eddie
See Alarm
MacDonald, Pat
See Timbuk 3
Macfarlane, Lora
See Sleater-Kinney
MacGowan, Shane
See Pogues, The
MacIsaac, Ashley **21**
Mack Daddy
See Kris Kross
MacKaye, Ian
See Fugazi
Mackey, Steve
See Pulp

MacNeil, Michael
See Simple Minds
MacPherson, Jim
See Breeders
Macy, Robin
See Dixie Chicks
Madan, Sonya Aurora
See Echobelly
Madder Rose **17**
Madness **27**
Madonna **16**
Earlier sketch in CM **4**
Mael, Ron
See Sparks
Mael, Russell
See Sparks
Magehee, Marty
See 4Him
Maghostut, Malachi Favors
See Art Ensemble of Chicago, The
Maginnis, Tom
See Buffalo Tom
Magnetic Fields, The **28**
Magnie, John
See Subdudes, The
Magoogan, Wesley
See English Beat, The
Mahavishnu Orchestra **19**
Maher, John
See Buzzcocks, The
Mahogany, Kevin **26**
Mahoney, Tim
See 311
Maida, Raine
See Our Lady Peace
Maillard, Carol
See Sweet Honey in the Rock
Maimone, Tony
See Pere Ubu
Maines, Natalie
See Dixie Chicks
Maïtra, Shyamal
See Gong
Majewski, Hank
See Four Seasons, The
Makeba, Miriam **8**
Makino, Kazu
See Blonde Redhead
Malcolm, Hugh
See Skatalites, The
Malcolm, Joy
See Incognito
Male, Johnny
See Republica
Malherbe, Didier
See Gong
Malin, Jesse
See D Generation
Malins, Mike
See Goo Goo Dolls, The
Malkmus, Stephen
See Pavement
Malley, Matt
See Counting Crows
Mallinder, Stephen
See Cabaret Voltaire
Malmsteen, Yngwie **24**
Malo, Raul
See Mavericks, The
Malone, Russell **27**
Malone, Tom
See Blood, Sweat and Tears
Malone, Tommy
See Subdudes, The
Mamas and the Papas **21**
Man or Astroman? **21**
Mancini, Henry **20**
Earlier sketch in CM **1**
Mandel, Johnny **28**
Mandrell, Barbara **4**
Maness, J. D.
See Desert Rose Band, The
Mangione, Chuck **23**
Manhattan Transfer, The **8**
Manic Street Preachers **27**
Manilow, Barry **2**
Mann, Aimee **22**
Mann, Billy **23**
Mann, Herbie **16**
Manninger, Hank
See Aqua Velvets
Manson, Shirley
See Garbage
Manuel, Richard
See Band, The
Manzarek, Ray
See Doors, The
March, Kevin
See Shudder to Think
Marie, Buffy Sainte
See Sainte-Marie, Buffy
Marilyn Manson **18**
Marini, Lou, Jr.
See Blood, Sweat and Tears
Marker, Steve
See Garbage
Marks, Toby
See De Gaia, Banco
Marley, Bob **3**
Marley, Rita **10**
Marley, Ziggy **3**
Marr, Johnny
See Smiths, The
Also see The The
Marriner, Neville **7**
Mars, Chris
See Replacements, The
Mars, Derron
See Less Than Jake
Mars, Mick
See Mötley Crüe
Marsalis, Branford **10**
Marsalis, Ellis **13**
Marsalis, Wynton **20**
Earlier sketch in CM **6**
Marsh, Ian Craig
See Human League, The
Marshal, Cornel
See Third World
Marshall, Amanda **27**
Marshall, Brian
See Creed
Marshall, Jenell
See Dirty Dozen Brass Band
Marshall, Steve
See Gene Loves Jezebel
Martensen, Vic
See Captain Beefheart and His Magic Band
Martha and the Vandellas **25**
Martin, Barbara
See Supremes, The
Martin, Barrett
See Screaming Trees
Martin, Carl
See Shai
Martin, Christopher
See Kid 'n Play
Martin, Dean **1**
Martin, Dewey
See Buffalo Springfield
Martin, George **6**
Martin, Greg
See Kentucky Headhunters, The
Martin, Jim
See Faith No More
Martin, Jimmy **5**
Also see Osborne Brothers, The
Martin, Johnney
See Mighty Clouds of Joy, The
Martin, Mary **27**
Martin, Phonso
See Steel Pulse
Martin, Ricky **26**
Martin, Ronnie
See Joy Electric
Martin, Sarah
See Belle and Sebastian
Martin, Sennie
See Kool & the Gang
Martin, Tony
See Black Sabbath
Martinez, Anthony
See Black Flag
Martinez, Cliff
See Captain Beefheart and His Magic Band
Martinez, S. A.
See 311
Martini, Jerry
See Sly & the Family Stone
Martino, Pat **17**
Martsch, Doug
See Built to Spill
Marvin, Hank B.
See Shadows, The
Marx, Richard **21**
Earlier sketch in CM **3**
Mascagni, Pietro **25**
Mascis, J
See Dinosaur Jr.
Masdea, Jim
See Boston
Mase **27**
Masekela, Hugh **7**
Maseo, Baby Huey
See De La Soul
Masi, Nick
See Four Seasons, The
Mason, Dave
See Traffic
Mason, Nick
See Pink Floyd
Mason, Stephen
See Beta Band, The
Mason, Steve
See Jars of Clay
Mason, Terry
See Joy Division
Masse, Laurel
See Manhattan Transfer, The
Massey, Bobby
See O'Jays, The
Massi, Nick
See Four Seasons, The
Massive Attack **17**
Mastelotto, Pat
See King Crimson
Master P **22**
Masur, Kurt **11**
Matchbox 20 **27**
Material
See Laswell, Bill
Mathis, Johnny **2**

Mathus, Jim
See Squirrel Nut Zippers
Matlock, Glen
See Sex Pistols, The
Mattacks, Dave
See Fairport Convention
Mattea, Kathy **5**
Matthews Band, Dave
See Dave Matthews Band
Matthews, Chris
See Shudder to Think
Matthews, Dave
See Dave Matthews Band
Matthews, Eric **22**
Matthews, Ian
See Fairport Convention
Matthews, Quinn
See Butthole Surfers
Matthews, Scott
See Butthole Surfers
Matthews, Simon
See Jesus Jones
Maunick, Bluey
See Incognito
Maurer, John
See Social Distortion
Mavericks, The **15**
Maxwell **22**
Maxwell, Charmayne
See Brownstone
Maxwell, Tom
See Squirrel Nut Zippers
May, Brian
See Queen
May, Phil
See Pretty Things, The
Mayall, John **7**
Mayfield, Curtis **8**
Mays, Odeen, Jr.
See Kool & the Gang
Mazelle, Kym
See Soul II Soul
Mazibuko, Abednigo
See Ladysmith Black Mambazo
Mazibuko, Albert
See Ladysmith Black Mambazo
Mazzola, Joey
See Sponge
Mazzy Star **17**
MC 900 Ft. Jesus **16**
MC Breed **17**
MC Clever
See Digital Underground
MC Eiht **27**
MC Eric
See Technotronic
MC Lyte **8**
MC Serch **10**
MC5, The **9**
MCA
See Yauch, Adam
McAloon, Martin
See Prefab Sprout
McAloon, Paddy
See Prefab Sprout
McArthur, Keith
See Spearhead
McBoutie, Rip
See Lane, Fred
McBrain, Nicko
See Iron Maiden
McBrayer, Jody
See Avalon
MCBreed **17**
McBride, Christian **17**
McBride, Martina **14**
McCabe, Nick
See Verve, The
McCabe, Zia
See Dandy Warhols
McCall, Renee
See Sounds of Blackness
McCann, Lila **26**
McCarrick, Martin
See Siouxsie and the Banshees
McCarroll, Tony
See Oasis
McCartney, Paul **4**
Also see Beatles, The
McCarty, Jim
See Yardbirds, The
McCary, Michael S.
See Boyz II Men
McClary, Thomas
See Commodores, The
McClennan, Tommy **25**
McClinton, Delbert **14**
McCluskey, Andy
See Orchestral Manoeuvres in the Dark
McColgan, Mike
See Dropkick Murphys
McCollum, Rick
See Afghan Whigs
McConnell, Page
See Phish
McCook, Tommy
See Skatalites, The
McCorkle, Susannah **27**
McCoury, Del **15**
McCowin, Michael
See Mighty Clouds of Joy, The
McCoy, Neal **15**
McCracken, Chet
See Doobie Brothers, The
McCrea, John
See Cake
McCready, Mike
See Pearl Jam
McCready, Mindy **22**
McCulloch, Andrew
See King Crimson
McCullough, Danny
See Animals, The
McCuloch, Ian **23**
McCurdy, Xan
See Cake
McCutcheon, Ian
See Mojave 3
McD, Jimmy
See Jimmie's Chicken Shack
McDaniel, Chris
See Confederate Railroad
McDaniels, Darryl "D"
See Run DMC
McDermott, Brian
See Del Amitri
McDonald, Ian
See Foreigner
Also see King Crimson
McDonald, Jeff
See Redd Kross
McDonald, Michael
See Doobie Brothers, The
McDonald, Richie
See Lonestar
McDonald, Steven
See Redd Kross
McDorman, Joe
See Statler Brothers, The
McDougall, Don
See Guess Who
McDowell, Hugh
See Electric Light Orchestra
McDowell, Mississippi Fred **16**
McElhone, John
See Texas
McEntire, Reba **11**
McErlaine, Ally
See Texas
McEuen, John
See Nitty Gritty Dirt Band, The
McFarlane, Elaine
See Mamas and the Papas
McFee, John
See Doobie Brothers, The
McFerrin, Bobby **3**
McFessel, Sean
See Cake
McGearly, James
See Christian Death
McGee, Brian
See Simple Minds
McGee, Jerry
See Ventures, The
McGeoch, John
See Siouxsie and the Banshees
McGinley, Raymond
See Teenage Fanclub
McGinniss, Will
See Audio Adrenaline
McGrath, Mark
See Sugar Ray
McGraw, Tim **17**
McGuigan, Paul
See Oasis
McGuinn, Jim
See McGuinn, Roger
McGuinn, Roger
See Byrds, The
McGuinness
See Lords of Acid
McGuire, Christine
See McGuire Sisters, The
McGuire, Dorothy
See McGuire Sisters, The
McGuire, Mike
See Shenandoah
McGuire, Phyllis
See McGuire Sisters, The
McGuire Sisters, The **27**
McIntosh, Robbie
See Pretenders, The
McIntyre, Joe
See New Kids on the Block
McJohn, Goldy
See Steppenwolf
McKagan, Duff
See Guns n' Roses
McKay, Al
See Earth, Wind and Fire
McKay, John
See Siouxsie and the Banshees
McKean, Michael
See Spinal Tap
McKee, Julius
See Dirty Dozen Brass Band
McKee, Maria **11**
McKeehan, Toby
See dc Talk
McKenna, Greg
See Letters to Cleo
McKennitt, Loreena **24**
McKenzie, Christina "Licorice"
See Incredible String Band

McKenzie, Derrick
See Jamiroquai
McKenzie, Scott
See Mamas and the Papas
McKernan, Ron "Pigpen"
See Grateful Dead, The
McKinney, William
See McKinney's Cotton Pickers
McKinney's Cotton Pickers **16**
McKnight, Brian **22**
McKnight, Claude V. III
See Take 6
McLachlan, Sarah **12**
McLagan, Ian
See Faces, The
McLaren, Malcolm **23**
McLaughlin, John **12**
Also see Mahavishnu Orchestra
McLean, A. J.
See Backstreet Boys
McLean, Dave **24**
McLean, Don **7**
McLean, John
See Beta Band, The
McLennan, Grant **21**
Also see Go-Betweens, The
McLeod, Rory
See Roomful of Blues
McLoughlin, Jon
See Del Amitri
McMackin, Bryon
See Pennywise
McMeel, Mickey
See Three Dog Night
McMurtry, James **10**
McNabb, Travis
See Better Than Ezra
McNair, Sylvia **15**
McNeilly, Mac
See Jesus Lizard
McNew, James
See Yo La Tengo
McPartland, Marian **15**
McPhatter, Clyde **25**
McPherson, Graham "Suggs"
See Madness
McQuillar, Shawn
See Kool & the Gang
McRae, Carmen **9**
McReynolds, Jesse
See McReynolds, Jim and Jesse
McReynolds, Jim and Jesse **12**
McReynolds, Jim
See McReynolds, Jim and Jesse
McShane, Ronnie
See Chieftains, The
McShee, Jacqui
See Pentangle
McTell, Blind Willie **17**
McVie, Christine
See Fleetwood Mac
McVie, John
See Fleetwood Mac
McWhinney, James
See Big Mountain
McWhinney, Joaquin
See Big Mountain
Mdletshe, Geophrey
See Ladysmith Black Mambazo
Meat Loaf **12**
Meat Puppets, The **13**
Medley, Bill **3**
Medlock, James
See Soul Stirrers, The
Meehan, Tony
See Shadows, The
Megadeth **9**
Mehldau, Brad **27**
Mehta, Zubin **11**
Meine, Klaus
See Scorpions, The
Meisner, Randy
See Eagles, The
Mekons, The **15**
Melanie **12**
Melax, Einar
See Sugarcubes, The
Mellencamp, John **20**
Earlier sketch in CM **2**
Melvin, Eric
See NOFX
Melvins **21**
Memphis Jug Band **25**
Memphis Minnie **25**
Menck, Ric
See Velvet Crush
Mendel, Nate
See Sunny Day Real Estate
Mendel, Nate
See Foo Fighters
Mengede, Peter
See Helmet
Menken, Alan **10**
Menuhin, Yehudi **11**
Menza, Nick
See Megadeth
Mercer, Johnny **13**
Merchant, Jimmy
See Frankie Lymon and The Teenagers
Merchant, Natalie **25**
Also see 10,000 Maniacs
Mercier, Peadar
See Chieftains, The
Mercury, Freddie
See Queen
Mercury Rev **28**
Merman, Ethel **27**
Merritt, Stephin
See Magnetic Fields, The
Mertens, Paul
See Poi Dog Pondering
Mesaros, Michael
See Smithereens, The
Messecar, Dek
See Caravan
Messina, Jim
See Buffalo Springfield
Messina, Jo Dee **26**
Metallica **7**
Meters, The **14**
Methembu, Russel
See Ladysmith Black Mambazo
Metheny, Pat **26**
Earlier sketch in CM **2**
Meyer, Eric
See Charm Farm
Meyers, Augie
See Texas Tornados, The
Mhaonaigh, Mairead Ni
See Altan
Michael, George **9**
Michaels, Bret
See Poison
Michel, Luke
See Emmet Swimming
Michel, Prakazrel "Pras"
See Fugees, The
Michiles, Malcolm
See Citizen King
Middlebrook, Ralph "Pee Wee"
See Ohio Players
Middleton, Mark
See Blackstreet
Midler, Bette **8**
Midnight Oil **11**
Midori **7**
Mighty Clouds of Joy, The **17**
Mighty Mighty Bosstones **20**
Mike & the Mechanics **17**
Mike D
See Diamond, Michael
Mikens, Dennis
See Smithereens, The
Mikens, Robert
See Kool & the Gang
Milchem, Glenn
See Blue Rodeo
Miles, Chris
See Northern Lights
Miles, Richard
See Soul Stirrers, The
Miles, Ron **22**
Millar, Deborah
See Massive Attack
Miller, Charles
See War
Miller, Glenn **6**
Miller, Jacob "Killer" Miller
See Inner Circle
Miller, Jerry
See Moby Grape
Miller, Kevin
See Fuel
Miller, Mark
See Sawyer Brown
Miller, Mitch **11**
Miller, Rice
See Williamson, Sonny Boy
Miller, Robert
See Supertramp
Miller, Roger **4**
Miller, Steve **2**
Milli Vanilli **4**
Mills Brothers, The **14**
Mills, Donald
See Mills Brothers, The
Mills, Fred
See Canadian Brass, The
Mills, Harry
See Mills Brothers, The
Mills, Herbert
See Mills Brothers, The
Mills, John, Sr.
See Mills Brothers, The
Mills, John, Jr.
See Mills Brothers, The
Mills, Mike
See R.E.M.
Mills, Sidney
See Steel Pulse
Mills, Stephanie **21**
Milsap, Ronnie **2**
Milton, Doctor
See Alien Sex Fiend
Mingus, Charles **9**
Ministry **10**
Minnelli, Liza **19**
Miss Kier Kirby
See Lady Miss Kier
Mitchell, Alex
See Curve
Mitchell, John
See Asleep at the Wheel

Mitchell, Joni **17**
Earlier sketch in CM **2**
Mitchell, Keith
See Mazzy Star
Mitchell, Mitch
See Guided By Voices
Mitchell, Roscoe
See Art Ensemble of Chicago, The
Mittoo, Jackie
See Skatalites, The
Mize, Ben
See Counting Crows
Mizell, Jay "Jam Master Jay"
See Run DMC
Mo', Keb' **21**
Moby **27**
Earlier sketch in CM **17**
Moby Grape **12**
Modeliste, Joseph "Zigaboo"
See Meters, The
Moerlen, Pierre
See Gong
Moffatt, Katy **18**
Moginie, Jim
See Midnight Oil
Mogwai **27**
Mohr, Todd
See Big Head Todd and the Monsters
Mojave 3 **26**
Molko, Brian
See Placebo
Molla, Chris
See Monks of Doom
Molland, Joey
See Badfinger
Molloy, Matt
See Chieftains, The
Moloney, Paddy
See Chieftains, The
Monarch, Michael
See Steppenwolf
Money B
See Digital Underground
Money, Eddie **16**
Monica **26**
Monifah **24**
Monk, Meredith **1**
Monk, Thelonious **6**
Monkees, The **7**
Monks of Doom **28**
Monroe, Bill **1**
Montana, Country Dick
See Beat Farmers
Montand, Yves **12**
Montenegro, Hugo **18**
Montgomery, John Michael **14**
Montgomery, Ken "Dimwit"
See D.O.A.
Montgomery, Little Brother **26**
Montgomery, Wes **3**
Monti, Steve
See Curve
Montoya, Craig
See Everclear
Montrose, Ronnie **22**
Moody Blues, The **18**
Moon, Doug
See Captain Beefheart and His Magic Band
Moon, Keith
See Who, The
Mooney, Malcolm
See Can
Mooney, Tim
See American Music Club
Moore, Alan
See Judas Priest
Moore, Angelo
See Fishbone
Moore, Archie
See Velocity Girl
Moore, Chante **21**
Moore, Johnny "Dizzy"
See Skatalites, The
Moore, Kevin
See Dream Theater
Moore, LeRoi
See Dave Matthews Band
Moore, Melba **7**
Moore, Sam
See Sam and Dave
Moore, Sean
See Manic Street Preachers
Moore, Thurston
See Sonic Youth
Morand, Grace
See Chenille Sisters, The
Moraz, Patrick
See Moody Blues, The
Also see Yes
Morcheeba **25**
Moreira, Airto
See Weather Report
Morello, Tom
See Rage Against the Machine
Moreno, Chino
See Deftones
Moreve, Rushton
See Steppenwolf
Morgan, Frank **9**
Morgan, John Russell
See Steppenwolf
Morgan, Lorrie **10**
Morissette, Alanis **19**
Morley, Pat
See Soul Asylum
Morphine **16**
Morricone, Ennio **15**
Morris, Keith
See Circle Jerks, The
Morris, Kenny
See Siouxsie and the Banshees
Morris, Nate
See Boyz II Men
Morris, Roger
See Psychedelic Furs
Morris, Stephen
See Joy Division
Also see New Order
Also see Pogues, The
Morris, Wanya
See Boyz II Men
Morrison, Bram
See Sharon, Lois & Bram
Morrison, Claude
See Nylons, The
Morrison, Jim **3**
Also see Doors, The
Morrison, Lindy
See Go-Betweens, The
Morrison, Sterling
See Velvet Underground, The
Morrison, Van **24**
Earlier sketch in CM **3**
Morrissett, Paul
See Klezmatics, The
Morrissey **10**
Also see Smiths, The
Morrissey, Bill **12**
Morrissey, Steven Patrick
See Morrissey
Morton, Everett
See English Beat, The
Morton, Jelly Roll **7**
Morvan, Fab
See Milli Vanilli
Mosbaugh, Garth
See Nylons, The
Mosely, Chuck
See Faith No More
Moser, Scott "Cactus"
See Highway 101
Mosher, Ken
See Squirrel Nut Zippers
Mosley, Bob
See Moby Grape
Moss, Jason
See Cherry Poppin' Daddies
Mothersbaugh, Bob
See Devo
Mothersbaugh, Mark
See Devo
Mötley Crüe **1**
Motörhead **10**
Motta, Danny
See Roomful of Blues
Mould, Bob **10**
Moulding, Colin
See XTC
Mounfield, Gary
See Stone Roses, The
Mouquet, Eric
See Deep Forest
Mouskouri, Nana **12**
Mouzon, Alphonse
See Weather Report
Moye, Famoudou Don
See Art Ensemble of Chicago, The
Moyet, Alison **12**
Moyse, David
See Air Supply
Mr. Dalvin
See Jodeci
Mudhoney **16**
Mueller, Karl
See Soul Asylum
Muir, Jamie
See King Crimson
Muir, Mike
See Suicidal Tendencies
Muldaur, Maria **18**
Mulholland, Dave
See Aztec Camera
Mullen, Larry, Jr.
See U2
Mullen, Mary
See Congo Norvell
Mulligan, Gerry **16**
Murcia, Billy
See New York Dolls
Murdoch, Stuart
See Belle and Sebastian
Murdock, Roger
See King Missile
Murph
See Dinosaur Jr.
Murphey, Michael Martin **9**
Murphy, Brigid
See Poi Dog Pondering
Murphy, Chris
See Sloan
Murphy, Dan
See Soul Asylum

Murphy, John
See Gene Loves Jezebel
Murphy, Michael
See REO Speedwagon
Murphy, Peter **22**
Also see Bauhaus
Murray, Anne **4**
Murray, Dave **28**
Murray, Dave
See Iron Maiden
Murray, Dee
See Spencer Davis Group
Murray, Jim
See Quicksilver Messenger Service
Mushroom
See Massive Attack
Musselwhite, Charlie **13**
Mustaine, Dave
See Megadeth
Also see Metallica
Mutter, Anne-Sophie **23**
Mwelase, Jabulane
See Ladysmith Black Mambazo
Mydland, Brent
See Grateful Dead, The
Myers, Alan
See Devo
Myles, Alannah **4**
Mystic Revealers **16**
Myung, John
See Dream Theater
'N Sync **25**
N.W.A. **6**
N'Dour, Youssou **6**
Na'dirah
See Arrested Development
Naftalin, Mark
See Quicksilver Messenger Service
Nagler, Eric **8**
Najee **21**
Nakai, R. Carlos **24**
Nakamura, Tetsuya "Tex"
See War
Nakatami, Michie
See Shonen Knife
Nana
See Rasputina
Narcizo, David
See Throwing Muses
Nas **19**
Nascimento, Milton **6**
Nash, Graham
See Crosby, Stills, and Nash
Nash, Leigh
See Sixpence None the Richer
Nashville Bluegrass Band **14**
Nastanovich, Bob
See Pavement
Naughty by Nature **11**
Navarro, David
See Jane's Addiction
Navarro Fats **25**
Nawasadio, Sylvie
See Zap Mama
Ndegéocello, Me'Shell **18**
Ndugu
See Weather Report
Near, Holly **1**
Neel, Johnny
See Allman Brothers, The
Negron, Chuck
See Three Dog Night
Negroni, Joe
See Frankie Lymon and The Teenagers
Neil, Chris
See Less Than Jake
Neil, Vince
See Mötley Crüe
Nelson, Brett
See Built to Spill
Nelson, Brian
See Velocity Girl
Nelson, David
See Last Poets
Nelson, Errol
See Black Uhuru
Nelson, Gabe
See Cake
Nelson, Nate
See Platters, The
Nelson, Rick **2**
Nelson, Shara
See Massive Attack
Nelson, Willie **11**
Earlier sketch in CM **1**
Nero, Peter **19**
Nesbitt, John
See McKinney's Cotton Pickers
Nesmith, Mike
See Monkees, The
Ness, Mike
See Social Distortion
Netson, Brett
See Built to Spill
Neufville, Renee
See Zhane
Neumann, Kurt
See BoDeans
Neurosis **28**
Nevarez, Alfred
See All-4-One
Neville, Aaron **5**
Also see Neville Brothers, The
Neville, Art
See Meters, The
Also see Neville Brothers, The
Neville Brothers, The **4**
Neville, Charles
See Neville Brothers, The
Neville, Cyril
See Meters, The
Also see Neville Brothers, The
Nevin, Brian
See Big Head Todd and the Monsters
New Grass Revival, The **4**
New Kids on the Block **3**
New Order **11**
New Rhythm and Blues Quartet
See NRBQ
New York Dolls **20**
Newman, Randy **27**
Earlier sketch in CM **4**
Newmann, Kurt
See BoDeans, The
Newsboys, The **24**
Newson, Arlene
See Poi Dog Pondering
Newsted, Jason
See Metallica
Newton, Paul
See Uriah Heep
Newton, Wayne **2**
Newton-Davis, Billy
See Nylons, The
Newton-John, Olivia **8**
Nibbs, Lloyd
See Skatalites, The
Nicholas, James Dean "J.D."
See Commodores, The
Nicholls, Geoff
See Black Sabbath
Nichols, Gates
See Confederate Railroad
Nichols, Todd
See Toad the Wet Sprocket
Nickerson, Charlie
See Memphis Jug Band
Nicks, Stevie **25**
Earlier sketch in CM **2**
Also see Fleetwood Mac
Nico
See Velvet Underground, The
Nicol, Simon
See Fairport Convention
Nicolette
See Massive Attack
Nielsen, Rick
See Cheap Trick
Nijholt, Nico
See Willem Breuker Kollektief
Nikleva, Steven
See Ray Condo and His Ricochets
Nilija, Robert
See Last Poets
Nilsson **10**
Nilsson, Harry
See Nilsson
Nirvana **8**
Nisbett, Steve "Grizzly"
See Steel Pulse
Nishino, Kohji
See Ghost
Nitty Gritty Dirt Band, The **6**
No Doubt **20**
Nobacon, Danbert "The Cat"
See Chumbawamba
Nocentelli, Leo
See Meters, The
NOFX **28**
Nolan, Jerry
See New York Dolls
Nomiya, Maki
See Pizzicato Five
Noone, Peter "Herman"
See Herman's Hermits
Norica, Sugar Ray
See Roomful of Blues
Norman, Jessye **7**
Norman, Jimmy
See Coasters, The
Norman, Patrick
See Rusted Root
Norris, Jean
See Zhane
Northern Lights **19**
Northey, Craig
See Odds
Norum, John
See Dokken
Norvell, Sally
See Congo Norvell
Norvo, Red **12**
Notorious B.I.G. **20**
Novoselic, Chris
See Nirvana
Nowell, Bradley James
See Sublime
NRBQ **12**
Nugent, Ted **2**
Nunn, Bobby
See Coasters, The
Nutter, Alice
See Chumbawamba

Nylons, The **6**
Nyman, Michael **15**
Nyolo, Sally
See Zap Mama
Nyro, Laura **12**
O'Brien, Brien
See D.O.A.
O'Brien, Darrin Kenneth
See Snow
O'Brien, Derek
See Social Distortion
O'Brien, Dwayne
See Little Texas
O'Brien, Ed
See Radiohead
O'Brien, Marty
See Kilgore
O'Bryant, Alan
See Nashville Bluegrass Band
O'Connell, Chris
See Asleep at the Wheel
O'Connor, Billy
See Blondie
O'Connor, Daniel
See House of Pain
O'Connor, Mark **1**
O'Connor, Sinead **3**
O'Day, Anita **21**
O'Donnell, Roger
See Cure, The
O'Hagan, Sean
See Stereolab
O'Hare, Brendan
See Mogwai
Also see Teenage Fanclub
O'Jays, The **13**
O'Reagan, Tim
See Jayhawks, The
O'Riordan, Cait
See Pogues, The
O'Riordan, Dolores
See Cranberries, The
Oak Ridge Boys, The **7**
Earlier sketch in CM **4**
Oakes, Richard
See Suede
Oakey, Philip
See Human League, The
Oakland Interfaith Gospel Choir **26**
Oakley, Berry
See Allman Brothers, The
Oasis **16**
Oates, John
See Hall & Oates
Ocasek, Ric **5**
Also see Cars, The
Ocean, Billy **4**
Oceans, Lucky
See Asleep at the Wheel
Ochs, Phil **7**
Odds **20**
Odetta **7**
Odmark, Matt
See Jars of Clay
Offspring, The **19**
Ofwerman, Clarence
See Roxette
Ofwerman, Staffan
See Roxette
Ogino, Kazuo
See Ghost
Ogletree, Mike
See Simple Minds
Ogre, Nivek
See Pigface
Also see Skinny Puppy
Ohanian, David
See Canadian Brass, The
Ohio Players **16**
Oje, Baba
See Arrested Development
Olafsson, Bragi
See Sugarcubes, The
Olander, Jimmy
See Diamond Rio
Olaverra, Margot
See Go-Go's, The
Olde-Wolbers, Christian
See Fear Factory
Oldfield, Mike **18**
Oldham, Jack
See Surfaris, The
Oldham, Sean
See Cherry Poppin' Daddies
Olds, Brent
See Poi Dog Pondering
Oliver, Joe
See Oliver, King
Oliver, King **15**
Olivia Tremor Control **28**
Olsdal, Stefan
See Placebo
Olson, Jeff
See Village People, The
Olson, Mark
See Jayhawks, The
Olsson, Nigel
See Spencer Davis Group
Onassis, Blackie
See Urge Overkill
Ono, Yoko **11**
Opokuwaa, Akua
See Sweet Honey in the Rock
Orange, Walter "Clyde"
See Commodores, The
Orb, The **18**
Orbison, Roy **2**
Orbital **20**
Orchestral Manoeuvres in the Dark **21**
Orff, Carl **21**
Organ, Chad
See Flying Luttenbachers, The
Orgy **27**
Orlando, Tony **15**
Örn, Einar
See Sugarcubes, The
Örnolfsdottir, Margret
See Sugarcubes, The
Orr, Benjamin
See Cars, The
Orr, Casey
See Gwar
Orrall, Frank
See Poi Dog Pondering
Ortega, Leonor "Jeff"
See Five Iron Frenzy
Ortega, Micah
See Five Iron Frenzy
Orton, Beth **26**
Orzabal, Roland
See Tears for Fears
Osborne, Bob
See Osborne Brothers, The
Osborne Brothers, The **8**
Osborne, Buzz
See Melvins
Osborne, Joan **19**
Osborne, Sonny
See Osborne Brothers, The
Osbourne, Ozzy **3**
Also see Black Sabbath
Osby, Greg **21**
Oskar, Lee
See War
Oslin, K. T. **3**
Osman, Mat
See Suede
Osmond, Donny **3**
Ostin, Mo **17**
Otis, Johnny **16**
Ott, David **2**
Otto, John
See Limp Bizkit
Our Lady Peace **22**
Outler, Jimmy
See Soul Stirrers, The
Owen, Randy Yueull
See Alabama
Owens, Buck **2**
Owens, Campbell
See Aztec Camera
Owens, Henry
See Golden Gate Quartet
Owens, Ricky
See Temptations, The
Oyewole, Abiodun
See Last Poets
P.M. Dawn **11**
Pace, Amedeo
See Blonde Redhead
Pace, Simone
See Blonde Redhead
Page, Jimmy **4**
Also see Led Zeppelin
Also see Yardbirds, The
Page, Patti **11**
Page, Steven
See Barenaked Ladies
Paice, Ian
See Deep Purple
Paliotta, Cherie
See Avalon
Palmer, Bruce
See Buffalo Springfield
Palmer, Carl
See Emerson, Lake & Palmer/Powell
Palmer, Clive
See Incredible String Band
Palmer, David
See Jethro Tull
Palmer, Jeff
See Sunny Day Real Estate
Palmer, Jeff **20**
Palmer, Keeti
See Prodigy
Palmer, Phil
See Dire Straits
Palmer, Richard
See Supertramp
Palmer, Robert **2**
Palmer-Jones, Robert
See King Crimson
Palmieri, Eddie **15**
Paluzzi, Jimmy
See Sponge
Pamer, John
See Tsunami
Pankow, James
See Chicago
Panter, Horace
See Specials, The
Pantera **13**
Papach, Leyna
See Geraldine Fibbers
Pappas, Tom
See Superdrag

Parazaider, Walter
See Chicago
Paris, Twila **16**
Park, Cary
See Boy Howdy
Park, Larry
See Boy Howdy
Parkening, Christopher **7**
Parker, Charlie **5**
Parker, Evan **28**
Parker, Graham **10**
Parker, Kris
See KRS-One
Parker, Leon **27**
Parker, Maceo **7**
Parker, Tom
See Animals, The
Parkin, Chad
See Aquabats, The
Parks, Van Dyke **17**
Parnell, Lee Roy **15**
Parsons, Alan **12**
Parsons, Dave
See Bush
Parsons, Gene
See Byrds, The
Parsons, Gram **7**
Also see Byrds, The
Parsons, Ted
See Prong
Parsons, Tony
See Iron Maiden
Parton, Dolly **24**
Earlier sketch in CM **2**
Partridge, Andy
See XTC
Parvo, Carpella
See Rasputina
Pasemaster, Mase
See De La Soul
Pash, Jim
See Surfaris, The
Pasillas, Jose
See Incubus
Pass, Joe **15**
Passons, Michael
See Avalon
Pastorius, Jaco
See Weather Report
Paterson, Alex
See Orb, The
Patinkin, Mandy **20**
Earlier sketch CM **3**
Patrick, Richard
See Filter
Patti, Sandi **7**
Patton, Charley **11**
Patton, Mike
See Faith No More
Paul, Alan
See Manhattan Transfer, The
Paul III, Henry
See BlackHawk
Paul, Les **2**
Paul, Vinnie
See Pantera
Paulo, Jr.
See Sepultura
Pavarotti, Luciano **20**
Earlier sketch in CM **1**
Pavement **14**
Pavia, John
See Four Seasons, The
Paxton, Tom **5**
Payne, Bill
See Little Feat
Payne, Scherrie
See Supremes, The
Payton, Denis
See Dave Clark Five, The
Payton, Lawrence
See Four Tops, The
Payton, Nicholas **27**
Pearl Jam **12**
Pearl, Minnie **3**
Pearls Before Swine **24**
Pearson, Dan
See American Music Club
Peart, Neil
See Rush
Pedersen, Chris
See Monks of Doom
Pedersen, Herb
See Desert Rose Band, The
Peduzzi, Larry
See Roomful of Blues
Peek, Dan
See America
Peeler, Ben
See Mavericks, The
Pegg, Dave
See Fairport Convention
Also see Jethro Tull
Pegrum, Nigel
See Steeleye Span
Pelletier, Mike
See Kilgore
Pence, Jeff
See Blessid Union of Souls
Pendergrass, Teddy **3**
Pendleton, Brian
See Pretty Things, The
Pengilly, Kirk
See INXS
Peniston, CeCe **15**
Penn, Michael **4**
Penner, Fred **10**
Pennywise **27**
Pentangle **18**
Pentland, Patrick
See Sloan
Pepper, Art **18**
Perahia, Murray **10**
Pere Ubu **17**
Peretz, Jesse
See Lemonheads, The
Perez, Danilo **25**
Perez, Louie
See Los Lobos
Perkins, Carl **9**
Perkins, John
See XTC
Perkins, Percell
See Five Blind Boys of Alabama
Perkins, Steve
See Jane's Addiction
Perko, Lynn
See Imperial Teen
Perlman, Itzhak **2**
Perlman, Marc
See Jayhawks, The
Pernice, Joe
See Scud Mountain Boys
Perry, Brendan
See Dead Can Dance
Perry, Doane
See Jethro Tull
Perry, Joe
See Aerosmith
Perry, John G.
See Caravan
Perry, Phil **24**
Perry, Steve
See Journey
Perry, Steve
See Cherry Poppin' Daddies
Perry, Virgshawn
See Artifacts
Persson, Nina
See Cardigans
Pet Shop Boys **5**
Peter, Paul & Mary **4**
Peters, Bernadette **27**
Earlier sketch in CM **7**
Peters, Dan
See Mudhoney
Peters, Joey
See Grant Lee Buffalo
Peters, Mike
See Alarm
Petersen, Chris
See Front Line Assembly
Peterson, Debbi
See Bangles, The
Peterson, Garry
See Guess Who
Peterson, Oscar **11**
Peterson, Vicki
See Bangles, The
Petersson, Tom
See Cheap Trick
Petkovic, John
See Cobra Verde
Petra **3**
Petri, Tony
See Wendy O. Williams and The Plasmatics
Petrucci, John
See Dream Theater
Petty, Tom **9**
Also see Tom Petty and the Heartbreakers
Pfaff, Kristen
See Hole
Phair, Liz **14**
Phantom, Slim Jim
See Stray Cats, The
Pharcyde, The **17**
Phelps, Doug
See Kentucky Headhunters, The
Phelps, Ricky Lee
See Kentucky Headhunters, The
Phife
See Tribe Called Quest, A
Phil, Gary
See Boston
Philbin, Greg
See REO Speedwagon
Philips, Anthony
See Genesis
Phillips, Chris
See Squirrel Nut Zippers
Phillips, Chynna
See Wilson Phillips
Phillips, Glenn
See Toad the Wet Sprocket
Phillips, Grant Lee
See Grant Lee Buffalo
Phillips, Harvey **3**
Phillips, John
See Mamas and the Papas
Phillips, Mackenzie
See Mamas and the Papas
Phillips, Michelle
See Mamas and the Papas

Phillips, Sam **5**
Phillips, Sam **12**
Phillips, Scott
See Creed
Phillips, Shelley
See Point of Grace
Phillips, Simon
See Judas Priest
Phish **25**
Earlier sketch in CM **13**
Phungula, Inos
See Ladysmith Black Mambazo
Piaf, Edith **8**
Piazzolla, Astor **18**
Picciotto, Joe
See Fugazi
Piccolo, Greg
See Roomful of Blues
Pickerel, Mark
See Screaming Trees
Pickering, Michael
See M People
Pickett, Wilson **10**
Pier, Fred
See D.O.A.
Pierce, Charlie
See Memphis Jug Band
Pierce, Marvin "Merv"
See Ohio Players
Pierce, Webb **15**
Pierson, Kate
See B-52's, The
Pigface **19**
Pilatus, Rob
See Milli Vanilli
Pilson, Jeff
See Dokken
Pinder, Michael
See Moody Blues, The
Pine, Courtney
See Soul II Soul
Pink Floyd **2**
Pinkus, Jeff
See Butthole Surfers
Pinnick, Doug
See King's X
Pires, Maria João **26**
Pirner, Dave
See Soul Asylum
Pirroni, Marco
See Siouxsie and the Banshees
Pisarri, Bill
See Flying Luttenbachers, The
Pixies, The **21**
Pizzicato Five **18**
Placebo **27**
Plakas, Dee
See L7
Plant, Robert **2**
Also see Led Zeppelin
Platters, The **25**
Pleasant, Alvin
See Carter Family, The
Ploog, Richard
See Church, The
Plouf, Scott
See Built to Spill
Pogues, The **6**
Pohom, Chris
See D.O.A.
Poi Dog Pondering **17**
Poindexter, Buster
See Johansen, David
Point of Grace **21**
Pointer, Anita
See Pointer Sisters, The
Pointer, Bonnie
See Pointer Sisters, The
Pointer, June
See Pointer Sisters, The
Pointer, Ruth
See Pointer Sisters, The
Pointer Sisters, The **9**
Poison **11**
Poison Ivy
See Rorschach, Poison Ivy
Poland, Chris
See Megadeth
Polce, Tom
See Letters to Cleo
Polci, Gerry
See Four Seasons, The
Police, The **20**
Pollard, Jim
See Guided By Voices
Pollard, Robert, Jr.
See Guided By Voices
Pollard, Russ
See Sebadoh
Pollock, Courtney Adam
See Aquabats. The
Polygon Window
See Aphex Twin
Pomus, Doc
See Doc Pomus
Ponty, Jean-Luc **8**
Also see Mahavishnu Orchestra
Pop, Iggy **23**
Earlier sketch in CM **1**
Popoff, A. Jay
See Lit
Popoff, Jeremy
See Lit
Popper, John
See Blues Traveler
Porter, Cole **10**
Porter, George, Jr.
See Meters, The
Porter, Jody
See Fountains of Wayne
Porter, Tiran
See Doobie Brothers, The
Portishead **22**
Portman-Smith, Nigel
See Pentangle
Portnoy, Mike
See Dream Theater
Posa, Dylan
See Flying Luttenbachers, The
Posdnuos
See De La Soul
Post, Louise
See Veruca Salt
Post, Mike **21**
Potter, Janna
See Avalon
Potts, Sean
See Chieftains, The
Povey, John
See Pretty Things, The
Powell, Baden **23**
Powell, Billy
See Lynyrd Skynyrd
Powell, Bud **15**
Powell, Cozy
See Emerson, Lake & Palmer/Powell
Powell, Kobie
See US3
Powell, Paul
See Aztec Camera
Powell, William
See O'Jays, The
Powers, Kid Congo
See Congo Norvell
Also see Cramps, The
Prater, Dave
See Sam and Dave
Pratt, Awadagin **19**
Prefab Sprout **15**
Presley, Elvis **1**
Pretenders, The **8**
Pretty Things, The **26**
Previn, André **15**
Price, Alan
See Animals, The
Price, Leontyne **6**
Price, Lloyd **25**
Price, Louis
See Temptations, The
Price, Mark
See Archers of Loaf
Price, Ray **11**
Price, Rick
See Electric Light Orchestra
Pride, Charley **4**
Priest, Maxi **20**
Prima, Louis **18**
Primal Scream **14**
Primettes, The
See Supremes, The
Primus **11**
Prince **14**
Earlier sketch in CM **1**
Prince Be
See P.M. Dawn
Prince, Prairie
See Journey
Prince, Vivian
See Pretty Things, The
Prine, John **7**
Prior, Maddy
See Steeleye Span
Proclaimers, The **13**
Prodigy **22**
Professor Longhair **6**
Promise Ring, The **28**
Prong **23**
Propatier, Joe
See Silver Apples
Propellerheads **26**
Propes, Duane
See Little Texas
Prout, Brian
See Diamond Rio
Pryce, Guto
See Super Furry Animals
Psychedelic Furs **23**
Public Enemy **4**
Puccini, Giacomo **25**
Puente, Tito **14**
Puff Daddy
See Combs, Sean "Puffy"
Pullen, Don **16**
Pulp **18**
Pulsford, Nigel
See Bush
Pusey, Clifford "Moonie"
See Steel Pulse
Pyle, Andy
See Kinks, The
Pyle, Artemis
See Lynyrd Skynyrd

Pyle, Pip
See Gong
Pyro, Howie
See D Generation
Q-Tip
See Tribe Called Quest, A
Quaife, Peter
See Kinks, The
Quasi **24**
Quasthoff, Thomas **26**
Queen **6**
Queen Ida **9**
Queen Latifah **24**
Earlier sketch in CM **6**
Queensryche **8**
Querfurth, Carl
See Roomful of Blues
Quicksilver Messenger Service **23**
R.E.M. **25**
Earlier sketch in CM **5**
Raaymakers, Boy
See Willem Breuker Kollektief
Rabbitt, Eddie **24**
Earlier sketch in CM **5**
Rabin, Trevor
See Yes
Radiohead **24**
Raekwon
See Wu-Tang Clan
Raffi **8**
Rage Against the Machine **18**
Raheem
See Geto Boys, The
Rainey, Ma **22**
Rainey, Sid
See Compulsion
Rainford, Simone
See All Saints
Rainwater, Keech
See Lonestar
Raitt, Bonnie **23**
Earlier sketch in CM **3**
Rakim
See Eric B. and Rakim
Raleigh, Don
See Squirrel Nut Zippers
Ralph Sharon Quartet **26**
Ralphs, Mick
See Bad Company
Rammstein **25**
Ramone, C. J.
See Ramones, The
Ramone, Dee Dee
See Ramones, The
Ramone, Joey
See Ramones, The
Ramone, Johnny
See Ramones, The
Ramone, Marky
See Ramones, The
Ramone, Ritchie
See Ramones, The
Ramone, Tommy
See Ramones, The
Ramones, The **9**
Rampage, Randy
See D.O.A.
Rampal, Jean-Pierre **6**
Ramsay, Andy
See Stereolab
Ranaldo, Lee
See Sonic Youth
Randall, Bobby
See Sawyer Brown
Raney, Jerry
See Beat Farmers
Rangell, Andrew **24**
Ranglin, Ernest
See Skatalites, The
Ranken, Andrew
See Pogues, The
Rankin, Cookie
See Rankins, The
Rankin, Heather
See Rankins, The
Rankin, Jimmy
See Rankins, The
Rankin, John Morris
See Rankins, The
Rankin, Raylene
See Rankins, The
Ranking, Roger
See English Beat, The
Rankins, The **24**
Rapp, Tom
See Pearls Before Swine
Rarebell, Herman
See Scorpions, The
Rasboro, Johnathen
See Silk
Rasputina **26**
Rat Fink, Jr.
See Alien Sex Fiend
Ravel, Maurice **25**
Raven, Paul
See Prong
Rawls, Lou **19**
Ray, Amy
See Indigo Girls
Ray Condo and His Ricochets **26**
Raybon, Marty
See Shenandoah
Raye, Collin **16**
Raymonde, Simon
See Cocteau Twins, The
Raynor, Scott
See Blink 182
Rea, Chris **12**
Read, John
See Specials, The
Reagon, Bernice Johnson
See Sweet Honey in the Rock
Red Hot Chili Peppers, The **7**
Redbone, Leon **19**
Redd Kross **20**
Redding, Otis **5**
Reddy, Helen **9**
Redman, Don
See McKinney's Cotton Pickers
Redman, Joshua **25**
Earlier sketch in CM **12**
Redpath, Jean **1**
Redus, Richard
See Captain Beefheart and His Magic Band
Reece, Chris
See Social Distortion
Reed, Herbert
See Platters, The
Reed, Jimmy **15**
Reed, Lou **16**
Earlier sketch in CM **1**
Also see Velvet Underground, The
Reef **24**
Reese, Della **13**
Reese, Joey
See Wendy O. Williams and The Plasmatics
Reeves, Dianne **16**
Reeves, Jim **10**
Reeves, Lois
See Martha and the Vandellas
Reeves, Martha **4**
Also see Martha and the Vandellas
Regan, Julianne
See Gene Loves Jezebel
Reich, Steve **8**
Reid, Charlie
See Proclaimers, The
Reid, Christopher
See Kid 'n Play
Reid, Craig
See Proclaimers, The
Reid, Delroy "Junior"
See Black Uhuru
Reid, Don
See Statler Brothers, The
Reid, Ellen Lorraine
See Crash Test Dummies
Reid, Harold
See Statler Brothers, The
Reid, Janet
See Black Uhuru
Reid, Jim
See Jesus and Mary Chain, The
Reid, Lou
See Seldom Scene, The
Reid, Vernon **2**
Also see Living Colour
Reid, William
See Jesus and Mary Chain, The
Reifman, William
See KMFDM
Reinhardt, Django **7**
Reininger, Blaine
See Tuxedomoon
Reitzell, Brian
See Redd Kross
Relf, Keith
See Yardbirds, The
Renbourn, John
See Pentangle
Reno, Ronnie
See Osborne Brothers, The
REO Speedwagon **23**
Replacements, The **7**
Republica **20**
Residents, The **14**
Restless Heart **12**
Revell, Adrian
See Jamiroquai
Reverend Horton Heat **19**
Rex
See Pantera
Reyes, Andre
See Gipsy Kings, The
Reyes, Canut
See Gipsy Kings, The
Reyes, Nicolas
See Gipsy Kings, The
Reynolds, Nick
See Kingston Trio, The
Reynolds, Robert
See Mavericks, The
Reynolds, Sheldon
See Earth, Wind and Fire
Reznor, Trent **13**
Rhodes, Nick
See Duran Duran
Rhodes, Philip
See Gin Blossoms
Rhodes, Todd
See McKinney's Cotton Pickers
Rhone, Sylvia **13**

Rhys, Gruff
See Super Furry Animals
Rice, Chris **25**
Rich, Buddy **13**
Rich, Charlie **3**
Rich, John
See Lonestar
Richard, Cliff **14**
Richard, Zachary **9**
Richards, Edward
See Shamen, The
Richards, Keith **11**
Also see Rolling Stones, The
Richardson, Geoffrey
See Caravan
Richardson, Kevin
See Backstreet Boys
Richey, Kim **20**
Richie, Lionel **2**
Also see Commodores, The
Richling, Greg
See Wallflowers, The
Richman, Jonathan **12**
Richrath, Gary
See REO Speedwagon
Rick, Dave
See King Missile
Ricochet **23**
Riebling, Scott
See Letters to Cleo
Rieckermann, Ralph
See Scorpions, The
Riedel, Oliver
See Rammstein
Rieflin, William
See Ministry
Also see Pigface
Rieu, André **26**
Riles, Kelly
See Velocity Girl
Riley, Kristian
See Citizen King
Riley, Teddy "Street" **14**
See Blackstreet
Riley, Timothy Christian
See Tony! Toni! Toné!
Rimes, LeAnn **19**
Rippon, Steve
See Lush
Ritchie, Brian
See Violent Femmes
Ritchie, Jean **4**
Ritchie, John Simon
See Sid Vicious
Ritchie, Robert
See Kid Rock
Ritenour, Lee **7**
Rivers, Sam
See Limp Bizkit
Rizzo, Joe
See D Generation
Rizzo, Peter
See Gene Loves Jezebel
Roach, Max **12**
Roback, David
See Mazzy Star
Robbins, Charles David
See BlackHawk
Robbins, Marty **9**
Roberts, Brad
See Crash Test Dummies
Roberts, Brad
See Gwar
Roberts, Dan
See Crash Test Dummies
Roberts, Ken
See Charm Farm
Roberts, Marcus **6**
Roberts, Nathan
See Flaming Lips
Robertson, Brian
See Motörhead
Also see Thin Lizzy
Robertson, Ed
See Barenaked Ladies
Robertson, Robbie **2**
Also see Band, The
Robeson, Paul **8**
Robi, Paul
See Platters, The
Robie, Milton
See Memphis Jug Band
Robillard, Duke **2**
Also see Roomful of Blues
Robinson, Arnold
See Nylons, The
Robinson, Chris
See Black Crowes, The
Robinson, Cynthia
See Sly & the Family Stone
Robinson, David
See Cars, The
Robinson, Dawn
See En Vogue
Robinson, Louise
See Sweet Honey in the Rock
Robinson, Prince
See McKinney's Cotton Pickers
Robinson, R.B.
See Soul Stirrers, The
Robinson, Rich
See Black Crowes, The
Robinson, Romye "Booty Brown"
See Pharcyde, The
Robinson, Smokey **1**
Roche, Maggie
See Roches, The
Roche, Suzzy
See Roches, The
Roche, Terre
See Roches, The
Roches, The **18**
Rockenfield, Scott
See Queensryche
Rocker, Lee
See Stray Cats, The
Rockett, Rikki
See Poison
Rockin' Dopsie **10**
Rodford, Jim
See Kinks, The
Rodgers, Jimmie **3**
Rodgers, Nile **8**
Rodgers, Paul
See Bad Company
Rodgers, Richard **9**
Rodney, Red **14**
Rodriguez, Rico
See Skatalites, The
Also see Specials, The
Rodriguez, Sal
See War
Roe, Marty
See Diamond Rio
Roeder, Jason
See Neurosis
Roeder, Klaus
See Kraftwerk
Roeser, Donald
See Blue Oyster Cult
Roeser, Eddie "King"
See Urge Overkill
Roessler, Kira
See Black Flag
Roger, Ranking
See English Beat, The
Rogers, Dan
See Bluegrass Patriots
Rogers, Kenny **1**
Rogers, Norm
See Jayhawks, The
Rogers, Roy **24**
Earlier sketch in CM **9**
Rogers, Willie
See Soul Stirrers, The
Rogerson, Roger
See Circle Jerks
Roland, Dean
See Collective Soul
Roland, Ed
See Collective Soul
Rolie, Gregg
See Journey
Rolling Stones, The **23**
Earlier sketch in CM **3**
Rollins, Henry **11**
Also see Black Flag
Rollins, Sonny **7**
Rollins, Winston
See Jamiroquai
Romanelli, Chris "Junior"
See Wendy O. Williams and The Plasmatics
Romano, Ruben
See Fu Manchu
Romm, Ronald
See Canadian Brass, The
Ronstadt, Linda **2**
Roomful of Blues **7**
Roots, The **27**
Roper, Dee Dee
See Salt-N-Pepa
Roper, Reese
See Five Iron Frenzy
Roper, Todd
See Cake
Rorschach, Poison Ivy
See Cramps, The
Rosas, Cesar
See Los Lobos
Rose, Axl
See Guns n' Roses
Rose, Felipe
See Village People, The
Rose, Johanna Maria
See Anonymous 4
Rose, Michael
See Black Uhuru
Rosen, Gary
See Rosenshontz
Rosen, Peter
See War
Rosenshontz **9**
Rosenthal, Jurgen
See Scorpions, The
Rosenthal, Phil
See Seldom Scene, The
Ross, Annie
See Lambert, Hendricks and Ross
Ross, Diana **1**
Also see Supremes, The
Ross, Malcolm
See Aztec Camera
Rossdale, Gavin
See Bush

Rossi, John
See Roomful of Blues
Rossington, Gary
See Lynyrd Skynyrd
Rossy, Jose
See Weather Report
Rostill, John
See Shadows, The
Rostropovich, Mstislav **17**
Rota, Nino **13**
Roth, C. P.
See Blessid Union of Souls
Roth, David Lee **1**
Also see Van Halen
Roth, Gabrielle **26**
Roth, Ulrich
See Scorpions, The
Rotheray, Dave
See Beautiful South
Rotsey, Martin
See Midnight Oil
Rotten, Johnny
See Lydon, John
Also see Sex Pistols, The
Rourke, Andy
See Smiths, The
Rowberry, Dave
See Animals, The
Rowe, Dwain
See Restless Heart
Rowe, Simon
See Mojave 3
Rowlands, Bruce
See Fairport Convention
Rowlands, Tom
See Chemical Brothers
Rowntree, Dave
See Blur
Roxette **23**
Roy, Jimmy
See Ray Condo and His Ricochets
Rubin, Mark
See Bad Livers, The
Rubin, Rick **9**
Rubinstein, Arthur **11**
Rucker, Darius
See Hootie and the Blowfish
Rudd, Phillip
See AC/DC
Rudd, Roswell **28**
Rue, Caroline
See Hole
Ruffin, David **6**
Also see Temptations, The
Ruffin, Tamir
See Dru Hill
Ruffy, Dave
See Aztec Camera
Ruffy, Dave
See Waterboys, The
Run DMC **25**
Earlier sketch in CM **4**
Run
See Run DMC
Rundgren, Todd **11**
RuPaul **20**
Rush **8**
Rush, Otis **12**
Rushlow, Tim
See Little Texas
Russell, Alecia
See Sounds of Blackness
Russell, Graham
See Air Supply
Russell, Hal
See Flying Luttenbachers, The
Russell, John
See Steppenwolf
Russell, Mark **6**
Russell, Mike
See Shudder to Think
Russell, Pee Wee **25**
Russell, Tom **26**
Rusted Root **26**
Rutherford, Mike
See Genesis
Also see Mike & the Mechanics
Rutsey, John
See Rush
Ryan, David
See Lemonheads, The
Ryan, Mark
See Quicksilver Messenger Service
Ryan, Mick
See Dave Clark Five, The
Rybska, Agnieszka
See Rasputina
Ryder, Mitch **23**
Earlier sketch in CM **11**
Ryland, Jack
See Three Dog Night
Rzeznik, Johnny
See Goo Goo Dolls, The
Sabo, Dave
See Bon Jovi
Sade **2**
Sadier, Laetitia
See Stereolab
Saffery, Anthony
See Cornershop
Saffron,
See Republica
Sage, Danny
See D Generation
Sager, Carole Bayer **5**
Sahm, Doug
See Texas Tornados, The
Saint Etienne **28**
Saint-Saëns, Camille **25**
Sainte-Marie, Buffy **11**
Sakamoto, Ryuichi **19**
Salazar, Arion
See Third Eye Blind
Salerno-Sonnenberg, Nadja **3**
Saliers, Emily
See Indigo Girls
Salisbury, Peter
See Verve, The
Also see Pizzicato Five
Salmon, Michael
See Prefab Sprout
Saloman, Nick
See Bevis Frond
Salonen, Esa-Pekka **16**
Salt-N-Pepa **6**
Saluzzi, Dino **23**
Sam and Dave **8**
Sambora, Richie **24**
Also see Bon Jovi
Sammy, Piazza
See Quicksilver Messenger Service
Sampson, Doug
See Iron Maiden
Sams, Dean
See Lonestar
Samuelson, Gar
See Megadeth
Samwell-Smith, Paul
See Yardbirds, The
Sanborn, David **28**
Earlier sketch in CM **1**
Sanchez, Michel
See Deep Forest
Sanctuary, Gary
See Aztec Camera
Sanders, Pharoah **28**
Earlier sketch in CM **16**
Sanders, Ric
See Fairport Convention
Sanders, Steve
See Oak Ridge Boys, The
Sandler, Adam **19**
Sandman, Mark
See Morphine
Sandoval, Arturo **15**
Sandoval, Hope
See Mazzy Star
Sands, Aaron
See Jars of Clay
Sanford, Gary
See Aztec Camera
Sangare, Oumou **22**
Sanger, David
See Asleep at the Wheel
Santamaria, Mongo **28**
Santana, Carlos **19**
Earlier sketch in CM **1**
Santiago, Herman
See Frankie Lymon and The Teenagers
Santiago, Joey
See Pixies, The
Saraceno, Blues
See Poison
Sargent, Gray
See Ralph Sharon Quartet
Sasaki, Mamiko
See Pulp
Satchell, Clarence "Satch"
See Ohio Players
Satie, Erik **25**
Satriani, Joe **4**
Savage, Rick
See Def Leppard
Savage, Scott
See Jars of Clay
Sawyer Brown **27**
Earlier sketch in CM **13**
Sawyer, Phil
See Spencer Davis Group
Saxa
See English Beat, The
Saxon, Stan
See Dave Clark Five, The
Scaccia, Mike
See Ministry
Scaggs, Boz **12**
Scaggs, Shawn
See Atomic Fireballs, The
Scallions, Brett
See Fuel
Scanlon, Craig
See Fall, The
Scarface
See Geto Boys, The
Schayer, Bobby
See Bad Religion
Scheidt, Dean Norman
See Lane, Fred
Schelhaas, Jan
See Camel
Also see Caravan
Schellenbach, Kate
See Luscious Jackson

Schemel, Patty
See Hole
Schenker, Michael
See Scorpions, The
Schenker, Rudolf
See Scorpions, The
Schenkman, Eric
See Spin Doctors
Schermie, Joe
See Three Dog Night
Scherpenzeel, Ton
See Camel
Schickele, Peter **5**
Schlesinger, Adam
See Fountains of Wayne
Schlitt, John
See Petra
Schloss, Zander
See Circle Jerks, The
Schmelling, Johannes
See Tangerine Dream
Schmid, Daniel
See Cherry Poppin' Daddies
Schmidt, Irmin
See Can
Schmit, Timothy B.
See Eagles, The
Schmoovy Schmoove
See Digital Underground
Schneider, Christoph
See Rammstein
Schneider, Florian
See Kraftwerk
Schneider, Fred III
See B-52's, The
Schnitzler, Conrad
See Tangerine Dream
Schock, Gina
See Go-Go's, The
Schoenbeck, Scott
See Promise Ring, The
Scholten, Jim
See Sawyer Brown
Scholz, Tom
See Boston
Schon, Neal
See Journey
Schramm, Dave
See Yo La Tengo
Schrody, Erik
See House of Pain
Also see Everlast
Schroyder, Steve
See Tangerine Dream
Schulman, Mark
See Foreigner
Schulz, Guenter
See KMFDM
Schulzberg, Robert
See Placebo
Schulze, Klaus
See Tangerine Dream
Schuman, William **10**
Schuur, Diane **6**
Schwartz, Will
See Imperial Teen
Sclavunos, Jim
See Congo Norvell
Scofield, John **7**
Scorpions, The **12**
Scott, Andrew
See Sloan
Scott, George
See Five Blind Boys of Alabama
Scott, Howard
See War
Scott, Jimmy **14**
Scott, Mike
See Waterboys, The
Scott, Ronald Belford "Bon"
See AC/DC
Scott, Sherry
See Earth, Wind and Fire
Scott-Heron, Gil **13**
Screaming Trees **19**
Scruggs, Earl **3**
Scruggs, Randy **28**
Scud Mountain Boys **21**
Seal **14**
Seales, Jim
See Shenandoah
Seals & Crofts **3**
Seals, Brady
See Little Texas
Seals, Dan **9**
Seals, Jim
See Seals & Crofts
Seaman, Ken
See Bluegrass Patriots
Sears, Pete
See Jefferson Starship
Sebadoh **26**
Secada, Jon **13**
Secrest, Wayne
See Confederate Railroad
Sedaka, Neil **4**
Seeger, Peggy **25**
Seeger, Pete **4**
Also see Weavers, The
Seger, Bob **15**
Segovia, Andres **6**
Seidel, Martie
See Dixie Chicks
Seldom Scene, The **4**
Selena **16**
Selway, Phil
See Radiohead
Sen Dog
See Cypress Hill
Senior, Milton
See McKinney's Cotton Pickers
Senior, Russell
See Pulp
Sensi
See Soul II Soul
Sepultura **12**
Seraphine, Daniel
See Chicago
Sermon, Erick
See EPMD
Sete, Bola **26**
Setzer, Brian
See Stray Cats, The
Severin, Steven
See Siouxsie and the Banshees
Severinsen, Doc **1**
Sex Pistols, The **5**
Sexsmith, Ron **27**
Sexton, Chad
See 311
Seymour, Neil
See Crowded House
Shabalala, Ben
See Ladysmith Black Mambazo
Shabalala, Headman
See Ladysmith Black Mambazo
Shabalala, Jockey
See Ladysmith Black Mambazo
Shabalala, Joseph
See Ladysmith Black Mambazo
Shabo, Eric
See Atomic Fireballs, The
Shade, Will
See Memphis Jug Band
Shadow, DJ **19**
Shadows, The **22**
Shaffer, James
See Korn
Shaffer, Paul **13**
Shaggy **19**
Shaggy 2 Dope
See Insane Clown Possee
Shai **23**
Shakespeare, Robbie
See Sly and Robbie
Shakur, Tupac
See 2Pac
Shallenberger, James
See Kronos Quartet
Shamen, The **23**
Shane, Bob
See Kingston Trio, The
Shanice **14**
Shankar, Ravi **9**
Shannon, Del **10**
Shannon, Sarah
See Velocity Girl
Shannon, Sharon
See Waterboys, The
Shanté **10**
Shapiro, Jim
See Veruca Salt
Shapiro, Lee
See Four Seasons, The
Shapps, Andre
See Big Audio Dynamite
Sharon, Lois & Bram **6**
Sharon, Ralph
See Ralph Sharon Quartet
Sharp, Dave
See Alarm
Sharp, Laura
See Sweet Honey in the Rock
Sharpe, Matt
See Weezer
Sharrock, Chris
See Lightning Seeds
Sharrock, Sonny **15**
Shaw, Adrian
See Bevis Frond
Shaw, Artie **8**
Shaw, Martin
See Jamiroquai
Shaw, Woody **27**
Shea, Tom
See Scud Mountain Boys
Shearer, Harry
See Spinal Tap
Shearing, George **28**
Sheehan, Bobby
See Blues Traveler
Sheehan, Fran
See Boston
Sheep on Drugs **27**
Sheila E. **3**
Shellenberger, Allen
See Lit
Shelley, Peter
See Buzzcocks, The
Shelley, Steve
See Sonic Youth
Shenandoah **17**

Shepherd, Hunter "Ben"
See Soundgarden
Shepherd, Kenny Wayne **22**
Sheppard, Rodney
See Sugar Ray
Sherba, John
See Kronos Quartet
Sherinian, Derek
See Dream Theater
Sherman, Jack
See Red Hot Chili Peppers, The
Shines, Johnny **14**
Shirelles, The **11**
Shirley, Danny
See Confederate Railroad
Shively, William
See Big Mountain
Shives, Andrew
See Fear Factory
Shock G
See Digital Underground
Shocked, Michelle **4**
Shocklee, Hank **15**
Shogren, Dave
See Doobie Brothers, The
Shonen Knife **13**
Shontz, Bill
See Rosenshontz
Shorter, Wayne **5**
Also see Weather Report
Shovell
See M People
Shuck, Ryan
See Orgy
Shudder to Think **20**
Siberry, Jane **6**
Sice
See Boo Radleys, The
Sidelnyk, Steve
See Aztec Camera
Siebenberg, Bob
See Supertramp
Siegal, Janis
See Manhattan Transfer, The
Sikes, C. David
See Boston
Silk **26**
Sills, Beverly **5**
Silva, Kenny Jo
See Beaver Brown Band, The
Silver Apples **23**
Silver, Horace **19**
Silver, Josh
See Type O Negative
Silverchair **20**
Silveria, David
See Korn
Simeon
See Silver Apples
Simien, Terrance **12**
Simins, Russell
See Jon Spencer Blues Explosion
Simmons, Gene
See Kiss
Simmons, Joe "Run"
See Run DMC
Simmons, Patrick
See Doobie Brothers, The
Simmons, Russell **7**
Simmons, Trinna
See Spearhead
Simms, Nick
See Cornershop
Simon and Garfunkel **24**
Simon, Carly **22**
Earlier sketch in CM **4**
Simon, Paul **16**
Earlier sketch in CM **1**
Also see Simon and Garfunkel
Simone, Nina **11**
Simonon, Paul
See Clash, The
Simons, Ed
See Chemical Brothers
Simple Minds **21**
Simpson, Denis
See Nylons, The
Simpson, Derrick "Duckie"
See Black Uhuru
Simpson, Mel
See US3
Simpson, Ray
See Village People, The
Simpson, Rose
See Incredible String Band
Sims, David William
See Jesus Lizard
Sims, Matt
See Citizen King
Sims, Neil
See Catherine Wheel
Sin, Will
See Shamen, The
Sinatra, Frank **23**
Earlier sketch in CM **1**
Sinclair, David
See Camel
Also see Caravan
Sinclair, Gord
See Tragically Hip, The
Sinclair, Richard
See Camel
See Caravan
Sinfield, Peter
See King Crimson
Singer, Eric
See Black Sabbath
Singer, Eric
See Kiss
Singh, Talvin
See Massive Attack
Singh, Tjinder
See Cornershop
Sioux, Siouxsie
See Siouxsie and the Banshees
Siouxsie and the Banshees **8**
Sir Mix-A-Lot **14**
Sir Rap-A-Lot
See Geto Boys, The
Sirois, Joe
See Mighty Mighty Bosstones
Siverton
See Specials, The
Sixpence None the Richer **26**
Sixx, Nikki
See Mötley Crüe
Sixx, Roger
See Less Than Jake
Skaggs, Ricky **5**
Also see Country Gentlemen, The
Skatalites, The **18**
Skeete, Beverley
See Bill Wyman & the Rhythm Kings
Skeoch, Tommy
See Tesla
Skillings, Muzz
See Living Colour
Skinny Puppy **17**
Sklamberg, Lorin
See Klezmatics, The
Skoob
See Das EFX
Skunk Anansie **27**
Slash
See Guns n' Roses
Slayer **10**
Sleater-Kinney **20**
Sledd, Dale
See Osborne Brothers, The
Sledge, Percy **15**
Sledge, Robert
See Ben Folds Five
Slick, Grace
See Jefferson Airplane
Slick Rick **27**
Slijngaard, Ray
See 2 Unlimited
Sloan **28**
Sloan, Eliot
See Blessid Union of Souls
Slocum, Matt
See Sixpence None the Richer
Slovak, Hillel
See Red Hot Chili Peppers, The
Sly & the Family Stone **24**
Sly and Robbie **13**
Sly, Randy "Ginger"
See Atomic Fireballs, The
Small, Heather
See M People
Smalls, Derek
See Spinal Tap
Smart, Terence
See Butthole Surfers
Smash, Chas
See Madness
Smash Mouth **27**
Smashing Pumpkins **13**
Smear, Pat
See Foo Fighters
Smelly
See NOFX
Smith, Adrian
See Iron Maiden
Smith, Bessie **3**
Smith, Brad
See Blind Melon
Smith, Chad
See Red Hot Chili Peppers, The
Smith, Charles
See Kool & the Gang
Smith, Chas
See Cobra Verde
Smith, Clifford "Method Man"
See Wu-Tang Clan
Smith, Curt
See Tears for Fears
Smith, Debbie
See Curve
Also see Echobelly
Smith, Elliott **28**
Smith, Fran
See Hooters
Smith, Fred
See MC5, The
Smith, Fred
See Blondie
Smith, Fred
See Television
Smith, Garth
See Buzzcocks, The
Smith, James, "Smitty"
See Three Dog Night

Smith, Joe
See McKinney's Cotton Pickers
Smith, Kevin
See dc Talk
Smith, Mark E.
See Fall, The
Smith, Michael W. **11**
Smith, Mike
See Dave Clark Five, The
Smith, Parrish
See EPMD
Smith, Patti **17**
Earlier sketch in CM **1**
Smith, Rick
See Underworld
Smith, Robert
See Cure, The
Also see Siouxsie and the Banshees
Smith, Robert
See Spinners, The
Smith, Shawn
See Brad
Smith, Simon
See Wedding Present, The
Smith, Smitty
See Three Dog Night
Smith, Steve
See Journey
Smith, Tommy **28**
Smith, Tweed
See War
Smith, Wendy
See Prefab Sprout
Smith, Will **26**
Also see DJ Jazzy Jeff and the Fresh Prince
Smithereens, The **14**
Smiths, The **3**
Smog **28**
Smyth, Gilli
See Gong
Smyth, Joe
See Sawyer Brown
Sneed, Floyd Chester
See Three Dog Night
Snoop Doggy Dogg **17**
Snouffer, Alex "Alex St. Clair"
See Captain Beefheart and His Magic Band
Snow **23**
Snow, Don
See Squeeze
Snow, Phoebe **4**
Snyder, Richard "Midnight Hatsize Snyder"
See Captain Beefheart and His Magic Band
Soan, Ashley
See Del Amitri
Sobule, Jill **20**
Social Distortion **27**
Earlier sketch in CM **19**
Solal, Martial **4**
Sollenberger, Isobel
See Bardo Pond
Soloff, Lew
See Blood, Sweat and Tears
Solowka, Peter
See Wedding Present, The
Solti, Georg **13**
Son Volt **21**
Sondheim, Stephen **8**
Sonefeld, Jim
See Hootie and the Blowfish
Sonic Youth **26**
Earlier sketch in CM **9**
Sonnenberg, Nadja Salerno
See Salerno-Sonnenberg, Nadja
Sonni, Jack
See Dire Straits
Sonnier, Jo-El **10**
Sonny and Cher **24**
Sorum, Matt
See Cult, The
Sosa, Mercedes **3**
Soucie, Michael
See Surfin' Pluto
Soul Asylum **10**
Soul Coughing **21**
Soul II Soul **17**
Soul Stirrers, The **11**
Soundgarden **6**
Sounds of Blackness **13**
Sousa, John Philip **10**
Southerland, Bill
See Kilgore
Spampinato, Joey
See NRBQ
Spampinato, Johnny
See NRBQ
Spann, Otis **18**
Sparks **18**
Sparks, Donita
See L7
Spearhead **19**
Spears, Britney **28**
Special Ed **16**
Specials, The **21**
Spector, Phil **4**
Spector, Ronnie **28**
Speech
See Arrested Development
Spellman, Jim
See Velocity Girl
Spence, Alexander "Skip"
See Jefferson Airplane
Also see Moby Grape
Spence, Cecil
See Israel Vibration
Spence, Skip
See Spence, Alexander "Skip"
Spencer Davis Group **19**
Spencer, Jeremy
See Fleetwood Mac
Spencer, Jim
See Dave Clark Five, The
Spencer, Jon
See Jon Spencer Blues Explosion
Spencer, Thad
See Jayhawks, The
Spice Girls **22**
Spin Doctors **14**
Spinal Tap **8**
Spindt, Don
See Aqua Velvets
Spinners, The **21**
Spirit **22**
Spiteri, Sharleen
See Texas
Spitz, Dan
See Anthrax
Spitz, Dave
See Black Sabbath
Sponge **18**
Spring, Keith
See NRBQ
Springfield, Dusty **20**
Springfield, Rick **9**
Springsteen, Bruce **25**
Earlier sketch in CM **6**
Sproule, Daithi
See Altan
Sprout, Tobin
See Guided By Voices
Squeeze **5**
Squire, Chris
See Yes
Squire, John
See Stone Roses, The
Squires, Rob
See Big Head Todd and the Monsters
Squirrel Nut Zippers **20**
St. Hubbins, David
See Spinal Tap
St. James, Rebecca **26**
St. John, Mark
See Kiss
St. Marie, Buffy
See Sainte-Marie, Buffy
St. Nicholas, Nick
See Steppenwolf
Stacey, Peter "Spider"
See Pogues, The
Stacy, Jeremy
See Aztec Camera
Staehely, Al
See Spirit
Staehely, J. Christian
See Spirit
Stafford, Jo **24**
Stahl, Franz
See Foo Fighters
Staley, Layne
See Alice in Chains
Staley, Tom
See NRBQ
Stanier, John
See Helmet
Stanisic, Ched
See Cobra Verde
Stanley, Bob
See Saint Etienne
Stanley, Ian
See Tears for Fears
Stanley, Paul
See Kiss
Stanley, Ralph **5**
Stansfield, Lisa **9**
Staples, Mavis **13**
Staples, Neville
See Specials, The
Staples, Pops **11**
Stapp, Scott
See Creed
Starcrunch
See Man or Astroman?
Starkey, Kathryn La Verne
See Starr, Kay
Starkey, Richard
See Starr, Ringo
Starks, Tia Juana
See Sweet Honey in the Rock
Starling, John
See Seldom Scene, The
Starr, Kay **27**
Starr, Mike
See Alice in Chains
Starr, Ringo **24**
Earlier sketch in CM **10**
Also see Beatles, The
Starship
See Jefferson Airplane
Statler Brothers, The **8**
Stax, John
See Pretty Things, The
Stead, David
See Beautiful South

Steaks, Chuck
See Quicksilver Messenger Service
Stebbins, Jone
See Imperial Teen
Steel, John
See Animals, The
Steel Pulse **14**
Steele, Billy
See Sounds of Blackness
Steele, David
See English Beat, The
Also see Fine Young Cannibals
Steele, Jeffrey
See Boy Howdy
Steele, Michael
See Bangles, The
Steele, Peter
See Type O Negative
Steeleye Span **19**
Steely Dan **5**
Stefani, Gwen
See No Doubt
Stefansson, Baldur
See Gus Gus
Steier, Rick
See Warrant
Stein, Chris
See Blondie
Steinberg, Lewis
See Booker T. & the M.G.'s
Steinberg, Sebastian
See Soul Coughing
Stephenson, Van Wesley
See BlackHawk
Steppenwolf **20**
Sterban, Richard
See Oak Ridge Boys, The
Stereolab **18**
Sterling, Lester
See Skatalites, The
Stern, Isaac **7**
Steve
See Fun Lovin' Criminals
Stevens, Cat **3**
Stevens, Ray **7**
Stevens, Roger
See Blind Melon
Stevens, Vol
See Memphis Jug Band
Stevenson, Bill
See Black Flag
Stevenson, Don
See Moby Grape
Stevenson, James
See Gene Loves Jezebel
Steward, Pat
See Odds
Stewart, Dave
See Eurythmics
Stewart, Derrick "Fatlip"
See Pharcyde, The
Stewart, Freddie
See Sly & the Family Stone
Stewart, Ian
See Rolling Stones, The
Stewart, Jamie
See Cult, The
Stewart, John
See Kingston Trio, The
Stewart, Larry
See Restless Heart
Stewart, Rex
See McKinney's Cotton Pickers
Stewart, Rod **20**
Earlier sketch in CM **2**
Also see Faces, The
Stewart, Sylvester
See Sly & the Family Stone
Stewart, Tyler
See Barenaked Ladies
Stewart, Vaetta
See Sly & the Family Stone
Stewart, William
See Third World
Stewart, Winston "Metal"
See Mystic Revealers
Stiff, Jimmy
See Jackyl
Stills, Stephen **5**
See Buffalo Springfield
Also see Crosby, Stills, and Nash
Sting **19**
Earlier sketch in CM **2**
Also see Police, The
Stinson, Bob
See Replacements, The
Stinson, Tommy
See Replacements, The
Stipe, Michael
See R.E.M.
Stockman, Shawn
See Boyz II Men
Stockwood, Kim **26**
Stoll
See Clannad
Also see Big Mountain
Stoller, Mike
See Leiber and Stoller
Stoltz, Brian
See Neville Brothers, The
Stoltzman, Richard **24**
Stonadge, Gary
See Big Audio Dynamite
Stone, Curtis
See Highway 101
Stone, Doug **10**
Stone Roses, The **16**
Stone, Sly **8**
Stone Temple Pilots **14**
Stookey, Paul
See Peter, Paul & Mary
Story, Liz **2**
Story, The **13**
Stotts, Richie
See Wendy O. Williams and The Plasmatics
Stradlin, Izzy
See Guns n' Roses
Strain, Sammy
See O'Jays, The
Strait, George **5**
Stratton, Dennis
See Iron Maiden
Strauss, Richard **25**
Stravinsky, Igor **21**
Straw, Syd **18**
Stray Cats, The **11**
Strayhorn, Billy **13**
Street, Richard
See Temptations, The
Streisand, Barbra **2**
Strickland, Keith
See B-52's, The
Stringer, Gary
See Reef
Strummer, Joe
See Clash, The
Stryper **2**
Stuart, Mark
See Audio Adrenaline
Stuart, Marty **9**
Stuart, Peter
See Dog's Eye View
Stubbs, Levi
See Four Tops, The
Styne, Jule **21**
Sub Commander Ras I Zulu
See Spearhead
Subdudes, The **18**
Sublime **19**
Such, Alec Jon
See Bon Jovi
Suede **20**
Sugar Ray **22**
Sugarcubes, The **10**
Suicidal Tendencies **15**
Sulley, Suzanne
See Human League, The
Sullivan, Jacqui
See Bananarama
Sullivan, Kirk
See 4Him
Summer, Donna **12**
Summer, Mark
See Turtle Island String Quartet
Summers, Andy **3**
Also see Police, The
Sumner, Bernard
See Joy Division
Also see New Order
Sun Ra **27**
Earlier sketch in CM **5**
Sundays, The **20**
Sunny Day Real Estate **28**
Sunnyland Slim **16**
Super DJ Dmitry
See Deee-lite
Super Furry Animals **28**
Superdrag **23**
Supertramp **25**
Supremes, The **6**
Sure!, Al B. **13**
Surfaris, The **23**
Surfin' Pluto **24**
Sutcliffe, Stu
See Beatles, The
Sutherland, Joan **13**
Suzuki, Kenji "Damo"
See Can
Svenigsson, Magnus
See Cardigans
Svensson, Peter
See Cardigans
Svigals, Alicia
See Klezmatics, The
Swanson, Dave
See Cobra Verde
Swarbrick, Dave
See Fairport Convention
Sweat, Keith **13**
Sweet Honey In The Rock **26**
Earlier sketch in CM **1**
Sweet, Matthew **9**
Sweet, Michael
See Stryper
Sweet, Robert
See Stryper
Sweethearts of the Rodeo **12**
Swing, DeVante
See Jodeci
SWV **14**
Sykes, John
See Whitesnake
Sykes, Roosevelt **20**
Sylvain, Sylvain
See New York Dolls

Sylvian, David **27**
T. Rex **11**
Tabac, Tony
See Joy Division
Tabor, Ty
See King's X
Tackett, Fred
See Little Feat
Tadlock, Tom
See Tuxedomoon
TAFKAP (The Artist Formerly Known as Prince)
See Prince
Taggart, Jeremy
See Our Lady Peace
Tait, Michael
See dc Talk
Taj Mahal **6**
Tajima, Takao
See Pizzicato Five
Takac, Robby
See Goo Goo Dolls, The
Takahashi, Maki
See Blonde Redhead
Takanami
See Pizzicato Five
Take 6 **6**
Takeda, Clint
See Bardo Pond
Takemitsu, Toru **6**
Takizawa, Taishi
See Ghost
Talbot, John Michael **6**
Talcum, Joe Jack
See Dead Milkmen
Talk Talk **19**
Talking Heads **1**
Tampa Red **25**
Tandy, Richard
See Electric Light Orchestra
Tangerine Dream **12**
Taree, Aerle
See Arrested Development
Tate, Geoff
See Queensryche
Tatum, Art **17**
Taupin, Bernie **22**
Taylor, Aaron
See MC Eiht
Taylor, Andy
See Duran Duran
Taylor, Billy **13**
Taylor, Cecil **9**
Taylor, Chad
See Live
Taylor, Courtney
See Dandy Warhols
Taylor, Dan
See Silver Apples
Taylor, Dave
See Pere Ubu
Taylor, Dick
See Rolling Stones, The
Taylor, Earl
See Country Gentlemen, The
Taylor, James "J.T."
See Kool & the Gang
Taylor, James **25**
Earlier sketch in CM **2**
Taylor, John
See Duran Duran
Taylor, Johnnie
See Soul Stirrers, The
Taylor, Koko **10**
Taylor, Leroy
See Soul Stirrers, The
Taylor, Melvin
See Ventures, The
Taylor, Mick
See Rolling Stones, The
Also see Pretty Things, The
Taylor, Philip "Philthy Animal"
See Motörhead
Taylor, Roger
See Duran Duran
Taylor, Roger Meadows
See Queen
Taylor, Steve **26**
Taylor, Steve
See Ray Condo and His Ricochets
Taylor, Teresa
See Butthole Surfers
Taylor, Zola
See Platters, The
Te Kanawa, Kiri **2**
Teagarden, Jack **10**
Tears for Fears **6**
Technotronic **5**
Teenage Fanclub **13**
Television **17**
Teller, Al **15**
Temirkanov, Yuri **26**
Tempesta, John
See White Zombie
Temple, Michelle
See Pere Ubu
Temptations, The **3**
Tench, Benmont
See Tom Petty and the Heartbreakers
Tennant, Neil
See Pet Shop Boys
Tepper, Jeff "Morris"
See Captain Beefheart and His Magic Band
Terminator X
See Public Enemy
Terrell, Jean
See Supremes, The
Terrie
See Ex, The
Terry, Boyd
See Aquabats, The
Terry, Clark **24**
Tesh, John **20**
Tesla **15**
Texas **27**
Texas Tornados, The **8**
Thacker, Rocky
See Shenandoah
Thain, Gary
See Uriah Heep
Thayil, Kim
See Soundgarden
The The **15**
Theremin, Leon **19**
They Might Be Giants **7**
Thibaudet, Jean-Yves **24**
Thielemans, Toots **13**
Thin Lizzy **13**
Third Eye Blind **25**
Third World **13**
Thirsk, Jason
See Pennywise
Thistlethwaite, Anthony
See Waterboys, The
Thomas, Alex
See Earth, Wind and Fire
Thomas, David Clayton
See Clayton-Thomas, David
Thomas, David
See Pere Ubu
Thomas, David
See Take 6
Thomas, Dennis "D.T."
See Kool & the Gang
Thomas, George "Fathead"
See McKinney's Cotton Pickers
Thomas, Irma **16**
Thomas, John
See Captain Beefheart and His Magic Band
Thomas, Mickey
See Jefferson Starship
Thomas, Olice
See Five Blind Boys of Alabama
Thomas, Ray
See Moody Blues, The
Thomas, Richard
See Jesus and Mary Chain, The
Thomas, Rob
See Matchbox 20
Thomas, Rozonda "Chilli"
See TLC
Thompson, Chester
See Weather Report
Thompson, Danny
See Pentangle
Thompson, Dennis
See MC5, The
Thompson, Dougie
See Supertramp
Thompson, Lee
See Madness
Thompson, Les
See Nitty Gritty Dirt Band, The
Thompson, Mayo
See Pere Ubu
Thompson, Porl
See Cure, The
Thompson, Richard **7**
Also see Fairport Convention
Thomson, Kristin
See Tsunami
Thoranisson, Biggi
See Gus Gus
Thorn, Christopher
See Blind Melon
Thorn, Stan
See Shenandoah
Thorn, Tracey
See Everything But The Girl
Also see Massive Attack
Thornalley, Phil
See Cure, The
Thornburg, Lee
See Supertramp
Thornhill, Leeroy
See Prodigy
Thornton, Big Mama **18**
Thornton, Kevin "KT"
See Color Me Badd
Thornton, Teri **28**
Thornton, Willie Mae
See Thornton, Big Mama
Threadgill, Henry **9**
Three Dog Night **5**
Throwing Muses **15**
Thunders, Johnny
See New York Dolls
Tickner, George
See Journey
Tiffany **4**
Tikaram, Tanita **9**
Tilbrook, Glenn
See Squeeze

Tiller, Mary
See Anointed
Tilley, Sandra
See Martha and the Vandellas
Tillis, Mel **7**
Tillis, Pam **25**
Earlier sketch in CM **8**
Tilson Thomas, Michael **24**
Timberlake, Justin
See 'N Sync
Timbuk 3 **3**
Timmins, Margo
See Cowboy Junkies, The
Timmins, Michael
See Cowboy Junkies, The
Timmins, Peter
See Cowboy Junkies, The
Timms, Sally
See Mekons, The
Tinsley, Boyd
See Dave Matthews Band
Tippin, Aaron **12**
Tipton, Glenn
See Judas Priest
TLC **15**
Toad the Wet Sprocket **13**
Toback, Jeremy
See Brad
Todd, Andy
See Republica
Tolhurst, Laurence
See Cure, The
Tolland, Bryan
See Del Amitri
Toller, Dan
See Allman Brothers, The
Tolliver, T.C.
See Wendy O. Williams and The Plasmatics
Tolson, Peter
See Pretty Things, The
Tom Petty and the Heartbreakers **26**
Tone-Loc **3**
Tong, Winston
See Tuxedomoon
Tontoh, Frank
See Aztec Camera
Tony K
See Roomful of Blues
Tony Williams **6**
Tony! Toni! Toné! **12**
Too $hort **16**
Toohey, Dan
See Guided By Voices
Took, Steve Peregrine
See T. Rex
Tool **21**
Toomey, Jenny
See Tsunami
Topham, Anthony "Top"
See Yardbirds, The
Tork, Peter
See Monkees, The
Torme, Mel **4**
Torres, Hector "Tico"
See Bon Jovi
Toscanini, Arturo **14**
Tosh, Peter **3**
Toure, Ali Farka **18**
Tourish, Ciaran
See Altan
Toussaint, Allen **11**
Towner, Ralph **22**
Townes, Jeffery
See DJ Jazzy Jeff and the Fresh Prince
Towns, Efrem
See Dirty Dozen Brass Band
Townshend, Pete **1**
Also see Who, The
Traffic **19**
Tragically Hip, The **18**
Trammell, Mark
See Greater Vision
Travers, Brian
See UB40
Travers, Mary
See Peter, Paul & Mary
Travis, Merle **14**
Travis, Randy **9**
Treach
See Naughty by Nature
Treadmill Trackstar **21**
Tremonti, Mark
See Creed
Tribe Called Quest, A **8**
Trick Daddy **28**
Tricky **18**
Tricky
See Massive Attack
Trimble, Vivian
See Luscious Jackson
Trimble, Vivien
See Luscious Jackson
Trimm, Rex
See Cherry Poppin' Daddies
Tripp, Art "Art Marimba"
See Captain Beefheart and His Magic Band
Tritsch, Christian
See Gong
Tritt, Travis **7**
Trotter, Kera
See C + C Music Factory
Trucks, Butch
See Allman Brothers, The
Trugoy the Dove
See De La Soul
Trujillo, Robert
See Suicidal Tendencies
Truman, Dan
See Diamond Rio
Trynin, Jen **21**
Trytten, Lorre Lynn
See Willem Breuker Kollektief
Tsunami **21**
Tubb, Ernest **4**
Tubridy, Michael
See Chieftans, The
Tucker, Corin
See Sleater-Kinney
Tucker, Moe
See Velvet Underground, The
Tucker, Sophie **12**
Tucker, Tanya **3**
Tucker, William
See Ministry
Also see Pigface
Tufnel, Nigel
See Spinal Tap
Tull, Bruce
See Scud Mountain Boys
Turbin, Neil
See Anthrax
Turgon, Bruce
See Foreigner
Turner, Big Joe **13**
Turner, Elgin "Masta Killa"
See Wu-Tang Clan
Turner, Erik
See Warrant
Turner, Ike
See Ike and Tina Turner
Turner, Joe Lynn
See Deep Purple
Turner, Mike
See Our Lady Peace
Turner, Sonny
See Platters, The
Turner, Steve
See Mudhoney
Turner, Tina **1**
Also see Ike and Tina Turner
Turpin, Will
See Collective Soul
Turre, Steve **22**
Turtle Island String Quartet **9**
Tutton, Bill
See Geraldine Fibbers
Tutuska, George
See Goo Goo Dolls, The
Tuxedomoon **21**
Twain, Shania **17**
Twist, Nigel
See Alarm
Twitty, Conway **6**
Tyagi, Paul
See Del Amitri
Tyler, Steve
See Aerosmith
Tyner, McCoy **7**
Tyner, Rob
See MC5, The
Type O Negative **27**
Tyson, Ian
See Ian and Sylvia
Tyson, Ron
See Temptations, The
U2 **12**
Earlier sketch in CM **2**
UB40 **4**
Ulmer, James Blood **13**
Ulrich, Lars
See Metallica
Ulvaeus, Björn
See Abba
Um Romao, Dom
See Weather Report
Underworld **26**
Unitt, Victor
See Pretty Things, The
Unruh, N. U.
See Einstürzende Neubauten
Uosikkinen, David
See Hooters
Upshaw, Dawn **9**
Urge Overkill **17**
Uriah Heep **19**
US3 **18**
Usher **23**
Utley, Adrian
See Portishead
Utsler, Joseph
See Insane Clown Possee
Vaché, Jr., Warren **22**
Vachon, Chris
See Roomful of Blues
Vai, Steve **5**
Also see Whitesnake
Valdès, Chucho **25**
Valens, Ritchie **23**
Valenti, Dino
See Quicksilver Messenger Service
Valentine, Gary
See Blondie

Valentine, Hilton
See Animals, The
Valentine, Kathy
See Go-Go's, The
Valentine, Rae
See War
Valenzuela, Jesse
See Gin Blossoms
Valli, Frankie **10**
Also see Four Seasons, The
Valory, Ross
See Journey
van Dijk, Carol
See Bettie Serveert
van Lieshout, Lars
See Tuxedomoon
Van Gelder, Nick
See Jamiroquai
Van Halen, Alex
See Van Halen
Van Halen, Edward
See Van Halen
Van Halen **25**
Earlier sketch in CM **8**
Van Hook, Peter
See Mike & the Mechanics
Van Rensalier, Darnell
See Shai
Van Ronk, Dave **12**
Van Shelton, Ricky **5**
Van Vliet, Don "Captain Beefheart"
See Captain Beefheart and His Magic Band
Van Zandt, Townes **13**
Van Zant, Johnny
See Lynyrd Skynyrd
Van Zant, Ronnie
See Lynyrd Skynyrd
Vandenburg, Adrian
See Whitesnake
Vander Ark, Brad
See Verve Pipe, The
Vander Ark, Brian
See Verve Pipe, The
Vandermark, Ken **28**
Also see Flying Luttenbachers, The
Vandross, Luther **24**
Earlier sketch in CM **2**
Vanessa-Mae **26**
Vangelis **21**
Vanilla Ice **6**
Vasquez, Junior **16**
Vaughan, Jimmie **24**
Also see Fabulous Thunderbirds, The
Vaughan, Sarah **2**
Vaughan, Stevie Ray **1**
Vazzano, Frank
See Cobra Verde
Vedder, Eddie
See Pearl Jam
Vega, Bobby
See Quicksilver Messenger Service
Vega, Suzanne **3**
Velocity Girl **23**
Veloso, Caetano **28**
Velvet Crush **28**
Velvet Underground, The **7**
Ventures, The **19**
Verdecchio, Andy
See Five Iron Frenzy
Verdurmen, Rob
See Willem Breuker Kollektief
Verlaine, Tom
See Television
Verta-Ray, Matt
See Madder Rose
Veruca Salt **20**
Verve Pipe, The **20**
Verve, The **18**
Vettese, Peter-John
See Jethro Tull
Vicious, Sid
See Sex Pistols, The
Also see Siouxsie and the Banshees
Vickers, Robert
See Go-Betweens, The
Vickrey, Dan
See Counting Crows
Victor, Tommy
See Prong
Vienna Choir Boys **23**
Vig, Butch **17**
Also see Garbage
Village People, The **7**
Vincent, Gene **19**
Vincent, Vinnie
See Kiss
Vinnie
See Naughty by Nature
Vinton, Bobby **12**
Violent Femmes **12**
Violent J
See Insane Clown Posse
Virtue, Michael
See UB40
Visser, Peter
See Bettie Serveert
Vito, Rick
See Fleetwood Mac
Vitous, Mirslav
See Weather Report
Voelz, Susan
See Poi Dog Pondering
Volodos, Arcadi **28**
Volz, Greg
See Petra
von Karajan, Herbert **1**
Von Bohlen, Davey
See Promise Ring, The
Von, Eerie
See Danzig
Vox, Bono
See U2
Vudi
See American Music Club
Waaktaar, Pal
See A-ha
Wachtel, Waddy **26**
Wade, Adam
See Shudder to Think
Wade, Chrissie
See Alien Sex Fiend
Wade, Nik
See Alien Sex Fiend
Wadenius, George
See Blood, Sweat and Tears
Wadephal, Ralf
See Tangerine Dream
Wagoner, Faidest
See Soul Stirrers, The
Wagoner, Porter **13**
Wahlberg, Donnie
See New Kids on the Block
Wailer, Bunny **11**
Wainwright III, Loudon **11**
Waits, Tom **27**
Earlier sketch in CM **12**
Earlier sketch in CM **1**
Wakeling, David
See English Beat, The
Wakeman, Rick **27**
Also see Yes
Walden, Narada Michael **14**
Waldroup, Jason
See Greater Vision
Walford, Britt
See Breeders
Walker, Clay **20**
Walker, Colin
See Electric Light Orchestra
Walker, Ebo
See New Grass Revival, The
Walker, Jerry Jeff **13**
Walker, Joe Louis **28**
Walker, Matt
See Filter
Walker, T-Bone **5**
Wallace, Bill
See Guess Who
Wallace, Ian
See King Crimson
Wallace, Richard
See Mighty Clouds of Joy, The
Wallace, Sippie **6**
Waller, Charlie
See Country Gentlemen, The
Waller, Dave
See Jam, The
Waller, Fats **7**
Wallflowers, The **20**
Wallinger, Karl
See Waterboys, The
Wallinger, Karl **11**
Wallis, Larry
See Motörhead
Walls, Chris
See Dave Clark Five, The
Walls, Denise "Nee-C"
See Anointed
Walls, Greg
See Anthrax
Walsh, Joe **5**
Also see Eagles, The
Walsh, Marty
See Supertramp
Walter, Weasel
See Flying Luttenbachers, The
Walters, Richard
See Slick Rick
Walters, Robert "Patch"
See Mystic Revealers
War **14**
Ward, Andy
See Bevis Frond
Also see Camel
Ward, Bill
See Black Sabbath
Ward, Michael
See Wallflowers, The
Ware, Martyn
See Human League, The
Wareham, Dean
See Luna
Wariner, Steve **18**
Warner, Les
See Cult, The
Warnes, Jennifer **3**
Warrant **17**
Warren, Diane **21**
Warren, George W.
See Five Blind Boys of Alabama
Warren, Mervyn
See Take 6
Warwick, Clint
See Moody Blues, The

Warwick, Dionne **2**
Was (Not Was) **6**
Was, David
See Was (Not Was)
Was, Don **21**
Also see Was (Not Was)
Wash, Martha
See C + C Music Factory
Washington, Chester
See Earth, Wind and Fire
Washington, Dinah **5**
Washington, Grover, Jr. **5**
Wasserman, Greg "Noodles"
See Offspring
Waterboys, The **27**
Waters, Crystal **15**
Waters, Ethel **11**
Waters, Muddy **24**
Earlier sketch in CM **4**
Waters, Roger
See Pink Floyd
Watkins, Christopher
See Cabaret Voltaire
Watkins, Tionne "T-Boz"
See TLC
Watley, Jody **26**
Earlier sketch in CM **9**
Watson, Doc **2**
Watson, Guy
See Surfaris, The
Watson, Ivory
See Ink Spots
Watt, Ben
See Everything But The Girl
Watt, Mike **22**
Also see fIREHOSE
Watters, Sam
See Color Me Badd
Watts, Bari
See Bevis Frond
Watts, Charlie
See Rolling Stones, The
Watts, Eugene
See Canadian Brass, The
Watts, Lou
See Chumbawamba
Watts, Raymond
See KMFDM
Watts, Todd
See Emmet Swimming
Weather Report **19**
Weaver, Louie
See Petra
Weavers, The **8**
Webb, Chick **14**
Webb, Jimmy **12**
Webb, Paul
See Talk Talk
Webber, Andrew Lloyd
See Lloyd Webber, Andrew
Webber, Mark
See Pulp
Webster, Andrew
See Tsunami
Wedding Present, The **28**
Wedgwood, Mike
See Caravan
Wedren, Craig
See Shudder to Think
Weezer **20**
Weider, John
See Animals, The
Weiland, Scott
See Stone Temple Pilots
Weill, Kurt **12**
Weir, Bob
See Grateful Dead, The
Weiss, Janet
See Sleater-Kinney
Also see Quasi
Weissman, Marco
See Waterboys, The
Welch, Bob
See Fleetwood Mac
Welch, Brian
See Korn
Welch, Bruce
See Shadows, The
Welch, Mcguinness
See Fleetwood Mac
Also see Lords of Acid
Welch, Sean
See Beautiful South
Welk, Lawrence **13**
Weller, Paul **14**
Weller, Paul
See Jam, The
Wells, Cory
See Three Dog Night
Wells, Junior **17**
Wells, Kitty **6**
Welnick, Vince
See Grateful Dead, The
Welsh, Alan
See Aztec Camera
Welty, Ron
See Offspring
Wenberg, Erik
See Emmet Swimming
Wendy O. Williams and The Plasmatics **26**
Wertz, Jenn
See Rusted Root
West, Brian
See Cherry Poppin' Daddies
West, Dottie **8**
West, Steve
See Pavement
Westerberg, Paul **26**
Also see Replacements, The
Weston, Randy **15**
Weston
See Orb, The
Wetton, John
See King Crimson
Wexler, Jerry **15**
Weymouth, Tina
See Talking Heads
Whalen, Katharine
See Squirrel Nut Zippers
Whalley, Dennis
See Captain Beefheart and His Magic Band
Wharton, Dianaruthe
See Sweet Honey in the Rock
Wheat, Brian
See Tesla
Wheeler, Audrey
See C + C Music Factory
Wheeler, Caron
See Soul II Soul
Wheeler, Harriet
See Sundays, The
Wheeler, Robert
See Pere Ubu
Whelan, Bill **20**
Whelan, Gavan
See James
Whitaker, Rodney **20**
Whitaker, Yolanda
See Yo Yo
White, Alan
See Oasis
White, Alan
See Yes
White, Barry **6**
White, Billy
See Dokken
White, Chris
See Dire Straits
White, Chris
See Zombies, The
White, Clarence
See Byrds, The
White, Dave
See Warrant
White, Dennis
See Charm Farm
White, Freddie
See Earth, Wind and Fire
White, Karyn **21**
White, Lari **15**
White, Mark
See Spin Doctors
White, Mark
See Mekons, The
White, Maurice
See Earth, Wind and Fire
White, Ralph
See Bad Livers, The
White, Roland
See Nashville Bluegrass Band
White, Verdine
See Earth, Wind and Fire
White, Will
See Propellerheads
White Zombie **17**
Whitehead, Donald
See Earth, Wind and Fire
Whiteman, Paul **17**
Whitesnake **5**
Whitfield, Mark **18**
Whitford, Brad
See Aerosmith
Whiting, Margaret **28**
Whitley, Chris **16**
Whitley, Keith **7**
Whitman, Slim **19**
Whittaker, Hudson **20**
Whitten, Chris
See Dire Straits
Whitwam, Barry
See Herman's Hermits
Who, The **3**
Wichnewski, Stephen
See Yo La Tengo
Wickham, Steve
See Waterboys, The
Widenhouse, Je
See Squirrel Nut Zippers
Wiedlin, Jane
See Go-Go's, The
Wiggins, Dwayne
See Tony! Toni! Toné!
Wiggins, Raphael
See Tony! Toni! Toné!
Wiggs, Josephine
See Breeders
Wiggs, Pete
See Saint Etienne
Wikso, Ron
See Foreigner
Wilborn, Dave
See McKinney's Cotton Pickers
Wilburn, Ishmael
See Weather Report

Wilco **27**
Wilcox, Imani
See Pharcyde, The
Wilde, Phil
See 2 Unlimited
Wilder, Alan
See Depeche Mode
Wildwood, Michael
See D Generation
Wilk, Brad
See Rage Against the Machine
Wilkeson, Leon
See Lynyrd Skynyrd
Wilkie, Chris
See Dubstar
Wilkinson, Geoff
See US3
Wilkinson, Keith
See Squeeze
Wilkinson, Kevin
See Waterboys, The
Willem Breuker Kollektief **28**
Williams, Andy **2**
Williams, Boris
See Cure, The
Williams, Cliff
See AC/DC
Williams, Dana
See Diamond Rio
Williams, Dar **21**
Williams, Deniece **1**
Williams, Don **4**
Williams, Eric
See Blackstreet
Williams, Fred
See C + C Music Factory
Williams, Hank, Jr. **1**
Williams, Hank, Sr. **4**
Williams, James "Diamond"
See Ohio Players
Williams, Joe **11**
Williams, John **28**
Earlier sketch in CM **9**
Williams, Lamar
See Allman Brothers, The
Williams, Lucinda **24**
Earlier sketch in CM **10**
Williams, Marion **15**
Williams, Milan
See Commodores, The
Williams, Otis
See Temptations, The
Williams, Paul
See Temptations, The
Williams, Paul **26**
Earlier sketch in CM **5**
Williams, Phillard
See Earth, Wind and Fire
Williams, Robbie **25**
Williams, Robert
See Captain Beefheart and His Magic Band
Williams, Rozz
See Christian Death
Williams, Terry
See Dire Straits
Williams, Tony
See Platters, The
Williams, Vanessa **10**
Williams, Victoria **17**
Williams, Walter
See O'Jays, The
Williams, Wendy O.
See Wendy O. Williams and The Plasmatics
Williams, Wilbert
See Mighty Clouds of Joy, The
Williams, William Elliot
See Artifacts
Williams, Yasmeen
See Sweet Honey in the Rock
Williamson, Gloria
See Martha and the Vandellas
Williamson, Robin
See Incredible String Band
Williamson, Sonny Boy **9**
Willie D.
See Geto Boys, The
Willis, Clarence "Chet"
See Ohio Players
Willis, Kelly **12**
Willis, Larry
See Blood, Sweat and Tears
Willis, Pete
See Def Leppard
Willis, Rick
See Foreigner
Willis, Victor
See Village People, The
Willner, Hal **10**
Wills, Aaron (P-Nut)
See 311
Wills, Bob **6**
Wills, Mark **27**
Wills, Rick
See Bad Company
Willson-Piper, Marty
See Church, The
Willsteed, John
See Go-Betweens, The
Wilmot, Billy "Mystic"
See Mystic Revealers
Wilson, Anne
See Heart
Wilson, Brian **24**
Also see Beach Boys, The
Wilson, Carl
See Beach Boys, The
Wilson, Carnie
See Wilson Phillips
Wilson, Cassandra **26**
Earlier sketch in CM **12**
Wilson, Chris
See Love Spit Love
Wilson, Cindy
See B-52's, The
Wilson, Dennis
See Beach Boys, The
Wilson, Don
See Ventures, The
Wilson, Eric
See Sublime
Wilson, Gerald **19**
Wilson, Jackie **3**
Wilson, Kim
See Fabulous Thunderbirds, The
Wilson, Mary
See Supremes, The
Wilson, Nancy **28**
Wilson, Nancy **14**
Also see Heart
Wilson, Orlandus
See Golden Gate Quartet
Wilson, Patrick
See Weezer
Wilson Phillips **5**
Wilson, Ransom **5**
Wilson, Ricky
See B-52's, The
Wilson, Robin
See Gin Blossoms
Wilson, Ron
See Surfaris, The
Wilson, Shanice
See Shanice
Wilson, Wendy
See Wilson Phillips
Wilson-James, Victoria
Also see Shamen, The
Wilton, Michael
See Queensryche
Wimpfheimer, Jimmy
See Roomful of Blues
Winans, Carvin
See Winans, The
Winans, Marvin
See Winans, The
Winans, Michael
See Winans, The
Winans, Ronald
See Winans, The
Winans, The **12**
Winbush, Angela **15**
Winfield, Chuck
See Blood, Sweat and Tears
Winston, George **9**
Winter, Johnny **5**
Winter, Kurt
See Guess Who
Winter, Paul **10**
Winthrop, Dave
See Supertramp
Winwood, Muff
See Spencer Davis Group
Winwood, Steve **2**
Also see Spencer Davis Group
Also see Traffic
Wire, Nicky
See Manic Street Preachers
Wiseman, Bobby
See Blue Rodeo
Wiseman, Mac **19**
WishBone
See Bone Thugs-N-Harmony
Withers, Pick
See Dire Straits
Witherspoon, Jimmy **19**
Wolf, Peter
See J. Geils Band
Wolfe, Gerald
See Greater Vision
Wolstencraft, Simon
See Fall, The
Womack, Bobby **5**
Wonder, Stevie **17**
Earlier sketch in CM **2**
Woo, John
See Magnetic Fields, The
Wood, Chris
See Traffic
Wood, Danny
See New Kids on the Block
Wood, Ron
See Faces, The
Also see Rolling Stones, The
Wood, Roy
See Electric Light Orchestra
Woodgate, Dan
See Madness
Woods, Gay
See Steeleye Span
Woods, Terry
See Pogues, The
Also see Steeleye Span
Woods-Wright, Tomica **22**

Woodson, Ollie
See Temptations, The
Woodward, Keren
See Bananarama
Woody, Allen
See Allman Brothers, The
Woolfolk, Andrew
See Earth, Wind and Fire
Worley, Chris
See Jackyl
Worley, Jeff
See Jackyl
Worrell, Bernie **11**
Wray, Link **17**
Wreede, Katrina
See Turtle Island String Quartet
Wren, Alan
See Stone Roses, The
Wretzky, D'Arcy
See Smashing Pumpkins
Wright, Adrian
See Human League, The
Wright, David "Blockhead"
See English Beat, The
Wright, Heath
See Ricochet
Wright, Hugh
See Boy Howdy
Wright, Jimmy
See Sounds of Blackness
Wright, Norman
See Country Gentlemen, The
Wright, Rick
See Pink Floyd
Wright, Simon
See AC/DC
Wright, Tim
See Pere Ubu
Wu-Tang Clan **19**
Wurzel
See Motörhead
Wyatt, Robert **24**
Wyman, Bill
See Rolling Stones, The
Also see Bill Wyman & the Rhythm Kings
Wynette, Tammy **24**
Earlier sketch in CM **2**
Wynne, Philippe
See Spinners, The
Wynonna **11**
Also see Judds, The
X **11**
Xefos, Chris
See King Missile
XTC **26**
Earlier sketch in CM **10**
Ya Kid K
See Technotronic
Yale, Brian
See Matchbox 20
Yamamoto, Hiro
See Soundgarden
Yamamoto, Seichi
See Boredoms, The
Yamano, Atsuko
See Shonen Knife
Yamano, Naoko
See Shonen Knife
Yamashita, Kazuhito **4**
Yamataka, Eye
See Boredoms, The
Yamauchi, Tetsu
See Faces, The
Yamazaki, Iwao
See Ghost
Yang, Naomi
See Damon and Naomi
Yankovic, "Weird Al" **7**
Yanni **11**
Yardbirds, The **10**
Yarrow, Peter
See Peter, Paul & Mary
Yates, Bill
See Country Gentlemen, The
Yauch, Adam
See Beastie Boys, The
Yearwood, Trisha **25**
Earlier sketch in CM **10**
Yella
See N.W.A.
Yes **8**
Yeston, Maury **22**
Yo La Tengo **24**
Yo Yo **9**
Yoakam, Dwight **21**
Earlier sketch in CM **1**
Yoot, Tukka
See US3
York, Andrew **15**
York, John
See Byrds, The
York, Pete
See Spencer Davis Group
Yorke, Thom E.
See Radiohead
Yoshida, Tatsuya
See Flying Luttenbachers, The
Yoshikawa, Toyohito
See Boredoms, The
Yoshimi
See Boredoms, The
Young, Adrian
See No Doubt
Young, Angus
See AC/DC
Young, Brian
See Fountains of Wayne
Young, Faron **7**
Young, Fred
See Kentucky Headhunters, The
Young, Gary
See Pavement
Young, Grant
See Soul Asylum
Young, Jeff
See Megadeth
Young, La Monte **16**
Young, Lester **14**
Young M.C. **4**
Young, Malcolm
See AC/DC
Young, Neil **15**
Earlier sketch in CM **2**
Also see Buffalo Springfield
Young, Paul
See Mike & the Mechanics
Young, Richard
See Kentucky Headhunters, The
Young, Robert "Throbert"
See Primal Scream
Youth, Todd
See D Generation
Youtz, Raif
See Built to Spill
Yow, David
See Jesus Lizard
Yseult, Sean
See White Zombie
Yule, Doug
See Velvet Underground, The
Zander, Robin
See Cheap Trick
Zankey, Glen
See Bluegrass Patriots
Zap Mama **14**
Zappa, Frank **17**
Earlier sketch in CM **1**
Zawinul, Josef
See Weather Report
Zender, Stuart
See Jamiroquai
Zevon, Warren **9**
Zhane **22**
Zilinskas, Annette
See Bangles, The
Zimmerman, Udo **5**
Ziskrout, Jay
See Bad Religion
Zombie, Rob
See White Zombie
Zombies, The **23**
Zoom, Billy
See X
Zorn, John **15**
Zoyes, Dino
See Charm Farm
Zuccaro, Steve
See Charm Farm
Zukerman, Pinchas **4**
Zulu, Ras I
See Spearhead
ZZ Top